USA by Rail
plus Canada's main routes

the Bradt Travel Guide

John Pitt

edition
9

www.bradtguides.com

Bradt Travel Guides Ltd, UK
The Globe Pequot Press Inc, USA

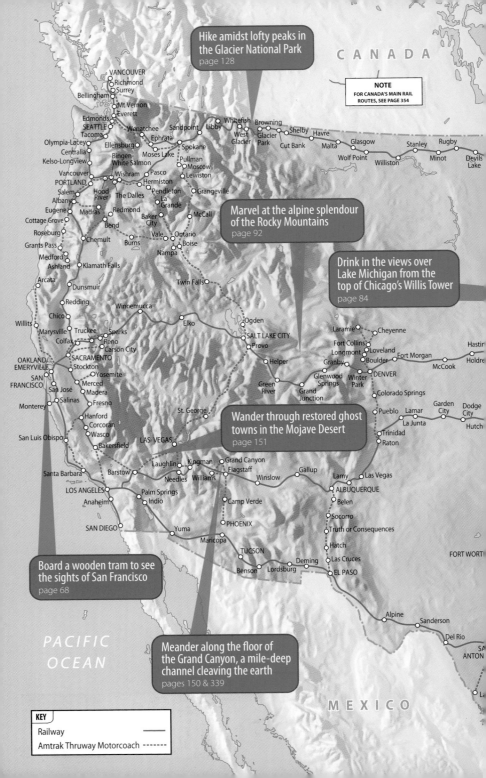

Hike amidst lofty peaks in the Glacier National Park
page 128

CANADA

NOTE
FOR CANADA'S MAIN RAIL
ROUTES, SEE PAGE 354

Marvel at the alpine splendour of the Rocky Mountains
page 92

Drink in the views over Lake Michigan from the top of Chicago's Willis Tower
page 84

Wander through restored ghost towns in the Mojave Desert
page 151

Board a wooden tram to see the sights of San Francisco
page 68

Meander along the floor of the Grand Canyon, a mile-deep channel cleaving the earth
pages 150 & 339

VANCOUVER
Richmond
Surrey
Bellingham
Mt Vernon
Edmonds
Everett
SEATTLE
Tacoma
Olympia-Lacey
Centralia
Kelso-Longview
Vancouver
PORTLAND
Salem
Albany
Eugene
Cottage Grove
Roseburg
Grants Pass
Medford
Ashland
Arcata
Dunsmuir
Redding
Chico
Willits
Marysville
Truckee
Colfax
OAKLAND/
EMERYVILLE
SAN
FRANCISCO
San José
Monterey
Salinas
Hanford
Corcoran
Wasco
San Luis Obispo
Bakersfield
Santa Barbara
LOS ANGELES
Anaheim
SAN DIEGO

Wenatchee
Ellensburg
Ephrata
Moses Lake
Wishram
Hood
River
The Dalles
Redmond
Madras
Bend
Chemult
Burns
Klamath Falls

Sandpoint
Libby
Whitefish
West
Glacier
Browning
Glacier
Park
Shelby
Havre

Spokane
Pullman
Moscow
Lewiston
Pasco
Hermiston
Pendleton
La
Grande
Grangeville
McCall
Baker
City
Vale
Ontario
Nampa
Boise

Twin Falls

Winnemucca
Elko
Ogden
SALT LAKE CITY
Provo
Sparks
Reno
Carson City
SACRAMENTO
Stockton
Yosemite
Merced
Madera
Fresno
St. George

Helper

Green
River
Grand
Junction
Glenwood
Springs
Winter
Park
DENVER
Colorado Springs

LAS VEGAS

Laughlin
Kingman
Needles
Williams
Grand Canyon
Flagstaff
Winslow
Gallup
Barstow
Palm Springs
Indio
Camp Verde
PHOENIX
Yuma
Maricopa
TUCSON
Benson
Lordsburg
Deming

Cut Bank
Malta
Wolf Point
Glasgow
Stanley
Rugby
Williston
Minot
Devils
Lake

Laramie
Cheyenne
Fort Collins
Longmont
Loveland
Granby
Boulder
Fort Morgan
McCook
Hastir
Holdre

Colorado Springs
Pueblo
Lamar
Garden
City
Dodge
City
La Junta
Trinidad
Raton
Hutch

Lamy
Las Vegas
ALBUQUERQUE
Belen
Socorro
Truth or Consequences
Hatch
Las Cruces
EL PASO

FORT WORT

Alpine
Sanderson
Del Rio
SA
ANTON

PACIFIC
OCEAN

M E X I C O

Le

KEY
Railway ———
Amtrak Thruway Motorcoach ------

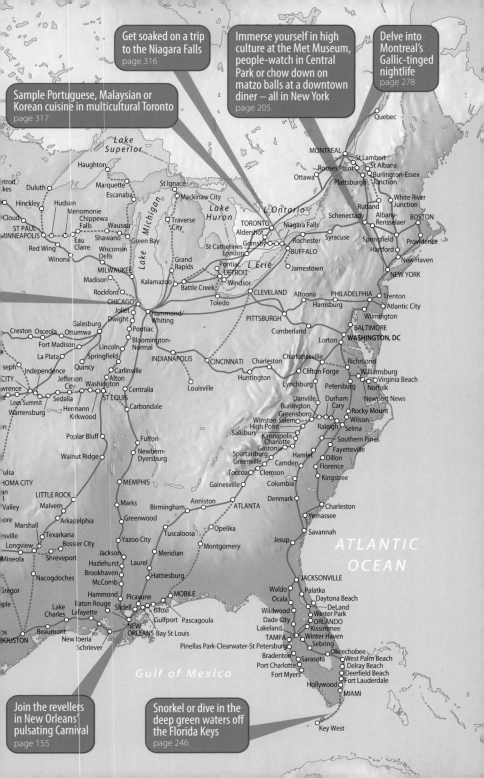

Get soaked on a trip
to the Niagara Falls
page 316

Immerse yourself in high
culture at the Met Museum,
people-watch in Central
Park or chow down on
matzo balls at a downtown
diner — all in New York
page 205

Delve into
Montreal's
Gallic-tinged
nightlife
page 278

Sample Portuguese, Malaysian or
Korean cuisine in multicultural Toronto
page 317

Join the revellers
in New Orleans'
pulsating Carnival
page 155

Snorkel or dive in the
deep green waters off
the Florida Keys
page 246

Lake Superior

Haughton

etroit
kes
Duluth
Hinckley
Cloud
ST PAUL
MINNEAPOLIS
Red Wing
Winona

Marquette
Escanaba

St Ignace
Mackinaw City

Lake Huron

Hudson
Menomonie
Chippewa
Falls
Eau
Claire
Wausau
Shawano

Traverse
City

Mackinaw City

L Ontario

Wisconsin
Dells
Green Bay

Madison
Rockford
CHICAGO

Grand
Rapids
Kalamazoo
Battle Creek

MILWAUKEE

Lake Michigan

TORONTO
Aldershot
St Catherines
London
Grimsby

Niagara Falls
Rochester

Syracuse

BUFFALO

Schenectady
Albany-
Rensselaer

Rutland

White River
Junction

BOSTON
Providence

Quebec

MONTREAL
St Lambert
St Albans
Rouses Point
Ottawa
Plattsburgh
Burlington-Essex
Junction

Springfield
Hartford
New Haven

NEW YORK

Creston Osceola
Fort Madison
La Plata
joseph
CITY
wrence
Lees Summit
Warrensburg

Galesburg
Ottumwa

Joliet
Dwight
Pontiac

Bloomington-
Normal

Hammond/
Whiting

Pontiac
DETROIT
Windsor

CLEVELAND
Toledo

Altoona

PHILADELPHIA
Harrisburg

Trenton
Atlantic City
Wilmington

BALTIMORE
WASHINGTON, DC

PITTSBURGH

Cumberland

Lorton

Lincoln
Springfield
Quincy

INDIANAPOLIS

CINCINNATI

Charleston

Charlottesville

Richmond
Williamsburg
Virginia Beach
Norfolk
Newport News

Carlinville
Alton

Independence
Jefferson
City
Sedalia
Hermann
Kirkwood
ST LOUIS

Washington
Centralia

Carbondale

Louisville

Huntington

Clifton Forge
Lynchburg

Petersburg

Danville
Burlington
Greensboro
Winston-Salem
High Point
Salisbury
Kannapolis
Charlotte
Gastonia

Durham
Cary

Rocky Mount
Wilson
Raleigh
Selma

Poplar Bluff

Fulton
Newbern-
Dyersburg

Walnut Ridge

MEMPHIS

Gainesville

Spartanburg
Greenville
Toccoa Clemson

Columbia

Denmark

Southern Pines
Fayetteville
Hamlet
Dillon
Camden
Florence
Kingstree

Charleston

ulsa
HOMA CITY
l
Valley
LITTLE ROCK
Malvern
Arkadelphia

Marshall
esville
Longview
Mineola

Texarkana
Bossier City
Shreveport

Nacogdoches

Gregor
ple

HOUSTON
Beaumont
New Iberia
Schriever

Lake
Charles
Lafayette

Hammond
Baton Rouge
Slidell
NEW
ORLEANS

Marks

Greenwood

Yazoo City

Jackson
Hazlehurst
Brookhaven
McComb

Picayune
Biloxi
Gulfport
Bay St Louis
Pascagoula

MOBILE

Birmingham

Tuscaloosa

Meridian

Laurel

Hattiesburg

Anniston

Opelika

Montgomery

ATLANTA

Yemassee

Savannah

Jesup

JACKSONVILLE

Waldo
Ocala
Wildwood
Dade City
Lakeland
TAMPA

Palatka
Daytona Beach
DeLand
Winter Park
ORLANDO
Kissimmee
Winter Haven
Sebring

Pinellas Park-Clearwater-St Petersburg
Bradenton
Port Charlotte
Fort Myers
Sarasota

Okeechobee
West Palm Beach
Delray Beach
Deerfield Beach
Fort Lauderdale

Hollywood

MIAMI

Key West

ATLANTIC
OCEAN

Gulf of Mexico

USA
by Rail
Don't
miss...

Grand Canyon
A mile-deep channel gouged
out of the earth, this surreal
landscape is the ultimate
American sight
(RC/DT) page 150

Niagara Falls
This dramatic natural wonder
straddles the USA and Canada
(EI/DT) page 316

San Francisco
With 43 hills, travelling on an iconic tram is a must for visitors to this laid-back city
(SE/DT) page 68

Rocky Mountains
Fantastic views abound in this range running through Colorado, Wyoming, Montana and Idaho
(MZ/DT) page 32

New York City
The Brooklyn Bridge affords a magnificent view of Lower Manhattan
(T/S) page 205

USA by Rail in colour

above left   San Diego is home to the first Franciscan mission in California, and contains many other restored early buildings (JB/DT) page 112

above right   Dating from 1907, Pike Place Market in Seattle is a labyrinth of shops, restaurants, galleries and stalls (S/DT) page 56

below   From the brooding presence of El Capitan to ranks of giant sequoias and shimmering alpine lakes, Yosemite National Park packs in an almost indecent number of breathtaking sights (MZ/DT) page 107

top   San Francisco's Chinatown, the largest outside Asia, is a city-within-a-city with numerous temples, restaurants and traditional shops (J/DT) page 68

above   Once the producer of many crops, today California's sunny Napa Valley is particularly renowned for its wine industry (SS) page 67

right   With its stylish buildings and coffee culture, Portland rivals Seattle for the accolade of 'America's most liveable city' (JRP/S) page 60

above   **The desolate landscapes of Monument Valley have starred in many westerns** (RA/DT) page 97

below   **The world's largest monorail system is in Walt Disney World, Florida, including Future World with its famous geodesic dome** (JK/S) page 241

AUTHOR

John Pitt studied economics and philosophy at East Anglia University before working at the Ministry of Defence and in local government. He has travelled extensively in the USA and Canada, including over 85,000 miles by train, and has written on travel for Thomas Cook as well as for magazines and newspapers such as the *Daily Mail*, *Daily Telegraph* and *The Sunday Times*.

AUTHOR'S STORY

Anything can happen on a train, and when Amtrak's *Pennsylvanian* paused early one evening at Lancaster a young Amish couple came on board. The man looked like Gary Cooper and had a neat beard, a wide-brimmed hat and a long, black coat. His wife wore traditional dark clothes, black boots and a bonnet, and carried their baby asleep in a black shawl. Suddenly we were in the middle of a scene from the film, *Witness*. All afternoon we had travelled among the flat fields and white farmhouses of Pennsylvania Dutch country, where the churches have wooden bell towers and cars are a rarity. Now and then a horse-drawn buggy would trot surreally along a dusty road or wait beside the tracks for the train to pass. By the time we reached Lancaster it seemed quite natural to have an Amish family join us and share their picnic.

Chance encounters are part of what makes an American train journey such a rewarding experience even when, as a writer, I'm trying to make notes for a book. One day it might be a group of schoolgirls heading for Niagara Falls, the next it's Australian backpackers in Arizona. US trains are friendly places so you are sure to run into someone interesting before very long, and you can learn a great deal by sitting next to a Kansas City mortician, Tennessee Williams's former chauffeur, or a drag artist on her way to entertain the troops in San Diego. Between the small towns and big cities you also appreciate the country's sheer size and variety, and understand what this land was like before McDonald's and Coca-Cola. As Homer Simpson has said, 'Nothing beats flying across the country on a train.'

PUBLISHER'S FOREWORD *Hilary Bradt*

A trip across America by train is surely one of *the* great romantic journeys: it is evocative of old movies, it has the scent of adventure, and it promises broad and beautiful landscapes. More practically, it also ensures that you're minimising your carbon footprint. Moving into its ninth edition, John Pitt's book has long established itself as the essential resource for those tourists who recognise that travelling is as much a part of the experience as arriving.

Ninth edition May 2019
First published 1992

Bradt Travel Guides Ltd
IDC House, The Vale, Chalfont St Peter, Bucks SL9 9RZ, England
www.bradtguides.com
Print edition published in the USA by The Globe Pequot Press Inc,
PO Box 480, Guilford, Connecticut 06437-0480

Text copyright © 2019 John Pitt
Maps copyright © 2019 Bradt Travel Guides Ltd
Photographs copyright © 2019 Individual photographers (see below)
Project managers: Felicity Laughton and Claire Strange
Cover research: Marta Bescos

ISBN: 978 1 78477 625 1

British Library Cataloguing in Publication Data
A catalogue record for this book is available from the British Library

Photographs Alamy Stock Photos: Jeff Greenberg (JG/A); Amtrak (A); Dreamstime.com: Ronald Adcock (RA/DT), Asterixvus (A/DT), Jay Beiler (JB/DT), Natalia Bratslavsky (NB/DT), Richard Charpentier (RC/DT), Elephantopia (E/DT), Serban Enache (SE/DT), Eric Inghels (EI/DT), Jerryway (J/DT), Dean Riley (DR/DT), Silvestrovairina (S/DT), Minyn Zhou (MZ/DT); Shutterstock.com: andersphoto (AP/S), Chantal de Bruijne (CdB/S), Danita Delmont (DD/S), GTS Productions (GTSP/S), Joshua Rainey Photography (JRP/S), Brian Kinney (BK/S), James Kirkikis (JK/S), Felix Lipov (FL/S), Stuart Monk (SM/S), Sue Stokes (SS/S), Taiga (T/S), Zhukova Valentyna (ZV/S), Chuck Wagner (CW/S), Ken Wolter (KW/S), Dima Zel (DZ/S); SuperStock (SS)

Front cover Coast Starlight: Seattle–Portland–Los Angeles (A)
Title page Amtrak train arriving in San Diego (KW/S); Union switch and signal at Fullerton (SS); Grand Central Station, New York City (SM/S)
Part openers page 53: Track running through Nevada desert (DZ/S); page 351: CN engine near Jasper in the Rockies (SS)
Back cover Monument Valley, Arizona (ZV/S); Mardi gras parade, New Orleans (GTSP/S)

Maps David McCutcheon FBCart.S

Typeset by Ian Spick, Bradt Travel Guides Ltd
Production managed by Jellyfish Print Solutions; printed in India
Digital conversion by www.dataworks.co.in

Acknowledgements

The author would like to thank the following for their generous help in the preparation of this book. Craig White, Barbara Bach, Ann Owens, Christine Suchy, Kathleen Gordon and Terry Rowley at Amtrak; Lyne Perreault and Guy Faulkner at VIA Rail; Kate Selley and Diana Cima at Rocky Mountaineer; Tamra L Hoppes at GrandLuxe Rail Journeys; Breanne Feigel at Canadian Pacific; Jim Williams at the USA Hostel Handbook; Kathryn Potter at the American Hotel & Lodging Association; Tim Thompson at the Alaska Railroad; Mark S Bassett at the Nevada Northern Railway Museum; Rebecca Laurie at the Colorado Historical Society; William W Sherrick at the New Hope & Ivyland Railroad; Paul Hammond at the California State Railroad Museum; Craig Lacey at the Heber Valley Railroad; Jerry Thull at the Grand Canyon Railway; Pam Butler at the Durango & Silverton Railroad; Joanne Hirasaki at Roaring Camp Railroads; Rebecca McGlynn at the Ontario Northland Railway; Craig S O'Connell and other Friends of Amtrak; Stephen Grande; Albert M Tannler in Pittsburgh; Wanie Biggs in San Francisco; Raymond Parker in New Orleans; Ann Terry in Washington, DC; Nelson Sanchez and Tom Bynum in New York; Heidi Gardner at Trailfinders; Anna Crew at BUNAC; Christopher Muller at RailServe.com; Rita Plahetka; Marjorie and Wayne Preston in Florida; Natasha Smith; Vangie S Palacios; Lynne Williams; Brian and Alison Henley; Michael B Gehl; George William; Eileen Rose; P J Bryant; Mitchell F Barker; Anne Cousins; Robert Moseley; Patrick Kidd at Amtrak's Great American Stations. Many thanks are also due to Felicity Laughton for her editorial expertise.

FEEDBACK REQUEST AND UPDATES WEBSITE

At Bradt Travel Guides we're aware that guidebooks start to go out of date on the day they're published – and that you, our readers, are out there in the field doing research of your own. You'll find out before us when a fine new family-run hotel opens or a favourite restaurant changes hands and goes downhill. So why not write and tell us about your experiences? Contact us on 01753 893444 or e info@bradtguides.com. We will forward emails to the author, who may post updates on the Bradt website at w bradtupdates.com/usa. Alternatively, you can add a review of the book to w bradtguides.com or Amazon.

Contents

LIST OF MAPS

HOW TO USE THIS BOOK

ACCOMMODATION Accommodation has been selected wherever possible for easy access from the rail station or from the downtown area. Consideration is also given to safety and value for money, hotels being listed in descending order of price per room.

TELEPHONE CODES Where a telephone code is separately listed in the information given for a town or city, unless otherwise noted it applies to all visitor attractions, places to stay, etc, included within that town's entry, whether these are actually situated within the city limits or some distance away.

THE MAPS The strip maps that illustrate the routes are inevitably schematic. They are not to scale and curves have been straightened, although the north indicators will show you roughly which direction you are travelling in. Please refer to the area maps on pages viii–xiii for a more accurate impression of the routes.

PRICES Prices given throughout this book are in US dollars ($) except where referring to Canadian dollars, in which case we specify Cdn$.

Introduction

ALL ABOARD! Ever since they came on the scene, American trains have had a strong hold on the popular imagination, inspiring countless stories, songs, scandals, films and legends. Their rugged charm sets them apart from more mundane means of transport and their ecological soundness is again in fashion. Trains pollute less, rarely suffer from weather delays and won't give you jet lag. You can choose your companions, read a book, let your thoughts unfurl, take a snooze, sleep horizontally and generally enjoy most of the comforts of home. One reason for travelling by train is especially compelling: it's much more fun.

Passenger trains go to most big cities as well as to Disney World, Niagara Falls and the Grand Canyon. Pampered by helpful attendants, you can travel from coast to coast, explore the Rocky Mountains and ride directly alongside two oceans. You cross many rivers, lakes and deserts, often seeing places which cannot be visited any other way. Less expensive than flying, more comfortable than the bus, trains keep you relaxed and in touch with an ever-changing landscape as the world becomes a moving picture, framed.

Amtrak coaches have generous reclining seats, air conditioning, bright observation domes and snug bunks. This may not be the fastest way to travel but the civilised pace is perfect for sightseeing. If the scenery palls you can always go for a stroll, enjoy a meal or make friends in the bar. At night a gentle rocking and the steady, muffled rhythm of the wheels are sure to lull you to sleep.

Not many people entertain fond thoughts about airports or enjoy the tedium of highways, but children still count freight cars and wave when a train goes by. Instead of leaving you exhausted and surly, trains create a sense of adventure and romance, so for many the sound of a locomotive whistle at midnight is a sure sign that it's time to move on. As the bell clangs and the conductor calls out 'All aboo-aard!', you soon discover why North American rail travel is such a beguiling experience.

FOLLOW BRADT

For the latest news, special offers and competitions, subscribe to the Bradt newsletter via the website **w** bradtguides.com and follow Bradt on:

- **f** BradtTravelGuides
- **🐦** @BradtGuides
- **📷** @bradtguides
- **P** bradtguides
- **▶** bradtguides

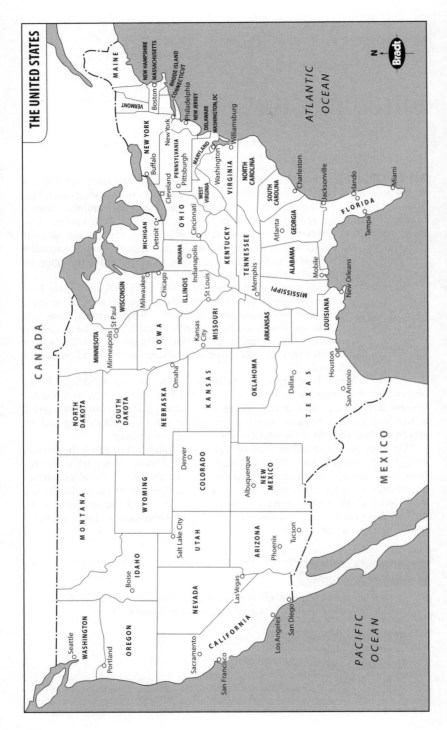

THE UNITED STATES

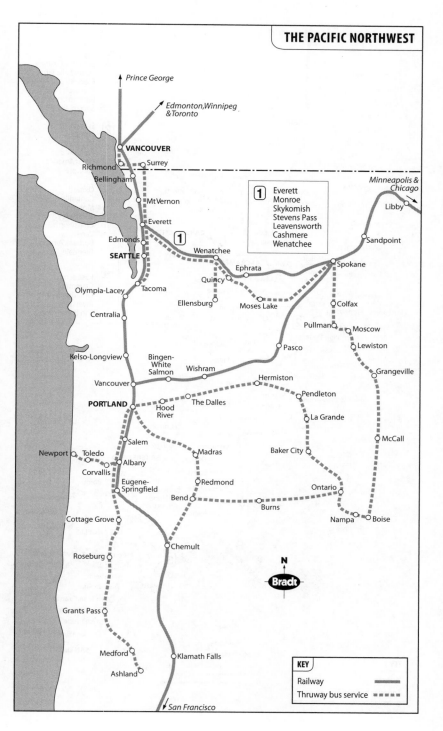

THE PACIFIC NORTHWEST

↑ Prince George

↗ Edmonton, Winnipeg & Toronto

VANCOUVER

Richmond ○ Surrey

Bellingham

Mt Vernon

Everett

Edmonds

SEATTLE

Olympia-Lacey

Tacoma

Centralia

Kelso-Longview

Bingen-White Salmon

Wishram

Vancouver

PORTLAND

Hood River

The Dalles

Salem

Newport ○ Toledo

Albany

Corvallis

Madras

Eugene-Springfield

Redmond

Bend

Cottage Grove

Roseburg

Chemult

Grants Pass

Medford

Klamath Falls

Ashland

↓ San Francisco

Wenatchee

Ephrata

Quincy

Ellensburg

Moses Lake

Pasco

Hermiston

Pendleton

La Grande

Baker City

Burns

Ontario

Nampa ○ Boise

①
Everett
Monroe
Skykomish
Stevens Pass
Leavensworth
Cashmere
Wenatchee

Minneapolis & Chicago

Libby

Sandpoint

Spokane

Colfax

Pullman ○ Moscow

Lewiston

Grangeville

McCall

N

Bradt

KEY
Railway ——————
Thruway bus service - - - - -

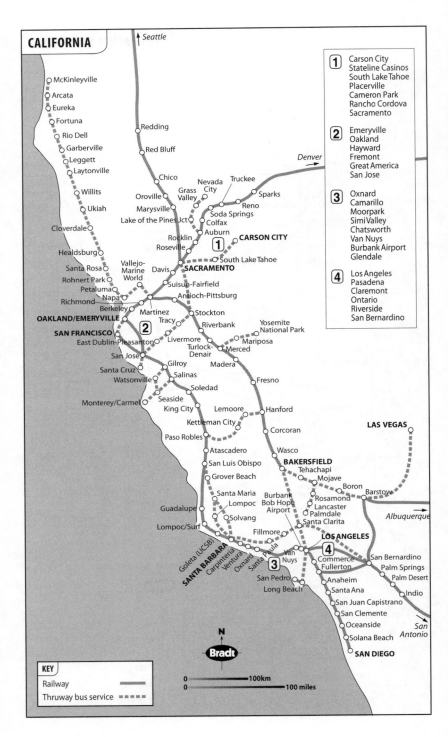

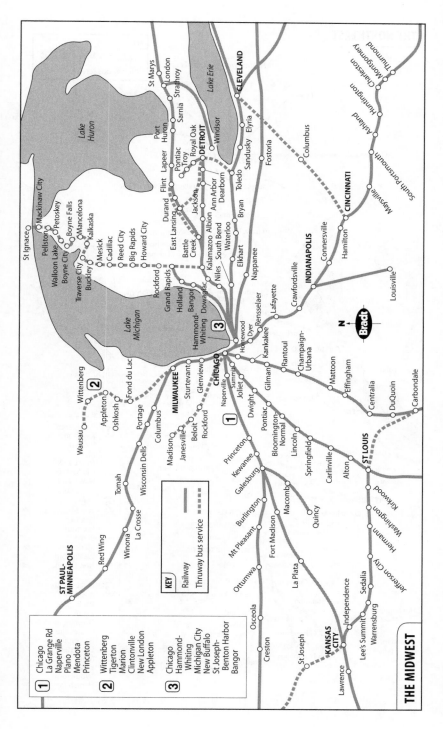

THE MIDWEST

KEY

Railway
Thruway bus service

1
Chicago
La Grange Rd
Naperville
Plano
Mendota
Princeton

2
Wittenberg
Tigerton
Marion
Clintonville
New London
Appleton

3
Chicago
Hammond-
Whiting
Michigan City
New Buffalo
St Joseph-
Benton Harbor
Bangor

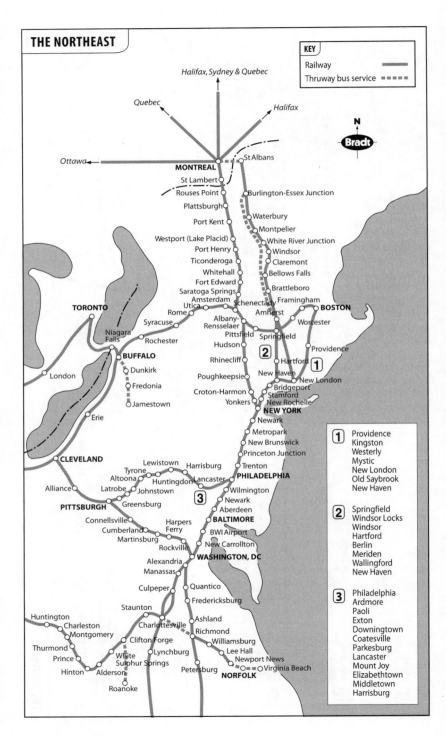

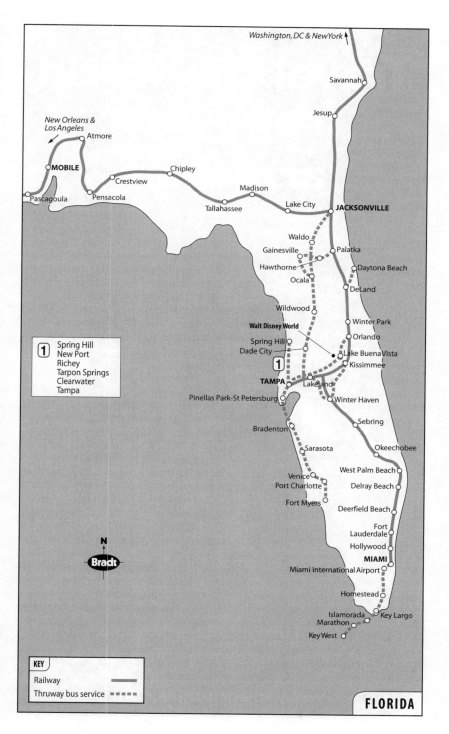

Part One

GENERAL INFORMATION

Location North America, bordering both the North Atlantic Ocean and the North Pacific Ocean
Neighbouring countries Canada and Mexico
Size/area 3,718,711 square miles (9,631,418km²)
Climate Mostly temperate, but tropical in Hawaii and Florida, arctic in Alaska, semi-arid in the great plains west of the Mississippi River, and arid in the Great Basin of the Southwest. Low winter temperatures in the Northwest are ameliorated occasionally in January and February by warm chinook winds from the eastern slopes of the Rocky Mountains.
Status Federal republic
Population 325,442,110 (December 2017)
Capital Washington, DC
Other main cities New York, Los Angeles, Chicago, Houston, Philadelphia, Phoenix, San Diego, Dallas, San Antonio, Detroit
Economy The largest economy in the world by nominal GDP, with a per-capita GDP of $57,436. Agriculture 1.1%; industry 19.4%; services 79.5% (2016).
GDP $19.3 trillion (2017)
Languages English is spoken by approximately 80% of the population; Spanish (12.4%) is regarded as the second national language
Religion Protestant 51%, Roman Catholic 24%, Mormon 2%, Jewish 2%, Muslim 1%, other 10%, none 10%
Currency US dollar; $1 = 100 cents
Exchange rate £1 = $1.29, €1 = $1.13 (February 2019)
International telephone code +1
Time There are four different time zones in the continental USA: Eastern Standard Time, Central Standard Time, Mountain Standard Time and Pacific Standard Time. Two further time zones apply in Alaska and Hawaii.
Electrical voltage 120V/60Hz standard plugs have two parallel flat pins ('American' type) or have two pins with an earth connector.
Weights and measures The USA is one of the few countries not to have adopted the International System of Units as its official system of weights and measures. Although the metric system has been lawful in the USA since 1866, it has been slow in displacing the adaptation of the British Imperial System known as the US Customary System (miles, gallons, etc).
Flag The Stars and Stripes has 13 horizontal stripes of red alternating with white. A blue rectangle in the upper hoist-side corner has 50 small, white, five-pointed stars arranged in nine offset horizontal rows of six stars alternating with rows of five stars. The 50 stars represent the 50 states; the 13 stripes represent the 13 original colonies.
National anthem 'Star Spangled Banner'
National flower American rose
National bird/animal Bald eagle
National sports Baseball, basketball, American football, ice hockey

RAILWAYS Seven Class I freight railroads operated over 95,264 miles (153,300km) of the 138,524 miles (222,933km) US standard-gauge network in 2016, with 152,702 employees, 26,719 locomotives and 1.63 million freight cars. They carried 1.554 billion US tons (1.41 billion tonnes) of freight.

1

From Horsepower to Amtrak

THE IRON HORSE

Railroad iron is a magician's rod, in its power to evoke the sleeping energies of land and water. – Ralph Waldo Emerson.

The development of the United States in the 19th and early 20th centuries largely coincided with the epic story of its railroads. Trains contributed hugely to prosperity and provided a sense of national identity, coming to symbolise the country's strength, optimism and pioneering spirit. For over 170 years Americans have been proud to call themselves 'locomotive people'.

It may be symbolic that one of the country's first railroads had as its purpose the hauling of granite for the Bunker Hill Monument, which was being built to commemorate a defining episode in America's War of Independence. Gridley Bryant's Granite Railway used horsepower to operate over 3 miles of track at Quincy, Massachusetts, in 1826. America's first steam-powered locomotive was the English-built *Stourbridge Lion*, inaugurated in August 1829 on the Delaware & Hudson Canal Company's line at Honesdale, Pennsylvania. But the story really began on 19 February 1827, when a group of Baltimore residents decided to build the country's first public railroad between their city and the Ohio River. Charles Carroll, by then the only surviving signatory of the Declaration of Independence, laid the cornerstone on 4 July 1828, and two years later the experimental engine *Tom Thumb*, weighing less than a ton and generating only 1.43hp, reached 18mph (29km/h) on 13 miles (21km/h) of Baltimore & Ohio track.

America's first (and the world's second) regular steam train service went into operation on Christmas Day 1830 on the South Carolina Canal & Railroad, when the *Best Friend of Charleston*, built at West Point Foundry in New York State, took a passenger train out of Charleston on a line built to transport cotton from central Georgia. US mail was first carried by train on the South Carolina Railroad in 1831. Completed three years later, the Charleston & Hamburg was for a time the world's longest railway (135 miles/217km).

Andrew Jackson became the first US president to travel by train when he boarded the Baltimore & Ohio in 1833. Two years later, the B&O opened the first route to Washington, DC. Author Charles Dickens would travel this route in 1842, as well as the Portage Railroad in central Pennsylvania, describing his experiences in *American Notes*:

'There is a gentleman's car and a ladies' car: the main distinction between which is that in the first, everybody smokes; and in the second, nobody does. As a black man never travels with a white one, there is also a negro car; which is a great, blundering, clumsy chest, such as Gulliver put to sea in, from the kingdom of Brobdingnag. The cars are like shabby omnibuses, but larger: holding thirty, forty, fifty, people. The seats, instead of stretching from end to end, are placed crosswise. Each seat holds two persons. There is a long row of them on each side of the caravan, a narrow passage up the middle, and a door at both ends. In the centre of the carriage there is usually a stove, fed with charcoal or anthracite coal; which is for the most part red-hot. It is insufferably close; and you see the hot air fluttering between yourself and any other object you may happen to look at, like the ghost of smoke.'

The Portage Railroad, the first to be built through the Allegheny Mountains, began operating in 1834. It included the first railroad tunnel in the United States, the Staple Bend Tunnel, 901ft (275m) long, located 4 miles (6km) east of Johnstown. Other lines soon followed, most notably the New York Central from Albany to Buffalo and the Philadelphia & Columbia (the first to be government-sponsored). Like most early lines, they served local needs and few people imagined the railway's full potential. Canal owners and road transport companies opposed them, partly on safety grounds, and doctors warned of the dangers inherent in such reckless speeds. Indeed, accidents did often happen. Few rights of way were fenced off and early railroad cars were little more than stagecoaches with flanged wheels, whose grip on the track was sometimes uncertain.

Despite these problems, total trackage increased to 3,000 miles by the early 1840s and to 9,000 miles (4,800–14,500km) by 1850 (when it was three times the length of the canal system). By the late 1850s, America had built half the world's railroad mileage in existence, and French traveller Guillaume Poussin wrote that 'the locomotive appears to be the personification of the American'. A railroad station was the first building in many towns and streets were often laid out parallel to the rail line.

Early locomotives such as *Tom Thumb* and the *Best Friend of Charleston* had upright boilers but these were soon replaced by engines using horizontal, English-style boilers which allowed greater capacity. Mid-century engines were most usually handsome American-type (4-4-0) wood burners, brightly painted and extravagantly decorated with polished brass. Other elegant innovations included a bell, whistle, headlight and pilot (or cowcatcher, invented by Charles Babbage and perfected by engineer Isaac Dripps). Bulbous chimneys reduced emissions and sparks, a cab gave weather protection to the crew and a sandbox was added to improve traction, allegedly after a plague of locusts on a line in Pennsylvania. Typical examples from this period can be seen in the 1903 silent film *The Great Train Robbery* and in D W Griffith's 1916 epic *Intolerance*.

The first ticket offices were at stagecoach stops or in hotels, but characteristic railroad depots soon developed, usually as one-storey buildings located parallel to the tracks. Large cantilevered canopies protected passengers and freight from inclement weather. Clock towers were often added at a later date as stations became more elaborate and companies adopted distinctive styles of architecture to make their railroads easily identifiable.

The New York Central brought together ten small railroads in the Northeast whose lines ran roughly parallel with the Erie Canal, later extending them to St Louis. The Erie Railroad went from the Hudson River north of New York to Lake Erie and Chicago, enabling New York City to enjoy fresh milk every day and consume more strawberries than anywhere else in the world. Chicago by this time had 11 railways and saw 70 trains a day, making it the busiest rail centre in the world.

From 1856, the Illinois Central linked Chicago to Cairo, at the junction of the Mississippi and Ohio rivers, with federal land grants assisting the line's construction through 700 miles (1,130km) of thinly populated country. The first railroad bridge across the Mississippi was at Davenport, Iowa. The Far West's first railway, the Sacramento Valley, opened in the same year between Sacramento and the gold mines at Folsom, after the locomotives *Sacramento* and *Nevada* arrived by sailing ship round Cape Horn. The first locomotive in the Pacific Northwest was the *Oregon Pony* (1862).

Southern railways made slower progress, but by the 1860s, 1,000 miles (1,600km) of track existed in each of Georgia, Tennessee and Virginia, and a network of lines served all states west of the Mississippi. This proved vital to both sides during the Civil War, when railroads and trains became major targets. In 1862, General Bragg's army of 30,000 men travelled nearly 800 miles (1,300km) to the key rail centre of Chattanooga from Mississippi by Confederate railway. The following year, 23,000 Union troops and their equipment journeyed 1,200 miles (1,900km) from Virginia to relieve Chattanooga. Their expedition took 12 days and required 30 trains with a total of 600 coaches. More than 35,000 lives were lost in bitter fighting before the battle ended. Later in the war, General Sherman's army of 100,000 men in Georgia needed 16 trains a day to keep it supplied. Without railways the North might never have broken Confederate resistance. Northern lines were better developed than those in the South and military traffic was given priority, but the Confederate government failed to take over responsibility for railroads in its territory. By the end of the Civil War, half the South's railroads were out of action while those in the North were more dominant than ever.

THE GOLDEN AGE

Even before the Civil War, railroads had come to represent unity for a country divided by geography and culture. In 1862, at a crucial time for the Union, President Lincoln signed the Pacific Railway Act making possible America's first transcontinental route. Abraham Lincoln had earlier played a part in railroad history in 1856, when as a young man he represented the Rock Island & Chicago Railroad, which had built the first bridge across the Mississippi River between Rock Island, Illinois, and Davenport, Iowa. Riverboat operators previously had a monopoly on the large-scale movement of passengers and goods and tried to block the bridge's construction (it was nicknamed 'Hell Gate of the Mississippi' in St Louis). Fifteen days after the bridge's gala opening, a steamboat, the *Effie Afton*, struck one of its piers and a stove on the boat overturned, setting fire to the bridge and causing extensive damage. The owners of the steamboat sued the railroad company but Lincoln brilliantly demonstrated that the accident occurred because the steamboat's starboard paddle wheel failed. He also stressed the vital importance of allowing railroads to span the Mississippi, saying that east-to-west travel was 'growing larger and larger, building up new countries with a rapidity never before seen in the history of the world'.

The Central Pacific Railroad set out to build a line eastwards from Sacramento, California, while the Union Pacific Railroad would go west from the Missouri River. Each company received generous federal loans and was given ownership of huge tracts of land – ten sections (each one mile square) for every completed mile. Despite experiencing the worst winter on record, with temperatures down to −40°C, track was laid at a phenomenal rate, using mostly Irish or ex-army labour on the Union Pacific and Chinese immigrants, paid between one and three dollars a day, on the Central Pacific (CP). The thousands of workers from Kwantung Province imported by the CP became known as 'Celestials' after their 'Celestial Kingdom' homeland. They were often lowered down sheer cliff faces in baskets attached to ropes to drill into rock, pack in explosives and light a fuse before making a rapid return up the rope. Many 'basket men' failed to make it to safety before the explosion took place. A total of 19 tunnels (15 of them on the Central Pacific) were blasted out of solid rock with black powder at the rate of 14 inches a day. Nitroglycerin was tried in 1867, but had to be abandoned when it was found to be dangerously unstable.

At ten spikes to the rail and 400 rails to the mile, it required approximately 21 million strokes of the hammer to complete the line. In 1867 alone, 235 miles of track were finished and in 1869 Charles Crocker's Central Pacific team won a $10,000 bet from Thomas Durant of the Union Pacific after 4,000 mostly Chinese workers each lifted more than 100 tons of steel using heavy tongs to lay 10 miles (16km) in a single day (still a record). Hundreds of horses and wagons were used in this well-drilled effort that required 25,800 ties (sleepers) and 3,520 rails. At one time the Union Pacific employed 10,000 labourers and an equal number of working animals. Hunters slaughtered vast quantities of buffalo to keep the workers supplied with meat and ramshackle tent towns sprang up along the way. These 'Hell on Wheels' settlements became notorious for land speculators, gambling, drinking and prostitution. Most collapsed as soon as the railroad moved on but some remained to become permanent towns.

Over 1,774 miles (2,860km) of track had been constructed by the time the two lines met ahead of schedule at desolate Promontory Point, north of Utah's Great Salt Lake. Half a million people, including newspapermen, dignitaries and railway employees (though Chinese labourers were specifically excluded), gathered on 10 May 1869 to watch the Golden Spike ceremony complete one of the greatest engineering feats of the century. The ceremony was rather disorganised, due partly to the size of the crowd. Leland Stanford of the Central Pacific had brought four ceremonial spikes, the famed 'Golden Spike' being presented by David Hewes, a San Francisco construction magnate. It was inscribed with the names of Central Pacific directors as well as the words 'The Last Spike' and 'May God continue the Unity of our Country as this Railroad unites the two great oceans of the world'.

A second gold spike was presented by the San Francisco *News Letter*, a silver spike by Nevada and a spike made from iron, silver and gold by Arizona. All four were dropped into a polished, pre-bored Californian laurel wood tie during the ceremony and at 12.47 the actual last spike – an ordinary iron one – was driven into a regular tie. The spike had been wired to send the sound of the strikes over the telegraph to the nation but Leland Stanford and the Union Pacific's Thomas Durant frequently missed their aim as they took turns to drive it home. A single word, 'done', was telegraphed to the nation anyway, resulting in widespread celebrations. Meanwhile, construction supervisors actually drove in the final spike. A beautifully engraved three-cent ultramarine stamp showing a Norris-type locomotive was issued in 1869 as part of a US Post Office 'pictorial' series. About 474 million were printed so this remains an affordable item for collectors.

The Central Pacific's *Jupiter* and the Union Pacific's *No 119* were present at the ceremony and replicas of both appear in the final scenes of John Ford's excellent 1924 pictorial history *The Iron Horse*. Cecil B DeMille told the story less convincingly in *Union Pacific*. The original 'Golden Spike' is now on display behind glass at Stanford University in Palo Alto, California. The temporary town of Promontory remained as a 'Hell on Wheels' settlement for a few weeks but never became a permanent city.

The first engines to cross the continent were the Central Pacific's *Success* and *Excelsior*, built by Rogers and delivered by rail. The first trains to carry passengers and cargo along the route ran on 11 May 1869, with emigrants travelling west and a consignment of Japanese teas going east. The *Jupiter* was scrapped for iron in

1901 and the Union Pacific's *No 119* went the same way two years later. The Lucin Cutoff took most traffic away from Promontory in 1904 and the last tie of laurel was destroyed in the 1906 San Francisco earthquake. The old rails over the 123-mile (197km) Promontory Summit line were salvaged in 1942 for the war effort in ceremonies marking the 'Undriving of the Golden Spike', when collectors picked over the area for ties and materials.

A re-enactment of the last spike ceremony took place in 1948, using miniature locomotives provided by the Southern Pacific, and in 1951 a monument to the event was erected at Ogden's Union Station. Congress established a seven-acre (2.8ha) piece of land as the Golden Spike National Historic Site and the National Golden Spike Society was formed to promote it. The site was enlarged to 2,176 acres (880ha) in 1965, and is now administered by the National Park Service. To mark the centennial of the transcontinental railroad, the Golden Spike Monument was moved 150ft (46m) northwest and the National Park Service began the reconstruction of two railroad and telegraph lines, together with switches and siding connections.

The engines used in the 1969 ceremonies were modified to resemble the originals and from then until 1980 the annual re-enactment used vintage locomotives on loan from Nevada. In 1980, with water from Liberty Island in New York Harbour and Fort Point in San Francisco Bay, two replica locomotives, built by Chadwell O'Connor Engineering of Costa Mesa, California, were introduced. Costing $1.5 million, these were the first steam engines to be manufactured in the United States for a quarter of a century, and today they operate from May until August and from Christmas to New Year's Day. Visitors can also walk and drive along the old grades and see exhibitions relating to the railroad's construction.

Elsewhere, the Southern Pacific linked southern California to New Orleans in 1883 and two years later the Atchison, Topeka & Santa Fe line ran from Kansas City to Los Angeles along the Southern Pacific route. Cross-country travel now took five days instead of a month. When the Santa Fe first reached Los Angeles only 10,000 people lived in southern California, but more soon arrived as competition brought fares from New York down to as little as $1. Many farmers in the South returned from the Civil War to find themselves homeless and impoverished and so took the only jobs they could find – building railroads. Being farmers, they were often referred to as 'hoe boys' or 'hobos'. Unable to settle, many later went on to wander the country, riding on the same rails they had built.

The Iron Horse began to open up the West and create rapid development in cities along the way, creating the foundations on which modern western states such as Washington, Idaho, Montana and Wyoming were constructed. The Union Pacific advertised five million acres (2,023,428ha) of farmland in Kansas and Colorado to prospective German immigrants. Colonisation agents were employed to recruit people in the East or from abroad, especially 'hard-working, thrifty' people from England, Scandinavia and the Netherlands, urging them to settle where the air was clean and the land dirt cheap. Some immigrants travelled west free, sharing a wagon with their personal belongings, livestock and machinery. Educational trains up to ten coaches long were sent out to teach farmers how to grow more and better crops – the Poultry Train featured a famous talking rooster. In a remarkably short time the railways transformed America's heartland into one of the most productive food-growing areas in the world.

Tourists also began to arrive as brochures promoted hunting and fishing trips as well as the scenery, abundant produce ('The King of Fruits – 150 recipes for Apple Dishes'), and settlement opportunities in the 'Golden West', 'where money grows on trees'. The Atchison, Topeka & Santa Fe Railway, commonly called the Santa

Fe, cleverly publicised its route along the Santa Fe Trail by naming its trains the *Chief* and *Superchief*. Their exotic interiors were decorated with rare woods such as Macassar ebony and African rosewood and the company used the slogan 'see Indian country by train' on its calendars and posters. Native Americans were recruited to present a romanticised picture of the West and artists were commissioned to paint both landscape and people. Detours were made, allowing urban Americans to see the outback for the first time and feel a sense of adventure as they overcame their fear of the West. The first brochures were published to tell passengers what they would be seeing en route. Koch and Oakley's *Railway and Navigation Guide*, published in the 1890s, advised: 'Keep your temper and don't get left at the water tank where you have alighted to enjoy the mountain scenery.'

Other railways tried different means to attract passengers, selling or giving away such items as ashtrays, letter openers, match safes, spoons and scissors. Almost anything which could be stamped with a name or slogan was tried, including paperweights in the shape of locomotives or, in one instance, an Idaho baking potato. Such promotional items are now greatly sought after by rail fans, as are early books, posters, timetables, railroad songs and train recordings. Some people collect hardware such as destination signs, lanterns, silverware, locks, keys, telegraph instruments and hand brakes, or even bricks from demolished stations.

The Northern Pacific Railroad opened up the Northwest in the 1880s and acquired more land than has been owned by any other single company in the United States. In 1883, the company's charismatic president, Henry Villard, spent nearly a quarter of a million dollars to celebrate the railway's completion. He invited financiers, newspaper reporters and dignitaries from Europe, as well as hundreds of American politicians, bankers, railroad officials, investors and journalists. Five trainloads of guests, including former president Ulysses S Grant, converged on Gold Creek, west of Helena, where a sign read 'Lake Superior 1,198 miles, Puget Sound 847 miles'. Sitting Bull spoke in Sioux through a translator in a speech that began: 'I hate all white people. You are thieves and liars.' The interpreter hastily improvised flowery compliments in English and the speech was greeted with rapturous applause, much to Sitting Bull's amusement.

James J Hill built a similar transcontinental route, the Great Northern, between St Paul, Minnesota and Seattle. Born in Rockwood, Ontario, the clever, determined and obsessive Hill arrived in St Paul by steamboat in 1856 and started working for the Mississippi River Steamboat Company, fixing freight and passenger rates. After the Civil War he joined the St Paul & Pacific Railroad, which he later bought. He also advised on the construction of the Canadian Pacific but resigned when he saw that it would become a competitor to his own transcontinental line, which he built without government funds or loans: 'Most men who have really lived have had their great adventure. The railway is mine.'

Construction of the Great Northern reached Great Falls in 1887, the fast rate of laying track being ensured by excellent planning and the use of 8,000 men and 3,300 teams of horses. Immigrants were carried west for $10 provided they agreed to settle along the route and farmers were offered free pedigree Angus cattle imported from Scotland. Boxcars full of the best seed grains were distributed to improve yields. More than 6 million acres (2,428,000ha) of Montana were settled in two years and the line reached Puget Sound in 1893. The success of his railroad meant that Hill was able to take over the Northern Pacific in 1896.

Unlike the Great Northern, most railroad construction west of the Mississippi received federal land grants, eventually totalling 131 million acres (53,000,000ha). Rail companies charged reduced rates for government traffic in return. As well as the four great transcontinental routes, many smaller lines were built throughout the West and by 1890, a network of 164,000 miles (264,000km) covered virtually the whole country. Few Americans then lived more than 25 miles (40km) from the track. Large, often grandiose, new stations opened at South Street, Boston (1890), St Louis (1894), Washington, DC (1907) and New York (Pennsylvania 1910, Grand Central 1913).

The Pennsylvania Railroad (PRR, sometimes known as the 'Pennsy') was established in 1846 in Philadelphia and began as a rail line connecting Harrisburg to Pittsburgh. By 1882 it was the largest railroad in the world, with a budget second only to the US government. During the first half of the 20th century, the PRR owned 10,000 miles (16,000km) of track, having acquired or merged with over 800 other lines, and carried three times more traffic than any other comparable railroad.

Standard-gauge track and Standard Time (adopted in 1883, replacing 100 local times) helped integration. The four time zones were eventually adopted more generally by Congress in 1918. Railroad timekeeping became so good that farmers set their clocks according to passing trains. Safety innovations included air brakes and automatic coupling. Trains became longer, faster and more efficient as coal-burning engines replaced less powerful wood burners. 'American' types gave way to heavier Atlantics (4-4-2) and Pacifics (4-6-2). Refrigerated wagons were introduced to ship beef from Chicago and oranges from Florida as the railways brought increasing control over nature.

Compressed gas and electricity superseded candlelight in passenger carriages and hot-water heating replaced wood-burning stoves after the Civil War, with corridors and steam heat arriving by the turn of the century. The paint on these new, 85ft-long (25m) coaches was varnished to make it shiny, and the word 'varnish' is still slang for a First-Class passenger car. Express services for passengers and special freight were introduced as the economy grew at an ever greater pace.

Sleeping and dining cars, rarely seen before the Civil War, afterwards became much more common. George Pullman's $20,000 *Pioneer* sleeper boasted thick carpets, chandeliers, polished walnut, crimson plush upholstery and marble wash-stands. Pullman, originally a cabinet maker by trade, instructed his craftsmen to build 'palaces on wheels' in which the wealthy would wish to travel. More than 2,000 were in operation by 1893. The owner of the Penn Railroad was one of the first to buy a lavishly equipped private coach complete with drawing room, dining room and private galley. Delmonico dining cars, introduced in 1868, meant passengers no longer had to snatch hurried meals at scheduled stops along the way. Parlour cars, forerunners of present-day lounge and club cars, also went into service at about this time. The first transcontinental train of Pullman cars took eight days to travel from Boston to San Francisco in 1870. The rich could buy their own lavish private luxury vehicle equipped as they chose, sometimes with marble baths, Venetian glass mirrors and a secret safe. J P Morgan had an open log-burning fire and rail baron Jay Gould's four private carriages included one for a cow that provided fresh milk. The super-rich could also hire an entire 'hotel train', complete with barber shop and dance floor.

Railroads became America's first big business, dominating economic life for three-quarters of a century, but the golden age had its less appealing aspects. Train routes made obsolete the Pony Express, the overland stagecoach, and much of the Mississippi riverboat trade. They devastated wildlife, brought the bison to near-extinction, and helped destroy a way of life for many Native Americans. Unionisation brought better pay, at least for train crews, but a dispute on the Baltimore & Ohio in 1877 spread to other companies and resulted in riots. Following wage cuts, a strike at the Pullman factory in 1894 led to sympathy action throughout the Midwest. Rail traffic in America came to a halt as the dispute turned violent. People were threatened, property burned and at least 34 people died when the government sent in 12,000 troops to break up the strike. Union leader Eugene Debs was jailed.

Fraud, corruption and coercion became commonplace. The huge profits attracted a profusion of crooks and bribery sometimes appeared the only way to get business done. Owners often bought up newspapers, politicians and even the law. Jay Gould, 'Commodore' Cornelius Vanderbilt ('the public interest be damned') and the Central Pacific's 'scrupulously dishonest' Collis Huntington were famous for their ruthlessness. 'Jubilee Jim' Fisk defrauded Erie Railroad stockholders of $64 million. Competition increased in some places but the railways too often exploited their monopoly and public opinion turned against them. The Interstate Commerce Commission was set up in 1887 to control their excesses and the financier Pierpoint Morgan, whose business fortune was said to total more than the combined value of all other property in the 22 states west of the Mississippi, was surprised and hurt when forced to break up his railroad empire. As Theodore Roosevelt commented: 'A man who has never gone to school may steal from a freight car; but if he has a university education, he may steal the whole railroad.'

In 1868, with the first transcontinental line near completion, the great American writer, politician and political economist Henry George predicted that trains would alter California for ever: 'It will not merely open a new route across the continent; it will be the means of converting a wilderness into a populous empire in less time than many of the cathedrals and palaces of Europe were built.' He foresaw that it would lead to great wealth concentrated in the hands of a relatively small number of people. The Central Pacific and Union Pacific were the two largest corporations in the country and the revered and reviled 'Big Four' grew immensely rich from their investment.

Nevertheless, the country had reason to be grateful for the railroads. They brought prosperity, opened up the West, carried the mail and helped turn the United States into a major world power. Ralph Waldo Emerson wrote that, 'the old universe was thrown on to the ash-heap and a new one created'. Railroads changed perceptions of time and space, measuring distance not by miles but by hours and minutes. They made many people rich and gave even penniless hobos a means of transport they could afford. Trains became an indelible part of national culture, inspiring countless stories and featuring in folk songs, blues, jazz, country and gospel music, from 1859's 'North Western Railway Polka' to Johnny Cash's 'Rock Island Line' and 'Wreck of The Old 97'. 'Midnight Special' was one of many songs in which a train symbolised the American desire for escape. 'Bound For Glory', 'Heavenbound Train' and 'Downbound Train' made the railway journey a metaphor for life. On 'The Black Diamond Express To Hell', Sin was the engineer, Pleasure the headlight and the conductor was the Devil. 'Big Rock Candy Mountain' was originally a hobo song, later sanitised for children, and it was down by the railroad track that Johnny B Goode learnt to play guitar so well.

The first American narrative film, *The Great Train Robbery*, was directed in 1903 by Edwin S Porter. Its action-packed plot was inspired by a real-life robbery that took place in August 1900, when four members of the 'Hole in the Wall' gang led by Robert Leroy Parker (Butch Cassidy) held up the *No 3* train on Union Pacific Railroad tracks near Table Rock, Wyoming. They made the conductor uncouple the passenger cars from the rest of the train, blew up the mail car safe and escaped with $5,000 in cash. Instead of the 10-minute-long film being made in Wyoming, it was shot at Thomas Edison's New York studio and on part of the Lackawanna and Western Railroad. *The Great Train Robbery* starred the world's first cinematic cowboy hero, Gilbert M 'Bronco Billy' Anderson, along with Billy Whiskers, Marie Murray and George Barnes.

Trains have featured in countless movies in the century since, including classics such as *Double Indemnity*, *Butch Cassidy and the Sundance Kid*, Alfred Hitchcock's *Strangers on a Train*, and 2004's IMAX 3D animation, *The Polar Express*.

THE 20TH CENTURY

By 1900, there were 1,000 railroad companies and 193,000 miles (310,600km) of track. More than a million people worked on the railroads – one out of every 23 Americans – and the USA probably had the best trains in the world. The New York Central's *Twentieth Century Limited* – 'a gentlemen's club on rails' – was inaugurated on the Water Level route in 1902, becoming the fastest and most luxurious way to travel between New York and Chicago. The *Twentieth Century* was the pride of the fleet and a national institution, its name synonymous with prestige and comfort. This train gave the world the expression 'red-carpet treatment', as at New York and Chicago stations a 260ft-long (79m) carpet bearing the New York Central's logo would be rolled out for passengers. Every other transcontinental route also had its prestige train intended to impress. Such rolling palaces on wheels included the Great Northern's *Oriental Limited* and later its *Empire Builder*. Northern Pacific's *North Coast Limited* boasted a clothes-pressing service, a barber, shower rooms and a buffet serving 'fine cigars and beverages'. The Union Pacific had its *City of Portland* and the Milwaukee Road's *Olympian* featured a Parlour car with a powerful moveable floodlight with which to view the scenery by night. The Florida East Coast Railway's *Florida Special* had a pre-dinner string quartet and swimsuited models to entertain passengers. Another luxury train, the *Overland Limited*, provided passengers with fresh flowers and Persian carpets and served champagne for breakfast.

By the late 1920s, most city-to-city travel was by rail, with more than 15,000 passenger trains running every day over 254,000 miles (405,000km) of track. The peak was reached in 1929, when 20,000 passenger trains operated every day – one for every 600 Americans – and nearly two million people were employed by the railroads. The 1932 film *Union Depot* gives a vivid picture of the atmosphere inside a busy station of the time. Traders gathered at stations to sell their wares and card sharps often made a living out of cheating naive passengers, resulting in notices warning people not to play cards with strangers – still good advice.

In the beginning, the Pullman Company would hire only African-American men for the job of porter, which was eventually to have significant cultural and political consequences when A Philip Rudolph used the power of the labour union to demand substantial social changes for African-Americans. The Brotherhood of Sleeping Car Porters, which he founded, became the first African-American union to gain a contract with a major US corporation. Rudolph later went on to become an important figure in the 1960s civil rights movement.

The 20th century brought other dramatic changes. In a sign of things to come, 1916 saw more than three million automobiles registered in the USA. Over-expansion by the railroads led to financial problems, though these were temporarily disguised when World War I made heavy demands for the movement of freight and people. President Wilson set up the Railroad Administration to put the whole network under government control. With this extra workload the unions became more powerful, demanding an 8-hour day and the end of piecework. Over 100,000 women were recruited, mostly in clerical positions, though nearly all would lose their jobs when the railroads became private again after the war.

Many of the women recruited during World War II were given more responsible jobs and some remained for another 40 years. A few women had worked on the railways ever since the mid-19th century, sometimes making a living as professional gamblers. Former slave women sold food to passengers on the Chesapeake & Ohio line and attractive women were always in demand to christen a new engine or stretch of track.

Engines continued to become more efficient as 'compounding' (using steam more than once) and 'articulation', together with huge Mallet-type locomotives, allowed prodigious numbers of freight cars to be moved in a single train. Larger fireboxes and 'superheating' also improved productivity. Steam railroads served almost every large community by 1920, and were augmented by many local electric and street railways providing passenger services and encouraging cities to expand.

As the 20th century progressed, diesel replaced steam as the chief source of power. Steam engine numbers reached a peak of 72,000 in the 1920s, but no more were put into service after 1953. The last regular service operating under steam was on the Norfolk & Western in April 1960. The first successful diesel service had been the streamlined *Pioneer Zephyr*, which in 1935 averaged 77.5mph (125km/h) on its inaugural run from Denver to Chicago. Streamliner designers boasted that they took their engines from trucks and their styling from automobiles. These trains were undeniably luxurious but rarely attracted enough passengers to pay their way.

Railroads were badly hit by the Great Depression. Passenger traffic in 1932 was less than two-thirds of the total in 1929. Freight tonnage and railroad employment almost halved. Increasing numbers of hobos rode boxcars and flats to search for work. A million Americans are thought to have 'caught out' (jumped) trains during the 1930s, although it was a dangerous pursuit and thousands died from being crushed between carriages or falling from moving trains. Around a quarter of a million teenagers hopped freight trains at the height of the Depression, joining the adult drifters who wandered from town to town. In makeshift hobo camps called 'jungles', these teenaged transients would often encounter prostitution, gambling and violence. The number of adolescents on freight trains became an epidemic that inspired the 1933 Hollywood film, *Wild Boys of the Road*, which aimed to show the dangers of such a life. For some, the movie had the opposite effect, encouraging them to catch the next freight train out of their home town.

Even today, 'riding the rods' offers the chance to travel free and hobo encampments can sometimes be seen alongside the track. 'First Class' hobo travel means a boxcar offering protection from the elements and great panoramic views through the open doors. A wise hobo stays near the front of the car so that he is not thrown out of the door if the train suddenly stops. He tries never to walk between the rails, cross under couplers or carriages, 'catch out on the fly' (jump on a moving train) or join anyone else in a boxcar. Other hobo slang includes: accommodation car – the caboose of a train; angelina – a young inexperienced hobo; banjo – a small portable frying pan; bindle stick – belongings wrapped in cloth and tied around a stick; bone polisher – a mean dog; cannonball – a fast train; catch the westbound – to die; cow crate – a railroad stock car; crums – lice; doggin' it – travelling by bus; road kid – a young hobo learning the ways of the road; rum dum – a drunkard; soup bowl – a place to get soup, bread and drinks; yegg – a travelling professional thief.

Being a hobo remains hazardous and many were horrifically murdered during the 1990s in a series of killings for which there have been few arrests. Hobos such as Danville Dan, Steamtrain Maury and Guitar Whitey continued to ride the rails in the 1960s and 1970s, sharing food, cigarettes and alcohol as they roamed 200,000 miles (320,000km) of track across the land. Evading the 'bulls' (railroad security guards), they became part of an underworld culture that would later attract students, accountants and other 'weekend riders' looking for thrills. Writer James Michener described this as 'the last red-blooded American adventure'.

As the century progressed, mass car ownership, improved highways and air travel took away rail traffic, reducing revenues. America was the world's first nation to transfer its affection from trains to the automobile. Almost 98% of intercity passengers travelled by rail in 1916, and in 1920 the US rail network carried a record 1.2 billion passengers. By 1975 numbers were down to 6% and falling. Freight traffic also declined, although less rapidly.

Despite improved efficiency and lower wages, railways increasingly ran into massive deficit. By the end of the Depression half were bankrupt and many of those which remained were only rescued, temporarily, by World War II. Military and civilian traffic in 1944 totalled an amazing 97 billion miles (155 billion kilometres), stretching resources to breaking point. Retired railway workers and old wooden railroad cars were brought back to help the war effort. After the war the locomotive fleet was mostly worn out and there was a dramatic fall in business. More streamlined trains were introduced, along with domed observation cars, high-level seating and economy sleepers. The Santa Fe slogan was: 'If you want to feel like a star, travel like a star', and for a while the railways continued to carry more traffic than all other means of transport put together. The Interstate Commerce Commission insisted that they operate passenger services but by 1970 only 500 intercity trains were left.

By 1962, freight traffic was lower than at any time since the Depression. Tracks started turning to rust as railways merged or were forced into bankruptcy. The greatest collapse was that of the Penn Central (formed only two years earlier) in 1970. Ironically, the last time many lines made a profit was when hauling concrete to build the new interstate highways. To stay in business, the Union Pacific halved its workforce and increased productivity by 55% in less than ten years. Federal government, under pressure to save America's trains, passed the 1970 Rail Passenger Service Act, and a year later the Railroad Passenger Corporation set up Amtrak (short for American Trackage) to take over most long-distance passenger routes. The Southern Railway, the Denver & Rio Grande Western, the Reading, the Georgia, the Chicago, South Shore & South Bend, and the Chicago, Rock Island & Pacific were the only lines to stay independent, but most gave up their passenger services soon afterwards. The Chicago, Rock Island & Pacific line, which last saw trains more than 20 years ago, has been leased by the Union Pacific Railroad to the Missouri Central Railroad, which hopes to restore freight and possibly passenger trains.

The dire state of the freight industry in the early 1970s also forced the government to set up Conrail (the Consolidated Rail Corporation) to take over six bankrupt railroads in the Northeast. An estimated $13 billion in subsidy was spent before the company was privatised in 1987. Like other private rail companies, Conrail shed labour, cut costs and sought new business. Services and revenues gradually improved, helped by a change in the government regulations which had put railroads at a disadvantage to truckers. Freight could now be transferred more easily between trains, trucks and ships. Containers gave faster delivery times and rates were cut by two-thirds. More powerful and efficient locomotives were introduced, train crew size reduced and unprofitable routes abandoned or sold, leaving the remaining lines more profitable. For the first time in decades, business found it could save on transport costs by using rail instead of road. Consequently, since the mid-1980s, haulage has increased by a third and revenues have reached more than $31 billion.

This remarkable recovery has led to a series of mergers, resulting in further cost savings as fewer freight cars need to be shunted into sidings or change trains before reaching their destination. From 31 rail companies in 1980 there are now seven, four of which control 90% of the traffic. The Burlington Northern and Santa Fe joined forces in 1995 to form the Burlington Northern Santa Fe Railroad (BNSF), and in 1996 the Union Pacific and Southern Pacific merged to create Union Pacific, the largest and most powerful transport organisation in the world. Conrail was valued at $10 billion in 1997 when its operations were competed for by the CSX and Norfolk Southern. In 2009, investment guru Warren Buffett paid $44 billion for the Burlington Northern Santa Fe, which owns 390 railroad lines in the United States. Each Burlington Northern train takes 280 trucks off the highways. Explaining his biggest ever deal, Buffett said that: 'Our country's future prosperity depends on its having an efficient and well-maintained rail system.'

Today's railroads employ 192,000 people to maintain and operate almost 200,000 miles of track, with 26,000 locomotives pulling 1.6 million freight and passenger cars. More rational line usage by freight companies should result in fewer delays for Amtrak passengers and the corporation's future seems much more assured. New equipment and other improvements continue to be introduced and Amtrak has received more than $15 billion from the government since 1971. Amtrak's management personnel numbers have been cut by over a third in recent years and the workforce as a whole by several thousand, making it one of the world's most efficient rail operators.

Even in the age of cyberspace, trains still have their uses. President Bill Clinton took a four-day train journey through West Virginia, Kentucky, Ohio, Indiana and Michigan on his way to the 1996 Democratic convention in Chicago, travelling aboard the *21st Century Express* on the kind of whistle-stop campaign not seen since the days of Harry Truman. The bullet-proof royal-blue car with gold curtains and dark wooden panelling had formerly been used by Franklin Roosevelt.

Before President-elect Barack Obama took office he made a point of using the same privately owned Georgia 300 railcar on his inaugural weekend to travel from Philadelphia to Washington, DC's Union Station, primarily because Abraham Lincoln also came by train along this route in 1861. Lincoln travelled for 12 days all the way to Washington, DC from the state capital of Springfield, Illinois, where Obama announced his presidential bid in 2007. President Obama always championed the railroads and voted to support state investment. When he was a senator, Vice President Joe Biden returned home to Wilmington from Washington, DC by train almost every night for three decades to be with his sons after his first wife and daughter were killed in a car crash.

President Obama's decision to make this symbolic journey was at first resisted by officials on security grounds as the ten-car 'Obama Express' stopped in Wilmington (where Joe Biden and his family boarded) and Baltimore (where 40,000 people turned out for a rally) and made several 'slow rolls' through places where large crowds of onlookers had gathered on a bitingly cold day. The coach was fitted with internet facilities for the trip, on which the new president was accompanied by his family, journalists and a number of hand-picked 'everyday Americans'.

When terrorists attacked and destroyed New York City's World Trade Center on 11 September 2001, Amtrak trains continued to operate throughout the crisis, bringing crucial emergency supplies and personnel to the scene. Trains also played a vital role in the recovery efforts after the devastation caused by Hurricane Katrina in 2005. The New Orleans terminal was spared major damage – at one point it was used as a temporary jail – and Amtrak was able to start moving residents from the city when a special 12-car train arrived from Baton Rouge able to carry 600 passengers. Food and water were loaded on to the train before it left for New

Orleans. By the Monday after the hurricane, Amtrak was able to operate four runs a day and would later provide the first commercial transportation out of the city with the departures of the *City of New Orleans* to Memphis and Chicago and the *Crescent* to Atlanta and New York.

President Donald Trump planned to end subsidies for long-distance trains but Richard White, President of the American Public Transportation Association, argued that the American economy and communities of all sizes would be losers. Opinion polls suggest that three out of four Americans support increased public transportation investment, and a November 2016 election poll found that 81% of Americans who voted for Donald Trump oppose any cuts to the current levels of public transportation investment. Amtrak covers an unprecedented 94% of its annual operating costs from revenue, so any change in policy would essentially be politically motivated.

As well as providing such essential services, environment-friendly trains relieve traffic congestion and conserve energy. They use fuel efficiently, are not greedy for land and encourage economic growth. They are also the most enjoyable way to see America, which has some of the world's finest long-distance routes, and by using them as often as possible you help ensure their survival and prosperity.

AMTRAK TRAINS TODAY

The system Amtrak inherited in 1971 was dilapidated after being starved of investment for many years. Rolling stock was falling apart, roadbeds were crumbling, stations were dangerous and staff, not surprisingly, felt demoralised. The corporation initially served just 340 cities, with 21 routes operating over 20,000 miles (32,000km) of track. Most employees still worked for the rail companies Amtrak had taken over and continuing losses seemed inevitable. Things improved surprisingly quickly, though, as extra trains were scheduled and modern equipment purchased. In 1971, Amtrak announced a schedule of 184 trains, serving 314 destinations, and services began on 1 May that year, when *Clocker No 235* departed New York Penn Station at 00.05 bound for Philadelphia. Train reservations and tickets were still laboriously written by hand until Amtrak introduced an automatic system with computerised ticketing, well before airlines caught on to the same development. In efforts towards greater efficiency Amtrak has also introduced a mobile satellite communications and tracking system to link trains and support facilities.

Since the beginning, most even-numbered trains have travelled north and east and odd-numbered trains travel south and west. Exceptions include *Pacific Surfliners*, which use the opposite numbering system inherited from their former operator, the Santa Fe Railway, and some Empire Corridor trains.

Amtrak's slogan – 'the tracks are back' – was emblazoned on everything from lapel badges to bumper stickers. Stations were spruced up and made secure, running times significantly improved and staff again had reason to be cheerful. In Amtrak's first year passengers travelled over 3 billion miles (4.8 billion kilometres), rediscovering historic trains like the *California Zephyr* and *Sunset Limited*. Many trains operate like first-class mobile hotels, with room service, overnight shoeshines and mints left on your pillow by the sleeping-car attendant.

Conrail (since acquired by CSX and the Norfolk Southern Railway) took over six bankrupt railroads in the Northeast in 1976 and allowed Amtrak to acquire its first tracks. The corporation today owns 730 route miles (1,175km; about 3% of the total nationwide). This primarily consists of the electrified Boston–New York–Washington, DC route and some routes in Michigan. In other parts of the country, Amtrak trains use tracks owned by freight railroads. Its largest hosts are BNSF (6.8 million train miles; 10.9 million kilometres), Union Pacific (6.19 million train miles; 9.96 million kilometres), and CSX (5.9 million train miles; 9.5 million kilometres). Amtrak owns 18 tunnels consisting of 24 miles (38km) of track and 1,414 bridges. In co-operation with contract railroads and local government, 30 new stations have been built and 35 others renovated.

Heavy maintenance facilities are located in Wilmington and Bear (Delaware) and Beech Grove (Indiana), and there are other maintenance facilities in Boston, Chicago, Hialeah (Florida), Los Angeles, New Orleans, New York City, Oakland, Rensselaer (New York), Seattle and Washington, DC.

Employee numbers have risen from 1,200 in 1972 to approximately 20,000 today. Amtrak has 20 *Acela Express* high-speed trainsets and 1,236 other railroad cars, plus 80 *Auto Train* vehicle carriers and 80 baggage cars, and operates 330 locomotives. Amtrak Cascades service operates with seven trainsets with cars owned by Amtrak and the states of Oregon and Washington. In 2016, Amtrak received the last of 70 new Amtrak Cities Sprinter electric locomotives ordered from Siemens for $466 million for use on the NEC and Harrisburg Line. Amtrak also anticipates arrival of new single-level dining and sleeping cars that are part of a 130-car order over five years in a $298.1 million contract awarded to the CAF assembly plant in Elmira, New York. The cars are similar to the Viewliner and will include 25 sleeping cars, 25 diners, 55 baggage cars and 25 baggage/dormitory cars. This is the first step in Amtrak's plan to replace its entire fleet of passenger cars and locomotives over the next 30 years.

In 2010, Amtrak announced a 30-year plan to invest $117 billion in deploying high-speed rail in the Northeast Corridor, narrowing the commuting time between Washington, DC and New York City from 162 minutes to 96 minutes and the commuting time between New York City and Boston from 215 minutes to 84 minutes. In 2016 it contracted with Alstom to produce 28 next-generation high-speed trainsets that will replace the equipment used to provide the *Acela Express* service. The contract is part of $2.45 billion that will be invested on the NEC as part of a modernisation programme to renew and expand the *Acela Express* service. The trainsets will operate initially at speeds up to 160mph (257 km/h) and will be capable of speeds up to 186mph (299 km/h). The manufacture of the trainsets will create 400 jobs in upstate New York. Parts for the new equipment will come from over 350 suppliers in more than 30 states, generating an additional 1,000 jobs. The first trainset should enter revenue service in 2021, and all trainsets are expected to be in service by the end of 2022. Amtrak is also investing in infrastructure, including significant improvements at Washington Union Station and Moynihan Station New York.

In 2021, Amtrak celebrates the 50th anniversary of its formation. It operates up to 300 trains on weekdays, excluding commuter trains, and carries more than 85,700 passengers, with trains running every minute of the year. In 2017, Amtrak posted record ridership (31.7 million passenger trips), revenue ($3.2 billion) and operating earnings ($194 million). It also achieved a new record for cost recovery, covering 94.7% of its operating costs with ticket sales and other revenues. On average nearly twice as many passengers travel on an Amtrak train than on a domestic airline flight. No country in the world operates a passenger rail system without some form of public support for capital costs and/or operating expenses. Amtrak was named in *Forbes* magazine's 2018 list of America's best employers, its fourth straight year of such recognition, based on the magazine's independent survey of 30,000 people who work for large firms or institutions who rated their willingness to recommend their own companies on a scale of 0 to 10.

Amtrak's customer-focused improvements underway include: refreshed trains (refurbishing the interiors of more than 450 coaches), new fare discounts, enhanced Wi-Fi, improved schedules, seat assignments allowing customers to select their preferred seat before travelling, better facilities at major stations, expanded communications (offering real-time and frequent information via social media, specifically ✈@AmtrakNEC), additional Thruway connections and expansion to more cities, and extra mobility options. Less welcome changes include discontinuing station agents in many towns across America. Amtrak's Northeast Corridor is the busiest railway in North America, carrying over 12 million passengers a year. More than 2,600 trains operate over some portion of the Washington, DC–Boston route each day. More than a quarter of a million riders every weekday generate more than 4.4 million daily passenger miles. The busiest Amtrak stations are in New York, Washington, DC, Philadelphia, Chicago, Los Angeles, Boston, Sacramento, Baltimore and San Diego.

In addition to its Northeast Corridor services, Amtrak carried 15 million passengers on state-supported services in 2017 and 4.6 million passengers on long-distance routes. Trains travel to most cities in 46 states and the District of Columbia. The states not served are Alaska, Hawaii, South Dakota and Wyoming, although Wyoming does have Amtrak Thruway buses. There are plans also to serve such places as Las Vegas, Abilene, Louisville, Boise and Nashville, and for a luxury transcontinental route (60 hours from coast to coast). Other possibilities include more Midwestern trains out of Chicago, an *Aztec Eagle* train from San Antonio to Monterey in Mexico, and the reintroduction of the *Pioneer* route between Chicago and Seattle.

More people each month are turning to trains as a convenient and enjoyable alternative to congested highways and crowded airports. Of the 510 communities currently served by Amtrak, 130 have no air service, 113 are without intercity buses and 35 have neither air nor bus services. Altogether, 65 million people a year in the USA travel by train and without them there would be 167,000 more cars on the road.

Amtrak is the country's largest provider of contract-commuter services for state and regional authorities, and an average of nearly 925,000 people every weekday depend on commuter rail services that use Amtrak-owned infrastructure or ride commuter trains operated by Amtrak under contracts with local or regional agencies. Commuter services are provided for Caltrain (California), Coasters (California), Maryland Area Regional Commuter (MARC), Metrolink (California), Shoreline East (Connecticut) and Virginia Railway Express (VRE).

Amtrak also provides maintenance services for the Sounder Commuter Rail system in the Seattle area.

An early economic-stimulus bill placed before Congress by President Obama included a commitment of $8 billion to construct high-speed rail systems – the most dramatic national pledge to rail since the Pacific Railway Act under President Lincoln. This was intended to be the first stage in a six-year, $53 billion high-speed rail investment plan to modernise the national system with intercity rail hubs. One prime corridor candidate for upgrading is the Chicago-centred Midwest network including St Louis, Cleveland, St Paul–Minneapolis and Detroit. Other candidates include the Pacific Northwest (Seattle–Portland–Eugene), South Central (San Antonio–Dallas–Tulsa), Florida (Miami–Orlando–Tampa), Northern New England/New York (Boston–Springfield–Albany–Buffalo) and Southeast–Gulf Coast (Raleigh–Charlotte–Atlanta–New Orleans–Houston).

In 2017, Amtrak appointed Richard H Anderson as President and co-Chief Executive Officer (with Wick Moorman), the 11th executive to lead America's railroad since the company began operations in 1971.

The Rail Passengers Association (RPA), formerly known as the National Association of Railroad Passengers (NARP), is the largest national advocacy organisation for train and rail transit passengers (w *railpassengers.org*). It aims to expand the quality and quantity of passenger rail in the United States and has around 20,000 members, whose benefits include excellent newsletters, 10% discounts on most Amtrak fares and the Grand Canyon Railway, and an 'I'd Rather Be On The Train' bumper sticker. The association acts as a voice for train passengers – particularly Amtrak customers, but also commuter rail and rail transit riders – on Capitol Hill, before the US Department of Transportation, and before Amtrak management. It has provided consistent backing for every positive development in American intercity passenger train service since the creation of Amtrak and its concerted efforts have saved routes like the *Texas Eagle* from what once seemed to be certain demise. The RPA is the only organisation with a broad vision for an expanded passenger train network.

Newsletters about current Amtrak activities can also be found on the websites of Friends of Amtrak (w *trainweb.org/crocon/amtrak.html*) and the National Corridors Initiative (w *nationalcorridors.org*).

SEND US YOUR SNAPS!

We'd love to follow your adventures using our *USA by Rail* guide – why not tag us in your photos and stories via Twitter (🐦 *@BradtGuides*) and Instagram (📷 *@bradtguides*)? Alternatively, you can upload your photos directly to the gallery on the USA destination page via our website (w *bradtguides.com/usa*).

Train Practicalities

AMTRAK FACILITIES AND SERVICES

TICKETS Coach Class is the standard Amtrak ticket. Business Class, available mainly on *Acela*/Northeast Corridor routes, and First-Class services, on *Acela* only, offer extra facilities (see *Equipment* later in this chapter, page 25). Sleeping-car accommodation is also First Class. Since most long-distance trains require advance reservations you normally have to reserve and purchase separate tickets if you wish to break your journey en route. Business Class, available on some trains in the Northeast, Midwest and on Empire services, provides coaches with more room around the seats and extra facilities such as changing rooms and telephones.

Fares naturally depend on the distance travelled and standard of service provided, though special offers, seasonal rates and excursion deals often provide big reductions. Ticket prices are often 50% or 75% less than the equivalent air fare, especially if you travel off-peak. This may be influenced by the season, day of the week or time of day, depending on the route. Check Amtrak's website (**w** *amtrak. com*) or your travel agent for news of the current special deals. Sleeping-car accommodation is always charged for in addition to the journey fare.

Up to two accompanied children aged two–12 pay half fare (limited to two half fares per adult) and those aged under two travel free if they share an adult's seat. Passengers 12 years of age and younger must travel with an adult passenger who is at least 18 years old. There are further reductions for group travel, a group being 20 people or more. You can buy one-way standard-rate tickets on board but a penalty will be added if the ticket office was open at the time of your departure. Passengers holding a valid **VetRewards Card** receive a 15% discount on most Amtrak trains. For information on discounts for children, students, senior citizens and group travel, see page 31. Where space is available you can upgrade accommodation on board, including sleepers and Business Class, and sometimes obtain a discount on the usual rate. Ask the conductor or chief of on-board services. Tickets can be delivered by mail if paid for by credit card but Amtrak accepts no responsibility for lost, stolen or destroyed tickets.

Quik-Trak self-service machines with touch-screen menus are now in use at most major stations. These accept credit and debit cards and enable you to purchase Coach-Class tickets to any city listed on the machine. You can also pick up tickets for previously made reservations by entering your reservation number.

All ticket information can be found on Amtrak's award-winning website.

RESERVATIONS Coach seating on unreserved trains is not guaranteed and is allocated on a first-come, first-served basis. Coach Class and all First Class and sleeping-car accommodation on all-reserved trains should be booked well in advance, particularly during summer when some routes may be very busy. If travelling overnight through particularly scenic areas try to make your departure

Each of the routes in this book gives details of a different long-distance Amtrak train. Scheduled stops are shown in ALL CAPITALS in black letters, followed by figures in parentheses giving the time from the previous stop and to the next stop. Other towns and places of interest en route are shown in lower case and are also followed by figures in parentheses but trains do not actually stop in these places, eg: Kent (↑20/32↓). This shows that when you are travelling in the direction described in the text you will pass through Kent 20 minutes after departing from the previous scheduled stopping station, SEATTLE. Going on from Kent it will be 32 minutes to the next stop at TACOMA (see page 57 for this example). Routes can therefore be read in either direction, changing left for right and arrival for departure as appropriate. However, you should note that the timetable means that some places can only be seen by day when you are travelling in one direction.

date just before a full moon. If you book your travel at least 14 days in advance on many routes you can save 20% on the regular adult fare.

Reservations can be obtained up to 11 months ahead via Amtrak's website, through any Amtrak station ticket office (try to avoid busy times) or at designated travel agents, including those abroad. Many travel agents in North America are connected into the Amtrak computer booking system. Alternatively, you can call 'Julie', Amtrak's state-of-the-art voice-recognition system (↖ *1 800 USA RAIL or* ↖ *1 800 872 7245; for group reservations,* ↖ *800 USA 1GRP).* You will be given a reservation number and hold date by which time you must collect your tickets. Tickets can be paid for when you make your reservations and picked up at any time prior to travel, but reservations will be cancelled if collection is not made by then. Telephone lines are open 24 hours a day, 365 days a year, but you may receive a faster service by calling early in the morning or late at night.

A service charge is made for prepaid tickets. If you need to upgrade and find no sleeper is available, try calling again at a later date, if possible early in the morning, as there are sometimes compartments and coach seats available as a result of cancellations or 'no-shows'.

AMTRAK VACATIONS Plan a rail vacation the easy way by calling Amtrak Vacations (↖ *1 800 268 7252 or 020 3327 3500).* This allows you to make all your arrangements for train tickets, hotel reservations, car rental and sightseeing.

MULTI-RIDE TICKETING OPTIONS Many Amtrak short-distance trains offer multi-ride ticket options. The monthly ticket is valid for unlimited travel between the origin and destination stations you select, and all stations in between, for one calendar month. The ten-ride ticket is valid for rides within a 45-day, 60-day or 180-day period depending on your origin and destination stations. The six-ride Downeaster College Pass (for students with college/university ID) is valid for a 365-day period on Downeaster trains between Boston, MA, and Brunswick, ME.

You can purchase multi-ride tickets with a credit or debit card on the Amtrak website as well as via the Amtrak App, at Amtrak station ticket offices and Quik-Trak kiosks and by telephone. Call ↖ 1 800 USA RAIL (↖ *1 800 872 7245)* to speak to a customer service representative and have a multi-ride ticket mailed to you. You must call every time you want a new ticket and allow at least ten days before your first intended travel date. Multi-ride tickets are not available for purchase on board trains.

AMTRAK MOBILE APP The Amtrak mobile phone app, available free to download, gives easy access to travel information.

You can check the status of a train stopping at any station by searching in Amtrak's app.

SECURITY Amtrak's security measures require customers to provide acceptable photo identification when purchasing/obtaining tickets – whether in stations or on board trains – or checking baggage. Acceptable forms of identification include a valid driver's licence, passport or government-agency ID.

USA RAIL PASS Amtrak rail passes enable you to visit any destination in Amtrak's system throughout the United States. They are available in three travel durations and travel segments: 15 days/eight segments, 30 days/12 segments and 45 days/18 segments. A travel segment is specified as any time you get on and then get off a vehicle (train, bus, ferry or other allowable leg) regardless of distance travelled. Each segment booked counts towards the total number of segments permitted for the pass. Travel must begin within 180 days of the date that your pass is purchased.

A USA Rail Pass entitles you to travel in regular Coach-Class seats and is valid on all Amtrak trains except the *Auto Train, Acela Express* and the Canadian portion of trains operated jointly by Amtrak and VIA Rail. Travel is restricted to four one-way trips between two cities, and to all cities in between, over the same route.

On some trains, you can upgrade to Business Class or sleeping-car accommodations for the appropriate surcharge. Children aged two to 12 years travel for half-price when accompanied by a full-fare-paying adult, and two children permitted per adult fare. One child under two years old may ride free with each fare-paying adult.

You can purchase a USA Rail Pass on Amtrak's website using a credit card or by contacting an international sales representative (page 381). Passes cannot be bought on board trains. The following prices currently apply:

15 days (eight segments) $459.00 (adult)
$229.50 (child aged 2–12)
30 days (12 segments) $689.00 (adult)
$344.50 (child aged 2–12)

45 days (18 segments) $899.00 (adult)
$449.50 (child aged 2–12)

The pass is not a ticket, so you must make reservations and pick up your ticket(s) before boarding any train. Seats available for USA Rail Pass passengers are limited so you should make reservations as far in advance as possible and not wait until the day of departure, since there is then a greater chance that seats may not be available on your desired train. If your plans are not flexible, non-USA Rail Pass seats may be available at an additional cost. For more information, call ✆1 800 USA RAIL (✆*1 800 872 7245*).

For travellers outside the United States, reservations can be made by sending your name, desired travel date(s), USA Rail Pass confirmation number and the train(s) on which you want to travel to ✉ inat5@sales.amtrak.com prior to arriving in the United States, or call ✆ (001) 215 856 7953 during regular business hours (*08.30–17.30 Mon–Fri EST*). If you are already in the United States, call ✆1 800 USA RAIL (✆*1 800 872 7245*) and speak to a reservations agent. You can pick up your pass and tickets at any staffed Amtrak ticket office in many Amtrak stations by showing your USA Rail Pass or pass confirmation number. Travel on Amtrak requires full identification so bring a valid passport or US-issued identification card, such as a driver's licence or picture ID card.

Refunds are only allowed before travel begins. The pass as well as all tickets issued with it must be turned into an Amtrak ticket agent no later than the day before the date of the first use written on the pass. A cancellation fee may apply, which might be substantial if sleeping-car accommodations are cancelled less than 24 hours in advance.

CALIFORNIA RAIL PASS The California Rail Pass allows up to seven days of travel in California over a consecutive 21-day period for $159 (adults) and $79.50 (children two–12). Eligible trains are the *Capitols*, *San Joaquin* and *Pacific Surfliner* corridor trains, most connecting Thruway services, and the *Coast Starlight* between Los Angeles and Dunsmuir, California. The California Rail Pass is not valid on long-distance trains, such as the *Sunset Limited*, the *Southwest Chief*, the *California Zephyr* and the *Texas Eagle*. On the *Coast Starlight*, travel to or from points outside California requires a separate fare, calculated between Dunsmuir and the out-of-state origin or destination. A pass holder is entitled to regular Coach-Class travel, which may be upgraded to Business Class or sleeping-car accommodations by paying an extra charge.

California Rail Passes are not available for purchase online so you need to call a travel agent or Amtrak at ☎ 1 800 USA RAIL (☎ *1 800 872 7245*). In addition to holding the pass, you must make reservations on all trains and obtain hard-copy tickets for all travel prior to boarding. The pass is not valid without a corresponding ticket. You should also carry identification as this may be requested.

Travel during any part of a calendar day counts as using that day and travel is limited to not more than four one-way journeys on a given route segment. The California Rail Pass is not transferable and must be used within one year of purchase. Refunds are only available if it has not been used, and if the pass and all tickets issued against it are returned to Amtrak. A penalty may apply to sleeping-car accommodations not cancelled at least seven days before departure. The pass cannot be combined with other offers, discounts or promotions unless specifically allowed under the terms of these offers.

PAYMENT You can pay for Amtrak tickets and dining-car meals with cash or by credit or debit card. Amtrak does not accept travellers' cheques, money orders or personal cheques, except for group travel by prior arrangement.

REFUNDS If you change your plans you should apply for a refund as soon as possible to avoid penalties. In most cases a fee will be charged. No change fees are charged as long as you buy another Amtrak ticket of equal or greater value or take a credit towards future travel. If a passenger does not take the entire trip paid for, a refund is paid based on the remaining ticket value calculated by subtracting the fare for any travel already taken from the total amount paid. Refund policy applies as soon as payment is made, whether or not any ticket is printed.

Sleeping accommodation cancelled 15 or more days before the scheduled departure is refundable less a 20% refund fee. If cancelled 14 days or fewer before the scheduled departure, fares are not refundable but the value may be applied to an eVoucher that can be used toward future travel within one year. If not cancelled before the scheduled departure from the origin (a 'no show'), the entire amount is forfeited. *Acela Express* First-Class and non-*Acela* Business-Class tickets cancelled before the scheduled departure date are refundable without a refund fee. If not cancelled before the scheduled departure from the origin, the ticket is refundable less a 20% fee.

Reserved Coach and *Acela Express* Business-Class refund rules vary based on the type of fare purchased. Those sold as a Value fare are fully refundable up to 48 hours prior to the scheduled departure from the origin; less than 48 hours' notice will incur a 20% fee. If not cancelled before the scheduled departure time, the entire amount is forfeited. Flexible fare tickets are fully refundable and will not incur a fee. Advance Purchase fare refundability is based on the rules applying to the particular fare and some (such as Saver fares) are not refundable. A 20% fee applies on refunds for all unreserved Coach tickets.

Reimbursement can be received from ticket offices, online or by mail from Amtrak Customer Refunds (*30th St Station, 2995 Market St, Philadelphia, PA 19104-2898*). Send your ticket via certified mail. Travel agency-sold tickets must usually be refunded through the agent, although Amtrak will make refunds on the spot if this is due to service disruption or downgrading.

TIMETABLES Amtrak ticket offices and travel agents can provide free timetables for individual routes, the Northeast and for the National network. You can get a complete view of Amtrak's train routes and learn about the cities they serve or the parts of the country they traverse by exploring the Interactive Travel Planning Map on the Amtrak website (**w** *amtrak.com*). Up-to-date timetables can also be found on the website and on the Amtrak mobile app. To access timetable information, and ticket prices, use the 'Book' feature located at the bottom of the app screen. Times shown are local, taking into account any zone changes en route. You should confirm your departure time the day before travelling, especially if the tickets were bought several weeks in advance. In the autumn, on the day clocks go back, trains may be deferred for an hour in order to arrive 'on time'. On the day clocks go forward in spring, a new timetable comes into effect and trains attempt to make up time lost before reaching subsequent stations. Arizona and parts of Indiana do not observe daylight saving time.

Generally speaking, Amtrak's timekeeping performance in recent years has compared favourably with that of airlines, although circumstances beyond the corporation's control can lead to delays. Freight trains sometimes have to take precedence and Amtrak trains crossing into Canada may be held up by customs and immigration inspections. Connections of less than 60 minutes are not guaranteed (90 minutes between arriving long-distance trains and local trains in the Northeast Corridor) so you should allow at least an hour between trains. Even a guaranteed connection may sometimes be missed. If this happens, alternative transport on Amtrak or another carrier will usually be provided and, in exceptional circumstances, overnight accommodation arranged.

If you have limited time to change trains ask the conductor on the train where you should go to get your next one when you reach the depot. This will save you having to hunt for signs or wait in a queue for information. Note that some cities have more than one station. Trains may not pause for as long as the timetable indicates at scheduled stops, so listen to the announcements or ask an attendant before deciding to stretch your legs on the platform. Stay within sight and hearing of the train and be prepared to reboard at a moment's notice or you may be left behind. Anyone intending to meet a train can check times of arrival and departure by calling 1 800 USA RAIL (*1 800 872 7245*) and listening to the automated information.

STATIONS America's train stations and depots are at the heart of many communities. They were often built on a grand scale, even in smaller cities, and many have been transformed into centres of economic activity while still accommodating train and bus services. These great stations are important historical and architectural expressions. Designed to embellish cities and towns and bring prestige to their builders, railroad stations play an important role in a community's collective memory. They have housed offices for the railroads, hotels, eating houses and other facilities, and are one of the last expressions of greatness in public architecture. Amtrak's busiest stations today are Penn Station in New York City (with over ten million passengers a year), Union Station in Washington, DC, 30th Street Station in Philadelphia, Chicago's Union Station, and Union Station in Los Angeles. The Great American Stations website at w greatamericanstations.com offers invaluable expertise, encouragement and inspirational stories. It is also highly recommended for comprehensive information about Amtrak's stations and their fascinating histories.

THRUWAY BUSES Some routes in the Amtrak system include Thruway services. These are co-ordinated transfers provided by bus, train, ferry, van or taxi through a variety of operators. Amtrak-dedicated Thruway bus services are accessible and lift-equipped. Services provided by partners are also accessible but may require up to 48 hours' advance notice. Where a Thruway bus is necessary to complete your journey the cost is included in the rail fare.

Timetables show some of the connecting services provided by other carriers to destinations not served by Amtrak or Thruway buses. Reservations and tickets for these services can be obtained from Amtrak but you should note that they may leave from another terminal.

AIRPORT CONNECTIONS Several Amtrak stations (including BWI Thurgood Marshall and Newark Liberty International) are adjacent to airports with connecting services provided by the airport. Others, especially in larger cities, have a range of transfer options available between the station and airport.

BOARDING You should arrive at least half an hour before departure time (or 2 hours for the *Auto Train*). It is important that you go to the right coach, so tell the gate attendant your destination and he will direct you. Red Caps (porters) are there to assist with luggage if required. Choose a window seat for a better view of the scenery, a little more privacy and a corner to lean against when sleeping. An aisle seat will give you more freedom to move without disturbing other passengers. Try not to sit too near the front as the view there may be restricted.

METROPOLITAN LOUNGE Chicago and Portland, Oregon, have Metropolitan waiting rooms located away from the crowds. They provide a staffed reception desk, comfortable chairs, television, telephones, internet access, a conference area, rest rooms, newspapers, luggage stores and a superior class of muzak. They also offer complimentary coffee, soft drinks and doughnuts, or you can even take a shower. In the large, two-floor Chicago Metropolitan Lounge, Amtrak representatives will check your baggage and later pre-board you from the lounge to your train.

Metropolitan Lounges are available (on arrival or departure) to sleeping-car-service passengers, Business-Class passengers and Amtrak Guest Rewards Select Plus or Select Executive members. If you would like to use the Chicago Metropolitan Lounge and you don't already have it included with your reservation, you can buy a day pass to get full access to all the lounge amenities for $50.

CLUBACELA First-Class ClubAcela lounges are located in Boston South Station, New York Penn Station, Philadelphia 30th Street Station and Washington Union Station. They are available to passengers travelling *Acela* First-Class or sleeping-car passengers, Single-Day Pass holders, Amtrak Guest Rewards Select Plus and Select Executive members. Business-Class passengers can purchase daily access passes for the ClubAcela locations at Philadelphia and Boston stations for $20 per day.

Facilities include complimentary soft drinks, juice, pastries and snacks; comfortable and quiet seating; reservations and ticketing assistance; newspapers and periodicals; internet, fax and photocopy services; conference room access; television; information on local dining and entertainment options; train information; advance boarding (where available); and Quik-Trak ticketing machines (where available).

FIRST-CLASS LOUNGE Unattended, separate sleeping-car passenger and Amtrak Guest Rewards Select Plus member waiting rooms are available in St Paul–Minneapolis, St Louis, New Orleans and Raleigh. Business-Class passengers may also use the First-Class Lounge in Raleigh.

CHICAGO UNION STATION LEGACY CLUB Open daily and located in the southwest corner of the Great Hall where coach passengers, commuters and others can enjoy a quiet, comfortable atmosphere to wait for trains or unwind after travelling, the Legacy Club has lounge seating, complimentary refreshments, free Wi-Fi and charging stations, satellite TV, train status displays and priority boarding. You can buy a day pass to get full access to all the lounge amenities for $20.

EQUIPMENT
Superliner Manufactured by the Pullman-Standard Company for Amtrak between 1979 and 1981, these spacious, twin-decked coaches operate on all long-distance routes west of the Mississippi as well as on some in the East. Designed to be 'the finest trains anywhere in the world', they have air-cushioned suspension and were built with extra sound-absorbing materials. Each Superliner car measures 85ft (26m) long and 16ft (5m) high, weighs 75 US tons (68 tonnes) and has large windows with excellent views, especially from the upper level. The reclining seats, about equivalent to flying First Class, provide leg and foot rests, folding trays and personal reading lights.

In the 1990s, a new generation of Superliner II cars, built by the Bombardier company, was introduced on the *Auto Train* and several western routes. These have bigger windows and larger compartments than the first range of Superliners.

Dining cars cater for up to 72 people and are on the upper level above the kitchen. Sightseer lounge cars and most kinds of sleeping accommodation are also usually available. Rest rooms (toilets) are mostly on the lower level, with at least one accessible to passengers travelling with a disability. Facilities include toilet, washbasin, mirror, infant changing table, soap, tissues and a 120V AC electric point. Luggage may be left at the lower level on entry or stored in overhead racks.

Amfleet Designed for short and medium journeys and operating mostly in the East, Amfleet coaches were built by the Budd Company of Philadelphia. They offer reclining seats, fold-down trays, overhead luggage racks and personal reading lights. Amfleet II coaches, intended for longer journeys, provide leg rests, slightly larger windows and more space. At least one rest room caters for disabled passengers. Dinette and lounge cars serve light meals which you can take to a table or back to your seat.

Business Class Business-Class cars have a double seat on one side of the aisle and a single on the other, with complimentary at-your-seat food and drinks service, including wine, as well as free newspapers and hot towels. Custom Class includes a newspaper and complimentary coffee, plus tea or juice in a café car shared only with Business-Class passengers.

California Fleet Bi-level coaches feature large picture windows, overhead luggage racks, reclining seats with tray tables and footrests, reading lights, rest rooms, AmtrakConnect Wi-Fi, 120V power outlets and a wheelchair ramp. These coaches operate on the *San Joaquin* route and elsewhere in southern California. They were purchased by the state and are operated by Amtrak in partnership with the California Department of Transportation.

Pacific Surfliner With aerodynamic styling and ultra-efficient engineering, these latest bi-level trains are operated in partnership with Caltrans in southern California. Each five-car train has 422 seats and includes one Business-Class car with personal audio and visual systems. Coach-Class cars have wide reclining seats, panoramic windows, electrical outlets for laptops, Railfone and a digital information display showing station arrivals. Surfliner trains are designed to be easily accessible, especially for mobility-impaired passengers.

Acela Pronounced 'Ah-cell-ah', the name combines the words 'excellence' and 'acceleration'. *Acela Express* trains have replaced most Metroliner services in the Northeast Corridor, using new equipment and making fewer stops. The sleek trains, built by Bombardier and Alstom in Vermont, New York and Quebec, use tilt technology to achieve speeds of up to 150mph and cut the time between New York City and Washington, DC, to 2¾ hours. *Acela Regional* trains serve more destinations.

Besides a faster trip with fewer stops, the *Acela Express* provides a superior on-board experience, with reserved First-Class and Business-Class seating and upmarket amenities such as upgraded Wi-Fi, an electrical outlet at your seat, adjustable lighting and a tray table large enough for a laptop. Meetings can be held at one of 32 conference tables and there is a bistro-like café car with an extensive menu.

The new *Acela* train cars being introduced to this fleet from 2021 will give passengers more room, more lighting and better Wi-Fi access. When the new fleet is released, a new seat reservation system will also come into effect. The interiors will include larger and more comfortable seats, and there will be handles secured to the seats to help passengers negotiate the aisles when the train is moving. A larger overhead compartment, enhanced Wi-Fi and USB ports will be available at every seat and each new car will have six LED screens that will broadcast real-time information pertaining to location, train speeds and announcements from the conductor. Bathrooms will be ADA-compliant and have a full 60 inches' (150cm) turnaround space. Amtrak has stated that this will become the new standard for train travel.

Regional *Regional* services offer coach-car accommodations with reclining seats, fold-down trays and overhead reading lights. Business-Class passengers have more leg room and receive complimentary non-alcoholic beverages in the café car.

Cascades Service Sporting distinctive, 7ft-tall (2m) tail fins, Amtrak's sleek Cascades trains were built in Spain by Talgo and in Seattle by General Motors. They incorporate tilt technology and consist of 12 cars, each half the length of a normal Amtrak car, including a bistro and a dining car. They were bought in partnership with the Washington State Department of Transportation (*PO Box 47407, Olympia, WA 98504-7407;* 1 *800 872 7245 or* 360 705 7901 *(in Olympia);* w *amtrakcascades. com*) to operate along the Northwest Corridor. For safety reasons they are currently limited to 79mph (127km/h) but improvements to the track will eventually allow them to reach speeds of up to 110mph (177km/h).

The comfortable coaches are painted in bold colours, officially known as Double Latte and Evergreen, and feature plush seats and Railfone as well as video and stereo services. Business Class includes wider seats, more leg room, television screens and laptop outlets, plus complimentary snacks, drinks and newspapers.

For more information, see contact details, above.

SLEEPING Reclining seats, dimmed lights and a free pillow from the attendant complement a gentle rocking and the hypnotic rumble of the wheels: obtaining a comfortable night's sleep is easy even when travelling Coach Class given a certain amount of practice. You also save money on hotels. For the best results you should choose a seat in the middle of the car, away from the noise of sliding doors, and take a coat or blanket to ward off sometimes over-enthusiastic air conditioning. Souvenir blankets are sold on most long-distance trains. The pillows provided by Amtrak are fairly small so you may wish to take a larger one of your own. Alternatively, you could take a pillow case and ask the attendant for two pillows to put inside.

All sleeping-car accommodation is designated First Class. Compartments are ingenious but small, and become no bigger as your journey progresses, so it helps if you enjoy camping. You do get extra privacy and there is a strange pleasure to be had from hurtling through the night in your personal travelling capsule. Try to obtain a compartment in the centre of the coach away from the vibration of the wheels. You can either make up your own bed or let the attendant do it for you, and he may even leave a goodnight sweet on your pillow. Towels, soap and bed linen are provided. Remember that sleeping-car walls are usually thin so keep the noise down at night.

Complimentary tea, coffee or fruit juice (plus a newspaper) are served 06.30–09.30 to passengers in sleeping-car accommodation and your fare includes all meals in the dining car. Sleeping-car passengers are entitled to make use of Amtrak's Metropolitan Lounge waiting rooms both before and after their journey.

Superliner bedrooms All Superliner bedrooms have adjustable climate controls, individual reading lights, a fold-down table, garment rack and an electrical outlet.

Roomette Ten roomettes on the upper level and four on the lower level each accommodate two adults. Two reclining seats face each other or slide together to form the lower berth, and a second berth folds out from the wall. Features include a picture window, narrow closet (wardrobe) and an aisle window with curtains. Rooms are compact so it pays to leave most of your luggage in the lower storage area and take only a small bag into your bedroom. Rest rooms are provided on the lower or upper level. Room dimensions: 3ft 7in by 6ft 6in (1.09 by 1.98m).

Bedroom Five bedrooms are located on the upper level, each sleeping two adults in berths which fold down. Daytime seating consists of a large sofa and an armchair. Adjoining rooms can sometimes be combined into a suite for up to four people. Features include a closet and an aisle window with curtains. There is space for two medium-sized suitcases. Rest-room facilities include a shower, washbasin and toilet. Room dimensions: 6ft 6in by 7ft 6in (1.98 by 2.28m).

Family bedroom One family bedroom on the lower level sleeps two adults and two children, with daytime seating consisting of two chairs and a long sofa. Only a few family rooms are available on each trip so book well in advance if possible. Upper and lower berths are for adults, with two short berths for children. Family bedrooms extend the full width of the car, giving windows on each side. The windows are smaller, though, which makes watching the scenery less easy. Being on the lower level puts you closer to the wheels so you may find travelling slightly noisier, although this should not affect sleeping. There is space for up to three suitcases and a rest room is provided on the lower level. Room dimensions: 5ft 3in by 9ft 6in (1.60 by 2.90m).

Accessible bedroom Each sleeping car has a bedroom on the lower level intended for up to two people, including one passenger with special mobility requirements. Features include an attendant call button. Two berths fold down for sleeping and for daytime use there are two reclining seats. There is space for two suitcases. The accommodation includes meals and drinks served in your room by the car attendant. Rest-room facilities (which are curtained off) include a toilet, washbasin and hand grips. Room dimensions: 6ft 6in by 9ft 6in (1.98 by 2.90m).

Viewliners These Amtrak-designed cars were the first single-level sleepers to be manufactured in the US for 40 years. Introduced on routes in the East and Midwest they have replaced the Heritage sleepers which pre-dated Amtrak. Viewliners are larger and give a smoother ride. Their modular design means that each bedroom is a separate structure, making them quieter, and there are more windows so that upper-berth passengers can have a view. All Viewliner bedrooms have adjustable climate controls, an electrical outlet, reading lights, built-in audio and a video screen for movies. A shower room is also available. Room dimensions: 6ft 8in by 7ft 1in (2.03 by 2.16m).

Standard bedroom Designed for one or two people. Two reclining seats convert into a bed at night and an upper berth drops down from the ceiling. There is a picture window and another window above for extra light. Rest-room facilities include a toilet, mirror and washbasin, and a shower is located nearby. If you are in a Viewliner by yourself, sleep in the top bunk, leaving more room to store your belongings below and access to the toilet. Room dimensions: 3ft 7in by 6ft 6in (1.09 by 1.98m).

Deluxe bedroom Extra space is provided for two people, with an armchair and a sofa. The sofa converts into a wide berth below an upper berth. Rest-room facilities include a private shower, toilet, mirror and washbasin. Two deluxe bedrooms can be combined into a suite for four people. Room dimensions: 6ft 6in by 7ft 3in (1.98 by 2.20m).

Accessible bedroom This is a deluxe bedroom equipped for passengers with special mobility requirements, with all facilities accessible by wheelchair. There is a reclining seat and upper and lower berths. Meals and drinks can be served to those with disabilities. Rest-room facilities include a private shower, toilet, mirror and washbasin. Room dimensions: 6ft 6in by 7ft 3in (1.98 by 2.20m).

DINING Most long-distance trains have a complete dining-car service, providing breakfast (*06.30–10.00*), lunch (*11.30–15.00*) and dinner (*17.00–21.30*). A meal service is generally available for passengers boarding 30 minutes before the end of each meal period.

Regional specialities such as barbecued spare ribs or fresh salmon are sometimes added to the standard steak, chicken and lasagne menu, and there are special meals for vegetarians and children. Dessert is usually a choice of fruit pie (à la mode if you wish), cake or cheesecake. Breakfast is likely to consist of fresh fruit, cereal, bagels and muffins with cream cheese, jelly and butter. You should let Amtrak know of any special dietary requirements at least 72 hours before travelling. Call 1 800 USA RAIL and ask for the Special Services desk.

Advance dinner reservations are normally taken by the chief of on-board services or dining-car attendant moving through the train. This minimises waiting time, since on arrival you can be seated straight away by the steward. The tables usually seat four so you may find yourself eating with strangers, which can be an entertaining and revealing experience. Amtrak uses china dishes and linen tablecloths on the *Capitol Limited*, *Coast Starlight* and *Southwest Chief*, and has plans to extend these civilised touches to other trains. *Auto Train* passengers receive a full dining-car service but buffet-style dining cars operate on most Florida routes.

Lunch is usually better value than dinner for those keeping to a tight budget. Meal prices start from about $12.50, and anything alcoholic tends to be expensive. Many people bring their own supplies of food and drink on board, but this is not encouraged and may be impractical for longer journeys. You can buy snacks such as sandwiches, pizza, soup, salad, drinks and sweets to take back to your seat or consume in the dinette or café car, which usually opens from 06.00 to midnight. Business Class provides a meal service to your seat.

LOUNGE AND DOME CARS Superliners have a Sightseer lounge car, giving views through huge windows that extend part way over the roof. Here you can mingle with fellow passengers, watch a movie (most likely a comedy or light drama) on the television monitor in the evening, get a drink at the bar, buy a sandwich or coffee, and watch the changing landscape pass by outside. Movies and sometimes cartoons or travelogues are also occasionally shown during the afternoon. You can also buy souvenir blankets, playing cards and postcards. Seating is on a first-come, first-served basis but it is good manners not to monopolise a seat all day.

Hospitality hour in the lounge is an excellent opportunity to sample exotic drinks, snack on hors d'oeuvres and break the ice by meeting new people. The relaxed atmosphere on board seems to encourage Americans in particular to tell their life stories to a complete stranger. This special kind of friendliness is encouraged by the thought that, unless you make a considerable effort, you are unlikely ever to see them again.

Amfleet lounge and Dome cars offer similar services to Superliners, with more 'land cruise' experience and wide-angle viewing on eastern and Midwestern routes.

Amtrak's charming Great Dome carriage is the only one of its kind still in service. It has windows on every side including the ceiling, so that passengers can enjoy a panoramic view from their seat. Previously used on the *Empire Builder* route when the train was operated by the Great Northern Railway and the Chicago Burlington & Quincy Railroad, the car was built in 1955 by the Budd Company for the Great Northern and carried the name *Ocean View*. Amtrak has brought back this classic Dome car on two of its most scenic routes, the *Downeaster* and *Adirondack*, during autumn so that you can immerse yourself in the changing tree colours and Lake Champlain vistas as you travel from Albany across the Canadian border to Montreal.

QUIET CAR Many Northeast and West Coast Corridor trains, as well as the *Hiawatha* service, have a Quiet Car where passengers are asked not to use mobile phones or the sound feature of laptops, and to speak only in subdued tones. Low overhead lighting creates a restful atmosphere, but reading lights are available. Seating is on a first-come, first-served basis and cannot be reserved specifically. There is no additional charge to sit in the Quiet Car.

BAGGAGE Trains can accommodate up to two items of carry-on luggage (maximum weight 50lb/22.7kg each) per passenger, but Amtrak encourages you to use its checked baggage service whenever possible. Carry-on bags with shoulder straps are easier to handle. All bags must be visibly tagged with the name and address of the passenger. There is storage space in overhead racks and at the end of the car. When occupying sleeping accommodation, you can bring on board as much as will safely fit into your bedroom, although sometimes this will not be much. Additional bags can be left in the storage area outside your room.

Amtrak usually accepts no liability for loss or damage to carry-on luggage but you should report any problems to the attendant as soon as possible. Although it's usually safe to leave things behind on your seat when you visit the diner or lounge car, you should take expensive cameras or other items of value with you just in case.

Where a check-in service is provided, you are allowed to check up to two items of baggage weighing no more than 50lb (22.7kg) each or 100lb (45.4kg) altogether. You pay a surcharge if this is exceeded but items slightly over the limit are usually permitted. Two additional bags can be checked in for $20 each. Well-secured boxes or cartons weighing less than 50lb (22.7kg) will also be accepted. If you require special assistance with your bags you should let Amtrak know when making reservations. Many stations provide free luggage trolleys. Others have handcarts for which a small charge is made, partly refunded when you return the cart to a vending machine.

Bags should be labelled with your name and address and checked in at least half an hour before departure. Checked baggage may be sent by a different route and get to your destination before you do. It will be held for up to two days without charge following your arrival. Amtrak's liability for checked baggage is limited to $500 per passenger, but you can purchase additional insurance up to $2,500. Claims for loss or damage must be submitted within 30 days to the Office of Customer Relations (*Attn: Baggage Claims, Amtrak, 60 Massachusetts Av NE, Washington, DC 20002-4285*). For more details call Amtrak at ☎1 800 USA RAIL (☎*1 800 872 7245*) and ask for Customer Relations.

An increasing number of trains now offer bicycle and ski racks. Space for bikes remains limited, though, so you should make reservations well ahead of your journey.

RED CAPS Assistance with baggage is provided by uniformed Red Cap porters at most large stations. Items handled by Red Caps are not checked baggage and are your responsibility once loaded on to the train. Make sure you obtain a claim check for each bag in case anything is mislaid. Red Caps will help passengers with disabilities, senior citizens and large groups navigate the station, operate wheelchair lifts and ramps, and provide general assistance. Red Cap service is free for Amtrak passengers, though you are welcome to tip if you wish ($3–5 is usual). Amtrak recommends you accept help only from a Red Cap.

SAFETY Try to arrive early in order to avoid rushing for your train. Don't leave luggage in the aisle or in the vestibules between cars. Always wear shoes when moving about the train and use handrails when boarding or climbing stairs. Only touch connecting doors on the 'press' plate to open them. Remain behind the yellow line on the platform while waiting for trains, which may stop very close to the edge or, in some cases, may not be scheduled to stop at all. When boarding, be mindful of the gap between the platform and the train. Always use handrails for support and hold small children by the hand.

SMOKING Smoking is prohibited on all Amtrak trains as well as on Thruway buses and in stations. This includes electronic smoking devices, such as e-cigarettes. The use or transportation of marijuana for any purpose is prohibited, even in states where recreational use is legal or permitted medically. If you smoke on a non-smoking train you may, without a warning, be asked to get off at the next stop. Some long-distance trains provide semi-official smoking stops announced by the train crew at certain stations along the way.

TIPPING You do not have to tip Amtrak personnel, although most people reward bar staff, waiters and sleeping-car attendants, especially after a long trip. The IRS taxes Amtrak officials based on what they expect the crew to receive in tips, so $1 at breakfast is usual and a few dollars at dinner. Red Caps should be tipped $2 per bag, or more where extra help has been provided. Train-operating personnel such as conductors are never tipped.

ALCOHOL Except in sleeping cars you are not officially supposed to consume your own supplies of alcoholic drinks.

PERSONAL ELECTRONIC DEVICES Earphones or headphones must be used when listening to radios, music or electronic viewing devices. Keep the volume down to prevent 'leakage'.

LAPTOPS Electrical outlets for use with computers are available in Metropolitan Lounges. Some trains also provide electrical sockets for use with laptops but train power current is not always stable so a surge protector should be used.

PETS Dogs and cats up to 20lb (9kg) can travel on trips of up to 7 hours on most routes. Go to w Amtrak.com, call a reservation agent on ↘1 800 USA RAIL or visit a staffed station to make a reservation. Pet owners must provide a suitable carrier, which counts as one piece of carry-on baggage. While in stations and on board trains, pets must remain inside their carrier placed under your seat. They can travel in Coach Class but not in other accommodation or food-service cars. They are not allowed to travel as checked baggage. The pet fare is $25 for each travel segment. Service animals are not considered pets and are welcome on all Amtrak services.

CHILDREN Even more than adults, children love to travel by train, especially since this is often a rare treat. When travelling with children you should take a good supply of books, games and other amusements, such as quiet toys. Children must always be supervised by an adult while in the lounge car and should never be left unattended. Most trains have rest rooms with infant changing facilities. Chicago's Union Station and the *Auto Train* have special play rooms and a private area for nursing mothers. Women are free to breastfeed anywhere in an Amtrak station, as well as on board trains (although breastfeeding in public has only recently become legal in Idaho and Utah!). However, for mothers who prefer more privacy, Amtrak has introduced 'lactation suites' in Washington, DC, Baltimore, Philadelphia,

Chicago and New York City's Penn Station. The suites include a bench, a fold-down table, an electrical outlet and a locking door. They are ADA-compliant (Americans with Disabilities Act Standards for Accessible Design), with enough room to bring luggage and other children inside.

Children aged 12 and under may not travel alone and must be accompanied by another person who is at least 18 years old. Children aged 13–15 may travel unaccompanied under certain conditions. Travel is permitted only on Amtrak trains and is not permitted on Thruway motorcoach services, or on any other connecting services. The full adult fare will be charged. Call ☎ 1 800 USA RAIL for more information.

SENIOR CITIZENS Travellers 65 years of age and over are eligible to receive a 10% discount on the lowest available rail fare on most Amtrak trains. On cross-border services operated jointly by Amtrak and VIA Rail Canada, a 10% senior discount is applicable to people aged 60 and over. The senior discount is not available on the *Auto Train* or *Acela Express*, and does not apply to Business Class, First Class or sleeping accommodation. Valid proof of age is required when purchasing your ticket and on board the train. For information on discounts for accommodation and other matters of interest contact Senior Service America, Inc (*8403 Colesville Rd, Suite 200, Silver Spring, MD 20910;* ☎ *1 301 578 8900*).

STUDENTS Those with a Student Advantage card or ISIC (International Student Identity Card) can get 15% off most Amtrak fares as well as reductions for hotels, car hire and theatres. Call ☎ 1 800 96 AMTRAK or visit w studentadvantage.com if you are a university or secondary-school student. You can keep up with Amtrak's latest deals and online promotions on Twitter (*@Amtrak*) and on Facebook (*Facebook. com/Amtrak*).

GROUP AND CONVENTION TRAVEL Generous extra discounts are available if you can rustle up a group of people to travel together between the same origin and destination. Amtrak offers discounts for groups of at least 20 people, and can even handle groups of 100 or more, depending on the train and time of year travel is taking place. You can choose from a 20% discount or one free escort ticket for each 20 paying passengers. Amtrak's 10% senior citizen and half-fare children's discounts may be applied to eligible members of the group. These discounts are not valid on all trains and further restrictions may apply.

To make reservations you can use the online group travel form on w Amtrak.com, call ☎ 1 800 USA 1GRP (☎ *1 800 872 1477*) or email e groupsales@amtrak.com.

TRAVELLING WITH A DISABILITY Except for the *Auto Train*, passengers with a disability are entitled to 10% off regular one-way coach fares. Amtrak also offers a 10% discounted companion fare for accompanying passengers. Disabled children pay half the disabled adult fare and guide dogs accompanying blind or deaf passengers travel free.

Wheelchair lifts are available at most stations. Passengers can receive special assistance at a station or on board provided 72 hours' notice is given. Most trains have special rest rooms and sleeping accommodation, and meals can usually be served at your seat by the attendant. Call ☎ 1 800 USA RAIL for details and ask for a copy of *Access Amtrak*, a guide to services for the elderly or disabled. Explain your needs when making reservations and remember to bring any medication you require.

Amtrak Thruway and other bus connections are not accessible by wheelchair, although folding chairs can be stored. Disabled passengers must occupy a standard seat and be able to board the bus unassisted.

Hearing-impaired people can obtain information or make reservations by teletypewriter (☏ 1 800 523 6590). The service operates nationwide 24 hours a day, seven days a week. Many states supply access details in their brochures and a wide range of materials for people with disabilities, including information sheets, are available from the Society for the Advancement of Travel for the Handicapped (SATH) (*347 Fifth Av, Suite 610, New York, NY 10016;* ☏ *1 212 447 7284;* w *sath.org*).

WI-FI Amtrak offers free basic Wi-Fi service in select trains and stations throughout the country on AmtrakConnect. Upgraded Wi-Fi technology is available free on *Acela* that is six times faster and more reliable. To ensure there is enough bandwidth for all onboard users, this amenity supports general web browsing activities only and does not support high-bandwidth actions such as streaming music or video or downloading large files.

MOBILE PHONES Cellular phones work along most portions of Amtrak routes, subject to expected coverage issues, though typically do not work well in long tunnels. Cell phone usage is restricted aboard the Quiet Car. To maintain your privacy, and for the enjoyment of your fellow passengers, you should speak as quietly as possible when using your phone. Amtrak recommends that you use your phone's silent alert or vibrate feature.

ENTERTAINMENT Movies, travelogues and card games are sometimes featured in the lounge car, as are games of trivia and scavenger hunts where you win a modest prize by giving the correct answers to a quiz or coming up with a specific object. Desperately competitive types should carry their birth certificate, a $2 bill and a photograph of their pet. Games of bingo are sometimes organised in the dining car.

On some routes an official guide will board the train to describe the history and wildlife of the landscape through which you are travelling.

PHOTOGRAPHY Seeing the country by train provides passengers with almost too many photo opportunities. For best results a medium-speed film (ASA 64 or above) is recommended for shooting scenery through the windows. If your camera's shutter speed is adjustable (and light conditions permit) set it at either 1/125sec or 1/250sec. Taking photographs from a moving train can result in blurred images, so to cope with this you should boost the shutter rate. If you have a digital camera with an auto-advance option, use this to take photographs continuously and try to use fast film, ideally 400 ISO. Most digital still cameras can also capture short video clips, though a video camera will produce better results. Keeping the lens close to the window will help eliminate glare and reflections, or you can use a polarising filter. For interior shots using flash you can avoid reflections by not pointing directly at the windows.

ON-BOARD SERVICE The conductor is in charge of the train's crew and responsible for collecting tickets, identifying stops and ensuring the safety of the train. The chief of on-board services supervises the attendants on overnight long-distance trains.

Each coach attendant looks after a particular car and is a good person to make your friend. He or she will help with boarding and leaving the train, arranging seats, answering questions, bringing pillows and generally making your journey more agreeable. You are assigned a seat when you board and should not change it without consulting the attendant.

The sleeping-car attendant will help with your luggage, make up rooms for day or night use and bring your orders from the lounge car. In the morning he/she will provide complimentary tea, coffee or fruit juice and deliver a copy of the latest local newspaper to your room.

Service crew members such as car attendants, waiters and chefs ride the train all the way (except on the *Sunset Limited*) and have their own sleeping accommodation. Train personnel, such as conductors and engine crew, change every six or eight hours on long-distance routes.

CROSSING BORDERS For US and Canadian citizens, a passport is strongly recommended and may be required for all crossings of the US–Canadian border. Citizens of other countries must have a passport. Citizens of many countries must also have a visa, a US Employment Authorisation Card (a temporary work permit), or a Canadian Form IMM 1000 (for naturalised Canadian citizens or permanent residents). No passengers under 18 are allowed to cross the US–Canadian border unaccompanied. Where a passenger under 18 years old is not accompanied by one or both parents, the accompanying adult must bring a letter from a parent or legal guardian giving permission to cross the border. Except for citizens of the United States and Canada, a valid visa is required for return to the US after visiting Mexico, even after a one-day trip (page 37).

If in doubt check with your US embassy or contact US Citizenship and Immigration Services in Washington, DC (pages 39 and 379). Passengers without proper documentation are prohibited from entering the US or Canada and will be detrained before reaching the US–Canadian border.

CHARTER SERVICES An entire train, or an exclusive Amtrak coach attached to a regular scheduled service, can be hired for group travel. Handsomely furnished, privately owned cars are also available, offering the chance to experience a different type of train travel. The *Overland Trail* uses a 1949 lounge car restored to its former glory, making monthly trips between Los Angeles and San Diego. The 39-seat passenger car, complete with barber shop and shower, was built by the Pullman-Standard Car Manufacturing Company for the Southern Pacific Railroad. It was specifically ordered for the *San Francisco Overland*, a train jointly operated by the Southern Pacific, Union Pacific and the Chicago & North Western railroads between Chicago and Oakland. The *2981* car travelled millions of miles during its railroad career until in 1966 the beautiful lounge was stripped and converted into a dance floor. Purchased by Amtrak in 1971, it finished its 'revenue' railroad career assigned to Amtrak's Reno *Fun Train*, serving as a bar/dance car running between Oakland in California and Reno, Nevada. For more information contact Overland Trail (*2054 S Halladay St, Santa Ana, CA 92707;* ☏*1 800 539 7245 or* ☏*1 714 546 6923;* w *overlandtrail.com*).

For other private railcars available for charter, contact the American Association of Private Railroad Car Owners Inc (*311 East Main St, Suite 512, Galesburg, IL 61401-4838;* ☏*1 706 326 6262;* w *aaprco.com*).

COMPLAINTS AND SUGGESTIONS If you have any comments, compliments or suggestions regarding Amtrak services you can write to Amtrak Customer Care (*Washington Union Station, 60 Massachusetts Av NE, Washington, DC 20002-4285*) enclosing your ticket receipt. Alternatively, contact the website (w *amtrak.com*).

In July 2000, on the same day it unveiled its new logo, Amtrak introduced a guarantee of commitment to passenger satisfaction by promising to compensate for unsatisfactory experiences. If you did not receive a safe, comfortable and enjoyable trip you would be entitled to a certificate good for future Amtrak travel at equal cost.

NON-AMTRAK SERVICES

Many cities have their own **suburban and commuter services**, either operating independently or in association with Amtrak, and these sometimes provide a more frequent or cheaper alternative for shorter journeys. The best metropolitan services operate out of Chicago, Houston, Denver and Seattle. Details can be obtained at the local Amtrak station or information bureau. City-operated services often use locally the same routes served by Amtrak's longer-distance trains, but the stops and timings may be different.

The **Alaska Railroad** (*Alaska Passenger Service, 327 West Ship Creek Av, PO Box 107500, Anchorage, AK 99510-7500;* ☏ *1 907 265 2494 or* ☏ *800 544 0552;* w *alaskarailroad.com*) operates to Denali, Seward and Fairbanks, using three large-windowed Vistadome cars, and is one of the few railroads in the USA to carry both freight and passengers. Trains travel through almost 500 miles (800km) of national park land and remote landscapes with pristine mountain scenery and wildlife that includes moose, caribou, grizzly bear and beaver. You pass close to Bartlett Glacier (named in 1907 after Frank Bartlett, the Alaska Central Railroad's civil engineer at the time) and cross the continental divide at its lowest rail pass point (2,363ft/720m) in the Rocky Mountains. You also cross the Mears Memorial Bridge, a 700ft (213m) steel structure which is one of the world's longest single-span bridges and which marked the completion of the Alaska Railroad in 1923.

Services operate daily from May to September, otherwise only at weekends. A Gold Star service is offered daily between Anchorage and Fairbanks. Two custom-made coaches currently operate – one southbound and the other on the northbound *Denali Star*. These unique railcars feature a viewing platform on the second level. A trip to Whittier, located at the head of the Passage Canal and gateway to Prince William Sound, follows the shore of Turnagain Arm, where you may be lucky enough to see beluga whales.

BRIGHTLINE Florida East Coast Industries, Inc is developing the only privately owned, operated and maintained passenger rail system in the United States. By connecting Orlando, the most-visited city in the United States, with south Florida's business and vacation destinations, this passenger rail project, called **All Aboard Florida**, will serve Florida's growing number of business travellers, as well as families and tourists travelling for pleasure. The 240-mile (386km) route combines 200 miles (322km) of existing tracks between Miami and Cocoa and the creation of 40 miles (64km) of new track to complete the route to Orlando. Eventually the system could be expanded with connections to the Tampa Bay Area and Jacksonville. Contact 161 NW 6 St, Suite 900, Miami, FL 33136; ☏ 305 520 2300 (West Palm Beach) and ☏ 305 521 4800 (Fort Lauderdale); w gobrightline.com.

Brightline's service currently runs between Miami and West Palm Beach with a single intermediate stop at Fort Lauderdale. The Fort Lauderdale–West Palm Beach segment opened in 2018, to be followed by Fort Lauderdale–Miami in 2019. An extension from West Palm Beach to Orlando via Cocoa is scheduled to open in 2021, with more extensions planned. Brightline's diesel-electric locomotive-hauled trains run alongside freight trains in a shared-use corridor that was upgraded from a pre-existing Florida East Coast Railway freight train corridor. The West Palm Beach–Cocoa segment will be constructed similarly, while 40 miles (64km) of new track will be constructed for the remainder of the extension, between Cocoa and Orlando International Airport. Between Miami and West Palm Beach, there are 11 round trips on weekdays with an additional late-night run, with eight trips on Saturdays and seven on Sundays. Weekday service will increase to 16 round trips daily, with trains running hourly most of the day. There are two classes of service. 'Select' offers two seats together or four-to-a-table seating with 21-inch (530mm)-wide seats and complimentary snacks and beverages. The slightly less expensive 'Smart' fare coaches have narrower 19-inch (480mm) seats, with snacks and beverages available for purchase.

The downtown Miami station, known as MiamiCentral is located just east of Miami-Dade County Hall, connecting Brightline with the Metrorail, Metromover, County bus and City of Miami trolley systems. The Fort Lauderdale station is at NW Second Avenue between Broward Boulevard and NW Forth Street, connecting to the Sun Trolley and Broward County Transit system. Brightline also plans to build a transit-oriented development to the east of the Florida East Coast Railway corridor. The West Palm Beach station is between Datura and Evernia streets, connecting with Tri-Rail, Palm Tran Downtown Trolley and Amtrak West Palm Beach station.

The future Orlando Station will be at the new Orlando International Airport Intermodal Terminal, providing direct access to theme parks, shopping and attractions via ground transportation, rental cars and future connections to the Central Florida commuter rail system and SunRail. An Automated People Mover will connect to the North Terminal.

3

Practical Information

WHEN TO VISIT

Most people choose summer, when days are warmer and longer and most of the attractions will be open, but this can create problems. Hotels are more expensive, restaurants more crowded and train reservations harder to come by. Large numbers of people, many as foreign as yourself, crowd around the very things you have come to see, and sometimes it can be too hot for comfort. Usually the weather is fine, though, and it can be exciting to travel when half the country seems on the move.

Train reservations, flights and accommodation are more readily available in winter, often at reduced prices. You see fewer tourists and more of the real America, with only an hour's wait for the Washington Monument elevator. The sun still often shines, at least in the South, and the skiing season is open. Landscapes, especially the Rocky Mountains, can look even more spectacular when sprinkled with snow.

For many people, spring and autumn (known as 'fall' to Americans) are probably the best times to visit. During spring, flowers bloom in the mountains and the countryside is at its greenest. New England's forests always put on a dazzling show for autumn 'peepers'.

CLIMATE The United States is a huge country with a diverse geography so the climate varies accordingly. Temperatures in some places can go well above 100°F (38°C) or as cold as –40°F (–40°C). Some places see dramatic differences between seasons; others scarcely change at all.

The North experiences European-type summers, but other regions, especially the Southwest, become considerably hotter. The South and Midwest are often humid. In winter the Northwest continues to follow a European pattern, while the Northeast and Midwest become much colder. Florida, southern California and the Southwest stay mostly warm throughout the year.

Although spring and autumn are good times to visit, these seasons can be quite short. In the Midwest, summer and winter sometimes swap places within a few days. Autumn is the hurricane season along the Gulf of Mexico and tornadoes can occur in central regions during the spring.

RED TAPE

Travellers to the US should have a full passport valid for at least six months after the intended date of return, although the US has an agreement with most countries, including the UK, automatically to extend the validity of a passport for six months past its expiration date. A British passport therefore needs to be valid only for the duration of your stay. Passport information (for the UK) is available on the website **w** gov.uk.

Children should have their own passport or be included in that of a parent or guardian. Canadians and permanent legal residents of the USA do not require a visa, nor do citizens of the UK, Australia, New Zealand, South Korea, Chile, Singapore, Brunei, Japan and most countries in Europe, provided you intend to stay for no more than 90 days. You must have an unexpired passport that is machine-readable, identified by the presence of two typeface lines printed at the bottom of the biographical page that can be read by machine. These lines electronically provide some of the information contained on the upper part of the biographic page. If you are in doubt as to whether or not your passport is machine-readable, you should check with the passport-issuing authority of your country. Families require individual passports for each traveller in order to travel visa-free, regardless of the fact that they may hold machine-readable passports. Travellers not in possession of machine-readable passports will require either B-1 (business) or B-2 (tourist) visas.

Passports issued on or after 26 October 2005 must include a 'biometric identifier'. If your passport is issued prior to this date, provided it is an individual machine-readable passport, you may continue to use the passport to travel visa-free even though it does not have the biometric identifier. If your passport was issued after 26 October 2006, you must have an e-passport containing an integrated computer chip to travel to the US on the Visa Waiver Program (VWP).

To travel visa-free you also require a return or onward ticket and a completed form I-94W, obtainable from airline and shipping companies en route. UK travellers to Canada planning to cross the land border into the USA no longer require a visa.

British passports must state that the holder is a British citizen. If the passport states 'British subject' the holder must apply for a visa, and visa-free travel does not apply if you intend to work, study or stay in the US for more than 90 days. You may then require either a B-1 (business) or B-2 (tourist) visa. Application forms are available from travel agents, airlines, US embassies and consulates. Applications must be made by post or through a travel agent or courier two weeks (preferably a month) before your departure date.

The VWP does not apply if you have been arrested for certain offences, even if a criminal conviction did not result, or if you are a dual national of Iran, Iraq, Sudan or Syria, or if you have travelled to Libya, Iran, Iraq, Somalia, Sudan, Syria or Yemen since March 2011. Certain exemptions apply on a case-by-case basis so you should see the website of the US Customs and Border Protection Agency or contact your nearest US embassy or consulate. You also need to show that you have sufficient funds available on arrival to support yourself during your stay, even if you are staying with family and friends.

Before you travel you should complete an online pre-registration form on the Electronic System for Travel Authorisation (ESTA) website (w *esta.cbp.dhs.gov/esta*). The US Customs and Border Patrol recommends that you do this at least 72 hours before departure. Applying for and securing an ESTA is a separate process to providing your airline with advance passenger information (details of your passport, country of residence, address of your first night's accommodation in the US, etc). For more information visit the official ESTA website (see above). Beware of fraudulent unauthorised websites which charge you for information about ESTAs and for submitting ESTA applications to the Department of Homeland Security (DHS) on your behalf.

Indefinite visas are no longer provided (the maximum is now ten years); those in existence remain valid for ten years from the date they were issued. A visa is still valid in an expired passport if you also have a current passport. Make sure that when your expired passport was cancelled it was not clipped by the authority in such a way as to damage the visa and thereby make it invalid. If you are travelling visa-free and your passport is valid for less than 90 days you will only be admitted until the date your passport expires. If you hold a visa of any classification you are not required to hold a return ticket and may enter the US on a one-way ticket.

If in doubt, contact your US embassy for the latest requirements. Visa information is also available on the website **w** travel.state.gov.

Where appropriate you should obtain in advance an International Student Identification Card, an American Youth Hostel Card and an international driver's licence.

IMMIGRATION Before passing through immigration control you are given a form to complete, asking where you will be staying and the date you intend to leave. This is attached to your passport and must be shown on your departure. If you lose the certificate or wish to extend your stay you should contact the nearest Citizenship and Immigration Services (USCIS) office. For more details contact US Citizenship and Immigration Services (*20 Massachusetts Av NW, Washington, DC 20529;* ℡*1 800 375 5283;* **w** *uscis.gov*).

Immigration officers may ask for some evidence that you can support yourself during your visit, usually reckoned on the basis of a minimum $150 per week. Take plenty of travellers' cheques and perhaps a copy of your latest bank statement or evidence of current employment. Resist any temptation to test the officers' sense of humour.

On arrival in the US, visitors are photographed with a digital camera and inkless prints are taken of your right and left index fingers with a scanner, to be checked against those of suspected terrorists and criminals. Assuming you are not one of these people, your details will be stored separately and you will be free to enter the US. This procedure applies to residents of all countries, including those in the Visa Waiver Program (VWP). People will also be asked to 'check out' when they leave the country, enabling the authorities to know whether someone is still in the US or staying longer than permitted.

All persons, including US citizens, entering the United States from the Americas, Canada, Mexico, the Caribbean and Bermuda are now required to have a passport or other accepted document that establishes the bearer's identity and citizenship. For more information, visit **w** travel.state.gov.

It's a good idea to keep copies of all your travel documents in your email account so that, if necessary, they can be accessed en route. If your passport is lost or stolen, for example, your embassy in the US should be able to issue a temporary one from a scanned copy.

CUSTOMS As well as personal belongings you can bring in 200 cigarettes and 100 cigars. If aged over 21 you can also import one litre of wine, beer or spirits for your own use or as a gift. Food, illegal drugs, firearms and endangered species products such as ivory are forbidden. If carrying prescribed drugs, only take the quantity a person in your condition would normally require, and keep them in their original containers. You are allowed to take in or bring out any amount of currency but if it comes to more than $10,000, including travellers' cheques, you should report it to customs. The penalty for not doing so could be severe.

For more information, contact the customs office of your US embassy or the US Customs Service (**w** *cbp.gov*).

GETTING THERE AND AWAY

Competition has reduced the cost of flights, particularly over the North Atlantic, but fares vary tremendously according to date and season. Low season generally runs from November to March, excluding Christmas. Midweek flights tend to be cheaper and it usually pays to fly into a gateway airport such as Boston, Los Angeles or New York (John F Kennedy and Newark), though places such as Cincinnati, served by Delta (❧ 1 800 221 1212; w delta.com) and Charlotte, served by British Airways (❧ 800 247 9297 in the UK) are worth considering.

The main airlines flying from Europe include American (w aa.com), British Airways (w britishairways.com), United Airlines (w united.com) and Virgin Atlantic (w virginatlantic.com). Air India, El Al and Kuwait Airlines may be cheaper to book through agents such as Trailfinders in the UK (❧ 020 7408 9000; w trailfinders.com).

Charter flights are not necessarily less expensive but may offer a greater choice of departure airports, especially to Florida. British operators include Thomas Cook Airlines (❧ 01733 224330; w thomascookairlines.com). For the latest deals check the internet, national press or teletext for flight-only advertisements.

HEALTH

REGULATIONS No inoculations or vaccinations are required for visitors from Europe. Visitors from elsewhere should check with their US embassy. If you have a medical condition that requires syringe-administered medications, carry a valid prescription signed by your doctor.

TRAVEL CLINICS AND HEALTH INFORMATION A full list of current travel clinic websites worldwide is available on w istm.org. For other journey preparation information, consult w travelhealthpro.org.uk (UK) or w wwwnc.cdc.gov/travel (US). Information about various medications may be found on w netdoctor.co.uk/travel. All advice found online should be used in conjunction with expert advice received prior to or during travel.

MEDICAL INSURANCE The USA has no free health service available to overseas visitors. A hospital room alone can cost over $1,500 per night so horror stories about people being financially ruined by illness or accident are not apocryphal. Make sure you take out sufficient insurance cover for your entire stay, including provision to be flown home for treatment if necessary ($2 million is recommended). Airlines and travel agents usually try to sell you their own policies but check the small print and compare prices. If you plan a long stay it may be cheaper to buy annual cover.

TREATMENT Hospital clinics will often provide simple treatments and some have a 24-hour emergency room. Most towns have a late-opening pharmacy. If you need regular medication you should be sure to take sufficient to last for your visit. For prescribed drugs you should obtain a letter from your doctor explaining why you need them. If you wear glasses, carry an extra pair.

SAFETY

WOMEN TRAVELLERS The United States is a relatively safe place and most crime victims are young single men, not female tourists. Nevertheless, women travellers are wise to take special care to avoid sexual harassment, physical assault or theft. Sleeping

LONG-HAUL FLIGHTS, CLOTS AND DVT   *Dr Felicity Nicholson*

Any prolonged immobility, including travel by land or air, can result in deep-vein thrombosis (DVT) with the risk of embolus to the lungs. Certain factors can increase the risk and these include:

- History of DVT or pulmonary embolism
- Recent surgery to pelvic region or legs
- Cancer
- Stroke
- Heart disease
- Inherited tendency to clot (thrombophilia)
- Obesity
- Pregnancy
- Hormone therapy
- Older age
- Being over 6ft (1.83m) or under 5ft (1.52m)

A DVT causes painful swelling and redness of the calf or sometimes the thigh. It is only dangerous if a clot travels to the lungs (pulmonary embolus). Symptoms of a pulmonary embolus – which commonly start three to ten days after a long flight – include chest pain, shortness of breath, and sometimes coughing up small amounts of blood. Anyone who thinks that they might have a DVT needs to see a doctor immediately.

PREVENTION OF DVT
- Wear loose comfortable clothing
- Do anti-DVT exercises and move around when possible
- Drink plenty of fluids during the flight
- Avoid taking sleeping pills unless you are able to lie flat
- Avoid excessive tea, coffee and alcohol
- Consider wearing flight socks or support stockings, widely available from pharmacies

If you think you are at increased risk of a clot, ask your doctor if it is safe to travel.

in train or bus stations is generally not accepted. Getting off a train late at night to look for lodging is not a good idea, so try to arrange your accommodations in advance. If you have to wait for a train alone, especially at night, find a group to stand near to or go to a café until it's time for the train to arrive. Avoid sitting or walking in empty areas, no matter what time of day. Be aware of the people around you and do not stand alone listening to your mobile phone or MP3 player. Budget considerations should not be allowed to prevent you from being safe, so consider upgrading to a better hotel or take a taxi if you need to get out of a bad area of town. Dress appropriately, preferably like a local, and avoid ostentatious jewellery. You may wish to stay clear of bars and other places with a predominantly male clientele. If you feel uncomfortable – leave.

CRIME Most people survive a visit to the United States without being mugged, assaulted or robbed, but sensible precautions should always be taken. Don't keep all your valuables in one place; then if some are stolen you still have an emergency fund. Keep to downtown or well-lit areas at night and avoid going to secluded places alone. Your hotel desk clerk will advise on safety for the part of town in which you are staying.

Try to be inconspicuous. Don't flash money around in public but carry a small amount to surrender if threatened. Carry your camera in a bag, use the hotel safe for valuables and always lock your hotel door. Watch over your belongings and be wary of pickpockets or bag snatchers in crowded places such as train and bus stations. Don't ask strangers to keep an eye on your things. At stations, only trust your bags to a uniformed member of staff. Report any theft to the police and ask for a reference number to show to your insurance company. Bags should be secured with a good lock, preferably a TSA-approved luggage lock.

When driving, don't stop if flagged down by anyone other than the police, and keep all windows and doors locked. If you get lost, drive to a well-lit area before asking directions. When leaving your car, lock any bags and packages in the boot and park in a busy place. Never hitchhike or pick up hitchhikers.

Many cities have residential areas which are effectively segregated by race so ask advice before venturing where your presence might be too distinctive. All policemen and some security guards carry guns. Do not run away if challenged.

DRUGS It is now legal to possess a small amount of marijuana for personal use in eight US states, including California and Nevada, but purchase usually remains illegal and the authorities take a dim view. Apart from the dangers inherent in dealing with shifty characters on street corners you are more than likely to be ripped off. If caught with illegal drugs the best you can hope for is to be put on the next flight home, and you will find it less easy to get into America another time. If you do run into trouble you should contact your nearest consulate, which will recommend a lawyer.

SEX The dangers of casual sex are well known. AIDS remains a serious problem in the USA, where upwards of 1.2 million people are thought to be HIV positive. In many cities a majority of prostitutes carry the virus and Nevada is the only state where prostitution is legal. Enjoy the bars and nightlife but save your affections for those you can trust.

Some states, particularly in the South and Midwest, have laws restricting certain types of sexual behaviour that may be permitted where you come from. In most places the age of consent is 16, although it may be up to 18. Statutory rape (consensual sex with a minor) is treated legally in the same way as any other rape.

INSURANCE Make sure your policy protects against cancellation or delays, loss of baggage or passport, and claims for negligence. SLI (Supplemental Liability Insurance) is a type of car-hire insurance that gives you third-party liability cover against bodily injury and property damage. PAI (Personal Accident Insurance) provides a one-off payment in the case of death or serious injury (page 40, for information on medical insurance). PEC (Personal Effects Coverage) will pay for lost or stolen items, including those stolen from a car. If you plan to indulge in adventurous sports such as skiing or white-water rafting you may have to pay an extra premium. For motor insurance, see page 44.

Take copies of all your insurance policies with you and make a separate note of their numbers and any emergency phone numbers.

WHAT TO TAKE

Pack as lightly as possible, especially the bags you carry on board. You may find it useful to take a pair of binoculars, a good book, a deck of cards, maps (preferably showing rail lines), a light blanket, a pillow or large pillow case, earplugs or an eyeshade if you are a light sleeper, bathing and grooming items, a pocket torch, sunglasses, a cheap digital watch with an alarm, a small first-aid kit, bottled mineral or spring water (which will probably taste better than that provided at the drinking fountain), fresh fruit, nuts and other snacks. Wear comfortable clothes, especially shoes. A neck wallet or money belt will allow you to keep money hidden safely beneath your clothes.

MONEY

The American dollar (or buck) is worth 100 cents. Coins are one cent (penny), five cents (nickel), ten cents (dime), 25 cents (quarter), 50 cents (half dollar) and one dollar. Dollar and half-dollar coins seem almost as scarce as two-dollar bills (now no longer printed). The most common denomination banknotes, all confusingly similar in size and colour, are for one, five, ten, 20 and 50 dollars. You need plenty of coins for telephones, buses, vending machines and tips so carry enough cash on arrival to last for two or three days. US dollars are widely accepted in Canada.

Travellers' cheques are safer than carrying large amounts of cash but the process of changing them can be inconvenient, especially in remote locations or at weekends. Debit and prepaid travel cards (or 'Money Cards') are now a more popular electronic alternative to travellers' cheques. Money cards can be pre-loaded with a set amount of money before you travel then used anywhere that Visa is accepted. As long as transactions are in the currency loaded on to the card, there is usually no transaction charge. There is a low-rate charge for cash withdrawals, in addition to ATM provider charges.

Charge and credit cards such as American Express, Visa and MasterCard are accepted throughout the USA. Handy when paying a deposit for hotels, car hire or tickets by phone, they can also be used to obtain cash at banks and bureaux de change. Always make a note of the card number and keep it separately. In case of loss or theft you should notify the police and call the card company's emergency number immediately. It pays to take two credit cards with you because hotels and car-hire companies often 'block' an amount for themselves as a deposit and do not release it for some time after you have paid the bill. A second card helps in emergencies or if your first card balance gets too low. You could also ask your card company for a higher limit before you travel.

Banks generally open at 09.00 on weekdays, closing at 15.00 on Monday–Thursday, or 17.00 on Friday. Not all of them will change foreign currency or travellers' cheques and, even if they do, the commission may be high. In an emergency you can have money transferred from your bank account at home to an associated US bank, or to an office of Thomas Cook. International money orders take about a week to arrive by airmail. If you become desperate, consulates will reluctantly help you to obtain money from home.

PRICES Unless you are rich or feeling extravagant you should reserve the uptown streets for window shopping, looking for bargains where tourists are less in evidence. Books and records are particularly good value and are often found at a discount. DVDs and computer games may not be compatible with your equipment at home but CDs should be fine. Clothing is also a good buy and New York's garment district has many bargain stores. American clothing and shoe sizes are different from British or European sizes, so try things on before you buy.

Car hire, gas (petrol) and cigarettes are often only a third the price of their European equivalents. You can save even more on petrol by using a self-service station and paying with cash. US gallons (3.8 litres) are five-sixths the volume of imperial gallons (4.5 litres).

Local buses and subways provide excellent value, especially with a travel pass. Tourist bureaux should have the details. Taxis, on the other hand, can be expensive, although occasionally there is no safe or reliable alternative.

In most states a sales tax usually ranging from 3% to 9% is added to retail prices except on some foods and other goods, and these taxes may also apply to hotel rooms, airline tickets and car rental. Municipalities often impose their own taxes, too, so prices shown are usually less than you actually have to pay.

TIPPING You may think that tipping is a class-conscious anachronism inappropriate for a country where everyone has been proclaimed equal. This is not a good line to adopt with the average cab driver. He expects 10% or 15%, as do bartenders and hairdressers, and in restaurants 20% is more usual. Follow the practice of other customers or you may notice an abrupt change in the standard of service. Tipping is not necessary in self-service cafés or fast-food restaurants.

Most hotels don't include a service charge so a tip is expected. Hotel, airport and railway porters receive $1–2 per bag. Of course, you don't have to tip anyone who is rude or unhelpful. Amtrak service is free but attendants should be rewarded for exceptional assistance (page 30).

GETTING AROUND

BY CAR Trains and buses may not take you everywhere you wish to go so you may need to hire a car. You are allowed to drive for up to a year in the USA provided you hold a valid licence in a country (such as the UK) which has ratified the Geneva Road Traffic Convention. An international driving licence is not essential but will be more readily accepted by a traffic cop than the home-country version. The speed limit is mostly 35mph (48km/h) in towns and 65mph (110km/h) on highways, freeways, interstates and major roads outside towns. Limits are strictly enforced. Always carry your licence when driving – it is a legal requirement.

Rental companies have a minimum age restriction (usually 21) and sometimes a maximum. Check the limits when booking and take your passport as proof. National firms have offices in most cities and can be reached on the following toll-free numbers or websites – **Hertz** (800 654 3131; w hertz.com); **Avis** (1 800 230 4898; w avis.com); **Budget** (1 800 214 6094; w budget.com); **Dollar** (1 800 800 3665; w dollar.com); **Thrifty** (1 800 847 4389; w thrifty.com). For cheap transport, companies with names like Rent-A-Wreck (1 877 877 0700; w rent-a-wreck.com) hire out battered but roadworthy cars past their prime.

Local companies may be less expensive but national ones allow you to rent a car in one place and leave it in another, though this may be expensive. Prices depend on location, size of vehicle and rental period. Economy cars are smallest, followed by compact and standard (the normal American size). Virtually all have automatic gears. The cheapest rates are obtained if you book well ahead, especially online.

Make sure you obtain third-party insurance of at least $0.5 million, and ask for a collision damage waiver (CDW) or loss damage waiver (LDW) that includes protection against vandalism and theft. Avoid 'fuel purchase plans' where you have to prepay for a full tank of petrol or pay for what you have used when you return the car with a part-filled tank. The hire company will charge an exorbitant amount (by US standards) for the refill fuel.

If you plan to drive extensively you may find it more economical to take out car insurance before leaving home. American policies don't always include third-party protection and in some states insurance is voluntary – two good reasons for having full medical cover (page 40). Members of affiliated organisations can obtain free assistance and route maps from the American Automobile Association (*1000 AAA Dr, Heathrow, FL 32746;* ✆ *1 800 222 4357;* w *aaa.com*).

Cars for travellers with a disability Some rental companies provide hand-controlled cars (call their toll-free numbers to check). For further information contact the Society for Accessible Travel & Hospitality (SATH) (*347 Fifth Av, Suite 605, New York, NY 10016;* ✆ *1 212 447 7284;* w *sath.org*).

ACCOMMODATION

All big cities have international-style hotels such as Hiltons and Hyatts where you can expect first-class service. Prices vary with the season but a double room is likely to cost upwards of $100 per night. Single rooms cost almost as much as doubles or triples so it pays to travel in company. Hotels may offer American plan (meals included) or European (without meals). Rates are lower if you book for a week or more and some chains offer discounts with prepaid vouchers.

Smaller hotels are more individual and charge $25–75 per night for a single room. The local tourist bureau will help you choose a place in a safe area convenient for sightseeing. Bed and breakfast is becoming easier to find, especially in rural areas. Standards are high and prices start at around $35. Check with the tourist bureau or contact one of the agencies or directories for details. Those covering the whole country include:

BedandBreakfast.com 700 Brazos St, Suite B-700, Austin, TX 78701; ✆ 1 512 322 2710 or ✆ 1 800 462 2632; w bedandbreakfast.com

Bed & Breakfast Inns ONLINE 909 N Sepulveda Bd, 11th Fl, El Segundo, CA 90245; ✆ 800 215 7365; w bbonline.com

BnBFinder ✆ 1 888 469 6663; w bnbfinder.com

Motels can cost as little as $25 a night but vary greatly in quality and service. Ask to see the room before accepting. The best motels will have a restaurant, a shop and possibly a swimming pool. Major chains include Holiday Inn, Travelodge, Marriott, Ramada and Best Western. Econo Lodge (✆ *1 877 424 6423;* w *choicehotels.com/econo-lodge*) and Super 8 (✆ *1 800 454 3213;* w *wyndhamhotels.com/super-8*) are

ACCOMMODATION CODING

Based on the price of a double room:

Exclusive	$$$$$	US$200+	£150+
Upmarket	$$$$	US$150–200	£100–150
Mid-range	$$$	US$100–150	£75–100
Budget	$$	US$50–100	£40–75
Shoestring	$	up to US$50	up to £40

among the most economical places to stay. Unfortunately, motels tend to be a long way from downtown, making them less convenient for rail travellers.

An alternative, particularly for young people, are the **YMCAs** (2,600 altogether) found in most large cities in the USA. Many have swimming pools, cafés, a library and sports facilities. Single and double rooms are usually available to men and women. For information contact YMCA of the USA (*101 N Wacker Dr, Chicago, IL 60606;* ✆*800 872 9622;* w *ymca.net*).

America also has more than 300 YWCA centres, for women only. Contact YWCA USA (*1020 19th St NW, Suite 750, Washington, DC 20036;* ✆*1 202 467 0801;* w *ywca.org*).

Hundreds of **youth hostels** provide some of the best-value and friendliest accommodation, often located in a historic building. Some have family rooms. Most hostels close during the day and operate a midnight curfew. Cooking facilities are provided but alcohol and drugs are forbidden. For about $26 a night you get a bed in a dormitory (segregated by sex) but must supply your own sleeping bag. Although no age restrictions apply you are more likely to enjoy your stay if you remain young at least in spirit. International Youth Hostel membership can be taken out before travelling or guest membership purchased on arrival.

For more information contact Hostelling International-USA (*8401 Colesville Rd, Suite 600, Silver Spring, MD 20910;* ✆*1 240 650 2100;* w *hiusa.org*).

For Canada contact Hostelling International-Canada (*205 Catherine St, Ottawa, ON K2P 1C3;* ✆*1 800 663 5777;* w *hihostels.ca*).

Camping sites, public and private, can be found in most parts of the country. Unrestricted camping is still possible in wilderness areas (with a permit from the nearest park rangers' office) and some youth hostels permit camping. Reservations are recommended for state sites and those in national parks. For information contact the Director, National Park Service (*1849 C St NW, Washington, DC 20240;* ✆*1 202 208 6843;* w *nps.gov*).

Kampgrounds of America is a private organisation with 75,000 campsites throughout North America. Contact KOA (*PO Box 30558, Billings, MT 59114;* ✆*1 406 248 7444;* w *koa.com*).

If staying in one place for a few weeks it might be worth checking the price of **apartments and rooms**. Usually you need to rent for at least a month. Ask around and check in local newspapers under 'furnished rooms'. For college rooms available for let during summer you should enquire at the university housing office or local visitors bureau.

EATING AND DRINKING

FOOD Americans dine out more than most people so finding somewhere to eat is rarely a problem. New York City alone boasts 15,000 places, from unpretentious cafés and hamburger bars to some of the finest restaurants in the world. Fast-food staples such as hot dogs, burgers, pizzas, KFC and McDonald's are sure to make you feel at home, although American versions are likely to be superior.

You may be lucky enough to find one of the few remaining 1940s-style diners. An authentic place should have chrome fittings, a jukebox, ornate mirrors, counter seats and booths. Like coffee shops, diners are great for sampling the traditional American breakfast of eggs (cooked your way), crispy bacon, pancakes (with maple syrup), sausage, buttered toast and hash browns (fried grated potato), all washed down with coffee, tea (for the adventurous) or the ubiquitous Pepsi or Coca-Cola. Some places serve breakfast 24 hours a day.

Desserts are a major temptation, from homemade apple pie to chocolate fudge. No country has fancier doughnuts or better Danish pastries, not to mention chocolate-covered, peanut-filled pretzel nugget ice cream. Other ice cream varieties you may meet include garlic, lobster and many more.

America's diverse population produces a formidable range of cuisines. Some of the world's best Chinese food can be found in the Chinatowns of cities such as San Francisco and Los Angeles. You can sample black-eyed peas and grits in the south, steaks in Texas, and lobster, crabs or clam chowder in New England. Chicago invented the deep-pan pizza and in New Orleans eating is a way of life.

Some restaurants offer all-you-can-eat for a fixed charge or have two-for-the-price-of-one deals. Lunch is usually better value than dinner, but look for early-bird specials where evening meals are discounted until 17.00–18.00. Mexican food is tasty and cheap and salad bars, delis and supermarkets provide the basis for an inexpensive picnic. Sandwich bars sell any filling or bread you can think of, including the famous bagels with cream cheese.

DRINK The water is safe to drink and Americans prefer it iced. If a glass is not delivered with your meal you only have to ask. Any soft drink is a soda. Pepsi and Coke come in small, medium (meaning large) and large (meaning gigantic) sizes. Sprite and 7-Up may be familiar but root beer is definitely an acquired taste.

Bars range from the seedy to the glamorous and from cheerful to film-noir gloomy. The clientele may consist of businessmen, sports fans, LGBTs, singles, television addicts or any other all-American type. Look for cut-price drinks during happy hour, which sometimes stretches much further than 60 minutes. Arrive looking respectable between 17.00 and 19.00 and you can often fill up on free hors d'oeuvres as you sample a margarita or mint julep.

Drinks served 'on the rocks' have ice added while those 'straight up' do not. If you fail to specify you will usually get the ice. Measures are generous and spirits often 90° proof (45% vol), so don't underestimate your consumption. Draught, canned and bottled beer will most likely be served well chilled, with brands such as Budweiser familiar to many non-Americans. Canadian or Mexican brands can also often be found. Various low-alcohol and alcohol-free 'Lite' beers are widely available. Groups can save money by ordering draught beer in a (usually half-gallon/2-litre) jug or pitcher. American wines, especially those from California, can be excellent.

Some states, including Utah, have laws restricting the sale of alcohol in various ways or in certain areas. The minimum legal age for the purchase of alcohol is 21, so if you look young enough you may be asked for identification. It is an offence in most cities to consume alcohol in a public place.

PUBLIC HOLIDAYS

Banks, post offices, businesses, museums and government agencies are likely to be closed on the following dates:

USA

New Year's Day	1 January
Martin Luther King's Birthday	Third Monday in January
Lincoln's Birthday	First Monday in February
Presidents' Day	Third Monday in February
Memorial Day	Last Monday in May

Independence Day	4 July
Labor Day	First Monday in September
Columbus Day	Second Monday in October
Election Day	4 November
Veterans Day	11 November
Thanksgiving	Fourth Thursday in November
	(the day after Thanksgiving is also effectively, if
	not officially, a holiday)
Christmas Day	25 December

Some states celebrate George Washington's Birthday (12 February) instead of Presidents' Day or make 12 October Columbus Day.

CANADA Public holidays in Canada include the following:

New Year's Day	1 January
Good Friday	
Easter Sunday	
Easter Monday	
Victoria Day	Next to last Monday in May
Canada Day	1 July
Labour Day	First Monday in September
Thanksgiving	Second Monday in October
Christmas Day	25 December
Boxing Day	26 December

Travelling on holidays, even when possible, is sure to be crowded. However, if it is unavoidable, remember to book tickets and accommodation well ahead.

SIGHTSEEING

CityPasses (☏ *1 888 330 5008;* w *citypass.com*) are available for visitors to 12 cities, including New York, Boston, Philadelphia, Chicago, Seattle, Dallas and San Francisco. The San Francisco programme includes unlimited rides aboard cable cars and all other Muni transportation. Each booklet contains actual tickets, not vouchers, to six of the most popular attractions and cultural institutions, together with information about the best times to visit. Tickets are valid for nine days once the booklet has been presented to the first attraction.

Passes can be purchased at any CityPass attraction as well as many US travel agencies, visitor centres and at the website.

STUDENT CARD

Students can claim discounts ranging from air fares to accommodation and sightseeing. An International Student Identity Card (ISIC) gives generous reductions for VIA Rail train travel in Canada and for hotel chains such as Travelodge and Howard Johnson throughout North America. Discounts are available on airlines and for airport shuttle services in New York, Boston, San Francisco and Washington, DC, as well as at Busch Gardens, Sea World, Elvis Presley's Graceland, and the Rock and Roll Hall of Fame and Museum in Cleveland. There is a 24-hour emergency assistance service which card holders can call toll-free from anywhere in the world.

Cards can be bought at w isic.org and at STA Travel (page 379). To be eligible you must be a full-time student. Ask for a directory when buying your card or look for current discounts on the ISIC website.

TIME ZONES

Mainland USA has four time zones. Seattle (Pacific Standard Time) is an hour behind Denver (Mountain Standard Time), 2 hours behind Chicago (Central Standard Time) and 3 hours behind New York (Eastern Standard Time). Amtrak schedules take account of this and show local times for arrival and departure. Canada has the same time zones, with the same names, as the USA. In addition, Canada has Atlantic Standard Time (AST), 1 hour ahead of EST, and Newfoundland Standard Time, 1½ hours ahead of EST.

Canada and most of the USA, apart from Arizona and some of Indiana, observe Summer Time (Daylight Saving Time). Clocks are set ahead an hour at 02.00 on the last Sunday in April. Standard Time returns when clocks go back an hour on the last Sunday in October.

MEDIA AND COMMUNICATIONS

TELEPHONES The US telephone system is famous for its efficiency and economy. Public phones are found in train and bus stations as well as in stores, hotels, restaurants and bars. You don't have to be a customer to use one. Read the instructions before making your call and have lots of change handy, or pay with a credit card by calling ⟍1 800 CALL ATT. Local calls usually cost 25 cents. Press '1' before the area code when calling from out of town, and for operator assistance press '0'.

If you need to find a local number and have no directory, call ⟍1 555 1212. For long-distance information call ⟍1 (area code) 555 1212. Directory enquiries are free from pay phones. The international dialling code for the USA and Canada is 1. No international code is required for calls from the US to Canada and vice versa. Simply use the area code in the usual way.

Calls prefixed 800 or 1 800 are toll-free and any toll-free number can be obtained by calling ⟍1 800 555 1212. Toll-free numbers can be dialled from outside the US but in that case they are charged at the same rate as any other international call. Use only the 800 part of the prefix, not the whole 1 800.

Calling home is cheaper from a public telephone than from a hotel, which may add a surcharge. It is easiest to call collect (reverse charges) and the international operator can be contacted by dialling 0170. Give the operator the name, country and number that you wish to call, and you will be connected. The international prefix for calls from the USA is 011, which must be followed by the relevant country code (eg: 44 for the UK). Use a private telephone and dial direct between 23.00 and 08.00 for the lowest call rates.

In most places the emergency number for police, fire or ambulance is ⟍911. No coin is required. If in difficulty call the operator on 0 or 01.

MOBILE TELEPHONES (CELL PHONES) Most modern smartphones will work on mobile networks in the USA if they support 3G or 4G. Some networks, such as Sprint USA and Verizon USA, won't work on a UK-purchased smartphone but your handset will normally connect to an alternative that does (such as AT&T or T-Mobile USA). Visitors from the UK can either set up a UK-based SIM card for roaming before leaving home (the recommended option) or buy a US-based SIM card on arrival. A

UK SIM card means you keep your UK phone number and will be charged for usage by your UK network. Pay As You Go SIM cards are available for about £10, with inclusive data and calls back home for up to one month. A US-based SIM card, either from AT&T or T-Mobile USA, costs about $50 and will give unlimited US calling plus an allowance for data (additional charges apply for calling back to the UK).

For information about international coverage, you should refer to your mobile network's website before travelling. Make sure your account is enabled for international roaming as some networks require you to opt in. The cost of using your phone will depend on your network and may include extra charges for sending or receiving calls, text messages and data. To prevent unexpectedly large bills, UK mobile networks are legally obliged to cut off your data roaming connection when the charges reach £53 per month. If you wish to go above this threshold you will need to opt out of the data roaming spend limit.

Using Wi-Fi can save money on calls and this is often available free in hotels, bars, restaurants, cafés and train stations. Be careful with the security of your data when transmitting over a public network. Making phone calls via WhatsApp and Skype means there will be no additional fees charged and Skype lets you call out to a regular phone number at rates that will be cheaper than through your mobile network. It's often cheaper to send an instant message using applications like iMessage, WhatsApp, Facebook Messenger and Snapchat rather than sending an SMS text message. To minimise the amount of data required, you can download maps, ideally before leaving home, by opening the Google Maps application and searching for the place you intend to visit (eg: New York City). These can then be viewed even when you don't have an internet connection.

INTERNET With an email account through an internet service provider, you can access your mailbox while travelling. You will need to know your email server name as well as your username and password. Free email providers include Gmail (w *google.com*), Outlook Mail (w *outlook.live.com/owa*) and Mail2Web (w *mail2web.com*). Do not leave your email account unused for more than two or three months or it may be closed.

POSTAL SERVICE The US mail service is less wonderful than America's telephones, so when sending postcards home you should allow at least a week for delivery. Either put them in the appropriate box or hand them over the counter at a post office, where you will find information on mailing rates. Post offices open 09.00–17.00 on weekdays and 09.00–noon on Saturdays. Large cities often have one branch that opens 24 hours a day. You can also buy stamps (at 25% extra cost) from shops or vending machines.

Street-corner mailboxes are dark blue and may be mistaken by the unwary for litter bins. Allow between two and four days for letters to be delivered within the US, or a day more without the Zip (area) code. The correct code can be obtained from the telephone directory, at a post office, or by calling ✎1 800 ASK USPS (✎ *1 800 275 8777*). This toll-free number also has details of mailing costs, post office hours and other information.

Packets or parcels weighing 16oz (0.5kg) or more must be presented to a postal clerk or mailing agent. This is a policy designed to eliminate the risk of terrorism on aircraft.

Mail can be delivered c/o General Delivery at any main US post office, which will keep it for up to a month. To collect your letters you will need a passport or other identification.

NEWSPAPERS America has more daily newspapers than any other country in the world. There is no national press apart from the *Wall Street Journal* and *USA Today*, but the *Los Angeles Times* and *New York Times* are widely distributed outside their own cities. Local papers are inexpensive (some only 50 cents), heavy (especially at weekends) and great value for the funny pages alone. You can buy them from station shops and street-corner vending machines. A local paper gives you insight into a town's character and provides up-to-date information about clubs, hotels, shops and theatres. Look for restaurant and cinema advertisements offering special deals.

Foreign newspapers are hard to find even in big cities, although public libraries should be able to track down a week-old copy of something reassuring.

WORKING

Working illegally can result in stiff penalties, including being deported and banned from re-entering the USA for up to five years. To work legally you must obtain a special visa (J-1 or J-2) prior to departure. Forms are available from US employer sponsors. For more information contact the Federal Citizen Information Center (FCIC), originally the Federal Consumer Information Center (❧1 844 872 4681).

If you get on well with children and are aged 18 or over you can apply to work at one of America's 12,000 summer camps. Most are in the Northeast but some can be found as far west as California and Oregon. Work starts in June and lasts for about nine weeks. You can also be employed as a family companion – providing child care and doing light household duties. You receive a return flight, the necessary work permit, pocket money, board and lodging, plus two months' free time for independent travel. Contact **Camp America** (*37A Queens Gate, London SW7 5HR;* ❧*+44 (0)20 7581 7373;* e *enquiries@campamerica.co.uk;* w *campamerica.co.uk*).

BUNAC (the British Universities North America Club) (*Priory Hse, 6 Wrights Lane, London W8 6TA;* ❧*+44 (0)33 3999 7516;* w *bunac.org/uk; in the USA: 585 N Juniper Dr, Suite 250, Chandler, AZ 85226;* ❧*1 866 220 7771;* w *bunac.org/usa*) has summer camp and other work programmes in the US and Canada. Jobs last for up to 12 months in Canada (US programmes run during the summer, typically from June to September) and are for students only. Early application is strongly advised. Support is provided from a New York office and there are good travel deals, loan plans and free job directories. **Real Gap Experience** (*121–123 Mount Pleasant Rd, Tunbridge Wells, TN1 1QR;* ❧*+44 (0)1892 277040;* e *info@realgap.co.uk;* w *realgap.co.uk*) has several programmes for visitors hoping to work in North America. The H-2B Seasonal Work Visa programme offers this visa to any UK resident aged 18–38 who is looking for the opportunity to work in the States. The visa is available for the summer and winter seasons yearly and offers jobs ranging from ski instructors to hotel and restaurant positions. For full jobs listings visit w realgap.co.uk/paid-work-abroad. The **J-1 Career Training Visa** is available to UK residents with a degree and one year of experience in their degree field, or to those without a degree but with five years' experience in the same field. They are available in Accounting, Advertising, Architecture, Business Administration, Computer Science, Engineering, Finance, Hospitality and Tourism, Information Media and Communications, Management, Marketing and Sales, Public Law and Public Relations. The Student Summer J-1 Visa is specifically designed for university students on their summer break. Work for up to four months and travel for a month afterwards. This visa allows students to take a job that Real Gap Experience has on offer or to find a job on their own. Real Gap also has volunteer jobs in America, conserving the environment in the national parks of the West, at a wildlife rehab centre in America's South or as a real-life cowboy on a ranch in Wyoming.

Part Two

TRAINS AND ROUTES IN THE UNITED STATES

4

The *Coast Starlight*
Seattle–Los Angeles

GENERAL ROUTE INFORMATION

One of Amtrak's most popular and scenic routes, this is a particular favourite with young people. Not surprisingly, a party atmosphere often develops, starting in the lounge car and spreading throughout the train. On the 35-hour, 1,377-mile (2,216km) journey you can see snow-covered mountains, deep forest valleys and long stretches of Pacific shoreline. When travelling south, choose a seat on the right of the train for the best views.

ESSENTIAL INFORMATION

HIGHLIGHTS As well as visiting some of America's most dynamic cities, the *Coast Starlight* travels alongside idyllic Puget Sound and stretches of dramatic Pacific Ocean shoreline. There are stops at desirable resort towns such as Santa Barbara and San Luis Obispo, from where you can visit Hearst Castle, Orson Welles's inspiration for *Citizen Kane*.

FREQUENCY Daily. The **southbound** service leaves Seattle mid-morning to arrive in Portland by early afternoon, Emeryville (for San Francisco) early next morning, Santa Barbara by early evening and Los Angeles mid-evening. Travelling **north**, trains leave Los Angeles mid-morning to reach Santa Barbara just after midday and Emeryville by mid-evening. You arrive in Portland the following afternoon and Seattle by mid-evening.

DURATION 35 hours

RESERVATIONS All reserved. Book well ahead during summer and at weekends. Passengers for San Francisco have bus transport from Emeryville included.

EQUIPMENT Superliner coaches

SLEEPING Superliner bedrooms

FOOD Complete meals, snacks, sandwiches and drinks. The dining car offers freshly prepared meals served on china plates and linen tablecloths. At-seat meal service is available to Coach-Class passengers.

LOUNGE CAR Movies, games, hospitality hour. The Arcade Room entertains children of all ages with arcade-style video games (parental supervision required). The Pacific Parlour car (for First-Class passengers) has a library, large-screen movies, wine tastings, fresh flowers and candlelit evenings. Parlour cars are refurbished Santa Fe Heritage coaches with polished wood panelling.

BAGGAGE Check-in service is available at most stations.

Between San Francisco and Los Angeles the *Coast Starlight* follows tracks formerly used by the Southern Pacific Railroad's *Coast Daylight*, and one of that train's last steam engines was brought out of retirement to haul the American Bicentennial Freedom Train. In the 1930s, five trains a day ran between the Northeast and California – the *Rouge River, Klamath, Oregonian, Shasta Limited* and the luxurious *Cascade*, which had sumptuous Pullman cars featuring the services of a barber, a valet or ladies' maid, showers and telephones. In the 1950s, the *Cascade* became a streamlined, two-tone-grey train with a Cascade Club lounge car and a bar serving the driest of Martinis.

Rangers from the Klondike Gold Rush National Historical Park provide a narrative commentary between Seattle and Portland on select trains from Thursday through to Monday, Memorial Day to Labor Day. Rangers from the Juan Bautista de Anza National Historic Trail between Santa Barbara and San Luis Obispo or Oakland also provide a commentary on certain days throughout the year.

As on some other routes, First-Class passengers on the *Coast Starlight* may be presented with a gift, such as a glass mug or an umbrella decorated with the train's logo, as well as a 'personal amenities' kit that includes shampoo, soaps and lotions, and can receive complimentary on-board internet access via AmtrakConnect.

JOINING THE TRAIN

SEATTLE (52↓) Surrounded by mountains, Lake Washington and Puget Sound, the Emerald City was named after Chief Sealth of the Damish and Suquamish tribes. Seattle sees only 56 days of sun a year but has less rainfall than New York or Atlanta, so the city is not quite so wet as outsiders may imagine. Water provides an important leisure resource, however, and countless marinas provide enough space for two boats to every three people.

Seattle was the birthplace of Jimi Hendrix (buried in Greenwood Cemetery in the suburb of Renton), Starbucks coffee, grunge rock and Microsoft. Lately one of America's most fashionable cities, famous for its coffee houses, Seattle has been the setting for movies such as *The Fabulous Baker Boys, Sleepless in Seattle, Captain Fantastic, Get Carter* and *Battle in Seattle*, as well as television's *Frasier*. A month-long film festival is held each spring and the Folklife music festival takes place around Memorial Day.

Seattle basics

Telephone code 206

Station (*Ticket office* 06.15–21.15; *waiting room* 06.00–23.00) Handsome King St Station at 303 S Jackson, with its distinctive 240ft (73m) clock tower modelled after Venice's campanile, was built by the Great Northern Railway in 1905 & is listed on the National Register of Historic Places. Designed by the architect firm Reed & Stem, which was involved with the building of Grand Central Terminal in New York, the building was part of a larger project that moved the main rail line away from the waterfront & into a 5,245ft long (1,599m) tunnel under downtown. In 2008, this impressive landmark building was purchased for $10 from the Burlington Northern Santa Fe Railway by the City of Seattle as part of a $56 million project to develop the area & restore the building's historic character & grandeur. Lockers, vending machines, newspapers, handcarts, Red Caps, ATM banking, taxi stand.

Connections Amtrak trains operate daily into Canada, & Thruway buses connect incoming & outgoing *Coast Starlight* trains with Vancouver, BC, in about 4hrs.

Local transport

Metro buses (553 3000) operate in the downtown area. Seattle has some of the worst traffic problems in the USA so it pays to use public transport. The Seattle monorail (905 2600) was built for the 1962 World's Fair &

SEATTLE
Olympia
Lacey
Tacoma
Centralia
Kelso-
Longview
Vancouver
PORTLAND
Salem
Albany
Eugene-
Springfield
Chemult
Klamath
Falls
Dunsmuir
Redding
Chico
Davis
Sacramento
Martinez
Emeryville
SAN   OAKLAND
FRANCISCO
San Jose
Salinas
Paso Robles
San Luis
Obispo
Santa   Burbank
Barbara   Bob Hope
             Airport
Oxnard
Simi Valley
Van Nuys   LOS
           ANGELES

operates a startling 2-min service between the downtown Westlake shopping mall & the Seattle Center.

🚕 **Taxis** Yellow 📞 622 6500; Farwest 📞 622 1717

🚗 **Car rental** Budget, 801 4th Av; 📞 682 8989

🚌 **Greyhound** 503 S Royal Brougham Way; 📞 624 0618

✈ **Seattle-Tacoma Airport** Located 14 miles south & accessible by Gray Line Downtown Airporter (📞 *626 6088*) & Metro bus #174

Tours City tours with Tours Northwest, 8219 7th Av S (📞 *1 888 293 1404*). Guided sea kayak tours with Alki Kayak (📞 *953 0237*).

ℹ **Visitors bureau** Seventh Av & Pike; 📞 461 5840; w visitseattle.org; ⊕ daily.

🏠 **Accommodation** Hotels include the Fairmont Olympic at 411 University; 📞 621 1700; w fairmont.com/seattle, **$$$$**; Sorrento, 900 Madison; 📞 622 6400, **$$$$**; Inn at Queen Anne, 505 First Av N; 📞 282 7357; w innatqueenanne.com, **$$$**; Sheraton Grand Seattle, 1400 Sixth Av; 📞 621 9000, w marriott.com; **$$$**; Days Inn Downtown, 2205 Seventh Av; 📞 441 6976, **$$**; Moore Hotel, 1926 Second Av; 📞 448 4851; w moorehotel.com, **$$**.

11th Avenue Inn Bed & Breakfast, 121 11th Av E Seattle, WA 98102; 📞 720 7161; w 11thavenueinn.com, **$$$$**.

Green Tortoise Hostel, 105 Pike; 📞 340 1222; w greentortoise.net, **$**. YMCA, 909 Fourth Av; 📞 382 5010. Incorporates the Traveller's Aid office. Over 200 rooms for men or women, **$**. YWCA, 1118 Fifth Av; 📞 461 4888. Women over 18 only, **$**.

Recommended in Seattle

Seattle Center 305 Harrison; 📞 684 7200 or 📞 684 7100; w seattlecenter.com. This legacy of the 1962 World's Fair, a min or so from downtown by monorail, has over 70 acres (28ha) of parkland & entertainments, dominated by the 605ft (198m) Space Needle (📞 *905 2100*; w *spaceneedle.com*). Take an elevator to the observation deck for lofty views of the city, Puget Sound & Mount Rainier.

The Waterfront Where gold arrived during the 1897 Klondike rush, ex-Australian streetcars now run along waterfront tracks. Ferries to Canada & Alaska go from Pier 48, & to Bremerton & Bainbridge Island from Pier 52 (Colman Dock), giving wealthy island commuters inspiring views of snow-capped mountains & an occasional whale.

Ye Olde Curiosity Shop Pier 54, sells souvenirs & has a museum of bizarre relics (📞 *682 5844*). Pier 55 has Argosy Cruises (📞 *623 1445*) & excursions from Pier 56 go to Tillicum Village on Blake Island (📞 *933 8600*).

Seattle Aquarium Pier 59, has coral reef & underwater dome (📞 *386 4300*; w *seattleaquarium.org*).

Pike Place Market Between downtown & the Waterfront at First & Pike; w pikeplacemarket.org; ⊕ daily; admission free. This 1907 market is a warren of shops, restaurants, galleries & stalls selling every kind of fish, fruit & vegetable. Great for street entertainment, people-watching & dodging the flying salmon.

Pioneer Square Covering 12 blocks from Second Av to the Waterfront. The square is where Seattle began in the 1850s with the setting up of a sawmill & where logs were skimmed along Skid Road. During the gold rush this became a dangerous place & in the Depression it was a refuge for down-and-outs (the original 'Skid Row'). Art galleries, restaurants & shops now occupy restored buildings & daily Underground Tours (✆682 4646) explore the basements of Old Seattle.

Klondike Gold Rush National Historic Park 319 Second Av S; ✆220 4240; ◷ daily; admission free. Depicting the excitement & hardship, with old mining photographs & clothes. Chaplin's *The Gold Rush* is shown on w/end afternoons.

Museum of Flight 9404 E Marginal Way S; ✆764 5700; w museumofflight.org; ◷ daily; admission charge. Chronicles the history of flying from the Wright Brothers up to the space age.

Northwest Railway Museum 38625 SE King in Snoqualmie; ✆425 888 3030; w trainmuseum.

org; ◷ daily; admission charge. One of the largest displays in the country, with steam locomotives, passenger & freight cars, & specialised railway equipment that built & maintained the right of way. Built in 1890, Snoqualmie Depot has been fully restored & there are train rides through the upper Snoqualmie Valley.

Seattle Art Museum Downtown 1300 First Av; ✆344 5275; w seattleartmuseum.org; ◷ daily; admission charge. The largest art museum in the region, with Native American paintings, African masks, old masters & contemporary works.

Pacific Science Center 200 Second Av N; ✆443 2001; w pacsci.org; ◷ daily; admission charge. Explore the tropical butterfly house & see robotic dinosaurs. IMAX films in 3D.

SEATTLE: ALL ABOARD! (52↓) The *Coast Starlight* leaves King Street Station with Smith Tower, once one of the city's tallest buildings, on your right. You pass the Kingdome sports stadium, also on the right, and for the next few miles travel through industrial scenes where factories are owned by the likes of Westinghouse, Nabisco and Ford.

Boeing Field (↑7/45↓) Seattle's largest manufacturing company is on your right. The airport is used for testing and sometimes by private planes. Boeing's original factory, a red-brick building seen across the runway, is now the Museum of Flight. With over 175 aircraft and spacecraft, this is the largest museum of its kind in the world (see above).

The *Coast Starlight* continues through residential areas, with the Green River on your right.

Kent (↑20/32↓) Look left for an interesting old train station built by the Puget Sound Shore Railroad, a subsidiary of the Northern Pacific Railway.

After the train crosses the Green River, half an hour from Seattle, the urban landscape begins to give way to small farms and dairies. The train crosses the White River and makes a long right turn towards the east, crossing the Puyallup River.

Puyallup (↑40/12↓) This town, like the river, was named after a Native American tribe. A pioneer named Ezra Meeker who had crossed the plains with an ox team in 1882 to set up home here returned to New York in 1906, marking the Oregon Trail with many monuments.

You go through downtown and attractive western suburbs then cross Clark's Creek, travelling southwest through tall pine forest. During the summer months, look for the bright, dandelion-like flowers of gosmore, or 'cat's ear'.

⚏ TACOMA (↑52/42↓) Note the eccentric domed Transit Center Building. Tacoma was chosen as the terminus of the North Pacific Railroad in 1873 and was transformed from rustic frontier outpost into a bustling commercial city with the finest hotel on the North Pacific shore. It became known as 'the city of destiny', where much of the state's lumber reached the sawmills. Tacoma's Beaux-Arts Union Station is no longer a working railroad facility but its 90ft-high (27m) copper dome still stands out on the city skyline. The rotunda houses a collection of glass by Tacoma artist Dale Chihuly and is used as part of the federal courthouse. The old Milwaukee, St Paul & Pacific Railroad freighthouse, located a few blocks south of Amtrak's station, has found a new life as Tacoma's public market. Timber is still an important industry here, along with shipbuilding. The **visitors bureau** is at 1516 Commerce (◥1 *800 272 2662;* **w** *traveltacoma.com*).

Tacoma overlooks Commencement Bay in the east and the Tacoma Narrows highway bridge to the west. **Point Defiance Park, Zoo and Aquarium** is famous for its sharks and giant Pacific octopuses (◥*253 591 5337;* **w** *pdza.org; admission charge*). The **State History Museum** can be found at 1911 Pacific Avenue (◥*888 238 4373;* **w** *wshs.org; admission charge*).

The *Coast Starlight* leaves Tacoma alongside the city waterway. Old City Hall, with its elaborate clock tower, can be seen perched beside the North Pacific Railroad building on cliffs to your left.

A few minutes later the train goes through a tunnel and turns due south, emerging on the shoreline of Puget Sound with the Olympic Mountains beyond. This idyllic coast with its evergreens and blue water has dozens of coves and piers, where pleasure boats come and go. Look also for herons and bald eagles gliding above the rivers, which have names such as Nisqually, Nooksack and Skookumchuck.

Stellacoom (↑26/16↓)

A ferry terminal serves Anderson and McNeal islands, visible across Henderson Bay to your right. Between early spring and late summer brilliant yellow broom grows beside the track.

⫸ OLYMPIA–LACEY (↑42/20↓)

Olympia is Washington's state capital, with a Capitol dome that claims to be the largest domed masonry building in the country. The 900,000-acre (360,000ha) Olympic National Park is accessible along US Highway 101. Amtrak's station is at 6600 Yelm Highway SE in Lacey, a suburb of Olympia. The wooden building was designed in the style of a classic early 20th-century station and opened in 1993. Passengers previously used a remote shelter at East Olympia.

Soon after pulling out of Olympia, the *Coast Starlight* crosses the Skookumchuck River.

⫸ CENTRALIA (↑20/45↓)

This food-processing and logging town was founded in 1875 by a former slave from Virginia called George Washington. Early settlers built the blockhouse in Fort Borst Park as a defence against marauding Indians. Amtrak's picturesque brick station (*ticket office* ⊕ *09.00–16.45*) is at 210 Railroad Avenue. Handsomely restored in the 1990s, it was opened by The Northern Pacific Railroad in 1912 to serve the city's booming population. As the train departs you glimpse the Mount St Helens volcano across fields to your left. A massive eruption in 1980 killed 57 people, together with thousands of birds, animals and fish. Traces of grey ash can still be seen, although grass and a few trees now grow on 'pumice plain'.

The train continues south through Chehalis then crosses the Newaukum River.

Winlock (↑18/27↓)

The former 'egg capital of the world' used to ship a quarter of a million cases of eggs to market each year, and the planet's largest egg nestles in a monument to your right. Winlock's once-mighty chicken industry is still celebrated with an annual festival.

Castle Rock (↑35/10↓) You cross the Toutle River, with the Cowlitz River on your right. Mud was pushed this far from the St Helens eruption 40 miles (64km) away in 1980. The volcano is now a 110,000-acre (45,000ha) park; you can take a flight over the summit and buy souvenirs sculpted from the debris.

KELSO–LONGVIEW (↑45/40↓) 'The smelt capital of the world', where vast numbers of these small fish swim up the Cowlitz River each year to spawn, Kelso also has a major lumber industry and deep-water port. The **Cowlitz County Historical Museum** (*405 Allen;* ☏ *360 577 3119;* w *www.co.cowlitz.wa.us/museum*) features a settler's log cabin built in 1884, Native American artefacts and other exhibits of local historical interest. Kelso's Multimodal Transportation Center was originally built in 1912 for the Northern Pacific Railroad and it became an Amtrak stop in 1981. The station underwent extensive renovation beginning in 1994 and now includes commercial and intercity bus services. In 1871–72, the Northern Pacific Railroad came to the Cowlitz Valley and built a short line from Kalama to Commencement Bay that later became part of the transcontinental rail system. This line carried passengers and freight both ways on the east bank of the Cowlitz, and at that time the stop was called Crawfordville. In 1884, Peter Crawford, of Kelso, Scotland, officially founded the town of Kelso, which was a rowdy place catering to local loggers and the lumber mills. The townspeople petitioned the Northern Pacific for a better station and the brick passenger and wooden freight depot was built. Kelso, the county seat, is on the eastern bank of the Cowlitz, directly across from Longview, the larger town. Timber baron Robert A Long founded Longview in 1924. A large brick station with a tall clock tower was built but the tracks were washed away in a flood in 1933. Longview remains an important town for the lumber industry and is the home of the largest pine nut collection in the United States, housed in the Northwest Nut and Conifer Preservation Center, owned and operated by a local enthusiast.

On a clear day, three of America's most impressive mountains can be seen as you leave. Mount St Helens (8,400ft/2,560m) and Mount Adams (12,307ft/3,750m) are to your left, and Mount Rainier (14,410ft/4,390m) to your right. Between May and October, Gray Line tour buses operate from Seattle to Rainier National Park.

Columbia River (↑8/32↓) To your right, the train joins the river which used to represent the border between the United States and Canada. The *Coast Starlight* route follows the Columbia River as far as Vancouver in Washington State, with Oregon on the opposite shore. Look for gigantic rafts of logs being transported downstream.

Trojan Power Plant (↑12/28↓) The site of this former nuclear energy plant stands on the Oregon side of the river. The plant was decommissioned in 1993 and finally demolished in 2006.

Kalama (↑15/25↓) Look right for the world's largest totem pole. The landscape begins to turn into marsh as you approach Lake Vancouver, meeting its shoreline on the right.

VANCOUVER (↑40/25↓) Not to be confused with Vancouver, Canada. The Hudson's Bay Company built Fort Vancouver as a trading post in 1824, making this the oldest non-Native American settlement in the northwest USA. Amtrak's station (*ticket office* ⏰ *08.30–20.30. Waiting room* ⏰ *08.15–21.00; information*

📞 *360 694 7307*) is at 1301 West 11th. In 1879, the Northern Pacific connected Vancouver to Puget Sound, and in the 1880s, a railroad ferry service crossed the Columbia River to link to Portland and California by rail. The wood-frame depot was constructed in 1907–08 for the Northern Pacific Railroad. Passengers board north–south-bound and east–west-bound trains on different sides of the building – the *Empire Builder* on the southeast side, *Coast Starlight* and Amtrak *Cascades* trains on the northwest.

The *Coast Starlight* leaves Vancouver and soon afterwards crosses the Columbia into Oregon by way of Hayden Island. You then cross the Willamette River near Portland before crawling among freight yards, industrial plants and ocean-going ships being loaded.

🚂 **PORTLAND (↑25/65↓)** Spread along the Columbia River between the Cascade Mountains and the Pacific, Oregon's only metropolis is a seaport famous for its many gardens, fountains and parks, and for having one of the country's largest bookstores, which covers an entire city block. The eco-friendly 'City of the Roses' considers itself a rival to Seattle for the accolade of 'America's most liveable city'.

Portland basics

📞 **Telephone code** 503

🚂 **Station** (*Ticket office & waiting room* ☉ 05.30–22.00; information 📞 *273 4864*) Union Station, at 800 NW Sixth Av, has been in continuous operation since it was built in 1896 on what had been a lake in an old part of town. The large echoing building boasts chandeliers, ceiling fans, evocative pictures & an antique weighing machine. It was constructed as part of the Northwest Pacific Terminal Company & owned jointly by the Northern Pacific, Union Pacific & Southern Pacific railroads. The centrepiece of the Romanesque & Queen Anne architecture is the landmark 150ft (45m) clock tower with its 4-sided Seth Thomas clock & a neon sign encouraging travellers to 'Go By Train'. In 2009, the city's downtown transit mall was remodelled to include Union Station on the green & yellow light-rail lines. Amtrak travellers now have rail-to-rail access from Union Station to Hillsboro, Wilsonville, Clackamas & Portland Airport. Metropolitan Lounge, vending machines, newspapers, handcarts, Red Caps, café/shop, restaurant, left-luggage room, taxi stand.

Connections Thruway buses go to Pendleton & Boise, Idaho

🚌 **Local transport** Portland is well served by TriMet buses (📞 *238 7433*) & the MAX light railway. Both are free downtown.

🚕 **Taxis** Green Cab 📞 *234 1414*; Broadway; 📞 *333 3333*

🚗 **Car rental** Enterprise, 445 SW Pine; 📞 *275 5359*

🚌 **Greyhound** 550 NW Sixth Av, close to Union Station; 📞 *243 2361*

✈ **Portland International Airport** Located 8 miles (13km) Northeast by MAX Red Line service train every 15 mins

Tours Gray Line 📞 *241 7373*; Rose-Smith 📞 *201 1921*. Whale-watching with Marine Discovery (📞 *541 265 6200*; w *marinediscovery.com*).

ℹ **Visitors bureau** 701 SW Sixth Av; 📞 *275 8335*; w *travelportland.com*; ☉ winter Mon–Sat, summer daily.

🏠 **Accommodation** Hotels include the Benson at 309 SW Broadway; 📞 *228 2000*, w *bensonhotel.com*, **$$$$$**; Hotel deLuxe, 729 SW 15th Av; 📞 *219 2094*; w *hoteldeluxeportland. com*, **$$$$**; Lucia, 400 SW Broadway; 📞 *225 1717*; w *hotellucia.com*, **$$$$**; Ace, 1022 SW Stark; 📞 *228 2277*; w *acehotel.com/portland*, **$$$**; Days Inn, 1530 NE 82nd Av; 📞 *253 1151*; w *wyndhamhotels.com/days-inn*, **$$**; Mark Spencer, 409 SW 11th Av; 📞 *224 3293*; w *markspencer.com*, **$$**.

White House B&B, 1914 NE 22nd Av; 📞 *1 800 272 7131* or 📞 *287 7131*; w *portlandswhitehouse.com*, **$$$$$**; Portland International Guesthouse, 2185 NW Flanders St; 📞 *224 0500* or 📞 *877 228 0500*; w *pdxguesthouse.com*, **$$**.

YMCA, 9500 SW Barbur Bd; 📞 *223 9622*; w *ymca-portland.org*, **$$**. YWCA, 10305 East Burnside; 📞 *988 6400*; w *ywcapdx.org*. Women only, **$**. AYH Youth Hostel, 3031 SE Hawthorne Bd; 📞 *236 3380*; w *portlandhostel.org*, **$**.

Recommended in Portland

Rose Festival ✆227 2681; **w** rosefestival.org. A week of mostly free parades, concerts, sporting events & bands honours the city's favourite flower in early Jun.

Washington Park 4033 SW Canyon Rd; ✆319 0999. Douglas firs, a Japanese garden & statues can be found here, along with 400 varieties of rose.

Oregon Zoo 4001 SW Canyon Rd; ✆226 1561; oregonzoo.org; ⊕ daily; admission charge. Only 2 miles (3km) from downtown by TriMet bus #63 or the Westside MAX. Beavers, otters & nocturnal cats live in natural settings. Steam & diesel trains operate around the zoo & through the forested hills to Washington Park.

Portland Art Museum 1219 SW Park Av; ✆226 2811; **w** portlandartmuseum.org; ⊕ daily; admission charge. One of the oldest & largest museums in the country, featuring works by Renoir & Monet as well as Native American art & English silver.

Pioneer Courthouse 701 SW Sixth Av; ✆223 1613; ⊕ daily; admission free. The oldest public building in the Northwest dates from the 1860s. You can climb a stairway up to the cupola & get a view of downtown & Pioneer Courthouse Sq.

Classical Chinese Garden 239 NW Everett; ✆228 8131; **w** portlandchinesegarden.org. Located in the middle of Portland, this is the largest urban Suzhou-style garden outside China. Rugged rocks & serpentine walkways are reflected in the lake.

Oregon History Center 1200 SW Park Av; ✆222 1741; **w** ohs.org; ⊕ daily; admission charge. State history comes to life in this spectacular building with interactive exhibits.

Oregon Museum of Science & Industry 1945 SE Water Av; ✆797 4000; **w** omsi.edu; ⊕ closed Mon; admission charge. Hands-on fun, with live demonstrations, a planetarium & laser shows. Visit the USS *Blueback* submarine, see the Omnimax cinema & check out the latest touring exhibitions.

PORTLAND: ALL ABOARD! (↑25/65↓) Departing Portland, the *Coast Starlight* quits the Burlington Northern Santa Fe (BNSF) route followed so far and switches to the Union Pacific (UP). You cross the Willamette River on a steel bridge then pass through Milwaukie, Gladstone and Chackamas suburbs. As the train heads into the fertile Willamette Valley, the Cascades and Mount Hood (11,235ft/3,425m) can be seen to your left. The Coast Range is on the right.

Oregon City (↑30/35↓) The original capital of Oregon Territory, this was the end of the Oregon Trail. More than 200,000 people travelled the 2,000-mile (3,218km) trail when 'Oregon fever' swept the country over 150 years ago. The first Protestant church and first Masonic lodge west of the Rockies were built here. An interpretive centre at 1726 Washington (✆ *503 657 9336;* **w** *historicoregoncity.org*) has films, exhibits and a multi-media show which explain the famous pioneer route.

Waterfalls appear on your right, with lumber factories and giant logs next to the river. In springtime, look for fields of daffodils and tulips near the city of Canby.

Aurora (↑45/20↓) Reached after the train crosses the Pudding River, Aurora was founded by Germans in the 19th century as America's first commune.

Woodburn (↑50/15↓) A nostalgic Southern Pacific steam engine stands on the left. As the train continues, you travel among fields of strawberries, raspberries, blackberries and loganberries.

▂▂▀ SALEM (↑65/28↓) Oregon's capital is one of the oldest cities in the state, with many historic buildings. Willamette University, the oldest in the west, can be seen to your right as the train arrives. Also look right for the white marble Capitol topped by a gold-plated statue of a man with an axe (the *Spirit of Oregon*). The 'cherry city' is the birthplace of the modern maraschino cherry industry, after Oregon State

University professor Ernest Wiegand perfected the art of preserving the cherry.

Salem's beautiful 1918 Beaux-Arts station building was originally constructed for the Southern Pacific Railroad and has been fully restored, with tall columns, decorative plasterwork, a black marble ticket counter and terrazzo and marble floors. Hanging light globes in the lobby were recast according to the original designs.

The *Coast Starlight* pulls out of Salem past the city airport to your left. Between the towns of Turner and Marion, 15 minutes later, look for a llama and alpaca farm on your right. Formerly kept for their wool, the animals are now used for pet therapy and as pack animals on expeditions into the mountains.

Jefferson (↑20/8↓) You cross the Santiam River.

₩₩ ALBANY (↑28/40↓) Founded in 1845, Albany was connected by railroad in 1870 after citizens paid the O & C company $50,000 to be included in the line. This agriculture and lumber town now supplies almost all the grass seed sold in America. It also hosts the world championship timber carnival, with everything from tree climbing to axe throwing. Amtrak's station at 110 Tenth Avenue SW was constructed for the Southern Pacific Railroad in 1909 and is one of the oldest continuously used passenger rail stations in the country. The building was restored in 2006 and a 60ft (18m) clock tower, that features two clocks and spells out 'Albany' in illuminated letters, was constructed.

The **visitors bureau** is at 110 Third Avenue (☏ *1 800 526 2256;* w *albanyvisitors.com*).

The *Coast Starlight* leaves Albany and crosses the Calapooia River, entering a region known as 'the plains of Lebanon'.

Tangent (↑15/25↓) The town was named after the long, straight stretch of track here. The buttes seen on the left, created by prehistoric volcanoes, contain fossils and mammoth bones. To your left are some of the fields producing grass seed. Between here and Eugene look out for farms growing mint, another local speciality.

Harrisburg (↑25/15↓) The distant snow-covered Three Sisters Mountains appear to the left before the train crosses the Willamette River. Southern Pacific rail yards and Lane County jail are seen to your right as you near Eugene and travel through Junction City.

₩₩ EUGENE–SPRINGFIELD (↑40/165↓) Home to the Nike Corporation, 'The lumber capital of the USA' is the westernmost city served by Amtrak. Look for huge stacks of timber being sprayed with water to reduce the fire risk. Named after a settler called Eugene Franklin Skinner, who built the first cabin here in 1846, Eugene is now the second-largest city in Oregon and the 'running capital of the universe' (home town of Mary Decker Slaney, America's greatest ever female middle-distance and distance runner; at one point, she held every American women's record from the 800 to 10,000 metres, setting 36 national and 17 world records). This region is famous for its mild climate and for fishing and boating on the McKenzie River. The ticket office of Amtrak's renovated station at 433 Willamette opens from 05.10 to 21.00. Now listed on the National Register of Historic Places, the depot and the park that originally surrounded it were part of the City Beautiful movement of the early 20th century.

The historic 1908 Southern Pacific station and 1955 mail shed addition have become a safe and convenient multimodal transportation facility, accommodating Amtrak passengers, motorists, bus users, cyclists and pedestrians, and local Amtrak staff. The $4.5 million project (including approximately $3.5 million in federal funds) was designed so that the station would meet the aesthetic and functional needs of a modern transit facility while preserving the building's historic features.

The *Coast Starlight* leaves past the University of Oregon campus on the right before crossing the tree-lined Willamette River into Springfield, the sister city to Eugene.

Tracks curve right as the train climbs slowly for 70 miles (112km) into the Cascade Mountains, winding through 22 tunnels and several snow sheds towards the source of the Willamette. Snow sheds are wooden or concrete structures built over the track to protect it from avalanches and accumulating snow. Spectacular waterfalls, wild flowers, rhododendrons and dense vegetation feature in the alpine scenery of Willamette National Forest on both sides.

Lookout Point Lake (↑30/135↓)
Lookout Point Dam (276ft/84m high) and the reservoir are on your left, with Diamond Peak (8,750ft/2,670m) to the south. The Three Sisters Mountains appear in the left distance.

Westfir (↑60/105↓)
Spanning the Willamette River to your right is one of the many covered bridges in this region.

Oakridge (↑65/100↓)
The train starts climbing 'the hill' to Cascade Summit, an ascent of 3,600ft in 44 miles (1,100m in 70km). You cross Salmon Creek then follow Salt Creek on the right.

Salt Creek Canyon (↑80/60↓)
The train follows the canyon for 25 minutes. Views of the tracks above and below dramatically demonstrate the steepness of your climb. There are another 2,700ft (800m) to go from the health resort of McCredie Springs to the summit along 30 more miles (48km) of track. The tops of tall trees appear beside the train windows and dense, dark evergreens cover the mountains to your right. In autumn, the occasional maple makes a spectacular splash of crimson or yellow.

Willamette Pass (↑120/45↓)
Source of the Willamette River, with the slopes of Willamette Path ski resort visible ahead.

Cascade Summit (↑140/25↓)
The line is 4,800ft (1,460m) above sea level here. Maiden Peak (7,811ft/2,380m) overlooks the deep-blue water of Odell Lake to your left. The purple and green Cascade Mountains are all around, giving breathtaking views as the train gently descends among Douglas firs, waterfalls and wild flowers towards the Oregon–California border. Look for quail creeping in the grass banks between tunnels.

▬▬ CHEMULT (↑165/70↓)
Diamond Peak (8,750ft/2,670m) can be seen on your right. Buses connect Chemult with Bend, a resort 60 miles (96km) to the northeast. Located off the Dalles–California Highway (US Route 97) in Fremont-Winema National Forest, the station consists of a platform and a small building containing a waiting room and welcome centre. A kiosk provides information to rail and car travellers passing through.

Chemult was established in 1924 as a stop for the Southern Pacific Railroad's Cascade Line. During construction, it was known as 'Knott' and the station's name was changed to Chemult when the line opened. The town's name comes from a Klamath chief who signed the Klamath Lake Treaty in 1864.

After Chemult you pass Mount Thielsen and Mount Scott (both over 9,000ft/2,750m) to your right. Diamond Lake is also on the right a few minutes later as you enter the Winema National Forest. Logging operations appear on both sides as you continue towards Klamath Marsh. Half an hour from Chemult the train joins the Williamson River on the right, following it intermittently through a canyon for the next 15 miles (24km) after crossing at Kirk.

Chiloquin (↑55/15↓) America's largest museum of logging is in nearby Collier State Park. The train continues down Calimus Hill to Modoc Point.

Upper Klamath Lake (↑60/10↓) One of the country's largest freshwater lakes, where in summer you may see white pelicans. You follow the eastern shore of the lake for 18 miles (29km), with Mount McLaughlin (9,495ft/2,894m) to your right. Mount McLaughlin has been known by a number of different names over the years, including Snowy Butte and Mount Pitt (after the Pit River).

▄▄▀ KLAMATH FALLS (↑70/160↓) Sawmills appear on your left near the station. Geothermal springs once used by Klamath Native Americans for cooking are now harnessed to heat homes, and the Klamath County Museum explains this underground activity along with pioneer history. Amtrak's grey stone station at 1600 Oak Avenue was built for the Southern Pacific Railroad in 1910. The waiting room features handsome wooden benches and white glass Art Deco hanging pendants.

The *Coast Starlight* departs with the Klamath River to your right then travels via two short tunnels and crosses the state line, 20 miles (32km) south, into California. You may catch a first glimpse of the Cascades' highest peak, Mount Shasta (14,160ft/4,453m), snow clad and ethereal by moonlight as the train speeds through the small Butte Valley communities of Dorris and Mount Hebron. Past Mount Shasta is an extinct volcano, the beautiful Crater Lake.

Grass Lake (↑80/80↓) This is the highest point on the route and from here the *Coast Starlight* descends around the base of Mount Shasta, cutting through solidified lava flows. Black Butte is seen on the left before you travel down via the alpine town of Mount Shasta City into the Sacramento River Canyon. The train follows this winding canyon for 32 miles (51km) and passes a spectacular waterfall.

▄▄▀ DUNSMUIR (↑160/100↓) A base for the Southern Pacific railway, Dunsmuir is also an all-year recreation centre. The Central Pacific Railroad (a Union Pacific predecessor) completed its line along the Siskiyou Trail in 1886, leading to the founding of a town to support its division point at Upper Soda Springs. The settlement was called Pusher but the first station – opened that year in a railroad boxcar – was called Dunsmuir. The station moved up to the engine house at Upper Soda Flats in 1887 and the town renamed itself Dunsmuir after a family of wealthy coal barons from British Columbia. They created the town's fountain, which can still be seen at the Dunsmuir Botanical Gardens.

Since 2006, Amtrak passengers have had access to the well-lit waiting room in the now-renovated railway building. The Dunsmuir Railroad Depot Historical Society has opened a display area for photographs, railroad memorabilia and equipment. The society participates in the annual Dunsmuir Railroad Days, held each July at the station. The depot museum is also home to the Southern Pacific (SP) Shasta Division archives, including maps, historic photographs, drawings and other memorabilia.

The train departs and continues its slow descent from the high tableland. The grey granite spires of Castle Crags appear to the right.

REDDING (↑100/70↓) Located at the north end of the Sacramento Valley, Redding is close to Lake Shasta and Lassen National Park. Shasta Dam, three times the height of Niagara Falls, backs up the Sacramento, McLoud and Pit rivers. Amtrak passengers use a platform next to a stone and stucco depot at 1620 Yuba, built by the Southern Pacific Railroad in 1923. The California & Oregon Railroad established a temporary end-of-line terminal and supply centre in Shasta County, known as the Railroad Reservation, in this area. The town grew up around it and the railroad called the stop Redding, after its railroad land agent, Benjamin B Redding. Local residents felt it should have been named after Pearson B Reading, an early California pioneer, and the name was changed in 1874. Confusion resulted as railroad officials and the post office refused to change, so the original spelling was returned a few years later. All that remains of the original Railroad Reservation is the Wells Fargo Building, also known as the SP Freight Station, the oldest building in Redding.

Look left as the train continues to see the Sierra Nevada, and right for views of the Coast Range.

CHICO (↑70/110↓) Home of one of California State University's campuses, Chico was originally settled by gold miners. Fortunes were later made by those who came to farm, since most things seem able to grow here, including rice, peaches and olives. General John Bidwell established the town and his mansion now forms part of a state park. Other famous residents have included abstract painter Jackson Pollock, astronomer Carolyn S Shoemaker, and Annie Bidwell, leader in women's suffrage and the temperance movement.

In 1996, the Olympic torch arrived at Chico's Amtrak station at 450 Orange, before being carried through the streets with thousands of citizens celebrating along its path to the summer Olympics in Atlanta. The station consists of a platform next to Chico's historic depot, built for the Southern Pacific in 1892. The city and its Chamber of Commerce saved the building from demolition and it now houses the Chico Art Center, with a coffee bar located inside a refurbished train car. The city has been used as a setting in 19 films, including 1947's *Magic Town*, when James Stewart stepped off the train at the Chico depot.

Nearby is Oroville Dam, the largest earth-filled dam in America.

Marysville (↑40/70↓) Another former gold prospectors' town, Marysville is a centre for agriculture, with Yuba City adjacent to the west. The 'Gateway to The Gold Fields' once had hopes of becoming 'The New York of the Pacific', but vulnerability to flooding from the Feather and Yuba rivers prevented this.

Roseville (↑90/20↓) The train turns southwest here, crossing the American River just before Sacramento.

SACRAMENTO (↑110/20↓) To the scorn of some who live in glitzier cities further south, Sacramento has been California's capital since 1854. The 1849 gold rush started nearby at Sutter's Mill (gold was actually first found in 1848) and the Pony Express ended its inaugural run here in 1860. A rail link over the Sierra Nevada soon afterwards brought the first trains.

Many 19th-century houses have been preserved and a reconstructed **Fort Sutter** stands on the east side of town. The 1869 **State Capitol** features ornate plaster and splendid oak staircases. Sacramento is the hub of a food-producing area specialising in almonds, peaches and pears, and the **visitors bureau** is at 1608 I (✆*916 808 7777;* w *cityofsacramento.org/Visitors*).

Amtrak operates from a historic station at 401 I. Opened by the Southern Pacific Railroad in 1926, it is part of a complex that dates back to the Central Pacific Railroad's construction of the western portion of the first transcontinental rail line. The imposing Renaissance Revival-style station has a red-tile roof and a waiting room with a 40ft-high (12m) barrel-vaulted ceiling, mahogany woodwork, marble floors and enormous arched windows. A mural by John A MacQuarrie depicts the 1863 groundbreaking ceremony of the Central Pacific Railroad.

The station today is part of a massive development to create a multimodal transportation hub, revitalise Sacramento's urban centre and end 150 years of railroad ownership over a large area adjacent to downtown. Prior to construction over the site, the rail yards must undergo environmental detoxification after more than a century of heavy industrial contamination. The station building is also being rehabilitated and conserved.

Close by and seen to your left at 125 I is the **California State Railroad Museum** (✆*916 323 9280 or*✆*916 445 5995 for train ride information;* w *csrmf.org;* ⊕ *daily; admission charge*). The Transcontinental and Sacramento Valley railroads began in Old Sacramento and this massive museum on an 11-acre (4.5ha) site displays 21 restored locomotives, railroad cars and 46 exhibits, including a 1929 St Hyacinthe Pullman sleeper. The Central Pacific Depot at First and J is a faithful reconstruction of Sacramento's 1876 depot and shows bustling train travel in the late 19th century. Steam trains travel on holidays and at weekends (April–September) on the **Sacramento Southern Railroad** for a 6-mile (10km) round trip through the Feather River Canyon. More nostalgia is on hand at the hardware store where the Central Pacific and Southern Pacific were planned by the Big Four, the men behind the building of the first transcontinental railway line – Leland Stanford, Charles Crocker, Mark Hopkins and Collis Huntington. Together with single-minded and clear-eyed designer Theodore Judah, these financiers and merchants had the idea for a transcontinental route which would make it easier to trade with the east coast and would encourage more trade with Asia. The store museum recreates the boardroom and has much archive material. The Southern Pacific Railroad eventually came to own a fifth of California's land.

The Capitol's gilded dome can be seen to your left as the train leaves, crossing the Sacramento River with a drawbridge on the left. As you travel through the flat landscape of the Sacramento Valley look for fields which are sometimes flooded to grow rice. The Coastal Range is to your right and the attractive Sierra foothills away to your left as you cross the Yolo Bypass on a long low trestle.

⊶ DAVIS (↑20/40↓) The town, originally called Davisville, was named after a local farmer who founded it in 1868. Part of the University of California is based here and Davis has enlightened policies promoting recycling and energy conservation. Bicycle pathways exist throughout the city to discourage car use. Amtrak's Spanish adobe-style station on the right is a historic landmark that dates from 1913 and carries a Southern Pacific logo. The beautiful concrete and stucco depot was designed in Mission Revival style, following a precedent set by the Santa Fe Railway.

As the *Coast Starlight* leaves past the university campus look right to see some of the research animals, including llamas and pygmy goats. You also pass fields of sunflowers.

Suisun-Fairfield (↑25/15↓) Note the pretty pink and cream station building
on your left, a scheduled stop for the *California Zephyr*. The white pillars of Solano County Courthouse are to your right at the end of Union Avenue. Large military transport aircraft can be seen at the Travis Air Force base on your left.

The train races on over flat agricultural land past a ridge on the right, beyond which is the Napa Valley. As you cross Suisun Marsh at up to 79mph (130km/h), look for ducks, herons and cattle. Boeing's pioneer wind farm generates electricity on your right.

Mothball Fleet (↑30/10↓) Across the bay lies a fleet of transport ships kept
in 'mothballs', officially known as the Suisun Bay Reserve Fleet. Only a few vessels remain but at its peak Suisun Bay had 340 ships lined up in neat rows. In the left distance is Mount Diablo (3,849ft/1,170m). The beacon on top of the mountain was extinguished after Pearl Harbor but is lit once a year by war veterans.

You cross the impressive Benicia–Martinez Bridge spanning the Carquinez Strait. Before the double-track steel bridge opened in 1930, trains had to be ferried across the water in sections. Benicia, on your right, was the state capital from 1853 to 1854. Look for oil tankers in the harbour as you near Martinez.

⚒ MARTINEZ (↑40/40↓) Named after a Spanish governor, Martinez was
the birthplace of baseball star Joe DiMaggio and the Martinez, forerunner of the Martini. It was also the home of John Muir, an early environmentalist and father of the modern conservation movement. Amtrak's station at 601 Marina Vista Avenue is the connecting point for services along the San Joaquin Valley. Opened in 2001, the architecture of this award-winning intermodal facility resembles an old-fashioned train station with high ceilings and canopied benches. A balcony overlooks the tracks and an 800ft (244m) platform. In 2003, the city constructed a memorial to those who died in the 9/11 attacks. The September 11 Memorial includes two pieces of steel girder from the World Trade Center and stands close to the station. The city's museum occupies an old house to the left of the building.

Amtrak Thruway shuttle buses make a 20-minute journey from Martinez to **Six Flags Marine World** (*1001 Fairgrounds Dr, Vallejo;* 707 644 4000; w *sixflags.com*). Marine World is home to thousands of animals, including tigers, sharks, dolphins, walruses, killer whales and a herd of elephants. Opened in 2018, the Harley Quinn Crazy Coaster is the world's first duelling looping ride.

The *Coast Starlight* continues along the rocky shore of Pablo Bay and Carquinez Strait to the right, with gulls, yachts and fishing boats. You go through Crockett and pass the California & Hawaii Sugar factory and several large oil refineries. Mare Island Shipyard and California's Maritime Academy are on the far side of the strait. To the right also are the Marin County Hills and Mount Tamalpais (2,604ft/791m).

Richmond (↑25/15↓) Over 100,000 people worked at Richmond's Kaiser
Shipyards during World War II. The town is now a San Francisco suburb, its modern station on the right linked to the Bay Area Rapid Transit system. Look for BART trains lined up on the left. Richmond is also a stop for Amtrak's *California Zephyr*, *San Joaquin* and *Capitol Corridor* trains.

San Francisco's skyline appears across the bay to your right as you leave and speed through Berkeley. The Golden Gate Bridge is to the north and Oakland Bay Bridge (8 miles/13km long, including approaches and toll plaza) to the south.

Golden Gate Fields (↑5/35↓) Look for this racetrack on your right, next to an aquatic park.

EMERYVILLE (↑40/5↓) Pixar Animation Studios as well as many biotech and software companies have their headquarters here. Passengers for San Francisco disembark at Amtrak's modern station at 5885 Horton for transfer by shuttle bus into San Francisco's downtown area, connecting via the Oakland Bay Bridge with the Transbay Temporary Terminal, Pier 39 on Fisherman's Wharf, the San Francisco Shopping Center at 835 Market and the Financial District (Hyatt Regency). Located between Berkeley and Oakland, Emeryville's train station was the first new one to be built in northern California in over 60 years when it opened in 1994.

SAN FRANCISCO (↑5/5↓) Free shuttle buses connect the Emeryville train station with downtown San Francisco in about 30 minutes.

The 'City by the bay' is famous for its Golden Gate Bridge, fog in the morning, vertiginous streets, elegant houses and Alcatraz. Home of Dashiell Hammett and Sam Spade, San Francisco was the birthplace of beatniks, hippies and the topless bar. Finance, industry and a large LGBT community coexist in the cosmopolitan atmosphere. With 'Silicon Valley' to the south, the city has become home to some of the world's most successful dot.com companies, creating hundreds of 25-year-old millionaires. Spaniards arrived here in 1776 but the city prospered only after it became a part of the United States. When gold was discovered in 1848, ships and wagon trains, then the railroads, began bringing thousands of settlers across the Sierra Nevada. San Francisco's Chinatown was founded (like the one in Vancouver, Canada) by immigrants who worked on the transcontinental railroad. Neither the 1906 earthquake nor the tremors of 1989 and more recently have dissuaded a million people from making the city their home.

San Francisco basics

Telephone code 415

Station (*Ticket office* ⏲ *06.00–22.20; waiting room* ⏲ *24hrs*) Amtrak no longer uses San Francisco's Ferry Building bus stop & has moved to a shiny new rail & bus station in downtown San Francisco. The Salesforce Transit Center takes up 3 blocks just south of Mission St in the South of Market neighbourhood & is now a stop for Muni buses & Amtrak. Named after the nextdoor skyscraper occupied by the cloud tech giant, this $2.2 billion, 1 million-square-foot (92,903m²) complex is expected to handle around 45 million passengers a year & will eventually be a high-speed rail & commuter train hub for the proposed California Light Rail system that is planned to connect northern & southern California.

This landmark building has an undulating crystalline 'skin' exterior & sun-flooded central entrance hall. The 5.5-acre (2.2ha) rooftop park is like a San Francisco High Line, with open grassy areas, a playground & kiosks with books, art supplies & board games should you want a game of Scrabble in the sun. An outdoor amphitheatre will host performances at night. Amtrak offers all the services that were available at the Ferry Building, including baggage check-in, ticketing, payphones & vending machines.

Connections Caltrain services operate to San Jose & Gilroy (1 800 660 4287). Thruway buses go to Santa Cruz. Futuristic BART trains leave from Market St & are a fast & inexpensive way to explore Oakland, Berkeley, Fremont & Concord (510 465 2278). Alameda-Contra Costa Transit District buses serve the East Bay area (510 891 4700).

Local transport San Francisco can best be seen on foot or by cable car. Or you can use buses & the Muni Metro, a light railway running partly underground. For information on buses, cable cars & Muni trains, 673 6864.

Taxis Luxor 282 4141; Yellow 333 3333

Car rental Hertz, 325 Mason; 771 2200

Greyhound 425 Mission, in the Salesforce Transit Center; ✆495 1569

San Francisco International Airport (SFO) 14 miles (22km) south on US Highway 101. American Airporter buses connect to a downtown terminal at 120 Willow (✆*202 0733*), or you can take a BART train or SamTrans bus #397 (✆*1 800 660 4287*).

Tours Tower Tours, 288 Beach; ✆345 8687. Bay cruises from the Blue & Gold Fleet at Pier 39 (✆*705 8200*). Air tours from Seaplane Adventures (✆*332 4843*).

Visitors bureau 900 Market; ✆391 2000; w sftravel.com; ⊕ daily

Accommodation Everything from expensive, classic hotels to downbeat rooming houses can be found, with budget accommodation in Japantown & Oakland.

Hotels include the Essex, 684 Ellis; ✆474 4664; w essex-hotel.sanfranciscotravelhotel.com, **$$**; Grant Plaza, 465 Grant Av; ✆ 434 3883; w grantplaza.com, **$$**; Music City, 1353 Bush; ✆816 6207; w musiccityhotel.org, **$$**; Mystic, 417 Stockton; ✆400 0500; w mystichotel. com, **$$**; Opal, 1050 Van Ness Av; ✆673 4711; w theopalsf.com, **$$**; Amsterdam, 749 Taylor; ✆673 3277; w hostelsf.com, **$**.

Bed & Breakfast San Francisco; ✆1 800 452 8249; w bbsf.com, or Red Victorian Bed & Breakfast, 1665 Haight; ✆864 1978; w red-victorian-bed-breakfast.san-francisco-hotels-ca.com, **$$$**.

Central (IYHF) Hostel, 312 Mason, 1 block from Union Sq; ✆788 5604; w hihostels.com/hostels/hi-san-francisco-downtown. Free continental b/fast & Wi-Fi. Max 4 beds per dorm room, private rooms with bathroom available, **$$**.

City Center Hostel, 685 Ellis; ✆474 5721; w hihostels.com/hostels/hi-san-francisco-city-center. Renovated, 75-room hostel offers both private rooms & 4- or 5-bed dorms, all with private bathrooms, **$**. International (IYHF) Hostel, Bldg 240, Fort Mason; ✆771 7277; w hihostels. com/hostels/hi-san-francisco-fisherman-s-wharf. Overlooks the Golden Gate Bridge. Mostly dormitory rooms, **$**.

Recommended in San Francisco

Golden Gate Bridge Linking the city with Marin County to the North is one of the world's best-known & most impressive landmarks. At 2 miles (3.2km) long – 7 miles (11km) including approaches – it incorporates 80,000 miles (128,000km) of cable & is painted orange rather than gold. Magical views of San Francisco from the Marin County side.

Golden Gate Park Between Fulton & Lincoln Way is one of the world's largest manmade parks, where many museums & the odd buffalo can be found among 1,000 acres (400ha) of lakes, redwoods & eucalyptus. Information from the office at McLaren Lodge, 501 Stanyan (✆*831 2700*).

Maritime Museum 2 Marina Bd; ✆561 7000; w maritime.org; ⊕ daily; museum free, pier admission charge. Photographs, models & relics showing west-coast seafaring life from sail to steam are located in a building shaped like a 1930s liner. Excellent ranger-guided tours of the historic ships moored at nearby Hyde St Pier.

Cable Car Barn & Museum 1201 Mason; ✆474 1887; w cablecarmuseum.com; ⊕ daily; museum admission free. Cable cars travel 9 miles (14.5km) of track at up to 9mph (14.5km/h) & are America's only historic landmarks with wheels. Observe this unique system in operation & see old cable cars (including the first, built in 1873), along with other exhibits & films.

Fisherman's Wharf On the waterfront between Taylor & the Embarcadero, the wharf has gift shops, salt air, cruise boats & hordes of tourists. Open-air stalls sell freshly cooked seafood while sea lions bark for fish & gulls glide above the water. Downmarket pleasures include a wax museum, the Guinness World of Records & Ripley's 'Believe It Or Not!'.

The Cannery 2801 Leavenworth ✆771 3112; w cannerycourtyard.com. Built in 1894 as a fruit-canning factory, the Cannery has been converted into a mall with dozens of shops, a comedy club, restaurants & art galleries. Jack's Cannery Bar boasts more beers on tap than almost anywhere in the country. There are stalls & cafés among century-old olive trees in the courtyard & street performers entertain on summer w/ends.

Coit Tower Located on top of Telegraph Hill, just east of North Beach; ✆249 0995; ⊕ daily; admission charge. The wealthy eccentric Lillie Hitchcock Coit left San Francisco $125,000 to build this memorial to volunteer firemen. Completed in

1933, the slender white concrete column has great views & impressive murals depicting California during the 1930s.

San Francisco Museum of Modern Art 151 Third; ✆357 4000; w sfmoma.org; ⊕ closed Wed; admission charge. One of the largest contemporary art museums in the world, San Francisco's Museum of Modern Art (SFMOMA) contains more than 33,000 modern works, including paintings by Henri Matisse, Georges Braque, Jackson Pollock, Marcel Duchamp, Frida Kahlo, Edward Hopper, Francis Bacon & Andy Warhol, as well as photographs by Ansel Adams.

Wells Fargo Museum 420 Montgomery; ✆396 2619; w wellsfargohistory.com/museums; ⊕ Mon–Fri; admission free. A history museum for one of California's largest banks, located on the site where Wells Fargo first opened for business in 1852. Among the hundreds of relics are a Concord Coach used by Wells Fargo in the 1860s, an impressive display of gold dust & ore, pistols, photographs, early posters & mining equipment.

Alcatraz ✆212 852 4822 (for ferry information & tickets); w alcatraz.us; admission charge. A million visitors every year come on boats from Pier 41 to the isle of pelicans, former residence of Al Capone, 'Machine Gun' Kelly & the 'Birdman'. The prison's first 53 inmates, including Capone, were brought on a 1,000-mile (1600km) journey in a train equipped with barred windows & reinforced doors. Each man was clamped in leg irons & chained to his seat. The rock closed as a federal penitentiary in 1963 but still has the power to freeze your spirit. Make reservations early (at least 1 week ahead during summer) & dress warmly for the excellent tours led by national park rangers.

Golden Gate Railroad Museum Formerly located on the naval base at Hunter's Point, the GGRM collection is now located at Niles Canyon Railway, 5550 Niles Canyon Rd, Sunol; ✆650 365 2472; e 2472info@ggrm.org; w ggrm.org; admission free. The museum started in 1975 when pharmacist Michael Mangini acquired an old steam engine he saw in the San Mateo Fairgrounds parking lot & began restoring & repairing the vintage ex-SP #2472 Pacific-type locomotive. In May 1991, #2472 steamed under its own power for the first time to make its debut at that year's Railfair & since then the GGRM has continued collecting artefacts & rolling stock & securing the machinery & parts needed to establish the museum as a 'hands-on' facility for the public. It also operates charters & excursions using #2472 as motive power.

SAN FRANCISCO: ALL ABOARD! (↑5/5↓)

Buses leave from the Ferry Building and cross the Oakland Bay Bridge, with great views to your left of the city, Alcatraz and the Golden Gate Bridge. To your right are Oakland and the tall Gothic tower of the University of California at Berkeley. The *Coast Starlight* continues south from Emeryville to Oakland.

Southern Pacific's *Daylight* train operated between the Bay area and Los Angeles from the 1930s to 1971. One of the world's most beautiful trains, it was painted red and black with an orange California sun emblem on the side. The night-time *Lark* ran through San Luis Obispo and Santa Barbara until the 1960s and was a stylish all-Pullman affair with the emblem of a winged silver moon. Southern Pacific's *Starlight* was a night-train version of the *Daylight*.

OAKLAND (↑5/70↓)

Known as 'the place where the trains stopped', Oakland lacks San Francisco's glamour but does have inexpensive accommodation less readily found on the other side of the bay. Amtrak's glass and stone station was built in 1994, replacing an older station built in 1912 at the terminus of the transcontinental railroad. The Southern Pacific's Beaux-Arts-style 16th Street Station (now called Central Station) was condemned as unsafe following an earthquake in 1989. The adjacent former superintendent's office was used as a waiting room until the tracks were moved further west in the 1990s. The building still stands and some Oakland residents hope that it can be salvaged and restored.

A pedestrian bridge takes you across from Amtrak's modernistic station to Jack London Square, named after Oakland's former resident and author of *The Call of the Wild*. Other notable citizens have included Gertrude Stein, Jessica Mitford and the Black Panthers. The **visitors bureau** is at 481 Water (☏ *510 839 9000;* w *oaklandcvb.com*).

The **Oakland Museum** (*1000 Oak;* ☏*510 318 8400;* w *museumca.org; admission charge*) features Californian art and a simulated journey from sea level to the Sierra Nevada. Nearby are the Victorian houses of Old Oakland and the **Pardee Museum** (w *pardeehome.org; admission charge*), built in 1868–69 by Enoch Pardee, a gold rush immigrant, and once the home of the 'earthquake governor', George Pardee. **Lake Merritt**, a unique fresh- and salt-water lake close to the city centre, has a wildlife refuge and boating.

The train leaves and gathers speed through industrial suburbs with the Bay Bridge still visible to your right.

Jack London Square (↑5/65↓)
Oakland's main tourist attraction on your right features the Jack London Museum, the USS *Potomac*, Franklin D Roosevelt's presidential yacht, and dozens of waterfront restaurants. Also on your right is the former Alameda base, one of the US Navy's busiest air stations during World War II, with 3,600 officers and 29,000 enlisted personnel.

Oakland Coliseum (↑20/50↓)
This massive circular construction on your right is home to the Oakland Athletics baseball team. The stadium hosted a record 66 shows by The Grateful Dead between 1979 and 1995. The BART train line is to your left.

You continue across mudflats via Drawbridge, an officially certified 'ghost town' which was formerly the home of railroad workers, bootleggers and duck hunters. The narrow-gauge South Pacific Coast Railroad opened a depot on Station Island in 1876 and ten passenger trains a day used to stop here. Two drawbridges were removed long ago so the only path leading into Drawbridge is the Union Pacific Railroad track. The sinking town is now part of the Don Edwards San Francisco Bay National Wildlife Refuge and no longer open to the public.

Moffett Field (↑50/20↓)
Beyond the lower end of San Francisco Bay are three giant hangars that are some of the largest unsupported structures in the country. The former naval air station is now owned and operated by the NASA Ames Research Center.

California's Great America Park (↑60/10↓)
Formerly known as Marriott's Great America Park. Look right for rollercoasters and other amusement rides as the mudflats are left behind. The new RailBlazer single-rail rollercoaster is one of only two of its kind in the world.

Santa Clara (↑65/5↓)
The enclosed sports stadium of Santa Clara University can be seen to your right in this computer industry centre of 'Silicon Valley'. Just south of town you travel among extensive Southern Pacific rail yards and pass a historic brick roundhouse.

⚏ SAN JOSE (↑70/70↓)
California's oldest city and first capital was founded in 1777 as Pueblo de San José de Guadalupe. Larger than San Francisco in area and population, San Jose has fruit and wine industries as well as many companies specialising in aerospace and computer technology, including Adobe Systems, Cisco and eBay, as well as Hewlett-Packard, IBM and Hitachi. The **Mission of Santa Clara de Assisi** is a reminder of earlier days.

Amtrak's restored station at 65 Cahill was designed by Southern Pacific Railroad architect John H Christie in Italian Renaissance Revival style (one of only four in California) and opened in 1935. The station was placed on the National Register of Historic Places in 1993 and its restoration completed a year later, when it was renamed the Diridon Station to honour former Santa Clara County Supervisor Ron Diridon, 'father' of the VTA light rail system. This multi-level building is planned as a future station on the BART extension to Silicon Valley and California high-speed rail, offering connections to BART, high-speed rail, Caltrain 'Baby Bullet', Amtrak, ACE and VTA light rail train and buses. The opening scene of Alfred Hitchcock's 1964 film *Marnie* was shot on the platform here. Caltrain commuter services operate to and from San Francisco.

The *Coast Starlight* travels on through the Santa Clara Valley, one of the richest farming regions in America. To your left are Mount Hamilton (4,430ft/1,350m) and the Diablo Mountains, with the beautiful Santa Cruz Range to your right.

Gilroy (↑30/40↓)

'The garlic capital of the world', where tons of garlic-laden food are cooked and eaten by devotees at the town's August festival. You can see and sometimes smell these plants growing near the tracks. Marilyn Monroe was once crowned as Gilroy's 'garlic queen'. To your right are St Mary's Church (with its gold bell) and the City Hall clock tower.

Pajaro Gap (↑40/30↓)

You cross the Santa Cruz Mountains, via Chittenden Pass and the San Andreas Fault on a bridge near Logan, into the Pajaro Valley – 'the valley of the birds'. Look for herons, divers and buzzards, as well as more of the Santa Cruz Range to your right. Exotic eucalyptus trees flourish beside the tracks.

Watsonville (↑45/25↓)

First settled during the 18th-century gold rush, Watsonville has many attractive Victorian houses. This area specialises in growing apples, lettuces and strawberries. Spanish explorer Don Gaspar de Portola was the first European to discover the nearby redwoods.

Castroville (↑60/10↓)

'The artichoke capital of the world', where tall, bushy plants grow in fields of black earth to your right. In 1949, an unknown Marilyn Monroe was named the town's first 'artichoke queen'.

⚏⚏ SALINAS (↑70/110↓)

The centre of America's salad bowl, where huge crops of strawberries, watermelons, spinach and other vegetables fatten in rich, black earth beneath a benevolent sun. More than 80% of the lettuce grown in the United States comes from here.

Salinas was the birthplace of John Steinbeck, who described his home town in *East of Eden*. His beautiful Victorian house at 132 Central Avenue is now a restaurant and museum, and the public library owns a collection of his manuscripts.

Amtrak's attractive Art Deco-influenced Spanish Revival-style station at 11 Station Place was built in 1942 by the Southern Pacific Railroad. The waiting room is embellished with decorative blue and yellow glazed tiles. Other original features include streamlined letters over the Amtrak desk reading 'Tickets' and a simple clock face on the opposite wall. Thruway buses serve Monterey (immortalised by Steinbeck in *Cannery Row*) and Carmel.

West of the depot stands a long, wooden SP freight house constructed in the early 1880s and recently restored. In 1919, the Railway Express Agency (REA) erected a building that was moved about 100ft (30m) west in the 1930s to make way for the creation of an underpass. During the move, the building was also turned around so that the track-side freight doors now face Railroad Avenue. Later abandoned, this building was restored in the 1990s and now houses the Monterey & Salinas Valley Railroad Museum, which includes exhibits tracing the history of the railroad in the region. An HO scale model railroad layout depicts Monterey County as it was in the spring of 1953.

Big Sur, where Jack Kerouac, Henry Miller and Orson Welles lived, is 15 miles (24km) to the west.

You leave Salinas past an incongruous Firestone factory standing in fields to your right then travel 100 miles (160km) along the Salinas River Valley. San Benito Mountain (5,258ft/1,600m) is the highest peak of the Diablo Range to your left. The rugged Santa Lucia Mountains are on your right.

Soledad (↑20/90↓)
Built as a mission town in 1791 – the name is Spanish for 'solitude' – Soledad was the setting for John Steinbeck's novel, *Of Mice and Men*. The large, modern prison to your left once held the Black Panther leader, Eldridge Cleaver.

The *Coast Starlight* continues along the Salinas Valley with the river to your right and Pinnacles National Monument on the left. Just before Rocky Point tunnel (1,305ft/400m long), look left for an airfield where light planes used for crop spraying are based.

King City (↑45/65↓)
'The most metropolitan cow town in the west', where many crates of agricultural produce await transportation on your right. John Steinbeck's father was the town's first railroad agent.

San Lucas (↑65/45↓)
A statue of Christ protects the cemetery seen to your right.

Camp Roberts (↑85/25↓)
The camp is the headquarters of California's National Guard.

San Miguel (↑95/15↓)
On your right among cactus plants is the 18th-century Mission San Miguel Arcángel, its two-storey, red-tiled adobe structure enclosing the best-preserved interior of all California's missions. *Coast Starlight* tracks from Oakland to Los Angeles closely follow the Spanish mission path, *El Camino Real* ('the Royal Road'), founded between 1769 and 1823 by Franciscan father Junípero Serra. The 21 missions and four chapels along the *Camino Real* from San Diego to Sonoma were each a day's journey apart.

PASO ROBLES (↑110/60↓)
The transportation centre at 800 Pine was built in 1998 and stands next to the original restored Southern Pacific Depot which now houses retail shops. The centre includes space for Amtrak, intercity buses, car rental agencies and local and regional buses.

The Southern Pacific Railroad arrived in 1886 to serve visitors coming to sample the area's famous curative hot springs and a magnificent new resort hotel began in 1889. In 1913, the renowned concert pianist Ignace Paderewski came to the springs for a successful treatment of his arthritis. He kept a private car with a piano at the train station, and townspeople would gather there to hear him play in the evenings. After resuming his concert tour, he returned to live at the hotel and bought two ranches just west of the city.

Paso Robles was once known as Almond City because local growers in the early 20th century created nearby the largest concentration of almond orchards in the world. Cattle and horse ranches, wheat, barley, garden produce, fruit and nut orchards have been important to the city. Today, much of this land is devoted to wineries and vineyards.

Atascadero (↑15/45↓)
The golf course on your right is bounded by the Santa Lucia foothills. Atascadero's red-brick City Hall houses a history museum.

Cuesta Pass (↑40/20↓)
A quintessential railroad experience begins as the train climbs into the Santa Margarita Mountains, negotiating five tunnels and giving magnificent views of the Santa Lucias. Los Osos Valley is below and Highway 101 opposite. Look for rocky outcrops, adventurous sheep, pine trees, eucalyptus and scrub oak. Splendid white oaks can be seen in the valley below.

The descent from Cuesta Grade represents a fall of more than 1,000ft in 11 miles (300m in 18km), with the old wooden trestle over Stenner Creek visible ahead.

Horseshoe Curve (↑55/5↓)
The *Coast Starlight* winds down to San Luis Obispo, taking two spectacular sweeping curves that bring the entire train into view. On your right is the California Men's Colony, a state penitentiary from which Timothy Leary once made his escape. As the train crosses Stenner Creek, look left for California's Polytechnic State University.

⟂⟂⟂ SAN LUIS OBISPO (↑60/125↓)
This oasis of palm trees, sunshine and Spanish architecture began in 1772 as the Mission San Luis Obispo de Tolosa. Many of the buildings on Marsh Street were built for rail workers' families when it was an important railroad town. **San Luis Obispo County Historical Museum at** *696 Monterey (✆ 805 543 0638; w historycenterslo.org; ⊕ Wed–Mon; admission free)* explores the history of the county. The **visitors bureau** is at 895 Monterey (✆ 805 541 8000; w visitsanluisobispocounty.com).

Amtrak's colourful Spanish Colonial Revival-style station is at 1011 Railroad Avenue, from where buses leave for the amazing **Hearst Castle** (*750 Hearst Castle Rd, in nearby San Simeon;* ✆ *1 800 444 4445; w hearst-castle.org; ⊕ daily. A charge is made for tours and reservations – up to 60 days in advance – are strongly advised*). California's main tourist attraction after Disneyland was the home of William Randolph Hearst, the real-life entrepreneur and newspaper tycoon who became Orson Welles's inspiration for *Citizen Kane*. The 'Mediterranean Revival' mansion boasts 130 telephones and is crammed with baths, swimming pools, marble statues, armour, Persian rugs and flamboyant furniture from around the world. Former guests have included Charlie Chaplin, George Bernard Shaw, Buster Keaton, Cary Grant and Winston Churchill.

As the train leaves San Luis Obispo note the historic locomotive turntable on your right.

Grover City (↑15/110↓)
Obsolete rail coaches to the right now house a restaurant. The *Coast Starlight* continues south, crossing the Santa Maria River.

Pismo Beach (↑20/105↓)
Eucalyptus trees and dunes to your right conceal the resort of Pismo Beach, famous for its clams.

The train climbs Callender Hill then travels through Guadalupe and the Santa Maria Valley before emerging from the Schuman Canyon.

Vandenberg Air Force Base (↑50/75↓) For half an hour the train proceeds through the Strategic Air Command western missile test range, home of B-52 planes and firing site for Minuteman missile tests. Minuteman Beach is to your right. Further south, at Purisma Point, several satellite launch pads can be seen on the right and Vandenberg airfield is to your left. The base is military territory so no photography is allowed.

Pacific Ocean (↑51/74↓) More peaceful scenes appear on your right as the train travels for over 100 miles (160km) through unspoiled heather moorland with splendid views out across the Pacific Ocean.

Surf (↑60/65↓) You cross the Santa Ynez River with more launch pads on your right and oil rigs out to sea.

Space Shuttle (↑65/60↓) The big white buildings on your left were used during the Space Shuttle development programme and are now abandoned.

Point Arguello (↑70/55↓) This has been the site of many wrecks and an automatic lighthouse on the cliffs warns passing ships of the danger. Look out for dolphins and migrating grey whales in spring and autumn. The train's tracks run over a trestle above Jalama Beach Park at the southern end of Vandenberg Air Force Base.

Point Conception (↑80/45↓) Note the historic lighthouse, one of the earliest in California, still in use on the bluff as you continue south along the cliff tops. Ocean views here are shared only with grazing cattle since this area is inaccessible to the public except by train. The Santa Ynez Mountains begin far off to the left and extend south beyond Santa Barbara.

Gaviota (↑95/30↓) The name is Spanish for 'seagull'. You cross on high trestles above Gaviota Pass and Tajiguas Creek.

Refugio State Beach (↑100/25↓) Picnic tables dot the beach to your right. Oil rigs and production platforms then come into view as the train accompanies the Santa Barbara Channel, discovered in 1542 by the Portuguese explorer Juan Cabrillo. He was buried on San Miguel Island, seen out to your right, after he died there the following year.

The *Coast Starlight* temporarily leaves the coast and goes inland towards Santa Barbara, passing on the right the bell tower of the University of California at Santa Barbara, which houses a carillon of 61 bells.

Santa Barbara Mission (↑123/2↓) The 'Queen of the Missions' on your left was founded in 1786 and has been in use ever since. The only mission with twin towers, its fountain is fed by an aqueduct.

⚫⚫⚫ SANTA BARBARA (↑125/45↓) Originally the home of Chumash Native Americans, this resort and retirement area is located invitingly between a palm-lined beach and the Santa Ynez foothills. Santa Barbara was discovered by Sebastián Vizcaíno on St Barbara's Day in 1602 and it was here in 1782 that Spain built its last New World fortress, the Presidio Real. Spanish influence continues in the white adobe and red-tiled architecture, much of which had to be reconstructed after a 1925 earthquake.

The **visitors bureau** is located at 500 E Montecito (☏*805 966 9222 or*☏*1 800 676 1266;* w *santabarbaraca.com*).

Amtrak's Spanish-style station at 209 State was designed by Santa Barbara architect Francis W Wilson. Built for the Southern Pacific in 1902, it was restored to its original grandeur in 2000. To the left of the station is the Moreton Bay fig tree, planted in 1877 and the largest of its kind in America. Branches spread more than 160ft (50m) to provide welcome shade. The **Museum of Art at** *1130 State* (☏*805 963 4364;* w *sbma.net*) has American and Impressionist works as well as art from Asia and a children's gallery.

The **South Coast Railroad Museum** is 7 miles (11km) west (*300 N Carneros Rd, Goleta;* ☏ *805 964 3540;* w *goletadepot.org;* ⊕ *Wed–Sun; donation*). Amtrak's *Pacific Surfliner* trains travelling north of Los Angeles serve Goleta station. A 1901 Southern Pacific wood-frame depot has been relocated in Lake Los Carneros Park and restored to house model trains, rare photographs and miniature train rides.

The *Coast Starlight* leaves Santa Barbara among some of the city's finest residential areas.

Andree Clark Bird Refuge (↑4/41↓) The wildlife sanctuary next to a freshwater lagoon on your right is home to 200 bird species including herons, egrets, cormorants and many migrating birds.

Miramar (↑5/40↓) The old station house to your left has been converted into a restaurant.

Summerland Beach (↑6/39↓) A few minutes later, you pass Bates Beach, where nude bathers are sometimes seen frolicking. From here to Ventura the train, like Highway 101, travels along the shoreline.

Look for surfers at Carpintera Beach and Emma Woods Beach, where on a clear day you can see out to the Channel Islands. At Mussel Shoals a causeway leads to the island on which oil production began in 1964. More oil platforms appear in the channel before you cross the Ventura River and again head inland.

Ventura (↑30/15↓) In 1542, Spanish explorer Juan Rodríguez Cabrillo was the first European to discover Ventura, though the area has been inhabited for thousands of years by Chumash Native Americans. The town was in independent Mexico until the Mexican–American War of 1845–48, which resulted in the cession of California and much of the Southwest to the United States. Its name changed when the Southern Pacific Railroad arrived in San Buenaventura in 1886 and mistakenly printed tickets calling the town 'Ventura'.

To your right are the fairgrounds, home of the Ventura County Fair and Ventura Raceway, 'the best little dirt track in America'. The 1782 San Buenaventura Mission is to your left. A quaint museum contains the original church doors and two unique, original wooden bells.

Ventura is a scheduled stop for some *Pacific Surfliner* trains. The *Coast Starlight* continues south, crossing the Santa Clara River on a long, low trestle.

▄▄▀ OXNARD (↑45/20↓) Founded by the four Oxnard brothers, who made their fortune out of raising sugar beet and built the world's largest beet-processing factory in 1897. The factory functioned until 1958 and the giant warehouse next to it still stands. Now a centre for citrus and other fruit production, Oxnard is the home of California's strawberry festival and ships millions of baskets worldwide.

The city is also home to two large US Navy bases, Port Hueneme and NAS Point Mugu, and has developed the new Channel Islands Harbor.

Amtrak now uses Oxnard's modern Transportation Center after moving from a former Southern Pacific passenger station on East Fifth Street. The *Coast Starlight* travels east from the station into the beautiful Simi Valley with the Simi Hills to your right and Santa Susana Mountains to your left.

Camarillo (↑10/10↓)
The railroad coast route came through in 1898 and built a station here. A mission-style St John's Seminary stands on the hill to your left.

⚏⚏⚏ SIMI VALLEY (↑20/30↓)
Ronald Reagan's Presidential Library is located in this predominantly white suburb of Los Angeles. In 1992, a local jury acquitted four white policemen of using excessive force to arrest a black motorist, Rodney King, and the verdict led to riots in cities across America.

The Pacific Coast Stage Line used to run over the Santa Susana Pass into Simi Valley on its route between Los Angeles and San Francisco. In the 1890s, the Southern Pacific Railroad built a tunnel through the Santa Susana Mountains and built a depot that served passengers and farmers in the Simi Valley for more than 60 years. After the Santa Susana Depot closed in the 1970s, it was moved 2 miles (3km) east and is now a park museum featuring railroad history in the region, with many artefacts and historical photos. An HO scale model railroad layout of the coast route between Los Angeles and Portland in the early 1950s is operated by the Santa Susana Railroad Historical Society. After Simi Valley the *Coast Starlight* tackles the imposing Santa Susana Mountains, where tunnels and passes take you through a stark landscape of rocks and cacti. Early silent films such as *The Squaw Man* and Buster Keaton's *Three Ages* were filmed here, as well as James Cagney's *White Heat* and Alfred Hitchcock's *North by Northwest*. Over 3,500 productions have been made at the Iverson family ranch, including Laurel and Hardy's *The Flying Deuces* and Westerns such as *The Cisco Kid*, *The Virginian*, *Lone Ranger*, *Bonanza* and *Gunsmoke*. After movie-making ended in the mid 1960s, part of the ranch was occupied by the notorious murderer Charles Manson as a base for his followers, known as The Family.

Chatsworth (↑20/10↓)
On the border of Los Angeles County, this is the San Fernando Valley – land of the swimming pool. Millions of Angelinos live the suburban life in an area the size of Chicago.

⚏⚏⚏ VAN NUYS (↑30/5↓)
Amtrak shares the modern glass-and-concrete station with Metrolink commuter trains, local buses and taxis. Look for factories formerly belonging to General Motors and Schlitz as the scenery becomes industrial. Van Nuys Airport appears to your right before the train passes beneath the San Diego freeway.

⚏⚏⚏ BURBANK-BOB HOPE AIRPORT (↑5/25↓)
Trains stop only to deposit passengers (travelling south) or receive passengers (going north). A shuttle bus service runs between Amtrak's station and the airport terminal. Under the Rail2Rail programme, Amtrak passengers with valid tickets can travel on Metrolink to Los Angeles Union Station from Burbank. There are plans for a Regional Intermodal Transportation Center here to combine bus, train and rental car traffic into one hub, with a people-mover connecting to the airport terminal. Burbank Airport is a test area for the Lockheed factory seen beyond runways to your left.

Burbank (↑5/20↓) The city of Burbank is to your left. The movie industry started in Burbank with First National Pictures in 1926 and among the many films made here since are *Casablanca*, *High Noon*, *Mary Poppins* and *Bonnie and Clyde*. Disney, Warners and Columbia film studios, as well as NBC Television, have facilities among the Santa Monica Hills on your right. This is where the helicopter scenes for television's *MASH* were shot.

Glendale (↑10/15↓) The ornamental Spanish-style 1920s station has starred in many movies and has recently been renovated.

Soon after Glendale you pass Forest Lawn Memorial Park (page 81), next to Griffith Park on your left. The *Coast Starlight* travels on deeper into the city of Los Angeles.

Los Angeles River (↑8/7↓) The train travels alongside the river for 10 minutes. The concrete channel to your right is another favourite film location, notably for *Point Blank*, *Chinatown* and *Repo Man*. The channel stays dry most of the year but at times of flooding becomes a river. The train crosses the channel then passes beneath the Golden State and Pasadena freeways before winding slowly towards Union Station.

Dodger Stadium (↑20/5↓) Perched on a bluff to your right is the home of epic baseball. Opened in 1962, this is the country's largest Major League Baseball stadium by seat capacity and the oldest MLB ballpark west of the Mississippi River. Also look right for Elysian Park and the impressive Los Angeles skyline. Los Angeles County Jail is on your left.

ᴴᴴᴴ LOS ANGELES (↑5) Palm trees, beaches, blondes, surfing, freeways, smog and David Hockney swimming pools: Los Angeles is a sprawling place with an atmosphere all of its own. Founded by the Spanish in the 18th century as El Pueblo de Nuestra Señora de la Reina de Los Ángeles (the City of Our Lady, Queen of the Angels) its name grew shorter as the town became bigger. Completion of the transcontinental railroad in 1869, together with oil, Hollywood and a near-perfect climate, brought millions of settlers in search of the good life.

America's second-largest city now spreads ten million people over an area as big as Rhode Island and true Angelinos would never live anywhere else. The sun really does shine 90% of the year, although smog can be a problem in summer.

Los Angeles basics

☏ Telephone code 213

ᴴᴴᴴ Station (*Ticket office & waiting room* ⊕ *24hrs*) Los Angeles Union Station at 800 N Alameda is one of the world's prettiest railway stations, built in Spanish Mission & Art Deco styles with a lofty wooden ceiling, leather sofas & gardens shaded by palm trees & fragrant magnolia. Terracotta-tiled floors in the waiting room are accented with inlaid marble & the walls are clad with beautiful travertine tiles. Now on the National Register of Historic Places, the station serves 60,000 travellers, commuters & visitors every day. Originally known as the 'Los Angeles Union Passenger Terminal', the station was built in the 1930s to consolidate the services of the Southern Pacific, Union Pacific & Atchison, Topeka & Santa Fe railroads in 1 facility, with construction costs shared among the railroads. Half a million people came in 1939 to the grand opening ceremony, which had the theme 'Railroads Build the Nation'. A historical parade showed the part railroads had made in building the west, & massive locomotives from the Santa Fe, Union Pacific & Southern Pacific carried flags & banners promising continued co-operation & future prosperity. The first train to leave the new station, seen off by George Raft & Cecil B DeMille, was a special to promote the recently released film, *Union Pacific*. The station was built on part of the original Chinatown & has starred in many movies, including *Blade Runner*, *Bugsy*, *Pearl Harbor* & *Silver Streak*.

It handled more than 60 trains a day during the 1940s & Hollywood royalty such as Gable, Garland & Monroe would often pass through after arriving on the *Super Chief* or *City of Los Angeles*. Others came on more everyday trains, such as the *Scout* or *Californian*. In 2011, the Los Angeles County Metropolitan Transportation Authority (LACMTA) bought the station for $75 million & its master plan for development aims to celebrate the building's history & design, improve the passenger experience, create a great destination that attracts not only transit users but also residents & visitors, & prepare for potential high-speed rail service. This epitome of southern California glamour marked its 75th anniversary in 2014 with a celebration of live music, dozens of exhibitors & a grand display of modern & vintage locomotives & railcars. Metropolitan Lounge, ATM banking, newspapers, handcarts, Red Caps, restaurant, left-luggage room, shop, taxi stand.

Connections Metrolink commuter trains connect Union Station with the Antelope Valley, downtown Burbank, Oxnard, Riverside, San Bernardino & Orange County. There are plans for a daily train service between Los Angeles & Las Vegas, Nevada, using Talgo equipment, which would restore part of the route once used by Amtrak's *Desert Wind* train.

Local transport Los Angeles used to boast the largest electric railway in the world, its *Pacific Red* streetcars often appearing in early silent films. As in other cities, the oil, tyre & car companies bought up the railway in order to close it down. Metro Rail's Blue Line (✆ *323 466 3876*) from Long Beach to Los Angeles opened in 1990 & the system has expanded to 6 rapid transport & light rail lines & 111 miles (178km) of track, carrying more than 350,000 passengers each weekday.

MTA buses take in most city attractions, with free maps from the customer service centre (*3183 Wilshire Bd*; ✆ *323 466 3876*). MTA bus #1 leaves from the corner of Broadway & Arcadia for Hollywood. Inexpensive DASH shuttle buses (✆ *808 2273*) connect Union Station with Chinatown & the downtown area. For Metrolink

commuter trains serving southern California ✆ 1 800 371 5465.

Taxis Independent ✆ 310 659 8294; United ✆ 1 800 822 8294

Car rental Budget (at the terminal) ✆ 617 2977; Beverly Hills Rent-A-Car, 9732 Little Santa Monica Bd; ✆ 310 274 6969. LA is the ultimate city of the automobile, with 6,500 miles (10,000km) of road & freeway & 24 million vehicle trips on an average day. Renting a car is no problem but finding your way around is more tricky. If you have the time & inclination, the Automobile Club will supply maps & advice.

Greyhound 1716 E Seventh; ✆ 629 8401

LAX Airport 16 miles (26km) southwest of downtown by the Super Shuttle (✆ *310 222 5500*). Alternatively, you can get there via MTA bus # 439.

Tours LA City Tours go to Hollywood, Beverly Hills & the film studios (✆ *888 800 7878*). Other companies include Starline (✆ *800 959 3131*) & Dearly Departed Tours (✆ *855 600 3323*), which provides morbid & sometimes irreverent tours to places where famous people have died or been involved in various scandals. These include the Highland Gardens/Landmark Hotel (Janis Joplin), the Knickerbocker Hotel (D W Griffith) & the Hollywood sign (where a failed English actress, Peg Entwistle, was the first person to commit suicide). The Los Angeles Conservancy (*523 W Sixth*; ✆ *623 2489; [www] laconservancy.org*) helps preserve historical buildings, structures, landscapes & neighbourhoods & offers many walking tours, including one of Union Station.

Visitors bureau 800 N Alameda & several other locations; ✆ 323 467 6412; w discoverlosangeles.com

Accommodation Los Angeles has 48 million visitors a year so there are plenty of rooms to choose from. Consult the local press for w/end rates & special offers.

Hotels include the Chamberlain West Hollywood, 1000 Westmount Drive; ✆ 310 657 7400; w chamberlainwesthollywood.com, **$$$$**; Metro Plaza, 711 N Main; ✆ 680 0200; w metroplazahotellosangeles.site, **$$$$**; Palomar, 10740 Wilshire Bd; ✆ 310 475 8711; w hotelpalomar-beverlyhills.com, **$$$$**; O Hotel, 819 S Flower; ✆ 623 9904; w ohotelgroup. com, **$$$**; Figueroa, 939 S Figueroa; ✆ 627 8971; w hotelfigueroa.com, **$$**; Macarthur, 607 S Park View; ✆ 381 6300; w themacarthur.

com, **\$\$**; Stillwell, 838 S Grand Av;☎627 1151;
w lahoteltravel.com, **\$**.

For B&B contact Baywood Inn Bed & Breakfast,
1370 Second St, Baywood Park, CA 93402-1112;
☎805 528 8888; w baywoodinn.com, **\$\$\$**.

Banana Bungalow-Hollywood, 5920 Hollywood
Bd;☎323 469 2500; w bananabungalows.com/
hollywood-hostel-los-angeles. Take the Metro
Redline to Hollywood & Vine. Dormitory rooms,

\$. International (IYHF) Hostel, 3601 S Gaffey;
☎310 831 8109; w hihostels.com/hostels/hi-los-
angeles-south-bay. Take MTA bus #246; **\$**. Santa
Monica AYH Hostel, 1436 Second;☎310 393 9913;
w hiusa.org/hostels/california/los-angeles/santa-
monica. Take MTA bus #33. Dormitory rooms, **\$**
(dbl, **\$\$**). Walk of Fame Hostel, 6820 Hollywood
Bd;☎323 463 2770; w walkoffamehostel.com.
Dormitory rooms, **\$**.

Recommended in Los Angeles

El Pueblo de Los Angeles State Park Opposite
Amtrak's station. Los Angeles began here in 1781
& the city's oldest house, the Avila Adobe, which
dates from 1818, is at 10 E Olvera. This street
also features Mexican restaurants & cheerfully
tacky souvenir shops. Look also for the Masonic
Hall (1858), Old Plaza Church (1822), Old Plaza
Firehouse (1884) & Sepulveda House (1884). Free
film & walking tours from the visitor centre (*125
Paseo de la Plaza;*☎*628 1274;* w *lasangelitas.org*).

Natural History Museum 900 Exposition Bd;
☎763 3466; w nhm.org; ☉ daily; admission
charge. 2 world-famous habitat halls show
African & North American mammals in their
natural environments, & the museum is home to
Megamouth, the world's rarest shark. The Lando
Hall of California History has fascinating exhibits
showing the Southwest from the 1500s through to
downtown Los Angeles in 1940.

Graumann's Chinese Theater 6925 Hollywood
Bd;☎323 461 3331. Match your favourite actor's
cement prints in front of this outlandish pagoda,
now officially known as the TCL Chinese Theatre.
Nearby, almost 2,500 bronze stars in the Walk
of Fame celebrate the great & not so great of
Tinseltown, including Elvis Presley, Marilyn
Monroe, Groucho Marx, Charles Chaplin, Donald
Trump & Donald Duck.

LA County Museum of Art 5905 Wilshire Bd;
☎323 857 6000; w lacma.org; ☉ Thu–Tue;
admission charge. LACMA is one of the finest art
museums in the country, with more than 135,000
works spanning the history of art from ancient
times to the present & major special exhibitions.

J Paul Getty Center 1200 Getty Center Dr;☎310
440 7300; w getty.edu; ☉ Tue–Sun; admission
free. With panoramic views of Los Angeles &
the Pacific Ocean, the museum has 54 galleries
to display one of the richest collections in the
world, including medieval manuscripts & 65,000

photographs, as well as paintings by Cézanne,
Goya, Leonardo, Michelangelo, Monet, Titian,
Turner & Van Gogh. Metro Rapid Line 761 stops
at the main gate on Sepulveda Bd. The Roman-
inspired Getty Villa at 17985 Pacific Coast Highway
in Malibu has Greek, Roman & Etruscan antiquities
arranged by themes. Take Metro bus #534.

La Brea Tar Pits 5801 Wilshire Bd;☎763 3499;
☉ daily; admission charge. Bubbling black
deposits contain hundreds of fossilised mammals,
seen at the Page Museum & observation pit. The
fossils are up to 40,000 years old & include camels,
mammoths & mastodons.

Griffith Park 4730 Crystal Springs Dr;☎323
913 4688; ☉ daily, admission charge to the
zoo & some other attractions. This 4,107-acre
(1,650ha) city park is the largest in the country
& incorporates a planetarium, bird sanctuary,
miniature railway, carousel & an old abandoned
zoo, now a picnic area & hiking trail. The modern
Los Angeles Zoo & Botanical Gardens, home to
more than 1,100 animals & 7,400 plants, is at 5333
Zoo Drive (☎*323 644 4200;* w *lazoo.org*).

Universal Studios 100 Universal City
Plaza, Universal City;☎1 800 864 8377;
w universalstudios.com; ☉ daily; admission
charge. The 2nd-biggest tourist attraction in
southern California has spectacular rides such as
Jurassic Park, King Kong in 3D & the Simpsons
Ride, with character voices performed by stars of
the TV show. You can enter the world of Shrek &
experience the chilling, machine-controlled future
with the Terminator, as well as The Wizarding
World of Harry Potter with its Forbidden Journey &
Flight of the Hippogriff.

Travel Town 5200 Zoo Dr, in the northwest
corner of Griffith Park;☎323 662 5874;
w traveltown.org; ☉ daily; admission free. Travel
Town has one of the largest collections of steam
locomotives west of the Mississippi. The historic

Southern Pacific steam locomotive *No 219* is being restored & will be the first steam locomotive to operate at the museum since 1964, travelling on the Crystal Springs & Caheunga Valley Railroad running between Travel Town & the LA Zoo. There are also many passenger cars, freight wagons & cabooses (brake cars).

Forest Lawn Memorial Park 1712 S Glendale Av, Glendale, near Griffith Park; ✆323 254 3131 or ✆888 204 3131; w forestlawn.com; ⊕ daily; admission free. Made famous as Whispering Glades in Evelyn Waugh's novel *The Loved One*, Forest Lawn is the burial place of Michael Jackson, Elizabeth Taylor, Clark Gable, James Stewart, Humphrey Bogart, WC Fields, Walt Disney, Buster Keaton, Stan Laurel, Chico Marx, Carole Lombard, Jean Harlow, Errol Flynn & many others from the Golden Age of Hollywood. Tasteful highlights include a stained-glass version of Leonardo's *Last Supper*.

Lomita Railroad Museum Just south of Los Angeles at 2137 W 250th, Lomita; ✆310 326 6255; w lomita-rr.org; ⊕ Thu–Sun; admission charge. Includes live steam engines, memorabilia & a replica of the Boston & Maine's Greenwood station at Wakefield, MA. On display is a Southern Pacific Railroad Mogul steam locomotive & oil tender, a 1910 Union Pacific caboose & a 1913 Southern Pacific wood boxcar.

5

The *California Zephyr* Chicago–Emeryville (for San Francisco)

GENERAL ROUTE INFORMATION

The original *California Zephyr* streamliner was inaugurated in 1949 on this route, operated collectively by the Chicago, Burlington & Quincy Railroad, Denver & Rio Grande Western Railroad and Western Pacific Railroad. Sold as a 'cruise train' to compete on spectacular scenery rather than speed, it had Vista-Dome cars, 'Zephyrette' hostesses and coast-to-coast sleeping cars in conjunction with the Pennsylvania Railroad. One of the world's great trains, Amtrak's revived *California Zephyr* travels for two days and nights over farmland, prairie, deserts, rivers and

ESSENTIAL INFORMATION

HIGHLIGHTS The *California Zephyr* starts in Chicago with its impressive architecture then travels across prairies and the spectacular Rocky Mountains to San Francisco, one of the world's most popular tourist destinations. There are stops in Salt Lake City, home of the Mormons, and Denver, where the sun shines 300 days of the year.

FREQUENCY Daily. The **westbound** service leaves Chicago early in the afternoon to arrive in Omaha late in the evening and Denver by early next morning. You reach Salt Lake City by midnight on the second evening, Reno the following morning and Emeryville (for San Francisco) mid-afternoon. Travelling **east**, you leave San Francisco early in the morning to arrive in Reno by late afternoon and Salt Lake City during the night. You reach Denver by early evening and Omaha early on the second day, arriving in Chicago mid-afternoon.

DURATION 51 hours 20 minutes

RESERVATIONS All reserved

EQUIPMENT Superliner coaches. Sightseer lounge car.

SLEEPING Superliner bedrooms

FOOD Complete meals, snacks, sandwiches, drinks

LOUNGE CAR Movies, games. A California State Railway Museum history guide provides a commentary between Reno and Sacramento. In spring and summer, National Park Service rangers provide a narrative between Grand Junction and Denver.

BAGGAGE Check-in service is available at major cities.

mountains. Western pioneers came this way, as did gold prospectors, the Pony Express and the first long-distance telegraph line. The *Zephyr* follows America's earliest transcontinental rail route for much of its 2,438-mile (3,922km) journey, and many people take this train just to explore the Rocky Mountains.

JOINING THE TRAIN

CHICAGO (30↓) The proclaimed capital of America's third coast is one of the country's largest and most ethnically diverse cities. Writers such as Saul Bellow, Nelson Algren and Sara Paretsky have lived in 'the city of big shoulders', as have Al Capone (gangster) and Mother Cabrini (first American saint). Poet Carl Sandburg called Chicago the 'Player with Railroads and the Nation's Freight Handler'. Harrison Ford and Raymond Chandler, whose father was a railway engineer, were born here, and Ernest Hemingway grew up in the middle-class suburb of Oak Park. Muddy Waters, Howlin' Wolf and John Lee Hooker made blues history on the South Side.

Chicago began in 1833 but stayed a village until railways connected it to the east coast in 1852. Destroyed by fire in 1871 soon after the rail link with San Francisco was completed, the city rebuilt itself as a centre for industry, finance and the arts. The Junction Railway's stockyards were where cowboys brought their cattle, and although these closed down long ago, Chicago retains a hard-headed commercial spirit. More mainstream and less pretentious than New York or Los Angeles, the city became the fashionable home of television's *ER* and *Oprah*.

The first 11-storey skyscrapers were erected here, leading to the Chicago School of Architecture and subsequently Frank Lloyd Wright and Mies van der Rohe. You can see three of the world's ten tallest buildings and superb architecture in every modern style, as well as outdoor sculpture, an elevated railway and the brooding Chicago River. Chicago boasts 29 miles (46km) of beaches but it can be bitingly cold in winter, when ice sometimes floats on Lake Michigan.

Chicago basics

Telephone code 312 downtown

Station (*Ticket office* ⏰ *06.00–21.20; the Great Hall waiting room* ⏰ *05.30–midnight*) Chicago has long been a port for ships arriving on Lake Michigan via the St Lawrence Seaway & once had 6 major railway stations with hundreds of passenger trains every day to all parts of the country. It has been called the railroad hub of the world, with Union Station at 225 S Canal the centre of America's rail network. Completed in 1925, the station was built by a partnership of 4 railroads: the Pennsylvania; Chicago, Burlington & Quincy; Michigan Central; &

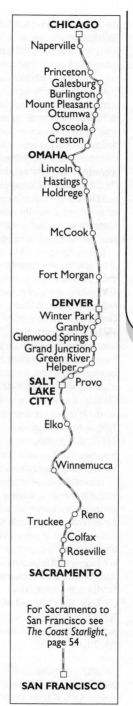

5

CHICAGO
Naperville
Princeton
Galesburg
Burlington
Mount Pleasant
Ottumwa
Osceola
Creston
OMAHA
Lincoln
Hastings
Holdrege
McCook
Fort Morgan
DENVER
Winter Park
Granby
Glenwood Springs
Grand Junction
Green River
Helper
SALT LAKE CITY   Provo
Elko
Winnemucca
Truckee   Reno
Colfax
Roseville
SACRAMENTO

For Sacramento to San Francisco see *The Coast Starlight*, page 54

SAN FRANCISCO

the Chicago, Milwaukee & St Paul. The Chicago & Alton Railroad also used the station as a tenant. The cathedral-like Great Hall features huge marble columns, statues, sweeping staircases, balconies, original wooden benches & a soaring arched ceiling. Sculptures by Henry Hering on its east wall show figures representing day (holding a rooster) & night (holding an owl). Amtrak has begun a $22 million project to restore the barrel-vaulted Great Hall skylight, installing an outer skylight above to protect the historic one. This magnificent waiting room has appeared in many films, including Brian de Palma's *The Untouchables*. *The Narrow Margin*, set mostly on board the Central Pacific's *Golden West Limited*, has intriguing shots of how the station looked in 1951. A separate waiting room is reserved for Amtrak passengers (*Metropolitan Lounge* ⊕ 06.00–21.00).

Amtrak also operates from a more modern part of the building, with a fountain into which you can throw pennies for luck. Lockers, vending machines, ATM banking, newspapers, handcarts, Red Caps, restaurants, shops, taxi stand.

Connections No Thruway bus connections.

🚐 **Local transport** Metra (⌁ 322 6777) runs commuter trains out of Union Station & City Transit Authority, the nation's 2nd-largest public transportation system, has buses covering the whole city, with a stop outside the Adams St exit. CTA buses & a subway augment the El railway, which has some great views of the city (⌁ 836 7000; w transitchicago.com). Pace buses (⌁ 847 364 7223; w pacebus.com) operate to the suburbs. Free maps from the tourist bureau & the Metra information window at Union Station.

Chicago also has an underground Pedway system of pedestrian walkways that makes navigation easy even in bad weather. From the Illinois Center at Michigan Av & the Michigan Av Bridge a network of walkways lead to stores in the Loop area & to major train stations, with an entrance elevator in Loop buildings & subway stations. Maps of the Pedway are available in hotels & at the Illinois Center.

🚕 **Taxis** Flash ⌁ 773 561 4444; Checker ⌁ 243 2537

🚗 **Car rental** Hertz, at Union Station; ⌁ 928 0539

🚌 **Greyhound** 630 W Harrison; ⌁ 408 5821. Also located at Union Station.

✈ **O'Hare Airport** One of the world's busiest, O'Hare is 20 miles (32km) northwest by coach or El train. GO Airport Express buses (⌁ 888 284 3826) run every few mins between downtown & the airport. CTA trains are as frequent & much cheaper ($2.25).

Tours Gray Line ⌁ 1 800 472 9546; Chicago Tours w chicagotours.us. Untouchable Tours visits infamous gangster scenes (⌁ 881 1195). For views of the city from Lake Michigan call Mercury (⌁ 332 1638) or Shoreline (⌁ 222 9328).

From May to Sep the Loop Train offers free 40min tours of downtown attractions. Tours are conducted each Sat afternoon by guides from the Chicago Architecture Foundation (⌁ 922 3432) & tickets can be obtained at the Chicago Cultural Center on the morning of the tour.

ℤ **Visitors bureau** The Cultural Center is located in what was once Chicago's first central library building at 77 E Randolph; ⌁ 744 3316; w choosechicago.com; ⊕ daily. The Visitor Center, also open daily, is located at 163 E Michigan Av in the pumping station adjacent to the water tower, sole survivors of Chicago's great fire.

🏠 **Accommodation** Call the Hotel Association (⌁ 346 3135). For discount hotel rates call Hot Rooms (⌁ 1 800 468 3500 or ⌁ 773 468 7666; e hotrooms@hotrooms.com; w hotrooms.com).

Hotels include Blackstone, 636 S Michigan Av; ⌁ 447 0955; w theblackstonehotel.com, **$$$**; The Drake, 140 E Walton Pl; ⌁ 787 2200; w thedrakehotel.com, **$$$**; River Hotel, 75 E Wacker Dr; ⌁ 777 0990; w chicagoriverhotel. com, **$$$**; Cass, 640 N Wabash Av; ⌁ 787 4030; w casshotel.com, **$$**; Kimpton Hotel Allegro, 171 W Randolph; ⌁ 236 0123; w allegrochicago.com, **$$**; Travelodge, 65 E Harrison; ⌁ 427 8000, **$$**.

Contact Chicago Bed & Breakfast; e info@ chicago-bed-breakfast.com; w chicago-bed-breakfast.com.

Getaway Hostel, 616 W Arlington Pl; ⌁ 773 929 5380; w getawayhostel.com. Private & dormitory rooms, **$**. International Hostel, 24 E Congress Parkway; ⌁ 360 0300; w hiusa.org/hostels/illinois/chicago/chicago. Members & non-members, **$**. Some hotels offer w/end & summer packages.

Recommended in Chicago

Willis Tower 233 S Wacker & Jackson, near the station; ⌁ 875 9447; w willistower.com; ⊕ daily; admission charge. Formerly the Sears Tower. Edward Sears, a former railway clerk, co-founded

Sears, Roebuck, the world's largest mail order company. Railways proved ideal for distributing the catalogue & its goods, including entire houses. This building, completed in 1973, was the world's tallest for 25 years, reaching 110 storeys & 1,454ft/443m (1,729ft/527m including added antennae). Ear-popping elevators shoot you to the 103rd-floor Skydeck (w *theskydeck.com*) for views of the city, Lake Michigan & 4 states. Go before sunset & watch the city come alight.

360 Chicago 875 N Michigan Av; ✆ 888 875 8439; w 360chicago.com; ☺ daily; admission charge. Even at 327ft (99.6m) lower than the Willis Tower, the John Hancock Center observation deck gives wonderful views of Lake Michigan & the city. The 94th-floor observatory is more than 1,000ft (300m) above Chicago & features an outside Skywalk, a virtual-reality tour of more than 80 city sites, 3D 'talking' telescopes & a Chicago history wall. TILT, 'Chicago's highest thrill ride', extends out & over the city's famous skyline to give unique, downward-facing views.

John Shedd Aquarium 1200 Lake Shore Dr; ✆ 939 2438; w sheddaquarium.org; ☺ daily; admission charge, free on community discount days. When the aquarium began in 1927, live specimens were transported here aboard a specially built fish car, the *Nautilus*, later replaced by the *Nautilus II* (now on display in the Railway Museum at Monticello, Illinois). Today's splendid building holds 32,000 animals, including thousands of fish as well as the largest indoor collection of marine mammals in the world, such as beluga whales, seals, sea otters & dolphins. Don't miss the penguins & the amazing alligator snapping turtle.

Art Institute 111 S Michigan Av; ✆ 443 3600; w artic.edu; ☺ daily; admission charge. One of the world's top galleries features Impressionist, American & Renaissance works alongside major exhibitions. Crowded at w/ends.

Museum of Science & Industry 57th & Lake Shore Dr; ✆ 773 684 1414; w msichicago.org; ☺ daily; admission charge. Includes a German U-Boat, a British Spitfire, robots, a real coal mine, the *Apollo 8* spacecraft & many automobiles, plus a theatrical adventure through the Amazon rainforest. Among the railroad engines is the New York Central's *No 999*, which in 1893 was the first locomotive to exceed 100mph (160km/h). The Great Train Story presents 2,200 miles (3,540km)

of scenery & stories from Chicago to Seattle along 1,400ft (427m) of winding track.

Navy Pier 600 E Grand Av; ✆ 595 PIER (7437) or ✆ 1 800 595 PIER (outside Chicago); w navypier. com. A city landmark with 50 acres (20ha) of parks, gardens, shops, restaurants & attractions, including a Ferris wheel, carousel, children's museum & Chicago's Shakespeare Theatre. The 3,000ft pier (914m) was one of several planned for the city but the only one actually to be constructed (in 1916).

Robie House 5757 S Woodlawn; ✆ 994 4000; w wrightplus.org; ☺ Thu–Mon; admission charge. Designed by Frank Lloyd Wright, this spectacular building features 174 art-glass windows & doors. Daily tours & special events. The house is managed by the Frank Lloyd Wright Foundation.

Pullman Community 11111 Forestville Av; ✆ 773 660 2341; w pullman-museum.org. America's earliest railway sleeping cars were made here by the businessman & inventor George Mortimer Pullman's Palace Company. Designed so that people could 'Travel and Sleep in Safety and Comfort', they were the first to have electric lights & folding berths. Pullman's company town was designed in 1885 by an English architect, Solon Beman, as a model community for 12,000 workers. Some were expert carriage makers who had arrived from Germany. Most of the town was built around the factory between 1880 & 1884, & included a church, school & library but no saloon. Workers lived in houses which reflected their level of skills. The company was sold to Canada's Bombardier in 1987.

Pullman is a designated landmark district & most of the original buildings in the town are still standing. The Hotel Florence, built in 1881, is the community's showpiece but hundreds of homes are undergoing restoration. Pullman is located about 14 miles (22km) south of downtown but can easily be reached by CTA bus #111 or Metra train on the Illinois Central Gulf Railroad.

The **Historic Pullman Foundation Visitor Center** is at 11141 S Cottage Grove Av (✆ *773 785 8901 for group tours of 20 or more people;* w *pullmanil.org*). Guided walking tours leave from the Visitor Center all year round.

A Philip Randolph/Pullman Porter Museum 10406 S Maryland; ✆ 773 850 8580; w aphiliprandolphmuseum.com; ☺ Thu–Sat;

admission charge. Located in the Pullman District, this museum gallery is named after Asa Philip Randolph, chief organiser of the Brotherhood of the Sleeping Car Porters (BSCP) & once regarded by some people in government as 'one of the most dangerous Negroes in America'. Wonderful photographs & memorabilia show the struggle between corporate power & disenfranchised workers in 1937, when Randolph chartered the first African-American labour union. On 19 February 2015, President Barack Obama designated the Historic Pullman district a National Monument & it is now a part of the National Park Service.

CHICAGO: ALL ABOARD! (30↓) The *California Zephyr* departs Chicago on BNSF Railway Company tracks with the city skyline diminishing to your right. You should pass the eastbound *Zephyr* a few minutes out of Union Station. The westbound train continues at a modest pace through industrial scenes followed by many miles of suburbs such as Hinsdale, Westmont and Downer's Grove.

⋙ NAPERVILLE (↑30/60↓) Established in 1831 by Captain Joseph Naper, Naperville grew after the Chicago, Burlington & Quincy (CB&Q) Railroad ran a line through town in 1864. Amtrak shares with Metra the station built in 1910. Chicago's main western suburb has attractive restored buildings and a 4-mile-long river walk that helped it rank second on CNN/*Money Magazine's* list of 100 best places to live in the United States. Commuter trains provide connections to La Grange, Cicero and Aurora.

Aurora (↑10/50↓) A stone roundhouse and other early railway buildings can be seen to your right. Double-decker commuter trains wait on your right. Aurora has been a transport junction since stagecoach days and in 1908 was the first American city to have electric street lights. The Chicago, Burlington & Quincy (CB&Q) Railroad was formed here in 1849. Not just a place but a state of mind, Aurora was the setting for the excellent *Wayne's World* in 1992.

Look right as the train leaves to see the Caterpillar Tractor company's water tower and factory; in 2017 the company announced the factory would close and began winding down production. You then cross the Fox River before travelling among corn fields and the small communities of Plano, Sandwich, Somonauk and Mendota.

⋙ PRINCETON (↑60/60↓) The former 'City of Elms' is now 'Where Tradition Meets Progress'. Princeton began as a New Englander settlement in 1833 and was later the home of John Bryant (1807–1902), a founder of the Republican Party. The anti-slavery Underground Railroad had a 'station' here and actor Richard Widmark grew up in Princeton and first began acting at Lake Forest College. An old caboose from the Burlington Railway can be seen to your left just before the handsome, renovated station, built by the CB&Q Railroad in 1911.

Wyanet (↑15/45↓) Look for some of the large local population of pigs and cattle.

Kewanee (↑30/30↓) Located next to the Spoon River, this was another early New Englander settlement. The town's name is a Native American word for 'prairie chicken'.

Galva (↑40/20↓) In the 19th century, Swedish dissidents set up the utopian community of Bishop's Hill among these wooden houses.

GALESBURG (↑60/50↓) Birthplace of the poet Carl Sandburg, whose father worked for the railroad here, Galesburg was also the home town of George Washington Ferris, creator of the original Ferris wheel, and Olmsted Ferris, who invented popcorn. The Marx brothers are said to have received their nicknames here during a poker game in 1914. The **National Railroad Hall of Fame** is at 200 East Main (✆ *309 345 4634;* w *nrrhof.org*) and Galesburg hosts the Railroad Days festival each June. To your right is the copper spire of Knox College. Galesburg was another station on the secret Underground Railroad for escaped slaves. A 1930s Hudson engine with its coach and caboose stands to the right of Amtrak's modern canopied station. This has original wooden pews salvaged from a former CB&Q Railroad depot, as well as historically styled wood panelling, ceiling fans and lamps. The CB&Q (now succeeded by BNSF) arrived here in 1854 and established a major rail yard with car shops, roundhouse, locomotive maintenance department, bridge department and stockyards. This is still active, and with seven main rail lines going in and out of the city, Galesburg remains an important transportation centre. Thruway buses connect with *Texas Eagle* trains stopping at Springfield.

Monmouth (↑20/30↓) Western lawman, gunfighter, gambler and boxing referee Wyatt Earp was born here in 1848 and the railway later brought a large block of granite to Monmouth to build a monument in his honour. You travel on through a region of cattle farms and corn fields. Nearing the Mississippi River you start to see woodland, marshes and wildfowl.

Mississippi River (↑45/5↓) The train crosses on a 2,000ft-long (600m) steel bridge, giving wonderful views of the river and its forested banks. A graceful highway bridge reflects in the water to your right. The Mississippi is the world's third-longest river, stretching 2,350 miles (3,780km) to the Gulf of Mexico and draining a third of the United States. Before the railway bridge opened in 1868, passengers crossed here by ferry. During winter they sometimes went over the ice on foot. Crossing the river takes you from Illinois into Iowa.

BURLINGTON (↑50/30↓) The nearby Shoquoquon Hills were one of the few places in this area where flint could be found, so Native Americans came to regard them as neutral territory. Strategically placed next to the river, Burlington became a natural railroad centre and capital of both Wisconsin and Iowa. Look for the steam locomotive to the left of Amtrak's streamlined station at 300 South Main, built in 1944 by the CB&Q Railroad. In the 1930s, the CB&Q ran its famous *Zephyrs* – articulated stainless-steel, streamlined passenger trains that epitomised a new era of glamour for the railroads. This location played an important part in the history of rail technology when George Westinghouse developed the air brake on adjacent Burlington Hill from 1863 onwards.

The *California Zephyr* passes slowly through an older part of town, with warehouses and an ammunition factory on the left, before travelling among wide fields of maize and oats.

Danville (↑15/15↓) Trees surround a town once used by stagecoaches and the Pony Express.

MOUNT PLEASANT (↑30/40↓) The Old Settlers & Threshers Reunion celebrates America's frontier heritage each September in this typical Midwestern town, known as the 'Athens of Iowa' for its emphasis on education. Vintage steam locomotives pull wooden coaches and cabooses on the **Midwest Central Railroad** (☎ *319 385 2912;* w *mcrr.org*).

The red building to your right is Iowa's Wesleyan College, the oldest college west of the Mississippi River, which was founded in 1842. Arabella Babb Mansfield graduated here in 1869, the first woman to pass the bar exam in the United States.

Soon after leaving Mount Pleasant the train crosses the Skunk River. Note the dilapidated Rock Island Line building on your right as you approach Ottumwa. Celebrated by Leadbelly and other balladeers, the Rock Island Line had a colourful history, beginning in 1852 when the first train out of Chicago sported a rainbow-painted locomotive and six bright-yellow coaches. Jesse James and his gang carried out their first hold-up on a Rock Island train, derailing its locomotive and killing the engineer. The railroad faced bankruptcy several times but somehow managed to struggle on over its weather-beaten tracks until the 1970s.

OTTUMWA (↑40/70↓) Named after a Native American tribe when this was a trading post on banks above the Des Moines River, Ottumwa subsequently became a business centre and 'home town' to *MASH*'s Radar O'Reilly. Three bridges span the river in Ottumwa, known as the 'City of Bridges'.

You leave Ottumwa and cross the Des Moines River on its way to join the Mississippi.

OSCEOLA (↑70/30↓) Settlers in the 19th century discovered the first 'Delicious' apple tree 30 miles (48km) to the north of here at Winterset, where John Wayne was born and christened Marion Morrison. Osceola was named after a Seminole warrior chief whose wooden statue stands on your left beyond the restored Prairie-style station built by the Chicago, Burlington & Quincy Railroad in 1907. Look in the adjacent park for a large lettered sign spelling out 'OSCEOLA'. This is Amtrak's busiest stop in Iowa and its nearest to Des Moines, 50 miles (80km) to the north. The first European-American settlers in this area were Mormons who were separated from their group as it moved from Illinois to Utah in the 1840s.

As the train travels east look for some of the covered wooden bridges made famous by Robert Waller's book *The Bridges of Madison County*, and by the subsequent film starring Clint Eastwood. The story takes place in Winterset and this small town has been invaded by romantics attempting to trace the steps of the star-crossed lovers.

CRESTON (↑30/105↓) This railroad town is set on a ridge between the Des Moines and Missouri valleys, hence the name 'Creston', and is the *Zephyr*'s highest point east of the Missouri River. It was originally settled in 1868 as a survey camp for the workers with the Burlington & Missouri Railroad. Amtrak's single-storey station was built in 1968 and is shared with the BNSF Railway. The beautiful, restored yellow-brick CB&Q rail depot seen to your right opened in 1899 and is a national landmark that now houses the Chamber of Commerce, an art gallery, a museum and Creston City Hall. Farmers' co-operatives' silos, also on your right, provide the town's best viewing platform.

The train continues among cornfields, neat towns, woods, quiet rivers, cattle and horse farms. Sometimes you may catch sight of a roving coyote.

Stanton (↑40/65↓) Look right for the famous water tower shaped like a coffee pot, complete with handle. Also to your right is the town's courthouse building.

Council Bluffs (↑75/30↓) This pioneer trading post became the eastern end of the Union Pacific Railroad leading to California. A red-roofed, former 1899 Rock Island depot at 1512 Main houses the **RailsWest Railroad Museum** and model railroad (☏ *712 323 2509*; **w** *thehistoricalsociety.org/museums/railswest.html*). The museum is located in the former waiting rooms and has displays of dining-car silverware, a telegraph office, memorabilia and a large collection of newspapers chronicling the rise and fall of the railroads.

The **Union Pacific Railroad Museum** is at 200 Pearl Street (☏ *712 329 8307*; **w** *uprrmuseum.org*; ☉ *Thu–Sat; donation*). Artefacts, photographs and documents trace the development of the railroad and the American West. The collection dates from the mid-1800s and features original editions of reports from survey teams that searched for the best land route for the construction of the nation's first transcontinental railroad.

Missouri River (↑80/25↓) From its source in the Montana Mountains (where the Gallatin, Jefferson and Madison rivers converge), the Missouri River comes through here to join the Mississippi at St Louis. Crossing 'Big Muddy' takes you from Iowa into Nebraska.

Offutt Air Force Base (↑90/15↓) The airfield and Strategic Air & Space Museum (page 90) are seen to your left before you approach Omaha through extensive freight yards.

✈ OMAHA (↑105/60↓) This was the birthplace of Fred Astaire, Marlon Brando, Montgomery Clift, Malcolm X and Henry Fonda, and is the home of businessman Warren Buffett, the 'Sage of Omaha'. Mormons wintered here in 1846 on their way to Utah, and Omaha played an important part in the great days of westward migration, being a stop on the first transcontinental railroad. The Union Stockyards have been in business since 1884 and the city deals mostly in grain and cattle raised on the prairies.

Omaha basics

☏ **Telephone code** 402

✈ **Station** (*Ticket office & waiting room* ☉ *21.30–06.30; information* ☏ *1 800 872 7245*) Omaha was chosen as the eastern terminus of the first transcontinental railroad in 1862, ensuring this would become a major transportation centre. Amtrak's modest brick station is 1 mile (1.6km) from downtown at 1003 S Ninth. Vending machines, handcarts, taxi stand. The Amtrak depot is located between the historic CB&Q & splendid Art Deco Union Pacific railroad stations. Until 1974, Amtrak used the historic CB&Q station. Next to the current Amtrak depot is a massive old Burlington Northern building opened in 1898 in time for the Trans-Mississippi Exposition that attracted visitors from around the world.

Connections Buses connect with Kansas City & St Joseph

🚌 **Local transport** Metro buses operate downtown as well as to Council Bluffs & Nebraska.

The ORBT rapid transit service starts on Dodge St (*2222 Cuming St*; ☏ *341 0800*; **w** *ometro.com*).

🚕 **Taxis** City ☏ *933 8700*; Checker ☏ *339 0110*

🚗 **Car rental** Midwest, 14116 W Center Rd; ☏ *333 3434*

🚌 **Greyhound** 1601 Jackson; ☏ *341 1906*

✈ **Eppley Airport** The Navigator Airport Express shuttle serves Eppley Airport; ☏ *1 800 888 9793*

Tours The *River City Star*, 151 Freedom Park Rd; ☏ *342 7827*; www.rivercitystar.com. The riverboat offers a wide range of day & night cruises along the Missouri River.

ℹ **Visitors bureau** 1001 Farnam; ☏ *444 4660*; **e** info@visitomaha.com; **w** visitomaha.com; ☉ closed Mon

🏠 **Accommodation** Hotels include the Doubletree, 1616 Dodge; ☏ *346 7600*; **w** doubletree3.hilton.com, **$$$$**; Hilton, 1001 Cass; ☏ *855 605 0316*; **w** hilton.com, **$$$**; Sheraton, 655 N 108th Av; ☏ *496 0850*; **w** marriott.

com, **$$$**; Best Western Plus Kelly Inn, 4706 S
108th;✆339 7400; w bestwestern.com, **$$**;
Old Mill Inn, 10960 W Dodge Rd;✆855 599 9710;
w bestwestern.com, **$**; Super 8, 7111 Spring;
✆390 0700; w wyndhamhotels.com/super-8, **$**.
For B&B contact the Cornerstone Mansion, 140
N 39th;✆558 7600; w cornerstonemansion1894.
com, **$$$**.

Recommended in Omaha

Durham Western Heritage Museum 801
S Tenth;✆444 5071; w durhammuseum.org;
⊕ Tue–Sun; admission charge. The museum
looks at the history of the region's culture, science,
industry & more through affiliation with the
Smithsonian Institution, Library of Congress,
National Archives & the Field Museum. The
Union Pacific collection, formerly housed in the
UP headquarters building at 12th & Dodge, is
now located here. Explore the railroad's long &
sometimes controversial history, including an
auditor's office, Abraham Lincoln's funeral car
with its original furnishings, & the surveying
instruments of General Grenville M Dodge,
who was the Union Pacific's chief engineer &
responsible for constructing some of America's
most vital early routes. The research facility &
library has a photograph collection containing an
estimated 1 million images. The famous picture of
the Golden Spike ceremony shows General Dodge
shaking hands with Samuel S Montague of the
Central Pacific. Union Pacific technicians today
control up to 2,000 trains simultaneously at the
largest computerised rail command centre in
the world.

Old Market Farnam to Jackson sts, Tenth to 13th
✆346 4445; w oldmarket.com. Bookstores, art
galleries, antique shops, pubs & more than 30
restaurants populate this historic neighbourhood.

Murdock Historical Society & Museum 9014
310th;✆867 3331; w murdockmuseum.com;
⊕ Sun; admission free. The settlement of
Murdock began in 1890 when it was a water
stop on the Rock Island Railroad. Many German
settlers moved to this area & the Historical
Society Museum tells their story.

Joslyn Art Museum 2200 Dodge;✆342
3300; w joslyn.org; ⊕ Tue–Sun; admission
free. Nebraska's only fine arts museum opened
in 1931. The encyclopaedic collection features
works from antiquity to the present with a
special emphasis on 19th- & 20th-century art
from Europe & America. Designed as a cultural
centre for the community, the museum was built
as a gift to Omaha from Sarah Joslyn in memory
of her husband George, a prominent Omaha
businessman & community leader.

Greenwood Depot Museum 440 N Broad,
in Greenwood;✆430 0238. Cass County's only
preserved depot is almost 130 years old & contains
history of the town & surrounding area.

Malcolm X Birthsite 3448 Evans;✆1 800 645
9287; w malcolmxfoundation.org; ⊕ daily;
admission free. Visit the house where the 1960s
civil rights activist Malcom X was born on 19
May 1925.

Henry Doorly Zoo 3701 S Tenth;✆733 8401;
w omahazoo.com; ⊕ daily; admission charge.
Gorillas, orang-utans & white tigers live beside
the Missouri River in Omaha's greatest tourist
attraction, which has the largest indoor rainforest
in the world. The aquarium features sharks & king
penguins. Union Pacific has funded a new engine
house from where steam trains chug through the
grounds on a 30in-gauge (76cm) line originally
laid with help from the Union Pacific in 1968.

Boys Town 14100 Crawford;✆498 1300
; w boystown.org; ⊕ daily; admission free.
Boys Town was founded in 1917 as a home for
underprivileged youngsters by Father Flanagan,
played in the *Boys Town* film by Spencer Tracy. Boys
Town is now a National Historic Landmark with
attractions that include Father Flanagan's House, a
working farm & 2 Gothic chapels.

Strategic Air & Space Museum 28210 W Park
Hwy in Ashland;✆944 3100; w sacmuseum.
org; ⊕ daily; admission charge. The museum
includes a flight simulator & has many aircraft
& missiles to show the entire development of
military aviation.

OMAHA: ALL ABOARD! (↑105/60↓) The *Zephyr* leaves past high-rises to the right
and rolls on across Nebraska, crossing the Platte River midway between Omaha
and Lincoln. The course of this river was followed west by Mormons, and later by
the Pony Express and settlers on the Oregon Trail.

LINCOLN (↑60/90↓) Nebraska University appears to your left as the train approaches the red-brick station, which has a mural depicting classic steam and streamlined locomotives. Amtrak used to occupy the north end of a handsome Chicago, Burlington & Quincy building, using a renovated waiting room called the Great Hall.

Lincoln's 400ft-high (120-m) State Capitol, known as the 'tower of the plains', can be seen on your left and is the only unicameral (single house) state legislature in the country. The statue on its gold dome represents a man scattering seed. Lincoln's **visitors bureau** is at 3 Landmark Centre (℡*402 434 5335;* w *lincoln.org/visiting*).

HASTINGS (↑90/50↓) Founded in 1872 at the junction of the Burlington & Missouri River and St Joseph & Denver City railways, the city was named after Colonel D T Hastings of the St Joseph. Amtrak occupies part of the renovated Spanish Colonial Revival-style station, built in 1902 and now on the National Register of Historic Places. The town is a centre for trade and manufacturing, especially of farm machinery and Kool-Aid, invented here in 1927. Grand Island, 30 miles (48km) north, is home to the **Stuhr Museum of the Prairie Pioneer** (*3133 W Hwy 34;* ℡ *308 385 5316;* w *stuhrmuseum.org;* ⊕ *daily; admission charge*). The cottage where Henry Fonda was born is one of 60 authentic buildings in Railroad Town, which recreates a prairie community of the late 19th century. The rail yard includes an 1890 depot, turntable, steam locomotives and rolling stock. The museum also has large collections of Native American and Old West memorabilia as well as antique auto and farm machinery.

The countryside becomes progressively drier as the *California Zephyr* pulls out of Hastings and travels west, moving gradually from farmland into predominantly cattle country.

Kenesaw (↑15/35↓) You cross the Oregon Trail once used by wagon trains.

HOLDREGE (↑50/70↓) Named after George Holdrege, a former manager of the Chicago, Burlington & Quincy Railroad. The handsome 1910 CB&Q Depot is another listed on the National Register of Historic Places.

McCOOK (↑70/115↓) The 'gem of the prairie' was established in 1882 following an agreement between the CB&Q and the Lincoln Land Company to form a new railroad centre. McCook was a division point on the railroad before becoming an oil town named after Alexander McDowell McCook, a Union Brigadier General.

Nebraska–Colorado state line (↑70/45↓) As you change from Central to Mountain Time, watches go back an hour (forward when travelling east). The *California Zephyr* leaves Nebraska and travels towards Denver over the high plains of eastern Colorado, which used to be buffalo territory.

FORT MORGAN (↑115/80↓) The fort dates from 1864, since when the town has grown rich on oil and cattle. Fort Morgan is the burial place of science fiction writer Philip K Dick and was the boyhood home of musician Glenn Miller, who formed his first band here.

Pike's Peak (↑60/20↓) This 14,110ft (4,300m) mountain is just visible on the far-left horizon. It was on top of Pike's Peak in 1893 that Katherine Lee Bates was inspired to write the words to 'America the Beautiful'. The Rockies are 80 miles (130km) away to your right.

Commerce City (↑65/15↓) Until the late 1920s this area was devoted to agriculture, including wheat fields, dairies and pig farms, before it became Denver's chief industrial suburb. A large refinery was established and grain elevators were built in the 1930s. The city's 15,000-acre (6,000ha) Rocky Mountain Arsenal National Wildlife Refuge is one of the few remaining short-grass prairies in existence, with more than 330 species, including coyotes, white pelicans, black-tailed prairie dogs, bison, owls, mule deer and bald eagles.

Riverside Cemetery (↑70/10↓) The pioneer graveyard to your right dates from 1876. As the train passes beneath Interstate 70, look for Denver's skyline on your left. The front of the train comes into view on the right, turning north before reversing into the station.

⚒ DENVER (↑80/120↓) 'The mile-high city' was a gold rush town founded in 1858, when flakes of gold were discovered at nearby Cherry Creek. Many narrow-gauge railroads were built to serve the camps and in 1876 a route was opened via the steep black rock walls of Clear Creek Canyon to the town of Central City. It was here that George Pullman was working as a miner when he thought of the idea for his sleeping car.

The Union Pacific bypassed Denver on its transcontinental route but citizens built their own railroad to meet it at Cheyenne, Wyoming. This line and the Kansas City railroad helped transform Denver from a frontier town (where Bat Masterson patrolled the saloons) into one of the fastest-growing cities in the United States, with a population of over two million (not counting the Carringtons). Skyscrapers glitter in the brilliant light and older parts of the city have been restored.

Denver invented the cheeseburger and brews more beer than anywhere else in the world, yet still claims to have America's thinnest residents. The dry climate and high altitude make this city unique, so treat its pure sunlight with respect and allow a few days to become acclimatised before undertaking anything too strenuous. Many ski resorts are close by and equipment can easily be hired.

Denver basics

☎ Telephone code 303

⚒ Station (*Ticket office* ⊕ *05.30–21.15; waiting room* ⊕ *05.30–21.00*) The first Union Station at 1701 Wynkoop opened in 1881. When the building was badly damaged by fire, a splendid replacement designed in Beaux-Arts style was opened in 1914. The new station featured high-arched windows, terrazzo floors, chandeliers & a barrel-vaulted ceiling in the Great Hall, known as 'Denver's Living Room'. In 2012, the station underwent a major renovation to become the centre of a new transit-oriented development built on former rail yards, reopening as a hotel, restaurants, shops & an open-air train hall housing tracks for Amtrak & future commuter rail lines. Lockers, ATM banking, Red Caps, newspapers, handcarts, taxi stand.

Connections Thruway buses connect with Gunnison, Alamosa & Vail, as well as Colorado Springs, Pueblo & Raton.

🚍 Local transport RTD light rail trains & buses (☎ 299 6000; w rtd-denver.com) serve downtown & the suburbs, with maps & schedules available from the station. A free MallRide shuttle service runs along 16th St, between RTD's Civic Center Station & Union Station.

🚕 Taxis Yellow ☎ 777 7777; Freedom ☎ 444 4444

🚗 Car rental Avis, 1900 Broadway; ☎ 839 1280

🚍 Greyhound 1055 19th; ☎ 293 6555

✈ Denver International Airport The airport cost $4.8 billion, covers an area twice the size of Manhattan & is the largest airport in the United

States by total land area. The RTD 'SkyRide' has frequent bus services from the airport to dozens of locations downtown & an electric commuter rail line runs from Union Station to the airport.

Tours Gray Line city & mountain excursions leave from 5855 E 56th Av (☏ *289 2841*). The Denver Tramway Heritage Society operates riverfront rides on summer w/ends (☏ *458 6255*). Walking tours can be taken with Denver History (☏ *720 234 7929*; w *denverhistorytours.com*).

🆔 **Visitors bureau** 1575 California; ☏ 892 1505; w denver.org. For a free guide to Denver, ☏ 1 800 233 6837 or visit the website.

🏨 **Accommodation** Hotels include Residence Inn, 2777 Zuni; ☏ 458 5318; w marriott.com, **$$$$$**; the Brown Palace, 321 17th; ☏ 297 3111; w brownpalace.com, **$$$$**; Fairfield Inn, 1680 S Colorado Bd; ☏ 691 2223; w marriott. com, **$$$**; Holiday Inn, 401 17th; ☏ 296 0400; w ihg.com/holidayinnexpress, **$$**; Metlo, 1111 Broadway; ☏ 905 0915; w themetlo.com, **$$**; Quality Inn Central, 200 W 48th Av; ☏ 296 4000; w qualityinndenver.com, **$**.

Adagio Bed & Breakfast 1430 Race; ☏ 870 0903; www.adagiobb.com, **$$$**.

Recommended in Denver

Larimer Square 1530 16th; ☏ 534 2367; w larimersquare.com. This historic part of the city, once the haunt of outlaws, has Victorian houses, courtyards, gaslights, craft shops, restaurants & nightclubs.

US Mint 320 W Colfax; ☏ 405 4761; w usmint. gov; ⊕ Mon–Thu; free tours (reservations are required & can be booked through the website). No free samples & the joke is wearing thin! Tours cover the present state of coin manufacturing & its history. The mint, located in an Italian Renaissance-style building, is the largest single producer of coins in the world, turning out around eight billion a year. It also boasts more gold bullion (an estimated $100 billion worth) than anywhere outside Fort Knox. Souvenir coins are on sale.

Denver Art Museum 100 W 14th Av Parkway; ☏ 720 865 5000; w denverartmuseum.org; ⊕ daily; admission charge. The spectacular 28-sided museum building houses over 70,000 works, including the world's finest Native American art collection. The New-World gallery has 5,000 pre-Columbian & Spanish colonial works, & there are pictures by Georgia O'Keeffe, Degas, Matisse, Monet, Picasso & Renoir. The spirit of the American West is captured by artists such as Frederic Remington & Norman Rockwell.

State Capitol 200 E Colfax; ☏ 866 2604; ⊕ Mon–Fri; free tours. Murals, unique Colorado onyx & a dome covered with gold leaf, plus balcony views towards the Rockies & north to the Wyoming border. The 15th step on the west side is exactly 1 mile (1.6km) above sea level.

Black American West Museum & Heritage Center 3091 California, near Amtrak's station; ☏ 720 242 7428; w bawmhc.org; ⊕ Fri–Sat; admission charge. A third of working cowboys in the Old West were African-Americans, often freed slaves who travelled west after the Civil War. This museum uses photographs, personal belongings, clothing & oral histories to tell the story of black pioneers, buffalo soldiers, African-American cowboys & businessmen who helped settle the west.

Coors Brewery 13th & Ford St in Golden; ☏ 277 2337; w coors.com; ⊕ Thu–Mon. The Coors Brewery has been in business since 1873 & this is the largest single brewing site in the world. Over 10 million people have taken the free tour, which guides you through the entire brewing process & lets you sample the products in the hospitality lounge.

Colorado Railroad Museum 17155 W 44th Av in Golden, 12 miles (19km) west of Denver; ☏ 279 4591; w coloradorailroadmuseum.org; ⊕ daily; admission charge. The replica 1880s-style masonry depot has 50,000 rare photographs & artefacts. The sprawling grounds contain more than 100 narrow- & standard-gauge steam & diesel locomotives, passenger cars & cabooses, including some of the oldest in the state. A large model railroad recreates local lines such as those at Cripple Creek, Telluride & Tennessee Pass. Over 2,000 miles (3,200km) of tracks once probed the local mountain canyons, & there are short steam-train rides at w/ends.

Forney Transportation Museum 4303 Brighton Bd; ☏ 297 1113; w forneymuseum.com; ⊕ daily; admission charge. The museum features locomotives, including a 1941 Union Pacific 'Big Boy', as well as horse-drawn vehicles & antique cars such as Amelia Earhart's Kissel Speedster (Gold Bug) & a flamboyant 1923 Hispano-Suiza once owned by Hollywood director D W Griffith.

DENVER: ALL ABOARD! (↑80/120↓) The *California Zephyr* departs Denver and travels all the way to Emeryville on Union Pacific tracks, having arrived on the BNSF line from Chicago. Look back to your right for terrific views of Denver.

Arvada (↑20/100↓) You pass through another major suburb with the Front Range of the Rockies ahead. Gold was first discovered here in the Rocky Mountain region in 1850, resulting in the Pike's Peak Gold Rush. Mount Evans (14,264ft/4,350m) is on your left and Long's Peak (14,255ft/4,345m) on your right. The road up to Mount Evans is the highest paved road in North America.

Rocky (↑40/80↓) The train takes an S-shaped curve to gain height among the foothills. Winds can reach 100mph (160km/h) here so the track is protected at Big 10 Curve by railroad cars anchored with sand. The *Zephyr* climbs a 2% gradient and enters the first of 29 tunnels, with Coal Creek Canyon on your left.

Plainview (↑50/70↓) Look for spectacular sightings of the barren Colorado plains 1,500ft (450m) below and the whole city of Denver back to your right. The site of the former Rocky Flats nuclear weapons factory can be seen in the foreground. It was closed in the 1990s and the last contaminated building was removed in 2003. Part of the site is now the Rocky Flats National Wildlife Refuge, where herds of elk are commonly seen. To your right are Colorado University and the city of Boulder. The train rumbles on into the Rockies through South Boulder Canyon.

Gross Reservoir (↑60/60↓) A 340ft-high (100m) dam provides Denver with 14 billion US gallons (52 billion litres) of water. An expansion project began in 2017 which will raise the level of the dam by 131ft (40m) by 2025 and result in an additional 25 billion US gallons (95 billion litres) of water storage capacity. Look out for deer and elk as you enter the Roosevelt National Forest with the continental divide ahead.

Moffat Tunnel (↑105/15↓) The tunnel was named after railroad pioneer David Moffat of the Denver, Northwestern & Pacific (DNW&P) and is over 6 miles (10km) long. This is the highest point (9,239ft/2,820m) on Amtrak's network. Before the tunnel opened in 1928, reducing the distance between Denver and Salt Lake City by 65 miles (100km), trains took 5 hours to cross the continental divide around James Peak (13,260ft/4,040m). Now the journey takes only 10 minutes before you emerge from darkness into dazzling light.

Winter Park Resort (↑115/5↓) Ski slopes appear close by on your left. This is one of the largest ski areas in Colorado and a free year-round shuttle is provided to/from Amtrak's Fraser/Winter Park station.

⚞ WINTER PARK (↑120/20↓) This is one of many mountain parks in a densely wooded region which is famous for pine trees, tourists and ranching. The train station, the highest served by Amtrak, is actually in Fraser – called 'the icebox of America' because temperatures sometimes get as low as –50°F (–46°C). The heated shelter built in the 1980s was recently renovated. Look on a ridge to your right to see the Devil's Thumb rock formation.

Tabernash (↑5/15↓) Before the Moffat Tunnel opened, helper (pusher) locomotives would be added here to enable trains to climb over Rollins Pass. The community is named after a Native American chief of the Ute tribe.

Fraser Canyon (↑10/5↓) For 5 minutes, the *Zephyr* accompanies the clear, trout-laden Fraser River, where President Eisenhower often came to fish.

⊷ GRANBY (↑20/180↓) Granby was founded as a railroad town in 1905 along the route of the Denver, Northwestern & Pacific Railway and was named after Granby Hillyer, a United States Attorney whom the railroad paid to plan and found the town. Granby today serves as an access point for the Arapaho National Forest and Rocky Mountain National Park, in this area of meadow lands known as Middle Park. Trail Ridge Road (the USA's highest car road) runs through Rocky Mountain Park to your right. Evidence has been found locally of people who pre-date all known Native American tribes.

After Granby the train joins the Colorado River near its source and accompanies it for more than 200 miles (320km), making this one of the longest stretches of river followed by a train route anywhere in the world.

Hot Sulphur Springs (↑15/165↓) Thermal springs heat the indoor swimming pool to your right. According to Ute legend, the springs are heated by the fire of an old Native American chief desolately awaiting the return of tribesmen who left on an ill-fated mission of glory. In 1997 the resort was renovated and a Ute spiritual leader blessed the waters at the opening ceremony.

Byers Canyon (↑16/164↓) Spiky rock formations tower above the track and Highway 40 can be seen on your left. Poles next to the track carry alarm wires that stop train traffic in the event of a rockslide. Watch for herds of deer and the occasional buffalo as the *Zephyr* picks up speed through prime cattle country.

Kremmling (↑35/145↓) After the Denver, Northwestern & Pacific Railway arrived in 1906, Kremmling became a central shipping point. The town is on your right and Mount Powell (13,534ft/4,125m) to your left.

Gore Canyon (↑40/85↓) The train follows the canyon for 55 minutes. Sheer rock walls reach 1,500ft (450m) and make the canyon accessible only by train. The Gore Range to your left touches 13,000ft (4,000m). Coming out of the canyon you travel through meadows and ranch land. Just before Bond you see remains of the old State Bridge to your left.

Bond (↑100/80↓) A historic railroad town where the Rio Grande branch line to Steamboat Springs can be seen above on the right. The cut-off line between Bond and Dotsero was built by the Denver & Salt Lake Railroad.

Red Canyon (↑110/65↓) The train follows the canyon for 5 minutes. Spaniards called this place Colorado (meaning red) after seeing the vivid colours of these strange rock formations.

Dotsero (↑140/40↓) An 1885 survey of the Colorado River marked this point '.0' or 'dot-zero' on its maps and this represents the midpoint of the *California Zephyr*'s journey. The Eagle River joins the Colorado on your left.

Glenwood Canyon (↑155/10↓) The train follows the canyon for 15 minutes. Brightly coloured rocks, cliffs, aspen trees and evergreens proliferate as you follow the river. Interstate 70, one of the longest highways ever built, is on the far shore.

GLENWOOD SPRINGS (↑180/100↓) A centre for fishing, hiking and white-water rafters who come to brave the rapids. The ski resorts of Snowmass and Aspen, where you might bump into Oprah Winfrey or Martina Navratilova, can be reached by bus. On your right is one of the world's largest outdoor swimming pools, heated all year round by Yampa Hot Springs. Beyond the pool is Theodore Roosevelt's favourite, Colorado Hotel. John Henry 'Doc' Holliday, the gambler, gunfighter and part-time dentist, lived and was buried here when he died at the age of 35. Sheriff Pat Garrett was also buried nearby.

Glenwood's Railroad Museum occupies the station's former ladies' waiting room and tells the story of railroading in the Roaring Fork River Valley. The station and the town featured in the BBC television series Michael Palin: *Around the World in 80 Days*. Amtrak's attractive station to your left has unusual, square, Chinese-style towers.

As the train leaves along a typical Rocky Mountain valley, look for rafters riding on the Roaring Fork River joining the Colorado to your left.

New Castle (↑30/70↓) Named after Newcastle, England. Massive oil shale deposits have been discovered in this area and some are visible in the cliffs to your right. Also to your right is Mount Baxter (11,188ft/3,410m). In 1896, 54 workers died in a local coal mine explosion and a second disaster in 1931 killed 37 more.

Parachute (↑70/30↓) In 1908, the name of the town Parachute was changed to 'Grand Valley' to lure travellers on their way to the Colorado River valley to the southwest. The name was changed back to 'Parachute' in the 1980s. The Parachute Mountains can be seen to your right.

De Beque-Palisade (↑80/20↓) The beautiful and majestic Grand Mesa on your left is the world's largest flat-top mountain (over 10,000ft/3,000m). This region produces great quantities of fruit, especially peaches and apricots. As you approach Grand Junction among fruit fields, vineyards and orchards, look for a goat farm on your right.

GRAND JUNCTION (↑100/85↓) Where the Gunnison and Colorado rivers met the Denver and Rio Grande railroads. Amtrak's station is on the left at 339 South First. Grand Junction is a centre for agriculture and the coal industry, as well as a base for visitors travelling to Mesa Verde National Park, Grand Mesa Forest and Colorado National Monument, whose red cliffs are visible to your left as you leave.

Ruby Canyon (↑20/65↓) Another splendid photo opportunity as the train winds through beautifully coloured rocks carved by the Colorado River out of the Uncompahgre Plateau. Bald and golden eagles ride currents of air along the canyon walls and above the river. Several sets of *moki* steps on your right show where Anastosia Native Americans used to climb, and a sign marks the Colorado–Utah border. Moki steps are small depressions carved into the rock by early inhabitants to make climbing easier.

At Westwater the Colorado goes south and enters a quite different landscape, travelling 150 miles (240km) through sandy desert. Watch for antelope as you cross the dried riverbeds of this arid region, which used to be below sea level. The massive eroding mesas to your right are the intricately carved Book Cliffs, made from sandstone and shale. La Sal Mountains can be seen far off to the left.

Thompson Springs (↑60/25↓) The white and green station on the left was formerly a flag stop where Amtrak trains halted on request. For many years previously the city had been served by D&RGW passenger trains such as the *Scenic Limited, Exposition Flyer, Prospector, California Zephyr* and *Rio Grande Zephyr*. Commercial coal mining in Sego Canyon north of town began in the early 20th century and the Ballard & Thompson Railroad was constructed to connect the mines with the railhead at Thompson. The railroad continued operating until the 1950s.

Rich in uranium, this part of Utah has dramatic and sometimes desolate scenery. Nearby are Arches National Monument, Dead Horse Point, Canyonlands National Park and Monument Valley (star of many John Ford Westerns, including *Stagecoach*).

GREEN RIVER (↑85/70↓) Look for fields of cantaloupes and watermelons before you cross the Green River and enter the town of the same name. Originally called Blake Station, the town was first settled in the 1870s. Amtrak has a platform only with no passenger shelter or services. Green River Bible Church is to your right. An altitude of 4,075ft (1,240m) makes this the lowest point on the line between Denver and Salt Lake City. To your left are Mount Marvine (11,600ft/3,540m) and Thousand Lake Mountain (11,306ft/3,450m).

HELPER (↑70/120↓) Named after the extra locomotives once attached here to westbound freight trains to enable them to climb the mountains, Helper, known as the 'Hub of Carbon County', remains a busy centre for shipping coal, of which this region has enough to supply America for hundreds of years. The **Western Mining and Railroad Museum** (*294 S Main;* ☏ *435 472 3009;* ☉ *closed Sun; free admission, donation requested*) is housed in the Old Helper Hotel building and tells the history of the railroad, mining and the lifestyles of the multi-ethnic immigrants who came to the area between 1880 and about 1936 to work on the railroad and in the coal mines. Union Pacific freight wagons stand on your right.

You leave past a western downtown district to your left, where a large brick building on the hillside belongs to the Utah Railway. As the train heads into the Wasatch Mountains by way of Soldier Summit it is joined on the left by the Price River. The conglomeration of machinery to your right, 10 minutes from Helper, is a coal-processing plant.

Castle Gate (↑15/105 ↓) So-called because the rock walls resemble a castle. Also high up on the right is Balancing Rock, topped by a flying flag. The train robber Butch Cassidy, alias of Robert Leroy Parker the 'Robin Hood of the West', lived in this area. In 1897, he and the Wild Bunch held up a train from Salt Lake City as it entered Castle Gate carrying the $8,800 payroll for the Pleasant Valley Coal Company. The gang then fled to Robbers Roost, cutting telegraph wires to prevent news of the robbery spreading along their escape route.

Soldier Summit (↑60/60↓) The 7,440ft (2,270m) peak's name commemorates Southern Army soldiers who were caught in a sudden snowstorm and buried here in 1861. Look for the abandoned mine to your right. The train descends sharply from this summit of the snow-capped Wasatch Mountains by a series of horseshoe curves into the Spanish Fork River Canyon. You may catch sight of deer and elk as you travel between the rusty red and white canyon walls.

Thistle (↑100/20↓) Heavy rains caused a mudslide in 1983 which deluged the village of Thistle along with the river and parts of the Rio Grande tracks. The route had to be closed for three months while a 3,000ft (910m) tunnel was constructed beneath Billy's Mountain. Old tracks can be seen below to your left and remnants of this ghost town are visible just before the tunnel. Thistle serviced trains for the Denver & Rio Grande Western Railroad during the era of steam locomotives, until the changeover to diesel started the town's decline.

Look for llamas and horses in fields to your right as the train approaches Springville.

Springville (↑115/5↓) The colonial building on the right was once a school. Springville is known as 'Art City' and its Museum of Art is the oldest in Utah.

⊶ PROVO (↑120/55↓) Founded by Mormons in 1849, Utah's third-biggest city is the headquarters of Brigham Young University (America's largest private college) as well as the Osmond family, famous since the 1970s. Provo's nondescript industrial buildings and car-wrecking yards are set among beautiful mountain ranges, with the Uinta and Manti La Sal national forests close by.

The *Zephyr* crosses the Provo River with the site of US Steel's Geneva Works to the right. Once one of the largest steel mills in the country, producing most of the steel used in the Western United States, the plant was shut down in 2002. Mount Timpanogos (11,750ft/3,575m) is also to the right and Mount Nebo on your left.

Utah Lake (↑15/40↓) The lake is to your left with the Tintic Mountains in the distance. The lake has more than 200 bird species, including sandhill crane, great horned owl, golden eagle and cinnamon teal duck.

Riverton (↑25/30↓) From 1913, the Salt Lake & Utah Railroad went through Riverton and was used as a commuter and freight line until 1945. Among the hills to your left is the Kennecott copper mine. Also known as the Bingham Canyon Mine, this is the largest manmade excavation in the world, producing more copper than any other mine in history. A thousand antiquated cars on the former Kennecott Utah Copper electric railroad have been replaced by conveyors and a 17-mile-long (27km) pipeline. Nearing Salt Lake City, look right for the Salt Lake Temple and domed State Capitol.

⊶ SALT LAKE CITY (↑55/250↓) Founded in 1847 by Brigham Young and other pioneers seeking to practise their beliefs in freedom, Mormon influence still dominates this pretty valley between the Wasatch Mountains and the Oquirrh Range. The Golden Spike ceremony which completed the first transcontinental rail route took place 40 miles (60km) north of here at Promontory Summit.

Salt Lake City is an attractive place with clean air, wide streets and downtown crossing signals that chirrup endearingly. Nearby ski resorts include Alta (America's second oldest) and Sundance (proprietor Robert Redford). Five national parks with dramatic rock scenery are within a single day's drive.

Salt Lake City basics

☏Telephone code 801

⊶ Station (*Ticket office & waiting room* ☺ *22.00–05.15*) The station used by Amtrak is at 340 S 600 W. Lockers, vending machines, payphones, handcarts, restaurant, taxi stand.

Connections Thruway buses go to Ogden, Utah, & Boise, Idaho, as well as south to Las Vegas, Nevada.

Local transport Amtrak operates from an island platform at the intermodal transportation hub (Salt Lake Central Station) also used by Greyhound & Utah Transit Authority buses that visit most tourist attractions (☎ 743 3882; w rideuta.com). UTA also provides an extensive bus & light rail (TRAX) service to the ski resorts & Provo as well as throughout the valley. FrontRunner commuter trains run between Salt Lake Central & the Ogden Intermodal Transit Center.

🚕 **Taxis** City ☎ 363 5550; Yellow ☎ 521 2100

🚗 **Car rental** Advantage, 72 N 2400 W; ☎ 1 800 777 5500

🚌 **Greyhound** 300 S 600 W; ☎ 355 9579

✈ **Salt Lake City International Airport** 5 miles west of the city by UTA bus #453. TRAX Green Line trains leave for the airport every 15mins on w/days & every 20mins at w/ends.

Tours Gray Line ☎ 433 6500. City Tours ☎ 531 1001. Ride an authentic Salt Lake Trolley through the historic streets of the city on a 90min trip (☎ 364 3333). Salt Lake City Guided Tours has minibus tours to the best tourist attractions as well as to the Great Salt Lake, Wasatch Mountains,

Big Cottonwood Canyon & Antelope Island (☎ 654 6763; w saltlakecityguidedtours.com).

🛈 **Visitors bureau** 90 S West Temple; ☎ 0800 541 4955; w visitsaltlake.com; ⊕ daily; admission free guide

🛏 **Accommodation** Hotels include the Peery, 110 W Broadway; ☎ 521 4300; w peeryhotel. com, **$$$**; Crystal Inn-Downtown, 230 W 500 S; ☎ 328 4466; w crystalinnsaltlake.com, **$$**; Little America Hotel, 500 S Main; ☎ 596 5700; w saltlake.littleamerica.com, **$$**; Motel 6, 315 W 3300 S; ☎ 486 8780; w motel6.com, **$$**; Red Lion, 161 W 600 S; ☎ 521 7373; w redlion.com, **$$**; Carlton, 140 E South Temple; ☎ 355 3418; w carltonhotel-slc.com, **$**.

For B&B contact Inn on the Hill, 225 N State St, Salt Lake City, UT 84103-4615; ☎ 328 1466, **$$$**. **Avenues Youth Hostel** 107 F; ☎ 359 3855; e Info@saltlakehostel.com; w avenueshostel.com. Located a few blocks from the heart of downtown. Take UTA bus from Amtrak's station. Members & non-members, **$**. Camelot Inn & Hostel, 165 W 800 S; ☎ 688 6196. Some private rooms. Dormitory rooms, **$**.

Recommended in Salt Lake City

Temple Square 50 W North Temple; ☎ 531 1000; w templesquare.com. The heart of the Church of Jesus Christ of Latter-Day Saints is a 6-spired temple which can only be entered by Mormon Church members. Film shows & tours take place elsewhere. The Mormon Tabernacle Choir broadcasts a TV & radio programme each Sun morning (*free*) & there are daily recitals on the temple's 11,623-pipe organ, complete with light effects. Free concerts take place in summer on Tue & Fri evenings in Brigham Young Historic Park (☎ 240 3323).

Buildings of interest within walking distance include the Lion House at 63 E South Temple, an elegant mansion named after the stone lion sculpted for the front porch, & the 1847 Deuel Pioneer Log Home, one of the first log houses built in the Salt Lake Valley. Brigham Young's Beehive House at 67 E South Temple (☎ 240 2681) provides free tours & traditional candy.

The Church Office Building 50 E North Temple ☎ 240 1000; ⊕ Mon–Fri; admission free. The second tallest structure in Salt Lake City is this world headquarters of the Church of Jesus Christ of Latter-Day Saints. An observation deck on the 26th floor gives spectacular views of the Great Salt

Lake, the Wasatch Mountains, the city skyline & the Oquirrh Mountains.

Family History Library 35 N West Temple; ☎ 240 6996; ⊕ Mon–Sat; admission free tours. Trace your family line among over 2 million rolls of microfilm, 727,000 microfiche & 356,000 books in the largest library of its kind in the world.

Family Search Center Joseph Smith Memorial Bldg, 15 E South Temple; ☎ 240 4085; w familysearch.org; ⊕ Mon–Sat; free. Another likely place to check out your ancestors, with a vast collection of compiled genealogical data on hundreds of computers & the aid of helpful staff.

The Capitol At the north end of State St; ☎ 538 1041; ⊕ Mon–Sat. This impressive Neoclassical, Corinthian-style state house, inaugurated in 1926, was constructed from marble & granite beneath a copper dome.

Pioneer Memorial Museum 300 N Main; ☎ 532 6479; ⊕ daily; admission free. Pioneer artefacts including clothes & vehicles are looked after by ladies every bit as formidable as those in the photographs.

Trolley Square 602 700 E; ☎ 521 9877; ⊕ Mon–Sat; admission free. Originally a fairground, this city block was the site of the Utah Light & Railway Company's trolley system carbarn complex. Now a registered historic place, it has been carefully converted into a shopping & entertainment centre. Walking tour highlights include the original 97ft-high (30m) water tower & a stained-glass dome from the First Methodist Church in Long Beach, California.

Gardner Mill 1100 W 7800 S; ✆566 8903; w gardnervillage.com; ☉ Mon–Sat; admission free. Scottish immigrant Archibald Gardner was one of the original settlers with Brigham Young & he set up mills here in the 19th century. His main mill is now a restaurant & many historic buildings have been moved here to recreate a village, complete with a stream winding among connecting pathways & covered bridges.

Clark Planetarium 110 S 400 W; ✆385 468 7827; w slco.org/clark-planetarium; ☉ daily; admission charge. The Clark Planetarium opened in 2003, replacing the historic 1904 Hansen Planetarium. It features 3 floors of hands-on, interactive exhibits to help you understand our world, space, the solar system, & beyond. Spectacular shows are programmed at the Hansen Dome & Orbital ATK IMAX Theatre.

Great Salt Lake State Marina PO Box 16658, Salt Lake City, Utah 84116; ✆250 1898; w stateparks.utah.gov/parks/salt-lake. Located about 16 miles (25km) west on Interstate 80, the lake was once part of Lake Bonneville & the water's high salt content makes swimming here a buoyant experience. The park is open all year round for picnics, boating & wildlife watching.

SALT LAKE CITY: ALL ABOARD! (↑55/250↓) The *California Zephyr* makes a long service stop before leaving on Union Pacific tracks, touching the edge of the Great Salt Lake before crossing Bonneville Salt Flats. The run between here and Elko is Amtrak's longest without a scheduled halt. As you pass from Mountain to Pacific Time, watches should go back an hour (forward when travelling east).

🚂 ELKO (↑250/120↓) Legend has it that Elko was named by Charles Crocker, a superintendent of the Central Pacific Railroad who liked elk. The name Elko is also a Native American word for 'white woman'. The town was founded as a railhead for the White Pine mines in 1869 and was a stop for wagon trains on the Humboldt River Overland Trail. It is now a base for the region's many sheep and cattle ranches. Each spring the town holds the world chariot race championships.

As the train travels west, look for the Ruby Mountains to your left and the Independence Range on your right.

🚂 WINNEMUCCA (↑120/175↓) The *Zephyr* makes a service stop in this town that changed its name from French Ford to that of a Paiute Native American chief. In 1900, Butch Cassidy, Kid Curry and the Sundance Kid robbed the town's First National Bank, brimming with cash for local gold, copper and silver mines. Formerly a trading post where wagons crossed the Humboldt River, Winnemucca is a distribution point for agriculture and livestock.

The *California Zephyr* continues on Union Pacific tracks and follows the Humboldt River.

Lovelock (↑80/95↓) This was a way station on the Humboldt Trail to California and prospered with the coming of the Southern Pacific Railroad in 1868. Edna Purviance grew up in Lovelock, where her parents owned a hotel, before going on to act in 30 classic Charlie Chaplin films. The Trinity Range is to your right and the Humboldt Mountains to your left. You cross the Humboldt Sink, a muddy region located in the middle of a desert.

Fernley (↑140/35↓) The Truckee River joins on the right and the train begins to trace it back to the High Sierras as far as Truckee.

Mustang Ranch (↑145/30↓) The red-tiled building to your left is Nevada's best-known brothel – the first to be legal in the United States.

Sparks (↑165/10↓) Settlement here remained low until 1904 when the Southern Pacific Railroad built a switch yard and maintenance sheds. The city was first called Harriman, after E H Harriman, President of the Southern Pacific, and was then renamed after John Sparks, then Governor of Nevada. Note the old wooden station with its canopy, tower and peeling cream paint. Sparks is a major distribution centre since the introduction of Nevada's tax-free warehousing scheme. Southern Pacific freight wagons stand on the left and the high-rise Nugget Casino on the right. Pyramid Lake's bird sanctuary, famous for its large colony of American white pelicans, is 30 miles (48km) to the north.

To your left as you leave Sparks and approach Reno is the massive Grand Sierra Resort, formerly known as the MGM Grand Casino.

⋙ RENO (↑175/55↓) 'The biggest little city in the world' tries hard to be Las Vegas but still retains its charm. What started as a Mormon settlement became more riotous once silver was discovered. Gambling was legalised in 1931, after which Reno began accumulating the neon-clad casinos which draw fun-seekers to Virginia Street, located on either side of Amtrak's Spanish-style station. If you plan to gamble, or just want to know what goes on behind the mirrors, you can take a behind-the-scenes tour. Reno has prospered in recent years and some of the downtown casinos are now being turned into condominiums. The large stucco-clad station was built in 1926 by the Southern Pacific Railroad and was also used by the Virginia & Truckee Railroad. The building is listed on the National Register of Historic Places and the City Council plans to renovate it as a heritage centre for local history. The station was enlarged in 2007 and trains now dip down through downtown in what is locally called 'The Trench'. A fountain that once stood in downtown Reno has been transferred to the Amtrak waiting room. The **visitors bureau** is at 4001 S Virginia (✆ 775 827 7600; w *visitrenotahoe.com*).

Gaming pioneer Bill Harrah's collection of antique cars reached approximately 1,400 and many of these are now housed in the **National Automobile Museum** (*10 S Lake;* ✆ *775 333 9300;* w *automuseum.org*). Lake Tahoe, North America's largest alpine lake, is 35 miles (56km) southwest.

The *Zephyr* departs with the dome of St Thomas Aquinas Church a calming presence on your left. You travel through ranch country into Tahoe National Forest then cross the Sierra Nevada Range, which climbs to over 7,000ft (2,100m). Gold prospectors were the first white men to follow this route, which later became a heroic challenge to pioneer railroad constructors.

The train accompanies the fast-running Truckee River most of the way to the town of Truckee. On weekends (daily during summer) a guide from the California Railroad Museum joins the train across the Sierras to describe the line's history and places of interest.

Verdi (↑15/40↓) A hydro-electric generator on the far side of the Truckee River is powered by water brought along wooden flumes from the mountains. The first train robbery took place here in November 1870, less than 18 months after the railroad arrived. Virginia City miner and businessman 'Big Jack' Davis was among five men who boarded the eastbound train as paying passengers when it stopped at Verdi around midnight. About 1 mile (1.6km) east of Verdi, the men put on masks, drew pistols, stopped the train and tied up the crew before scooping $41,800 in gold pieces and $8,800 in silver bars from the baggage car. After dividing the loot between them they escaped individually into the hills and along the banks of the Truckee River. Within a week, they were all caught and jailed in Nevada State Penitentiary, though $3,000 (worth more than a million today) is still missing, buried somewhere along the Truckee or on the slopes of Peavine Mountain. The same *Atlantic Express* was robbed again less than 24 hours later in Independence, Nevada.

Nevada–California state line (↑20/35↓) Look right for the border mark. Wooden flumes on the cliffs to your left are relics of the mining industry.

Floriston (↑30/25↓) A splendid yellow mansion stands on the left.

Boca (↑40/15↓) The small town of Boca was demolished when the earthfill dam to your right was built to create a reservoir. Only a few foundations and a cemetery remain of the town. Boca formerly earned a living by supplying ice packed in sawdust to San Francisco and by brewing California's first lager. It once registered California's lowest-ever temperature (–45°F/–42°C) and became known as 'the coldest place in the nation'.

⚞ TRUCKEE (↑55/125↓) Named after Paiute Winnemucca's father, Chief Trukizo, and located on the banks of the Truckee River, the town had 14 lumber mills by the time the railroad arrived. Truckee managed to burn down six times between 1871 and 1882, but Chaplin filmed some of the remaining wooden buildings on Main Street for *The Gold Rush*.

Truckee is a gateway to Lake Tahoe and the ski resorts of Squaw Valley and Sugar Bowl. Pullman railway cars used to run from Oakland to Lake Tahoe but the branch line, abandoned in the 1940s, is now a cycle track. Amtrak's long, low station is on the right at 10065 Donner Pass Road. An old SP railroad car caboose, used by crew when coupled at the end of a freight train, now stands next to the station and houses the Truckee Railroad Museum. For **tourist information**, the Truckee California Welcome Center is inside the station (☏ *530 587 8808*).

After leaving town the train starts to ascend the Donner Pass in a sequence of horseshoe curves, providing fine views of the Truckee River basin below. All the trees are less than 100 years old because the original forest was demolished to feed wood-burning locomotives.

Donner Lake (↑15/110↓) Blizzards in 1846 trapped 87 Illinois settlers who had been travelling to California. By the time a relief party arrived here on 19 February 1847, nearly half the settlers, including five women and 14 children, had frozen to death or died from starvation. Others were reduced to cannibalism or had gone mad in the greatest single natural disaster of America's westward expansion. The place became known as Donner Pass after the Donner family, who were among the settlers. The Donner Memorial State Park and Emigrant Trail Museum at 12593 Donner Pass Road (☏ *530 582 7892;* w *parks.ca.gov/?page_id=503*) commemorates those who emigrated to California in the mid-1800s. It tells moving and inspiring stories of the Donner Party, the Land of the Washoe, Chinese construction of the railroad, and early motoring adventures over Donner Pass.

Mount Judah (↑25/100↓) Nearing Judah's summit the slopes of Sugar Bowl ski resort, one of the oldest in California, can be seen on both sides of the track, joined by an overhead trestle. The train then enters a tunnel through the mountain named after the Central Pacific's designer, Theodore Judah.

Norden (↑35/90↓) Snowfall averages 34ft (10m) a year so building and maintaining this track is a remarkable achievement. The *City of San Francisco* was once snowbound here for four days but today's trains are often able to run when the nearby highway becomes impassable.

There used to be 37 miles (60km) of snow sheds between Truckee and Sacramento, leading some to describe the route as 'like railroading in a barn'. Sheds were usually made from wood and often caught fire during the days of steam power. Special fire trains had to be kept in readiness and only 4 miles (6.5km) of sheds now remain. On a mountain to your left is the small box which was once a fire lookout point.

Soda Springs (↑40/85↓) Lake Van Norden and the Soda Springs ski resort are to your left. On the other side of the valley to your right is Castle Peak, shaped like a fortress. Beside it is Black Butte Mountain (8,030ft/2,450m).

Emigrant Gap (↑65/60↓) Lake Spalding's irregular outline appears to your right as the train crosses Interstate 80. Trees sometimes grow almost horizontally in the alpine scenery. Pioneers used to lower wagons by rope into the beautiful Bear Valley on your right after travelling through Emigrant Gap.

Blue Canyon (↑70/55↓) Named after the blue haze produced by sawmills, this was a gold rush town and a servicing stop for steam trains.

American River Canyon (↑90/35↓) Astonishing views appear to your left as the train inches along evergreen-covered cliffs 1,800ft (550m) above the north fork of the American River. The remains of gold mine workings can be seen opposite in a valley that stretches all the way to Sacramento.

Alta (↑100/25↓) A red fire station stands on the right. Among the hills are flumes originally constructed by gold miners and which are now used to carry water to the farms below.

Gold Run (↑105/20↓) Note the old post office building to your left. Until it became illegal in 1884, hydraulic gold mining washed away huge sections of the hillside. The *California Zephyr*'s tracks run alongside the old mine site.

Cape Horn (↑118/7 ↓) This is the steepest slope on the *Zephyr*'s entire journey. Chinese labourers constructing the route were lowered on ropes to hack out a rocky ledge for the track. Lewis Metzler Clement was hired by Theodore Judah as one of the Central Pacific's chief assistant engineers and was primarily responsible for designing and building the section of the line between Truckee and Colfax, including Cape Horn, all the tunnels and the snow sheds. Although not present at the Golden Spike ceremony he is shown in the famous Thomas Hill painting standing behind Judah (who was by then dead) and Charles Crocker. Clement later worked on constructing the cable-car system in San Francisco.

Colfax can be seen ahead to your left as the train curves left over a highway.

⫶⫶⫶ COLFAX (↑125/60↓) Amtrak passengers use a platform next to the 1906 'Colonnade'-style wood depot, which now houses the Colfax Historical Museum and a visitor centre. Look left for a flea market and an ancient Southern Pacific railroad car housing a bank. During the gold rush, goods were brought to Colfax by mule for transfer into the mountains. The town became the Central Pacific's 'end of track' in 1865. Barlett pears, Hungarian prunes and Tokay grapes are grown around this former 'mother lode' town, now known as the 'Gateway to the High Sierra Mountains'.

As the *Zephyr* eases down the western side of the Sierra Nevada (the snowy mountains) look for drifts of wild lupins and red and yellow poppies.

Auburn (↑25/35↓)

When gold was discovered at Coloma, just south of here, Auburn supplied the camps and administered claims. Among several preserved buildings is the 1893 fire house on your right, which boasted the first volunteer fire department west of Boston. Outlaws used to be publicly hanged in the grounds of the beautiful gold-domed Placer County Courthouse on a hill to your right.

As you leave, the town cemetery can be seen on a hill to your right before the train descends through less mountainous terrain and enters the fields, ranches and orchards of the Sacramento Valley.

Rocklin (↑45/15↓)

In 1912, 22 granite quarries operated in Rocklin and 2,000 train carloads of granite were sent out to become part of the State Capitol and be used for buildings such as Fort Mason in San Francisco. Local granite was also used as ballast (for laying railroad tracks). The last quarry closed in 2005 and more recent growth has come with residential development and hi-tech companies.

⋘ ROSEVILLE (↑60/25↓)

The *California Zephyr* picks its way carefully among the complexities of the Southern Pacific's rail yards. Note the large locomotive-maintenance shop next to a wooden station building to your left.

McClellan Air Force Base (↑10/15↓)

The airfield and depots can be seen on your right. Closed in 2001, this former logistics and maintenance facility is now a civil-military airfield and business park. The Aerospace Museum of California displays military aircraft in one of the hangars and on the runway. Approaching Sacramento, both sides of the track are engulfed by the Blue Diamond Company – the largest almond-processing plant in the world. Most of California's yearly crop of more than two billion pounds (907,184 tonnes) find their way here and groves of almond trees can often be seen. Valued at over $5 billion, this is California's largest food export.

⋘ SACRAMENTO (↑25/20↓)

For Sacramento and the rest of the *California Zephyr* route to San Francisco, see pages 65–8). The *Zephyr* makes a scheduled stop at Richmond.

6

The *San Joaquin*
San Francisco–Bakersfield
(via Emeryville/Oakland)

GENERAL ROUTE INFORMATION

With fig trees, vineyards, date palms, orchards and oil wells, the San Joaquin Valley is definitive California: a heady blend of warmth and almond blossom. *San Joaquin* trains travel more than 300 miles (480km) between Emeryville/Oakland and Bakersfield, giving access to several national parks and some of the richest farm country in America. Amtrak has plans for nine more stations on this busy route by 2023, including one for midtown Sacramento.

JOINING THE TRAIN

SAN FRANCISCO: ALL ABOARD! (25↓)   For San Francisco, Emeryville/Oakland and the route to Martinez, see pages 67–8. *San Joaquin* trains initially travel north

ESSENTIAL INFORMATION

HIGHLIGHTS The *San Joaquin* explores California's finest agricultural region, bordered in the west by mountain ranges and in the east by the magnificent Yosemite, Kings Canyon, Sequoia and Death Valley national parks. Stops include Martinez, with its many preserved old buildings, and Modesto, George Lucas's hometown immortalised in his film, *American Graffiti*.

FREQUENCY Five trains operate daily in each direction. Departure times are early morning, mid-morning, noon, mid-afternoon and early evening.

DURATION Six hours 15 minutes

CONNECTIONS Connecting buses link Emeryville with San Francisco, and Bakersfield with Los Angeles and Santa Barbara. An extensive Amtrak Thruway bus system operates in the Bay Area and throughout the Sacramento Valley. Trains and buses are funded by Amtrak and Caltrans (the California Department of Transportation) and are a good way to explore some of the less well-known parts of the state. Schedules are available from Amtrak agents and information about Amtrak services in California can also be found on the website **w** amtrakcalifornia.com.

RESERVATIONS All reserved

EQUIPMENT Bi-level California coaches. Wi-Fi available.

FOOD Complete meals, snacks, sandwiches, drinks

BAGGAGE Check-in service is available on all trains. Bicycle racks.

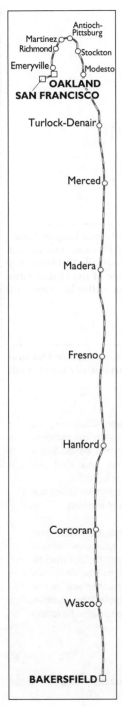

Antioch-
Pittsburg
Martinez
Richmond
Stockton
Emeryville
Modesto
OAKLAND
SAN FRANCISCO

Turlock-Denair

Merced

Madera

Fresno

Hanford

Corcoran

Wasco

BAKERSFIELD

from Oakland towards Martinez, stopping en route at Richmond (described in the *Coast Starlight* chapter).

MARTINEZ (↑25/22↓) Amtrak Thruway coaches serve McKinleyville via Vallejo, Napa, Santa Rosa, Ukiah, Garberville and Eureka. As the train leaves Martinez it parts company with the *California Zephyr* and *Coast Starlight* tracks, which continue over the bridge to your left. Storage tanks and a Shell oil refinery appear on the right.

Mothball Fleet (↑12/10↓) Across the bay to your left lies a fleet of transport ships kept in 'mothballs', officially known as the Suisun Bay Reserve Fleet. Only a few vessels remain but at its peak Suisun Bay had 340 ships lined up in neat rows.

Between here and Antioch-Pittsburg, *San Joaquin* trains change from Southern Pacific tracks to those of the Santa Fe Railroad.

ANTIOCH-PITTSBURG (↑22/35↓) You begin to escape the Bay Area's influence as the Sacramento and San Joaquin rivers converge to your left. Look for the deep-water channel linking Stockton, 80 miles (128km) from the sea, with San Francisco. Amtrak's stop is a modern shelter beside the platform.

STOCKTON (↑35/25↓) The Magnolia District has 19th-century houses and this inland port and distribution centre was the location for John Huston's *Fat City*. The University of the Pacific here has been a location for films such as *Raiders of the Lost Ark* and *Indiana Jones and the Last Crusade*, and is home to the Brubeck Institute, named for jazz piano legend and former student Dave Brubeck. The Stockton **visitors bureau** is at 125 Bridge Place (↳*209 938 1555;* w *visitstockton.org*).

From the 1860s, both the Western Pacific and Central Pacific railroads served Stockton, with the CP providing a link to the first transcontinental rail line in 1869. Amtrak's station is at 735 South San Joaquin, from where Thruway buses go north to Sacramento. Additional train and Thruway connecting bus services are available at the Robert J Cabral Station, 949 East Channel Street. Amtrak passengers use a concrete platform with shelters next to a restored 1930 Southern Pacific Railroad depot built in Italian Renaissance and Spanish Revival style.

After leaving town the train travels through a landscape where hundreds of vineyards supply local wineries. You cross the Stanislaus River.

MODESTO (↑25/15↓) *Star Wars* creator George Lucas grew up in Modesto and the film *American Graffiti* was based on his teenage years here. Served by ferries during the 1880s gold rush, further development came to neighbouring Riverbank with the arrival of the Santa Fe Railway.

Hetch Hetchy Aqueduct (↑3/12↓)
The train crosses a concrete-lined aqueduct which supplies the Bay Area with water from the Sierra Nevada. A few minutes later you cross the Tuolumne River.

₩ TURLOCK-DENAIR (↑15/22↓)
The station is at Santa Fe Avenue in Denair, named after a Santa Fe Railway employee who owned land in the area. Adjacent Turlock is much larger. The Diablo Mountains can be seen in the right distance.

As the *San Joaquin* crosses the Merced River, look for the numerous almond trees growing on both sides – an especially wonderful sight when they blossom in late winter.

Atwater (↑15/7↓)
Preserved World War II planes can be seen at the Castle Air Museum to your left. As you approach Merced the town's 1875 courthouse is on your right.

₩ MERCED (↑22/30↓)
Built in Renaissance style and restored, the **Courthouse Museum** at 21st and North streets (☏ *209 723 2401;* w *mercedmuseum.org*) dominates the main square with a figure of Justice perched on its cupola. Amtrak's modern Arts and Crafts-style station is at 324 West 24th, from where Thruway buses will take you east to one of America's finest experiences, **Yosemite National Park**. Highlights include El Capitan (a granite dome twice as tall as the Rock of Gibraltar) and Yosemite Falls (2,425ft/740m). Late spring and early summer are the best times to visit. A visitor centre opens daily in the park or you can contact PO Box 577, Yosemite National Park, CA 95389 (☏ *209 372 0200;* w *nps.gov/yose*).

Planada (↑5/25↓)
Kadota fig trees grow raggedly on your left as you continue through some of America's most productive land. Other local specialities to look for include pistachio nuts, rice, tomatoes, peaches and grapes. Back to your left before the train crosses the Fresno River you can see the Sierra Nevada's Cathedral Mountains (13,000ft/4,000m).

₩ MADERA (↑30/25↓)
A busy farming town, Madera is located in the geographical centre of California and is famous for its wines and olives. The Madera County Historical Society operates a local history museum in the old Madera County Courthouse.

San Joaquin River (↑10/15↓)
A golf course is on your right as you cross the river.

Fresno State College (↑20/5↓)
The campus is seen to your right before the train enters Fresno, passing a water tower and the Santa Fe Railway offices.

₩ FRESNO (↑25/30↓)
This is the 'raisin capital of the world', where Sun-Maid's packing facility covers 73 acres (30ha). Grapes grown south of here are mostly turned into raisins while those produced further north become wine. The Meux Mansion (w *meux.mus.ca.us*), located a block from the station at 1007 R, is a charming, ornate Victorian house originally built for a doctor.

Fresno's station is Amtrak's busiest stop between Emeryville and Bakersfield, and also the nearest station to **Sequoia** and **Kings Canyon national parks** in southern Nevada. These are quieter than Yosemite but still have fantastic mountains, caves, meadows and sequoia trees (the largest living things in the world). For **information** contact 47050 Generals Highway, Three Rivers, CA 93271 (✆ *559 565 3341;* w *nps. gov/seki*).

The *San Joaquin* leaves Fresno with the beautiful water tower of Sun-Maid's old plant on your right, once dubbed the 'finest factory building west of Detroit'.

You continue among sun-baked vineyards and cross the Kings River.

HANFORD (↑30/20↓) Named after James Hanford, a Southern Pacific paymaster who sometimes paid his company's employees in gold. Hundreds of Chinese came to work on constructing the railroad and left behind the Taoist temple in China Alley. You can also visit Hanford's Neoclassical courthouse and the Courthouse Square jail, which resembles the Bastille in Paris. Amtrak's single-storey station is at 200 Santa Fe Avenue, from where Thruway buses connect to San Luis Obispo and Visalia, the central valley's first settlement.

The train travels on, making good time through the flat landscape of orchards, vineyards and alfalfa fields. Irrigation means prolific crops can be grown over an area the size of the Netherlands.

CORCORAN (↑20/25↓) Note the grain elevators and cotton gin to your right beyond Amtrak's Spanish Revival-style station at the corner of Whitley and Otis Avenue. Corcoran is the home of a California state prison built on what was once Tulare Lake, home of the Yokut Native American people.

Allensworth Park (↑10/15↓) The park on the right is in the middle of the Tulare Lake region.

WASCO (↑25/22↓) This is another predominantly agricultural town, famous for growing half of America's roses. A Rose Queen is crowned each year at Wasco's Festival of Roses. Amtrak's modern open-air station is at 700 G and Highway 43.

Shafter (↑2/20↓) Look for more grapes and almond trees before the *San Joaquin* passes through Kern County's densely developed oilfield, where pumps can be seen working on both sides of the track. The area's largest refinery is to your left as you near Bakersfield. A few minutes from town, the train crosses a canal then enters the Santa Fe yards with an old roundhouse to your right.

BAKERSFIELD (↑22) Home of country music's Merle Haggard and Glen Campbell, Bakersfield rapidly expanded when oil was discovered at the turn of the century. **Kern County Museum** (*3801 Chester Av;* ✆ *661 437 3330;* w *kerncountymuseum.org*) has more than 50 buildings dating from 1865 to World War II, including a one-room school, a general store and a jail.

The strikingly modern station is at 601 Truxtun Avenue. Opened on 4 July, 2000, it has vast walls of glass, a veneer of rich India red sandstone and unique fountains that announce the arrival of trains. Amtrak buses link with Palm Springs, Pasadena and many places in the Los Angeles area, as well as with trains to Los Angeles and San Diego.

7

The *Pacific Surfliner*
Los Angeles–San Diego

GENERAL ROUTE INFORMATION

Pacific Surfliner (formerly *San Diegan*) trains travel one of Amtrak's busiest routes, serving two major cities and a growing population. For part of the journey the *Pacific Surfliner* hugs the Pacific shoreline and other pleasures include Disneyland, San Juan Capistrano and the Tijuana Trolley.

JOINING THE TRAIN

LOS ANGELES: ALL ABOARD! (32↓) For Los Angeles city information, see page 78.

As the *Pacific Surfliner* leaves Los Angeles look for City Hall's white tower dominating the skyline to your left. Between here and Fullerton the train passes through the residential and industrial suburbs of Los Angeles County.

ESSENTIAL INFORMATION

HIGHLIGHTS This journey along the southern California coast takes in alluring beaches as well as tourist and cultural attractions such as Disney World and the adobe homes of San Capistrano. In San Diego you can visit outstanding museums housed in Spanish-style buildings in Balboa Park and cross the border into neighbouring Mexico.

FREQUENCY Departures are approximately every two hours in both directions from early morning until late evening (a total of 11 daily round trips, with many trains continuing to Santa Barbara, Sacramento or San Luis Obispo).

DURATION Three hours

CONNECTIONS Amtrak Thruway buses and some local trains, as well as the *Coast Starlight*, connect Los Angeles with Santa Barbara along the San Fernando Valley. The Pacific Surfliner Transit Transfer Program provides free transfers to connecting transit providers at most stations. Just show your Amtrak *Pacific Surfliner* paper ticket or e-ticket when you board the bus or shuttle. You can also purchase a discounted one-day transit pass for Metro (Los Angeles) and MTS (San Diego) in the Café Car.

RESERVATIONS Unreserved except for Pacific Business-Class passengers, who have access to the Amtrak Metropolitan Lounge in Los Angeles.

EQUIPMENT Bi-level Surfliner coaches. Business Class. Railfone.

FOOD Snacks, sandwiches, drinks in the Sea View Café Car

BAGGAGE Check-in service is available on most trains. Bicycle and surfboard racks.

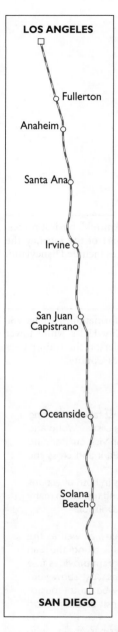

LOS ANGELES

Fullerton

Anaheim

Santa Ana

Irvine

San Juan
Capistrano

Oceanside

Solana
Beach

SAN DIEGO

Los Angeles River (↑5/27↓) The train accompanies a
concrete channel to your left. Designed for flood control
and usually dry, the channel has been a location for
dozens of movie chases.

Redondo Junction (↑10/22↓) Amtrak Superliners
for the *Coast Starlight*, *Sunset Limited* and *Southwest Chief*
are set up in the yards and roundhouse to your right.

Commerce (↑15/17↓) This was formerly a stop for
two passenger trains a day in each direction. Commerce
is the 'water polo capital of the world', with a large aquatic
centre that has trained successful players such as four-
time Olympic medallist Brenda Villa.

Santa Fe Springs (↑22/10↓) Oil wells, tanks and
derricks gradually accumulate on both sides.

⚞ FULLERTON (↑32/9↓) The attractive restored
1930 Santa Fe station on your left has pink stucco walls,
a red-tiled roof, graceful arches, quatrefoil windows
and decorative metalwork. Next to it is a 1923 Mission
Revival-style Union Pacific Depot, which was moved to
this site and is now a restaurant. Fullerton is a suburban
stop as well as the station for two of the state's most
popular venues.

Recommended near Fullerton
Disneyland 1313 Harbor Bd, Anaheim; ☎714 781 4636 or 714 781
4565 (for tickets); w disneyland.disney.go.com; ◷ daily; admission
charge. Opened in 1955, the original fun park has been added to ever
since. California's largest tourist attraction features Big Thunder Mountain
Railroad, the Haunted Mansion, the Indiana Jones Adventure, Splash
Mountain (the world's longest flume ride) & a twice-nightly Fantasmic!
light show. Disneyland's Victorian-style railroad train circles the park every
few mins.
   Walt Disney's inspiration for Disneyland came when he lived on his
Carolwood Estate in Los Angeles. Steam enthusiast Walt built a one-
eighth-scale backyard steam train around the grounds in 1950 & soon
got carried away with his pet project, developing a huge control room
in a barn as he expanded the train's route until it became known as the
Carolwood Pacific Railroad. With 2,615ft (797m) of track, a 46ft (14m)
trestle & a 90ft-long (27m) tunnel under his wife Lillian's flowerbeds,
Disney wondered whether he could develop rides & amusements
further. Disneyland was opened 5 years later with a full-size steam train
similar to the one on the Old Disney Estate. Walt's barn was donated to
the Live Steamer's Museum at Griffith Park. With picnic tables & Disney memorabilia, it can be visited
free & tells the story of its effect on Disney's business plan.
Knott's Berry Farm 8039 Beach Bd, Buena Park; ☎714 220 5200; w knotts.com; ◷ daily. This recreated
ghost town comes with shops, restaurants & a hundred rides, including Montezooma's Revenge (0–55mph
(88km/h) in 5secs) & the *GhostRider* (largest roller coaster in park history & the longest, tallest & fastest

wooden roller coaster on the West Coast). Steam engines & equipment formerly owned by the Denver & Rio Grande Western & Rio Grande Southern operate over a 36in-gauge (91cm) track. Train rides included in the admission charge.

FULLERTON: ALL ABOARD! (↑32/9↓) As the *Pacific Surfliner* pulls out of Fullerton you can just make out Disneyland's replica Matterhorn to your right. Approaching Anaheim, look right also for the enormous sports stadium located beyond the station.

ANAHEIM (↑9/9↓) One of the country's fastest-growing cities, this was the birthplace of Leo Fender, pioneer of the electric guitar. Founded by German settlers and former gold miners from San Francisco, Anaheim's name combines the nearby Santa Ana River with *heim* (German for 'home'). The Rams (football) and Angels (baseball) perform in the stadium next to a stunning, ultra-modern railway station opened in 2014 at 2626 E Katella Avenue. Part of a $184.2 million development, it has a 120ft-tall (37m) glass wall entrance and a 'dynamic holographic experience' by artist Mikyoung Kim.

The train leaves for another brief run to Santa Ana through Orange County, famous for Valencia oranges.

Orange (↑4/5↓) Seen away to your right with an old station building on the left.

SANTA ANA (↑9/10↓) This was the birthplace of Michelle Pfeiffer. The restored downtown area and more recent developments feature traditional Spanish architecture. Amtrak's beautiful Mediterranean Revival-design station at 1000 East Santa Ana Boulevard features arcades, decorative tiles and a fine coffered ceiling.

As the train leaves, look right for the two giant hangars which accommodated World War II air balloons and now house US Marine helicopters. The Santa Ana Mountains are to your left.

El Toro Base (↑8/2↓) The former Marine Corps Air Station on your left was used by all post-World War II US presidents, especially Richard Nixon. The base closed in the 1990s and is being converted to a regional park.

IRVINE (↑10/10↓) In 1888, the Santa Fe Railroad extended its line north of San Diego and named a station here after local rancher and businessman James Irvine. The Irvine Historical Society, housed in the former cooking wing of the cattle and sheep camp, preserves the history of the ranch and offers tours of Old Town.

You continue south from here through a land of orange groves interspersed with the occasional small town.

SAN JUAN CAPISTRANO (↑10/30↓) The station at 26701 Verdugo features a restaurant and live jazz performances. Amtrak passenger areas are housed in vintage boxcars. The 1776 mission where Juanero Native Americans converted to Christianity was damaged by an earthquake but part of the adobe building still stands in neatly kept grounds to your left. The famous San Juan Capistrano swallows leave in October, returning (fairly) punctually on 19 March each year.

Soon after leaving town, the train joins the Pacific Ocean on your right, staying in touch with its shoreline until Del Mar. Enviable houses cling to cliffs on your left.

San Clemente (↑10/20↓) Three trains a day stop in San Clemente, where Richard Nixon lived at Casa Pacifica for some of his time as president. The beach is one of the prettiest in California.

San Onofre Nuclear Plant (↑16/14↓) Look right for this ominous presence next to the beach. Extra-warm water once attracted heedless surfers but the plant closed in 2013 and is waiting to be decommissioned. Its interestingly shaped containment shields are referred to in Leslie Nielsen's 1987 film, *The Naked Gun*.

Camp Pendleton (↑25/5↓) One of many naval facilities to be found in this part of the state, Camp Pendleton is a large Marine Corps training base. Yachts and pleasure boats bob in the busy marina to the right.

⊶ OCEANSIDE (↑30/17↓) Amtrak and Greyhound share the busy transit centre, a major railway interchange allowing easy transfers among Amtrak, commuter rail lines and intercity and local buses. Mission San Luis Rey is on nearby Mission Avenue. Oceanside is the home of the Legoland Museum, featuring a castle, miniature Lego cities, a safari adventure complete with Lego animals, and a 4D New Adventure movie.

Carlsbad (↑5/12↓) Look out for a military boys' school to your right before the train passes a gigantic Encina power plant, also to the right. The plant, with its looming 400ft (120m) smoke stack, will be shut down when a new 500-megawatt power station is completed next to the current site.

Del Mar Racetrack (↑15/2↓) The racetrack immediately to your left was built by a partnership that included Bing Crosby, Pat O'Brien, Gary Cooper, Joe E Brown and Oliver Hardy, and boasted the slogan: 'Where The Turf Meets The Surf'. Del Mar is famed for its conservatism and exclusive beach apartments. A hundred annual events take place at the Del Mar fairgrounds, where Thoroughbred Club meetings are popular with today's big Hollywood names.

⊶ SOLANA BEACH (↑17/30↓) The light-filled Amtrak depot opened in 1994. Inspired by the shape of the Quonset hut, a semicircular prefabricated structure used by the army, the building anchors the Cedros Avenue Design District.

The *Pacific Surfliner* shifts away from the ocean at this point and travels inland through rugged country towards its final destination. Look out for the celebrated Torrey Pines on both sides as you descend through Soledad and Rose canyons.

University of San Diego (↑20/10↓) The campus is to your left.

San Diego International Airport (↑25/5↓) Formerly known as Lindbergh Field, the runways and buildings appear on your right.

⊶ SAN DIEGO (↑30) The state's oldest city has smog-free sunshine, Spanish architecture and an easy-going atmosphere. Portuguese explorer Juan Cabrillo discovered this bay in 1542, but settlement began much later when a garrison and California's first Spanish mission were built. San Diego became part of the United States in 1847, after which the Santa Fe Railway brought rapid expansion to a city which continues to grow. It is now the seventh-biggest city in the country and has the world's largest military complex (125,000 acres/50,500ha).

Railroad tycoon Elisha Babcock opened his massive Hotel del Coronado across the bay in Coronado in 1888, when it was the largest resort hotel in the world. Celebrated guests have included Thomas Edison, Charlie Chaplin, Babe Ruth, Katharine Hepburn, George Harrison, Brad Pitt, Barbra Streisand and Oprah Winfrey, as well as presidents from Benjamin Harrison and William McKinley to John F Kennedy, Jimmy Carter and Barack Obama. Now a National Historic Landmark and a California Historical Landmark, this is the second-largest wooden building in the USA and 'the talk of the western world' still prospers, though most guests no longer arrive by train.

San Diego basics

Telephone code 619

Station (*Ticket office & waiting room* closed between 01.00 & 03.00) Amtrak's station at 1050 Kettner Bd is a beautiful, spacious, twin-domed building close to the waterfront in an older part of downtown. Union Station, also known as the 'Santa Fe Depot', was built in a mixture of Spanish Mission & Colonial Revival styles by the Atchison, Topeka & Santa Fe Railway for passengers arriving at the 1915 Panama–California Exposition, replacing the California Southern Railway's 1887 Victorian depot. From 1916 to 1951, the depot also served the San Diego & Arizona Railway (later SD & AE) & the San Diego Electric Railway until 1949.

Luggage store, ATM, Red Caps, taxi stand. Listed on the National Register of Historic Places, the station also houses the downtown branch of the Museum of Contemporary Art San Diego, the research library of the San Diego Railroad Museum & the Santa Fe Historical Society library.

Connections The station is also served by the San Diego Coaster, the San Diego Trolley & the San Diego Metropolitan Transit System (buses).

Local transport The city is easy to negotiate on foot or by bicycle. San Diego Transit buses (233 3004) operate a comprehensive service. Passes can be used on all routes as well as the San Diego Trolley (downtown & from the station to San Ysidro on the Mexican border) & the Bay Ferry from Broadway Pier to Coronado. Coaster runs commuter rail services to Oceanside (760 966 6500). Orange County Transportation Authority provides bus transit service throughout Orange County including *Pacific Surfliner* stations in Fullerton, Anaheim, Santa Ana, Irvine, San Juan Capistrano & San Clemente (714 636 7433; w octa.net).

Taxis Yellow 444 4444; San Diego Taxi 566 6666

Car rental Avis, 3355 Admiral Boland Way; 688 5000

Greyhound 1313 National Av; 515 1100

San Diego Airport 3 miles (5km) north of downtown by MTS bus #992 from the station

Tours Harbour cruises from Hornblower (686 8700) & trips to Santa Catalina Island with Princess (0344 338 8663)

Visitors bureau 996-B N Harbor Dr; 737 2999; w sandiego.org; daily

Accommodation Hotels include the Bristol, 1055 First Av; 232 6141; w thebristolsandiego. com, **$$$$**; Indigo, 509 9th Av; 906 4809; w ihg.com/hotelindigo, **$$$$**; Sofia, 150 W Broadway; 234 9200; w thesofiahotel.com, **$$$$**; Days Inn, 543 Hotel Circle S; 297 8800; w daysinnhc.com, **$$$**; Comfort Inn, 660 G; 238 4100; w comfortinngaslamp.com, **$$**; Red Roof Inn, 4545 Mission Bay Dr; 858 483 4222; w innatpacificbeach.com, **$**.

For B&B contact Carole's Bed & Breakfast Inn, 3227 Grim Av; 280 5258; w carolesbnb.com, **$$$**; The Cottage, 3829 Albatross; 299 1564, **$$**.

The San Diego Hostel, about 10mins' walk from Amtrak's station, is at 726 Fifth Av; 232 3100. Dormitory, **$**, sgl, **$$**. AYH Hostel, 3790 Udall, Point Loma; 223 4778; w hiusa.org/hostels/california/san-diego/point-loma. Take bus #35. Members & non-members, **$**.

The nearest campsite is Campland On The Bay, 2211 Pacific Beach Dr; 1 800 422 9386; w campland.com, **$$**. Take bus #30.

Recommended in San Diego

Balboa Park 2125 Park Bd. The park information centre is in the House of Hospitality building, near the Plaza de Panama, in the heart of Balboa Park (239 0512; w balboapark.org). The park has well over 1,000 acres (400ha) of gardens, trees & lawns, as well as the world's largest outdoor pipe organ. The California–Pacific Exposition succeeded the Panama–California Exposition here in 1935, & Spanish-style buildings house 17 excellent art galleries, museums & theatres. A pass gives access to all the museums, most of which are free on the 1st Tue in the month to residents & military personnel; a free tram service operates around the park.

San Diego History Center 1649 El Prado in Balboa Park; ☎ 232 6203; w sandiegohistory.org; ☺ daily; admission charge. Changing exhibits & lectures are used imaginatively to interpret San Diego's regional history.

Aerospace Museum 2001 Pan American Plaza in Balboa Park; ☎ 234 8291; w aerospacemuseum. org; ☺ daily; admission charge. Aviation history from the Wright Brothers to the space age is brought to life with over 65 aircraft, including a replica of the *Spirit of St Louis* monoplane in which Charles Lindbergh made his first flight in 1927 from a San Diego airfield & the *Apollo 9* Command Module. The first transcontinental flight, from New York to San Diego, took place in 1923.

Museum of Contemporary Art 1100 & 1001 Kettner Bd; ☎ 234 1001; w mcasd.org; admission charge. The museum has 2 distinct, complementary locations – in the heart of downtown & in the coastal community of La Jolla. MCASD in downtown shows contemporary art in a historic setting – the Jacobs Building, formerly the Santa Fe Depot baggage building. MCASD in La Jolla gives a fabulous ocean view from the Edwards Garden Gallery & houses the Museum's X Store, filled with contemporary art books, clothes & innovative design objects.

Model Railroad Museum 1649 El Prado, on the lower level of the Casa de Balboa in Balboa Park; ☎ 696 0199; w sdmodelrailroadm.com; ☺ daily; admission charge, but children under 15 enter free. At 28,000 square feet (2,600m^2), this is the world's largest of its kind, with 4 enormous scale & model layouts depicting railroads of the Southwest in 0, HO, & N scales. The museum has detailed recreations of beautiful train routes, including Tehachapi Pass, the Cabrillo Southwester, San Diego & Arizona Eastern & the Pacific Desert lines.

San Diego Zoo 2920 Zoo Dr, Balboa Park, north of the museums; ☎ 231 1515; w sandiegozoo.org; ☺ daily; admission charge. Koalas, tigers, giant pandas, rhinos & gorillas are among the 3,500 rare & endangered animals (over 500 species) living in one of the world's best zoos. Children's area, tours & an aerial tramway.

Old Town Historic Park 4002 Wallace (information centre); ☎ 220 5422. Restored buildings, galleries & restaurants occupy the site of the first (1769) Spanish settlement. Highlights include the Machado y Silvas Adobe, San Diego's first schoolhouse & the Casa de Estudillo, built in 1827 by a *presidio* commander who would watch bull & bear fights from its cupola.

Whaley House Built in 1856 on a former gallows site, this was the first 2-storey brick building in southern California & has been officially designated as a haunted house by the US Department of Commerce. Free walking tours leave daily from the information centre. For Old-Town trolley tours, ☎ 298 8687.

Gaslamp Quarter 614 Fifth Av; ☎ 233 5227; w gaslamp.org. Many of the buildings in this area from Broadway to the waterfront were erected in the late 19th century & have been returned to their former glory, serving now as shops, restaurants & nightclubs. You can take a walking tour narrated by the former Gaslamp Quarter saloon owner & gunslinger, Wyatt Earp. Call the Gaslamp Quarter Foundation (☎ 233 4692) for information & reservations.

La Jolla This affluent northern suburb is famous for its beaches, scuba diving & chic residents. Raymond Chandler used La Jolla as the setting, renamed Poodle Springs, for his last novel *Playback*. Chandler's former home can be seen at 6005 Camino de la Costa. La Jolla's racetrack also features in the film of Jim Thompson's novel *The Grifters*, along with several shots of San Diegan trains.

San Diego Railroad Museum Located at 750 Depot St in Campo, 50 miles (80km) to the east; ☎ 478 9937 (w/ends); w sdrm.org; admission charge. Over 80 pieces of railroad equipment, including steam & diesel locomotives of the Southern Pacific & California Western railroads, passenger cars, freight cars & cabooses can be seen at the restored depots at La Mesa & Campo.

Steam train excursions using vintage equipment over parts of the San Diego & Arizona Railway take place at w/ends, & diesel-powered trains travel to Tecate in Mexico.

Tijuana Not classic Mexico, and less wild than it used to be, but 'the world's most visited city' is an easy trip from San Diego. From the Santa Fe Depot cross Kettner Bd to America Plaza Station for the MTS Blue Line Trolley that will take you the 17 miles to the border, although beggars and the concrete walkway make crossing on foot a bleak experience. San Ysidro is the world's busiest international border crossing, with about 25,000 pedestrians (and 50,000 motorists) passing through daily. Try to avoid peak times, such as weekends, and return after 19.00. An alternative westside pedestrian crossing, commonly referred to as PedWest, opened in 2016 and has increased capacity, providing travellers with an additional crossing option located near the Virginia Avenue Transit Center (VATC) in West San Ysidro.

Tijuana offers cheap drinks, accommodation, food, shopping and bullfights. US dollars are welcome as you shop for blankets, leather goods, jewellery and tequila. For more information visit the website **w** tijuana.com.

Note: except for citizens of the US and Canada, a valid visa is required for return to the United States, even after a one-day visit. US citizens can cross the border coming back from Tijuana with a valid passport or a US passport card. Americans without passports can also return from Tijuana with two proofs of citizenship, such as a driver's licence or birth certificate. Non-US citizens must have a valid passport as well as form I-94 and a multiple-entry visa. More information can be obtained from the US Department of State online at **w** travel.state.gov or by calling ✆202 647 5225.

USA BY RAIL ONLINE

For additional online content, articles, photos and more on travelling in the USA by rail, why not visit **w** bradtguides.com/usa?

8

The *Empire Builder* Chicago–Seattle

GENERAL ROUTE INFORMATION

The *Empire Builder* crosses the Mississippi River and travels more than 2,200 miles (3,500km) past wheat fields, cattle ranges, forests, mountains and glacial lakes. America's northern plains were mostly wilderness until the freewheeling tycoon James J Hill built his Great Northern Railway between St Paul, Minnesota and Seattle. Amtrak's *Empire Builder* takes its name from the train called after him, which ran on this route during the heyday of rail travel.

ESSENTIAL INFORMATION

HIGHLIGHTS This journey through awe-inspiring wilderness areas follows in the footsteps of early pioneers, with fine views of the Mississippi River and night skyline of Minneapolis/St Paul. After crossing North Dakota's plains you skirt the Missouri and reach the Big Sky country of Montana, stopping at Glacier National Park with its rugged mountains and pristine lakes.

FREQUENCY Daily. The **westbound** service leaves Chicago mid-afternoon to arrive in Milwaukee by late afternoon and St Paul–Minneapolis late in the evening. You reach Havre on the second afternoon, West Glacier by mid-evening and Spokane during the night, arriving in Seattle or Portland by mid-morning. Travelling **east**, trains leave Seattle or Portland late in the afternoon to reach Spokane at midnight and West Glacier early next morning. You reach Havre by early afternoon and St Paul–Minneapolis early the following morning, arriving in Milwaukee early afternoon and Chicago by late afternoon.

DURATION 46 hours

RESERVATIONS All reserved

EQUIPMENT Superliner coaches

SLEEPING Superliner bedrooms

FOOD Complete meals, snacks, sandwiches, drinks

LOUNGE CAR Movies, games, hospitality hour. During the spring and summer months, National Park Service guides from the Klondike Gold Rush National Historic Park provide a narrative commentary between the stations of Seattle and Shelby. Rangers from the Fort Union Trading Post are similarly on board between Williston and Shelby stations, and rangers from Knife River Indian Villages between Minot and Malta or Shelby (from Memorial Day until Labor Day).

BAGGAGE Check-in service is available at most stations.

JOINING THE TRAIN

CHICAGO: ALL ABOARD! (24↓) For Chicago city information, see page 83. The *Empire Builder* leaves on the complex tracks of the Chicago, Milwaukee, St Paul & Pacific Railroad (also known as the Soo Line or Milwaukee Road), following what was a plank road in the days of horse-drawn wagons.

Some of the fastest-ever trains, capable of well over 100mph (160km/h), ran between Chicago and Milwaukee in the 1930s when this route was known as 'the world's greatest steam railroad speedway'.

On your right as the train pulls out of Chicago is the Chicago River, the massive Art Deco Merchandise Mart Building, which was the largest building in the world when it opened in 1930, and the cylindrical towers of Marina City, which was the tallest residential building in the world when completed in 1968. Also to your right are a former Rock-Ola jukebox factory and the tapered John Hancock Center. The Willis Tower is to your left. You continue among the older buildings and spired churches of Chicago's northside.

Niles (↑4/20↓) The Niles half-size version of Pisa's leaning tower appears on your left. The beautiful 1892 Michigan Central Railroad station here is listed on the National Register of Historc Places.

⋈ GLENVIEW (↑24/60↓) The attractive modern station's tall clock tower is a community landmark. When the train stops at this busy suburban station, traffic along Glenview Road has to wait, so there are plans to move Amtrak's stop to the Metra station in North Glenview. The train pauses before changing from Metra tracks to those of Canadian Pacific (CP) to continue north through residential areas, farms and industrial plants. Look for the patriotic water tower to your left.

The Glen (↑2/58↓) Glenview air base was once the largest primary training facility for the US Navy. Since it closed in 1995, the area seen on the left has been transformed into a commercial and residential development known as The Glen.

Gurnee (↑15/45↓) Look right for the Six Flags' Great America Amusement Park. The *Goliath* ride set three world records for wooden roller coasters when it opened in 2014: the longest and steepest drop and the fastest speed.

Wadsworth (↑20/40↓) This rural village was named after Elisha Wadsworth, a major stockholder for the

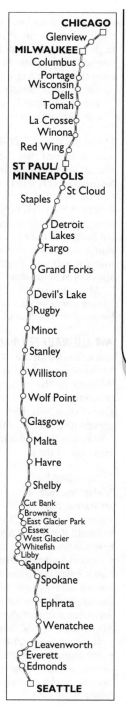

CHICAGO
Glenview
MILWAUKEE
Columbus
Portage
Wisconsin
Dells
Tomah
La Crosse
Winona
Red Wing
ST PAUL/
MINNEAPOLIS
St Cloud
Staples
Detroit
Lakes
Fargo
Grand Forks
Devil's Lake
Rugby
Minot
Stanley
Williston
Wolf Point
Glasgow
Malta
Havre
Shelby
Cut Bank
Browning
East Glacier Park
Essex
West Glacier
Whitefish
Libby
Sandpoint
Spokane
Ephrata
Wenatchee
Leavenworth
Everett
Edmonds
SEATTLE

Chicago, Milwaukee, St Paul & Pacific Railroad, which was a big influence on the local economy. Trains stopped here to take on water and coal for their steam engines, and the depot had an agent and a telegraph operator as well as other railroad employees. Farmers shipped milk to Chicago and would take the milk train there once a month to collect their milk money from the dairies. By the mid-1930s, trains no longer stopped in Wadsworth.

The Des Plaines River comes into view on your left, and a few minutes later the *Empire Builder* crosses the Illinois–Wisconsin state line into 'America's dairyland'.

Franksville (↑40/20↓)
Contrary to popular belief, 'the kraut capital of the world' was not named after the Frank Pure Food Company (makers of sauerkraut), seen on the left, but after either pioneer surveyor Frank Brandecker or Frank Drandieker, foreman of a crew that laid the railroad tracks through the area.

General Mitchell Airport (↑50/10↓)
The international airport can be seen to your right. As the train nears Milwaukee and crosses the Monomonee River, look left for two of the city's finest churches. The opulent **St Josaphat's**, with its distinctive dome, was North America's first Polish basilica, built in 1901 by immigrants using material salvaged from the post office building in Chicago. Next to it are the gold spires of **St Stanislaus Cathedral**.

Also on your left as the train snakes into the station are the octagonal dials and square tower of an enduring local landmark, the **Allen-Bradley clock**, the world's largest four-faced clock.

▲▼ MILWAUKEE (↑60/70↓)
'The Genuine American City' is Wisconsin's largest and is famous for the 1970s TV series *Happy Days*, Miller beer and Harley-Davidsons. Milwaukee stands on a Lake Michigan bay which Potawatomi Native Americans called 'Millioki' or 'the gathering place by the waters'. In the 19th century, many thousands of immigrants came from Italy, Ireland, Poland, Scandinavia and especially Germany. One of them was the future Israeli premier, Golda Meir. Milwaukee's different ethnic groups give the city a lively cultural atmosphere and its annual Summerfest on the lakefront is the largest music festival in the world, hosting over 800 bands and 900,000 fans over 11 days.

Milwaukee basics

Telephone code 414

▲▼ Station (*Ticket office* ⊕ *05.30–21.00; waiting room* ⊕ *05.00–23.59*) Milwaukee Intermodal Station at 433 W St Paul Av is served by Amtrak as well as by bus companies Wisconsin Coach Lines, Greyhound, Jefferson, Indian Trails, Lamers, Badger Bus, Tornado & Megabus. The station is also a stop for the new Milwaukee Streetcar, known as The Hop. Wisconsin's Department of Transportation, which owns the MIS, reconstructed its 400ft-long (122m) train passenger concourse in 2016 in a $22 million project designed to harmonise with the station's modern, minimalist aesthetic. ATM, vending machines, payphones, newspapers, Red Caps, restaurant, taxi stand.

Connections No Thruway bus

Local transport Many attractions are within walking distance of the Milwaukee River & a skywalk system means you can get around easily without going outdoors. Milwaukee County Transit at 1942 N 17th (✆ *937 3218*; w *ridemcts.com*) operates an extensive near-24hr bus service.

Taxis Yellow ✆ 271 1800; TaxiMKE ✆ 220 5000

Car rental Avis, 916 E State; ✆ 272 0892; Budget, 603 N Fourth St; ✆ 276 1634

Greyhound 433 W St Paul Ste 150; ✆ 272 2156

✈ General Mitchell Airport 6 miles (10km) from downtown by MCTS GreenLine or bus #80

Tours MCT has summer excursions to historic sights & the lakeshore. Walking tours are available from Historic Milwaukee (📞 277 7795). Boat trips are offered by Milwaukee Boat Line (📞 294 9450; www.mkeboat.com).

🛈 **Visitors bureau** 400 W Wisconsin Av; 📞 273 7222 or 📞 1 800 554 1448; **w** visitmilwaukee.org; ⊕ daily

🏨 **Accommodation** Hotels include the Intercontinental, 139 E Kilbourn Av; 📞 276 8686; **w** ihg.com/intercontinental, **$$$$$**; Metro, 411 E Mason; 📞 272 1937; **w** hotelmetro.com, **$$$$$**; Pfister, 424 E Wisconsin Av; 📞 273 8222;

w thepfisterhotel.com, **$$$$**; Astor, 924 E Juneau Av; 📞 1 800 558 0200; **w** theastorhotel. com, **$$$**; Radisson, 2303 N Mayfair Rd; 📞 257 3400; **w** radisson.com. **$$$**; Residence Inn Milwaukee Downtown, 648 N Plankinton Av; 📞 224 7890; **w** marriott.com, **$$$**; Courtyard Milwaukee Downtown, 300 W Michigan; 📞 291 4122; **w** marriott.com, **$$**.

Contact Manderley Bed & Breakfast, 3026 W Wells St; 📞 459 1886; **w** bedandbreakfastmilwaukee.com, **$$$**.

Recommended in Milwaukee

Milwaukee Art Museum 700 N Art Museum Dr; 📞 224 3200; **w** mam.org; ⊕ Tue–Sun; admission charge. Over 30,000 works of art from ancient to contemporary are housed in the city's 'masterpiece on the lakefront', designed by Eero Saarinen. The museum has a large collection of works by Wisconsin-born Georgia O'Keeffe, as well as by Fragonard, Rodin, Degas, Monet, Toulouse-Lautrec, Picasso, Rothko & Andy Warhol. A $63 million expansion with its spectacular wing-like *brise soleil* design gave the city skyline a new profile when it opened in 2001. A new $34 million building, designed by Milwaukee architect James Shields, opened in 2015 & includes a section devoted to light-based media, photography & video installation.

Milwaukee Public Museum 800 W Wells; 📞 278 2728; **w** mpm.edu; ⊕ daily; admission charge. A recreation of Old Milwaukee, a tropical rainforest & the first known total habitat diorama are included among 4 million objects & specimens in one of the largest museums in the United States.

Mitchell Park Conservatory 524 S Layton Bd; 📞 257 5600; **w** milwaukeedomes.org; ⊕ daily; admission charge. 3 giant glass domes, each 85ft high & 140ft wide (26m by 43m), house collections of plants in desert, tropical & temperate environments. Brightly coloured birds & iguanas live among the exotic rainforest flowers of the tropical dome.

Milwaukee County Zoo 10001 W Blue Mound Rd; 📞 256 5412; **w** milwaukeezoo.org; ⊕ daily; admission charge. Around 3,300 creatures, including endangered trumpeter swans & black rhino, live in 200 wooded acres (81ha). There are

377 species of mammals, birds, reptiles, fish & invertebrates plus a children's zoo, guided tours & a miniature train safari ride (*mid-Apr–mid-Oct*). Take bus #10.

Pabst Mansion 2000 W Wisconsin Av; 📞 931 0808; **w** pabstmansion.com; ⊕ daily; admission charge. Built by the sea captain, beer baron & philanthropist Frederick Pabst in 1892, the mansion boasts 37 rooms, 14 fireplaces & 12 baths as well as stained glass, carved woodwork & ornamental iron. The mansion was the home of Roman Catholic archbishops for 67 years & is now being restored to its original splendour. Guided tours.

Old World Wisconsin Off Hwy 67 at nearby Eagle; 📞 262 594 6301; **w** oldworldwisconsin. org; ⊕ daily; admission charge. This open-air museum captures the lifestyles, ideas & challenges of 19th- & early 20th-century rural immigrants. The world's largest museum about rural life has more than 60 historic structures rescued from throughout Wisconsin, painstakingly dismantled & rebuilt here. They include ethnic farmsteads with furnished houses & rural outbuildings as well as the 1880s village with traditional small-town institutions.

Historic Cedarburg Located 20mins north of Milwaukee at Washington Av & Spring in Cedarburg; 📞 1 800 237 2874; **w** cedarburg.org. First settled by Irish immigrants in the 1840s, Cedarburg prospered with the coming of the railroad in 1870 & German families who built dams & mills along the fast-running Cedar Creek. Over 100 main-street businesses, many of them antique shops, occupy registered historic buildings surrounded by attractive limestone houses. Special events & festivals take place all year round.

MILWAUKEE: ALL ABOARD! (↑60/70↓) As the *Empire Builder* departs Milwaukee, look for the Mitchell Park Conservatory's three graceful domes. The site of the demolished County Stadium to your left is now a car park for the new Miller Park stadium. The Miller Brewery, which made Milwaukee famous, is on your right. The train travels through city suburbs for 20 minutes towards America's heartland of lakes and farms.

Pewaukee Lake (↑30/40↓) The shoreline and town are visible to your left before you cross the Rock River three times. Lake Oconomowoc also comes into view on the left, with Pine and Okauchee lakes to your right. Look for wheat fields, silos, cattle and horse-drawn farm wagons.

Watertown (↑50/20↓) The steeple of St Bernard's Church pokes above trees on your right just before the campus of Marantha College Baptist university. The train then crosses the Crawfish River.

🚂 COLUMBUS (↑70/30↓) The neat, well-preserved Ludington Street Station originally had separate waiting areas for men and women and the benches inside are still in use. The Zion Evangelical Lutheran Church is to the left of the station. Its steeple bell, presented by Germany's emperor, was cast from pieces of French cannon captured during the Franco-Prussian War. Beside the church stands the 1892 City Hall, which originally housed the police department, the fire department, the jail and the city library.

Wyocena (↑25/5↓) Wyona Lake (Wyocena Millpond) is a 96-acre (39ha) lake famous for fishing for panfish, largemouth bass and northern pike. Between here and La Crosse are marshes and woodlands.

🚂 PORTAGE (↑30/20↓) The town was founded as a stopover between the Fox and Wisconsin rivers to serve traders and settlers. They had to *portage* (carry) goods across this strip of land when going from Lake Michigan to the Mississippi. Milwaukee Road freight cars gather on the left of Amtrak's small square brick station at 400 W Oneida. State capital Madison is 25 miles (40km) to the south.

Wisconsin River (↑15/5↓) The river on your left cuts through many miles of finely streaked rock. A Baptist Native American church and cemetery can be seen high up to your right.

🚂 WISCONSIN DELLS (↑20/45↓) Situated in a sandstone canyon created by the winding Wisconsin River, natural beauty and an amusement park combine to make this one of the state's chief attractions. Rafting and boat trips are popular pastimes along the river.

Amtrak's tan-brick station at 100 LaCrosse Street is a 1989 replica of a former Chicago, Milwaukee, St Paul & Pacific Railroad depot. **Park Lane Model Railroad Museum** (✆ 608 254 8050) in nearby Reedsburg features 2,000 model trains of various vintages. Also in Reedsburg is the **Riverside & Great Northern Railway**, a 15-inch-gauge (38cm) railroad museum offering live steam train rides through scenic canyons, woods and rocks beside the Wisconsin River (✆ 608 254 6367; w dellstrain.com).

The *Empire Builder* continues northwest and crosses the Wisconsin River.

Mauston (↑20/25↓) The spire of St Patrick's Church is to your right. Lake Decorah, also to your right, was formed by a dam built across the Lemonweir River.

Camp Douglas (↑30/15↓) The village was named after a logging camp established by James Douglas in 1864 to supply wood to steam locomotives. The flow of the Wisconsin River over centuries has produced the splendid red sandstone rock formations seen in Mill Bluff State Park to your left.

TOMAH (↑45/40↓) The area around Tomah has a large Amish population so a horse and buggy can sometimes be seen parked outside the station. Cartoonist Frank King, creator of the long-running US comic strip *Gasoline Alley*, grew up in Tomah. Competitors from the whole Midwest come here for Wisconsin's annual dairyland truck and tractor pull – 'Not just a pull … but an experience!'.

Tomah Lake is to your left as the *Empire Builder* leaves town and suddenly enters a landscape of steep hills.

Tunnel City (↑5/35↓) Named after a tunnel which was used by the Chicago & North Western Railway (track now abandoned west of the tunnel) and the Milwaukee Road, the train runs along a single track through the 1,350ft (410m) tunnel.

Sparta (↑15/25↓) Look right for Sparta/Fort McCoy Airport, used for public and military aviation. You join the La Crosse River on your right and follow it for the next 25 miles (40km) until it joins the Mississippi.

Bangor (↑25/15↓) Many early settlers here came from Bangor in Wales, hence the name. An imposing village hall appears on your right before the train crosses the river.

LA CROSSE (↑40/40↓) Situated at the junction of the Mississippi, Black and La Crosse rivers, the town was named after a term French trappers gave to a game they saw being played by Native Americans. Amtrak's large station at 601 St Andrew was built in 1926. Now renovated and listed twice on the National Register of Historic Places, the waiting room has marble surfaces, its original benches and a handsome wooden ticket counter.

After leaving La Crosse, the *Empire Builder* crosses the Mississippi River for the first time, going from Wisconsin into Minnesota. Islands in midstream divide the Mississippi into three channels. Once across the river you enter one of the route's most attractive stretches, accompanying the Mississippi into hardwood forest. The train bowls along for 40 miles (64km) past farmland and riverboat towns, with the river at times becoming as wide as a lake.

Number 7 Dam (↑5/35↓) The dam and lock system on your right, forming Lake Onalaska, is one of several built in attempts to tame the river.

Number 6 Dam (↑20/20↓) Another dam constructed in the mid-1930s appears on the right.

WINONA (↑40/60↓) The city's name is a Sioux word for 'first-born daughter'. Sugar Loaf Mountain, rising 500ft (150m) to your left, was a ceremonial meeting place for the Sioux. Chief Wa-Pa-Sha's outline could be seen there before quarrying altered the mountain's shape. Winona has grown from its early sawmill days to become a centre for shipping and manufacturing. It hosts the Great River Shakespeare Festival (w *grsf.org*), and the Merchants National Bank is one of many masterpieces of Prairie School architecture. Actress Winona Ryder was born in nearby Olmsted County and named after the city.

Winona has had a rich railroad heritage ever since the 1850s and Amtrak's dark red-brick station dates from 1888. Look out for the large grain elevators standing on your right as the train leaves the station.

Number 5 Dam (↑10/50↓) Another dam built in the federally financed series. Completed in 1935, this concrete structure is 1,619ft (493.5m) long.

Weaver (↑15/45↓) This area is 'the white bass capital of the world', and has many nearby fishing camps. The *Empire Builder* crosses the Zumbro River.

Wabasha (↑30/30↓) At the 1856 Anderson House (the oldest hotel in the state) services used to include free shoeshines, hot bricks to warm your bed and pet cats to keep you company. The hotel closed due to the economic slowdown in 2009 and reopened two years later with a new owner and a museum, but no more cats in the rooms.

Lake Pepin (↑35/25↓) This is where the Chippewa River joins the Mississippi to form the largest lake on the river. Lake Pepin is home to eagles and claims to be the place where water skiing was invented by Ralph Samuelson in the 1920s. Watch for the romantic *Pearl of the Lake* paddle-wheel riverboat.

Frontenac (↑50/10↓) This small town dates back to a French fort built in 1723. The ski runs have been closed at Mount Frontenac ski resort to your left, which is now part of a golf course.

As the train nears Red Wing look left for the 1891 Minnesota State Training School, resembling a German castle. Bob Dylan's song, 'The Walls of Red Wing', is a harrowing portrait of this juvenile reform facility.

⚡ RED WING (↑60/65↓) The name came from a Dakota chief whose emblem was a swan's wing dyed scarlet. Red Wing today is famous for shoes and pottery. In 1905, the Milwaukee Road built a station which the city acquired from the Milwaukee's successor, the Soo Line, and Amtrak leases a waiting room restored to its original condition. The luxurious St James Hotel is to your left. Built in 1875, when Red Wing was the wheat-trading centre of the world, the hotel is located between the Red Wing train depot and the steamboat docks. St James's chefs dining rooms developed such a fine reputation that the railroad adjusted its timetables to allow passengers time to disembark and enjoy dinner here and the hotel still has an excellent reputation.

Cannon River (↑5/60↓) Look right to see the Prairie Island nuclear power station next to the Prairie Island Indian Community Reservation, before you cross the Vermillion River.

Hastings (↑20/45↓) The domed City Hall on your left was formerly the 1871 Dakota County Courthouse. Another lock and dam system can be seen to your right. The *Empire Builder* continues north, again crossing the Mississippi River.

St Paul Airport (↑45/20↓) The airport appears across the river to your left, with the city skyline on palisades to the right.

Harriet Island (↑50/15↓) During summer, picturesque riverboats go from the island on your right to Fort Snelling. As you approach St Paul, look right for the cathedral and left for the castle-like Schmidt Brewery. The brewery shut down in 2002 but the building is being renovated and turned into a community centre with studio space and lofts for artists.

⋙ ST PAUL–MINNEAPOLIS (↑65/80↓) The 'Twin Cities' began as frontier towns on the banks of the Mississippi, settled by immigrants from Scandinavia, Germany and Great Britain. Over three million people now live in the metropolitan area, which has hundreds of lakes and parks.

Prince Rogers Nelson (aka Prince) was born in Minneapolis and state capital St Paul was the birthplace of F Scott Fitzgerald, burlesque striptease artist Lili St Cyr, Monty Python's Terry Gilliam and Charles M Schulz, creator of the comic strip *Peanuts*. St Paul almost became Silicon Valley after World War II when an elite group of navy code breakers created a company whose top-secret work helped launch the world's computer industry.

Twin City basics

Telephone codes 612 in Minneapolis; 651 in St Paul

⋙ Station (*Ticket office* ⊕ *07.00–22.30; Waiting room* ⊕ *24hrs*) Union Station at 240 Kellogg Bd East is a landmark building in the Lowertown neighbourhood of St Paul. Empire Builder Lounge, payphones, lockers, vending machines, handcarts, taxi stand. The Beaux-Arts station with its imposing 150ft-long (45m) Doric colonnade was completed in 1926 & at its peak hosted the passenger trains of 9 railroads, with 282 trains stopping here daily in the 1920s. The concourse is dominated by a barrel-vaulted ceiling with decorative plasterwork interspersed with skylights. A repeating frieze made of creamy brown terracotta runs around 'the living room of Saint Paul' & depicts transportation over time, including an early locomotive pulling carriages.

Connections Amtrak Thruway buses connect with Rochester, Winona, La Crosse & Duluth, birthplace of Robert Allen Zimmerman (better known as Bob Dylan)

⋙ Local transport Minneapolis & St Paul have glass-covered skyways which make it easy to get about on foot, even in winter. Metro Transit bus maps & timetables are available from 560 Sixth Av N (✆ *373 3333; w metrotransit.org*). On buses marked 'Free Ride' you pay no fare when boarding along Nicollet Mall for travel between the Convention Center & the METRO Blue & Green lines on Fifth St.

Metro Transit also operates the METRO Blue Line light-rail service between Mall of America

& Target Field, the Red Line on Cedar Av for Bus Rapid Transit (BRT) between Apple Valley & Mall of America, & the Green Line between downtown Minneapolis & downtown St Paul.

⋙ Taxis (St Paul) Saint Paul Taxi ✆ 600 2906; Yellow ✆ 222 4433

⋙ Car rental Alamo, 7150 Humphrey Dr; ✆ 794 3977 (Minneapolis) & 4650 Glumack Dr; ✆ 713 6277 (St Paul)

⋙ Greyhound (St Paul) 4300 Glumack Dr; ✆ 1 800 231 2222

⋙ Greyhound (Minneapolis) Union Depot; ✆ 1 800 231 2222

✈ Minneapolis–Saint Paul International Airport 8 miles (13km) from downtown by METRO Blue Line & Metro bus #54

Tours Gray Line, 22750 Pillsbury Av, Lakeville (✆ *952 985 7514*) Metro Connections, 1650 West 82nd St, Minneapolis (✆ *333 8687*). Mississippi stern-wheel riverboats leave from Harriet Island (✆ 651 227 1100).

⋐ Visitors bureau 250 Marquette Av S; ✆ 612 767 8000; w minneapolis.org. Also at 175 W Kellogg Bd in St Paul; ✆ 1 800 627 6101; w visitsaintpaul.com; ⊕ daily.

⌂ Accommodation St Paul hotels include the St Paul, 350 Market; ✆ 292 9292; w saintpaulhotel.com, **$$$$$**; InterContinental Riverfront, 11 E Kellogg Bd; ✆ 292 1900; w ihg.com/intercontinental, **$$$$**; Motel 6, 1739 Old Hudson Rd; ✆ 771 5566; w motel6.com, **$$**.

For B&B contact The New Victorian Mansion Bed & Breakfast, 325 Dayton Av, St Paul; ✆321 8151; w newvicbb.com, **$$$$**. The University of Minnesota housing office often has inexpensive rooms during summer; ✆624 2994; w housing. umn.edu/guest-housing, **$$**. Minneapolis International Hostel is at 2400 Stevens Av S;

✆522 5000; w minneapolishostel.com, **$**.

Minneapolis hotels include the Crowne Plaza Northstar, 618 Second Av S; ✆338 2288; w ihg. com, **$$$$**; Renaissance Minneapolis, 225 Third Av S; ✆375 1700; w marriott.com, **$$$$**; DoubleTree, 1101 La Salle Av; ✆332 6800; w doubletree3.hilton.com, **$$$**.

Recommended in the Twin Cities

Minneapolis Institute of Arts 2400 Third Av S; ✆888 642 2787; w artsmia.org; ⊕ Tue–Sun; admission free. Among 89,000 exhibits spanning 20,000 years are Chinese jade, Roman sculptures, an Egyptian mummy & paintings by Rembrandt. Tours, films & lectures.

American Swedish Institute 2600 Park Av, Minneapolis; ✆871 4907; w asimn.org; ⊕ Tue–Sun; admission charge. This chateauesque mansion, built in 1908 for the newspaper publisher Swan J Turnblad, has wooden panels & carvings, Swedish art, glassware, furniture & a reference library. The *Svenskarnas Dag*, one of the largest festivals in the United States, takes place each Jun in Minnehaha Park.

Landmark Center 75 W Fifth; ✆292 3225; w landmarkcenter.org; ⊕ daily; admission free. St Paul's 1902 Federal Court building has been restored to its Romanesque splendour, with guided tours of the chambers & courtrooms.

James Hill House 240 Summit Av, St Paul; ✆297 2555; w mnhs.org/hillhouse; ⊕ Wed–Sun; admission charge. Canadian-born James Jerome Hill owned the St Paul-Pacific Railroad & was closely involved with the building of the Canadian Pacific. He gained control of the Great Northern Railroad (later to become the Burlington Northern) after a stock exchange battle, & no expense was spared when he constructed this mansion in 1891. The house is one of many fine residences on Summit Av, where F Scott Fitzgerald lived.

The James J Hill Library owns a vast & complete collection of Hill's business & private papers, including thousands of letters. As well as financing & constructing railroads, he ran experimental farms, helping to increase livestock & crop yields for those who came to settle along the line. In 1915, the Panama–Pacific Exposition in San Francisco named him 'Minnesota's greatest living citizen'.

Hill retired in 1907, handing over the Great Northern to his son, Louis W Hill, but he

continued to go into the office to supervise business until his death in 1916. He left a fine modern French art collection & $53 million, much of it to the Church. Every train & steamship on the Great Northern came to a stop for 5mins in his honour on the day of his funeral.

Twin City Model Railroad Museum 668 Transfer Rd, St Paul; ✆647 9628; w tcmrm. org; ⊕ Fri–Tue; admission charge. The museum opened in 1934 & found a long-term home in the old Union Depot before moving into former Northern Pacific maintenance shops in Bandana Sq. It features a scale model of the Minneapolis riverfront skyline, with a Northern Pacific passenger train heading across the Stone Arch Bridge. During Night Trains season the lights are turned down & buildings & street lights glow warmly, setting the scene for lighted models of vintage passenger trains.

Minnesota Transportation Museum 193 Pennsylvania Av E, St Paul; ✆228 0263; w transportationmuseum.org. The museum operates the Jackson St Roundhouse in St Paul, vintage bus rides & the Minnehaha Depot, or 'Princess' depot, a jewel on the former Milwaukee Rd railway.

The museum also runs the Osceola & St Croix Valley Railway, 114 Depot Rd, Osceola (✆*651 228 0263*). The railway is located east of the St Croix River, about a 1hr drive from the Twin Cities, & has steam & diesel train rides Jul–Oct.

Lake Superior Railroad Museum Lovingly restored steam engines & coaches (including the *Gallery Car* exhibit with its works of art rescued from the ashes of a fire that destroyed the old Union Depot in Ashland, WI) are housed in an old railway depot at 506 W Michigan in Duluth (✆*218 727 8025*; w *lsrm. org*). There are also daily train rides on the North Shore Scenic Railroad (✆*218 722 1273*; w *northshorescenicrailroad.org*).

TWIN CITIES: ALL ABOARD! (↑65/80↓) After a service stop, the *Empire Builder* leaves St Paul on Burlington Northern Santa Fe (BNSF) tracks for the rest of its journey to Seattle/Portland. Minneapolis can be seen in the left distance, dominated by the 57-storey IDS Tower, the tallest building in Minnesota.

ST CLOUD (↑80/60↓) Located on the shores of the Mississippi, St Cloud ships granite from local mines. To your right is the largest granite wall in the world, surrounding the Romanesque St Cloud Reformatory, now the Minnesota Correctional Facility, completed by inmates in 1889.

STAPLES (↑60/60↓) Built by the Northern Pacific Railway in 1909, the two-storey brick depot is owned by the Staples Historical Society and will eventually house a local history museum and shops in addition to the passenger waiting room. This former railroad town became run-down but has lately attracted new industries, from manufacturing to health care.

DETROIT LAKES (↑60/55↓) The 400 lakes nearby are a popular venue for fishing and other outdoor pursuits. Amtrak's buff-brick station at 116 Pioneer was built by the Northern Pacific Railroad in 1908 and renovated in 2010.

Red River (↑53/2↓) You cross the river and go from Minnesota into North Dakota, the Sioux State.

FARGO (↑55/60↓) Named after William Fargo of the Wells Fargo Express Company, North Dakota's largest city is at the heart of the Red River Valley. In the late 19th century, this was the main hub of the North Pacific Railroad and became known as the 'Gateway to the West'. Amtrak's station at 420 Fourth Street N also serves Moorhead in Minnesota. The waiting room is in the old American Railway Express Agency building next to a former Great Northern Railway depot, now home to the Great Northern Bicycle Co. Both buildings were completed in 1906. **Bonanzaville USA** (☏ *701 282 2822;* w *bonanzaville.com*), in West Fargo, relives pioneer days with a village reconstructed from original buildings, including two rail depots.

GRAND FORKS (↑60/80↓) Located where the Red Lake River meets the Red River, Grand Forks is the home of North Dakota University. Buses connect downtown with Amtrak's modern station at 5555 DeMers Avenue.

DEVIL'S LAKE (↑80/60↓) The brick-built Devil's Lake depot opened in 1907 at a cost of $50,000. Catchily nicknamed 'the goose- and duck-hunting capital of America', the town stands next to North Dakota's largest lake. Sioux and Chippewa Native Americans called this the Evil Spirit Lake, telling of water monsters, thunderbirds and overturned canoes.

The *Empire Builder* continues its way across the vast yellow and gold expanses of the northern plains, above which can often be seen eagles and huge flocks of wild geese.

RUGBY (↑60/65↓) The geographical centre of North America boasts a stone monument and museum to support its claim. The Canadian border is less than 50 miles (80km) from Amtrak's one-and-a-half-storey Tudor-style station on your left.

Look for crops of sunflowers from midsummer and fields of ploughed black earth as the train travels on over the plains. Near Minot look left for the converted green railroad car used as part of a plant nursery. Also to your left are several picturesque railway buildings and a large letter 'M'.

MINOT (↑65/50↓) Located on the Souris River and named after Henry D Minot, a railroad investor and friend of James J Hill, this service stop was called the Magic City as it seemed to grow overnight when the Great Northern Railroad arrived in 1886. Minot remains an important railway divisional point with extensive marshalling yards, and the city prospers thanks to oil and the military. Amtrak's recently renovated station is on your left.

The landscape opens out dramatically as immense prairie fields of wheat stretch to the horizon on all sides. Look for scattered farms and small towns with grain elevators and brick or white clapboard depots.

STANLEY (↑50/65↓) The town's economy is based mainly on grain and livestock production. Mountrail County Courthouse can be seen to the right of the white wooden station with its fading green sign.

WILLISTON (↑65/80↓) Oil discoveries at the western edge of Lake Sakakawea during the 1950s turned Williston into a boom town. Several wells with patiently nodding pumps can be seen along the train's route. Look also for the *Mikado* steam locomotive standing in the shade of tall trees to your right just before the renovated 1910 station. The locomotive was given to the town in 1958 at the end of the steam era.

The *Empire Builder* joins the Missouri River on the left and follows it along the Missouri Breaks for the next 60 miles (96km). Garrison Dam on the Missouri greatly increased this region's farming activity and rows of tall grain elevators stand next to many small stations along the way.

Fort Buford (↑15/65↓) This is where Chief Sitting Bull surrendered in 1881 after the Battle of the Little Bighorn in Montana (1876). The army officers' quarters, a cemetery and other relics can be seen at the fort.

Fort Union (↑20/60↓) On your left is one of the 19th century's liveliest fur-trading posts, where Assiniboine and other Northern Plains tribes exchanged buffalo robes (over 25,000 a year) and smaller furs for cloth, guns, blankets and beads. Wild West excitement returns each June with the Fort Union Rendezvous.

North Dakota–Montana state line (↑22/58↓) The state line is the official entry to Big Sky country and the change from Central to Mountain Time. Watches go back an hour (forward when travelling east).

For most of the next 700 miles (1,100km) the train makes its way across the gently rolling brown, gold and green grassland plains of northern Montana, where you'll see more cattle than people and more sheep than cattle. The train passes many abandoned passenger depots, such as Baineville, Savoy, Rudyard, Devon and Dunkirk. Watch out also for woodchuck, occasional wolverine and herds of antelope.

Culbertson (↑50/30↓) Just west of town the *Empire Builder* crosses Big Muddy Creek into Fort Peck Indian Reservation, home to the Assiniboine and Nakota Sioux tribes of Native Americans. Sitting Bull lived here after surrendering at Fort Buford in 1881.

The train crosses the Poplar River. Two forks of the Poplar combine here before flowing south-southwest to join the Missouri River.

WOLF POINT (↑80/45↓) This small town is set among hundreds of thousands of acres of Montana's high plains. Wolf Point is located on the Hi-Line of the BNSF Railway and is a major shipping point for grain to West Coast and Great Lakes ports. Amtrak's blue-painted depot, built in 1963, has a wolf sculpture that commemorates the town's frontier-era role in trapping and trading. Each July, Wolf Point hosts the Wild Horse Stampede at 'the granddaddy of Montana rodeos'.

Fort Peck Dam (↑30/15↓) Built in 1940, the earth-filled dam is the highest of six major dams along the Missouri River, 250ft (75m) tall and forming a 383-square-mile (990km²) lake. As the train leaves Fort Peck Reservation and approaches Glasgow, look right for a large letter 'G' on the hillside.

GLASGOW (↑45/55↓) The neat station stands to your left and a church to your right. Fossils and dinosaur bones discovered nearby are displayed at the Fort Peck Museum. The Valley County Pioneer Museum traces the region's rich history through the lives of its residents.

The train accompanies the Milk River west to Havre (pronounced 'Have-er') and somewhere between here and Malta, assuming both trains are on time, you should pass the eastbound *Empire Builder*.

Tampico (↑15/40↓) Named after Tampico, Mexico, the small town to your right was originally a siding on the main Great Northern line across northern Montana.

Sleeping Buffalo Hot Springs (↑35/20↓) The only hot springs in northern Montana, Sleeping Buffalo has attracted bathers since the 1920s. A large bell hangs in a tower on the Saco Methodist Church to your right. The town of Saco got its start because of the need of a place for a Great Northern Railroad water tank. Railroad agents could not decide on a name, so they spun a globe and a finger landed on Saco, Maine. The *Empire Builder* passes Nelson Reservoir and part of Lake Bowdoin, also to your right. The wildlife refuge on the left is a resort for waterbirds.

MALTA (↑55/70↓) The town's name is also said to have been determined by a spin of the globe when a Great Northern official's finger came to rest on the island of Malta in the Mediterranean. Local cattle empires inspired the western artist Charles Russell and ranching is still big business.

The *Empire Builder* leaves Malta's Swiss chalet-style depot and makes a fast run to Havre, passing many more grain elevators alongside the track.

Wagner (↑10/60↓) The Wild Bunch dynamited the Adams Express car on Great Northern's *Oriental Limited* here in 1901 and stole $68,000. Gang members Butch Cassidy and the Sundance Kid took no part in the robbery as both had already set sail for Buenos Aires to escape the law.

You travel beside the northern edge of Fort Belknap Indian Reservation, with the Bear Paw Mountains ahead to your left. In 1877, Chief Joseph of the Nez Perce Native Americans surrendered to the US Army after a 1,700-mile (2,700km) retreat with the words: 'From where the sun now stands I will fight no more forever.' On your left beyond the highway are the Little Rocky Mountains.

HAVRE (↑70/95↓) Located between downtown and the Milk River, the depot was built in 1904 by the Great Northern Railway. A statue of 'Empire Builder' James J Hill stands in front. This is an Amtrak service stop so you should have plenty of time to detrain and inspect the Northern Class S-2 steam locomotive standing on a pedestal to the left of the station. It was one of the last 14 steam engines acquired from the Baldwin works for main-line service by the Great Northern in 1930. They were the most powerful steam locomotives built until then. Some continued in freight service after the previous *Empire Builder* was streamlined and switched to diesel power in 1947.

Native Americans used to hunt buffalo by driving them over nearby cliffs, and a museum at the site shows some of the animals' skeleton remains. Havre has expanded greatly since the discovery of natural gas in this area.

Fort Benton, located 70 miles (112km) south of Havre, has a larger-than-life bronze statue of Old Shep, a sheepdog who appeared at the town's Great Northern railway station one day in 1936 as the casket of his dead master was being loaded on a train to be sent back east to relatives. The dog watched the train depart and for the next 5½ years he maintained a vigil at the station, scanning passengers alighting from the four trains that arrived each day as he waited for his master to return. Tragedy struck in 1942, when the old and deaf Shep failed to hear the 10.17 and slipped on an icy rail trying to get away, disappearing under the engine. He was buried on a lonely bluff looking down on the depot and the Great Northern Railroad put up an obelisk, with a painted wooden cut-out of Shep next to it and white stones spelling out 'SHEP'. Lights illuminated the display at night, and it can still be seen today.

Milk River (↑5/90↓) The river departs to the north, entering Canada before finding its source in Montana's Glacier National Park. The gradient starts to rise as the *Empire Builder* route approaches the Rockies.

SHELBY (↑95/30↓) This region produces most of the state's barley and wheat, as well as almost all the mustard seed grown in the United States. Named after Peter Shelby, General Manager of the Montana Central Railroad, this characteristic prairie town is located at the heart of Montana's oil region. Look for freight wagons and grain elevators standing beside the track. A railway branch line goes north from the station on your right through the Crowsnest Pass to Lethbridge in Alberta.

Shelby was the unlikely venue in 1923 for a heavyweight boxing championship fight between Jack Dempsey and Tom Gibbons. Chaos ensued when the match was cancelled before being reconvened in front of 7,000 fans and 17,000 gatecrashers, many of whom arrived by chartered train. Dempsey won but received no prize money after his manager vanished with $300,000. Several banks failed as a result and the city never hosted another fight.

Between Shelby and Cut Bank look for more old stations with names such as Gunsight, Sundance, Bison and Rising Wolf.

CUT BANK (↑30/32↓) Winter temperatures in this small, oil-producing town are among the nation's coldest. Sweetgrass Hills and the Canadian border are only 25 miles (40km) away to your right.

The *Empire Builder* departs on tracks supported by a trestle across Cut Bank Creek and you get your first views ahead of the Rocky Mountains. This horizon becomes increasingly impressive as you near Glacier National Park, but if you wish to be sure of seeing this section of the route by daylight you should travel during summer or take an eastbound train.

Lewis and Clark Monument (↑20/12↓) An obelisk on your left commemorates Lewis and Clark's search for a pass through the mountains when they made the first overland journey across North America during 1804–06.

⚒ BROWNING (↑32/20↓) The train stops here when East Glacier Park Station is closed during winter. Browning is at the heart of the Blackfeet Indian Reservation and a good place to shop for Native American goods. The **Museum of the Plains Indian** (✎ *406 338 2230;* **w** *blackfeetcountry.com*) features the art and history of many Northern Plains tribal peoples including the Blackfeet, Crow, Northern Cheyenne, Sioux, Assiniboine, Arapaho, Shoshone, Nez Perce, Flathead, Chippewa and Cree. Every July, Browning hosts the North American Indian Days celebration, one of the largest gatherings of Native American and First Nations Canadians in the Northwest.

The train continues towards the Rockies, approaching East Glacier Park Station on a high trestle over Two Medicine River.

⚒ EAST GLACIER PARK (↑20/60↓) The rustic station opens in summer to provide a gateway into one of America's most stunning national parks, which opened in 1910 and features 200 lakes, 10,000ft (3,000m) mountains and 50 living glaciers. For **information** on boating, hiking and skiing, call ✎ 406 888 7800, **w** nps.gov/glac.

Timber was brought from Oregon and Washington by the Great Northern to build Glacier Park Lodge, seen to your right beside the 1912 station. When the station closes out of season, access to the park may still be possible via Browning or Essex. Having enjoyed relatively easy conditions so far the *Empire Builder* now has to tackle the jagged barrier ahead.

Marias Pass (↑15/45↓) The continental divide at this point is lower (5,216ft/1,590m) than anywhere else between Canada and New Mexico. Native Americans may have crossed Mystery Pass but Meriwether Lewis and William Clark were unable to chart an accurate route. It was John Stevens, working as a surveyor for the Great Northern, who finally discovered a passage in 1889. Almost freezing to death in temperatures of –40°F (–40°C), he fully earned the statue dedicated to him on the summit to your right.

Also on the right is a fence constructed to keep out grizzly bears. The monument to your left honours President Theodore Roosevelt, after whom the adjacent highway was named.

As the train descends the western side of the pass the scenery becomes even more breathtaking, with waterfalls and deep gorges cutting through the rugged mountains.

Flathead River (↑45/15↓) Joining from your left, the river is crossed on another trestle.

⚒ ESSEX (↑60/35↓) Essex was originally home to a rail yard for the Great Northern Railway. Large snowploughs were stationed here in the 1930s to deal with an average downfall of 240 inches (6m) and these days Amtrak's long concrete platform has embedded heating coils for automatic snow clearance. On your right is the Izaak Walton Inn, built at a cost of $40,000 in 1939 to house railroad personnel and named after the English writer and angler. It was also intended to serve as an entrance to Glacier National Park but this plan never materialised, leaving Essex with a hotel that seems disproportionate to its modest needs.

WEST GLACIER (↑35/35↓) This is the entrance to the western part of **Glacier National Park**, where yearly snowfall can reach over 200 inches (5m). The *Empire Builder* leaves and again crosses the Flathead River.

Columbia Falls (↑20/15↓) Look for the preserved steam engine on your left and the site of a closed aluminium plant at the base of Teakettle Mountain to your right.

WHITEFISH (↑35/110↓) A German-style station on the left complements the alpine scenery. Built in 1928, the Whitefish depot is listed on the National Register of Historic Places and was restored in the 1990s to house a waiting room, railroad offices and the Stumptown Historical Society. A Great Northern locomotive is preserved on show at the station. Whitefish is located in a valley of the Flathead National Forest close to the resorts of Whitefish Lake and Big Mountain. Flathead Lake, the greatest expanse of water west of the Mississippi, is 25 miles (40km) to the south.

Flathead Tunnel (↑40/70↓) You travel 7 miles (11km) through one of the longest tunnels in the United States. The east portal has a door that can be closed and fans to ventilate the tunnel.

LIBBY (↑110/55↓) The town is in the middle of the beautiful 2.2-million acres (8,900km²) **Kootenai National Forest**, popular with nature lovers, hunters and fishermen. Libby's sawmills and log-processing plants are sometimes open to visitors.

Between here and Sandpoint the train goes from Montana into Idaho, changing from Mountain to Pacific Time. Watches go back an hour (forward when travelling east).

SANDPOINT (↑55/80↓) This is Amtrak's only operating station in Idaho and the red-brick Gothic Revival-style station building is the oldest remaining active passenger depot of the former Northern Pacific Railway. Built in 1916, it was fully renovated in 2015 and all passengers now use the elegant former ladies' retiring room as a waiting room. Sandpoint is next to Lake Pend Oreille and close to the Schweitzer ski area.

Travelling on through the night, the *Empire Builder* leaves Idaho for Washington, the Evergreen State.

SPOKANE (↑80/120↓) 'The monarch of the inland empire' stands next to the Spokane River and is surrounded by farmland. An important railroad junction, this is where the Great Northern route meets the Spokane, Portland & Seattle line. The old Great Northern clock tower remains a prominent downtown landmark.

Bing Crosby attended Spokane's Gonzaga University and the library owns related photographs, memorabilia and a bronze statue. The **Northwest Museum of Arts and Culture** (*2316 W First Av;* ☎ *509 456 3931;* w *northwestmuseum.org*) has fine art, historic regional paintings and a huge collection of American Plateau Indian culture. Its collection numbers over one million artefacts and ephemera, including art from the Americas, Europe and Asia. The **Grand Coulee Dam**, one of the largest concrete structures in the world, is 80 miles (128km) east. Famously sung about by Woody Guthrie, the dam was begun in 1933 as part of President Roosevelt's New Deal.

As the *Empire Builder* divides into two trains, in this chapter we continue to Seattle. For the route to Portland, see page 133.

EPHRATA (↑120/65↓) Known as a gateway to the Columbia River Basin, Ephrata is set among fertile land irrigated by water from the Columbia River project. Amtrak's basic Transportation Center is also used by local buses.

Rock Island Dam (↑35/30↓) The hydro-electric dam to your left holds back the Columbia River, which the *Empire Builder* crosses 5 minutes later. Built near the geographical centre of Washington between 1929 and 1933, this was the first dam to span the Columbia.

WENATCHEE (↑65/25↓) The city was named after a Salish word that means 'river which comes from canyons' or 'robe of the rainbow'. Wenatchee is one of the apple capitals of the world, and orchards in the Cascades foothills have perfect weather conditions for producing a seventh of the country's crop. Since 1920 it has hosted the annual Washington State Apple Blossom Festival, which includes a carnival and parade. The **Wenatchee Valley Museum and Cultural Center** (*127 Mission;* ✆509 888 6240; w *wenatcheevalleymuseum.org*) shows the rich history of north central Washington and has spirited demonstrations of apple sorting.

The train pulls out past warehouses and lumber yards then accompanies the Wenatchee River to your left. To enjoy the best scenery for the next hour or so you should stay on this side of the train. This region is one of the last refuges for the endangered spotted owl, a source of conflict between conservationists and loggers.

Cashmere (↑15/10↓) Look for more apple warehouses. Turkish delight-type sweets called aplets (made from apples) and cotlets (from apricots) are local specialities.

The train crosses the Wenatchee River several times as it approaches the Cascade Mountains.

LEAVENWORTH (↑25/150↓) Bavarian-style buildings appear among the orchards as the *Empire Builder* starts a long, steep climb, entering the first of many tunnels before again crossing the river.

Merritt (↑35/115↓) The train slows further as it gains height among streams, mountains and marshland.

Icicle Canyon (↑40/110↓) The best views are now to your right. Keep a look out for goats, elk, deer and perhaps beaver.

Cascade Tunnel (↑50/100↓) Completed in 1929, the tunnel is another of the world's longest, at 7.79 miles (12.53km). It helped replace 43 miles (69km) of stiff grades with an easier 34-mile (54km) route. Stevens Pass is 500ft (150m) higher, at 4,061ft (1,225m). The tunnel lasts 15 minutes before the train emerges to begin a 65-mile (105km) descent to Everett, giving delightful views of the Cascades and Puget Sound.

The *Empire Builder* crosses the Skyomish River, which it follows to Everett. A waterfall appears on the left but the best scenery remains to your right. This is *Twin Peaks* country, with wooden houses, cloud-topped mountains, misty evergreen pine forests, fast-running streams and huge logging trucks. The modest towns look as if they belong in a Norman Rockwell painting.

You cross the Skyomish River on another dramatic high trestle, with the Mount Baker-Snoqualmie National Forest ranger station to your right.

Skyomish (↑75/75↓) A logging town which has an interesting Burlington Northern station that is on the National Register of Historic Places, as is the entire historic centre of the town.

Sunset Falls (↑90/60↓) The falls are to your left before you again cross the river. Look also for Indian Falls, Table Rock and Index Mountain.

Grotto (↑92/58↓) A small village stands among the mountains to your right. The train crosses the river twice more, leaving the Cascades for less demanding terrain.

Monroe (↑125/25↓) Note the old station building away from the tracks to your right. This was once an important stop on the rail line and was known for the GN Greenhouses, which grew flowers for passengers to purchase.

EVERETT (↑150/25↓) As a natural inland port, Everett was a focal point for the fishing and lumber industries even before the railroad came. Boeing's 747/767 assembly plant is contained here in what may be the world's largest building.

South of the city you join Puget Sound on your right for the next 15 miles (24km), with the Olympic Mountains in the distance. Forest comes down to the sea and yacht basins dot the shoreline. Islands in the sound include Bainbridge and Whidbey, linked to the mainland by ferry.

EDMONDS (↑25/30↓) 'The gem of the Puget Sound', Edmonds is mostly residential and its Old Milltown shopping arcade was developed inside an old Ford garage. The *Empire Builder* stops at a Modernist 1956 depot.

Shilshole Bay (↑15/15↓) Innumerable boats are moored in the marina to your right. Bainbridge Island, where Michael Douglas lived in the movie *Disclosure*, is across the water. You cross Salmon Bay inlet then travel briefly inland past Chittenden Locks to your left, part of a waterway system linking the bay with Lake Washington. On your right is a statue of the 10th-century Norse explorer Leif Ericsson.

The train returns to the shoreline by way of a US Navy reservation, then travels along Seattle's waterfront. Pier 70 to your right is America's largest restored wooden building. The former warehouse has 40 shops and restaurants and is connected to downtown by a trolley running on tracks beside the train. Seattle's Space Needle comes into view on your left before the *Empire Builder* passes through a mile-long (1.6km) tunnel to complete its journey at King Street Station.

SEATTLE (↑30) For Seattle city information, see page 55.

UPDATES WEBSITE

You can post your comments and recommendations, and read feedback and updates from other readers online at **w** bradtupdates.com/usa.

9

The *Empire Builder*
Spokane–Portland

JOINING THE TRAIN

SPOKANE: ALL ABOARD! (150↓) For Spokane, the route from Chicago and onward to Seattle, see the previous chapter (page 116).

Through-coaches for this branch of the *Empire Builder* service to Portland continue via Pasco.

🚂 PASCO (↑150/115↓) This is the furthest seagoing vessels can voyage up the Columbia River. The Columbia and Snake rivers meet in this territory, which was claimed by the British until it became part of the United States in 1846. Before a railroad bridge was built across the Columbia in 1883, connecting Pasco with railroad tracks leading over the Cascade Range to Puget Sound, steel barges were used to transport Northern Pacific railroad cars across the water. The barges were operated by the Pacific Steamship Company, which gave the town its name. An alternative explanation is that Virgil Bogue, a construction engineer for the Northern Pacific, named the town after Cerro de Pasco, a city in the Peruvian Andes where he had helped build a railroad.

North McNary (↑30/85↓) Named after Charles Linza McNary, who was a US senator for Oregon from 1917 to 1944.

Columbia River (↑75/40↓) The state of Oregon can be seen on the opposite side as you travel the water-level route through the Columbia River Gorge – a land of stone cliffs, lakes, streams, meadows and woods.

Roosevelt (↑80/35↓) Barges shipping grain are a common sight on the river between here and Vancouver.

John Day Dam (↑100/15↓) The concrete dam is 5,900ft (1,800m) long and was completed in 1968 at a cost of $487 million. Masses of pylons take away enough

---

ESSENTIAL INFORMATION

HIGHLIGHTS After following the *Empire Builder* route to Spokane, this train travels down the Columbia River Gorge for glorious views of Mt Hood, Beacon Rock and Multnomah Falls, the second-highest waterfall in the country. In Portland you can visit the acclaimed art museum, with work by native peoples of North America, and enjoy the city's Rose Festival in June.
DURATION 7 hours 15 minutes

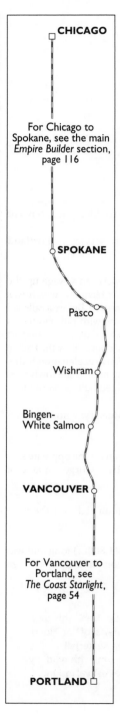

CHICAGO

For Chicago to Spokane, see the main *Empire Builder* section, page 116

SPOKANE

Pasco

Wishram

Bingen-White Salmon

VANCOUVER

For Vancouver to Portland, see *The Coast Starlight*, page 54

PORTLAND

electricity to supply Portland three times over. The locks carry eight million tons of shipping a year and incorporate one of the highest (113ft/35m) single lifts in the world. Look for fish ladders on both sides.

Maryhill (↑105/10↓) Just past an emu and ostrich farm to your left, look right for a glimpse of the Maryhill Castle Art Museum and a replica of Stonehenge. Entrepreneur Sam Hill named Maryhill after his wife, who was the daughter of James J Hill. He built the first paved roads in the Pacific Northwest, the Maryhill Museum (originally intended as a grand family mansion) and the concrete Stonehenge monument to honour the Klickitat County troops who died in World War I.

WISHRAM (↑115/30↓) Named after a Native American settlement known to 19th-century explorers Lewis and Clark, Wishram is the site of a legendary 'beanery' – one of the cheap restaurants built and operated by the railway for its workers. Although Wishram is one of the smallest places served by Amtrak, this is an important gateway to recreational opportunities on the Columbia River.

On the far side of the Columbia are the Union Pacific tracks used until 1997 by Amtrak's *Pioneer* train from Seattle and Salt Lake City. A bridge ahead takes the Burlington Northern line south to Klamath Falls.

Avery (↑2/28↓) The pyramid of Mount Hood can be seen to the south as you continue through the Columbia Gorge.

Dalles Dam (↑10/20↓) Dalles, a French word for 'trough', describes the narrow channel formed by the river. The 8,700ft (2,650m) zigzag-shaped dam provides irrigation and power. The reservoir behind the dam is named Lake Celilo and runs 24 miles (39km) up the river to the foot of John Day Dam. The town of Dalles is on the opposite shore.

Mount Hood (↑15/15↓) Look left for another view of Oregon's tallest mountain, 11,235ft (3,425m) and permanently snow-capped.

Lyle (↑25/5↓) Originally called Klickitat Landing, the town was named in 1866 after its first postmaster, James O Lyle. The train crosses the Klickitat River, with the Native American burial ground of Memaloose Island to your left. Until recent times, Native American tribes of the Columbia River did not bury their dead. Instead, they were wrapped in robes or furs and deposited in canoes or burial vaults in woods or on islands such as Memaloose. The name is derived from the Chinook word memalust, which means 'to die'.

BINGEN-WHITE SALMON (↑30/80↓) Jointly named after the White Salmon River and a German town called Bingen. The orange-yellow station bears the name of both communities but is located in Bingen. White Salmon is a mile (1.6km) away on a bluff overlooking the Columbia River. The city of Hood River can be seen on the far shore.

For the next 55 miles (88km) the landscape changes from near-desert to rainforest as the *Empire Builder* travels through the Columbia Gorge, carved into ancient rocks by the river. Explorers Lewis and Clark were the first white people to venture this far in 1805 and settlers on the Oregon Trail would often refuse to risk crossing the powerful river.

Wind Mountain (↑15/65↓)
Around 1,000 years ago, young members of local tribes began walking up the slopes of Wind Mountain (2,500ft/760m), seen to your right. They fasted, made piles of rocks and waited for visions from their guardian spirits. Today the mountain is a recreational area for hikers, though tribal members continue to visit the sacred site.

One of this region's few remaining log flumes transports lumber to a sawmill beside the river.

Stevenson (↑30/50↓)
Located on a low bluff above the river, the first settlers built a water-powered sawmill here in 1852. George Stevenson bought the land in 1893 and expanded the original dock to serve daily sternwheelers unloading passengers and cargo and loading logs. A ferry connected to Cascade Locks, on the Oregon shore of the river. In 1894, the town survived the largest recorded flood on the Columbia River, and when the Spokane, Portland & Seattle Railway reached Stevenson in 1908, the town moved up the hill to make way for the tracks. The railway called their station 'Stevenson's Spur', later shortened 'Stevenson'. Amtrak's *Pioneer* train formerly stopped at Cascade Locks.

Bridge of the Gods (↑33/47↓)
The bridge ahead to your left replaced a stone bridge which Native Americans say their god destroyed when he was angered by his sons arguing over a maiden. The sons became Mount Hood and Mount Adams and the maiden was transformed into Mount St Helens. In 1927, Charles Lindbergh flew the *Spirit of St Louis* over the recently opened bridge then turned to fly back under the bridge to Portland.

Sheridan's Point (↑35/45↓)
Philip Sheridan, a cavalry officer and later a ruthless Civil War general, defended settlers from Native American marauders here in 1855 when he was a young officer. He allegedly remarked that the only good Indians he ever saw were dead ones. The final spike was driven nearby in 1908 to complete the route of the Spokane, Portland & Seattle Railway, otherwise known as 'The North Bank Railroad', 'The North Bank Road', 'Columbia River Scenic Route' or 'The Northwest's Own Railway'.

Bonneville Dam (↑36/44↓)
This was the Columbia's first great dam, worked on by Woody Guthrie. The half-mile (0.8km) feat of engineering created Lake Bonneville. Look for the fish ladder which allows migrating salmon to swim upstream.

Beacon Rock (↑40/40↓) The 840ft (255m) Beacon Rock is claimed to be the second-largest free-standing monolith in the northern hemisphere, just behind the Rock of Gibraltar. El Capitan in Yosemite National Park is twice as tall but the term 'monolith' usually defines a 'single rock'. Named by Lewis and Clark, it was an unmistakable guide for travellers.

Multnomah Falls (↑42/38↓) The second-highest waterfall in the country cascades 620ft (190m) on the Oregon side. According to Native American lore, Multnomah Falls was created to win the heart of a young princess who wanted a discreet place to bathe. Look also for rafts of logs, paper mills and sawmills.

Cape Horn (↑48/32↓) The train leaves the Columbia Gorge by way of a 2,369ft (720m) tunnel through the western Cascades. Just before Vancouver you can glimpse a smart Spokane, Portland & Seattle railroad car to your left.

VANCOUVER (↑80/22↓) For Vancouver and the rest of the *Empire Builder* route to Portland, see page 59.

FOLLOW BRADT

For the latest news, special offers and competitions, subscribe to the Bradt newsletter via the website **w** bradtguides.com and follow Bradt on:

 BradtTravelGuides

 @BradtGuides

 @bradtguides

 bradtguides

 bradtguides

10

The *Southwest Chief* Chicago–Los Angeles

GENERAL ROUTE INFORMATION

Amtrak's fastest trip from Chicago to the Pacific is along part of the Santa Fe Trail first used by Native Americans and Spanish *conquistadors*, then by mule caravans, wagon trains, stagecoaches and gold prospectors. The train travels 2,265 miles (3,645km) through eight states, passing wheat fields, ranches, missions, pueblos, mountains and deserts. Sometimes the canyons you go through are only a few feet wider than the train. Close by this route are Santa Fe, Taos and the Grand Canyon.

The *Southwest Chief* follows a Santa Fe Railway line which the *Super Chief* first took in 1937, cutting 15 hours from the time of its predecessor, the *Chief*. The *Chief* in turn had succeeded two other luxury trains, the *Southwest Limited* and the *Santa Fe De Luxe*. Even as late as the 1970s, Frank Sinatra was inclined to hire a luxury private car to travel with his friends between San Bernadino and Chicago.

ESSENTIAL INFORMATION

HIGHLIGHTS The *Southwest Chief* takes in the grandeur of the American West as you cross the Mississippi River and travel through landscapes with unspoilt views not visible from any highway. From Lamy you can visit the art galleries of Santa Fe and from Flagstaff take a tour of the magnificent Grand Canyon.

FREQUENCY Daily. The **westbound** service leaves Chicago mid-afternoon to arrive in Kansas City late in the evening and Dodge City early next morning. You reach Albuquerque late in the afternoon, Flagstaff (for the Grand Canyon) by mid-evening and Los Angeles early on the third day. Travelling **east**, trains leave Los Angeles early in the evening to reach Flagstaff early next morning, Albuquerque by early afternoon and Dodge City about midnight. You arrive in Kansas City early on the third day and Chicago by mid-afternoon.

DURATION 40+ hours

RESERVATIONS All reserved

EQUIPMENT Superliner coaches

SLEEPING Superliner bedrooms

FOOD Complete meals, snacks, sandwiches, drinks

LOUNGE CAR Movies, travelogues, hospitality hour. National Park Service guides are on board between Albuquerque and La Junta, Colorado, as follows: From Bent's Old Fort (La Junta), from the Pecos National Historic Park (Pecos, New Mexico) and from Petroglyph National Monument (Albuquerque).

BAGGAGE Check-in service is available at most stations.

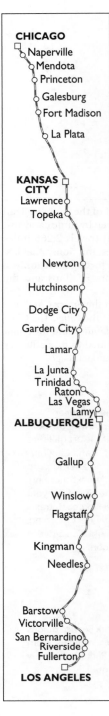

CHICAGO
Naperville
Mendota
Princeton
Galesburg
Fort Madison
La Plata

KANSAS
CITY
Lawrence
Topeka

Newton
Hutchinson
Dodge City
Garden City
Lamar
La Junta
Trinidad
Raton
Las Vegas
Lamy
ALBUQUERQUE

Gallup

Winslow
Flagstaff

Kingman
Needles

Barstow
Victorville
San Bernardino
Riverside
Fullerton
LOS ANGELES

JOINING THE TRAIN

ALL ABOARD! CHICAGO (42↓) For Chicago city information and the route as far as Galesburg, see pages 83–7. In addition to the stops made by the *California Zephyr*, the *Southwest Chief* serves the renovated station in Mendota. The station now houses the **Union Depot Railroad Museum** (✆815 539 3373; w *mendotamuseums. org/UDRR*) with a working HO model of the Mendota depot in the 1930s, and a steam engine, tender and caboose from the CB&Q, now BNSF Railway. The *Southwest Chief* travels all the way to Los Angeles on BNSF tracks.

⚒ GALESBURG (↑42/45↓) Settled by Presbyterians from Oneida, New York, Galesburg was the scene of a Lincoln–Douglas debate in 1858. This was also the home of George Washington Ferris (creator of the first Ferris wheel) and Olmsted Ferris (inventor of popcorn). Amtrak's modern station at 225 S Seminary Street has original wooden seats salvaged from its predecessor.

Mississippi River (↑35/10↓) North America's greatest waterway appears to your right. A few minutes later the train crosses the river from Illinois into Iowa by means of the longest (3,347ft/1,020m) double-track, double-decked bridge in the world. The structure pivots to allow larger boats to pass beneath.

Approaching Fort Madison, note the Santa Fe steam engine on your left.

⚒ FORT MADISON (↑45/65↓) The train's only stop on its brief passage through Iowa is this industrial city. US soldiers set fire to the original fort in 1813 to divert attacking Native Americans while settlers escaped through a tunnel to the Mississippi. This event is commemorated by One Chimney Monument to your right.

Fort Madison is Amtrak's closest stop to Keokuk, 5 miles (8km) south along the river. The station was built in 1968 by the Atchison, Topeka & Santa Fe Railway, otherwise known as the 'Santa Fe'. Fort Madison's historic Mission Revival-style Santa Fe Depot is being restored and will be used as a future Amtrak station.

Nauvoo (↑10/55↓) The old Mormon town seen across the Des Moines River has been restored as a monument and features an exact copy of the original temple on the same site. Soon after Nauvoo you cross the Des Moines River from Iowa into Missouri.

⚒ LA PLATA (↑65/130↓) This small farming town is in a region famous for deer, pheasant and turkey hunting.

La Plata Lake is on your left and Kirksville, home of Northeast Missouri University, 10 miles (16km) to the north. Amtrak's restored Art Deco-style station has a rail cam which can be viewed on YouTube.

Marceline (↑35/95↓)
Walt Disney's childhood home was in Marceline, and he invented Mickey Mouse while riding on the *Southwest Chief*. Walt Disney Park to your right features a steam locomotive from the Santa Fe Railway.

Mendon (↑45/85↓)
Waterfowl migrate to Canada from Swan Lake Game Reserve, seen on your right. Hunters account for several hundred thousand birds each year.

Bosworth (↑50/80↓)
You cross the Grand River, bordered by pecan trees.

Missouri River (↑105/25↓)
The train crosses on a 135ft-high (40m) bridge. To your right are the remains of Fort Osage, built in 1808.

Sugar Creek (↑120/10↓)
The town was a haunt of the outlaw Jesse James, who died in 1882 at nearby St Joseph after being shot by fellow gang member Robert Ford. James held up his first train in 1873 near Adair, Iowa. His tombstone reads, 'Jesse W. James, Died April 3, 1882, Aged 34 years, 6 months, 28 days, Murdered by a traitor and a coward whose name is not worthy to appear here'.

⋙ KANSAS CITY (↑130/50↓)
Birthplace of Harry S Truman, Jean Harlow and Charlie Parker, the larger and better-known Kansas City is in Missouri rather than Kansas. Kansas City, Kansas, is immediately across the Missouri River but is politically separate. 'The heart of America' was named after Kanza Indians who traded with the city's founder, John Calvin McCoy. A settlement on a bend in the river later became the place where wagon trains were equipped for the Santa Fe, California and Oregon trails. After the Civil War, with the coming of the railroad, Kansas City turned to agriculture and transport for a living.

The stockyard district reflects Cowtown history and the Royal Livestock Show has been held here every year since 1899. Around the turn of the 20th century, the architect George Kessler set out to create 'one of the loveliest cities on earth'. Today's Kansas City rivals Paris for boulevards and claims to have more fountains than Rome. It has been 'the home of the barbecue' since the 1920s and has more than 60 barbecue restaurants. The city is also famous for its jazz tradition, which flourished in the 1930s Prohibition era when the authorities still allowed alcohol to be served in this 'wide-open town'.

Kansas City basics

☏ **Telephone code** 816, for Kansas City, Missouri; 913 for Kansas City, Kansas. All numbers given in this section are 816 code unless otherwise noted.

⋙ **Station** (*Ticket office & waiting room* ☺ *06.30–23.00*) Amtrak trains again began operating out of Kansas City's Beaux-Arts masterpiece Union Station at 30 W Pershing Rd in December 2002, with a new $4.6 million passenger ticketing & boarding facility. The 2,000ft² (186m²) waiting room features 5 of the splendid original wooden benches from the station's North Waiting Room. An elevated walkway leads to stairs & an elevator provides access to the boarding platform. Kansas City outgrew its old Union Depot by the 1880s & Jarvis Hunt, an advocate of the City Beautiful movement, was commissioned to design a new building. His grandiose 'Great Gateway to the West' opened in 1914, becoming the 2nd-largest train station in the country (with almost 80,000 trains visiting in 1917). Among the building's features were an ornate 95ft (29m) ceiling with oak leaf clusters in the Grand Hall, 3 huge chandeliers, a clock over 6ft (2m) in diameter, & terracotta floors in elegant geometric designs. Warm rose-brown marble decorated the separate male & female lounges, & the North Waiting Room was longer than a football field.

The station also housed fine restaurants, the city's largest barbershop, a post office, a drug store, a small jail, a Harvey House coffee shop & an emergency hospital. The complex was lit, heated & cooled by its own power plant, & 3 sub-levels smoothed traffic between passengers, baggage transportation & local citizens using the station's services.

Union Station became notorious in 1933 for the Kansas City Massacre in which 5 people died in an attempt by Charles Arthur 'Pretty Boy' Floyd and others to free the notorious underworld figure Frank 'Gentleman' Nash from Federal custody. Floyd became Public Enemy Number One as a result, with a $23,000 dead-or-alive reward on his head. After fleeing Kansas City, he made his way to Ohio, where he died after being shot by FBI agents in 1934. Floyd's body left East Liverpool in a baggage car & 20,000 people attended his funeral. To some people of his home state, Oklahoma, he was a folk hero – the 'Robin Hood of the Cookson Hills' – & was written into legend through Woody Guthrie's ballad.

During World War II, half of all military personnel passed through Kansas City on troop trains but rail travel declined in the 1950s. The North Waiting Room was closed, the grand structure began to deteriorate & Amtrak temporarily relocated to a small boarding office nearby. Local preservationists, with help from Kansas & Missouri taxpayers, raised the necessary funds & Union Station reopened in 1999 after a $118 million renovation. Now an entertainment centre, it has a hands-on Science City for children, theatres, a 5-storey cinema, KC Rail (a hands-on journey through the history of the American railroad), a free Model Railroad Experience, restaurants, shops & offices. For information about programming & events, ☏ 460 2020; w unionstation.org.

Connections Thruway buses go to St Louis & Jefferson City

Local transport Kansas City covers 300 square miles (770km²), so most people get around by car. KCTA (☏ 221 0660; w kcata.org) operates local & express buses.

Taxis Yellow ☏ 471 5000; Checker ☏ 444 4444

Car rental Thrifty, 2001 Baltimore Av; ☏ 842 8550

Greyhound 1101 N Troost; ☏ 221 2835

✈ **Kansas City International Airport** 20 miles (32km) northwest by Champion Shuttle Bus (☏ 888 245 7844) or Metro bus #129

Tours Self-guided walking tours from the Historic Kansas City Foundation, 234 W 10th (☏ 931 8558; w historickansascity.org)

Visitors bureau 1321 Baltimore Av; ☏ 691 3800; w visitkc.com; ⊕ closed Sun

Accommodation Downtown hotel rates can be expensive but look for w/end deals. Hotels include the Raphael, 325 Ward Parkway; ☏ 756 3800; w raphaelkc.com, **$$$$**; Westin Crown Center, 1 Pershing Rd; ☏ 474 4400; w marriott. com, **$$$$**; Best Western Seville Plaza, 4309 Main; ☏ 913 561 9600; w bestwesternsevilleplaza. com, **$$$**; Intercontinental, 401 Ward Parkway; ☏ 756 1500; w www.ihg.com, **$$$**; Drury Inn-KC Stadium, 3830 Blue Ridge Cut-off; ☏ 923 3000; w druryhotels.com, **$$**; Super Inn, 1600 Parvin Rd; ☏ 453 5210, **$$**.

For B&B contact 1812 Overture Bed & Breakfast at 1812 Washington; ☏ 645 2405, **$$$**.

Recommended in Kansas City

The parks Among the city's 300 parks is America's 2nd largest, Swope Park, with its Starlight Theatre, the Kansas City Zoo & 2 golf courses. Others include Loose Park (famous for its roses) & Shawnee Mission Park.

Crown Center 2405 Grand Bd, opposite the station; ☏ 274 8444; w crowncenter.com; ⊕ daily; free concerts in summer. This complex of shops, offices & hotels incorporates an indoor waterfall & the Hallmark Cards Visitors Center.

Country Club Plaza 2 miles (3.2km) south of Crown Center at 4745 Central; ☏ 753 0100; w countryclubplaza.com. This was America's 1st (1922) shopping precinct & has pretty Spanish-style architecture, fountains & sculpture. The Plaza Art Fair takes place here each Sep.

Kansas City Museum 3218 Gladstone Bd; ☏ 460 2020; ⊕ Tue–Sun; donation. Housed in the mansion of lumber tycoon R A Long, the museum includes a replica trading post.

Science City Union Station, 30 W Pershing Rd; ☏460 2020; w sciencecity.com. The beautiful, restored 1914 train station features this interactive science museum where you can experience the world of science first-hand through fun & engaging exhibits.

American Jazz Museum 18th & Vine; ☏474 8463; w americanjazzmuseum.com; ⊕ closed Mon; admission charge. The story of jazz & performers such as Louis Armstrong, Charlie 'Bird' Parker, Duke Ellington & Ella Fitzgerald is celebrated in one of the country's most interactive museums. This building is shared with a theatre & the Negro Leagues Baseball Museum (*1616 E 18th*; ☏221 1920; w nlbm.com; admission charge). The museum opened in 1991 & is located in the historic Lincoln Building.

1859 Jail Museum 217 N Main, Independence; ☏252 1892; w jchs.org/1859-old-jail; ⊕ daily; admission charge. Frank James was a resident within the massive, limestone walls of the jail during Wild West days. As well as the 2-storey County Jail, with its barred windows & double iron doors, the museum features a schoolhouse & marshal's office.

KANSAS CITY: ALL ABOARD! (↑130/50↓) The *Southwest Chief* departs Kansas City, Missouri, and crosses the state line into Kansas City, Kansas.

⊬⊬ LAWRENCE (↑50/32↓) This was a 'station' on the Underground Railroad founded by abolitionists before the Civil War. In 1863, Quantrill's pro-Confederate guerrillas attacked the peaceful town, killing 150 of its citizens. Kansas University began here in 1866.

Opened in 1956, the train station was built by the Atchison, Topeka & Santa Fe Railroad and is a prime example of mid-century modern architecture, with clean lines and minimal ornamentation. Improved and restored, it has been listed on the National Register of Historic Places. The 1906 Santa Fe Depot at Baldwin, 12 miles (19km) south, has vintage equipment, memorabilia and diesel-powered trips from May to October, travelling through scenic eastern Kansas farmland and woods on the historic **Midland Railway** (☏913 721 1211; w *midlandrailway.org*).

⊬⊬ TOPEKA (↑32/130↓) The capital of Kansas was home to the Menninger Foundation, a world leader in the treatment of mental illness, until the clinic moved to Houston, Texas, in 2003. Menninger is now affiliated with Baylor College of Medicine.

Emporia (↑65/65↓) This is the home of Emporia State University and the *Emporia Gazette*, founded in 1890. The newspaper's iconic former editor and spokesman for middle America, William White, gave the city its Peter Pan Park.

⊬⊬ NEWTON (↑130/35↓) One of the country's largest Mennonite settlements, Newton was founded in 1872 by immigrants from Russia. Seed they brought for winter wheat helped Kansas become 'the world's breadbasket'. This is the 'bull's eye' of North America, located at the intersection of the railroad and Main Street – US Highway 81. The two-storey brick Tudor Revival-style station, inspired by Shakespeare's house in Stratford-on-Avon, was built in 1930. Thruway buses link with Wichita and Oklahoma City.

⊬⊬ HUTCHINSON (↑35/95↓) A centre of trade for farmers in the area, Hutchinson has a large wheat market and some of the biggest grain elevators in the world. Nearby is one of the world's biggest salt mines, giving Hutchinson the nickname 'Salt City'.

Between here and Dodge City the train travels through oil country, with nodding pumps seen on both sides of the track.

Kinsley (↑65/30↓) A sign to your right states that Kinsley is exactly 1,561 miles (2,510km) from both San Francisco and New York.

⚡ DODGE CITY (↑95/42↓) This former trading post and army fort began to prosper when the Santa Fe Railway arrived in 1872. Dodge soon became the cowboy capital of the world, shipping longhorn steers brought on cattle drives from Texas and the south. Lawlessness took hold of 'the wickedest little city in America' until Bat Masterson, Wyatt Earp and Doc Holliday restored order. The hangman's tree still survives and many gunfighters and outlaws who died were buried on Boot Hill to your left. The rail yards still ship great quantities of cattle and wheat. Front Street, to your right, looks much as it always did, although calmer these days. The **tourist bureau** is at 400 W Wyatt Earp Boulevard (↖620 225 8186; w *visitdodgecity.org*). Two sundials on your right signify a change of time zone which actually takes place further west.

Cimarron (↑15/27↓) This is where the Santa Fe Trail crosses the Arkansas River, seen to your left.

⚡ GARDEN CITY (↑42/75↓) Apparently named by a passing hobo who admired the garden of its founder's wife, Garden City is an agricultural centre famous for wheat, sugar beet and alfalfa crops. It claims to have the world's largest swimming pool and most capacious grain elevator. Nearby are the world's biggest buffalo herd and a massive natural gas field.

Holcomb (↑5/70↓) The murders described in Truman Capote's 'non-fiction novel' *In Cold Blood* took place here in 1959. This part of the Sunflower State has many fields and roadsides filled with these impressive plants, which are a yellow blaze in September.

Coolidge (↑50/25↓) The train leaves Kansas and enters Colorado, changing from Central to Mountain Time, so watches go back an hour (forward when travelling east).

The *Southwest Chief* crosses the Arkansas River, which it then follows west to La Junta. The valley produces vegetables and fruit, especially cantaloupe melons.

⚡ LAMAR (↑75/45↓) As the train nears the station in 'the goose hunting capital of America', look left to see the Madonna of the Trails statue erected in the 1920s by the National Society of Daughters of the American Revolution. A series of 12 monuments dedicated to the spirit of pioneer women were commissioned by the NSDAR and installed in the 12 states along the National Old Trails Road, extending from Cumberland in Maryland to Upland, California.

Lamar began as a stockyard siding on the Santa Fe Railway.

John Martin Dam (↑10/35↓) The dam forms a reservoir frequented by herons and cranes.

Las Animas (↑25/20↓) Named after the Río de las Ánimas Perdidas (the river of lost souls) where a wagon train of settlers camped and disappeared overnight, presumed to have been attacked by Native Americans.

Bent's Old Fort (↑35/10↓) The settlement seen among the trees to your right was built in the 1840s to protect fur traders and service wagon trains on the Santa Fe Trail. Frontier legend Kit Carson worked at the adobe fort, which has been authentically reconstructed and is open to the public.

⋙ LA JUNTA (↑45/75↓) The Santa Fe Trail meets the Cimarron cut-off here and La Junta is the Santa Fe Railway's divisional headquarters. Outlaws such as the notorious Belle Star inscribed their names on nearby rocks. On a clear day you can see Pike's Peak on your right even though it stands 100 miles (160km) north. The modern station was built in 1955.

After La Junta the *Southwest Chief* leaves the valley and swings south to make a fast run across the Comanche National Grassland.

Sunflower Valley (↑50/25↓) Farms in this region produce enormous crops of wheat, corn and sugar beet. As the train approaches Trinidad, look right for the snow-covered Sangre de Cristo Range and the twin Spanish Peaks of the Colorado Rockies. Native Americans called these mountains 'the breasts of mother earth'.

⋙ TRINIDAD (↑75/65↓) The name (meaning 'trinity') appears to your right on the hill known as Simpson's Rest, after the pioneer who was buried there. Fisher's Peak (10,000ft/3,038m) is also to your left.

Trinidad became known for the battle fought between Spanish and US settlers on Christmas Day in 1867, and the town's **history museum** (☏*719 846 7217*) reveals the struggles of early settlement life. Amtrak's temporary station is at 110 West Pine Street.

Purgatoire River (↑5/60↓) The *Southwest Chief* crosses the river and begins the steep climb to Raton Pass.

Morley (↑20/45↓) Look for an old coal mine and the ruins of a Spanish mission on the hill to your right.

Wootton Ranch (↑35/30↓) On your right is the ranch owned by 'Uncle Dick' Wootton, a noted frontier scout, Indian fighter, mountain man and trapper, paid for by the Raton Pass toll road he established. The road became obsolete when the Atchison, Topeka & Santa Fe Railroad was built in 1879 and bought the right of way, paying Wootton and his wife a lifetime pension as part of the purchase price.

The original Santa Fe Trail can be seen to your right and Interstate 25, which the train accompanies most of the way to Albuquerque, is off to your left.

Raton Pass (↑40/25↓) The highest point (7,588ft/2,310m) on the *Southwest Chief*'s journey, the ascent to this pass is the steepest (3.5%) on the route. Entering a half-mile-long (0.8km) tunnel, you go from Colorado into New Mexico.

⋙ RATON (↑65/105↓) Thruway buses connect with Colorado Springs and Denver's Union Station. A railroad and mining town nestled in the foothills of the Sangre de Cristo Mountains, Raton is Amtrak's nearest stop to the Philmont Ranch, a 137,441-acre (55,600ha) estate owned by the Boy Scouts of America. The historic 1903 depot is staffed during summer when tourism for the Philmont Scout Ranch and National Rifle Association (NRA) Whittington Center is at its peak.

Clifton House Ruins (↑5/100↓) To your left is the site of a house built in 1867 and known as the Red River Hotel. The grand three-storey building was once a resting place on the Santa Fe Trail.

Maxwell (↑20/85↓) In the mid 1800s, rancher and former hunter and trapper Lucien Maxwell, a friend of frontiersman Kit Carson, owned a staggering 2,680 square miles (6,941km²) of land in New Mexico and lower Colorado. Today this has been divided into a state park, a national forest and several huge ranches. The Maxwell wildlife refuge is a beautiful migratory waterfowl sanctuary.

Springer (↑35/70↓) After following the Canadian River, the train crosses the Cimarron River with Baldy Peak (12,441ft/3,795m) on the far right. Keep a look out for antelope.

Wagon Mound (↑60/45↓) The butte to your left, shaped like a covered wagon and horses, was one of many landmarks on the Santa Fe Trail.

Shoemaker Canyon (↑80/25↓) The train crosses then follows the Mora River. Pines and cottonwoods flourish in what was once a trade route for Plains and Texas Native Americans.

Watrous (↑85/20↓) To your left are the impressive adobe ruins of Fort Union, founded in 1851 as one of the largest forts in the Southwest. Ahead to your right are the higher Sangre de Cristo Mountains, called 'the blood of Christ' in 1719 by Spanish explorer Antonio Valverde y Cosío, who was impressed by the red-tinted hue of the snowy peaks at sunrise.

⊶ LAS VEGAS (↑105/100↓) This is not to be confused with any other Las Vegas. Look right just before the station to see La Casteñada Hotel, a former Harvey House. The first of Englishman Fred Harvey's dining rooms opened at Topeka, Kansas, in the spring of 1876 on the Atchison, Topeka & Santa Fe line. Orders taken on the train were ready to be served as soon as passengers arrived. Theodore Roosevelt joined his Rough Riders at La Casteñada for a reunion in 1899 following their exploits in Cuba during the Spanish–American War of the previous year.

Native Americans knew this region for thousands of years before Coronado discovered it in 1541. White settlers began to arrive in the 1830s, and the town grew faster when the railroad came in 1879. Prosperity also attracted outlaws such as Jesse James and Billy the Kid. At least 70 films from the early days of cinema to the present have been made here. Actor Tom Mix had a studio in Las Vegas in the 1910s and The Casteñada Hotel features in both the 1983 version of *Red Dawn* and 1994's *Speechless*. Other movies filmed in Las Vegas include parts of *Easy Rider* (1969), *No Country for Old Men* (2007) and *Wild Hogs* (2007).

As the train pulls out, look for an old railway roundhouse to your right.

Bernal (↑20/80↓) The ruins of a Las Vegas–Santa Fe stagecoach relay station can be seen off to your right. Martinez Canyon is to your left.

Starvation Peak (↑30/70↓) Legend claims that a band of around 30 early 19th-century Spanish settlers climbed the small, flat-topped mesa ahead on your left to defend themselves from Navajo Indians by throwing rocks, but were eventually starved to death.

S-Curve (↑35/65↓) The *Southwest Chief* descends a zigzag sequence of curves. Both ends of the train come into view as you travel through a wild landscape of dry riverbeds and pink earth.

Pecos River (↑45/55↓) The Mission of San Miguel is to your left. Called the oldest church in the United States, San Miguel Chapel can be traced back to the founding of Santa Fe in the early 17th century. The building seen today dates from 1710.

Rowe (↑65/35↓) Pecos Native Americans lived here in New Mexico's largest pueblo. After conversion to Christianity by the Spanish in 1617, they built the adobe mission seen in ruins across the valley to your right. Known as the **Pecos National Monument**, it rests on land donated by the actress Greer Garson. Pink pillars on the right mark the entrance to the Forked Lightning Ranch that she owned with her husband, Texas oilman Elijah 'Buddy' Fogelson. As well as being a working cattle ranch, Forked Lightning was used for entertaining Hollywood celebrities, politicians, artists and philanthropists, including Art Linkletter, Merle Oberon, Vincent Minnelli, David O Selznick, Winthrop Rockefeller and Georgia O'Keeffe. The ranch is now part of Pecos National Historical Park.

The *Southwest Chief* travels on past Glorieta Mesa to your left, with Santa Fe National Forest on your right.

Glorieta (↑80/20↓) One of the Civil War's most westerly battles took place here in 1862, when a Texan supply train was destroyed by Union forces. A Baptist retreat centre can be seen to the right.

Between Glorieta and Lamy the train descends Glorieta Pass – a 1,000ft drop over 10 miles (300m in 16km). The route twists through dry, red-rock canyons and hills thick with juniper, tamarisk, scrub oak and ponderosa pine.

Apache Canyon (↑95/5↓) A narrow granite gorge cuts into one of the oldest parts of the Rocky Mountains, where the rock face is sometimes only inches from the train as it snakes through the canyon.

⚶ LAMY (↑100/65↓) Named after Jean Baptiste Lamy, a 19th-century missionary, whose school, in ruins, can be seen to your left as the train arrives. Roadrunner Shuttle buses connect with the train and you can book through-tickets to Santa Fe (☎ *505 424 3367*). Amtrak's beautiful Spanish Mission-style adobe station has featured in many Western-themed films, including Billy Bob Thornton's 2000 version of *All the Pretty Horses*.

Connections from Lamy
Santa Fe The Southwest's oldest city was founded in 1610 and is the country's highest (7,000ft/2,100m) state capital. Crooked streets follow the contours of the earth and the flat-roofed buildings come in every shade of adobe. Formerly the royal city of the *conquistadors*, known as La Villa Real de Santa Fe de San Francisco de Asís, Santa Fe still has fine Spanish architecture, along with opera, art galleries, restaurants and probably too many tourists. In 1896, the Fred Harvey Company built the luxurious El Ortiz Hotel here when Lamy became an important railroad junction.

Handmade silver jewellery is sold by Native Americans on the pavement outside the Palace of the Governors and you can visit San Miguel Mission, the oldest house in the United States. The Loretto Chapel's Miraculous Staircase was built by a mysterious man who arrived from nowhere and left without payment after completing his task. Santa Fe's **visitor centre** is at 66 East San Francisco (✆*505 955 6215 or*✆*1 800 777 2489; w santafe.org*).

Taos Some 75 miles (120km) further north, Taos has an adobe pueblo culture going back at least 900 years, and it was here that D H Lawrence and his wife Frieda came in the 1920s to seek mystical enlightenment. His ashes are buried in a shrine on their former ranch, which has spectacular views across the desert to distant mountains. For **visitor information** about Taos, call ✆575 751 8800 or visit w taoschamber.com.

LAMY: ALL ABOARD! (↑100/65↓) As the *Southwest Chief* leaves Lamy and travels through tracts of barren countryside you begin to lose sight of the Sangre de Cristo Mountains back to your right.

Los Cerrillos (↑15/50↓) The Ortiz Mountains are in the left distance. This area is rich in minerals, including silver and turquoise, and was the site of the earliest (1830s) US gold mine. The 1988 film *Young Guns*, telling the story of Billy the Kid and the Lincoln County War, was made on location in Los Cerrillos. Amtrak scenes for the first *Superman* film (1978) were also shot here on one of the network's fastest sections of track.

Santo Domingo (↑30/35↓) The settlement on your right dates from 1598. Look for the beehive-shaped *hornos* – traditional pueblo adobe ovens used for baking bread.

San Felipe (↑35/30↓) This pueblo was established around 500 years ago. A Catholic church and a Native American *kiva* (religious council chamber) can be seen to your right.

Sandia Crest (↑55/10↓) The mountain over on your left in the **Cibola National Forest** is 10,678ft (3,250m) high. These 'watermelon mountains' go bright red at sunset, when trees on the slopes resemble seeds.

As the train nears Albuquerque, look right to see the tower and gold globe of the Federal Office building.

▰▰ ALBUQUERQUE (↑65/140↓) A centre for business, government and the military, Albuquerque is popular for its dry, invigorating climate. Named after a Portuguese duke, the city was ruled by Spain and Mexico before being won for the United States in 1846. The railroad arrived in 1880, after which Albuquerque became the site of the main locomotive works of the Santa Fe Railway. Today's population of more than half a million represents a quarter of the total figure for the entire state of New Mexico.

Albuquerque basics

✆**Telephone code** 505

▰▰ **Station** Amtrak uses the attractive Alvarado Transportation Center (ATC) at 320 First St SW (*Ticket office & waiting room* ⊕ *09.45–17.00*). ATM, payphones, baggage store, vending machines, handcarts, taxi stand. This is the site of Albuquerque's first train station, opened in the 1880s, & of the famous Mission Revival-style Alvarado Harvey House, a luxurious hotel named after Hernando de Alvarado of the 1540 Francisco Vásquez de Coronado expedition. The current ATC complex was completed in 2006 &, as well as

Amtrak, it serves ABQ Ride, Greyhound & the New Mexico Rail Runner Express commuter rail line. Tiwa Native Americans sell pretty silver & turquoise jewellery on the platform.

Connections Thruway buses travel to Las Cruces & El Paso

🚍 **Local transport** ABQ Ride is Albuquerque's public bus system. The free D-RIDE downtown service runs every 7mins on w/days (✆ 243 7433; w cabq.gov/transit). The Rail Runner Express is a way for rail passengers to travel to some of the area's most popular destinations after arriving at the Alvarado Transportation Center. Travel part of legendary Route 66 by taking a bus down Central Av, Albuquerque's 'main street'.

🚕 **Taxis** Yellow-Checker ✆ 247 8888; Albuquerque ✆ 340 8967

🚗 **Car rental** In a city 20 miles long by 25 miles wide (32km by 40km), a car can be essential. Hertz, 3400 University SE; ✆ 842 4235.

🚍 **Greyhound** 320 First St, next to the Amtrak station; ✆ 243 4435

✈ **Albuquerque International Sunport Airport** 5 miles (8km) from downtown by ABQ bus #50 or the Sunport Shuttle (✆ 883 4966)

Tours ABQ City Tour has open-air trolley rides for an overview of all that Albuquerque has to offer

(✆ 200 2642; w abqtrolley.com). Walking tours of the Old Town start from the Albuquerque Museum of Art & History (✆ 243 7255).

🛈 **Visitors bureau** 20 First Plaza; ✆ 1 800 284 2282; w visitalbuquerque.org; ⊕ Mon–Fri

🏠 **Accommodation** Hotels include the Andaluz, 125 Second; ✆ 242 9090; w wyndhamhotels. com, **$$$**; Hotel Albuquerque, Old Town, 800 Rio Grande; ✆ 843 6300; w hotelabq.com, **$$$**; Hotel Parq Central, 806 Central Av SE; ✆ 242 0040; w hotelparqcentral.com, **$$$**; MCM Eleganté, 2020 Menaul; ✆ 884 2511, **$$$**; Hotel Blue, 717 Central NW; ✆ 924 2400; w thehotelblue.com, **$$**; Rio Grande Inn, 1015 Rio Grande Bd NW; ✆ 843 9500; w riograndeinn.com, **$$**; Rodeway Inn, 2108 Menaul; ✆ 884 2480, **$$**.

For B&Bs contact Adobe & Roses Bed & Breakfast, 1011 Ortega NW, Albuquerque, NM 87114; ✆ 898 0654; w adobeandroses.com, **$$**; or the Mauger Estate, 701 Roma; ✆ 242 8755; w maugerbb.com, **$$**.

KOA's nearest campsite is at 12400 Skyline NE; ✆ 296 2729. Route 66 Hostel, 1012 Central Av SW; ✆ 247 1813; w route-66-hostel.hotels-albuquerque.com, **$**. The hostel is within walking distance of the train station, & there are free pickups from Albuquerque & El Paso.

Recommended in Albuquerque

Old Town Off Central Av & Rio Grande Bd; ✆ 248 1087. Colourful activity around the plaza with artists, craft shops, good food & adobe architecture. The most impressive building is the 1706 San Felipe de Neri Church.

Albuquerque Museum of Art & History 2000 Mountain Rd, in Old Town; ✆ 243 7255; w cabq. gov/culturalservices/albuquerque-museum; ⊕ Tue–Sun; admission charge, free Sun morning & 1st Wed in every month. Shows the history of Albuquerque & the Middle Rio Grande Valley from the founding of early Spanish settlements to the present. The art collection concentrates on works by regional artists, contemporary & historical.

Indian Pueblo Cultural Center 2401 12th; ✆ 843 7270; w indianpueblo.org; ⊕ daily; admission charge. Traditional food, crafts, fetishes, carvings & dancing. The shop has a wide range of posters, music & books relating to Native American culture. Take bus #36.

Sandia Peak East of Albuquerque off Interstate 25. As well as mountains & desert you can see the

impressive lights of night-time Albuquerque & Santa Fe. Look too for wildlife such as mule deer, black bear, racoons, bobcats & various types of squirrel. Birds include golden eagles, hawks, jays, ravens & canyon wrens.

The Sandia Peak Tram (✆ 856 7325; w sandiapeak.com) travels up the longest (14,657ft/4,467m) tramway in the world, rising 4,000ft (1,200m) in 15mins. Sandia Crest (10,680ft/3,255m) is 300ft (90m) higher & can be reached by road from the east. The tramway closes for 2 weeks each spring & autumn for maintenance.

National Museum of Nuclear Science & History 601 Eubank Bd SE; ✆ 245 2137; w nuclearmuseum.org; ⊕ daily; admission charge. Documentary film & exhibitions reveal how atomic bombs were developed for use at Hiroshima & Nagasaki. Much of the early atom research was carried out at Los Alamos, 60 miles (96km) to the north. The museum incorporates robotics & nuclear medicine exhibits as well as information about

atomic timekeeping, micro worlds, nuclear arms control & renewable energy.
New Mexico Museum of Natural History & Science 1801 Mountain Rd; ☎841 2800; w nmnaturalhistory.org; ☉ daily; admission charge. Meet New Mexico's giant dinosaurs, walk through a volcano or explore the solar system. Footprint fossils date back to animals that lived in New Mexico 280 million years ago – 60 million years before dinosaurs. See Dynamax 3D movies on a huge 5-storey screen.

ALBUQUERQUE: ALL ABOARD! (↑65/140↓) The *Southwest Chief* departs this service stop and starts to leave the Rio Grande Valley behind to enter New Mexico's desert country. A guide from the Inter-Tribal Indian Ceremonial Association describes some of the route's highlights, including the Ladron Mountains to your right and the Manzano Range on the far-left horizon. As you cross the Rio Grande, look for lavender-coloured tamarisk trees (salt cedars).

Isleta Indian Reservation (↑15/125↓) St Augustine Church to your left dates from 1613 and is still in use. Away to your right is an extinct volcano, Mount Taylor (11,301ft/3,445m).

The train crosses the Puerco River, a tributary of the Rio Grande, and begins a 3,000ft (900m) climb to the continental divide.

Kneeling Nuns (↑48/92↓) The distinctive rock formation on your right resembles two nuns praying at an altar.

Route 66 (↑50/90↓) Crossing the track on a wooden bridge is the road which ran for 2,000 miles (3,200km) between Chicago and Los Angeles. The last official Route 66 marker was taken down in 1977, but the highway lives on in Bobby Troup's song and Jack Kerouac's *On the Road*.

Mesita Pueblo (↑55/85↓) The pueblo to your left is one of several seen as you cross the Laguna Indian Reservation. Gypsum cliffs on the right reveal local uranium workings. The *Southwest Chief* joins the San José River on the left before crossing it several times ahead.

Laguna Pueblo (↑60/80↓) This is the youngest and largest of the pueblos on this route. Ancestors of the Pueblo Native Americans have occupied these same lands since AD1300 and possibly as far back as 3000BC.

Paraje Pueblo (↑63/77↓) Look for the mission building to your left.

Acomita (↑65/75↓) An adobe church stands on the left. Just to the south of here, 850 years ago, Acoma Indians built a pueblo on top of a 365ft (110m) mesa.

McCartys (↑68/72↓) This village just off Route 66 on the Acoma Indian Reservation was built at the same time as the railroad and was named after a construction boss. The simple stone building of the Santa Maria Mission, built in 1933 in Spanish Colonial style with two square towers, overlooks Route 66 from the hill.

Anzac (↑75/65↓) Mount Taylor produced the black lava beds to your left, much favoured by warmth-loving rattlesnakes.

From here to Gallup the *Southwest Chief* travels among the Red Cliffs, some of which are 7,000ft (2,100m) high. The desert sun can produce spectacular changes of colour. Native Americans say that the hills became red after a wounded stag shed blood while escaping from hunters.

Grants (↑90/50↓) This railroad town became 'the carrot capital of the USA'. This area has the second-largest uranium ore reserves of any state in the USA and was a centre for uranium mining until 1998. The remains of an Anaconda uranium smelter can be seen to your right.

Bluewater (↑100/40↓) Mount Taylor is on the right. The Atlantic & Pacific Railroad, later the Atchison, Topeka & Santa Fe, built a station in Bluewater in 1881 and named it after a local creek. This is now almost a ghost town, with Bowlin's Old Crater Trading Post among the abandoned buildings.

Continental divide (↑110/30↓) The train crosses at Campbell's Pass.

Fort Wingate Depot (↑124/16↓) From 1918 until it closed in 1993, this army installation stored ammunition in bunkers securely hidden in the hillside to your right. Half of the base is now used jointly with the local tribes and the other half is retained for missile testing.

Pyramid Rock (↑130/10↓) Behind this landmark on your right is the spire of Church Rock, where a jilted Native American maiden is said to have jumped to her death.

Red Rock State Park (↑132/8↓) Trails in the park wind through manzanita and juniper to the banks of Oak Creek, framed by native vegetation and hills of bright red sandstone.

⚉ GALLUP (↑140/90↓) 'The Indian capital of the world', where more than half the population are Native Americans, is a good place to buy silver jewellery, baskets, pottery, rugs and blankets. The tribes include Acoma, Zuni, Hopi, Navajo and Apache. This stop gives access to the Four Corners region comprising the Painted Desert, Petrified Forest, Mesa Verde National Park and South Colorado Mountains.

Amtrak's two-storey station at 201 East Highway 66 also houses the Gallup Cultural Center, which has a museum dedicated to Native American culture, an art gallery, a cinema and a visitor centre. The station was built in the Mission Revival style in 1918.

New Mexico–Arizona state line (↑10/80↓) Arizona does not observe Daylight Saving Time, so watches go back an hour (forward when travelling east) only from November to April.

The train continues through stark desert country of mystical beauty, the wide plains interrupted by mesas and buttes. Sharp winds have carved the red and yellow sandstone into wonderful spires and caves. Part of the Painted Desert and Petrified Forest can be seen to your left.

Holbrook (↑70/20↓) The train makes a street crossing at Holbrook, trading place for Hopi, Navajo and Apache. To your right is the Blevins House where in 1887, Perry Owens, Sheriff of Apache County, shot a horse thief and three other men. The flamboyant Owens later became a US deputy marshal and businessman in Seligman. It was said that the memory of the shoot-out haunted Owens to his grave and he often saw the ghosts of the men he killed.

The *Southwest Chief* accompanies the Little Colorado River for the next few minutes. The giant electricity-generating plant you see on your right consumes four million tons of coal a year.

WINSLOW (↑90/60↓) Mentioned in the Eagles' song 'Take It Easy' and named after Edward Winslow, President of the St Louis & San Francisco Railroad, Winslow is the destination for visitors to Apache Sitgreaves National Forest, Homolovi Ruins State Park and Clear Creek Reservoir. About 20,000 years ago, a meteor hit the earth 23 miles (37km) west of here, causing a crater 600ft deep and 4,000ft wide (180m by 1,200m). 'Meteor city' is another trading post for Hopi and Navajo.

Amtrak's 1930 pink stucco station with red clay-tile roof at East Second Street is a fine example of Spanish-style architecture. Currently being transformed into the Route 66 Art Museum, this was the work of acclaimed designer Mary Colter as part of La Posada Harvey House hotel that she considered her masterpiece. Lovingly restored amid beautiful gardens, the hotel has a restaurant rated by Condé Nast as one of the top three in the United States. The hotel is owned by artist Tina Mion, whose paintings can be seen in the former ballroom.

Canyon Diablo (↑30/30↓)
The train crosses on a 544ft-high (165m) bridge, with a trading post and store ruins to your right, then continues through further canyons and high desert country. In the days of steam power, tank cars of water had to be hauled into this arid region to feed the locomotives.

You continue through Padre Canyon. Approaching Flagstaff, look right among the San Francisco Peaks for Mount Agassiz (12,340ft/3,760m) and the highest mountain in Arizona, Humphrey's Peak (12,670ft/3,860m).

FLAGSTAFF (↑60/155↓) Situated almost 7,000ft (2,100m) above sea level, the town was named after local settlers who celebrated America's 100th birthday by making a flagstaff out of a pine tree stripped of branches. Amtrak's picturesque station, is at 1 East Route 66. Next to it is an 1886 solid red sandstone freight depot built by the Atlantic & Pacific Railroad. Thruway buses connect with Sedona, Phoenix, Williams and the Grand Canyon. The station also houses Flagstaff's visitor centre. Open Road Tours (☎602 997 6474 or ☎855 563 8830; w openroadtoursusa.com) offers a Colorado River Float Trip, a Grand Canyon Railroad excursion that includes a 23-mile (37km) east rim tour, travel through the Painted Desert and a stop at the Cameron Trading Post on the Navajo Reservation. You can take a 30-minute helicopter ride (optional) as an inclusion to the Grand Canyon tour. Additional services include shuttles between Phoenix Sky Harbor Airport and Flagstaff's Amtrak station.

The Colorado River, which from the rim of the **Grand Canyon** looks little more than a thin green thread of water, created this natural wonder revealing two billion years of geological history. The canyon is about 190 air miles (306km) long and ranges between 600 yards (549m) and 18 miles (29km) wide, averaging 10 miles (16km). This 1,900-square-mile (4,921km²) phenomenon is actually 600 interlinked smaller canyons and much of the rain which falls here has evaporated in the heat before it reaches the bottom.

The best way to appreciate the Grand Canyon is to walk one of its trails, that on the south rim being easiest. You can also go down into the canyon itself, but temperatures often reach 100°F (38°C) in summer and fall below freezing in winter, so take sensible precautions.

Five million people visit the canyon each year. Mule-back rides need to be booked well in advance and flights are available from Grand Canyon Airlines

(☏*866 235 9422;* w *grandcanyonairlines.com*). For tours and lodge accommodation contact the Reservations Department, Grand Canyon National Park (*PO Box 129, AZ 86023;* ☏*928 638 7888;* w *nps.gov/grca*).

The *Southwest Chief* leaves Flagstaff to travel among some of the Coconino Forest's many ponderosa pines. Lowell Observatory, from where the planet Pluto was discovered in 1930, stands on a hill to your right. Also nearby are Sunset Crater and the Walnut Canyon National Monument.

Williams Junction (↑35/120↓)
Located in the Kaibab National Forest, Williams Junction was formerly a stop for the Grand Canyon Railway, which operated steam trains from the 1908 depot at nearby Bill Williams Avenue to the edge of the canyon on a line built by the Atchison, Topeka & Santa Fe Railway (page 339).

Seligman (↑45/110↓)
This mining and cattle-trading town was founded by the railroad in 1882 at the junction of the Santa Fe line and a route south to Prescott.

₩₩ KINGMAN (↑155/64↓)
The town was founded in 1882 and named after Lewis Kingman, who helped develop the Atlantic & Pacific Railroad route from Albuquerque to Needles, California. Kingman became a shipping and trading centre for precious metals and cattle. The Atchison, Topeka & Santa Fe Railway built a Spanish Colonial Revival-style depot here in 1907. Following extensive restoration work, this now houses a passenger waiting room and a railroad museum. Thruway buses link Kingman with Laughlin and Las Vegas in Nevada.

Arizona–California state line (↑50/14↓)
As the train crosses the Colorado River near Lake Havasu you change from Mountain to Pacific Time. Since Arizona does not observe Daylight Saving Time, watches go back an hour (forward when travelling east) only from November to April.

₩₩ NEEDLES (↑64/160↓)
California's easternmost city was named after jagged peaks of the nearby Sacramento Mountain Range. Cartoonist Charles Schulz attended school in Needles and it became the home of Snoopy's cousin, Spike. This part of the Mojave Desert often registers the country's hottest temperatures.

₩₩ BARSTOW (↑160/35↓)
Capital of the Mojave, Barstow began as a station on the Santa Fe Trail before becoming a BNSF railroad town. Named after William Barstow Strong of the Santa Fe Railway, Barstow's earliest railroad lines were built through the town to connect with nearby silver mines. On your right, set among cypress trees, is one of the few surviving Harvey House buildings, the 1911 Casa del Desierto (house of the desert). This elegant restored building is now home to Amtrak's station, the Chamber of Commerce, the **Mother Road Route 66 Museum** (w *route66museum.org*) and the **Western America Railroad Museum** (w *barstowrailmuseum.org*).

English immigrant Fred Harvey built 47 restaurants and hotels in the 19th century to service the railways and help civilise the West. Hundreds of people would leave the train, enjoy 'the best food and lodging anywhere', and be back on board inside an hour. Waitresses, chosen for their youth and attractiveness, wore immaculate black dresses and lived in dormitories guarded by matrons. They had to forgo half their salary if they married in the first year of employment but 5,000 still found Western husbands. Judy Garland made the waitresses immortal in *The*

Harvey Girls. Barstow is now a tourist centre, with military bases and NASA's Goldstone satellite station close by.

Leaving the station, the train manoeuvres through a complex of Santa Fe marshalling yards before setting out towards the San Bernardino Mountains.

Edwards Air Force Base (↑15/20↓) Beyond the Kramer Mountains to your right is the landing site for NASA's space shuttle. Craig Breedlove chose this 6-mile (9.6km) runway in 1996 to test his *Spirit of America* vehicle for an attempt at the land speed record and sound barrier. The late Francis Vincent (Frank) Zappa, who was born in Baltimore, Maryland, moved with his parents to the nearby desert town of Lancaster because of his childhood asthma.

Oro Grande (↑25/10↓) Wrightwood Mountain is to your left, along with several cement mines and processing plants.

⊷ VICTORVILLE (↑35/65↓) Founded in 1895, the town was named after California Southern Railroad general manager Jacob Nash Victor. The Transportation Center is served by Amtrak, Greyhound, the Victor Valley Transit Authority and military shuttles to Fort Irwin.

You cross the Mojave River, which runs 20ft (6m) below ground and forms dangerous quicksand. Another cement plant appears on the right before the *Southwest Chief* starts a long climb among spectacular rocks and Joshua trees to Cajon Pass. The Union Pacific Railroad also uses this route to approach Los Angeles from the East. At their highest point the tracks reach more than 3,800ft (1,160m) as they travel the border between the San Bernardino and San Gabriel Mountains. The San Andreas Fault is seen as a raised blue line along the hills.

Stunning rock formations feature on both sides as the train begins a slow, twisting 2,743ft (835m) descent towards San Bernardino. Desert scenes give way to a greener country of jacarandas, palm trees and bougainvillaea.

⊷ SAN BERNARDINO (↑65/20↓) Note the handsome grounds and Spanish Mission-style station to your right, with its four imposing domed towers. When opened by the Atcheson, Topeka & Santa Fe in 1918, this was the largest railway station west of the Mississippi River. A unique mail tube system replaced boy couriers and the station had an intricate telephone system for dispatching trains. A Harvey House was added soon afterwards and this was declared 'the finest station in the West'. A new elevator, platforms, tracks and an overpass were built in 2017 as part of the Downtown San Bernardino Passenger Rail Project.

Other Spanish buildings blend with modern architecture and the heritage of Mormon settlers who came here from Salt Lake City 100 years ago. A citrus fruit industry has existed since the first navel orange crop was grown locally in 1873, and the McDonald brothers opened their first hamburger stand in San Bernardino during the 1930s.

To your left as the train leaves is southern California's highest peak, Mount San Gorgonio (11,502ft/3,500m).

⊷ RIVERSIDE (↑20/50↓) Amtrak's modern station replaced the previously used Santa Fe depot. Built in 1927, this closed in 1984 but still stands a few blocks north of the present station. The March Air Reserve Base in Riverside is the largest air mobility wing of the Fourth Air Force.

Santa Ana Mountains (↑25/25↓) You travel through a canyon formed by the Santa Ana River on your left. Prado Dam was built at the head of the canyon to control flooding.

Yorba Linda (↑30/20↓) This is the birthplace of Richard Nixon, where the modest house constructed by his Quaker father stands next to the presidential library, which contains 46 million pages of official White House records.

🚂 FULLERTON (↑50/35↓) Amtrak uses the 1930 Santa Fe station with pink stucco and red tiles seen on your right. This masterpiece of Spanish Colonial Revival style has graceful arches, quatrefoil windows, decorative metalwork and a Monterey-style balcony. Next to it is a grand 1923 Union Pacific depot which was moved to this site and converted into a restaurant. Both depots are on the National Register of Historic Places.

Fullerton is a suburban stop as well as being the station for **Disneyland** and **Knott's Berry Farm**. For details of these attractions, see the *Fullerton* entry on page 110.

From here to Los Angeles the train passes through residential and industrial suburbs of Los Angeles County.

Santa Fe Springs (↑10/25↓) Oil wells, tanks and derricks abound on both sides.

Redondo Junction (↑25/10↓) Amtrak superliners are set up for the *Coast Starlight*, *Sunset Limited* and *Southwest Chief* in the yards and roundhouse to your left.

Los Angeles River (↑30/5↓) The train accompanies a concrete channel on your right. Designed for flood control and normally dry, the channel has been a location for dozens of movie chases. As the *Southwest Chief* nears Los Angeles, look for City Hall's white tower dominating the skyline to your right.

🚂 LOS ANGELES (↑35) For Los Angeles city information, see page 78.

The *Sunset Limited*
New Orleans–Los Angeles

GENERAL ROUTE INFORMATION

The *Sunset Limited* used to be the only way to travel almost from coast to coast on a single train, taking three days to make the 2,764-mile (4,472km) journey from Orlando to Los Angeles. Unfortunately, Hurricane Katrina damaged railroad tracks along the Gulf Coast in 2005, since when no passenger trains have run between New Orleans and Orlando. Freight trains have been rolling on this route since 2006 so it's hoped that Amtrak passenger service will also be restored and Congress authorised a $500,000 study of reinstating the line from the Southern Rail Commission. In the meantime, the *Sunset Limited* operates between New Orleans and Los Angeles, flirting with the Mexican border and crossing Texas range lands before you see mountains, deserts and the orange groves of California. The original *Sunset Limited*

ESSENTIAL INFORMATION

HIGHLIGHTS New Orleans is famous for its music, food and relaxed charm – the perfect place to let *les bons temps* roll. In San Antonio you can enjoy the romantic Riverwalk and see the sacred Alamo Mission. From Tucson you can take a trip to Tombstone and watch the gunfight at the OK Corral brought to life.

FREQUENCY Three trains a week in each direction. The **westbound** service leaves New Orleans early on Monday, Wednesday and Saturday morning to reach Houston by early evening and San Antonio during the night. You reach El Paso early afternoon, Tucson mid-evening and Los Angeles early on Wednesday, Friday or Monday morning. Travelling **east**, trains leave Los Angeles late on Sunday, Wednesday and Friday evening, reaching Tucson by early morning and El Paso mid-afternoon. You arrive in San Antonio mid-afternoon, Houston at midday and New Orleans mid-evening.

DURATION 48 hours

RESERVATIONS All reserved

EQUIPMENT Superliner coaches

SLEEPING Superliner bedrooms

FOOD Complete meals, snacks, sandwiches, drinks

LOUNGE CAR Sightseer lounge car with movies, games, hospitality hour. National Park Service guides from the Amistad National Recreation Area travel between New Orleans and Houston to provide a narrative along this part of the route.

BAGGAGE Check-in service is available at main stations.

began in 1895 as a Southern Pacific all-Pullman service, complete with silver finger-bowls, operating between San Francisco and New Orleans. Passengers could continue to New York by steamship. The current shortened route takes two days.

JOINING THE TRAIN

NEW ORLEANS (70↓) The 'Big Easy' features jazz, blues, Mardi Gras, voodoo and creole cooking, and more churches per person than anywhere else in the country. Immortalised by Tennessee Williams and William Faulkner, New Orleans was founded by the French in 1718, taken over by the Spanish, then bought by the US for $15 million in 1803. Settlers from France, Spain, Britain, Germany and the Caribbean have given it a uniquely cosmopolitan atmosphere.

Relaxed charm and a ragged beauty make New Orleans the perfect place for letting *les bons temps* roll. Apart from Las Vegas, this is one of the few places in America without a closing-time law. Louis Armstrong and Fats Domino were born here and blues, soul and Cajun music are played in hundreds of music clubs. **Jazz venues** include Mahogany Hall at 309 Bourbon Street and Preservation Hall at 726 St Peter.

The effect of Hurricane Katrina on New Orleans in August 2005 was catastrophic because of the failure of the levees that should have protected the city. Over 200,000 properties were damaged or destroyed by the floodwaters and more than 1,500 people died. Reconstruction and recovery work still continues in some areas, especially the Ninth Ward that was worst affected. Despite this, the most celebrated and historic parts of the city, including the French Quarter, Garden District and St Charles Avenue, remain intact and are thriving.

New Orleans basics

Telephone code 504

Station (*Ticket office* ☉ *05.45–21.45; Waiting room* ☉ *05.00–22.00*) Amtrak shares with Greyhound the modern Union Passenger Terminal at 1001 Loyola Av, also served by Megabus & NORTA, with direct connections to the Rampart– St Claude Streetcar Line. Lockers, ATM, payphones, vending machines, handcarts, restaurant, shop, taxi stand. Opened in 1954 to consolidate the city's passenger rail operations, the station features a colourful 120ft-long (37m) mural depicting the history of Louisiana from the age of exploration to the mid-20th century. At the time, this was the only AC station in the country, serving 7 railroads

& 44 passenger trains, including the fine *Southern Belle* to Kansas City, the *Gulf Wind* to Jacksonville & the *Humming Bird* to Cincinnati. Following Hurricane Katrina, a locomotive was used to power the building & Amtrak provided the first commercial transportation out of New Orleans. During the recovery efforts, the station was briefly used as a justice centre & jail.

Connections Thruway buses go to Baton Rouge & Montgomery

Local transport The RTA (☎ *248 3900;* w *norta.com*) operates buses & streetcars, including those along the Riverfront &

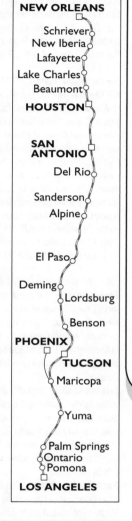

NEW ORLEANS
Schriever
New Iberia
Lafayette
Lake Charles
Beaumont
HOUSTON

SAN ANTONIO
Del Rio
Sanderson
Alpine

El Paso
Deming
Lordsburg
Benson
PHOENIX
TUCSON
Maricopa

Yuma

Palm Springs
Ontario
Pomona
LOS ANGELES

St Charles Av. A new mile-long (1.6km) streetcar line connects the Union Passenger Terminal with Canal St, the Central Business District & destinations such as the Superdome.

🚖 **Taxis** Nawlins Cab ☎ 522 9059; United ☎ 522 9771

🚗 **Car rental** Budget, 1317 Canal; ☎ 565 5600

🚌 **Greyhound** 1001 Loyola Av; ☎ 525 6075

✈ **Airport** The RTA Airport Express has 9 daily trips to & from New Orleans (Louis Armstrong) International Airport at Kenner, 15 miles (24km) west of downtown. Additionally, Jefferson Transit (☎ 818 1077) offers an airport bus (E2) that connects with the RTA system.

Tours City & plantation tours, as well as excellent Hurricane Katrina tours from Dixie (☎ 877 615 7998) & Gray Line (☎ 569 1401). Steamboat river cruises on the *Creole Queen* (☎ 529 4567) & the *Natchez* (☎ 569 1401). Walking tours leave from Jean Lafitte Historical Park, 419 Decatur St (☎ 589 3882).

🛈 **Visitors bureau** 2020 St Charles Av; ☎ 1 800 672 6124; w neworleans.com; ⊕ daily

🛏 **Accommodation** A wide range of hotels is available, from ultra modern to historic. Call the Tourist Commission (☎ 566 5011). Hotels include the Roosevelt, 130 Baronne; ☎ 648 1200; w therooseveltneworleans.com, $$$$; Bourbon Orleans, 717 Orleans; ☎ 523 2222; w bourbonorleans.com, $$$; Cornstalk, 915 Royal; ☎ 523 1515; w thecornstalkhotel.com, $$$; French Quarter Landmark, 920 N Rampart; ☎ 524 3333; w bestwestern.com, $$$; Creole Inn, 2471 Dauphine; ☎ 941 0243; w creoleinn.com, $$; Studio 6, 12330 I-10 at Bullard Av; ☎ 240 9778; w staystudio6.com, $$.

Hostels include India House Hostel, 124 S Lopez; ☎ 821 1904; w indiahousehostel.com, $. Marquette House AYH Hostel, 2249 Carondelet; ☎ 523 3014. Members & non-members, $.

Recommended in New Orleans

French Quarter (w *frenchquarter.com*) The Vieux Carré (Old Square) centres on Jackson Sq, where the first settlers arrived in 1718. The finely decorated wrought iron on the houses was made in Birmingham, England. You can soak up the atmosphere best at the French Market & along Bourbon St.

Jackson Square Originally the Place d'Armes, where soldiers marched & public executions took place. Later it became a park & was renamed after General Andrew Jackson, whose statue stands opposite the cathedral. See artists, street musicians & entertainers free & have your future told by tarot cards.

Pontalba Apartments Constructed on 2 sides of Jackson Sq over 100 years ago for the Baroness Micaela Pontalba, these buildings have handsome balconies & ironwork, eg: the 1850 House at 523 St Ann (☎ 568 6968; ⊕ *Tue–Sun; admission charge*).

Louisiana State Museum 751 Chartres St; ☎ 568 6968; w louisianastatemuseum.org; admission charge. The museum oversees a complex of 5 national landmarks reflecting Louisiana's history & culture. The properties, all located in the French Quarter, are the Cabildo, Presbytère, 1850 House, Old US Mint & Madame John's Legacy. 2hr walking tours through the Vieux Carré start at the 1850 House Museum Store on Jackson Sq.

Old US Mint 400 Esplanade Av; ☎ 568 6993; w nolajazzmuseum.org; ⊕ Tue–Sun; admission charge. This 1835 building is the only one to have served as both a Confederate & a US mint. It now houses carnival exhibits & the New Orleans Jazz Collection, including Louis Armstrong's first trumpet, as well as a history of coins.

The Cabildo 701 Chartres; ☎ 568 6968; w louisianastatemuseum.org/museums/the-cabildo; ⊕ Tue–Sun; admission charge. This was the site of the Louisiana Purchase Transfer & was built between 1795 & 1799 as the seat of the Spanish city council in New Orleans. The building has also served as the Louisiana Supreme Court & became part of the Louisiana State Museum in 1911. Reopened in 1994 after being damaged by fire, the Cabildo focuses on Louisiana's early history.

Mardi Gras The greatest free show on earth takes place during the month before Lent, with parades, bands & every kind of revelry. Book your accommodation in good time. Mardi Gras World (*1380 Port of New Orleans Pl;* ☎ *361 7821;* w *mardigrasworld.com*) has a collection that includes thousands of carnival props & giant figures.

Confederate Civil War Museum 929 Camp; ☎ 523 4522; w confederatemuseum.com; ⊕ Tue–Sat; admission charge. The 2nd-largest collection of Confederate memorabilia in the world, & the oldest continually operating museum in Louisiana, housed in Memorial Hall. The collection includes uniforms, guns, swords, photographs, paintings & 125 battle flags.

Texas-Pacific Depot 739 Third St, Gretna, just across the river. This landmark was built in 1905 to replace a pre-Civil War wood structure & was the starting point of all Texas-Pacific rails going north & west of the Mississippi. After passengers boarded in New Orleans, the cars were ferried across the river & assembled into a train in front of Gretna Station. It became redundant once a rail bridge was opened in 1935 but has been restored.

The Ogden Museum of Southern Art University of New Orleans, 925 Camp; ✆ 539 9650; w ogdenmuseum.org; ◷ daily; admission charge. The largest & most comprehensive collection of Southern art in the world tells the story of the South through its art, music & education. Among many artists represented in the museum's collection are Benny Andrews, William Dunlap, Ida Kohlmeyer, Will Henry Stevens, Kendall Shaw & George Ohr. 'Ogden After Hours' on Thu evenings features live performances of Southern music in an intimate setting.

NEW ORLEANS: ALL ABOARD! (70↓)

As the *Sunset Limited* departs, look right for the Mercedes-Benz Superdome arena, the largest fixed domed structure in the world, capable of housing a crowd of more than 70,000 people. The buildings on your left belong to *The Times-Picayune* and Xavier University.

Huey P Long Bridge (↑20/50↓)

Seen ahead to your left, the bridge was named after a state governor and US senator prominent in Louisiana and national politics during the 1930s. Before the 4.4-mile (7.1km) bridge opened in 1935, trains had to cross the river on barges. The *Sunset Limited* inches carefully over the Mississippi with views of the Avondale Shipyard and other industrial plants to your right. The New Orleans skyline becomes visible as the river curves away to your left, showing how the Crescent City earned its name.

The train slowly descends from the bridge and enters a bayou country of swamps, forests, mansions, Spanish moss, and streams famous for crayfish. Alligators can sometimes be seen sunning themselves beside the track. 'Bayou' comes from a Choctaw word meaning 'sluggish stretch of water'. The French-born pirate and smuggler Jean Lafitte hid in this region during the early 19th century. In summer, Jean Lafitte National Park Service guides join the train between here and Lafayette.

Harahan (↑30/40↓)

The cemetery to your right has graves above the ground to accommodate the swampy conditions.

Mississippi River (↑40/30↓)

Look for grain-loading facilities next to the river as you travel beside the levees.

Highway 90 (↑45/25↓)

To your left is the highway which the train will accompany for 1,100 miles (1,770km) to El Paso. You pass an oil refinery on the right then lose sight of the Mississippi to the north.

Des Allemands (↑50/20↓)

The name is French for 'of the Germans' after this colony was settled in 1721 by immigrants from Alsace and Lorraine. The bayou is on your right, and to your left are the first of many sugarcane fields. The land is so wet that much of this line had to be constructed on pilings.

Bayou LaFourche (↑65/5↓)

You cross the bayou at the town of the same name.

Bayou Blue (↑67/3↓)

The train crosses just before Schriever.

SCHRIEVER (↑70/80↓) Amtrak's platform station is next to a building that houses the Burlington Northern and Santa Fe Gulf Division office. It was originally built by the Texas & New Orleans Railroad at a junction that once provided service to the Southern Pacific Railroad (SP) as well as the Louisiana & Delta Railroad. This stop also serves Thibodaux and Houma.

Schriever is an industrial town and a base for offshore oil drilling. In 2010, an explosion on the *Deepwater Horizon* oil rig in the Gulf of Mexico killed 11 men working on the platform. The huge oil spill that followed caused extensive damage to marine and wildlife habitats as well as to the Gulf's fishing and tourism industries.

The *Sunset Limited* crosses Chacahoula Swamp, its graceful cypress trees decorated with Spanish moss.

Bayou Boeuf (↑15/65↓) A few minutes after leaving Bayou Boeuf you cross Bayou Chene.

Morgan City (↑25/55↓) Named after Charles Morgan, who built this section of the line when it belonged to the Louisiana & Texas Railroad. The intercoastal waterway to your left stretches from Brownsville, Texas, to New York, giving inland industries access to the Gulf.

Atchafalaya River (↑26/54↓) Over 200ft (60m) deep, the river has busy embankments on both sides.

Garden City (↑40/40↓) Look for a plantation house and estate to your right.

Jeanerette (↑65/15↓) A church and another above-the-ground cemetery can be seen on the right. As the train approaches New Iberia, several mansions and the towers of St Peter's Church appear to your right.

NEW IBERIA (↑80/22↓) Founded by Spanish colonists, New Iberia is famous for its annual Mardi Gras celebrations, Sugarcane Festival and World Championship Gumbo Cook-Off. The Romanesque red-brick station, listed on the National Register of Historic Places, was built in 1900. Commercial activity coexists with French and Spanish heritage among the town's ante-bellum homes. Edward McIllhenny, founder of the Tabasco Sauce Company, created Avery Island as a sanctuary for egrets, herons and ibises.

Between here and Lafayette you travel through typical southern Louisiana countryside, with more mansions and sugarcane fields in evidence after you cross the Vermillion River.

LAFAYETTE (↑22/80↓) Henry Longfellow called these bayous, forests and flowers 'the Eden of Louisiana'. The French-speaking locals arrived when the British took over Nova Scotia, then called Acadia, from France during the colonial wars of the 18th century, and Cajuns are their descendants.

Lafayette is 'the capital of Acadiana' and home to many oil companies, as well as the University of Southwestern Louisiana. Amtrak's restored station was built in 1902 by the Buckeye Chum Company for the Lake Erie & Western and Cleveland, Cincinnati, Chicago & St Louis (the Big Four) Railroads. The 550-US ton (500-tonne) building was relocated here from three blocks away in 1994 after being placed on 18 sets of wheeled dollies and rolled over in four days. Amtrak passengers cross above the rail line on an elevated pedestrian bridge to reach the platform.

Rayne (↑15/65↓) 'The frog capital of the world' holds jumping contests at its annual frog festival on the second weekend in November, attracting thousands of visitors.

Mermenteau River (↑40/40↓) You cross the river connecting Lake Charles with the intercoastal waterway. Between here and the lake, look for rice paddies and the flooded cages of crayfish farms.

⚞ LAKE CHARLES (↑80/80↓) The neat brick station with a gabled roof opened in 1999. Iron brackets supporting the roof were salvaged from the original Southern Pacific passenger station. Although barely 16ft (5m) above sea level, the deep-water port at Lake Charles ships vast quantities of oil, chemicals and cement.

In the nearby town of DeQuincy, the historic Kansas City Southern Depot now serves as the DeQuincy Railroad Museum (w *dequincyrailroadmuseum.com*). The museum has a large collection of memorabilia, including a restored 1913 steam locomotive, a 1947 passenger coach and two vintage cabooses. Also on display are many model trains and an extensive collection of Gauge 1 model steam and diesel engines.

Calcasieu River (↑5/75↓) As the *Sunset Limited* crosses the river note the duelling pistol design on the highway bridge to your left, a reminder that pirates once operated here.

Orange (↑40/40↓) You cross the Sabine River and enter the Lone Star State of Texas. The landscape remains Louisiana-like for a while, with cypresses, rice fields and the odd alligator. Between Orange and El Paso the train travels for 941 miles (1,500km) across Texas.

⚞ BEAUMONT (↑80/100↓) The town produces many professional footballers and was the home of Mildred 'Babe' Didrikson-Zaharias. When 18 years old, this remarkable athlete won six events in 3 hours during trials for the 1932 Los Angeles Olympics, subsequently setting two world records in the Games. In the 1940s and 1950s, she was the world's top woman golfer, winning 17 tournaments in a row. Nearby, the Lucas Gusher began delivering 75,000 barrels of oil a day in 1901 at Spindletop Field. Port Arthur, birthplace of Janis Joplin, is 5 miles southeast.

The red-brick station and adjacent police substation opened in 2012 on the site of an earlier station building damaged by Hurricane Rita in 2005. Look for irrigated rice fields to your right about half an hour after the train leaves Beaumont.

Trinity River (↑50/50↓) You cross the river as the train approaches the small town of Liberty.

San Jacinto River (↑70/30↓) You cross the river (on its way to Galveston Bay) and see in the far left distance the 570ft (170m) San Jacinto Monument.

Approaching Houston, the train passes Santa Fe rail yards to the left, busy with long lines of freight wagons. As the city skyline comes into view, note the Wells Fargo Plaza, currently the 20th-tallest building in the United States, and the chisel-shaped towers of Pennzoil Place.

⚞ HOUSTON (↑100/250↓) The largest city in Texas covers more than 500 square miles (1,300km²) and is a brash, bustling place where both international banker and redneck can feel at home. Houston was founded in 1836 by New York property developers who called their creation 'Baghdad on the bayou'. The boom in oil subsequently brought prosperity and many tall buildings.

A 50-mile (80km) ship canal links 'Bayou City' to Galveston on the coast. The oil business has its ups and downs but Houston remains hot in more ways than one, sharing the same latitude as the Sahara. For most of the year the weather is subtropical, but air conditioning prevails.

Houston basics

☎ Telephone code 713

🚅 Station (*Ticket office & waiting room* ☺ *10.00–19.30*) Opened by the Southern Pacific Railroad in 1960, the depot has wall panels tracing the history of railroading in the city & region. The wooden benches were salvaged from the much more attractive 1934 Grand Central Station nearby, which now houses Houston's main post office. The station has lockers, vending machines, handcarts, taxi stand.

Connections Thruway buses connect to Galveston

🚌 Local transport Metro buses (☎ *635 4000; w ridemetro.org*) operate throughout the city & to outlying places. METRORail is a fast, convenient way to travel to downtown, midtown & the Museum District.

🚕 Taxis Yellow ☎ 236 1111; Fiesta ☎ 225 2666

🚗 Car rental Budget, 6021 E Sam Houston Parkway; ☎ 281 454 4479

🚌 Greyhound 2121 S Main; ☎ 759 6565

✈ George Bush Intercontinental Airport 25 miles (40km) north by SuperShuttle (☎ *1 800 258 3826*) or Metro bus #102. Hobby Airport (formerly Howard R Hughes Airport & used for domestic flights) is 8 miles (13km) southeast.

Tours Discover Houston Tours at 912 Prairie St (☎ *222 9255; w discoverhoustontours.com*) has w/ day walking tours featuring Texas history & Art Deco architecture

ℹ Visitors bureau The main visitor centre is at 701 Av de las Americas; ☎ 853 8100 or ☎ 800 4HOUSTON; w visithoustontexas.com; ☺ daily

🏠 Accommodation Hotels include the Hilton, 2001 Post Oak Bd; ☎ 961 9300; w hilton.com, **$$$$**; Icon, 220 Main; ☎ 224 4266, **$$$$**; Sheraton Brookhollow, 3000 N Loop W; ☎ 688 0100; w marriott.com, **$$$$**; Westin Galleria, 5060 W Alabama; ☎ 960 8100; w marriott.com, **$$$$**; La Quinta Inn, 1625 W Loop S; ☎ 355 3440; w laquintahoustongalleriaarea.com, **$$$**; Econo Lodge, 6630 Hoover St US 290 & Bingle Rd; ☎ 956 2828; w choicehotels.com, **$$**.

Contact Sara's Bed & Breakfast Inn, 941 Heights Bd; ☎ 868 1130; w saras.com, **$$$$**.

The International Hostel is at 5302 Crawford St; ☎ 523 1009; w houstonhostel.com. Members & non-members, **$**.

Recommended in Houston

Port of Houston 111 East Loop North; ☎ 670 2400; w porthouston.com. The Houston Ship Channel has been a catalyst for growth ever since the first journey of a steamship up Buffalo Bayou in 1837. You can watch the non-stop activity in America's 2nd-largest & rather polluted port from a platform on Kirby Dr. Boat trips are available from Houston Historical Tours; ☎ 392 0867; w houstonhistoricaltours.com. Free 90min tours on the MV *Sam Houston*, for which you require reservations; w porthouston.com/sam-houston-boat-tour.

NRG Stadium 1 NRG Parkway; ☎ 832 667 1400; w nrgpark.com. Formerly known as Reliant Park, this 350-acre (141ha) complex includes the NRG Center, Arena, Stadium & Astrodome, home to the Houston Texans football team & the Houston Livestock Show & Rodeo. The stadium hosted the Super Bowl in 2004 & 2017. Billed as 'the 8th wonder of the world' when it opened in 1965, the original 'Dome' was the world's first large (45,000 seats) indoor venue for a major league field sport.

Sam Houston Park 1100 Bagby & Lamar; ☎ 655 1912; w heritagesociety.org; ☺ daily; museum free, admission charge to tour the historic buildings. A green space in the midst of downtown, with historic buildings such as the 1847 Kellum-Noble House (the oldest brick house in Houston) & an 1891 Lutheran Church. The Texas History Museum features items from the 16th century to the present.

Space Center Houston 20 miles (32km) south at 1601 Nasa Parkway off I-45 in Clear Lake; ☎281 244 2100; w spacecenter.org; ⊕ daily; admission charge. Better known as the headquarters of the manned space programme, the Center has rockets, lunar vehicles, moon samples & training simulators. Film shows & tours daily. Take bus #246 or 249.

San Jacinto Battleground 20 miles (32km) southeast on TX 225; ☎281 479 2421; w sanjacinto-museum.org; museum ⊕ daily; admission free, admission charge to film shows. Sam Houston defeated General Antonio López de Santa Anna here in 1836 to create an independent Texas. Great views from the world's tallest (570ft/170m) monument tower (elevator admission charge). Plans are underway to save the World War I/II battleship USS *Texas*, commissioned in 1914.

HOUSTON: ALL ABOARD! (↑100/250↓)

After Houston the *Sunset Limited* embarks on its longest run without a scheduled stop. The landscape changes as you begin to leave the Gulf Coast's green humidity for drier conditions. Cacti replace live oaks and Spanish moss, and there are fields of soya beans and cotton. Look also for some of this region's many birds, including flocks of delicate white egrets.

Sugarland (↑50/200↓)

A large former Imperial Sugar processing plant appears to your right just before you cross the Brazos River.

Richmond and Rosenberg (↑60/190↓)

These towns were infamous in Prohibition days for their brazen gambling and fast women. A brick courthouse stands on the right. Soon after Richmond, look right for rice elevators storing some of the local crop.

Colorado River (↑110/140↓)

The train crosses the Texas Colorado River – no relation of its larger namesake.

Columbus (↑111/139↓)

The dome and clock of a historic courthouse can be seen to your left. Approaching the station, look left also for the ancient live oak which was once the town's hanging tree, where in 1935 a 700-person lynch mob hanged two young African-American men accused of raping and murdering a white woman. The county attorney called their act 'the expression of the will of the people.'

Weimar (↑125/125↓)

The old train depot on your left is now a public library with an adjacent caboose used as a library office. One of the first annual celebrations in Weimar was the Cucumber Carnival, held in 1940 and 1941. The Texas Pickle Company operated here for over 30 years and more than 300 acres (120ha) of cucumbers were planted in the area.

Randolph Air Force Base (↑220/30↓)

Look for runways on your left and a Mission-style tower to your right. The base serves as headquarters of the Air Education and Training Command (AETC) as well as the Air Force Personnel Center (AFPC) and is known as 'the Showplace of the Air Force' because of the Spanish Colonial Revival-style architecture in which even the hangars were constructed.

⋙ SAN ANTONIO (↑250/185↓)

This modern, relaxed city is the place where 20 million tourists (including other Texans) come to unwind. Only 160 miles (250km) from the border, it has sometimes been called the northernmost town in Mexico.

Named by explorer Domingo Terán when he arrived on St Anthony's Day in 1691, San Antonio has lived under six flags. Influences are evident in the Spanish missions, Mexican ambience, fiestas and cattle stockyards – not forgetting the Alamo. April's fiesta is a Mexican Mardi Gras featuring a river parade, rodeos and a 'night in Old San Antonio'.

San Antonio basics

☏ Telephone code 210

⊷ Station (*Ticket office & waiting room* ⊕ *21.15–07.15*) The modern station is at 350 Hoefgen next to the Alamodome, where in 2013 country music singer George Strait set an all-time attendance record for the largest concert ever played in San Antonio. Amtrak previously used the adjacent Southern Pacific station, also known as the Sunset Station, built in 1902 in elegant Spanish Mission style with a vaulted ceiling, colourful stained glass & an imposing black marble staircase. It was known as the 'Building of 1,000 Lights', & featured in the 1975 Steve McQueen film, *The Getaway*. The station is now an entertainment complex with nightclubs, an outdoor dance hall & scores of shops. San Antonio's other surviving station, built by the International & Great Northern (I&GN) Railroad, has been restored, complete with a bronze Native American statue on top of its dome, & is home to the Generations Federal Credit Union.

Connections Megabus operates between San Antonio & Austin

🚍 Local transport VIA buses & a streetcar (☏ *362 2020*; **w** *viainfo.net*) serve the metropolitan area as well as downtown & are an inexpensive way to explore all the major attractions

🚕 Taxis Yellow ☏ 222 2222; National ☏ 434 4444

🚗 Car rental Budget, 430 Sandau Rd; ☏ 248 3313

🚌 Greyhound 500 N St Mary's; ☏ 270 5868

✈ San Antonio International Airport 8 miles (13km) north by bus #5

Tours Alamo (☏ *492 4144*) & San Antonio Detours (☏ *632 7839*) tour the Alamo & missions. The trolley makes a 45min circuit of downtown. San Antonio River Tours (☏ *244 5700*) offers 2½-mile (4km) trips by boat along the River Walk.

🛈 Visitors bureau 317 Alamo Plaza; ☏ 1 800 447 3372; **w** visitsanantonio.com; ⊕ daily

🏠 Accommodation Hotels include Menger, 204 Alamo Pl; ☏ 223 4361; **w** mengerhotel. com, **$$$$**; Drury Pl, 105 S S Mary's; ☏ 270 7799; **w** druryhotels.com, **$$$**; O'Brien Historic Riverwalk, 116 Navarro; ☏ 527 1111; **w** choicehotels.com, **$$$**; America's Best Value Inn, 900 N Main; ☏ 223 2951; **w** redlion.com/ abvi-riverwalk, **$$**; Crockett, 320 Bonham; ☏ 877 958 6030, **$$**; Economy Inn, 2434 S W Loop; ☏ 670 9455; **w** economyinnsanantonio.com, **$$**; Rose Park Inn & Suites, 312 South W W White Rd; ☏ 359 6767; **w** roseparkinn.com, **$$**.

Contact A Yellow Rose Bed and Breakfast, 229 Madison; ☏ 229 9903; **w** a-yellow-rose-bed-and-breakfast, **$$$**. International Hostel, 621 Pierce; ☏ 223 9426. Members & non-members, **$**. Take bus #20.

Recommended in San Antonio

Paseo Del Rio 110 Broadway; ☏ 227 4262; **w** thesanantonioriverwalk.com. A 2-mile (3.2km) downtown walk through parkland beside canals & the meandering river, with music, bars, floating restaurants, boat rides & a cosmopolitan parade of people. At twilight, fireflies & lanterns glow while cicadas hum among the pecan trees & palms. In 2009, a $72 million extension opened to reach the San Antonio Museum of Art at 200 W Jones Av (☏ *978 8100*; **w** *samuseum.org*; ⊕ *Tue–Sun; admission charge*). SAMA houses the largest collection of ancient Egyptian, Greek, Roman & Asian art in the southern United States. It also has

a fine collection of Latin American art, from pre-Columbian times to the present, & a wide range of contemporary works.

The Alamo 300 Alamo Plaza; ☏ 225 1391; **w** thealamo.org; ⊕ daily; donation. Mission San Antonio de Valero (The Alamo) is one of the city's oldest buildings & the most-visited attraction in Texas. In 1836, 189 defenders (including Davy Crockett & Jim Bowie) died fighting General Santa Anna's overwhelming forces after a 13-day siege which came to symbolise the Texan battle for independence.

The cool, rectangular chapel is set among subtropical gardens surrounded by high stone walls. Museum & guided tours organised by the doughty Daughters of the Republic of Texas, who rescued the mission from dereliction in 1905 & have looked after it ever since.

King William District These imposing Victorian houses on the southern edge of downtown were built for German merchants. The Steves Homestead, built in 1876, is at 509 King William (☎225 5924; ⊕ daily; admission charge). The Guenther House at 205 E Guenther (☎227 1061; ⊕ daily; admission free) was built for the founder of Pioneer Flour Mills.

Spanish Governor's Palace 105 Plaza De Armas; ☎224 0601; ⊕ daily; admission charge. 'The most beautiful building in San Antonio' once housed officials of the Spanish province of Texas. It was completed in 1749 & features period furnishings, a cobblestone patio & a fountain.

Botanical Gardens 555 Funston Pl; ☎536 1400; w sabot.org; ⊕ daily; admission charge. A miniature representation of the Texas landscape, from Hill Country wild flowers to formal rose gardens. Includes an exhibition hall, tropical house, desert house, palm house, fern room & orangery.

Tower of the Americas 739 E Cesar E Chavez Bd; ☎223 3101; w toweroftheamericas.com; ⊕ daily; admission charge. This 750ft (228m) tower, built for the HemisFair in 1968, symbolises progress made by Western civilisations. Glass-walled elevators take you over 500ft (152m) to the restaurant & observation level for panoramic views of the city & surrounding area.

Texas Transportation Museum 11731 Wetmore Rd, McAllister Park; ☎490 3554; w txtransportationmuseum.org; ⊕ Fri–Sun; admission charge. Featuring locomotives, rolling stock, a Southern Pacific station & a model railroad. Short steam train rides operate on the Longhorn & Western railroad.

The Missions Apart from the Alamo, 4 others can be seen on the Mission Trail starting at S Alamo & Market (all missions ⊕ daily; admission free). The visitor centre (☎932 1001; w nps.gov/saan) is next to Mission San José & has a free film showing early life at the mission.

Mission Concepción 807 Mission Rd; ☎534 1540. The oldest unrestored mission, dating from 1731, still has original frescoes.

Mission San José 6701 San José Dr; ☎932 1001. Largest & most impressive, with a church, granary & aqueduct. Mariachi mass on Sun. The 'Queen of the Missions' also has impressive carvings & the famous Rose Window.

Mission San Juan 9101 Graf Rd; ☎534 0749. Quiet, with a pretty bell tower & guided nature trail, the mission was established in 1731 after relocation from east Texas.

Mission San Francisco de la Espada 10040 Espada; ☎627 2064. The dam & aqueduct built in the 1730s between this remote mission & Mission San José are still in working order.

SAN ANTONIO: ALL ABOARD! (↑250/185↓)
The *Sunset Limited*, accompanied by through-cars of the *Texas Eagle*, continues from San Antonio into prairie country. Cactus plants, sage and yuccas thrive in these arid conditions as the train descends from the Anacacho Mountains to the Rio Grande Valley. Native Americans used the spiked leaves of yucca plants to make shoes and baskets.

Laughlin Air Force Base (↑175/10↓)
Away to your left across the flatlands is the largest and busiest pilot-training base in the US Air Force.

▄▄▄ DEL RIO (↑185/160↓)
The Queen City of the Rio Grande, otherwise known as 'the wool and mohair capital of the world', Del Rio is famous for sheep, goats and the Val Verde winery (the oldest continuously running in Texas). Immediately to the south is the Mexican sister town of Ciudad Acuña, visible on bluffs across the river. The 1920s brick station in Del Rio, with large, round-arch windows and classical detailing, was built in the 1920s. It also serves as the transportation centre for local buses.

The train is joined on the left by the Rio Grande, the 'big river' separating the United States from Mexico.

Amistad Reservoir (↑15/145↓) *Amistad* is Spanish for 'friendship', and the reservoir was a joint project between the US and Mexican governments. About 30 miles long and 20 miles wide (48km by 32km), it dams the Rio Grande near its junction with the Devil River to provide flood control, water conservation, irrigation, hydro-electric power and recreation.

As the *Sunset Limited* climbs 3,500ft (1,000m) over the next 200 miles (320km), watch for prickly pear cacti, more yuccas and the woolly grandpa's beard. Between April and June, prickly pears produce bright magenta flowers. Persimmons, mesquite and greasewood (the creosote bush) also grow here.

Pecos River (↑50/110↓) The train crosses a dramatic river canyon on a steel deck truss bridge up to 275ft (84m) high. Completed in 1944, it replaced the famous Pecos River High Bridge built by the Southern Pacific Railroad in 1892, when it was the highest bridge in the United States as well as the third highest in the world (321ft/98m). This amazing feat of engineering was 1,390ft (420m) long and formed part of the nation's first southern transcontinental railroad. Also known as the Pecos Viaduct, it was kept as a standby for nearly five years following the completion of the new bridge. The Southern Pacific then dismantled it, selling individual spans to several states and local governments for use as shorter bridges.

Eagle Rock Canyon (↑70/90↓) In 1883, the last spike was driven nearby to complete America's second transcontinental railway. Look for strange rock formations jutting from the canyon wall.

Langtry (↑71/89↓) This is where 'Judge' Roy Bean ran the 'Jersey Lilly' saloon and dispensed his version of justice west of the Pecos. It was claimed that his reverence for the British actress Lily Langtry caused him to change the town's name from Vinegaroon. In fact, the town was named after George Langtry, foreman of the immigrant Chinese crew working here to build the Southern Pacific Railroad.

Dryden (↑140/20↓) Look for parts of a wall that was built to keep out Pancho Villa's raiders.

⚡ SANDERSON (↑160/100↓) This is the 'Cactus Capital of Texas'. Roy Bean owned another saloon here when the town had a wild reputation as outlaws and rustlers mingled with cattle ranchers and sheep men. The last train robbery in Texas took place in 1912, when two masked men boarded the Southern Pacific's train #9 and forced it to stop midway between Dryden and Sanderson. They were Ole Hobek and Ben Kilpatrick, the latter sometimes being known as The Tall Texan when he rode with Butch Cassidy's 'Hole in the Wall' gang. Both men died during the robbery and were displayed in Sanderson before being buried in the town's Cedar Grove cemetery.

Amtrak's station at 201 W Downey is one of the least-used Amtrak stops in its national system, sometimes with only one passenger per day.

The train leaves with the ruined brick walls of Sanderson's Wool Commission to your right. Wool remains an important industry, but sheep and goat ranching become impractical further west because of predators such as coyotes, pumas, bobcats and eagles. An Apache cave and cooking mound can be seen away to your right.

Haymond (↑60/40↓) The former cow camp is now a ghost town, with its cemetery and deserted buildings on your right.

Warwick Flat (↑65/35↓) This crossing place on the Comanche War Trail ran for 1,000 miles (1,600km) from upper Texas to Chihuahua. As the train travels among the Glass and Del Norte Mountains, look for deer, pronghorn antelope, jackrabbits and javalina (wild pigs). Mount Ord (6,814ft/2,075m) is to your left and Altveda Mountain (6,860ft/2,090m) on your right.

Approaching Alpine, you see the town's rodeo grounds to your right. The letters 'SR' engraved on a hill signify Sul Ross University.

▲▲▲ ALPINE (↑100/220↓) The town is now capital of Texas's largest county, Brewster, with Mitre Peak (6,100ft/1,860m) on your right. When the Southern Pacific (SP) Railroad arrived in 1882, Alpine sprang up as a 'jerk-water' post where steam engine firemen would jerk a cord to release water from a water tower into the tender behind the locomotive. Alpine's water tower still stands. The Spanish-style station at 102 W Holland is used by tourists visiting **Big Bend National Park**, the largest protected area of Chihuahuan Desert ecology in the country.

The *Sunset Limited* continues through colourful canyon lands to Paisano Pass, the highest point (5,074ft/1,550m) on this journey. Chinati Peak (7,730ft/2,350m) is ahead to your left.

Marfa Ghost Lights (↑20/200↓) For many years mysterious usually yellow-orange lights have appeared among the Chinati Mountains and across the desert to your left.

Marfa (↑25/195↓) The town was founded in the early 1880s as a railroad water stop and named after Marfa Strogoff, a character in Jules Verne's novel, *Michael Strogoff*. The domed, stone building to your right is a Presidio County courthouse dating from 1886. The adobe walls of a World War II POW camp for Germans can be seen to your left. Also on your left, a few minutes west of Marfa, is the wooden windmill that was used as a location in the James Dean film, *Giant*. The 2007 drama There Will Be Blood and the Coen Brothers' *No Country for Old Men* were also filmed in Marfa.

Valentine (↑60/160↓) Bear Mountain (7,247ft/2,208m) and Mount Livermore (8,332ft/2,540m) are to your right. As the train descends further from the high plains, fields begin to appear and Van Horn is ahead in the right distance.

Quitman Mountains (↑90/130↓) You change from Central to Mountain Time, so watches go back an hour (forward when travelling east). For the first time in 24 hours the train parts company with Highway 90, which continues further north.

Hot Wells (↑100/120↓) A ruined adobe school appears on the right and the Eagle Mountains to your left.

Sierra Blanca (↑120/100↓) Look for the last adobe courthouse still functioning in Texas. Built in 1919, the courthouse is on the National Register of Historic Places and is a Recorded Texas Historic Landmark. The Sierra Blanca Peak (6,970ft/2,070m), located among mountains to your right, looks lighter because it contains soapstone.

Fort Hancock (↑150/70↓) The fort's remains are to your right and beyond them can be seen the Finlay Mountains. A fort was first established here in 1882 before being abandoned in 1895.

As the train approaches Fabens, look right for cheerful decorations displayed year-round on the graves in a Mexican cemetery.

Fabens (↑180/40↓) A splendid Mission-style church stands on the left next to a cotton gin. The town was named after George Wilson Fabens, an attorney for the Southern Pacific Railroad, and was a location for the Sam Peckinpah film *The Getaway*, starring Steve McQueen and Ali MacGraw.

Ysleta (↑190/30↓) Texas's longest-surviving ethnic group, the Tigua Native Americans, live in Ysleta, which has the second-oldest (1682) church in the country.

The train travels through industrial scenes towards El Paso, with oil and copper refineries on both sides. The attractive shell-shaped building to your left is the civic auditorium.

EL PASO (↑220/85↓) Encircled by the mile-high (1,600m) Franklin Mountains, this laid-back city was named after a pass (El Paso del Río del Norte) formed by the Rio Grande. Nearby are **Carlsbad Canyon National Park**, Las Cruces and Cloudcroft ski resort, the most southern ski area in New Mexico. The **tourist bureau** is at 1 Civic Center Place (☏ *915 534 0600 or* ☏ *1 800 351 6024*; w *visitelpaso.com*).

El Paso's population expanded rapidly with the arrival of the Southern Pacific, Texas & Pacific and the Atchison, Topeka & Santa Fe railroads in 1881. Seven companies owned stations here by 1902 so a 'union' station became necessary to unite them. Amtrak's Neoclassical Union Station at 700 San Francisco was completed in 1906, with a marble floor, pillars and pilasters, a second-storey gallery, and large Diocletian windows that allow sunlight to flood the waiting room. Thruway buses link with Las Cruces and Albuquerque.

El Paso maintains close links with Ciudad Juárez in Chihuahua, Mexico, seen above palisades to your left as the train departs. To your right are the campus and stadium of the University of Texas. On top of the Sierra de Cristo Rey, formerly known as the Cerro de los Muleros ('Mule Drivers Mountain') ahead to your left is a 33ft (10m) limestone statue of the crucifixion known as the *Christ of the Rockies*. Pilgrims climb 4 miles (6.4km) to the 4,576ft (1,390m) summit to celebrate the Feast of Cristo Rey at this meeting place of Texas, Mexico and New Mexico.

Rio Grande (↑5/80↓) The city holds the March record high for the United States at 108°F. A cement plant appears to your right and a mineral refinery to your left before the train crosses the river and enters New Mexico.

Sunland Park (↑7/78↓) The casino and race track, home of the Sunland Derby, is on your right.

US–Mexican border (↑10/75↓) A white post 30ft (10m) to the left of the tracks indicates the border line. The mountains on both sides are the Portillos. It was just to the north of here that the infamous Lincoln County cattle wars were fought in 1881, resulting in the shooting of Billy the Kid by Pat Garrett at Mesilla.

In 1916, this barren land witnessed the passage of Pancho Villa's marauders on their way to attack the town of Columbus and provoke a brief US–Mexico conflict.

Florida Mountains (↑75/10↓) Florida Peak is prominent close by to your left. A hole in the ridge at 7,300ft (2,200m) is known as the Window Peak. On your right the Cooke's Peak Range rises to 8,408ft (2,560m). The train crosses the Mimbres River near Deming, with the clock tower of Luna County Courthouse to your left.

DEMING (↑85/50↓) The city was named after Mary Ann Deming Crocker, wife of Charles Crocker, one of the Big Four of the railroad industry. A silver spike was driven here in 1881, to commemorate the meeting of the Southern Pacific and Atchison, Topeka & Santa Fe railroads, completing the second transcontinental railroad in the United States. Deming was formerly close to the Butterfield Overland Stagecoach route which ran to the north of the town.

Deming is the venue each August of the world's only duck races. Over 70,000 irrigated acres (28,000ha) nearby produce wine, peanuts, pecans, beans, cotton and grain sorghum. A mild climate among the Cooke's and Florida mountains makes this a popular retirement town. Similar secluded resorts can be found further north near Silver City, where Billy the Kid grew up. Amtrak's station in Deming is a small shelter with benches at 400 E Railroad Avenue, close to Rock Hound State Park.

Continental divide (↑25/25↓) The lowest elevation (4,587ft/1,400m) for any rail crossing of America's divide, where water falling to the west flows into the Pacific and to the east into the Atlantic.

LORDSBURG (↑50/110↓) Lordsburg began as a railroad town in a hollow between the Burro and Pyramid mountains. The US government bought this land from Mexico in 1854 to enable the rail line to be built to California.

On your right soon after Lordsburg you pass a dry lake where mirages transform the sand into sheets of water.

Steins (↑20/90↓) In 1878, Southern Pacific built a track through Steins Pass and the town was established as a work station for the railroad. Named after US Army Major Enoch Steen (sometimes spelled 'Steins'), who was killed by members of an Apache tribe in 1873, the town had three saloons, two bordellos, a post office, a school, a boarding house and a general store. A rock-crushing plant was built to produce track ballast for the railroad. Steins had no natural source of water, so all of it had to be brought in by train. After World War II the station was closed and the railway offered inhabitants free transport elsewhere with whatever they could carry. Most accepted and the town was abandoned, eventually becoming the ghost town it is today.

New Mexico–Arizona state line (↑25/85↓) Arizona does not observe Daylight Saving Time, so watches go back an hour (forward when travelling east) only between April and October.

Cochise's Face (↑35/75↓) On a ridge of the tawny Chiricahua Mountains rising 9,795ft (2,985m) to your left is the commanding outline of Cochise, gazing at the sky. The Peloncillo Mountains away to your right are rich in gold, silver and copper.

Dos Cabezas (↑60/50↓) Look in the Sulphur Hills to your left for this 'two heads' rock formation, named after Cochise and the Indian agent Thomas Jeffords.

Willcox (↑65/45↓) The town was founded in 1880 as a whistlestop on the Southern Pacific Railroad and later named in honour of a visit by General Orlando B Willcox in 1889. Willcox became a national leader in cattle production and agriculture remains important to the local economy to this day. From this altitude of 4,167ft (1,270m) the *Sunset Limited* will descend 3,000ft (900m).

Willcox Playa (↑70/40↓) A dry lake creates convincing mirages, even reflecting the mountains to your left.

Dragoon (↑95/15↓) During wars with the US Army between 1861 and 1872, Cochise and the Chiricahuas occupied the Dragoon Mountains to your left. The train crosses the San Pedro River.

◢◣◤ BENSON (↑110/55↓) Formerly a stop on the Butterfield stagecoach run from St Louis to San Francisco, a 2,800-mile (4,500km) journey which took 55 days. When the railway came in 1880, Benson developed as a shipping point for mines around Tombstone, 25 miles (40km) to the south. Amtrak's small metal shelter next to the tracks is a stop often used by visitors to the natural wonders of Kartchner Caverns State Park, Coronado National Forest and Texas Canyon.

The *Sunset Limited* leaves past the Rincon Mountains on the right and travels through a series of canyons down the Pantano Wash. To your right, 15 minutes from Benson, is where the television series *Little House on the Prairie* was filmed.

East- and westbound trains proceed on different lines for part of the way between Benson and Tucson, allowing the eastbound *Sunset Limited* an easier climb. Tracks are sometimes half a mile (0.8km) apart.

Vail (↑27/28↓) You travel the higher of two overlapping bridges – eastbound trains use the one below – and catch sight of the train ahead as you continue down into the rose-coloured Texas Canyon.

Santa Rita Shrine (↑37/18↓) A pink Catholic church is surrounded by desert to your right. The shrine of Santa Rita in the Desert was built in 1935 in memory of Dr Jokichi Takamine by his widow, Caroline, and is the only Catholic church in the United States built in memory of a Japanese citizen. The church has many beautiful stained-glass windows and was built to serve Mexican labourers who worked on the railroad and on nearby ranches.

Davis Monthan Air Force Base (↑47/8↓) Thousands of planes stand mothballed to your right, preserved by high altitude and dry desert air in the world's largest aircraft boneyard. Beside the track is the **Pima Air Museum** featuring World War II bombers (*6000 E Valencia Rd;* ✆ *520 574 0462;* w *pimaair.org*).

As the train nears Tucson it enters the rail yards of the Santa Fe Pacific (formerly the Southern Pacific).

University of Arizona (↑50/5↓) Look for the stadium and campus to your right. Low down on the southern horizon is the Santa Rita Range.

◢◣◤ TUCSON (↑55/60↓) The city began in 1776 as a supply station for the Mission San Xavier del Bac, located on the banks of the Santa Cruz River. Today it is a centre for farming, government and high-tech industry. It was capital of Arizona from 1867 to 1877, and Spanish, Mexican and Confederate flags have flown here at various times.

Tucson is 60 miles (96km) from the Mexican border and surrounded by mountains – the Santa Ritas to the south, Santa Catalinas to the north, Rincons in the east and Tucsons to the west. Being 1,000ft (300m) higher than Phoenix, temperatures are slightly cooler.

Tucson basics

✎Telephone code 520

⚊ Station (*Ticket office & waiting room* ⊕ *06.15–21.00 Mon, Thu & Sun, 08.15–21.00 Wed, 13.45–21.00 Tue, 06.15–13.30 Fri–Sat*) The Mission-style station at 400 N Toole Av was originally built in 1907 in Spanish Colonial style. In 1941, it was enlarged, modernised & streamlined, with colourful tiles & handsome wooden benches in the waiting room.

In 1882 Frank Stilwell, suspected in the murder of Morgan Earp, was killed by Wyatt Earp in the company of Doc Holliday at the previous Tucson depot. A statue of them now commemorates the spot where the revenge killing took place. **Connections** The Old Pueblo Trolley extended their historic streetcar line to the depot & is run by Sun Link

🚍 Local transport Sun Tran (✎*792 9222; *w* suntran.com*) operates an award-winning network of buses. The Sun Link Streetcar links the University of Arizona to the Mercado neighbourhood by way of downtown Tucson.

🚕 Taxis Yellow ✎300 0000; John's Taxicab ✎409 3215

🚗 Car rental Budget, 4570 N Oracle Rd; ✎544 6118

🚌 Greyhound 801 E 12th; ✎214 849 8966

✈ Tucson International Airport 6 miles (10km) south by bus #6

Tours Gray Line; ✎622 8811. Lost Souls Tours (✎*867 2037*) meet at the Amtrak train station behind Hotel Congress & visit haunted downtown Tucson.

🖼 Visitors bureau 811 N Euclid Av; ✎624 1817; *w* visittucson.org; ⊕ daily

🏠 Accommodation Hotels include the Doubletree, 445 S Alvernon Way; ✎881 4200; *w* doubletree3.hilton.com, **$$$$$**; Best Western Royal Sun Inn, 1015 N Stone Av; ✎844 325 8508; *w* bwroyalsun.com, **$$$**; Congress 311 E Congress; ✎622 8848; *w* hotelcongress. com, **$$$**; Homewood Suites by Hilton, 4250 N Campbell Av; ✎577 0007; *w* homewoodsuites3. hilton.com, **$$$**; Country Inn & Suites, 705 N Freeway; ✎867 6200; *w* countryinns.com, **$$**; Tucson City Center, 475 N Granada Av; ✎622 3000; *w* hoteltucsoncitycenter.com, **$$**.

Recommended in Tucson

Presidio Historic Park Located 45 miles (72km) south of Tucson at 1 Burruel, Tubac; ✎398 2252; *w* azstateparks.com/tubac. Tucson became a walled city (or *presidio*) when the Spanish built a barrier against Native Americans. Arizona's first State Park contains the ruins of the Spanish *presidio* founded in 1752 as the first European settlement in what later became Arizona. The Park showcases every culture (Native American, Spanish, Mexican, Pioneer American & Arizonian) and brings 2,000 years of history to life. Tubac Presidio Historic Park was named one of 14 must-see destinations in the world by *Condé Nast Traveler*. Many other historic places can be seen within walking distance of Amtrak's Tucson station, including the Pima County courthouse which preserves a small part of the wall, has a mosaic-tiled dome & a courtyard fountain. El Tiradito (the wishing shrine) makes dreams come true for believers who light a candle.

Arizona State Museum 1013 E University Bd; ✎621 6302; *w* statemuseum.arizona.edu;

⊕ daily; admission charge. The oldest & largest anthropological museum in the Southwest features the history of the American Southwest & northern Mexico. Combines prehistoric, historic & contemporary items with high-tech displays.

Arizona History Museum 949 E Second St ✎882 8607; *w* arizonahistoricalsociety.org; ⊕ Mon–Sat; admission charge. Southern Arizona history from the Spanish colonial to the territorial eras. The exhibits include Geronimo's rifle & 18th-century Spanish silver sculptures. Other Arizona Historical Society museums include the Sosa-Carrillo-Frémont House (✎*882 8607*; ⊕ *daily; admission free*). One of Tucson's oldest adobe houses has been restored using period furniture of the 1880s. Walking tours on Sat.

Saguaro National Monument 3693 S Old Spanish Trail; ✎733 5153; *w* nps.gov/sagu; ⊕ daily; admission charge. Located in 2 sections, east & west of the city. The eastern section has older & taller stands of the giant saguaro cactus,

11

which can live for 200 years & grows in only 2 states. White saguaro blossom, the state flower, appears in May & Jun.

Mission San Xavier del Bac 9 miles (15km) southwest of Tucson at 1950 W San Xavier Rd; ☏294 2624; w sanxaviermission.org; ⊕ daily; donation. Father Eusebio Kino arrived in 1692 & built a church 2 miles (3km) to the north. This mission, the most elaborate & beautiful in America, was completed 100 years later. Sometimes called 'The White Dove of the Desert', the mission is located on the Tohono O'dham Indian Reservation, where you can also sample Native American fry bread.

Pima Air & Space Museum 6000 E Valencia Rd; ☏574 0462; w pimaair.org; ⊕ daily; admission charge. 5 hangars contain more than 350 military, civilian & commercial aircraft, including President John F Kennedy's Air Force One & a replica of the Wright brothers' *Flyer*. Experience simulated space flights & a full motion simulator. Walking & tram tours.

Tombstone 65 miles (105km) southeast on Route 80. The Old Courthouse State Historic Park is at 223 Toughnut (☏457 3311; w azstateparks. com/tombstone). 'The town too tough to die' began as a mining settlement & was the scene of the 1881 OK Corral shoot-out between Wyatt Earp, 'Doc' Holliday & the Clantons. Tombstone is quieter now but looks little different from when it was 'the next best thing to hell on earth'. Big Nose Kate's saloon, the church, Boot Hill cemetery & the Epitaph Building are intact, & the OK Corral appears much as it did on the day of the gunfight. The Tourist Association is at PO Box 995, Tombstone, AZ 85638-0995 (☏888 457 3929).

TUCSON: ALL ABOARD! (↑55/60↓)

To your right as the *Sunset Limited* pulls out of Tucson are the Santa Catalina Mountains, including Mount Lemmon (9,157ft/2,790m). Half an hour from Tucson, the Little Owl Head Mountains are to your left and the Tortolita Range directly ahead. In this fertile country you see fields of cotton, pecans, cabbage and broccoli.

Picacho Pass (↑40/20↓)

Picacho Peak (3,382ft/1,030m) is to your left and the Picacho Range to your right.

Look for stands of candelabra-like saguaro cactus on both sides of the track for the next few miles as desert predominates. A saguaro can grow to 50ft (15m) and store 2,000 gallons (9,100 litres) of water. Look also for the portly barrel cactus, prickly pears, tangling chollas and the spindly ocotillo shrub. The last acquired its name (from ocotl, the Nahuatl for 'little torch') because of the bright-red flowers it sprouts after winter rain.

⚶ MARICOPA (↑60/180↓)

Amtrak's station on N John Wayne Parkway in Maricopa serves Phoenix, 25 miles (40km) to the north, as well as the surrounding area. Thruway buses travel to Tempe and Phoenix. On display is an elegant restored round tail observation car originally brought here from Los Angeles Union Station to serve as a ticket office and waiting room, since replaced by a more prosaic station building.

Maricopa is one of the country's fastest-growing cities, with access to Phoenix as well as the Him-Dak Eco-Museum preserving aspects of the Ak-Chin Native American heritage (w ak-chin.nsn.us), and the Casa Grande Ruins Monument, which has remains of structures built by people of the Hohokam period who farmed the Gila Valley in the early 13th century. In 1892 this was the first cultural and prehistoric site to be protected by the United States government.

Nearby Superstition Mountains were sacred to the Apache thunder god and a search for Apache gold has been going on here ever since. Hundreds of miners and their guards were massacred in the 1860s after being sent to look for the treasure by a Mexican cattle rancher. The Lost Dutchman mine, believed to be located somewhere in the canyons to your right, was never found again after its German prospector was shot trying to return to his find. An Apache girl reputedly had her tongue cut out for showing him the gold.

⚐ PHOENIX (↑180) Passenger rail service to Phoenix Union Station was discontinued in 1996 due to poor track conditions along the Southern Pacific line west of the city. *Sunset Limited/Texas Eagle* trains were rerouted to the south along the Southern Pacific main line and Maricopa became the closest station to Phoenix, 25 miles (40km) to the north.

Arizona's capital sprawls over 393 square miles (1,020km²), surrounded by impressive mountains. The original settlement was built on the ruined villages of Anasazi and Mogollon Native Americans, who lived here from before the time of Christ until the 15th century and used irrigation to tame the desert. The Anasazi grew maize, made fine pottery and constructed sophisticated architecture, but their civilisation was mysteriously destroyed. Settlers prophesied that a city would rise again like the legendary phoenix bird. Roosevelt Dam, 75 miles (112km) to the north, harnessed the Salt River in 1911 and helped fulfil the prophecy.

Phoenix boasts the highest water fountain in the world at 560ft (171m) and has 300 days of sunshine a year, with only 7 inches (17cm) of rain and summer temperatures sometimes up to 120°F (49°C).

Phoenix basics

☎ Telephone code 602

⚐ Station The magnificent Mission Revival-style Union Station on Harrison St at Fourth Av was built by the Santa Fe & the Arizona Eastern (Southern Pacific) railroads in 1923. A milestone in the city's development, Union Station brought tourism on a grand scale. At its peak after World War II, this station was served by 18 trains a day, including Southern Pacific's *Sunset Limited* between Los Angeles & New Orleans, & the *Golden State Limited* on the Los Angeles–Chicago route. The *Golden State* made its last run in 1968 & Amtrak rerouted the *Sunset Limited* away from Phoenix in 1996. Since then, the *Olympic Torch* train has stopped here twice & GrandLuxe tourist trains have occasionally used Union Station.

Connections Greyhound buses link Tucson with Phoenix & Thruway buses connect Phoenix with Amtrak's Maricopa Station in 1½hrs.

🚌 Local transport Valley Metro (☎ *253 5000;* w *valleymetro.org*) operates buses as well as a light rail service. The 44th St PHX Sky Train Station has rail services to the airport as well as Tempe & Mesa.

🚕 Taxis Paul's Taxi ☎ 222 2227; Great Value ☎ 332 3362

🚗 Car rental Enterprise, 1225 S 7th; ☎ 257 4177

🚌 Greyhound 2115 E Buckeye Rd; ☎ 389 4200

✈ Sky Harbor International Airport 4 miles (6.5km) southeast. Valley Metro bus routes 1, 13, 32 & 44 connect with the Airport at the PHX Sky Train Station. The free Sky Train runs regularly & is only mins from Sky Harbor terminals.

Tours Phoenix Rising; ☎ 842 1656. The Capitol walking tour includes the Capitol Museum & Confederate Monument. Detour has tours to the Grand Canyon, Sedona & the Apache Trail (☎ *866 438 6877*).

ℹ Visitors bureau 125 N Second; ☎ 254 6500; w visitphoenix.com; ⊕ Mon–Fri

⌂ Accommodation Hotels often have low-rate specials during summer, if you can take the heat. They include the Crescent, 2620 Dunlop Av; ☎ 943 8200; w marriott.com, **$$$**; Hyatt Regency, 122 N Second; ☎ 252 1234; w hyatt.com, **$$$**; Ramada Midtown, 212 W Osborn Rd; ☎ 595 4444; w wyndhamhotels.com, **$$$**; Wyndham Garden, 3600 N 2nd Av; ☎ 1 800 207 4421; w wyndhamhotels.com, **$$$**; San Carlos, 202 N Central Av; ☎ 253 4121; w hotelsancarlos.com, **$$**.

For B&B contact Maricopa Manor, 15 W Pasadena Av, Phoenix, AZ 85013; ☎ 1 800 292 6403; w maricopamanor.com, **$$$**.

Metcalf House Youth Hostel, 1026 N Ninth; ☎ 254 9803. Dormitory rooms; w phxhostel.org, **$**.

Recommended in Phoenix

Heritage Square 113 N Sixth St; ☎262 5070; ⊕ daily; admission charge. Restored 19th-century houses give an idea how Old Phoenix looked, eg: the 1895 Rosson House.

Encanto Park 2605 N 15th Av; ☎261 8991; ⊕ daily. An oasis in the middle of the city, featuring a lake, nature trails & a swimming pool.

Desert Botanical Garden 1201 N Galvin Parkway in Papago Park; ☎480 941 1225; w dbg.org; ⊕ daily; admission charge. The garden is an important conservation institution with 169 rare, threatened or endangered plant species from the world's deserts, especially the southwestern US & northern Mexico. Over 1,350 varieties of cactus are among the 50,000 plants located in 145 acres (58ha), 5 miles (8km) east of downtown. Take bus #3.

Phoenix Art Museum 1625 N Central Av; ☎257 1880; w phxart.org; ⊕ closed Mon; admission charge. The largest visual arts museum between Denver & Los Angeles features 14,000 exhibits, including art from Asia, the Americas & Europe to 1900, along with contemporary works.

Heard Museum 2301 N Central Av; ☎252 8840; w heard.org; ⊕ daily; admission charge, free tours. One of the best places to experience the cultures & art of Native Americans of the Southwest. 10 galleries & outdoor courtyards feature traditional & contemporary Native American art.

Phoenix Zoo 455 N Galvin Parkway, near the Botanical Garden; ☎286 3800; w phoenixzoo.org; ⊕ daily; admission charge. Approximately 3,000 animals & birds live in replicated natural habitats here, including rare Arabian oryx; there are also 2½ miles (4km) of walking trails.

Arizona Railway Museum 330 E Ryan Rd in Chandler, 20 miles (32km) southeast; ☎480 821 1108; w azrymuseum.org; ⊕ Sat/Sun from Labor Day to Memorial Day; donation. Located in a building resembling a train depot, the museum tells the history of southwestern railways.

Verde Canyon Railroad North of Phoenix at 300 N Broadway in Clarkdale; ☎1 800 582 7245; w verdecanyonrr.com; ⊕ daily; admission charge. A 20-mile (32km) round trip takes you to the ghost-town depot at Perkinsville over a line built in 1911 for the United Verde Copper Company. You travel through North Verde River Canyon & the Sycamore Wilderness area, which can only be visited by train. You cross the SOB Canyon on a 175ft-high (50m) trestle, then go through a 680-ft (200m) tunnel blasted with 20,000lb (9,000kg) of dynamite.

Parts of the 1962 film *How the West Was Won* were shot among the canyon's Sinagua ruins & abandoned gold mines. You can see cacti, wild flowers, bald eagles, javalinas, blue herons & deer, & sometimes beavers, mountain lions & black bears. The line was formerly operated by the Santa Fe, Prescott & Phoenix Railroad, which hauled freight until 1988.

MARICOPA: ALL ABOARD! (↑60/180↓) As the *Sunset Limited* leaves Maricopa and continues across the Sonoran Desert, home of the gila monster lizard, look for distant rocks eroded into natural sculptures. The flat rectangular ones are known as mesas. Others have been carved into recognisable figures, such as a praying monk and a weeping Apache.

🚂 YUMA (↑180/135↓) Amtrak's downtown stop is a platform next to the site of an old Southern Pacific passenger station that was destroyed by fire in 1995. Yuma is a resort set in farmland irrigated from the Colorado River and close to many wildlife refuge and wilderness areas. It is the sunniest place on Earth according to *Guinness World Records*. The former Yuma Prison is now a state park.

Colorado River (↑20/115↓) Crossing the river takes you from Arizona into California. Since Arizona does not observe Daylight Saving Time, watches go back an hour (forward when travelling east) only from October to April.

Indio (↑110/25↓) The city of Indio came about because it was a halfway point where engines needed to be refilled with water for the Southern Pacific route between Yuma, Arizona, and Los Angeles. After the railroad's arrival in 1876, the first permanent building was the Craftsman-style Southern Pacific Depot station and hotel with its fancy dining room and Friday-night dances. Indio became an agricultural centre as onions, cotton, grapes, citrus and dates thrived in the arid climate, watered through the valley's branch of the All-American Canal. 'The date capital of the world' still hosts a date festival each February.

⚲ PALM SPRINGS (↑135/75↓) Originally famous for its mineral springs, the city has become better known since the 1920s as a fashionable refuge for Hollywood stars. Half of Palm Springs is owned by the Cahuilla tribe, who were given a vast area of desert by the US government in return for the right to build a railroad. The Cahuillas thought they already owned the land, which subsequently became some of the world's most exclusive real estate and made them America's richest Native Americans. The Palm Springs Aerial Tramway travels more than 2 miles (3km) up into the cool surrounding mountains for views of the Coachella Valley. Amtrak's station is 8 miles (13km) from downtown, with connecting taxi service.

Colton (↑65/10↓) The train crosses the Santa Ana River, with the San Gabriel Mountains to your right. Look for giant, electricity-generating turbines seen from both sides of the train.

⚲ ONTARIO (↑75/10↓) Built in Spanish Revival style in 1991, Amtrak's shady open-air pavilion is surrounded by palm trees. Ontario is part of Southern California's Inland Empire region, located 37 miles (59km) inland of the Pacific Ocean. It was developed as a model colony by four brothers from Ontario, Canada, and is famous for its former All-States Picnic celebrating the origins of the town's first settlers. This started in 1916 and became an annual event that reached its heyday in the early 1960s, when around 100,000 people would attend the picnic and parade. The international airport is on your left.

⚲ POMONA (↑10/45↓) Although it was named after the Roman goddess of fruit, residential development has mostly replaced orchards and vineyards. Singer Tom Waits was born in the back of a taxi just outside the hospital here in 1949. Los Angeles County Fair, held in September, attracts more people than any other similar event in the country. Amtrak trains board at the north platform of a Spanish-style station built in 1940 with stuccoed walls and red clay-tile roof.

The train leaves with St Joseph's Church to your left and St Paul's Mission-style church on the right, next to the California Polytechnic.

San Gabriel River (↑15/30↓) You cross this often dried-out riverbed.

San Gabriel Valley Airport (↑17/28↓) The airport to your right was formerly named El Monte Airport after nearby Mount Wilson (5,700ft/1,730m).

The train crosses the concrete-lined Rio Hondo then enters a short tunnel to Temple City, dramatically emerging along the centre strip of the San Bernadino Freeway.

California State University (↑33/12↓) The campus is to your right as you part company with the freeway.

LA County Hospital (↑37/8↓) Look right for the tall buildings of one of the largest public hospitals and medical training centres in the United States. On your

left is the concrete channel of the Los Angeles River, with Dodger Stadium visible ahead on a hill. The *Sunset Limited* crosses the river then passes the post office building's twin domes and the tower of City Hall on the right. LA's county jail is to your left just before the station.

LOS ANGELES (↑45) For Los Angeles city information, see page 78.

The *Texas Eagle*
Chicago–San Antonio
(for Los Angeles)

GENERAL ROUTE INFORMATION

From Lake Michigan to the Alamo, the *Texas Eagle* makes a 1,306-mile (2,100km) journey down the centre of America, travelling through Lincoln land then crossing the Mississippi before continuing through the Ozarks to Arkansas and Texas. Pine

ESSENTIAL INFORMATION

HIGHLIGHTS The *Texas Eagle* travels deep in the heart of Texas, from Austin with its vibrant music scene to St Louis with its Saarinen Arch (twice the height of the Statue of Liberty) and cosmopolitan Dallas. You see the Land of Lincoln, the Mississippi River, the Ozark Mountains and the beautiful pine woods of east Texas.

FREQUENCY Daily. The **southbound** *Texas Eagle* leaves Chicago mid-afternoon to reach St Louis by mid-evening and Little Rock early next morning. You arrive in Dallas early in the afternoon and San Antonio by late evening. On some days (see below) coaches continue to Los Angeles by joining the *Sunset Limited* (pages 161–74). Travelling **north**, trains leave San Antonio early in the morning to reach Dallas by late afternoon and Little Rock late evening. You arrive in St Louis early next morning and Chicago by mid-afternoon. A through service west of San Antonio operates tri-weekly, departing on Sunday, Tuesday and Thursday. Eastbound trains departing Los Angeles on Sunday, Wednesday and Friday arrive in Dallas on Tuesday, Friday and Sunday, and stations between Walnut Ridge and Chicago on Wednesday, Saturday and Monday.

DURATION 32 hours 25 minutes (Chicago–San Antonio); 65 hours 20 minutes (Chicago–Los Angeles)

RESERVATIONS All reserved

EQUIPMENT Superliner coaches

SLEEPING Superliner bedrooms

FOOD Complete meals, snacks, sandwiches, drinks

LOUNGE CAR Movies, games, hospitality hour. A guide from the San Antonio Missions National Historical Park provides a narrative on select weekends from Memorial Day through Labor Day.

BAGGAGE Check-in service is available at main cities.

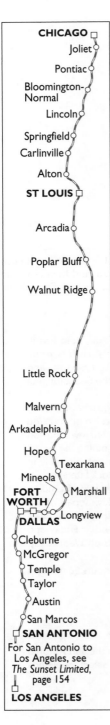

CHICAGO □
Joliet
Pontiac
Bloomington-
Normal
Lincoln
Springfield
Carlinville
Alton
ST LOUIS □

Arcadia

Poplar Bluff

Walnut Ridge

Little Rock

Malvern
Arkadelphia
Hope
Texarkana
Mineola
FORT
WORTH
Marshall
DALLAS
Longview
Cleburne
McGregor
Temple
Taylor
Austin
San Marcos
SAN ANTONIO

For San Antonio to
Los Angeles, see
The Sunset Limited,
page 154

LOS ANGELES

forest and lakes north of Dallas give way to cattle country as you approach San Antonio, where through-coaches to Los Angeles join the *Sunset Limited*. The *Texas Eagle* has one of the highest passenger growth rates of all the Amtrak routes.

JOINING THE TRAIN

CHICAGO: ALL ABOARD! (45↓) For Chicago city information, see page 83. The *Texas Eagle* operates between Chicago and Joliet over the Canadian National Railway, travelling initially through industrial suburbs.

Look back for fine views of the city as you cross the Chicago River, which provided French explorers with a passage from Lake Michigan almost as far as the Mississippi River. A few minutes out of Union Station the *Texas Eagle* crosses the Chicago Sanitary Ship Canal, a waterway which reverses the Chicago River's flow. The canal forms part of an inland system which runs 30 miles (48km) from Chicago to Lockport, linking the Great Lakes with the Mississippi.

Bridgeport (↑15/30↓) First settled by Irish immigrants who built the Illinois & Michigan (I & M) Canal, Bridgeport was the home of Chicago's influential former mayor, Richard J Daley.

Willow Springs (↑30/15↓) Look left for deer hiding in a wooded enclave. Willow Springs was a location for the 2006 film *The Lake House*, starring Keanu Reeves, Sandra Bullock and Christopher Plummer.

Lambert (↑32/13↓) The train crosses the Calumet Sag Channel joining Lake Michigan with the Sanitary Ship Canal. You then continue to Joliet through the urban parkland of the I & M National Corridor.

Lockport (↑38/7↓) Restored buildings can be seen to your right as the *Texas Eagle* accompanies a towpath. Lockport is 'the city that made Chicago famous' thanks to its strategic position on the I&M Canal, which had its headquarters here. This is a station on Metra's Heritage Corridor, with weekday rush hour rail service between Joliet and Chicago Union Station.

Illinois State Prison (↑41/4↓) The prison to your right was built by convict labour with limestone quarried on the site. The notorious correctional centre became the main execution site in Illinois but closed in 2002. It features in the film *The Blues Brothers*, the *Prison Break* television show, and in recordings by Memphis Minnie and Bob Dylan.

JOLIET (↑45/52↓) Named after the 17th-century French-Canadian explorer Louis Jolliet, this manufacturing town has busy rail and water connections, including two riverboat casinos. Amtrak's *Lincoln Service* and *Texas Eagle* trains have moved to the new $42 million Joliet Regional Multimodal Transportation Center completed in 2018 next to Joliet's old Union Station.

From Joliet to Fort Worth, the *Texas Eagle* operates on tracks of the Union Pacific Railroad. You continue with the Des Plaines River and conservation area to your right, next to the I & M Canal. To your left are a limestone quarry and a former US Army arsenal where munitions were stored underground.

Kankakee River (↑15/37↓) The train crosses this tributary of the Illinois River.

Braidwood (↑20/32↓) The tall towers on your left are part of a Con-Edison nuclear energy plant that provides much of the electricity used in the Chicago area.

Dwight (↑35/17↓) The town was named after Henry Dwight, who funded most of the building of this part of the Chicago & Mississippi Railroad, soon to become the Chicago & Alton Railroad. The station to your right, designed by Henry Ives Cobb, was continuously in use from 1892 until 2016. It now houses the Dwight Historical Society museum and the Chamber of Commerce. Beyond it is a brick building with a clock – the only one of three banks designed by Frank Lloyd Wright still in existence.

In 1860, the then Prince of Wales came incognito to Dwight on a hunting trip and visited the small, white pioneer church, built in 1857 and a rare example of wooden Carpenter Gothic church building. An impressive windmill can be seen to your left before the train crosses the Vermillion River.

PONTIAC (↑52/30↓) The town was named after a Native American chief of the 18th century. Amtrak serves a recently completed station with red brick, angled walls and large expanses of glass. Part of the original Route 66 was constructed right next to the tracks here.

Normal (↑25/5↓) Established in 1857, Illinois Normal School was a teachers' college which became the State University. Dormitories and other campus buildings appear to your right.

BLOOMINGTON-NORMAL (↑30/33↓) Abraham Lincoln delivered his final speech here on his way to becoming president in 1860. George Mortimer Pullman, designer and manufacturer of the Pullman sleeping car, lived here. His luxury Pioneer car proved too wide for some railroads until Mrs Lincoln used one following her husband's assassination in 1865, when alterations were made so that his body could be transported across country to Springfield. The journey took two weeks in order to let the nation pay its respects along the route. A reconstruction of the Washington *Night Flyer* train of 1861 can be seen in a Dick Powell film called *The Tall Target*, where Lincoln is saved from assassination by 'John Kennedy' during a fraught journey.

Amtrak uses the Uptown Station, a $47 million intermodal transportation centre opened in 2012. This is one of the busiest Amtrak stations in the greater Midwest, with Thruway buses going to Davenport, Galesburg, Peoria, Champaign/Urbana and Indianapolis. The prominent corner clock tower of Uptown Station is a local landmark and environmentally friendly features include a green roof planted with vegetation to absorb rainwater and cool the building.

Funk's Grove (↑8/25↓) Illinois's only tract of virgin timber, mostly maple, was donated to the state by Eugene Funk of Funk Seeds. Just before Lincoln you cross Kickapoo Creek.

⚏ LINCOLN (↑33/30↓) This is the only town named after Lincoln before he became president, and he christened it in 1853 using melon juice. Lincoln returned on a whistle-stop campaign tour in 1860, and in 1865 his funeral train stopped in the town overnight before going on to Springfield. A 'slice of watermelon' statue stands to the left of the station. Also to your left is the domed Logan County Courthouse where Lincoln practised law.

The *Texas Eagle* crosses the Sangamon River near Springfield, with the Illinois Fairgrounds to your right.

⚏ SPRINGFIELD (↑30/40↓) Lincoln spent 25 years in Springfield before becoming president. You can visit the only house he ever owned, the place where he was married and the grave in which he and his family are buried. He made his farewell address on leaving town in 1861 at a rail depot a short distance from the present station and gave his 'house divided' speech at the Old State Capitol. The present Capitol and Supreme Court can be seen to your right. The **Illinois Visitor Center** is at 1 SW Old State Capitol Plaza (☏*217 557 4588;* w *visitspringfieldillinois. com;* ⊕ *daily*).

Amtrak's renovated station features a quote from Abraham Lincoln: 'May our children and our children's children to a thousand generations continue to enjoy the benefits conferred upon us by a united country.'

Lake Springfield (↑10/30↓) The *Texas Eagle* crosses the western tip of the lake, a 4,260-acre (17.2km²) reservoir formed in the 1930s by building Spaulding Dam across Sugar Creek , a tributary of the Sangamon River.

⚏ CARLINVILLE (↑40/30↓) A new depot opened in 2017, built of cast stone with large glass walls. The silver-domed Macoupin County Courthouse on your left dates from when Carlinville hoped to become the state capital. The 'Million Dollar Courthouse' cost precisely $1,342,226.31 when completed in 1870. When Standard Oil operated local coal mines the company's workers lived in Sears, Roebuck houses which were prefabricated and transported in sections by train. The mines are closed but some of the houses remain.

Macoupin Creek (↑5/25↓) The *Texas Eagle* crosses at Beaver Dam State Park. Although beaver have almost gone from this area, the park was named after a beaver dam that created its lake.

⚏ ALTON (↑30/40↓) Birthplace in 1926 of the legendary jazz musician, Miles Davis. This Mississippi River port's newspaper editor, Elijah Lovejoy, was lynched in 1838 by a mob opposing his anti-slavery views. The town later became a supply point for the Union Army.

Unseen to your right as you cross the Wood River is Lewis and Clark State Park, where the Missouri and Mississippi rivers meet. Lewis and Clark's expedition wintered here before beginning their explorations west.

Cahokia Diversion Canal (↑10/30↓) Levees on both sides try to prevent flooding when the Mississippi rises. During the summer of 1993, the worst floods in history brought chaos to this region, covering 16,000 square miles (41,000km²) of crops in eight states and killing at least 40 people.

The Native American city of Cahokia stretched across 2,200 acres (890ha) and was inhabited from around AD700 to 1400. The inhabitants, known as Mississippians, had a culture based on cosmology and built sacred ritual mounds as large as Egypt's Great Pyramid. It is thought that deforestation caused devastating floods which ruined crops and made the population flee their 'Native American Jerusalem'.

Lenox (↑11/29↓) The train travels next to tracks which run between St Louis and Detroit and were used by the celebrated *Wabash Cannonball* train.

Granite City (↑14/26↓) Steel and other heavy industries accumulate as you approach St Louis.

Mississippi River (↑22/18↓) You cross high above the river on the Merchants Railroad bridge, leaving Illinois for Missouri. Look for barges on the river and the St Louis skyline to your left.

Eads Bridge (↑30/10↓) The train passes beneath the city's oldest bridge, which had the longest steel spans anywhere when it was completed in 1874 and was built high enough for steamboats to travel underneath.

Gateway Arch (↑35/5↓) The landmark to your right is America's tallest monument (630ft/192m), with a cathedral at its base. Old riverboats can be seen moored on your left.

Busch Stadium (↑38/2↓) To your right is Busch Stadium III, home of the St Louis Cardinal baseball team, on the site of the former Busch Memorial Stadium, demolished in 2005.

⚏ ST LOUIS (↑40/130↓) This gateway to the west was founded by Pierre Laclede in 1764 on high ground where the Mississippi River joins the Missouri. Named after King Louis IX of France, St Louis was acquired by President Jefferson as part of the 1803 Louisiana Purchase. The original fur-trading post became a place for wagon trains to gather before heading west, so the massive 630ft (192m) stainless-steel Gateway Arch designed by Eero Saarinen makes an appropriate symbol.

Scott Joplin invented ragtime when he lived here and W C Handy's 'St Louis Blues', one of the most recorded songs of all time, also helped put the city on the music map. Jazz musicians came by riverboat and train from New Orleans to join blues artists from the Mississippi Delta to create new musical styles. Their influence can still be heard in the many live music clubs and bars. Other famous St Louisans include singer/guitarist Chuck Berry, dancer Josephine Baker, actor Vincent Price and *Beat Generation* writer William S Burroughs.

St Louis basics

⚲ Telephone code 314

⚏ Station (*Ticket office* ☉ *03.30–23.30; waiting room* ☉ *24hrs*) Amtrak's Gateway Station at 430 South 15th is part of a state-of-the-art facility that also serves light rail, regional & local buses. ATM, payphones, First-Class lounge, taxi stand.

Connections No Thruway buses

⚍ Local transport Metro (☎231 2345; w metrostlouis.org) operates buses, including the Levee Line between Union Station & the river. The MetroLink light rail system extends 38 miles (61km) from Lambert-St Louis International

Airport to Shiloh-Scott (Air Force Base), Illinois College, stopping along the line at major retail, business, recreational & cultural centres, as well as the Convention Center. Passengers can travel from Union Station to Laclede's Landing & all points in between. The Metro also has a 2nd line that goes to the St Louis Galleria & to Shrewsbury.

🚖 **Taxis** County Cab & Yellow Cab ☎656 6705
🚗 **Car rental** Enterprise, 9305 National Bridge Rd; ☎427 7757
🚌 **Greyhound** 430 S 15th; ☎231 4485
✈ **Lambert-St Louis International Airport** 14 miles (22km) northwest by MetroLink train or Metro bus
Tours Gray Line; ☎241 1224. The St Louis Trolley has narrated tours of the most popular sights (w *stlouisfuntours.com*). 2 replica 19th-century steamboats, the *Tom Sawyer* & *Becky Thatcher*, offer 1hr narrated trips on the river (☎*877 982 1410*).

🛈 **Visitors bureau** At the Old Courthouse & 701 Convention Plaza; ☎1 800 916 8938; w explorestlouis.com; ⊕ daily
🏠 **Accommodation** Hotels include the Westin St Louis, 811 Spruce; ☎621 2000; w marriott. com, **$$$$$**; Fleur-de-Lys Mansion, 3500 Russell Bd; ☎773 3500; w thefleurdelys.com, **$$$$**; Drury Inn Union Station, 201 S 20th, adjacent to Union Station; ☎231 3900; w druryhotels. com, **$$$**; Holiday Inn Express, 4630 Lindell Bd; ☎361 4900; w ihg.com/holidayinnexpress, **$$$**; Napoleon's Retreat, 1815 Lafayette Av; ☎772 6979; w napoleonsretreat.com, **$$$**; Pear Tree Inn Union Station, 2211 Market; ☎241 3200; w druryhotels.com, **$$$**.
    Contact Lehmann House Bed & Breakfast, 10 Benton Pl, St Louis, MO 63104; ☎422 1483; w lehmannhouse.com, **$$$**.

Recommended in St Louis

City Museum 750 N 16th; ☎231 2489; w citymuseum.org; ⊕ daily; admission charge. Located in a factory built in 1909 for the International Shoe Company, the museum is an eclectic mix of children's playground, funhouse, surrealistic pavilion & architectural marvel made out of unusual, found objects.
National Museum of Transportation 2933 Barrett Station Rd; ☎965 6212; w transportmuseumassociation.org; ⊕ daily; admission charge. America's greatest collection of railway engines & equipment, including 70 locomotives, plus streetcars, buses & aircraft.
Union Station 18th & Market; ☎421 6655. Opened in 1894, this splendid Romanesque-style building with its great clock tower was once the world's largest & busiest train station. Now a National Historic Landmark, the station has been restored & transformed into a hotel, shopping mall & entertainment venue. More renovations are underway that will include a $45 million aquarium. The Memories Museum, located on the upper level of the train shed, features the history of St Louis Union Station & rail travel in the United States. The Grand Hall has a superb barrel-vaulted gilt ceiling, Tiffany stained glass, scale models of trains, & statues. The impressive 'Allegorical Window' above the main entrance shows 3 women representing the main US train stations during the 1890s – New York, San Francisco & St Louis. Union

Station's past & present can be discovered on self-guided walking tours. Actor Kurt Russell filmed part of *Escape from New York* in Union Station.
Old Courthouse 11 N 4th; ☎655 1700. Built between 1839 & 1862, this architectural masterpiece has restored courtrooms where enslaved African-Americans Dred & Harriet Scott sued for their freedom & suffrage activist Virginia Minor fought for women's right to vote. Special exhibits show St Louis's role in early settlers' movement into western America.
Laclede's Landing On the riverfront, between the Eads & Martin Luther King bridges; ☎241 5875; w lacledeslanding.com. This historic district stands next to the site of Pierre Laclede's original encampment. Dozens of shops & restaurants line 19th-century cobblestone streets decorated with cast-iron lamps.
Cupples House 221 N Grand Bd; ☎977 6630; w slu.edu/samuel-cupples-house; ⊕ Tue–Sat; admission charge. This restored Romanesque mansion dates from 1888 & has 42 rooms, 22 fireplaces, wooden floors, gargoyles & elegant stone carvings, as well as an art gallery.
Missouri History Museum In the Jefferson Memorial Bldg, Forest Park; ☎746 4599; w mohistory.org; ⊕ daily; admission free. Missouri Historical Society displays include Charles Lindbergh's flight suit & items from the 1904 World's Fair.

Scott Joplin State House 2658 Delmar Bd; ☏ 340 5790; ☉ daily; admission charge. Dating from just after the Civil War, this was the home of the composer Scott Joplin in the early 1900s.

Anheuser-Busch Brewery 12th & Lynch; ☏ 577 2626; w budweisertours.com; ☉ daily; admission free. Tour the world's largest brewery, admire the Clydesdale horses & sample a free beer. Take bus #40.

ST LOUIS: ALL ABOARD! (↑40/130↓) The *Texas Eagle* departs on the Missouri Pacific section of the Union Pacific Railroad for a run of almost 4 hours through Mark Twain country to Poplar Bluff.

Mississippi River (↑30/100↓) The shipyard to your left constructs boats for use on the river.

Jefferson Barracks (↑35/95↓) Chief Blackhawk of the Sac Native Americans was imprisoned at this 18th-century post, the oldest operating US military installation west of the Mississippi River.

Pevely (↑70/60↓) The *Texas Eagle* parts company with the Mississippi River.

Big River (↑120/10↓) You cross to the north of Ironton in an area that has some of the world's largest lead and iron ore mines.

⛟ ARCADIA (↑130/110↓) Amtrak's Arcadia station opened in 2016. Passengers in the beautiful Arcadia Valley were once served by St Louis, Iron Mountain & Southern and Missouri Pacific railways but the service ended in 1965. The 1941 MoPac Depot has been renovated but is not used for Amtrak passengers.

⛟ POPLAR BLUFF (↑110/50↓) Winner of the 'all American city' award, 'The Gateway to the Ozarks' is a manufacturing centre located among farmland. Mid-Continent Steel and Wire, America's largest nail manufacturer, is located here and accounts for half of US nail production. Nearby are the Ozark Mountains and Wappapello Lake. The **visitors bureau** is at 1111 W Pine (☏ *573 785 7761;* w *poplarbluffchamber.chambermaster.com*).

Amtrak stops at the historic station with its impressive steps. Built in 1910 by the St Louis, Iron Mountain & Southern Railway, it was renamed the Union Pacific Depot in 1983 and later added to the National Register of Historic Places. The **Mo-Ark Regional Railroad Museum** (*303 Moran St;* ☏*573 785 4539;* ☉ *Sat afternoons*) has photographs of early railroading days, an early steam engine and dining car display, as well as a large model train layout. For many years, train crews would stay in the hotels and boarding houses that once lined the city's streets.

Missouri–Arkansas state line (↑20/30↓) You cross into the smallest state west of the Mississippi.

⛟ WALNUT RIDGE (↑50/106↓) The city is situated at the junction of the Missouri Pacific (now Union Pacific) and the St Louis & San Francisco (now BNSF) railroads. The restored 1908 Italianate–Mediterranean-style train station, originally belonging to the Missouri Pacific, is located in a downtown park. The building is also used by the local Chamber of Commerce and serves the nearby cities of Jonesboro, Paragould and Pocahontas. Close by are Lake Charles State Park and one of Arkansas's first settlements, Old Davidsonville. The US government opened Walnut Ridge Flying School to train World War II pilots and part of the base was later turned into an airport.

Newport (↑26/80↓) Newport prospered after the Cairo & Fulton Railroad arrived. At neighbouring Jacksonport, Confederate troops massed beside the White River during the Civil War.

Arkansas River (↑105/1↓) You cross the river dividing North Little Rock from Little Rock then see the Capitol dome and city skyline to your left.

⊶⊷ LITTLE ROCK (↑106/45↓) French explorers called this 'La Petite Roche' but the biggest city in Arkansas has been the state capital since 1821. Until Governor Bill Clinton ran for president, Little Rock was best known for its strict 1950s segregationism.

The present Capitol is a smaller version of the one in Washington, DC. An older, Greek-style **state house** at 300 W Markham features Arkansas history and a display in honour of President Clinton, whose Presidential Center opened in 2004. Little Rock hosts the annual autumn state fair and is dominated by the Simmons Tower formerly called the TCBY tower (after The Country's Best Yogurt). At 547ft (167m), the 40-storey skyscraper is the tallest building in Arkansas. Amtrak's depot is at Union Station Square and the **visitors bureau** at 615 E Capitol Avenue (✆*501 371 0076;* w *littlerock.com*).

The *Texas Eagle* leaves with the Capitol again to your left. The train eases through suburbs before entering hillier country covered with forests of pine and hardwood.

Benton (↑30/15↓) The city was named after colourful Missouri Senator Thomas Hart Benton in 1836 when Arkansas became a state. For many years, most of America's aluminium came from local bauxite mines before the high-grade ore gave out. You cross the Saline River soon after leaving Benton.

⊶⊷ MALVERN (↑45/21↓) Malvern was founded in 1870 by the Cairo & Fulton Railroad. The original town of Rockport, located on the Ouachita River, transferred here and changed its name to Malvern Station. Known as 'the brick capital of the world', Malvern has three Acme brick plants and hosts an annual 'Brickfest'. Amtrak's stop at 200 E First also serves **Hot Springs National Park**, established in 1832 and formerly served by a narrow-gauge railroad called the Diamond Jo that replaced the previous stagecoach connection. Hot Springs **visitors bureau** is at 134 Convention Boulevard (✆*1 800 SPA CITY or*✆*501 321 2835;* w *hotsprings.org*).

Ouachita River (↑20/1↓) You cross the river, with Arkadelphia to your right.

⊶⊷ ARKADELPHIA (↑21/40↓) The former steamboat landing stage is famous for its educational establishments, including Ouachita Baptist University and Henderson State University. The restored Italianate/Mediterranean-style station now houses the Clark County Museum, preserving local history from prehistoric times to the present. Amtrak passengers use a covered outdoor waiting area.

A few minutes before reaching Prescott, the *Texas Eagle* crosses the Little Missouri River.

Prescott (↑25/15↓) Note the red-roofed station on your right. This 1912 Missouri Pacific Railroad building now houses the Nevada County Depot & Museum, with exhibits about Civil War battles, railroads and other local history. To the west is the 'Trail of Tears' travelled by Cherokees. Forced by the US Army to move to Oklahoma reservations, a quarter of the Cherokee nation died from inadequate food and clothing in the winter of 1838.

HOPE (↑40/40↓) Look right for an old brick-kiln chimney. 'The watermelon capital of the world' claims the all-time record (265lb/120kg). Richard Ford, author of Pulitzer Prize-winning novel *Independence Day* (1995), lived here while working on the Louisiana–Pacific Railroad in the 1960s.

The town became famous as the birthplace of America's 42nd President, William Jefferson Clinton. The red-brick Mediterranean-style depot was built in 1912 by the St Louis, Iron Mountain & Southern Railroad, and remained in passenger use until 1968. It was renovated following the election of Bill Clinton in 1992 and Amtrak service began in 2013. As well as a visitor centre, the station has a museum featuring the president's life and career. The family house on nearby South Hervey Street is also open to visitors.

Between Hope and the Red River you can see boisdarc trees, often with enormous green seed pods. Otherwise known as the Osage orange, hedge apple or monkey ball, the tree's exceptionally hard wood was used for fence posts and horse-drawn farm implements.

Red River Valley (↑15/25↓) You cross the river on its way south, eventually to join the Mississippi. The valley's red earth washes into the water and gives the river its name. Soya beans and grain now grow on land which once raised cotton.

Homan (↑25/15↓) Pecan trees on both sides of the track prove this really is the South.

Texarkana Airport (↑30/10↓) The runways and buildings of Texarkana Regional Airport, also known as Webb Field, appear to your left.

TEXARKANA (↑40/75↓) When the train stops, its front end is in Texas while the rear remains in Arkansas. Texarkana's unique position calls for two mayors and two police departments, and the post office is the only federal building to straddle a state line. Texarkana was the birthplace of one-time presidential candidate Henry Ross Perot, whose medals are displayed at the local Boy Scout Center. Amtrak passengers use the east end of Union Station, an imposing beige brick structure built in 1930.

The *Texas Eagle* departs, travelling south along the Texas border.

Sulphur River (↑20/55↓) Look left for a paper mill as you cross.

Atlanta (↑30/45↓) Prehistoric Native American settlements have been found nearby.

Jefferson (↑50/25↓) This is one of the state's earliest steamboat ports, where an old cemetery can be seen on the right. Nearby Caddo Lake has a water garden of bayous, cypress trees, Spanish moss, lotuses and water lilies.

MARSHALL (↑75/25↓) Marshall was an important centre for the Texas & Pacific Railway Company (the T&P) from the 1870s. Lady Bird Johnson, First Lady of the United States as wife of President Lyndon B Johnson, and George Foreman, entrepreneur and former heavyweight boxing champion respectively, were born here. When Texas seceded from the Union in 1861, this became one of its largest cities, making ammunition and saddles for the Confederate army. After the fall of Vicksburg, Marshall became the Missouri governor capital. Shreveport, Louisiana, is 25 miles (40km) to the west.

LONGVIEW (↑25/45↓) A railroad surveyor for the Southern Pacific Railroad changed the town's name from Earpville in 1870 after admiring the view from a farmer's front porch. Rail service arrived two years later, when Longview became the head of the former Southern Pacific line.

In 1930, the city's fortunes were transformed dramatically with the discovery of the East Texas Oilfield, the largest in the United States outside Alaska. Longview's population tripled as people came in search of work and prosperity. Amtrak stops at the solid red-brick Colonial Revival depot built in 1940 and lovingly restored; it serves as a multimodal transport centre while retaining its historic features. Thruway buses connect with Houston, Nacogdoches, Galveston and Shreveport.

Gladewater (↑20/25↓)

Gladewater was founded by the Texas & Pacific in 1873 and is located in the middle of east Texas oil country, where the industry expanded hugely after the first major discovery of 1931. Residents from the nearby communities of Point Pleasant and St Clair moved to Gladewater when the railroad announced that this would be the only mail stop in the area.

MINEOLA (↑45/95↓) The depot has been carefully restored to its original 1906 appearance.

The train's route follows the Sabine River for the next 50 miles (80km) through country famous for beef cattle and Quarter Horses.

Big Sandy (↑10/85↓)

Evangelist Garner Ted Armstrong's former Ambassador College is bounded by white-fenced fields on your right.

Grand Saline (↑20/75↓)

Named after the 700ft-deep (210m) salt mine seen to your left.

Mesquite (↑45/50↓)

A large building to your left houses the Mesquite Rodeo and other events. Thorny mesquite scrub trees are a common sight throughout the Southwest.

As the Dallas skyline appears to your right, look for the Texas fairground's Ferris wheel in the distance.

DALLAS (↑95/65↓) The train halts opposite the Hyatt Regency Hotel, mesmerised by its reflection in the glass façade familiar from television's *Dallas*. 'The city that should never have been' had few natural resources and no proper transport links until the railroad arrived. Founded as a log-cabin trading post in 1841, it became a utopian colony of artists and scientists.

Today's Dallas specialises in banking, oil and transport. The city has more shops, Cadillacs and divorces than anywhere else in the world. Neighbouring Fort Worth is more relaxed.

Dallas basics

Telephone code 214

Station (*Ticket office & waiting room* ⏰ 09.00–16.30) Eddie Bernice Johnson Union Station at 400 S Houston is a splendid renovated building decorated with white marble. Opened in 1916, this Beaux-Arts building was constructed by the Union Terminal Company to consolidate 5 Dallas rail stations into 1. At its peak, 80 trains a day stopped at the station. The station has been renovated to serve as an events space & intermodal centre used by DART light rail, TRE commuter trains & local buses as well as Amtrak. Lockers, payphones. vending machines, newspapers, handcarts, restaurant, shops, information centre, taxi stand. A walkway leads to the Hyatt Regency Hotel & Reunion Tower.

Connections Thruway buses serve Shreveport, Vicksburg, Jackson & Meridian

🚌 **Local transport** Dallas is primarily designed for cars but DART commuter rail, light rail, streetcar & bus services (🗲 *979 1111;* w *dart.org*) operate downtown & to the suburbs. The McKinney Av heritage streetcar operates daily, connecting to the Cityplace Station on the DART rail system (🗲 *855 0006;* w *mata.org*).

🚕 **Taxis** Yellow 🗲 426 6262; Ranger Cab 🗲 421 9999

🚗 **Car rental** Hertz, 1200 Ross Av; 🗲 979 9494

🚌 **Greyhound** 205 S Lamar; 🗲 849 6831

✈ **Dallas/Fort Worth Airport** Larger than Manhattan, the airport is 16 miles (25km) west, with bus connections to both downtown areas. Take the Super Shuttle (🗲 *972 615 2410*). The Trinity Railway Express (or TRE) commuter rail line serves Union Station & Dallas/Fort Worth Airport Station (🗲 *817 215 8600*).

Tours Discover Dallas 🗲 521 3737. City Tour (🗲 *310 0700*) has tours around Dallas, including the JFK Experience.

🎫 **Visitors bureau** Old Red Courthouse, 100 South Houston; 🗲 571 1316; w *visitdallas.com*; ⊕ daily

🏠 **Accommodation** Hotels include the Hyatt Regency, 300 Reunion Bd; 🗲 651 1234; w *hyatt. com*, **$$$$**; Lumen, 6101 Hillcrest Av; 🗲 219 2400; w *thelumendallas.com*, **$$$$**; Crowne Plaza, 1015 Elm; 🗲 742 5678; w *ihg.com/ crowneplaza*, **$$$**; Stoneleigh, 2927 Maple Av; 🗲 871 7111; w *marriott.com*, **$$$**; Knights Inn Market Center, 1550 Empire Central; 🗲 638 5151; w *knightsinn.com/dallas-tx*, **$$**.

Corinthian Bed & Breakfast, 4125 Junius St; 🗲 818 0400; w *corinthianbandb.com*, **$$$$**.

Recommended in Dallas

Reunion Tower 300 Reunion Bd; 🗲 712 7040; w *reuniontower.com*; ⊕ daily; admission charge. The best views of Dallas are from the restaurant & observation deck of this 50-storey building next to Union Station. Spectacular light displays from the high geodesic dome after dark.

Old City Park 1515 S Harwood; 🗲 421 5141; w *dallasheritagevillage.org*; ⊕ Tue–Sun; admission charge. Historic buildings relocated from the surrounding area include a blacksmith's shop, general store, railway depot, church & pre-Civil War mansion.

Fair Park 2 miles (3km) east of downtown at 1121 First Av; 🗲 426 3400; w *fairpark.org*. Fair Park has one of the world's largest collections of Art Deco art & architecture, with Texas centennial buildings dating from 1936. The 277-acre (92ha) park has been the site of the annual Texas state fair since 1887 & has symphony concerts, opera, rollercoaster rides & 8 museums.

Museum of the American Railroad 6455 Page St in nearby Frisco; 🗲 428 0101; w *museumoftheamericanrailroad.org*; ⊕ Wed–Sun; admission charge. Features locomotives, passenger cars, freight wagons & 10 cars manufactured by the Pullman Company, including 4 'heavyweight' sleeping cars. Guided tours.

Perot Museum of Nature & Science In Victory Park at 2201 N Field; 🗲 428 5555;

w *perotmuseum.org*; ⊕ daily; admission charge. 5 floors house 11 exhibit halls containing state-of-the-art video & 3D computer animation with thrilling, life-like simulations. The building & outdoor space serve as a living science lesson, offering provocative illustrations of engineering, technology & conservation.

Southfork Ranch About 30mins' drive north of Dallas at 3700 Hogge Dr, Parker; 🗲 972 442 7800; w *southforkranch.com*; ⊕ daily; admission charge. Tour the ranch where TV's *Dallas* was filmed & see the gun that was used to shoot J R Ewing. Lucy's flamboyant wedding dress is among the other memorabilia. Guided tours.

World Aquarium 1801 N Griffin; 🗲 720 2224; w *dwazoo.com*; ⊕ daily; admission charge. Wander safely through a jungle filled with rare plants, monkeys, toucans, crocodiles & jaguars. The aquarium features a 22,000-gallon walk-through tunnel with views of giant catfish, cichlids, huge turtles, stingrays & sea dragons.

Dallas Zoo 650 South R L Thornton Frwy; 🗲 469 554 7500; w *dallaszoo.com*; ⊕ daily; admission charge. View more than 2,000 animals from a monorail train as you travel through the wilds of Africa. The new $14 million Hippo Outpost is an immersive African waterhole habitat that includes an underwater viewing area.

The Sixth Floor Museum at Dealey Plaza 411 Elm; ☎747 6660; w jfk.org; ☉ daily; admission charge. The old Texas schoolbook depository now contains a museum which recreates the southeast window area as it looked on 22 Nov 1963 when President John F Kennedy was assassinated. The museum uses films, photographs, radio broadcasts & reconstructions to tell the story. Dramatic views of Dealey Plaza & tours.

DALLAS: ALL ABOARD! (↑95/65↓)

You leave Dallas with Dealey Plaza to your right. President Kennedy was shot here and the familiar scene still provokes a shiver. The train goes over the overpass that JFK's motorcade sped under after he was shot.

The *Texas Eagle* crosses the Trinity River.

Grand Prairie (↑25/40↓)

The former Dallas naval air station on your left is now an Armed Forces Reserve Complex for military training.

Arlington (↑35/30↓)

Part of the University of Texas can be seen to your right, with Six Flags Over Texas amusement park in the distance.

Handley (↑45/20↓)

Look left for the manmade Arlington Lake. Lee Harvey Oswald, John F Kennedy's alleged assassin, was buried in Rose Hill Cemetery to your right.

⊷ FORT WORTH (↑65/40↓)

The sister city of Dallas became a shipping point for cattle when citizens financed a 26-mile (42-km) link to the Texas & Pacific Railroad in 1876. After this line opened, cattle no longer had to be driven north to Kansas. Fort Worth has acquired other industries since but its old Cowtown flavour still persists. Amtrak uses the Intermodal Transportation Center (ITC), located near Sundance Square and the Botanical and Water Gardens. The **visitors bureau** is at 508 Main, Sundance Square (☎817 698 3300; w fortworth.com).

The **Grapevine Vintage Railroad** (☎1 800 457 6338; w grapevinetexasusa.com) operates steam trains with vintage 1920s coaches from Thursday to Saturday, starting from the Fort Worth stockyards. Formerly known as the *Tarantula Train*, it travels over a 21-mile (34km) route to Grapevine on tracks of the St Louis Southwestern Railway (sometimes called the 'Cotton Belt'), going through the centre of town with excellent views of the skyline as you cross the Trinity River on massive trestles and follow part of the Chisholm Trail. The stockyards station at 140 E Exchange Avenue is the largest train station in the Southwest.

The *Texas Eagle* goes south from Fort Worth on a Burlington Northern/Santa Fe Railroad line towards the small towns and villages of Texas hill country. This area has an exciting history of Comanche raids and cattle drives.

⊷ CLEBURNE (↑40/60↓)

The town was named after Confederate General Pat Cleburne in 1867, having previously been known as Camp Henderson. Cleburne deals in agricultural crops and livestock, especially longhorn cattle. Amtrak stops at the Intermodal Transportation Depot built in 1999 to replace an 1898 two-storey brick depot. For many years, Cleburne was the site of a major locomotive backshop of the Santa Fe Railroad and some its buildings can be seen on the east side of the track.

Balcones Fault (↑15/45↓)

Limestone hills suddenly rise out of the prairie as the train follows this fault line to San Antonio.

Brazos River (↑17/43↓) After crossing the Noland River you cross the Brazos, which runs to your left into Lake Whitney (15,000 acres/6,000ha of water created by a dam).

Meridian (↑28/32↓) Watch for Angora goats being raised for their mohair. Look also for fields of cotton, still a commonplace sight in the South.

Bosque River (↑30/30↓) You cross the river then accompany it for the next 30 miles (48km).

Clifton (↑40/20↓) Founded by Swedish and Norwegian settlers, the town was originally named Cliff Town after the surrounding limestone cliffs. To your right is one of the region's many limestone quarries.

Middle Bosque River (↑55/5↓) The *Texas Eagle* crosses the river shortly before Crawford, where former president George W Bush has his Prairie Chapel Ranch.

⚞ McGREGOR (↑60/32↓) This is Amtrak's stop for McGregor's bigger neighbour Waco, 20 miles (32km) to the east. McGregor was established in 1882 at the intersection of the Gulf, Colorado & Santa Fe (now BNSF) and St Louis Southwestern (Cotton Belt, now Union Pacific) railroads.

The area hit international headlines when David Koresh and his henchmen allegedly shot dozens of Branch Davidian cult members in 1993 during a siege by federal agents at nearby Mount Carmel. Many members died as fire swept through their ranch.

In 1896, Missouri, Kansas & Texas Railroad agent William G Crush decided as a publicity stunt to take two obsolete 35-US ton (31-tonne) locomotives, paint one green and one red, and put them on a track facing each other a few miles apart on a wide stretch of Texas prairie near Waco. The crews fired up the engines, each pulling seven boxcars, set them moving then jumped off as the trains raced towards each other, picking up speed to 45mph (72km/h) until they met in a spectacular crash. The trains were completely destroyed as the boiler of one locomotive exploded into a cloud of steam, sending iron and debris into the crowd. The publicity stunt was a great success, attracting more than 40,000 paying spectators, but the debris killed two people and seriously injured others. Crush was fired from his job, though he was rehired the following day. Scott Joplin immortalised the disaster with a march, 'The Great Crush Collision'.

Moody (↑10/22↓) Established in 1881 when the Gulf, Colorado & Santa Fe Railway arrived, Moody was named after Lt Colonel William Louis Moody of the Seventh Texas Infantry during the Civil War, who became a director of the GC&SF. This small town boasts a very large (1,679-ft/512-m) television transmission tower.

⚞ TEMPLE (↑32/55↓) The Gulf, Colorado & Santa Fe Railroad connects with the Missouri, Kansas & Texas here, making this a key junction. Thruway buses go to nearby Killeen and Fort Hood.

The town was named after a Santa Fe surveyor in 1880, and the 'Prairie-Beaux Arts' depot was completed in 1911, featuring the Santa Fe trademark (a cross in a circle) formed in brick. In 1989, Santa Fe vacated the depot and by the early 1990s, it was completely abandoned. The city of Temple bought the building and approved $2.4 million for its restoration, which was completed in the year 2000.

The **Santa Fe Depot Railroad and Heritage Museum** (*315 West Av B;* ✆ *254 298 5172;* w *templerrhm.org;* ⊕ *Tue–Sat; admission charge*) has vintage furniture and equipment, including a working telegraph machine.

The *Texas Eagle* continues on the Union Pacific line through ranch land and tree-covered hills.

Little River (↑25/30↓) You cross the river near the town of the same name.

San Gabriel River (↑40/15↓) As you cross look right for pecan trees growing on the river's banks.

₩₩ TAYLOR (↑55/42↓) Founded in 1876 pending the arrival of the International & Great Northern Railroad, this rail town was named Taylor Station then Taylorsville after Edward Moses Taylor, a railroad official. In 1882, the Missouri, Kansas & Texas Railroad was extended to Taylorsville and was joined with the Missouri Pacific to link east and west. The town officially became Taylor in 1892 and still ships much of the prairie's ranch and farm produce. This was the birthplace of cartoonist and voice actor Frederick Bean 'Tex' Avery, creator of such animated greats as Daffy Duck and Bugs Bunny.

Round Rock (↑22/20↓) This is a residential town for many people who commute to Austin.

Camp Mabry (↑35/7↓) The US Army base seen to your right was established in 1892 and houses the headquarters of the Texas Military Forces as well as its museum.

₩₩ AUSTIN (↑42/40↓) Capital of Texas and a former capital of the Texas Republic, Austin was founded in 1839 on hills beside the Colorado River. Richard Linklater's 1991 film *Slacker* was set in Texas University at Austin and the city has become an important film-making centre. The official 'live music capital of the world' is home to thousands of musicians and has more music venues per capita than anywhere else in the country. Austin is also home to the Lyndon Johnson Library and the Harry Ransom Center, where among nine million manuscripts are three versions of *Lady Chatterley's Lover*. This being Texas, the Capitol Building is 7ft (2m) taller than the one in Washington, DC.

The **tourist bureau** is at 602 East Fourth (✆ *512 474 5171;* w *austintexas.org*). Amtrak's brick depot was built in 1947 for the Missouri Pacific Railroad. The Houston & Texas Central Railroad came to Austin in 1871 and the stone Old Depot Hotel was the state's first railroad station, operational from 1871 to 1872. Known as Railroad House, it still stands on Fifth Street and houses an Italian Restaurant.

Colorado River (↑2/38↓) Look back to your left as you cross for views of Austin's skyline, dominated by the Capitol's ornate pink dome.

Aquarina Springs (↑37/3↓) The clear springs to your right are the source of the San Marcos River, which you cross as you enter San Marcos.

₩₩ SAN MARCOS (↑40/85↓) Home of Southwest Texas State University, alma mater of Lyndon Johnson, the town hosts an annual cooking contest for chilli aficionados. The intermodal centre opened in 2001 and serves Amtrak, Greyhound, intercity and local buses.

The train crosses the Guadalupe River.

New Braunfels (↑20/65↓) This town was founded in 1845 by a German prince called Carl von Solms-Braunfels.

San Antonio International (↑50/35↓) The airport can be seen to your right.

Olmos Park (↑52/33↓) The train travels through the middle of a golf course with Trinity University away to your left.

As San Antonio comes into view on the left, look for the 750ft (225m) Tower of the Americas and the green-roofed Tower Life Building (San Antonio's oldest skyscraper).

King William District (↑75/10↓) Victorian houses appear to your left beyond the Pioneer flour mill.

Lone Star Brewery (↑78/7↓) The brewery building is now a museum, seen on your right just before you cross the San Antonio River.

SAN ANTONIO (↑85) For San Antonio city information and through-travel to Los Angeles, see pages 161–74. For passengers between Chicago and Los Angeles, the train pauses to accommodate train-coupling operations. Access to train cars may be limited and temporary power outages will occur, including loss of air conditioning.

USA BY RAIL ONLINE

For additional online content, articles, photos and more on travelling in the USA by rail, why not visit **w** bradtguides.com/usa?

The *City of New Orleans*
Chicago–New Orleans

GENERAL ROUTE INFORMATION

The *City of New Orleans* train divides the United States neatly into two as it travels more than 900 miles (1,450km) from the Great Lakes to the Gulf of Mexico. Between Chicago and New Orleans are prairies, farms, plantations and the Mississippi Basin where Civil War history was made. You also visit Memphis, birthplace of the blues and rock and roll.

The Illinois Central – 'The Mainline of America' – ran from Chicago to New Orleans and, when completed in 1856, was the longest railroad in the world. A previous overnight train on this route was the Illinois Central's premier 'All-Pullman' *Panama Limited*, which had top-class dining and a club car that stocked 42 brands of bourbon. So called in 1911 in anticipation of the opening of the Panama Canal, it replaced the Chicago & New Orleans Limited. The company's original *City of New Orleans* was an all-coach streamliner daytime train and Amtrak revived this name after Steve Goodman's 1970s song became a hit for Arlo Guthrie, Joan Baez and Johnny Cash.

JOINING THE TRAIN

CHICAGO: ALL ABOARD! (↓45) For Chicago city information, see page 83.

ESSENTIAL INFORMATION

HIGHLIGHTS This train takes you on a journey through the heart of America's music heritage, from Chicago with its Symphony Orchestra and electric blues, to Beale Street in Memphis, and New Orleans, birthplace of jazz. You can visit Elvis Presley's Graceland in Memphis and pause in Hazlehurst, where blues legend Robert Johnson was born.

FREQUENCY Daily. The **southbound** service leaves Chicago mid-evening to reach Memphis early next morning and New Orleans by mid-afternoon. Travelling **north**, the train leaves New Orleans mid-afternoon to reach Memphis by late evening and Chicago by early morning.

DURATION 19 hours

RESERVATIONS All reserved

EQUIPMENT Superliner coaches

SLEEPING Superliner bedrooms

FOOD Complete meals, snacks, sandwiches, drinks

LOUNGE CAR Movies, games, hospitality hour. A National Park Service guide provides commentary along the route during summer.

BAGGAGE Check-in service is available at main stations.

The *City of New Orleans* leaves Union Station then reverses for a few minutes before continuing forward with the city's skyline to your left. This train travels on Canadian National (CN) tracks for its entire journey. After crossing the Chicago River, look left for Soldier Field football stadium and a view of Lake Michigan.

Chicago State University (↑20/25↓) Campus
buildings appear on your right just before you cross the Calumet River.

◀◀ HOMEWOOD (↑45/30↓)
This leafy suburb has a neat red-tiled station building seen to your right. The Illinois Central Railroad built this Spanish Colonial-style depot in 1923 to serve the *City of New Orleans* and *Seminole Limited* trains. Homewood is also a suburban Metra station and bus connections are provided by Pace Transit.

You continue through several more attractive suburbs interspersed with stretches of farmland.

◀◀ KANKAKEE (↑30/65↓)
This is one of many flag stops for the *City of New Orleans*, served only when passengers have tickets to or from Kankakee. The former 1898 Illinois Central station has been restored to its former glory and now houses the **Kankakee Railroad Museum** (w *kankakeerrmuseum.com*). Chicago's best-known architect, Frank Lloyd Wright, once lived here and many of the houses feature elaborate stonework, domes and spires.

You travel on through an increasingly rural landscape. Look for farmhouses and gently rolling fields of mostly cotton and soya beans.

Gilman (↑20/45↓)
This agriculture and railroad town used to be a scheduled stop for *City of New Orleans* trains travelling north and is now served by Illini and Saluki trains.

Rantoul (↑45/20↓)
Originally known as Neipswah, an Illiniwek word for 'where the minks are'. This also used to be a stop for the *City of New Orleans* and is served by Illini and Saluki trains.

Chanute Field (↑47/18↓)
The abandoned former US Air Force training base was the largest military centre in the country before the Pentagon was built.

◀◀ CHAMPAIGN-URBANA (↑65/35↓)
Opened in 1999, the Illinois Terminal provides intermodal service to Champaign and nearby Urbana. Thruway buses go

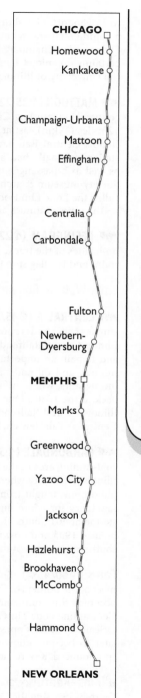

CHICAGO
Homewood
Kankakee

Champaign-Urbana
Mattoon
Effingham

Centralia
Carbondale

Fulton
Newbern-Dyersburg

MEMPHIS
Marks

Greenwood

Yazoo City

Jackson

Hazlehurst
Brookhaven
McComb

Hammond

NEW ORLEANS

to Davenport, Galesburg, Peoria, Bloomington and Indianapolis. Champaign is a commercial and manufacturing centre and the inspiration for an obscure Bob Dylan song, 'Champaign, Illinois', written with the rockabilly great Carl Perkins: 'I certainly do enjoy Champaign, Illinois.' Less industrial Urbana has been home to the University of Illinois since 1867.

MATTOON (↑35/22↓) Another manufacturing town set among Illinois farm country. Lincoln Log Cabin State Park is close by and Eastern Illinois University 12 miles (19km) east at Charleston. The flag stop station is housed in the former Illinois Central Railroad Depot, completed in 1918. This three-storey red-brick station originally had a power plant, mail room, luggage room and restaurant, as well as a passenger hall. Now restored, it houses the Coles County Historical Society museum & archives, Mattoon Tourism & Arts Office and an events space called the Lone Elm Room.

The train continues among more fields, trees, farmhouses and barns.

EFFINGHAM (↑22/45↓) Grain elevators and industrial scenes dominate both sides of the track. The 1924 union station is served by daily Illini and Saluki trains and is a flag stop for the *City of New Orleans*.

Little Wabash River (↑8/37↓) You cross this tributary of the Ohio.

CENTRALIA (↑45/50↓) A new brick depot was built in 2003 to replace a simple shelter and is another flag stop. Centralia was founded by and named after the Illinois Central Railroad in 1853. The yards are among this region's most impressive and remain an important part of the local economy along with agriculture, coal mining, and oil and natural gas production. The town was settled by German immigrants, whose influence is still present today in a historic downtown dating back to the 1880s. One of two remaining 2500-Class steam locomotives from the Illinois Central Railroad (among the largest locomotives ever built) is displayed in Centralia's Fairview Park (the other is in McComb, Mississippi).

CARBONDALE (↑50/105↓) The town acquired its name as the centre of a coal-mining area in the Shawnee Hills region. Carbondale is the home of Southern Illinois University where Buckminster Fuller, pioneer of modern architecture and philosophy, taught from 1959 to 1970. Nearby Crab Orchard wildlife refuge is a sanctuary for wintering birds such as Canada geese. Opened in 1981, Amtrak's station at 401 South Illinois is near the traditionally styled Illinois Central Depot, built in 1903 and now restored. Thruway buses serve St Louis. Carbondale is the southern terminus of the Illini and Saluki routes.

Cairo (↑60/45↓) 'Little Egypt' stands where the Mississippi and Ohio rivers meet at the borders of three states – Illinois, Missouri and Kentucky. General Grant occupied this commanding position during the Civil War. Before that the Illinois Central line ended in Cairo and passengers had to continue their journey to New Orleans by Mississippi steamboat. One of the river pilots then was Samuel Clemens, later to become known as Mark Twain. He said that the south began in Cairo (pronounced 'Kay-ro') and included the town in *The Adventures of Huckleberry Finn*.

Illinois–Kentucky state line (↑62/43↓) You cross the border southeast of Cairo by crossing the Ohio River.

FULTON (↑105/50↓) The city stands directly beside Fulton, Tennessee. Amtrak's modest flag stop station is unstaffed. Huge South and Central American banana cargoes used to be distributed by refrigerated railcar from this 'banana crossroads of the USA'.

Kentucky–Tennessee state line (↑2/48↓) The *City of New Orleans* crosses into the Volunteer State just south of Fulton.

NEWBERN-DYERSBURG (↑50/90↓) Named after William Dyer, a colonel in the War of 1812, Dyersburg processes cotton and other farm produce. Amtrak's Newbern Depot was constructed by Illinois Central in 1920 and also houses a museum commemorating the town's railroading past. Next to the depot is a cotton-loading platform where bales of cotton were taken off wagons and transferred to railcars in the days when Newbern was a major centre for the cotton ginning and the shipment of cotton. With the arrival of the Newport News & Mississippi Valley Railroad in 1884 and the Dyersburg Northern branch line linking the city to Tiptonville, economic expansion boomed as Dyersburg became a railroad hub for three lines.

After travelling most of the way from Chicago in darkness, the train nears Memphis around dawn. As you travel beside the Mississippi River look right for the shiny 32-storey Great American Pyramid which connects to Mud Island. Built in 1991, this former sports and entertainment venue ('the tenth-tallest pyramid in the world') is now a shopping complex.

On your left is Confederate Park and beyond that the old Cotton Row market. Immediately before the station, look left to see the Beale Street District.

MEMPHIS (↑90/60↓) The train trundles through a nondescript part of the city before making a service stop at Amtrak's beautifully restored Central Station, built in 1914. After falling into disrepair, the Central Station was acquired by Memphis Area Transit Authority, which completed a massive renovation project in 1999. On the Main Street side of the station is the Memphis Railroad & Trolley Museum, which includes a history of railroad bridges over the Mississippi River at Memphis and a live steam model of IC Hudson-type locomotive *No 2499*.

Set on bluffs overlooking the Mississippi, Memphis was named by Andrew Jackson in 1819 after the capital of ancient Egypt. It soon became a port and the largest city in Tennessee, with the world's biggest mule-trading market.

Memphis's railroads and a strategic position on the river made it an ideal supply base during the Civil War. The Memphis to Charleston railroad was taken over by Union forces after victories at Fort Pillow and Shiloh. In 1862, eight Confederate steamers were sunk here on the Mississippi River within an hour.

The city remains a major port but hardwoods, soya and other agricultural products have replaced cotton as the chief cargo. Birthplace of Tennessee Williams and the Piggly Wiggly supermarket, Memphis was officially named by *American Heritage* magazine as a 'Great American Place', only the second US destination to be given this award. The first went to Saratoga Springs and subsequent awards have been given to Tucson, Arizona, and Hampton Roads, Virginia. The **visitors bureau** is at 3205 Elvis Presley Boulevard (✆ *901 543 5333*; w *memphistravel.com*).

A free shuttle bus service runs every hour between Graceland, the Sun Studios and Beale Street. **Tours** can be had from Blues City (✆ *901 522 9229*; w *bluescitytours.com*) and riverboat cruises on the *Memphis Queen* (✆ *901 527 2628*; w *memphisriverboats.net*). The room and balcony where Martin Luther King was killed at the Lorraine Motel in 1968 are kept as a memorial.

Blues and Dixieland jazz feature in the handsomely restored Victorian **Beale Street** buildings (☏ *901 526 0115;* w *bealestreet.com*) of W C Handy's home town, which was also the birthplace of Stax Records. Elvis Presley, Roy Orbison, Johnny Cash, the Everly Brothers, Dolly Parton and many others made their earliest recordings at Sam Phillips's **Sun Records studio** (*706 Union Av;* ☏ *1 800 441 6249;* w *sunstudio.com*), a brownstone building preserved in its original state.

Graceland (*3734 Elvis Presley Bd;* ☏ *901 332 3322 or* ☏ *1 800 238 2000;* w *graceland.com*), where 'The King' died in August 1977, is 10 miles to the south. This is the country's second most-visited residence (after the White House). Go early and avoid a grilling wait in summer humidity for a tour of the mansion's surprisingly modest rooms, admire Elvis's 1955 pink Cadillac and put flowers beside his bronze gravestone.

The **Peabody Hotel** (*149 Union Av;* ☏ *901 529 4000;* w *peabodymemphis.com*), where the Tom Cruise film *The Firm* was made, has been restored to its original ornate splendour. Live ducks fed on strawberries and lettuce leaves are paraded from their rooftop home each day to splash in the lobby's marble fountain.

The train pulls out of Memphis among freight and storage facilities then travels through wooded, undulating country. Between here and New Orleans you mostly accompany the route of Interstate 55.

After 25 minutes, the Mississippi River appears again to your right beyond a line of trees as the train enters delta country – a flat land of cotton fields, woods, sluggish streams with Native American names, swamps, Spanish moss, and small towns with dirt roads and Baptist churches. This is the land of William Faulkner's fictional Yoknapatawpha County and Will Percy's *Lanterns on the Levee*. It was here that early blues singers such as Charley Patton and Robert Johnson played and made their first recordings. Others later took the train and their music north to Chicago.

🚉 MARKS (↑60/60↓)

The town was named after Leopold Marks, who left Germany in 1868 to avoid conscription by the German army. He acquired large holdings on the banks of the Coldwater River and became Quitman County's first representative to the state legislature. He encouraged the Yazoo & Mississippi Valley Railroad to come here by giving the company free right of way through his plantation plus 10 acres (40,000m^2) of land. Marks was the starting point in 1968 of Dr Martin Luther King Jr's Poor People's Campaign.

Amtrak's \$1.2 million rail passenger facility, opened in 2018, has a concrete platform and open-air shelter with benches and heating elements. The station is downtown, within walking distance of the domed Quitman County Courthouse.

You continue south through North Money, with extensive cotton fields seen on both sides. As you approach Greenwood, look left to see a lake and church among the trees.

🚉 GREENWOOD (↑60/55↓)

The *City of New Orleans* holds up traffic as it pauses across the town's main street. Amtrak's neat brick station is to your right, with the town beyond. Built in 1917 by the Yazoo & Mississippi Valley Railroad, the station is in Greenwood's Railroad Historic District, added to the National Register of Historic Places in 1985.

Named after Choctaw Chief Greenwood Leflore, Greenwood became known in the 19th century as the 'Cotton Capital of the World', shipping to Vicksburg, St Louis, Memphis and New Orleans. The cotton industry declined after the Civil War but Greenwood was saved by the arrival of the railroad in the 1880s, when two lines intersected: the Columbus & Greenville Railway and the Illinois Central. The city again became an important cotton shipping point and Front Street was known as Cotton Row. Little Richard recorded a song called 'Greenwood, Mississippi' and other local musicians have included Mississippi John Hurt, B B King and Walter 'Furry' Lewis. Blues legend Robert Johnson has three memorial gravestones in the Greenwood area.

You leave past a decaying railway building to your left then pass modern houses before seeing more cotton fields, processing plants and mansions. The train moves deeper into the South, passing small towns with white clapboard churches. There are houses with verandas, dusty roads, abandoned shacks and muddy, meandering rivers lined with trees. Woods and green fields start to predominate as you near Yazoo City.

⬆⬇ YAZOO CITY (↑55/60↓) The town was named in 1839 by French explorer Robert La Salle after a Native American word meaning 'River of Death'. Parts of the Coen Brothers' film, *O Brother, Where Art Thou?* were filmed in Yazoo City. Note the impressive church to your left and an abandoned railway building to your right. Amtrak's platform station is an unstaffed flag stop.

The train departs through attractive forest and crosses several narrow, almost dry streams. You see cypress trees, sleepy towns and sun-bleached barns. Look also for log stacks being sprayed with water to keep them cool.

One of America's most famous train wrecks occurred just east of here on a rainy night in April 1900. The *Cannonball Express*, speeding to make up time between Memphis and Canton, ploughed into the back of a stationary freight train at Vaughan. The train's headstrong engineer, John Luther 'Casey' Jones, died on board *No 382* but his skill saved others' lives. A friend of his wrote the well-known song and sold it for a case of gin. Vaughan's depot has a museum in Casey Jones's honour.

⬆⬇ JACKSON (↑60/28↓) Named after Andrew Jackson, Mississippi's capital and largest city began as a trading post beside the Pearl River and had to survive being burned down during the Civil War. You can tour the gold-domed Capitol and Greek-style Governor's Mansion. Amtrak's Georgian Revival-style station was built in 1927. Train service first came to Jackson in 1840, when the Clinton & Vicksburg Railway arrived, and the city became a prominent rail hub after the Civil War as a stop for the Illinois Central. The **visitors bureau** is at 111 E Capitol (☎ *1 800 354 7695;* w *visitjackson.com*).

As you depart, look left for the old 1840 Capitol (now a history museum) and the Arts Center Planetarium.

Crystal Springs (↑24/4↓) 'The tomato capital of the world' is famed for its bumper crops. This is also a well-known turkey-hunting area.

⬆⬇ HAZLEHURST (↑28/19↓) Birthplace in 1911 or 1912 of Robert Johnson, the most influential blues artist of all time, Hazlehurst hosts a **Robert Johnson Blues and Heritage Festival** each May to celebrate the birthday of the man who some claim 'sold his soul to the devil' at the crossroads. The city was named after George Hazlehurst, chief engineer and surveyor for the New Orleans, Jackson & Great Northern Railroad. Lumber and other freight wagons gather to your left with the station and town to your right.

You leave among pine forests, massive lumber yards and processing plants. As well as timber, this region produces pine oil and turpentine.

Wesson (↑13/6↓) Wesson used to have a hotel casino where passengers could while away their time and money between trains.

⚶ BROOKHAVEN (↑19/22↓) A recruiting town during the Civil War, Brookhaven deals in oil, timber and farm produce. The *City of New Orleans* stops at the Godbold Transportation Center, opened in 2011 in the city's handsome former power plant with its tall smokestack. Large expanses of glass allow natural light to flood the waiting room and the wooden benches were once in the 1907 Illinois Central depot downtown, now occupied by the Military Memorial Museum.

This is Amtrak's nearest stop to **Natchez**, home of 'King Cotton'. Natchez is considered the prettiest town on the Mississippi, with many of its ante-bellum homes furnished in authentic style. Visitors are escorted around by brisk society matrons during the Natchez Pilgrimage (four weeks in March/April, three weeks in October).

You leave Brookhaven among the town's older residential suburbs, with the Bogue Chitto River to your left.

⚶ McCOMB (↑22/50↓) Amtrak's flag stop is at the single-storey McComb depot built by the Illinois Central in 1901 as a 'combination' depot that included passenger and freight functions under one roof. Look for the IC's green diamond emblem etched in coloured masonry. The restored station also houses the **McComb Railroad Museum** (☏ *601 684 2291; w mcrrmuseum.com*), which has more than 1,500 catalogued items. Outside can be seen a 200-US ton (181-tonne) steam locomotive, one of the two largest steam engines in the Illinois Central Railroad fleet, as well as the only aluminium refrigerator car ever built and a 1966 cupola-style caboose. The town was named after Colonel Henry McComb, who took charge of rebuilding the New Orleans, Jackson & Great Northern Railroad after the Civil War.

McComb is the birthplace of blues musician Bo Diddley, pop singer Britney Spears, and of Sim Webb (Casey Jones's fireman). The camellias and azaleas are especially fine during spring and the city has more varieties than anywhere else in the country.

Illinois Central freight yards appear to your left as the train travels past lines of wagons loaded with logs.

Magnolia (↑10/40↓) The state's official flower, the giant magnolia, gave its name to the town. Look right for colonial mansions hiding among the trees.

Tangipahoa River (↑12/38↓) You cross the river, which continues to your left.

Mississippi–Louisiana state line (↑20/30↓) The border is crossed just south of the small town of Osyka. You travel among beautiful ranches and pine trees, with modest houses fronted by porches and rocking chairs.

Kentwood (↑27/23↓) Look left soon after Kentwood for the Camp Moore Cemetery and Museum. The camp was a training ground for Confederate troops during the Civil War.

Amite (↑36/14↓) New Orleans-type ironwork decorates some of the houses. This area, known as the Florida Parishes, belonged to Florida until 1810. Strawberry plantations appear on both sides until the train approaches Hammond through thick forest.

Independence (↑45/5↓) On your right are Southeastern Louisiana College and an above-the-ground cemetery, or 'city of the dead'.

⊶ HAMMOND (↑50/60↓) Vast quantities of fruit used to be sent aboard the *Crimson Flower* train to Chicago and New York from Hammond, the so-called 'strawberry capital of the world'. The red-brick station with its pointed octagonal tower was built in Queen Anne Revival style by the Illinois Central in 1912.

You depart past warehouses, a flea market and freight cars loaded with wood chippings. Note the rusting Illinois Central caboose to your left just before Ponchatoula.

Ponchatoula (↑6/54↓) A *Louisiana Express* locomotive stands on the left at the picturesque station building. You pass three large greenhouses and, a few minutes later, enter Cajun country. In this eerily beautiful land of forests, swamps and water hyacinths, egrets fly among the evergreen live-oaks and cypress trees are draped with Spanish moss. During earlier days, trains sometimes had to stop for the engineer to remove an occasional alligator sunning itself on the rails.

Interstate 55 (↑7/53↓) The highway to your right strides across the wet wilderness on two arched bridges supported by concrete pillars. Look right for water lilies among the reeds, rushes and trees. You may also see alligators and such exotic birds as pelicans, black herons and egrets.

The *City of New Orleans* curves left around oceanic Lake Pontchartrain, the state's largest expanse of water, as the train travels for 49,884ft, or 9½ miles (15km), on the longest continuous railway curve in the world.

Pass-Manchac (↑10/50↓) You cross the waterway linking Lake Pontchartrain with Lake Maurepas to your right.

Louis Armstrong Airport (↑33/27↓) Formerly known as Moisant Field, New Orleans's international airport appears on the left beyond factories and warehouses.

Xavier University (↑51/9↓) Look right for campus buildings as you approach New Orleans with the skyline ahead to your left featuring the massive Superdome.

The train continues to crawl towards the city before making a safety stop and reversing into the station.

⊶ NEW ORLEANS (↑60) Thruway buses connect with Baton Rouge, Mobile and Montgomery. For New Orleans city information, see page 155.

14

The Northeast Corridor
Boston–Washington, DC

GENERAL ROUTE INFORMATION

This is the fastest and busiest route in the country and the only one where Amtrak owns most of the track and stations. Since 1986, Amtrak has been the dominant carrier, moving more passengers between New York and Washington, DC than any airline. The main line of the Northeast Corridor (NEC) is 457 miles (735 km) long between Boston and Washington, DC, and it also serves major cities such as New York, Baltimore and Philadelphia. Connecting corridors take you to Harrisburg, PA, Springfield, MA, Albany, NY and Richmond, VA, covering a total of 899 miles (1,447km). This intricate railroad system is one of the most complex and heavily used in the world.

More than 260 million passenger trips are made on the NEC each year, of which 17.1 million are made by Amtrak passengers. More than 2,100 passenger trains and 60 freight trains operate on some portion of the NEC every day.

Acela Express trains capable of 150mph (240km/h) have been introduced on Amtrak's 'main street' and services are frequent and fast. En route you encounter cities, rural scenery and splendid seascapes. Some trains go all the way between

ESSENTIAL INFORMATION

HIGHLIGHTS Visit exciting and culturally rich cities such as Washington, DC, with its grand public buildings and Smithsonian Institute, the historic monuments of Philadelphia, vibrant New York City and sophisticated Boston, where you can follow the Freedom Trail to some of America's most significant landmarks.
FREQUENCY Over 40 trains daily, running almost 24 hours a day out of New York. *Northeast Regional* trains operate hourly between New York and Washington, DC, taking six hours for the journey. *Acela Express* trains take an hour less.
DURATION Seven hours (*Acela*); eight hours (Regional)
RESERVATIONS Most trains are reserved. First-Class *Acela* train passengers have the benefit of assigned seating, allowing seat selection and reservation ahead of time. You can select a single seat, a double seat or a two- or four-person conference table arrangement. Reservations can be made with your travel agent or on the Amtrak app or website. Seats can be changed only prior to boarding and there is no associated fee.
EQUIPMENT Amfleet and *Acela* coaches. Through-trains from Boston to Washington, DC have Club cars. Wi-Fi.
FOOD Most trains provide snacks, sandwiches and drinks
BAGGAGE No check-in service is available on this route.

Boston and Washington, DC while others operate over just part of the line. Pennsylvania Railroad services used to rejoice in names such as *Constitution*, *Judiciary*, *Potomac* and *President* but Amtrak's trains are now more prosaically given mere numbers. Trains may not stop at every station indicated, so check when buying your ticket.

More economical *Northeast Regional* trains have reduced the time between Boston and New York by as much as 90 minutes, making the journey in 4½ hours. The *Acela Express* cuts this by another hour. *Acela Express* trains operate hourly between New York, Washington, DC, and intermediate cities, as well as round trips between New York and Boston. *Northeast Regional* trains serve more stations. *Northeast Regional* coaches have been refurbished with improved seats and overhead lights and have a more modern colour scheme. They also give a much smoother ride. The motive power is mostly provided by Bombardier/Alstom 8,000-horsepower locomotives capable of up to 125mph (200km/h).

Acela-Express trains consist of one First-Class and four Business-Class cars, with a total seating of 304 passengers. First and Business Class are more comfortable than *Northeast Regional* coaches, with lumbar support, moveable armrests and headrests, laptop outlets, conference tables, extra telephones, deluxe rest rooms and personal controls for lights and audio. The current *Acela Express* equipment will be replaced by new Avelia Liberty trainsets beginning in 2021 and Amtrak will retire all current trainsets by the end of 2022.

ClubAcela is available in Washington, DC, Philadelphia, New York and Boston for travellers with First-Class *Acela Express* or sleeping-car tickets. These lounges offer a comfortable, quiet environment with complimentary soft drinks, juice, coffee and snacks, newspapers, periodicals, Wi-Fi, use of photocopy machines, conference rooms, television, advance boarding, and personal assistance with reservations and ticketing.

Acela Express trains reach up to 150mph (240km/h) on their 231-mile (372km) sprint between Boston and New York, and travel at 135mph (216km/h) from New York to Washington, DC, taking 6½ hours for the whole 457-mile (735km) Boston–Washington, DC run on 'America's Super Railroad'.

Many Northeast Corridor trains have a Quiet Car, where passengers are asked not to use mobile phones, pagers, or the sound feature of their laptops, and to speak only in subdued tones. There is no additional charge, but seating is first come, first served and cannot be reserved specifically. Announcements are made in stations and on the trains as to the location of the Quiet Car.

𝆄 BOSTON (5↓) English Puritans arrived in the 17th century, and the Revolution began here when British troops fired on colonists during the 'Boston Massacre' of 1770. New England's largest city became the hub of the solar system, where 'the Lowells spoke only to Cabots and the Cabots spoke only to God'.

Today's Boston is one of America's most sophisticated and attractive cities. Modern buildings, green spaces and the Cheers bar mingle successfully with older parts of the city.

Boston basics

✎Telephone code 617

𝆄 Station (*Ticket office* ☺ *04.45–21.40; waiting room* ☺ *24hrs*) Amtrak's restored South Station at Atlantic Av & Summer was Boston's first Beaux-Arts building. When completed in 1899, this was the largest structure in Boston & the busiest railway station in the world, serving nearly 40 million passengers a year. It was built to combine the services of the 5 passenger lines in the city's crowded south side: the Boston & Albany, New England, Boston & Providence, Old Colony, & New York, New Haven & Hartford railroads. With its curved façade & eagle-topped clock, this historic building is today a major intermodal transport hub serving the Greater Boston region & the midwestern & northeastern United States. ClubAcela Lounge. Lockers, payphones, Wi-Fi, newspapers, Red Caps, restaurants, shops, ATM banking, taxi stand.

Connections Amtrak *Downeaster* trains to New Hampshire & Maine arrive & depart from Boston's renovated North Station at 126 Causeway St (*North Station ticket office* ☺ *07.30–18.00 Mon–Fri, 08.00–19.30 Sat–Sun; waiting room* ☺ *05.00–01.00*)

All other Amtrak services in Boston depart from South Station & Back Bay Station. Passengers transferring between the *Downeaster* & other Amtrak services must arrange their own transfer between stations in Boston. Passengers travelling with significant luggage or young children should transfer by taxi to their continuing Amtrak train at South Station. Other passengers should connect to their continuing Amtrak train at Back Bay Station using the Orange Line subway.

🚍 Local transport MBTA (*10 Park Plaza;* ✆*222 3200;* w *mbta.com*) operates commuter trains from South Station to points south & west, & to points north & northwest from North Station.

You can see the city best on foot, with help from an MBTA system that includes bus, trolley &

subway (the 'T'). A subway stop is located in the station & a 'T passport' offers unlimited travel on buses & the subway as well as discounts at various attractions.

🚕 Taxis Red Cab ✆734 5000; Zride ✆431 3908

🚗 Car rental Thrifty ✆457 8157; Budget ✆248 0128

🚌 Greyhound 700 Atlantic Av, South Station; ✆526 1801

✈ Logan Airport East Boston, easy to reach by bus, car, taxi, the MBTA's Blue Line subway & Boston Express buses, as well as the Logan Express bus service

Tours Brush Hill Tours; ✆720 6342. National park rangers lead Black Heritage Trail walking tours, beginning at the Robert Gould Shaw & 54th Regiment Memorial on the corner of Park & Beacon (✆*617 742 5415*). Harbour & island trips from Bay State Cruises (✆*748 1428*).

🛈 Visitors bureau 2 Copley Pl; ✆536 4100 or ✆888 733 2678; w bostonusa.com. There is an information booth on Boston Common at Tremont & Park (☺ *daily*), & the National Historical Park Service is at 15 State (✆*242 5642;* w *nps.gov/bost*).

🏠 Accommodation For discount rates contact Citywide Reservation Services, 839 Beacon; ✆859 8880.

Hotels include the Copley Square, 47 Huntington Av; ✆536 9000; w copleysquarehotel.com, **$$$$$**; Eliot, 370 Commonwealth Av; ✆267 1607; w eliothotel. com, **$$$$$**; Lenox, 61 Exeter; ✆536 5300; w lenoxhotel.com, **$$$$$**; Park Plaza, 50 Park Pl; ✆426 2000; w bostonparkplaza.com, **$$$$$**; Studio Allston, 1234 Soldiers Field Rd; ✆206 1848; w hotelstudioallston.com, **$$$$**; Courtyard, 275 Tremont; ✆426 1400; w marriott. com, **$$$**; Ramada, 800 Morrissey Bd; ✆287 9100; w wyndhamhotels.com/ramada, **$$$**.

Contact the B & B Agency of Boston, 47 Commercial Wharf, Boston, MA 02110; ☎720 3540; w boston-bnbagency.com.

International (IYHF) Hostel, 19 Stuart; ☎536 9455; w bostonhostel.org. Members & non-members, **$**.

Recommended in Boston

Museum of Fine Arts 465 Huntington Av; ☎267 9300; w mfa.org; ⊕ daily; admission charge. Includes art from Egypt, Asia & Europe, with more than 450,000 works of art, including 40 by Monet, as well as portraits of eminent Americans such as George Washington. The Art of the Americas wing features paintings, sculpture & decorative arts created throughout North, Central & South America over 3,000 years.

Museum of Science Science Park; ☎723 2500; w mos.org; ⊕ daily; admission charge. The museum has a planetarium with laser displays, a butterfly garden, dinosaurs & a theatre showing films on a giant IMAX screen.

Freedom Trail 44 School; ☎357 8300; w thefreedomtrail.org; ⊕ daily. Most of Boston's historic buildings can be explored by following the Freedom Trail, marked somewhat erratically in red on the pavements. Information & a free map are available from the booth on Boston Common. 13 of the 16 places on the trail are free or by donation (except for The Old South Meeting House, Old State House and Paul Revere House). The USS *Constitution* is usually berthed at the former Charlestown Navy Yard. Launched in Boston in 1797, the oldest commissioned warship now afloat earned her nickname 'Old Ironsides' during the War of 1812 when she fought the British frigate HMS *Guerriere*.

Bunker Hill Monument A 221ft (67m) obelisk memorial erected between 1827 & 1843 to commemorate the battle fought nearby during the War of Independence. The granite was brought from Quincy, MA, to the site on the Granite Railway, built specially for that purpose. There are 294 steps to the top for excellent views of the city & harbour.

Museum of Afro-American History 46 Joy; ☎725 0022; w afroammuseum.org; ⊕ daily except Sun; admission free. Located in what was once the first publicly funded school for African-Americans, the museum has many exhibits showing their contribution to the city's history.

John F Kennedy Library & Museum Near the University of Massachusetts in Dorchester; ☎514 1600; w jfklibrary.org; ⊕ daily; admission charge. Photographs, films & memorabilia trace the Kennedy family history. You can listen to JFK's speeches & review the Nixon–Kennedy debates in an impressive building designed by I M Pei.

Isabella Stewart Gardner Museum 25 Evans Way; ☎566 1401; w gardnermuseum.org; ⊕ closed Tue; admission charge. Built in 1903 around a courtyard in the style of a 15th-century Italian palace, the museum's art collection includes Renoirs & many Renaissance works.

Harvard University Art Museums 32 Quincy in Cambridge; ☎495 9400; w harvardartmuseums. org; ⊕ daily; admission charge (1 admission covers all 3 museums), Sat free before noon. The Sackler has Roman, Egyptian & Islamic antiquities. The adjacent Fogg Museum features European, Asian & American art, & the Busch-Reisinger Museum specialises in art from Germany.

14

BOSTON: ALL ABOARD! (5↓) The Capitol, seen high above the city as the train departs, is topped by a marble dome and a statue of 'the independent man'. For the best coastal views choose a seat on the left of the train when travelling south.

⚊⚊ BACK BAY STATION (↑5/10↓) A subterranean station serves Copley Square, the Prudential Center and downtown hotels and is also a stop for many commuter trains. Amtrak trains pause only to receive passengers (or discharge them if travelling north). Back Bay Station was built in 1987 to replace the New Haven Railroad's 1928 station.

You leave and continue for several minutes below ground, occasionally surfacing amid concrete car parks for glimpses of Boston's skyline back to your right.

⚊⚊ ROUTE 128 (↑10/28↓) Trains pause only to receive passengers (or discharge them if travelling north) at this south suburban halt. Route 128 is one of Amtrak's main weapons in its battle with the airline shuttle services, being closer to New York and more convenient than Logan Airport for most people in southern and western Boston. The New Haven Railroad opened Route 128 station in the suburb of Westwood in 1953 as one of the first passenger rail facilities designed for travellers arriving by car. The current bright and spacious building, opened in 2000, has a glass-fronted waiting room facing the tracks.

You pass freight and warehouse facilities on your right, then travel through suburbs and woodland before entering the flat landscape of eastern Massachusetts.

Attleboro (↑20/8↓) Jewellery manufacturing began here in 1913 with the Balfour Company and many firms still operate in 'The Jewelry Capital of the World'. The **Attleboro Arts Museum** is at 86 Park Street (↘ 508 222 2644; w *attleboroartsmuseum.org*). Look left as you depart to see an imposing white church and steeple.

Approaching Providence you cross the border into Rhode Island. The city's green-domed Capitol and skyscrapers are ahead with freight yards to the right.

▄▟▛ PROVIDENCE (↑28/22↓) The capital of America's smallest state (Rhode Island) has many interesting 18th- and 19th-century buildings. The 1786 John Brown House at Benefit and Power is furnished in period style. The Roger Williams Memorial is located on the site of the original 1636 settlement. Other highlights include the Capitol and the Athenaeum Library where Edgar Allan Poe courted Sarah Whitman (his inspiration for Annabel Lee). The **visitors bureau** is at 1 Sabin (↘*401 751 1177 or*↘*1 800 233 1636;* w *pwcvb.com*).

Located near the statehouse grounds, the station opened in 1986 and is a masterpiece of Brutalist architecture with a large square clock tower.

Note the impressive Postmodern apartment block to your left as the train pulls out from next to the Capitol.

East Greenwich (↑12/10↓) The old seaport's 1773 General Varnum House and garden are preserved in their original condition (w *varnumcontinentals.org*). Narragansett Bay and its colourful yachts come into view to your left before the train departs temporarily inland through wooded countryside.

▄▟▛ KINGSTON (↑22/10↓) Some of the buildings in this quiet town date from when it was an 18th-century trading centre for plantation owners. The George Fayerweather House was built by the blacksmith son of a slave. Look for the lumber company mural to the right of a picturesque yellow clapboard station flanked by evergreens. Located in West Kingston, this is Amtrak's nearest stop to Newport, famous for its naval base, mansions and jazz festival (*connections by van/car;* ↘*401 295 1100*). Other sights in this former colonial seaport include the Friends Meeting House (1699) and the Old Colony House (1739). A seasonal ferry service from Kingston serves the island of Martha's Vineyard (↘ *401 295 4040;* w *vineyardfastferry.com*).

You continue west among woods, streams and marshes.

▄▟▛ WESTERLY (↑10/10↓) This 18th-century town is situated on the border between Rhode Island and Connecticut. Ancient industrial buildings stand on the opposite side of the track from the renovated station.

Between Westerly and New Haven the train accompanies an attractive shoreline to your left.

Stonington (↑5/5↓) This well-preserved coastal town boasts Connecticut's first lighthouse (now a museum) erected in 1823. You can tour vineyards in summer and take boat trips to the Isle au Haut.

As you depart past a marina and dry dock, look right for a Christmas tree plantation and several old railroad cars converted into unusual homes.

⊷ MYSTIC (↑10/10↓) Built in 1905, the charming wooden shingle-style station on your right has been restored to its pink and yellow glory. The town is on the banks of the Mystic River and owes its existence to the sea and shipbuilding. Vessels constructed here include one of America's first ironclad warships, the *Galena*, and the clipper *Andrew Jackson*, which sailed to San Francisco round Cape Horn in a record 89 days in 1859–60. **Mystic Seaport Museum** (✆ *860 572 0711;* w *mysticseaport.org*) has one of the largest outdoor displays in the country, with a 19th-century whaling ship, the *Charles Morgan*, moored in a recreated New England village. This was the last wooden whaler ever built (in 1841) and you can tour it, cramped conditions, ghoulish vats and all.

You pass another marina then continue along an embankment where water and pleasure craft can be seen on both sides. The pretty shoreline ahead features many inlets, trees and herons.

⊷ NEW LONDON (↑10/20↓) Trains cross the River Thames (rhymes with 'shames') on a steel bridge before entering a large Romanesque Union Station, the last and largest designed by Henry Hobson Richardson and built in 1887. One of Amtrak's first major restoration projects, this is an important transit centre for southeastern Connecticut, with connections to local and intercity buses as well as ferries to Long Island, Fishers Island and Block Island. Thruway buses link with Foxwoods Casino.

New London, among North America's earliest settlements, grew rich on whaling. The **Lyman Allyn Museum** (*625 Williams;* ✆ *860 443 2545;* w *lymanallyn.org*) is dedicated to a whaling captain and the seagoing tradition continues at the US Coastguard Academy. The training vessel *Eagle* can usually be seen either moored to your left or in full sail on the river. New London's shipyards launched the world's first nuclear submarine, *Nautilus*.

From here to Old Saybrook, trains run mostly alongside the beach, with the waters of Niantic Bay just a few feet from the track. Look for sunbathers, fishing boats and enviable homes.

Connecticut River (↑14/6↓) You cross the river on a drawbridge then continue among marshes.

⊷ OLD SAYBROOK (↑20/30↓) The elegant clapboard station was constructed in 1873.

Long Island Sound and some of its small islands can be seen to your left as the train speeds along this coastal stretch. Approaching New Haven you see a power plant and docks to your left before the train crawls through rail yards into the station.

⊷ NEW HAVEN (↑30/25↓) The first planned city in the USA, this is where the first sulphur matches and Colt revolvers were made. Other firsts claimed are the hamburger, pizza and frisbee, named after apple-pie plates from the Frisbie Pie Company. Founded in 1638 as Quinnipiac and renamed two years later, New Haven became one of the strictest Puritan towns. Dr Benjamin Spock was brought up here, where his father was a lawyer with the New Haven Railroad. The **visitors bureau** is at 127 Washington Avenue (✆*203 777 8550;* w *visitnewhaven.com*).

Amtrak's restored Union Station was designed by architect Cass Gilbert and opened in 1920. The grand four-storey building symbolised New Haven's position as the main passenger and freight carrier in lower New England and serves the city today as a busy intermodal centre with Amtrak, commuter rail and bus connections. It is also a planned stop on the route of the New Haven–Hartford–Springfield (NHHS) Rail Project, aimed at creating new commuter and intercity passenger services for cities along Amtrak's Springfield Line. Look right for Amtrak trains from Springfield and Hartford joining the main Northeast Corridor line as Metro-North trains wait on your left.

New Haven surrounds a green with three historic churches and you can take a cruise on the sound from Long Wharf dock. Nearby are Fort Nathan Hale, the Pardee-Morris House and **Yale University**, named after its early benefactor, Elihu Yale. Bill and Hillary Clinton first met here at Law School. Free guided tours of Yale include the 1752 Connecticut Hall, the Harkness Tower (221ft/66m tall) and the Center for British Art. A Gutenberg Bible is one of 400,000 books in the Beinecke Library.

You leave among rail yards, houses and factories to continue through southern Connecticut.

Milford (↑5/20↓) Milford is the scene of an annual oyster festival. As you travel southwest you cross the Housatonic and Pequonnock rivers.

▄▄▀ BRIDGEPORT (↑25/24↓) Connecticut's largest city contains 1,300 acres (525ha) of parkland and the state's largest zoo. City Hall was named after a socialist mayor, Jasper McLevy (in office 1933–57). Amtrak trains stop at the Bridgeport Transportation Center, with connections to intercity passenger and commuter rail lines, intercity and local bus routes, and an interstate ferry service.

To your right as you leave is the **Barnum Museum** (✆*203 331 1104;* w *barnum-museum.org*), containing an Egyptian mummy and the clothes worn by General Tom Thumb. Showman Phineas Taylor Barnum (also a Bridgeport mayor) was buried in Mountain Grove Cemetery, where Tom Thumb's grave is marked by a supposedly life-size 2ft (60cm) statue. Ocean-going ships can be seen in the harbour to your left.

▄▄▀ WESTPORT (↑10/14↓) The fanciful Victorian depot was opened by the Delaware & Hudson Company in 1876 and added to in later years. A handful of New Yorkers commute further north but Westport is as far as most will travel. Houses here and along the coast to Stamford are among this area's most expensive and fashionable. Nearby Sherwood Island is popular for swimming and boating on Long Island Sound.

As the train nears Stamford, look ahead to your right for the most modern part of the city.

▄▄▀ STAMFORD (↑24/18↓) Research City claims to have more international corporations than anywhere except New York or Chicago. Smart new office blocks and malls have transformed the downtown skyline.

The $40 million station, opened in 1987, is one of the busiest commuter stops between New York's Grand Central Terminal and New Haven's Union Station. Amtrak shares the building on Washington Boulevard with Metro-North trains, seen to your left, and a walkway links the platforms.

Greenwich (↑6/12↓) First settled by the Dutch, Greenwich is the home of many film and television stars and is possibly the richest town in Connecticut. Places of interest include the Bush-Holley House, of colonial 'saltbox' design (w *greenwichhistory.org*).

From here the train loses touch with Long Island Sound and travels through an increasingly urban and bleak landscape towards New York City.

NEW ROCHELLE (↑18/30↓) Located on the north shore of Long Island Sound, New Rochelle is a sought-after New York suburb easily accessible from midtown Manhattan by Amtrak, Metro-North trains and Bee-Line buses. The restored station was built in 1887 and is listed on the National Register of Historic Places. Amtrak trains part company here with Metro services, which operate out of New York's Grand Central Station.

Pelham Bay (↑4/26↓) Massive Co-op City apartment blocks appear to your right as you cross the bridge. Calvary Hospital is to your left.

The train crosses the Hutchinson River then slows down as it passes through a deprived South Bronx before entering Hell Gate Viaduct. The Hell Gate Bridge, 320ft (96m) above the East River, was the world's largest steel-arch bridge when completed in 1917, and it served as a model for the bridge across Sydney Harbour in Australia. The Hell Gate Route (or New York Connecting Railroad) was built to link the New York, New Haven & Hartford line with the Pennsylvania Railroad.

Manhattan State Hospital (↑10/20↓) Look right for this sombre 1930s building and your first views of Manhattan. The train crosses Randalls and Wards islands before going through Astoria. Rail yards and commuter trains extend on both sides as you enter a tunnel on Long Island, burrowing beneath the East River and Manhattan to reach Pennsylvania Station.

NEW YORK CITY (↑30/15↓) *Manhattan*, *Wall Street*, *42nd Street*, *West Side Story* and *Breakfast at Tiffany's* – everyone has visited New York in the movies. The birthplace of Bogart and Bacall is a world leader in fashion, finance and the arts, inspiring admen and bankers as much as painters, writers, filmmakers and musicians. Nowhere else has such energy and style.

New Amsterdam began in 1625, and the following year Peter Minuit bought Manhattan Island from the Native Americans for $24. Today its population is three million, plus 11 million commuters.

New York City basics

☏ Telephone codes 212 for Manhattan; 718 for Queens, Brooklyn, the Bronx & Staten Island. All numbers given in this section have Manhattan codes unless otherwise stated.

Pennylvania Station (*Ticket office* ⊕ *05.10– 21.00; waiting room* ⊕ *24hrs; information* ☏ *630 6400*). ClubAcela lounge (⊕ *05.15–21.30 Mon–Fri, 07.00–21.00 Sat–Sun*) is particularly swish – a welcome respite from the busy waiting room outside. Amtrak uses Pennsylvania Station at Seventh Av & 32nd, beneath Madison Square Garden, a poor substitute for the building it

replaced in the 1960s. With more than half a million passengers each day, New York Penn Station is the busiest rail hub in North America. As well as *Acela Express* & *Northeast Regional* trains it is served by Amtrak's short- or long-distance trains to places that include Chicago, Miami & New Orleans, as well as Long Island Rail Road (LIRR) & New Jersey Transit (NJ Transit) commuter rail, & is accessible from 14 lines of the New York City subway (MTA). The Port Authority Trans-Hudson (PATH) rapid transit system has a station 1 block away at 33rd & Sixth Av. The original Pennsylvania Station, which took the name of its owner & builder, the Pennsylvania Railroad (PRR), opened in 1910 & was a masterpiece of Beaux-Arts architecture designed by creative genius Charles Follen McKim. Thomas Wolfe described it as 'vast enough to hold the sound of time' & it can be seen in the 1942 film *The Palm Beach Story* as well as Alfred Hitchcock's thriller *Strangers on a Train* which was partly filmed at Penn Station (as it looked pre-1964). The building was demolished in an act of monumental vandalism to make way for Madison Square Garden sports & entertainment arena & an office building. Trains continued to run 50ft (15m) below street level, accessed by a warren of tunnels, but New York's Senator Daniel Patrick Moynihan proposed using the beautiful old post office building – renamed the James A Farley Building – as the grand ceremonial entrance to Penn Station. It wasn't until after the senator died in 2003 that the concept of transforming the post office into Moynihan Station began. Amtrak, in partnership with the ESDC & the Moynihan Station Development Corporation, is now creating a future home for its passenger operations within a new train hall in Moynihan Station. Together with the renovation of the existing Penn Station, this will offer improved passenger facilities, comfort & security. Phase I was completed in 2017 & Phase 2, currently under construction, will create a sunlit atrium, combined ticketing & baggage area, an Amtrak Metropolitan Lounge, a reserved customer waiting room, casual waiting space & retail & food shops. The Moynihan Train Hall is expected to be complete by late 2020 in time for the arrival of Amtrak's next-generation high-speed *Acela Express* trainsets. Baggage room, newspapers, restaurants, snack bars, shops, ATM banking, taxi stand, subway. **Connections** The Long Island Railroad (☏ 718 217 5477) & New Jersey Transit (☏ 973 275 5555) also operate from Penn Station

Grand Central Station The magnificent, atmospheric Grand Central Terminal at 89 E 42nd & Park Av is where John Barrymore won Carole Lombard after their cross-country train journey in the 1934 film *Twentieth Century*. Completed in 1913 by Cornelius Vanderbilt, the largest train station in the world replaced a smaller 1898 station which had proved to be unable to cope with increased traffic.

In 1902, an explosion in the open rail yards had killed 15 people with fumes, smoke & steam. It was decided therefore to electrify the trains & construct a roof over the entire complex, excavating 48ft (14m)

into Manhattan Island to create 3 separate levels. 8 underground tracks carried 700 trains per day while above ground a new New York grew, including all the buildings on Park Av. The $180 million station had been financed by selling air space above.

A 'city within a city', Grand Central originally had tennis courts, an art gallery, a bakery, a betting parlour & a hospital. Restored in magnificent style & rededicated in 1998, the station has 5 brass chandeliers (each with 100 lights), Tennessee marble floors, frescoes, grand balustraded staircases & triumphant arched windows where people walk in a wall of glass. Look for the Vanderbilt family's oak leaves emblem incorporated into the vaulted ceiling of the main concourse. The Oyster Bar, located in the bowels of the station, continues to serve shellfish stew, pan roasts & oysters across splendid marble counters & a new steakhouse occupies the north balcony. A murmur from the 'whispering gallery' outside the Oyster Bar's entrance can be heard clearly in the far corners of the cavernous hall.

By 1946, more than 65 million passengers a year were using Grand Central & rush hour can still be frantic. Metro-North (☏ 877 690 5114) operates over 500 commuter trains daily to the suburbs of New Jersey & Connecticut. Sadly, Amtrak stopped using Grand Central in April 1991. Despite attempts to deal the building a similar fate to the old Penn Station, campaigners such as Jackie Kennedy kept this spectacular building safe. The Municipal Art Society (☏ 935 3960) offers tours every afternoon at 12.30.

🚌 **Local transport** Manhattan's logical grid of streets & avenues makes it easy to find your way around, although driving or finding a place to park can be a nightmare. The visitors bureau has maps & schedules for public transport & more details are available from MTA NYC Transit Authority (*347 Madison Av, NY 10017-3739*). A MetroCard provides a week's unlimited travel on the subway & buses throughout the city for $32. For all bus & subway information, ☏ 718 330 1234. John Tauranac produces excellent subway guides & maps.

🚕 **Taxis** A taxi stand is located on 31st St between Seventh & Eighth avs. Otherwise look for a yellow cab with a lighted sign & hail it by raising your arm. In case of complaints or lost property contact the Taxi Commission (☏ 311).

🚗 **Car rental** National, 332 W 44th; ☏ 575 5400

🚌 **Greyhound** Port Authority Terminal, 625 Eighth Av; ☏ 971 6789

✈ **Airports** Call Air-Ride (☏ 1 800 247 7433) for

recorded information about transport to all 3 New York airports.

The largest is John F Kennedy in Queens, which can be reached by taxi, bus or limousine. Airlink shuttle buses operate between JFK, the Port Authority & Grand Central Station, with transfers to Penn Station from Grand Central (✆ 812 9000; w goairlinkshuttle.com). Journey time from JFK to Grand Central is about 1hr.

AirTrain JFK is an 8.1-mile (13km) light rail system that connects JFK to the New York City area's mass transit system. A trip from JFK to Jamaica or Howard Beach subway will average about 12mins, plus 60–75mins for the subway journey to midtown Manhattan.

LaGuardia Airport in Queens is served by several MTA bus lines, including the M60, linking LaGuardia to the New York City Subway & Long Island Railroad. A proposed extension of the subway system would allow a 'one seat' ride to LaGuardia from Manhattan.

Newark Airport is 14 miles (22km) southwest & was briefly, in the 1930s, the world's busiest airport. Express Shuttle buses (✆ 908 354 3330) connect to midtown Manhattan. AirTrain Newark Links (✆ 435 7000) is a light rail service to the Newark Liberty International Airport Train Station.

Tours Gray Line; ✆ 445 0848. Harlem Heritage walking tours (✆ 280 7888) are conducted by people who live & work in Harlem, giving an insider's view of the community. 3hr boat cruises around Manhattan from Circle Line at Pier 83, W 42nd at the Hudson River (✆ 563 3200). Helicopter flights from Liberty (✆ 1 800 542 9933). Food tasting & cultural walking tours with Foods of New York (✆ 855 223 8684; w foodsofny.com). The Staten Island ferry (✆ 718 815 2628) chugs around the harbour & Statue of Liberty, making 50 crossings each way on w/days between the Whitehall ferry terminal in Lower Manhattan & St George ferry terminal on the island. The 5-mile (8km) journey takes 25mins & is free to foot passengers.

The Jazz Trail takes place about once a month around Queens, visiting the former houses of musicians such as Louis Armstrong, Dizzy Gillespie,

Lena Horne & James Brown. Take the subway from Times Sq or the Long Island Railroad from Penn Station to Flushing Town Hall (137–35, Northern Bd; ✆ 718 463 7700).

🛈 Visitors bureau 810 Seventh Av, between 52nd & 53rd; ✆ 484 1200; w nycgo.com. Official NYC information centres are open daily at Macy's Herald Sq, 151 W 34th; Times Sq Pl, between 44th & 45th; & City Hall, southern tip of City Hall Park.

🏠 Accommodation Hotel room prices are often very high apart from some w/end rates.

Hotels include the Algonquin, 59 W 44th; ✆ 840 6800; w algonquinhotel.com, **$$$$$**. Hotel 41 at Times Sq, 206 W 41st; ✆ 703 8600; w hotel41nyc.com. Close to theatres & central Manhattan sights, **$$$$$**. Sofitel, 45 W 44th; ✆ 354 8844; w sofitel.com. An upmarket hotel with marble bathrooms & elegant Art Deco style, **$$$$$**. Hilton New York, 1335 Av of the Americas; ✆ 586 7000; w hilton.com. Close to Central Park & MOMA. Almost 2,000 rooms & 3 ballrooms, including the biggest in New York, **$$$$**. Hotel 414, 414 W 46th; ✆ 399 0006; w 414hotel.com. Pretty courtyard for guests. Great value, with continental b/fast included, **$$$**. Stewart, 371 Seventh Av; ✆ 563 1800; w stewarthotelnyc.com, **$$$**.

Contact B&B Lodges, 1598 Lexington Av; ✆ 917 345 7914; w bblodges.com. Located in the Upper East Side close to Central Park & the #6 subway on 103rd – 10mins to central Manhattan. 12 comfortable apts & suites with private kitchens & bathrooms, from **$$$**.

HI-New York Hostel, 891 Amsterdam Av; ✆ 932 2300; w hiusa.org/hostels/new-york. The world's largest hostel, with 672 beds. Family rooms available. Members & non-members, **$**. Vanderbilt YMCA, 224 E 47th; ✆ 912 2500; w ymcanyc.org/vanderbilt. A classic-style building on the fashionable East Side. TV, AC, swimming pool, gym & restaurant (with room service). For men & women, **$$**. West Side YMCA, 5 W 63rd; ✆ 912 2600; w ymcanyc.org/westside. Located off Central Park West in a European-style building close to Upper West Side attractions. TV, AC, swimming pool, fitness facilities, restaurant, **$$**.

Recommended in New York City

Statue of Liberty On Liberty Island, reached by Circle Line ferry from Battery Park; ✆ 363 3200; w nps.gov/stli. 'Liberty enlightening the world'

was designed by Frederic Bartholdi & paid for by the French. The statue reopened in 2004 after being closed for security reasons. Visitors can now view inside the structure through a glass ceiling & have access to the observation deck for panoramic views of New York City & the harbour. There is a choice of 2 tours: the Statue of Liberty Observatory Tour & the Statue of Liberty Promenade Tour. Both include a guided tour through the Statue of Liberty Museum which includes the Lady's original torch. To climb the staircase within the statue to the crown you should purchase a special ticket from Statue Cruises, which can be reserved up to a year in advance. Only 240 people a day are permitted to ascend the strenuous 354 steps. Reservations for all visits can be made with Statue Cruises (✆877 523 9849; w statuecruises.com).

Immigration Museum On nearby Ellis Island; ✆363 3200; w nps.gov/elis; ⊕ daily; admission free. The museum now occupies the building which 12 million immigrants passed through between 1892 & 1954.

Museum of the City of New York 1220 Fifth Av at 103rd; ✆534 1672; w mcny.org; ⊕ daily; admission charge. Housed in a beautiful Georgian Colonial-Revival-style building, the museum has over 750,000 objects, including paintings, historic photographs of New York City & its residents (with work by Percy Byron, Jacob Riis & film director Stanley Kubrick), costumes, antique toys, rare books & manuscripts, as well as a theatre collection celebrating the golden age of Broadway. Among the notable exhibits are several of Eugene O'Neill's handwritten manuscripts, a complete room of Duncan Phyfe furniture, a man's suit worn to George Washington's Inaugural Ball, & a dollhouse containing a miniature work by Marcel Duchamp.

The Frick Collection 1 East 70th; ✆288 0700; w frick.org; ⊕ Tue–Sun; admission charge. The collection, housed in an elegant mansion built by Henry Clay Frick, one of America's most successful steel & railroad tycoons, includes masterpieces of Western painting, sculpture & decorative art, displayed in a serene & intimate setting. Among the 16 galleries are the Fragonard Room & the Living Hall, with works by Holbein, Titian, El Greco & Bellini.

Empire State Building 350 Fifth Av; ✆736 3100; w esbnyc.com; ⊕ daily; admission charge. The people's favourite skyscraper was the world's tallest building when completed in 1931 & kept the record for 40 years. The 86th- & 102nd-floor observation decks still give great views of New York, but arrive early to miss the crush.

St Patrick's Cathedral Fifth Av & 50th; ✆753 2261; w saintpatrickscathedral.org; ⊕ daily; admission free. The Gothic towers of New York's Roman Catholic Cathedral contrast with the adjacent Rockefeller Center's Art Deco.

Central Park Bounded by 59th & 110th sts, & by Fifth Av & Central Park West; w centralparknyc. org; ⊕ daily. Watch New York at play, listen to concerts & enjoy free Shakespeare performances. The 843 acre (3.41km²) park has America's oldest carousel, a zoo & Strawberry Fields, dedicated to John Lennon. Free maps & details of latest events from the Mid-Park Visitor Center at 65th (✆794 6564; ⊕ daily).

Metropolitan Museum of Art 1000 Fifth Av at E 82nd; ✆535 7710; w metmuseum.org; ⊕ daily; admission charge. More than 4 million people each year visit this vast Victorian Gothic building to see the largest art collection in the USA. More like a dozen museums in one, with great works by Picasso, Rembrandt, Vermeer & French Impressionists, Egyptian art, a Chinese Ming-period courtyard, the Frank Lloyd Wright room & a terrific sculpture garden on the roof. For concerts & lecture tours, ✆570 3949. The Met is always busy so go early, although some galleries do not open until late on Sun morning.

Museum of Modern Art 11 W 53rd, between Fifth & Sixth avs; ✆708 9400; w moma.org; ⊕ daily; admission charge. One of the world's finest collections containing almost 200,000 works of modern & contemporary art. Includes Monet's Water Lily room & works by Picasso, Matisse, Miró & Jackson Pollock.

United Nations First Av & 46th, overlooking the East River; ✆963 8687; w un.org; ⊕ daily; admission charge for tours, free tickets to observe meetings. Take a guided tour of the Secretariat Bldg, General Assembly Hall & Hammarskjold Library.

The High Line ✆206 9922; w thehighline. org. This public park is built on a 1.45-mile-long (2.3km) elevated freight rail structure on Manhattan's West Side, stretching from Gansevoort St in the Meatpacking District to West 34th St. Originally built in 1934, the line lifted train traffic 30ft (9m) in the air to carry mostly food & agricultural goods to the upper storeys of factories & warehouses. Train traffic decreased in the 1950s & stopped altogether in 1980. The park is now a very pleasant walk for pedestrians, its design inspired by the vegetation that grew up during the 25 years after the trains stopped. Grasses, perennials, trees & bushes were chosen for their hardiness, texture & colour, with a focus on native species. In many places, the railroad tracks have been returned to their original locations & integrated into the planting beds.

Stock Exchange 20 Broad St; ☎656 5165; w nyse.com. Formed in 1792 when a group of brokers met at the junction of Wall & William sts, where kerbside brokers sold railroad stocks in the 1860s. The Stock Exchange is currently closed to visitors but the Wall Street Experience (☎608 0130; w thewallstreetexperience.com) has revealing tours designed & guided by insiders. Tours start opposite the Exchange at 15 Broad St.

NY Transit Museum Located in an authentic 1930s subway station at the corner of Boerum Pl & Schermerhorn St in downtown Brooklyn; ☎718 694 1600; w nytransitmuseum.org; ☺ Tue–Sun; admission charge. The first New York subway opened in 1904 & 2.4 billion people a year now ride the subways, buses & railroads. The museum has many subway cars, including early wooden ones, as well as photos & interactive exhibits showing how the city's subways & railroads were built. The museum also has a gallery annex with exhibitions at Grand Central Station.

NEW YORK CITY: ALL ABOARD! (↑30/15↓) The train pulls out of Pennsylvania Station by way of a 2.5-mile (4km) tunnel beneath the Hudson River, surfacing 3 minutes later in New Jersey. The Hudson tunnels were the first structural links across the river between New Jersey and New York City. Train services began when Penn Station opened in 1910.

The city's outline on the far left features the Empire State Building and, to your right, the MetLife Stadium is beyond a New Jersey Turnpike bridge.

Hackensack River (↑10/5↓) You cross with an impressive bridge to your left and lose sight of New York. The train follows then crosses the Passaic River before going through a New Jersey Transit depot at Harrison.

⚒⚒ NEWARK (↑15/14↓) New Jersey's largest city is one of the country's great manufacturing centres. It was the birthplace of the novelist Stephen Crane, author of *The Red Badge of Courage*. The Thomas Edison Historic Site in the suburb of West Orange preserves Edison's laboratory, his early gramophone and the first movie camera. Edison was once a newsboy on the Grand Trunk Railway.

Amtrak's echoing Art Deco Pennsylvania Station at Raymond Plaza W opened in 1935 and has a beautifully restored waiting room featuring a colourful terrazzo floor, sculpted wall medallions, metalwork and chandeliers decorated with signs of the Zodiac. The train leaves Newark past PATH trains, warehouses and brick-built factories, picking up speed as it travels through commuter stops such as Lincoln.

⚒⚒ NEWARK LIBERTY AIRPORT (↑14/10↓) Featuring large expanses of glass, this bright and airy station links Newark Liberty International Airport with Amtrak and New Jersey Transit rail services via monorail. The monorail fare is included in Amtrak tickets to and from the Newark Airport Rail Station and passengers with tickets showing Newark Airport as the destination or boarding point can scan the barcode on their e-ticket travel document (smartphone or paper) at the AirTrain fare gate. You must have an Amtrak ticket before boarding trains from this station.

Elizabeth (↑2/8↓) The former New Jersey capital, an influential town during the American Revolution, is bound to Newark by continuous suburbs and was named one of 'America's greenest cities' by *Popular Science* magazine.

Rahway (↑6/4↓) Interesting old brownstone buildings appear on both sides. Rahway grew because of its location next to the Rahway River and on stagecoach and railroad lines between New York City and Philadelphia. Among its many manufacturers was Nikola Tesla's Electric Light & Manufacturing company. More recently the downtown area has seen the development of new restaurants and art galleries as well as the old Rahway Theatre ('America's first million dollar movie palace'), now reopened as the Union County Performing Arts Center.

ᴬᴹᵀ METROPARK (↑10/15↓) Amtrak's renovated station at 100 Middlesex-Essex Turnpike opened in 1971 as a stop for park-and-ride commuters. You cross the Garden State Parkway and continue among industrial plants owned by some of America's biggest companies. The scene is occasionally brightened by a stretch of farmland and near New Brunswick you cross the Rariton River.

New Brunswick (↑7/8↓) A scheduled stop for some Amtrak trains, New Brunswick has frequent New Jersey Transit services to Newark and Trenton. Look right for Rutgers University (founded in 1776) and the headquarters of Johnson & Johnson.

The train continues through semi-rural scenes until factories, chemical plants and warehouses take over again on the approach to Trenton.

ᴬᴹᵀ PRINCETON JUNCTION (↑10/5↓) Princeton Junction's origins can be traced back to the United New Jersey Railroad & Canal Company, which built the original station in 1864. Albert Einstein used to enjoy sitting at the station and watching the trains go by; he even used trains to explain his General Theory of Relativity. The university's ivy-clad campus to your right features Einstein's house. Other inhabitants have included future presidents Woodrow Wilson and Aaron Burr. The art museum features pictures by Cézanne, Van Gogh and Picasso, and panels in University Chapel are carved from Sherwood Forest wood. For **visitor information**, call ✆609 258 6115. A few Amtrak trains stop at Princeton Junction and New Jersey Transit trains go to Princeton from Penn Station in New York City.

ᴬᴹᵀ TRENTON (↑15/32↓) This is home of New Jersey's State Museum and the 1792 Capitol Building. A major reconstruction project has replaced a rather lived-in station with the Trenton Transit Center, providing frequent NJ Transit high-speed rail service to New York's Pennsylvania Station. Public art installations include colourful handmade tiles decorated with historic Trenton scenes.

Look right for the Capitol's gold dome as you leave through older parts of the city.

The train slows down to cross the Delaware River near the place where Washington crossed in 1776 to attack a garrison of British-financed mercenaries. The bridge to your right proclaims that 'Trenton makes, the world takes'. Crossing the river transports you from New Jersey into Pennsylvania.

Holmesburg Junction (↑20/12↓) Holmesburg Prison is to your right. Built in 1896 and in use until 1995, the prison is now mostly abandoned after a history of riots, unsolved murders, inhuman punishments and death-defying escape attempts. Between 1951 and 1974, 'volunteers' were used for chemical and toxicology studies, including the injection of dioxin into prisoners. The Tacony-Palmyra Bridge arches across the Delaware River, seen beyond trees to your left.

Schuylkill River (↑30/2↓) You pass two spired churches then cross the river and enter Philadelphia through Fairmount Park. The zoo is on your left.

above   Amtrak's *Empire Builder* provides a gateway into Montana's stunning Glacier National Park, where the wildlife includes grizzly bears, moose and mountain goats (DD/S) page 130

below   Despite its desolation, Death Valley is visited every year by nearly a million visitors, who flock to see its salt flats, valleys, canyons and dunes (SS) page 105

Badwater
ELEV. - 282 ft.

top left	The residents of San Antonio unwind on the Paseo del Rio, a riverside walk offering music bars, floating restaurants and people-watching galore (A/DT) page 162
top right	Albuquerque has a distinctly Mexican feel with its brightly painted houses (NB/DT) page 146
above	Jazz comes alive on the streets during Mardi Gras in the French Quarter of New Orleans, birthplace of Jelly Roll Morton and Louis Armstrong (CW/S) page 156
left	The Amtrak station at Glenwood Springs has unusual square Chinese-style towers (SS/S) page 96

above The nightclubs and beaches of Miami's South Beach Art Deco district are a byword for glamour (E/DT) page 246

below Barely connected to mainland Florida, there's one road in and one road out of Key West, passing through Bahia Honda Key (JG/A) page 248

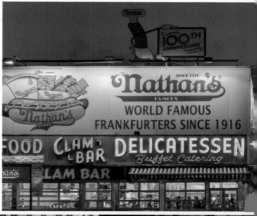

above   Designed by Santiago Calatrava, the interior of the World Trade Center Transportation Hub in Manhattan was completed in 2016 (AP/S) page 205

right   Nathan Handwerker's original restaurant has been selling its famous hot dogs on Coney Island in Brooklyn for more than a hundred years (FL/S) page 205

below   Built at the height of the Great Depression, the Rockefeller Center is a vast Art Deco complex that includes Radio City Music Hall, an array of public artwork and several outdoor plazas (SS) page 208

above   **A male grizzly bear near Prince Rupert, British Columbia** (SS) page 364

right   **Vancouver's Stanley Park is home to a large collection of monuments, including totem poles, statues and plaques** (SS) page 363

below right   **The *Rocky Mountaineer* offers a magnificent view of Mount Robson, the highest peak in the Canadian Rockies** (SS) page 369

The *Alberni Pacific*, an ex-logging locomotive, winds its way through forests up to the McLean Hill National Historic Site (SS) page 376

An old signalbox mural announces 'the city of brotherly love' as the train crawls among freight yards and half-derelict buildings, with Philadelphia's skyline in the left distance. Nearing the station, look left for Boathouse Row and the Parthenon-style Museum of Art with its famous *Rocky* steps.

PHILADELPHIA (↑32/22↓) 'On the whole I'd rather be in Philadelphia' was W C Fields's malign epitaph on his birthplace when he thought he was dying. The city has also been the home of Benjamin Franklin, Sammy Davis Jr, Dizzy Gillespie and Live Aid. Elfreth's Alley, occupied since 1772, is America's oldest street and the Walnut Street Theatre claims to be the oldest continuously operating theatre in the English-speaking world.

William Penn founded Philadelphia on a peninsula between the Schuylkill and Delaware rivers in 1682. It became America's capital from Independence until 1800, by when it was the world's second-largest English-speaking city. Apart from historic buildings and museums, Philly is famous for its cheesesteaks, pretzels and sometimes alarming crime rate.

Philadelphia basics

Telephone code 215

Station (*Ticket office* ☺ *05.15–21.35 Mon–Fri, 06.10–21.35 Sat–Sun; waiting room* ☺ *24hrs; ClubAcela Lounge* ☺ *06.00–21.00*) Stately 30th St Station at 30th & Market is one of Amtrak's busiest terminals, restored at great expense. Built between 1929 & 1933 by the Pennsylvania Railroad, this enormous, 8-storey steel Neoclassical-style frame building features 71ft-high (21.6m) Corinthian columns forming impressive porticoes rendered in Alabama limestone. The opulent main concourse has a high coffered ceiling, Art Deco chandeliers, gilded & ornamented columns, cathedral-like windows & a Tennessee marble floor. Electronic train information, Wi-Fi, payphones, newspapers, Red Caps, restaurants, shops, ATM banking, taxi stand.

Connections SEPTA trains operate to the suburbs & Philadelphia Airport (☏ *580 7800*). PATCO high-speed trains to New Jersey leave from Eighth & Market (☏ *922 4600*). For New Jersey Transit trains to Atlantic City & southern New Jersey, ☏ 1 800 772 2287. You can travel by commuter train between 30th St & downtown Penn Center Station at 1617 John F Kennedy Bd.

Local transport The historic district is best explored on foot & SEPTA (Southeastern Pennsylvania Transit Authority) operates buses, trolleys & the subway (☏ *580 7800*)

Taxis All Threes Taxi Cabs ☏ 333 3333; Streamline ☏ 439 5936

Car rental Avis ☏ 386 2332; Budget ☏ 222 4262. Both located in 30th St Station.

Greyhound 1001 Filbert; ☏ 931 4075

Airport The international airport is 8 miles (13km) southwest by SEPTA Airport Regional Rail Line from 30th St Station (call SEPTA for times).

Tours Philadelphia Sightseeing; ☏ 922 2300. Free Tours by Foot has walking & food tours (☏ *267 712 9512*). Philadelphia Trolly & The Big Bus Tours (☏ *389 8687*) take in most sights. Water cruises on the *Spirit of Philadelphia* (☏ *923 1419*) & the riverboat *Philadelphia Belle* (☏ *717 1617*).

Visitors bureau 1700 Market; ☏ 563 2970; w philadelphiausa.travel; ☺ 09.00–17.00 daily

Accommodation Hotels include the Penn's View, Front & Market; ☏ 922 7600; w hiepennslanding.com, **$$$$$**; Chestnut Hill, 8229 Germantown Av; ☏ 242 5905; w chestnuthillhotel.com, **$$$$**; Logan, 1 Logan Sq; ☏ 963 1500; w curiocollection3.hilton.com, **$$$$**; Alexander Inn, 12th & Spruce; ☏ 923 3535; w alexanderinn.com, **$$$**; Best Western, 1225 Vine; ☏ 398 3080; w bestwestern.com, **$$$**; Holiday Inn Midtown, 1305 Walnut; ☏ 735 9300; w ihg.com/holidayinnexpress, **$$$**; Holiday Inn Penns Landing, 100 N Christopher Columbus Bd; ☏ 627 7900; w hiepennslanding.com, **$$$**.

Contact La Reserve Bed & Breakfast, City Center, 1804 Pine, Philadelphia, PA 19103; ☏ 735 1137; w lareservebandb.com, **$$$**.

HI Hostel, Chamounix Mansion, a historic building in Fairmount Park; ☏ 878 3676; w philahostel.org. Some family rooms. Members & non-members, **$**.

Recommended in Philadelphia

Museum of Art 26th & Benjamin Franklin Parkway; ✆763 8100; w philamuseum.org; ⊕ Tue–Sun; admission charge (donation on 1st Sun of month). 300,000 works, including Van Gogh (*Sunflowers*), Picasso, Renoir, Rubens & Cézanne (*Bathers*), plus American crafts, a Japanese tea house & an Indian temple. Guided tours.

Fairmount Park Covering 4,500 acres (1,800ha) from downtown to the city's northwest boundary, the park features forests, waterways, sports fields & museums. Highlights include Boathouse Row (19th-century buildings used by rowing clubs), Strawberry Mansion & Memorial Hall (dating from the 1876 centennial).

Christ Church Beyond Franklin Court to Market. The pews in this church have been occupied by such luminaries as George Washington & Benjamin Franklin. Services are held on Sun.

City Hall Broad & Market; ✆514 4757; ⊕ Mon–Fri. Completed in 1900 & topped by a 37ft (11m) bronze statue of William Penn, this 548ft (166m) tower is one of the world's tallest & largest all-masonry, load-bearing structures without a steel or iron frame. Tours of the interior & observation deck.

Franklin Institute Science Museum 222 N 20th St; ✆448 1200; w fi.edu; ⊕ daily; admission charge. Includes a science centre, planetarium & theatre. The museum has many hands-on & walk-through exhibits, & the garden features high-tech displays & a maze. Climb aboard a steam locomotive & imagine yourself as the engineer of this massive engine in a simulated train factory. The 350-US ton (317-tonne) Baldwin 60000 arrived at the Institute in 1933, taking 5 days to move 5 blocks from 24th & Vine St to the museum.

Independence Park The national park visitor centre is at Sixth & Market; ✆1 800 537 7676; w independencevisitorcenter.com; ⊕ daily. This historic square mile draws 5 million tourists every year & buildings (*most ⊕ daily; admission free*), include the following:

Independence Hall Chestnut St. Opened in 1732, this is where the Declaration of Independence (1776) & Constitution (1787) were adopted. You can tour the Assembly Room & Old City Hall, where the US Supreme Court held sessions from 1791 to 1800.

Liberty Bell Pavilion Market St. Cast in England in 1751, the State House Bell hung in Independence Hall for 200 years before moving to its new glass-walled home.

Old City Hall On Chestnut at Fifth. This was the home of the US Supreme Court between 1791 & 1800. See the prisoner's dock & jury box as well as restored furniture.

Rodin Museum 2151 Benjamin Franklin Parkway; ✆568 6026; ⊕ Wed–Mon; donation; w rodinmuseum.org; free tours. The largest collection of Rodin drawings & sculptures (including *The Thinker*) outside Paris.

PHILADELPHIA: ALL ABOARD! (↑32/22↓) The train departs Philadelphia past the National Publishing Company Building to your left and the ivy-league university's Franklin Field to your right. You continue among residential suburbs and smokestack industry, with the former Pennsylvania Shipbuilding yard on your left.

Commodore Barry Bridge (↑11/11↓) The imposing steel structure to your left spans the Delaware River between Chester, Pennsylvania and New Jersey. It was named after American Revolutionary War hero and Philadelphia resident John Barry. Look for ships being loaded below.

Pennsylvania–Delaware state line (↑15/7↓) The Delaware River is to your left as you enter the Small Wonder State at Marcus Hook.

Brandywine Creek (↑18/4↓) You cross the creek, flowing into the Christina River to your left. The Christina eventually joins the Delaware.

From here to Wilmington the train progresses through Fort Christina Park, site of the first (1638) Swedish settlement. The **Holy Trinity (Old Swedes) Church** and graveyard on your right date from 1698 and are still in use. As you travel among more factories look right near Wilmington for the station's decorative clock tower.

WILMINGTON (↑22/25↓) Located at the confluence of the Christina River and Brandywine Creek, Wilmington became 'The chemical capital of the world', where Eleuthère du Pont founded a gunpowder mill in 1802. The site is now occupied by the **Hagley Museum and Library** (☏*302 658 2400; w hagley.org*), which collects and interprets the history of American enterprise. Wilmington's 1871 opera house boasts a splendid cast-iron façade. Amtrak's large, refurbished Victorian-style station at 100 S French Street, formerly known as Pennsylvania Station, was designed in 1907 by Frank Furness. The 12th-busiest station in the country, it boasts terracotta window arches, marble steps and a clay-tiled roof. Train travel is close to the heart of former US Vice President Joe Biden, who famously commuted between his home in Wilmington to Washington, DC on Amtrak during his 36-year Senate career, taking over 7,000 round trips. He was also the driving force behind Wilmington Station's $37.7 million renovation project, and in 2011 he cut a ribbon to dedicate the renamed Joseph R Biden Jnr Railroad Station. Two years earlier, he announced that Amtrak would receive $1.3 billion in federal stimulus money to expand passenger rail capacity, calling the system 'an absolute national treasure and necessity'.

The train leaves past freight yards and a Berger Brothers office furniture building before travelling beneath a highway bridge with a twin-spired church to your right.

Newark (↑8/17↓) A scheduled stop for a few trains but not to be confused with Newark, New Jersey. The University of Delaware appears to your right. To your left is the site of a vast former Chrysler plant which originally manufactured tanks. This is now owned by the University of Delaware, which plans to develop it as a Science, Technology and Advanced Research campus.

Delaware–Maryland state line (↑14/11↓) You cross into Maryland, exotically sculpted by Chesapeake Bay and the Potomac River. At the town of Hancock the state of Maryland is only 5 miles (8km) wide. Stone markers (one white, one black) in a field to your right indicate the state boundary, which is also the Mason–Dixon Line. This divided, and some people say still divides, north and south.

Elkton (↑15/10↓) Wedding chapels here witnessed thousands of quickie marriages during the 1930s. In 1913, the state of Delaware passed a new law requiring that people wanting to get married had to wait four days between getting a licence and having the ceremony. New York and Pennsylvania already had waiting periods, so couples in a rush looked further south for alternatives. The closest county seat in Maryland was Elkton and in 1936 this 'Gretna Green of the East' issued an astonishing 11,791 marriage licences. As late as the 1970s, even though the law had changed, Elkton was still marrying 6,000 couples a year, but only one wedding chapel now remains.

You pass a quarry to your right before continuing through a colonial countryside of streams, woods and traditional buildings.

Northeast River (↑16/9↓) The tree-lined river to your left flows towards Chesapeake Bay.

Perryville (↑20/5↓) The train slows down to cross the Susquehanna River. Look left for a marina and Chesapeake Bay, with sailboats and the supports of a former bridge. Three more bridges span the river upstream to your right.

Havre de Grace (↑23/2↓) This neat town on the south shore of the bay was burned by the British during the War of 1812.

⚡ ABERDEEN (↑25/22↓) This is a popular stop for Aberdeen Proving Grounds and the US Army Ordnance Museum.

The train gathers speed as it travels southwest and crosses the mile-wide (1.6km) Bush River, with attractive houses and boat jetties ranged along the banks. **Susquehanna Wildlife Refuge** can be seen to your left as green fields, forests and grain silos appear.

Edgewood (↑9/13↓) William Paca, one of the signatories to the Declaration of Independence, was born near this prosperous small town. You cross the Gunpowder River, also a mile (1.6km) wide, and pass the Maryland National Guard headquarters on your left.

Industrial scenes return as the train nears Baltimore and travels beneath Interstate 40. Look for an old brownstone district to your right and Baltimore's downtown skyline ahead to your left before the train curves left into a tunnel.

⚡ BALTIMORE (↑22/12↓) Birthplace of the American railroad and one of the country's busiest ports, Baltimore has been the home of Billie Holliday, F Scott Fitzgerald, Babe Ruth, *Homicide – Life on the Street* and *The Wire*. The great writer and satirist H L Mencken – the 'Sage of Baltimore' – was born here in 1880 and lived most of his life at 1524 Hollins Street. During the 1830s, Edgar Allan Poe lived in poverty at 203 N Amity. When he died in 1849, he was buried in the grounds of Westminster Church. Lexington Market, the world's largest continuously running market, has been in operation in Baltimore since 1782. You can experience panoramic views of the revived city and its harbour from the World Trade Center, the world's tallest regular pentagonal building, which was designed by I M Pei. The **visitor centre** is at 401 Light (✆ *877 225 8466; w baltimore.org; ⏰ 10.00–17.00 daily*).

Amtrak's renovated Beaux-Arts-style station, opened in 1911, stands on your left at 1500 N Charles. In the plaza of this beautiful $1 million building is a 51ft-tall (15.5m) aluminium sculpture by artist Jonathan Borofsky named *Male/Female*, depicting two intersecting human forms with a glowing heart. Nearby are the celebrated Walters Art Museum, the Peabody Conservatory of Music and the Inner Harbor, with the National Aquarium, historic sailing ships and great views of the waterfront.

The **Baltimore & Ohio Railroad Museum** (*901 W Pratt;* ✆ *410 752 2490; w borail. org; ⏰ daily; admission charge*) is the oldest, most comprehensive American railroad collection in the world. A huge restoration project took place after a record-breaking 2003 snowstorm devastated the museum's national landmark Roundhouse, the largest circular building in the world when it was built in 1884. The 'birthplace of American railroading' displays engines (including the original *Stourbridge Lion*), rolling stock, replicas and model trains, as well as the Mount Clare station. This is the oldest passenger and freight station in the United States and had the country's first railroad manufacturing complex. The first Mount Clare station was erected in 1830, when the first railroad was completed over 13 miles (20km) to Ellicott's Mills (now Ellicott City). The first passenger car to make the trip was the horse-drawn *Pioneer* on 25 May 1830, in 1 hour and 5 minutes. On August 28, the first American locomotive, *Tom Thumb*, made its debut run on the same route, taking 10 minutes longer.

The train continues through a tunnel to another district of traditional brownstones. Look for the pretty Renaissance-style church to your left and a Calvert whiskey distillery to your right before the train speeds up through a more wooded landscape. The water tower at Piney Orchard is balanced on stilts.

BALTIMORE/WASHINGTON INTERNATIONAL AIRPORT (↑12/10↓) Concrete platforms and an overhead walkway are set among attractive trees. Opened in 1980 as America's first intercity air-rail-ground transportation facility, the BWI offers free shuttle buses which transport passengers between the station, located at the edge of the airport, and the terminal – 24 hours a day.

NEW CARROLLTON (↑10/10↓) This key transport junction is in Washington, DC's northern suburbs, where the station and yards of Metro Rail can be seen beside Amtrak's depot.

After New Carrollton you enter the District of Columbia across the narrow Anacostia River and see the 555ft (170m) **Washington Monument** to your right. Also on your right, beyond Amtrak's maintenance facility, are the dome and tower of the **Shrine of the Immaculate Conception**. The train creeps among extensive rail yards before finally entering Union Station.

WASHINGTON, DC (↑10) 'Southern efficiency and northern charm' was President Kennedy's mischievous description of Washington, DC, an elegant Neoclassical city designed by Pierre Charles L'Enfant on what had been a swamp. The architecture, boulevards and green spaces provide a fine setting for Washington, DC's main business – government.

Events include the cherry blossom festival in April and an Independence Day parade in July. Tourist areas are clean and impressive but the nation's capital has a darker side. Drugs and other crime make parts of the city unsafe, so stay on the beaten track. Summer can be oppressively humid.

Washington, DC basics

Telephone code 202

Station (*Ticket office* ⏰ *04.30–22.10 Mon–Fri, 05.00–22.10 Sat–Sun; waiting room* ⏰ *24hrs for Amtrak ticket holders; ClubAcela lounge* ⏰ *04.45–21.30*) Union Station is at 50 Massachusetts Av (☎ *289 1908;* w *unionstationdc. com*). The station, built with white granite from Vermont, is as grand as Washington, DC's other public buildings & is one of Amtrak's showpieces. The most-visited destination in the city, with over 32 million visitors a year, it is also downtown's most impressive shopping centre. Ancient Rome's Baths of Diocletian inspired Daniel Burnham's waiting room design, the 96ft (29m) ceiling decorated with 70lb (32kg) of gold leaf. The main concourse, with its marble floor & glazed terracotta columns, is long enough (750ft/225m) to hold the Washington Monument horizontally. Over 37 million passengers, tourists & shoppers pass through Washington Union Station every year.

The station was completed in 1908 at a cost of more than $25 million, with the cost to construct the station building alone being $4 million. It originally included a bakery, butcher's shop, bowling alley, YMCA, hotel, ice house, liquor store, Turkish baths, nursery, police station & mortuary. The dining room could handle 1,000 people at one sitting & there were separate men's & women's waiting rooms, each with heavy mahogany benches & built-in steam heaters. Union Station employed 5,000 people & became known as the 'crossroads of America'. It was made a National Historic Landmark in 1964 but, as the railroads declined, the building fell into decay. It was reopened in 1988 after America's largest-ever restoration project, which took 2 years & cost $160 million. Major exhibitions & cultural events are hosted here & private events such as the Presidential Inaugural Ball & citywide galas are celebrated in the grand halls.

The station has dozens of shops & restaurants, ClubAcela lounge, Wi-Fi, lockers, vending machines, ATM banking, payphones, newspapers, handcarts, Red Caps, taxi stand, subway. There are

14

plans to add several new lower-level concourses, new entrance points & more passenger amenities.
Connections No Thruway bus
🚐 **Local transport** Washington, DC is best appreciated on foot, most places of interest being within walking distance of the station, although the length of the mall can be deceptive. Metrobus operates throughout the city as well as into Maryland & northern Virginia, & the expanding Metrorail subway (📞637 7000; w wmata.com) has a stop at the station & services as far as northern Virginia & Maryland. MARC commuter trains (📞866 743 3682) & the Virginia Railway Express (📞703 684 1001) operate on w/days from Union Station.
🚗 **Taxis** DC Taxi 📞412 7049; Yellow 📞546 7900
🚗 **Car rental** Avis 📞682 2983; Budget 📞289 5374. Both located in Union Station.
🚐 **Greyhound** Located at Union Station; 📞289 5141
✈ **Airports** Dulles International Airport, 25 miles (40km) west, is the main international flight centre. Ronald Reagan National Airport is in Arlington, Virginia, 4 miles (6.5km) from downtown by subway. Baltimore/Washington International Thurgood Marshall (BWI) is 45 miles (72km) northeast by bus, Amtrak & MARC trains. For Washington Flyer buses to all airports, 📞888 WASHFLY (📞888 927 4359).
Tours The Old Town Trolley (📞832 9800; w trolleytours.com/washington-dc) visits the main attractions, including Arlington Cemetery & Union Station. Unlimited stops are permitted en route. Gray Line coach tours (📞779 9894; w graylinedc.com/tours) operate from the station.
ℹ **Visitors bureau** 901 Seventh NW; 📞789 7000; w washington.org; ⏱ 09.00–16.30 Mon–Fri, 09.00–16.00 Sat. Also at the Capitol.
🏠 **Accommodation** Washington DC Hotels (📞1 800 847 4832; w washingtondchotels.com) has special rates & package deals among the 40,000 hotel rooms.

Hotels include the Phoenix Park, 520 N Capitol NW; 📞638 6900; w phoenixparkhotel.com, **$$$$$**; The River Inn, 924 25th; 📞335 9880; w theriverinn.com, **$$$$**; Hotel Hive, 2224 F St NW; 📞849 8499; w hotelhive.com, **$$$**; Liaison Capitol Hill, 415 New Jersey Av; 📞638 1616; w jdvhotels.com, **$$$**; Madera, 1310 New Hampshire Av; 📞296 7600; w hotelmadera.com, **$$$**; Comfort Inn Downtown, 1201 13th NW; 📞682 5300; w dcdowntownhotel.com, **$$**.

For Bed & Breakfast accommodations, contact PO Box 12011, Washington, DC 20005; 📞328 3510; w bedandbreakfastdc.com.

AYH Hostel, 1009 11th NW; 📞737 2333; w hiwashingtondc.org. Dormitory rooms, free tours & movies, **$**. The city's oldest continuously operating hotel, the Hotel Harrington, is at 436 11th & E (📞628 8140 or 📞1 800 424 8532). Handily located for the museums & monuments, it has AC, a restaurant & cable TV with HBO. Large family rooms are also available; w hotel-harrington.com, **$$$**.

Recommended in Washington, DC

The Capitol At the east end of the mall; 📞226 8000; w visitthecapitol.gov; ⏱ Mon–Sat; free tours. The nation's most important building was completed in 1800, when the Senate & House of Representatives met in joint session on 22 Nov. The familiar white dome is a later addition. In addition to its use by Congress, the Capitol is a museum of American art & history.
Supreme Court First & E Capitol; 📞479 3000; w supremecourt.gov. Housed in a white marble building, the court sits for 2 weeks each month from Oct to Jun (you are invited to watch). At other times, members of staff give free lectures on w/days.
White House 1600 Pennsylvania Av; 📞456 7041; w nps.gov/whho. This official residence has been occupied by every US president since George Washington. Tours (for US citizens) can be arranged by contacting your Member of Congress & reservations must be confirmed at least 1 month prior to the visit. For more information, 📞456 7041. Visits to the White House by non-US citizens must be made through their embassies in Washington, DC.
Washington Monument On the Mall at 15th & Constitution Av; 📞426 6841; w nps.gov/wamo. The tallest (555ft/170m) structure in the city & the highest free-standing masonry edifice in the world. A line in the marble a quarter of the way up shows where building work stopped during the Civil War. Finally completed in 1888, the monument provides stunning views from narrow slits in the observation deck. The elevator is being repaired & trips to the top should resume in 2019.

Lincoln Memorial At the west end of the mall; ☏426 6841; w nps.gov/linc/index.htm; ◷ daily; admission free. A classical Greek-style temple overlooks a reflecting pool. The walls around Abraham Lincoln's 19ft (5.8m) statue are inscribed with the words of his Gettysburg Address. Appropriately, this is where Martin Luther King made his 'I have a dream' speech.

National Archives 700 Pennsylvania Av; ☏866 272 6272; w archives.gov; ◷ Mon–Fri; admission free. A Classical-style building which contains over 3 billion items, including the Declaration of Independence, the Constitution & the Bill of Rights.

Smithsonian Institution The Castle visitor centre is at 1000 Jefferson Dr; ☏633 1000; w si. edu/visit; ◷ daily; admission free. This complex of 18 museums & galleries, mostly located between Sixth & 14th, include the following:

National Postal Museum 2 Massachusetts Av, next to Union Station; ☏633 5555; w postalmuseum.si.edu; free admission. The story of the US Mail service is entertainingly demonstrated with motor vehicles, aircraft, a stagecoach & a reproduction railroad mail car (the last one was retired in 1977). You can print & mail a free personalised postcard.

Air & Space Museum Independence Av & Sixth; ☏633 2214; w nasm.si.edu; free admission. The most-visited museum in the world features the Wright Brothers' *Flyer*, Lindbergh's *Spirit of St Louis*, the *Apollo 11* command module & a piece of moon rock billions of years old. IMAX film shows, planetarium & tours.

Museum of American History 14th & Constitution Av; w americanhistory.si.edu; free admission. Includes the original *DeWitt Clinton* locomotive & *John Bull*, America's oldest working steam locomotive. Built in England, the parts for the engine were purchased by New Jersey entrepreneur & engineer Robert Stevens in 1931 & shipped to the United States. Isaac Dripps, a skilled mechanic from Belfast, was hired to assemble the locomotive, which was later used on Stevens's successful Camden & Amboy Railroad in New Jersey. The engine got its famous cowcatcher, whose real function was not to deflect livestock but to add a new pair of wheels up front for better traction, thanks to the invention of Isaac Dripps.

The rugged *John Bull* was in service for 35 years & was acquired by the Smithsonian in 1885. Look also for a gold crescent moon on the cylinder of a 1926 Pacific engine from the Southern Railway's *Crescent Limited*. Passengers on the *Crescent Limited* could pay extra for valet or ladies' maid services & its Pullman cars were trimmed with real gold leaf. The museum also has Henry Ford's Model T, Edison's phonograph, Washington's false teeth, Muhammad Ali's gloves, Dorothy's ruby slippers from The *Wizard of Oz* & the flag which inspired the national anthem.

Museum of Natural History Tenth & Constitution Av; w mnh.si.edu; free admission. T-Rex bones, the 45.5-carat Hope Diamond (biggest blue diamond in the world) & the Fenykovi African elephant (largest ever recorded) are among 60 million exhibits.

14

15

The Northeast Corridor
New Haven–Springfield
(for Boston)

JOINING THE TRAIN

Several Northeast Corridor trains branch north at New Haven to travel inland through some of Connecticut's most appealing countryside.

NEW HAVEN: ALL ABOARD (17↓) For New Haven city information and the main Northeast Corridor route, see page 198.

🚂 WALLINGFORD (↑17/7↓) Look for a spired church to your right. Wallingford is a sought-after residential community whose older neighbourhoods have houses in many architectural styles. Nearby is Sleeping Giant State Park. Amtrak's $21 million station opened in 2017 as part of a New Haven–Hartford–Springfield (NHHS) Rail Project partnership. The new brick building is 1 mile (1.6km) north of the town's historic depot completed in 1870 by the Hartford & New Haven Railroad (H&NH) and used by Amtrak until 2017. The depot now serves as a hub of town life, with an adult education centre and New Haven's Society of Model Engineers Railroad Club.

🚂 MERIDEN (↑7/10↓) Located between Mount Beseck and the Hanging Hills, the town's name means 'pleasant vale' and Meriden is famous for its spring Daffodil Festival (the last weekend in April), culminating in a parade and the crowning of Little Miss Daffodil. **Meriden's Heritage Museum** recreates life in the 1700s and you can see Long Island Sound from the tower of **Castle Craig**, accessible through Hubbard Park. Amtrak's smart red-brick station opened in 2017 as another part of the NHHS Rail Project. When the H&NH first opened in the 1830s, passengers would transfer to steamships in New Haven to reach New York City.

ESSENTIAL INFORMATION

HIGHLIGHTS In Hartford, you can visit the Connecticut state Capitol with its gold-plated dome and the Library and Supreme Court to see where Abraham Lincoln signed the emancipation document. The homes of Mark Twain and Harriet Beecher Stowe (*Uncle Tom's Cabin*) are preserved here. In Springfield you can visit America's Basketball Hall of Fame and the Amazing World of Dr Seuss, who was born here.
DURATION 1 hour 30 minutes

Beaver Pond (↑4/6↓) The pond is to your left and Silver Lake to your right.

↭ BERLIN (↑10/10↓) Cradled between two ranges of hills, the city hosts the Berlin Fair each fall. Berlin was famous in the 18th century for brickmaking as well as its many blacksmiths and metal industries, especially the manufacture of tinware using sheets of tin imported from England.

↭ HARTFORD (↑10/8↓) This is the birthplace of actor Katharine Hepburn and singer/songwriter Gene Pitney. Founded in 1633, the former landing post known as Sucking became Connecticut's capital in 1875. Look for the Capitol's gold-plated dome high up to your right as the train arrives. The white-domed **Old State House**, designed by Charles Bulfinch, is now a museum. Hartford's Library and Supreme Court are opposite the Capitol Building and contain the table where Abraham Lincoln signed the emancipation document. Amtrak operates out of a building immediately west of Hartford's impressive Romanesque Union Station, completed in 1889 and now renovated. Hartford is a planned stop on the route of the NHHS Rail Project. The **tourist bureau** is at 800 Main (✆ 860 522 6766; w *visitconnecticut.com/ hartford_central*).

When Hartford's English colonists displaced the Dutch, the latter called them *jankes* (thieves), so inventing the word 'Yankee'. Around 50 companies now make this the 'insurance capital of the world' and the Travelers Insurance skyscraper on the site of the Charter Oak is one of America's tallest buildings at 527ft (160m). The homes of Mark Twain (*Tom Sawyer*) and Harriet Beecher Stowe (*Uncle Tom's Cabin*) are preserved at Nook Farm.

Connecticut River (↑5/3↓) The river is to your right. Between here and Old Saybrook it runs through one of America's prettiest valleys.

↭ WINDSOR (↑8/5↓) The town was originally settled in 1663 among colonial tobacco farms. Rail passengers use the platform next to Windsor's beautiful French Second Empire-style station, built by the Hartford & New Haven Railroad in 1870. The restored depot is leased by the Windsor Art Center, which supports local artists, actors and musicians. A former freight house across the tracks is used for exhibitions and other events.

You continue north across the Farmington River.

↭ WINDSOR LOCKS (↑5/20↓) The 19th-century canal to your right supplied water for Dexter and Sons, a paper

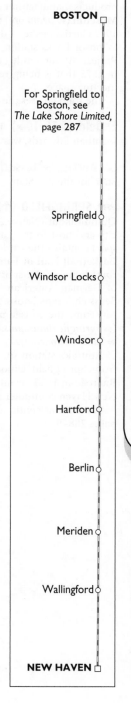

BOSTON

For Springfield to Boston, see
The Lake Shore Limited,
page 287

Springfield

Windsor Locks

Windsor

Hartford

Berlin

Meriden

Wallingford

NEW HAVEN

15

products manufacturer established here in 1871. Windsor Locks' **New England Air Museum** (w *neam.org*) owns more than 100 aircraft, including a 1909 Bleriot and a 1912 Curtiss pusher – the oldest surviving Connecticut-built airplane. The spartan Windsor Locks station is due to be improved as another stop for the NHHS Rail Project. About a mile (1.6km) away in downtown is a historic H&NH depot built in 1875 that is being rehabilitated as a visitor centre, art gallery and community meeting space.

The train crosses the Connecticut River.

Enfield (↑10/10↓) Theologian and future president of New Jersey College, Jonathan Edwards, was a Revivalist preacher here in colonial days.

Connecticut–Massachusetts state line (↑15/5↓) You leave the Constitution State for the Bay State.

⌗ SPRINGFIELD (↑20) A 17th-century trading post on the banks of the Quinnitukqut (Native American for 'long tidal') River has become an industrial city and host to the Eastern States Exposition. Springfield's **Armory** (w *nps.gov/ spar*) contains the world's largest collection of historic American firearms and the **Basketball Hall of Fame,** at 1000 Hall of Fame Av (☏ *877 446 6752;* w *hoophall. com*) honours the sport's inventor, James Naismith. This was also the birthplace of German-American Theodor Seuss Geisel, the much-loved author of the Dr Seuss children's books. Sights downtown include the Amazing World of Dr Seuss Museum, the Museum of Springfield History, and the Museum of Fine Arts (w *springfieldmuseums.org*). The **visitors bureau** is at 1441 Main (☏ *413 787 1548;* w *valleyvisitor.com*).

Amtrak's station sits on a railroad viaduct above street level, across the tracks from Springfield Union Station, which was opened by the Boston & Albany Railroad in 1926. It will become a stop for Amtrak trains and the new Springfield–New Haven commuter rail service.

Some trains continue from Springfield to Boston. For this part of the route, see pages 288–9.

16

The *Crescent*
New York–New Orleans

GENERAL ROUTE INFORMATION

Southern hospitality envelops staff and passengers as Amtrak's friendliest train travels the Northeast Corridor route then passes through Civil War country to Atlanta, Birmingham and the South. You pass through 12 states and the District of Columbia.

The *Crescent* began in 1891 as the Washington & Southwestern *Vestibule Limited*, an overnight train between Washington, DC and Atlanta. Operated by the Richmond & Danville Railroad, the predecessor of the Norfolk Southern (whose line the present train uses south of Washington, DC), the *Vestibule Limited* offered luxurious staterooms, a library and an observation car. It became a through-train from New York City to New Orleans in 1906, and was later renamed the *Crescent*. Extra amenities included a valet or ladies' maid and its Pullman cars were named

ESSENTIAL INFORMATION

HIGHLIGHTS From the Big Apple to the Big Easy, the *Crescent* explores the American South. You can tour Thomas Jefferson's exquisite Monticello home, enjoy wine tasting in the delightful town of Charlottesville, explore Atlanta's dynamic shopping and dining scene, and have fun in New Orleans with its jazz clubs, Cajun restaurants and Mississippi riverboat rides.

FREQUENCY Daily. The **southbound** train leaves New York early in the afternoon, reaching Washington, DC by early evening and Greensboro just after midnight. You arrive in Atlanta early next morning, Birmingham by late morning and New Orleans mid-evening. Travelling **north**, trains leave New Orleans early in the morning to reach Birmingham by early afternoon, Atlanta mid-evening and Greensboro during the night. You arrive in Washington, DC early on the second day and New York by early afternoon.

DURATION 30 hours

RESERVATIONS All reserved

EQUIPMENT Amfleet coaches

SLEEPING Viewliner bedrooms

FOOD Complete meals, snacks, sandwiches, drinks

LOUNGE CAR A National Park Service guide accompanies the train to provide passengers with a commentary along part of the route. An interpretive guide from the Martin Luther King Jr National Historic Site provides a narrative between Atlanta and New Orleans from Memorial Day to mid-August.

BAGGAGE Check-in service is available at most stations.

NEW YORK CITY

For New York City to Washington, DC, see *The Northeast Corridor*, page 198

WASHINGTON, DC

Alexandria

Manassas
Culpeper

Charlottesville
Lynchburg

Danville
Greensboro
High Point
Salisbury

Charlotte
Gastonia

Spartan-
Greenville burg
Clemson
Toccoa
Gainesville
ATLANTA

Anniston
Birmingham
Tuscaloosa

Meridian
Laurel
Hattiesburg
Picayune
Slidell

NEW ORLEANS

after distinguished people from southern states. The green-painted locomotives carried gold star-studded crescents and one can still be seen in Washington, DC's Smithsonian collection (page 217). In 1925, it travelled 1,362 miles (2,192km) between New York and New Orleans in 37 hours (today's route is 15 miles (24km) longer and 7 hours quicker). After World War II, it was re-equipped as a streamliner. The Southern Railway (logo 'The Southern Serves the South') continued this service until Amtrak took over in 1979.

JOINING THE TRAIN

NEW YORK CITY For New York City information and the route to Washington, DC, see page 198.

WASHINGTON: ALL ABOARD! (15↓) The *Crescent* departs by way of a tunnel, emerging with the Capitol Building to your right. Also to your right are the Bureau of Engraving, the Washington Monument and the Jefferson Memorial. To your right as you cross the Potomac River is the 14th Street road bridge.

The Pentagon (↑5/10↓) The nerve centre of America's military network employs 23,000 personnel and occupies the world's largest office building (3.7 million square feet or 340,000m²). Nearby Arlington Cemetery was the last resting place for General Pershing, Admiral Byrd and the boxer Joe Louis. President John F Kennedy's grave is marked by an eternal flame.

You pass the Ronald Reagan Washington National Airport to your left then a large Crystal City hotel and office development to your right, built on former railroad property. As the train approaches Alexandria, look left for long lines of Metro trains.

ALEXANDRIA (↑15/30↓) The massive grey stone building to your right is the George Washington Memorial Masonic Temple. Amtrak's attractive dormered Union Station at 110 Callahan Drive is one of many on this line which have been renovated. The station is in Old Town, which has the oldest continuously operating marketplace in the country.

Alexandria, 'the cradle of history', began in the 1740s as a port on the Potomac River. A million visitors each year now come to see the hundreds of restored buildings, a cobblestone waterfront and the nation's second-oldest apothecary shop. Gadsby's Tavern in Market Square was the traditional focus for business and social gatherings. Tours of **Old Town Alexandria** start at the Ramsay House (*221 King;* ✆*703 746 3301;* w *visitalexandriava.com*). The

Spirit of Mount Vernon travels along the Potomac River to George Washington's colonial estate, where you can visit his grand farmhouse, smokehouses and slave quarters.

After Alexandria, the *Crescent* changes from CSX tracks and travels on to New Orleans with the Norfolk Southern (NS).

MANASSAS (↑30/30↓) The town was fiercely fought over during the Civil War, when two battles around a strategic rail junction in 1861 cost 24,000 lives and earned Thomas 'Stonewall' Jackson his nickname. The present red-brick station on your right dates from 1914 and has original wood panelling in the waiting room. The platform and its sign can be seen on the cover of the Stephen Stills 1972 album, *Manassas*. The restored station houses the offices of Historic Manassas, a tourist information centre, and a railroad exhibition gallery.

Bristow Air Park is to your left as the *Crescent* passes a cemetery and grain elevators on the right before travelling among forests and farms.

Remington (↑20/10↓) Look right for a farmers' market before you cross the Rappahannock River. Factories and warehouses accumulate on the right as you approach Culpeper.

CULPEPER (↑30/60↓) The attractive downtown area of Culpeper can be seen beyond the red-brick station to your right. During the Revolutionary War, a pro-independence militia group called the Culpeper Minutemen formed in the town, and during the Civil War the Union Army had a headquarters here when this was an important crossroads and supply station for the troops. The current station dates from 1904 and has been renovated and is now used as a tourist information centre. It also houses the **Museum of Culpeper History** (*113 S Commerce;* ✆*540 829 1749;* w *culpepermuseum.com; admission charge*).

The *Crescent* continues southwest, accompanying the Blue Ridge Mountains and Shenandoah National Park to your right.

Rapidan River (↑15/45↓) More Civil War battles were fought at nearby Cedar Mountain, Port Republic and the Wilderness. You travel through lush farmland adorned with dogwoods and apple trees.

Orange (↑30/30↓) The James Madison law office appears to your left just before the town. Also look left for Montpelier Station and President Madison's estate.

CHARLOTTESVILLE (↑60/65↓) Named after King George III's wife, Charlotte, the last Queen of America, this is where Thomas Jefferson founded the University of Virginia and created his Monticello home on a nearby hill. Other residents have included explorer Meriwether Lewis, writer and Nobel laureate William Faulkner, actor Sissy Spacek and Presidents James Madison and James Monroe, whose **Ash Lawn Estate** is open to the public. The **visitors bureau** is at 610 E Main (✆*434 293 6789;* w *visitcharlottesville.org*).

In 2017, Charlottesville hit the news when one person died and 19 others were injured after a car rammed a crowd of people opposing a far-right rally. The march was called to protest against plans to remove a statue of a general who had fought for the pro-slavery Confederacy during the US Civil War.

To your right as you leave town is the University of Virginia Medical Center, then other academic buildings and the distinctive rotunda.

Monroe (↑55/10↓) Sweet Briar College is across the highway to your right as the train continues past rolling green fields with hedgerows, cattle, barns and streams. You cross the James River on a high trestle then enter Rivermont Tunnel.

₩ LYNCHBURG (↑65/65↓) Named after John Lynch, who founded a ferry service here after the town grew rich on tobacco, Lynchburg has many Victorian houses and is one of Virginia's chief industrial and education centres. Appomattox Courthouse, where Robert E Lee surrendered to General Grant, is 21 miles (33km) east.

The *Crescent* continues through mellow Piedmont countryside and the forests of the Blue Ridge Mountains, which extend from Pennsylvania down to Georgia as part of the Appalachian Range.

₩ DANVILLE (↑65/60↓) Located beside the Dan River, Danville once boasted 'the world's best tobacco market' and the largest textile mill in the world. The initials WBTM remain the call letters of the local radio station and the Tobacco Warehouse and Residential District includes over 500 buildings reflecting the late 19th- and early 20th-century development of Danville. The town became (briefly, in 1865) the Confederate capital, and was later the birthplace of Lady Astor.

A marker on Riverside Drive commemorates the 'wreck of the old 97' in 1903, when a mail train crashed at 90mph on the grade between Lynchburg and Danville. Thirteen people were killed, including engineer Joseph Broady. Three crates of canaries escaped and were found flying surreally in the wreck's smoky aftermath. Amtrak's fancy gabled station was built for the Southern Railway in 1899. The station was subsequently damaged by fire, reconstructed and is now renovated to include a market, a park with amphitheatre, a science centre, a community meeting and recreation facility, and a transport centre.

Virginia–North Carolina state line (↑5/55↓) The train crosses the border as it continues into the night.

₩ GREENSBORO (↑60/25↓) The grand train station was built in 1927, its waiting room having an impressive mural of the Southern Railway network of the time. Greensboro is famous for its annual Wyndham Championship golf tournament (**w** *wyndhamchampionship.com*) and for a crucial Revolutionary War battle where British general Lord Charles Cornwallis defeated General Greene at Guilford Courthouse in 1781 but lost a quarter of his army.

₩ HIGH POINT (↑25/40↓) So named because it represents the highest point on the NCRR route between Charlotte and Goldsboro where it intersected the Great Western Plank Road. The Romanesque brick and stone station was built in 1907 and in the 1990s was saved from demolition and restored. High Point is the 'home furnishings capital of the world', with 60% of all furniture produced in the United States made in the region. The biannual International Home Furnishings Market is the largest of its kind in the world, and the 'world's largest chest of drawers' is a 38ft-tall (11.5m) office building designed to look like a Goddard-Townsend block front chest. Revolutionary jazz saxophonist John Coltrane was born in Hamlet, NC, and soon after birth moved to High Point, where he attended high school.

₩ SALISBURY (↑40/50↓) Pioneer and frontiersman Daniel Boone, one of America's first folk heroes, grew up in this colonial town set among pretty hills and lakes. Amtrak's Spanish Mission-style station at Depot and Liberty opened in 1908 and was restored in the 1990s. An Arts Walk connects the station to downtown and a Rail Walk links other downtown buildings to the station.

A short distance to the north, at 411 S Salisbury Avenue in Spencer, is the **North Carolina Transport Museum** (↖ *704 636 2889;* w *nctrans.org;* ⊕ *closed Mon; admission charge*). Located on the site of what was once the Southern Railway Company's largest steam locomotive repair facility, the museum features an authentic train depot, antique automobiles and a 37-bay Roundhouse that includes 25 locomotives, dozens of railcars and other exhibit areas with memorabilia from Native American times to the present. The museum also offers seasonal train rides.

CHARLOTTE (↑50/25↓)　Another city named after George III's wife, Charlotte became the first place in America where gold was found. Railroads converged on what is now the largest city in the Carolinas.

Charlotte became rich as America's main producer of cotton cloth and is now the second-largest banking headquarters in the country, after New York City. Each May the **World 600 Auto Races** take place at the Motor Speedway and you can visit the NASCAR Hall of Fame at 400 E Martin Luther King Boulevard (↖*704 654 4400;* w *nascarhall.com*).

Charlotte was the birthplace, in a log cabin, of President James Polk, who secured the Oregon Territory for the United States. You can take a self-guided tour of the Old City from the **visitor centre** at 501 S College (↖*1 800 231 4636;* w *charlottesgotalot. com*). Highlights include a settlers' cemetery and the blushing pink splendour of Overcarsh House, a Queen Anne-style frame house completed in 1898. Latta Plantation Park, located within the Latta Plantation Nature Preserve, has costumed guides and a 19th-century merchant's house (w *lattaplantation.org*).

GASTONIA (↑25/55↓)　The *Crescent* makes a slight detour west to take in this industrial town, one of the largest centres for textile production in the world. A Revolutionary War battle was fought at Kings Mountain, nearby.

North Carolina–South Carolina state line (↑5/50↓)　You cross between the

two Carolinas and enter the Palmetto State, travelling through countryside famous for peaches.

SPARTANBURG (↑55/40↓)　This manufacturing town was named after the Spartan regiment of the South Carolina militia. Spartanburg's once-busy Union Station on Magnolia Street was saved from decline by local residents and was restored to house a passenger waiting area as well as the Hub City Railroad Museum, exploring this region's railroad, textile and agricultural industries.

GREENVILLE (↑40/35↓)　Another former textile city, known as 'The Textile Capital of the World', Greenville is now headquarters for Michelin and other major companies as well as a centre for research into emerging technologies. Bob Jones University became established in 1927, and Greenville was the birthplace of actor Joanne Woodward and Baptist minister turned politician Jesse Jackson. The small station is part of a large modern building containing offices of the Norfolk Southern Railroad.

CLEMSON (↑35/35↓)　Built for the Southern Railway in 1916, Clemson's station was originally in the town of Calhoun, named after the 19th-century politician John Calhoun. When the railroad track expanded the depot was moved, then relocated again in 2001 and restored to its early 20th-century appearance. Calhoun officially became part of the university town of Clemson in 1943.

South Carolina–Georgia state line (↑20/15↓) As the *Crescent* travels deeper into the south through wooded countryside, look for examples of the fast-growing *kudzu* vines. These were imported from Japan to combat soil erosion but have become a menace throughout the South, spreading over the ground to smother all in their path.

▟▛ TOCCOA (↑35/40↓) In 1870, Dry Pond was a stop on the Air-Line Railroad between Atlanta and Charlotte before, in 1875, the town changed its name to Toccoa, a Cherokee word for 'beautiful'. It is the home of Toccoa Falls (186ft/56m) and a college of the same name. Note the colourful station building to your right and an impressive spired church on your left. The 1915 Southern Railway Depot has been restored and houses, among other things, the Stephens County Historical Society, and the Currahee Military Museum.

The *Crescent* departs past warehouses and freight trains to travel among tree-covered hills, lumber yards, orchards and occasional fields. Near Gainesville, factories and freight trains gather on both sides.

▟▛ GAINESVILLE (↑40/55↓) The town is on the eastern edge of Lake Sidney Lanier, Georgia's largest lake. The Lake Lanier Islands are a popular recreation area with beaches, campsites, fishing and boating. Amtrak's charming brick station at 116 Industrial Boulevard also serves Athens, home of the University of Georgia (America's oldest state college). The depot was built by the Southern Railway in 1910 and is now owned by the Norfolk Southern. Gainesville's 1914 Midland Railroad station has been restored as an arts centre.

The train pauses across a barriered road junction before continuing among more factories, lumber yards and freight wagons. Look right for a flea market after you pass beneath a highway bridge.

As the day becomes lighter you begin to travel through less mountainous scenery, with cattle, horses and dark ploughed fields.

Norcross (↑35/20↓) Industry returns as MARTA commuter trains assemble. Look for the old green Pullman car sidelined to your left.

Oglethorpe University (↑40/15↓) The campus is to your right. The university is home to The Crypt of Civilization, the world's first buried time capsule, officially sealed in 1940 and due to be opened in the year AD8113. As you near Atlanta, the city's imposing skyscrapers can be seen ahead to your left.

▟▛ ATLANTA (↑55/130↓) Birthplace of Spike Lee, Julia Roberts and Kanye West, Atlanta was the venue for the 1996 Olympic Games and is one of America's fastest-growing cities. The unofficial capital of the South has the most affluent black middle class in the country and one of the country's highest crime rates. Magnolias still bloom along the older streets and spring fills Atlanta's parks with flowering azaleas and dogwoods.

The city began in 1837 as a railroad town after the Georgia General Assembly voted to build the Western & Atlantic Railroad as a trade route with the Midwestern United States. Following the forced removal of the Cherokee Nation, the area was opened up for settlement and railroad construction. The eastern railroad terminus, originally called 'Marthasville', was renamed 'Atlantica-Pacifica' by the Georgia Railroad's chief engineer, then shortened to 'Atlanta'. By the time of the Civil War, more rail lines converged here than anywhere else in the South and the city became a prime target for General Sherman's Union forces. The war's destruction failed to halt growth for long and many large corporations are now resident, including Coca-Cola, Delta Air Lines and CNN. The glass building to the left of the station belongs to AT&T.

Atlanta basics

Telephone code 404

Station (*Ticket office & waiting room* 07.30–21.30) Amtrak's renovated Brookwood (Peachtree) station is at 1688 Peachtree, 3 miles (5km) north of downtown (take bus #23). Built by the Southern Railway in 1918 as a small suburban halt, the station is barely adequate today & Amtrak is hoping to relocate to a larger facility. It opened at a time of segregation & originally had separate waiting rooms & rest rooms for white & African-American passengers. Lockers, payphones, vending machines, handcarts.

Connections No Thruway buses

Local transport MARTA operates buses & subway trains (848 5000; w itsmarta.com)

Taxis Atlanta Cab 935 9555; Checker 351 1111

Car rental Avis, 143 Courtland; 659 4814

Greyhound 232 Forsyth; 584 1728

Hartsfield Airport The world's busiest airport, both in terms of passengers & number of flights, is 10 miles (16km) south by MARTA train (848 5000) & ATL Shuttle bus (641 0962)

Tours American Coach Line; 1 800 593 1818. Walking tours from the Preservation Center, 327 St Paul Av (688 3353; w atlantapreservationcenter. com).

Visitors bureau 233 Peachtree; 521 6600; w atlanta.net; 08.30–17.30 Mon–Sat

Accommodation Hotels include the Artmore, 1302 West Peachtree; 876 6100; w artmorehotel.com, $$$$; Barclay, 89 Luckie; 524 7991, $$$; Holiday Inn, 111 Cone NW; 524 7000; w ihg.com/holidayinnexpress, $$$; Marriott Buckhead, 3405 Lenox Rd; 261 9250; w marriott.com, $$$; Wyndham Atlanta Galleria Center, 2762 Cobb Pkwy; 678 813 1915; w wyndhamhotels.com/wingate, $$$; Howard Johnson, 1551 Phoenix Bd; 770 996 4321; w wyndhamhotels.com/hojo, $$; Motel 6, 311 Courtland; 659 4545; w motel6.com, $$.

For B&B contact Sugar Magnolia Bed & Breakfast, 804 Edgewood Av NE; 222 0226; w sugarmagnoliabb.com, $$$.

Atlanta Hostel, 908 Tift Av SW; 643 5584; w theatlantahostel.com, $.

Recommended in Atlanta

State Capitol 206 State Capitol; 656 2846; w libs.uga.edu/capitolmuseum; Mon–Fri; free tours. Topped by a dome of gold leaf mined in north Georgia, the 1889 building houses state offices, Confederate flags & the Georgia History Museum.

Stone Mountain Park & Village 16 miles (25km) east of Atlanta on US 78; 1 800 401 2407; w stonemountainpark.com; daily; admission charge. This 3,200-acre (1,296ha) park attracts 6 million visitors a year, the 3rd-largest attendance in the United States (after the Disney parks). The site includes the world's largest granite outcrop, where you can see carved figures of Jefferson Davis, Robert E Lee & Stonewall Jackson on horseback.

Antebellum Plantation & Farmyard Featuring 19 restored historic buildings from around the state of Georgia, built between 1783 & 1875. This is the largest collection of period furniture & decorations in the South, reflecting the diverse lifestyles of 18th- & 19th-century Georgia residents.

Stone Mountain Scenic Railroad The railroad takes visitors on a 5-mile (8km) excursion around the mountain's base aboard a full-size locomotive. Opened in 1962, the railroad features diesel engines, built in 1950 & 1956, pulling newly renovated 1940s open-air train cars. The train departs from a scale replica of the Main Train Depot from late 19th-century downtown Atlanta.

Governor's Mansion 391 W Paces Ferry Rd; 261 1776; Tue–Thu; admission free. Built in Greek Revival style, the mansion has a fine collection of federal period furnishings.

Martin Luther King Center & Historic District The King Center at 449 Auburn Av (✆*526 8900;* w *thekingcenter.org;* ☉ *daily; admission free*) was established in 1968 by Coretta Scott King & has a library, films & museum. Atlanta was a focal point for the 1960s civil rights movement. You can visit Dr King's birthplace & see the Ebenezer Baptist Church (☉ *daily; donation*) where he preached.

Jimmy Carter Library 441 Freedom Parkway; ✆*865 7100;* w *jimmycarterlibrary.gov;* ☉ *daily;* admission charge. The Jimmy Carter Library is the only presidential library in the southeastern United States. Documents & memorabilia, including some of the nation's historic treasures, are on exhibit.

Southeastern Railway Museum 3595 Buford Hwy in Duluth, 20 miles (32km) northeast of Atlanta; ✆*770 476 2013;* w *train-museum.org;* ☉ Thu–Sat; admission charge. Among the rolling stock are vintage steam engines, wooden cars & Pullmans such as the 1911 car *Superb* used by President Harding. Train rides in restored coaches. In 2008, the former Southern Railway System depot previously used in downtown Duluth was relocated to the museum & is being restored.

Southern Museum of Civil War & Locomotive History 2829 Cherokee, Kennesaw; ✆*427 2117;* w *southernmuseum.org;* ☉ daily; admission charge. 25 miles (40km) north of Atlanta, Kennesaw is the only town in America where it is illegal for citizens not to own a gun. The museum

features *The General*, an 1855 Rogers steam engine that was stolen at Big Shanty by northern soldiers in 1862 along with 2 cars of a Western & Atlantic passenger train. *The General* was captured halfway to Chattanooga after being pursued at 60mph (96km/h) by southern troops aboard the locomotive *Texas*. The 'great locomotive chase' inspired the classic 1926 film, *The General*, starring Buster Keaton, who was born close to the sounds of a rail junction & had a lifelong obsession with trains.

Chattanooga Located 110 miles (176km) northwest of Atlanta; w choochoo.com. Chattanooga is dominated by Lookout Mountain, the top of which can be reached on the world's steepest passenger railway line. The 1909 Southern Railway terminal has been renovated, its magnificent 85ft (24m) dome becoming the lobby of a hotel where you can spend the night in restored Victorian passenger cars & eat in an original dining car (✆*423 266 5000*). The station also holds the largest HO-gauge model railway in the world.

The original 'Chattanooga Choo-Choo' was a passenger train which first operated from Cincinnati in 1880. Almost all trains going south passed through Chattanooga then, & this one later encouraged Glenn Miller to make a million-selling record. A vintage wood-burner locomotive resembling *The General* used on that first run is displayed at the terminal. The state has plans to reopen a regular train route between Chattanooga & Atlanta.

ATLANTA: ALL ABOARD! (↑55/130↓) The *Crescent* leaves Atlanta through western industrial suburbs. Extensive freight yards sprawl to your right and the derelict site of the former Chattahoochee Brick Company is to your left. In the 1800s, the company used free convict labour to produce hundreds of thousands of bricks a day, with high mortality rates. Many want the site to become an educational memorial and parkland to respect those abused workers.

The train crosses Interstate 75 and the Chattahoochee River before re-entering a landscape of tree-covered hills and ridges.

Douglasville (↑35/95↓) One of many quiet towns encountered on this section of the route, Douglasville was founded in 1874 when the railroad came to this area. It was originally known as 'Skint Chestnut', after a large tree which Native Americans stripped of its bark to use as a landmark.

Villa Rica (↑50/80↓) Look right among pine trees and dogwoods for the old Golden Hosiery Mills cotton warehouse, now transformed into apartments.

Bremen (↑65/65↓) The former Hubbard Slacks Company building is seen to your right before the *Crescent* moves slowly out of Bremen. You pass a church on your left then start climbing a series of S-shaped curves into the hills.

Tallapoosa (↑75/55↓) Note one of Georgia's finest golf courses on your left as you approach town. The *Crescent*'s tracks run on an island along the centre of Main Street and an ancient steam engine can be seen on display.

The train picks up speed as it crosses the attractive Tall River then climbs further into forested hills. Look for logs being loaded aboard railway wagons on your left before you cross the Tallapoosa River.

Georgia–Alabama state line (↑90/40↓) You pass from Eastern to Central Time, so watches go back an hour (forward when travelling east). The landscape becomes ever more densely wooded as you enter Talladega National Forest at the southern end of the Appalachian Mountains.

Heflin (↑105/25↓) This was once a gold rush town. In the left distance is Alabama's highest mountain, Mount Cheaha (2,407ft/735m).

ᴴᴴᴴ ANNISTON (↑130/90↓) The town's name is derived from 'Annie's Town', after Annie Scott Tyler, wife of railroad president Alfred L Tyler. This is one of the state's main manufacturing centres, with an attractive red-brick station on the right. Also on the right is the Lee Brass Foundry, one of the largest in the world.

Anniston Depot (↑10/80↓) World War II Sherman tanks guard silos at one of the US Army's largest military facilities for the production and repair of ground-combat vehicles, stretching away to your right.

Lincoln (↑15/75↓) Look for a modest blue railroad building on your right.

Pell City (↑30/60↓) The town was founded in 1890 by railroad investors and named after Jonathan H Pell of the Pell City Iron and Land Company, one of the railroad's main financial backers.

The train enters Chula Vista Mountain Tunnel, the only tunnel on this line.

Gahaba River (↑65/25↓) You cross by means of two high bridges. The river continues on your left as undulating, forest-covered hills give way to industrial scenes near Birmingham.

Irondale (↑70/20↓) Freight wagons assemble on the right. Look right also for the Sloss furnace, which operated as a pig iron-producing blast furnace from 1882 to 1971. After closing, it became one of the first industrial sites in the country to be preserved and is a designated National Historic Landmark. To your left is a large former Dr Pepper Company building, now housing a design centre, farmers' market, theatre, restaurants, shops and art galleries.

Red Mountain (↑85/5↓) A 55ft (17m) statue on the mountain to your left represents Vulcan, the Roman god of fire and forge. Made for the 1904 St Louis World's Fair, this is the largest (60 tons/54,000kg) cast-iron statue ever constructed. A stairway inside leads to an observation deck at the top.

BIRMINGHAM (↑90/60↓)   Located on the southern end of downtown, Birmingham's modern station stands next to Railroad Park, former industrial land transformed into a 19-acre (8ha) green space with hills, a lake and more than 600 trees. 'Birmingham's Living Room' is a historically rich venue for recreation, family activities, concerts and cultural events. A walking path follows the ridge of the hills and rises to the level of a viaduct giving rail enthusiasts great views of passing freight and passenger trains. Wood-panelled structures such as the park office and café were designed to look like railroad boxcars.

Alabama's biggest city has been the home of Willie Mays (of baseball fame), Nat King Cole and Hank Williams Jr. Founded in 1871 at the crossing of two railroad lines, Birmingham rapidly became the South's leading industrial centre, based on iron and steel production. Named after its English equivalent, the city also has parks and gardens filled with roses and dogwood trees. The **visitors bureau** is at 2200 Ninth Avenue N (↖*205 458 8000*; **w** *birminghamal.org*).

The *Crescent* departs among rail yards, with Vulcan still dominating the skyline to your left.

Bessemer (↑22/38↓) To your right are the Royster Guano Company building and a former Pullman-Standard factory. Assuming both trains are on time, you should soon be passing the northbound *Crescent*.

TUSCALOOSA (↑60/90↓) Named after a Choctaw chief, Tuscaloosa used to be Alabama's capital. The University of Alabama, home of the 'Crimson Tide' football team, is to your right as you approach the beautiful brick and stucco station, built in 1911 for the Southern Railway.

The train skirts a golf course to your left then travels southwest through swamp country. Sleepy towns, sunburned houses and characterful general stores appear between the forest plantations and logging sites.

Mound State Monument (↑15/75↓) Prehistoric mounds to your right were used by Native Americans for ceremonial purposes, although the temple on the highest one is more recent.

Black Warrior River (↑35/55↓) The *Crescent* slows down to clank across a steel drawbridge into further swamp country. Another track runs along the raised bed to your left.

Tombigbee River (↑45/45↓) Note the white cliffs as you cross this part of the Tenn-Tom project which links the Tennessee, Ohio and Upper Mississippi rivers with the Gulf of Mexico.

Livingston (↑70/20↓) Named after Edward Livingston, who negotiated the Louisiana Territory purchase in 1803.

York (↑75/15↓) Look for picturesque stores to your right and a sawmill to your left.

Alabama–Mississippi state line (↑80/10↓) The train continues south among cotton fields and magnolias.

MERIDIAN (↑90/60↓) Meridian was established in 1860 and the town prospered until much of it was burned to the ground by General Sherman during the Battle of Meridian in 1864. This was the birthplace of delta country blues artist Jimmie Rodgers, the 'singing brakeman' whose memory lives on at a museum and the town's music festival. Rodgers worked on the railroad and wrote many songs about his experiences. 'Waiting for a Train' told the story of a hobo who jumped freights to look for work during the 1930s Depression.

Meridian is still an important rail junction, where tracks radiate in six directions. In the shunting yards beyond the remodelled station you can see rolling stock from many lines, including the Southern Railway, the Delaware & Hudson and the Illinois Central Gulf. The splendid 1907 station was built in traditional style and is remarkably large, considering it sees only two Amtrak trains a day (one in each direction). As the *Crescent* leaves, look for a faded Gulf Mobile Sohio Railroad building falling apart to your left.

Key Field (↑8/52↓) Light aircraft are housed in the hangars to your right and other planes belong to the Mississippi National Guard. You cross Chunky Creek and pass a natural gas facility to your left.

⚞ LAUREL (↑60/30↓) This is a trading centre for farmers, with a fire station on the left and disused tracks that run into the trees. Laurel is a crew-change point for the *Crescent*. Amtrak has a waiting room at the north end of the neat brick station building, originally built in 1913 by the New Orleans & Northeastern Railroad and recently restored with its original wooden benches.

The *Crescent* crosses the Leaf River just before Hattiesburg Station, where an old baggage car can be seen confined between two steam locomotives.

⚞ HATTIESBURG (↑30/60↓) Home of Southern Mississippi University and the Magnolia Classic golf tournament, Hattiesburg was founded on the railroad and lumber industries. The New Orleans & Northeastern Railroad, built from Meridian through to New Orleans, came through Hattiesburg in 1884. Completion of the Gulf & Ship Island Railroad from Gulfport to Jackson, Mississippi, arrived in Hattiesburg in 1897, when this crossing of the rail lines earned Hattiesburg the title of 'Hub City'. The impressive restored station at 308 Newman was opened in 1910 and has been in continuous use ever since. Built in Italian Renaissance style, the 14,000ft² (1,300m²) brick structure is located in the Newman-Buschman Railroad Historic District, Hattiesburg's oldest neighbourhood.

You leave past a square-towered church on your left.

Poplarville (↑40/20↓) Birthplace of Theodore Bilbo, a US senator and segregationist who was Governor of Mississippi in the 1920s–40s.

⚞ PICAYUNE (↑60/15↓) Picayune was founded in 1904 by Eliza Jane Poitevent Nicholson, poet and publisher of the *New Orleans Times-Picayune* newspaper, named after a Spanish coin used throughout colonial America. The town received little damage from Hurricane Katrina so became a permanent home for many who relocated from the Mississippi Gulf Coast and New Orleans. Amtrak's modern station was built in the style of a classic early 20th-century passenger station, including a *porte-cochère* (covered carriageway) and waiting room. Note the old open wooden pavilion to provide shelter for waiting passengers.

Pearl River (↑5/10↓) Crossing the river takes you into the flat, lush subtropical landscape of southern Louisiana.

SLIDELL (↑15/55↓) Slidell was founded around 1882 during construction of a major new railroad from New Orleans to Meridian, Mississippi, connecting there with Cincinnati, Ohio, and eventually with New York City. The New Orleans & Northeastern Railroad established a building camp at the first high ground north of Lake Pontchartrain which eventually grew into the city. In 2005, Slidell suffered extensive damage from the effects of Hurricane Katrina, experiencing a massive storm surge from Lake Pontchartrain. It remains a residential suburb for many who commute into New Orleans and Main Street is to your left beyond the renovated station. Built around 1903, the depot connects to Olde Towne Slidell with its popular Robert's Landing Park. Nearby Bayou Liberty featured in the James Bond film, *Live and Let Die*.

Lake Pontchartrain (↑10/45↓) Taking the *Crescent* is worthwhile just to experience this spectacular 6-mile (10km) crossing of Lake Pontchartrain's eastern tip. The train runs along a causeway immediately above the lake's surface, giving sensational views across 630 square miles (1,630km²) of water. The scene is especially wonderful at sunset (or sunrise if travelling east). Look for fishing shanties on stilts and a road bridge to your left. In 1832, a steam engine built in England was shipped to New Orleans. Named Pontchartrain, it operated a 5½-mile (8.8km) route to the lake as the Pontchartrain Railroad.

Soon after leaving Lake Pontchartrain, you glimpse the New Orleans skyline ahead to your left. Look also for Tulane University and the Greenwood Cemetery with above-the-ground graves. On arrival in New Orleans the *Crescent* pauses before reversing into the station.

NEW ORLEANS (↑55) For New Orleans city information, see page 155.

UPDATES WEBSITE

You can post your comments and recommendations, and read feedback and updates from other readers online at **w** bradtupdates.com/usa.

The *Silver Star*
New York–Miami

GENERAL ROUTE INFORMATION

Another train with a party atmosphere, the *Silver Star* travels between the great north and Florida's subtropical resorts, passing through historic Virginia, tracts of pine forest and Old Savannah. Beyond Lake Okeechobee you head down the coast to Miami, the furthest south that you can travel by train in the US.

JOINING THE TRAIN

NEW YORK For New York City and the *Silver Star* route to Washington, DC, see page 198. For the route from Washington, DC to Alexandria, see page 222.

ALEXANDRIA: ALL ABOARD! (90↓) Soon after leaving Alexandria the *Silver Star* crosses the first of several inlets leading to the Potomac River.

Lorton (↑14/76↓) Amtrak's northern *Auto Train* depot is to your right. The *Silver Star* crosses the Occoquan River and Neabsco Creek.

ESSENTIAL INFORMATION

HIGHLIGHTS This train connects New York City and Miami with stops at exciting places in between, including stylish Savannah and Orlando for the thrills of Disney World and the inspiring Kennedy Space Center. At the end of the line are the beautiful beaches, colourful neighbourhoods and Latin-influenced food and music of Miami.

FREQUENCY Daily. The **southbound** service leaves New York mid-morning to reach Washington, DC mid-afternoon, Richmond late afternoon and Raleigh by mid-evening. You arrive in Savannah and Jacksonville early next morning, Orlando by mid-morning and Miami early evening. Travelling **north**, trains leave Miami mid-morning to reach Orlando early evening, Jacksonville late evening and Savannah during the night. You arrive in Richmond around midday, Washington, DC mid-afternoon and New York by early evening.

DURATION 30+ hours

RESERVATIONS All reserved

EQUIPMENT Amfleet coaches

SLEEPING Viewliner bedrooms

FOOD Complete meals, snacks, sandwiches, drinks

BAGGAGE Check-in service is available at most stations.

NEW YORK CITY □

For New York City and
the Silver Star route to
Washington, DC, see
The Northeast Corridor,
page 198

WASHINGTON, DC □

For the route from
Washington, DC to
Alexandria, see
The Crescent, page 222

Alexandria

Richmond

Petersburg

Rocky Mount

Raleigh

Cary

Hamlet — Southern Pines

Camden

Columbia

Denmark

□ **SAVANNAH**

□ **JACKSONVILLE**

Palatka

Deland

Winter Park

TAMPA □ **ORLANDO**

Lakeland — Kissimmee

Winter Haven — Sebring

Okeechobee

West Palm Beach

Delray Beach

Deerfield Beach

Fort Lauderdale

Hollywood

MIAMI

Possum Point (↑20/70↓) A huge Virginia Power electricity-generating plant appears on the peninsula to your left.

Quantico Base (↑30/60↓) Amtrak's *Carolinian* train makes a stop inside this 60,000-acre (24,000ha) US Marine Corps base, where the museum features World War II tanks and aircraft. Look left for the airfield and assault course.

You continue with the Potomac away to your left and travel south among forests and rivers.

Falmouth (↑36/54↓) Soon after this small residential and manufacturing town you cross the muddy Rappahannock River, across which George Washington famously threw a silver dollar. A highway bridge is to your right.

Fredericksburg (↑40/50↓) Another stop for the *Carolinian*. Washington lived in Fredericksburg as a boy and Mary Washington's garden at 1200 Charles still has the box hedges she planted. George's brother, Charles, owned the Rising Sun Tavern. The **visitors bureau** is at 706 Caroline (✆ 540 373 1776; w visitfred.com) and Amtrak's station at Caroline and Lafayette Boulevard. Nearby Fredericksburg and Spotsylvania Military Park explains events at four Civil War battlefields.

The train leaves with Fredericksburg's airport and runways to your left.

Meade Pyramid (↑45/45↓) This memorial to the Civil War general George G Meade can be seen to your left. This granite structure was completed in 1898 to commemorate the battles fought around Fredericksburg (1862). This is America's battleground, where the Civil War reached its bloody climax and more than 15,000 people died, buried mostly in unknown graves.

Jackson Shrine (↑55/35↓) Stonewall Jackson died in the modest white house to your left at Guinea. You cross the Mattaponi and Pamunkey rivers as the train travels through pleasant countryside. Logging operations and marshes are often close to the sides of the track.

Ashland (↑80/10↓) As the train runs carefully beside the town's main street look left for picturesque Randolph-Macon College. Dating from 1830, it was originally for women only and is the second-oldest Methodist-run college in the country.

🚂 RICHMOND (↑90/30↓) State capital since 1779, Richmond was the Confederate capital for much of the

Civil War. The old tobacco town has recently revived after a period of decline, and the Cultural Link trolley takes in 35 historic landmarks. Richmond's **tourist bureau** is at 401 N Third (✆ *804 783 7450;* w *visitrichmondva.com*).

The **Museum of the Confederacy** owns the world's largest collection of Civil War memorabilia, including General Lee's sword and Stonewall Jackson's forage cap (*1201 E Clay;* ✆ *855 649 1861;* w moc.org; admission charge). There are free tours of the Capitol, which Thomas Jefferson helped design, and of the Virginia Museum of Fine Arts (*200 N Bd;* ✆ *804 340 1405;* w *vmfa.museum*). Richmond's Renaissance Revival-style station (opened in 1901) with its ornate, domed clock tower is a city landmark.

The train curves right through massive yards bustling with goods traffic. As you near the James River, the University of Richmond can be seen to your left.

James River (↑14/16↓) You cross the rock-strewn waterway with an Interstate 95 highway bridge to your right. As you approach Petersburg, houses begin to replace the trees.

Centralia (↑20/10↓) The town is so named because it is in the central part of a county which is also at the geographic centre of West Virginia.

Chester (↑24/6↓) Several battles were fought here during the Civil War and the Battle of Chester Station started as a Union expedition against the Richmond & Petersburg Railroad. Look for the remains of an 1863 campsite to your left.

🚂 PETERSBURG (↑30/80↓) The *Silver Star* stops at the single-storey South Street Station on your right at Ettrick. The Civil War ended 75 miles (128km) west of here when Grant accepted Lee's surrender at Appomattox Courthouse. The actor Joseph Cotton was born in Petersburg.

Virginia University appears high up to your left as the train departs Ettrick. You cross another muddy river, the Appomattox, into Petersburg proper. Just to the south was Fort Hell, a large Civil War fort officially called Fort Sedgwick.

The train continues through Carson and Stoney Creek then crosses the Nottoway River.

Meherrin River (↑30/50↓) After you cross the river near Emporia look for fields producing prolific crops of peanuts.

Virginia–North Carolina state line (↑35/45↓) The Georgia Pacific Plywood factory straddles the border to your right. The train enters the Tar Heel State, so named after a promise Jefferson Davis made to tar the heels of soldiers to make them stand their ground.

Roanoke River (↑45/35↓) You cross the river on its way from the Blue Ridge Mountains to the Atlantic. This area around Weldon was the setting for the Sally Field film *Norma Rae*.

Enfield (↑65/15↓) Peanut storage warehouses appear on both sides before the train travels through a region of swamps renowned for their oversized crocodiles. North Carolina Wesleyan College can be seen to your right at Battleboro. Approaching Rocky Mount, you cross over the Tar River.

ROCKY MOUNT (↑80/80↓) North Carolina grows the largest tobacco crop in America and much of it comes here to be marketed, along with cotton and other produce. In the old days most of the tobacco was transported from here by rail. Amtrak's red-brick station is at 101 Hammond.

Wilson (↑20/60↓) This is a scheduled stop for *Palmetto* and *Carolinian* trains. The town of Wilson was named after General Louis Dicken Wilson, a state senator and early advocate of public schools. Years ago, Wilson was the world's largest tobacco market and it remains the largest in North America by volume. Warehouses and curing facilities feature on both sides of the track.

Selma (↑45/35↓) This modest town serves adjacent farm communities and is another stop for the *Palmetto* and *Carolinian*. Selma was born as a railroad town and Union Depot was built in 1924 for the Atlantic Coast Line and Southern railways. Several houses have pictures of locomotives painted on their sides and the annual 'Railroad Days' celebration each October commemorates the town's rail heritage.

The *Silver Star* travels on past oil storage tanks then crosses the Neuse River before going through Wilson Mills. Look for more tobacco plants and peanut fields. Fox hunters, or chasers, can sometimes be seen during spring and autumn.

RALEIGH (↑80/14↓) The 'city of oaks' was named after its founder, Sir Walter Raleigh, and proclaimed North Carolina's unalterable seat of government. Raleigh's statue takes pride of place near the Capitol, completed in 1840 and restored for the US bicentennial. Beautifully preserved Victorian houses stand on streets lined with oak trees, magnolias and dogwoods. Raleigh has many educational establishments and high-tech industries, and *Money* magazine voted it the best place to live in America.

The **North Carolina Museum** depicts life from the first settlements through Revolutionary days to the Civil War (*2110 Blue Ridge Rd;* ✆ *919 839 6262;* w *ncartmuseum.org; admission free*). use. For information on the Victorian neighbourhoods contact the **visitor centre** at 500 Fayetteville (✆ *0800 849 8499;* w *visitraleigh.com*).

North Carolina Central Prison (↑5/9↓) The jail to your left is bounded by a double wire fence with a razor ribbon on top.

North Carolina State University (↑7/7↓) The university is seen to your right before the train continues among lakes, streams and hills thick with pine trees.

CARY (↑14/61↓) Located in the heart of the Research Triangle region, this is one of the fastest-growing cities in the US, with more PhDs per capita than any city larger than 75,000 people. Begun in 1750 as a settlement called Bradford's Ordinary, the coming of the North Carolina Railroad (NCRR) 100 years later placed it on a major transportation route. Amtrak's modern station was built in 1996 after Cary's historic station had been demolished in the 1970s.

You continue through the small communities of Merry Oaks and Moncure. On the approach to Southern Pines look left for the corrals where racehorses are prepared.

SOUTHERN PINES (↑61/30↓) The train holds up traffic among manicured bushes at a road junction. The large building beyond Amtrak's wooden station is an arts centre.

HAMLET (↑30/70↓) A proud sign proclaims this 'the all-American city'. This was the birthplace of jazz saxophonist John Coltrane, and is located at a major junction of two CSX rail lines. Log trains are set up in rail yards to the right of canopied Main Street Station, which is a registered historic building. Dating from 1900, it was originally called the Seaboard Air Line Passenger Depot. 'Air Line' implies an absolutely straight direct line. Between 2001 and 2004, its Queen Anne-style station house was moved across a set of tracks for safety reasons and converted into a museum. The station was jacked up, rotated 90° and moved 210ft to its new foundation. Hamlet's **National Railroad Museum and Hall of Fame** is at 120 E Spring Street (✆ *910 582 3555*).

After Hamlet, industry gives way again to forests, fields and white-spired churches.

Carolinas state line (↑7/63↓) You move from North into South Carolina then cross the Pee Dee River north of Cherub and enter the Sand Hills.

Bethune (↑50/20↓) Located just south of the Lynches River, Bethune is one of the country's chief egg producers. The annual Bethune Chicken Strut is a three-day festival in August that includes a parade down Main Street, a classic car show, carnival rides and musical performances.

CAMDEN (↑70/30↓) Home of three racetracks and the Colonial Cup steeplechase, Camden is among South Carolina's oldest cities, often fought over during the Revolution. A stage of Alexander Graham Bell's first transcontinental telephone call was completed here in 1915.

COLUMBIA (↑30/55↓) The state capital since 1786, when government moved to the banks of the Congaree River from Charleston. The Hampton-Preston Mansion shows how Confederate general and statesman Wade Hampton lived in the 19th century. The **visitors bureau** is at 1110 Lincoln (✆ *803 545 0102*; w *experiencecolumbiasc.com*). Nearby are Fort Jackson and the state fairgrounds. Constructed in 1991 and featuring a delicate cupola, Amtrak's station is 3 miles (5km) from downtown. Look for the stationary red caboose.

The **South Carolina Railroad Museum** is 25 miles (40km) to the north at 110 Industrial Park Road, Winnsboro (✆ *803 635 9893*; w *scrm.org*). Locomotives and rolling stock include a Seaboard office car and a hospital/command car. The museum's railroad, known today as the Rockton, Rion & Western, began life in 1883 as the Rock City Railway. Some of America's last steam trains ran between Rockton and Greenbrier, and on Saturdays from June to August you can take a ride along the restored line.

DENMARK (↑55/80↓) This railroad town is situated in the middle of swampland. In 1830, Captain Z G Graham sold 17 acres (7ha) of land for a turnout and station to the South Carolina Canal & Railroad Company, which ran the *Best Friend of Charleston*, the first steam locomotive-driven passenger service in the United States, along the Charleston–Hamburg line. This passed through Graham's Turnout but never made it to Hamburg, as the *Best Friend of Charleston* exploded in a boiler accident less than a year later. Graham's Turnout was established as a town in 1837, and was later renamed after Captain Isadore Denmark, an official of the Seaboard Air Line.

South Carolina–Georgia state line (↑55/25↓) You enter what was once Great Britain's 13th colony.

▰▰▰ SAVANNAH (↑80/130↓) General James Oglethorpe and a group of English colonists founded Savannah on a bluff next to the river in 1733. Tobacco and cotton wealth soon resulted in great warehouses, mansions and a booming cotton exchange. America's first planned city was designed by Oglethorpe, who laid out a grid of streets and filled the squares with mountain laurel, oaks, azaleas and dogwoods. In *Treasure Island*, Robert Louis Stevenson refers to Savannah as a place of beauty and style. It was here, despite the rarity of snow, that James L Pierpoint composed *Jingle Bells*.

The cotton market and prosperity suffered after the Civil War, but 1,000 buildings have been restored. More recently Savannah gained fame by appearing as the setting for movies such as *Glory* (1989), *Midnight in the Garden of Good and Evil* (1997) and *Forrest Gump* (1994). Bus and carriage tours are available from the **Historic Savannah Foundation** at 321 E York (☎ *912 233 7787;* **w** *myhsf.org*). The **visitor centre** is in a former Central of Georgia railway station at 301 Martin Luther King Boulevard (☎ *912 944 0455;* **w** *visitsavannah.com*).

The **history museum** next to the visitor centre occupies a railway shed on the site of the Siege of Savannah in 1779 (*303 Martin Luther King Jr Bd;* ☎ *912 651 6840;* **w** *chsgeorgia.org; admission charge*). There are presentations of the siege as well as displays of historic train engines and dining cars. Amtrak's clean-lined station, built in 1962 by the Savannah District Authority, is 4 miles (6.5km) from downtown at 2611 Seaboard Coastline Drive.

The *Silver Star* departs through freight yards and travels among swampland, trees, farms and villages. Watch out for egrets and anglers along the banks of the many streams.

Hunter Airfield (↑5/125↓) A US Army establishment is seen to your left just before you cross the Ogeechee River.

Richmond Hill (↑10/120↓) The car magnate Henry Ford once owned the Richmond Plantation here and used this as a winter home.

Altamaha River (↑45/85↓) You cross a river which flows into the intracoastal waterway.

Jesup (↑50/80↓) The town formed at the intersection of two railroads, the Macon & Brunswick and the Savannah, Florida & Western, and was named after Morris K Jesup, who financed the line that is now part of the Seaboard Coast Railroad. Others argue that the town's name originated from General Thomas S Jesup, a hero from the American Indian War. Jesup is a scheduled stop for *Silver Meteor* trains. Nearby are Brunswick and St Simons Island. Look for the Jesup Shrimp Inc Building to your right and a very old freight wagon to your left as you pass through town.

After Jesup, the train travels inland through eastern Georgia among more logging operations.

Big Satilla Creek (↑70/60↓) You cross the creek and a few minutes later cross the Satilla River.

Folkston (↑85/45↓) Up to 50 trains a day pass through 'The Folkston Funnel', drawing many rail fans to the town's specially built viewing platform. West and south of here is the 650-square-mile (1,683km²) Okefenokee Swamp and wildlife refuge, where the beguiling scenery and animal life can best be seen from a canoe or by walking the canal trails. Campsites are raised on platforms to outwit alligators.

Georgia–Florida state line (↑95/35↓) The *Silver Star* crosses high above the St Mary's River into the Sunshine State, which grows by around 1,000 people a day.

⊶ JACKSONVILLE (↑130/60↓) This industrial centre is the largest US city by area, reaching from the St John's River to the Atlantic. The most attractive part of the city is down by the river, with its boardwalk and park. The **Cummer Art Gallery** is in a former lumber baron's mansion and **Jessie Ball du Pont Park** features the 250-year-old *Treaty Oak* tree under which, according to apocryphal stories, settlers and Native Americans concluded a truce. The **visitors bureau** is at 208 N Laura (☎ 1 800 733 2668; w visitjacksonville.com).

Sunset Limited trains used to travel west from Amtrak's station at 3570 Clifford Lane to New Orleans and Los Angeles, as well as south to Orlando. The *Silver Star* crawls out of Jacksonville among rail yards, crossovers, warehouses and loading facilities. The St John's River to your left is one of the few which flow 'up' from south to north.

You continue past Doctor's Inlet and Black Creek, then travel through a constantly changing countryside of hardwood forests, lakes and rivers. Palm trees start to appear among the hills.

Ortega River (↑16/44↓) You cross with the St John's River still to your left and a marina to your right. Beyond the river you can see the extent of Jacksonville.

US Naval Air Station (↑20/40↓) The base is across the highway to your left, alongside an armed forces' reserve centre.

St John's River (↑35/25↓) The river appears again among trees to your left as the train goes through a land of woods, Spanish moss, small lakes and alligators. More than 300 bird species live in this area, including bald eagles, black rails, bridled terns and yellow-breasted chats. Just before Palatka you cross a tributary of the St John's River.

⊶ PALATKA (↑60/52↓) The name is a Native American word for 'forbidding place'. Exotic palm trees grace the station to your left as the *Silver Star* stops twice to accommodate the train's length. This is Amtrak's closest station to St Augustine, the oldest European settlement in the United States.

The train leaves past azalea bushes, blooming mostly in spring, and holds up traffic at a road crossing – something which happens often on this part of the route. As you cross the St John's River, dairy farms and orchards begin to appear.

Pierson (↑35/17↓) 'The fern capital of the world' grows most of America's crop, much of it exported around the world.

DeLeon Springs (↑46/6↓) The town was named after Juan Ponce de León, a Spanish explorer who discovered Florida in 1512 while on a quest for the fountain of perpetual youth.

DELAND (↑52/40↓) Founded by Henry DeLand in 1876 and the home of Stetson University (named after the hat maker). A ferry goes to Hontoon Island, famous for Timucuan settlements that are thousands of years old. The 'Craftsman-style' station at 2491 Old New York Avenue was built in 1918 and has been restored to its original condition by Amtrak, receiving an award from the Florida Trust for Historic Preservation. DeLand has had many depots since the first railroad. One was constructed in the 1890s for the orange grower and university founder, John B Stetson, so that he could ship oranges more easily. The current Amtrak station is the sixth and only surviving depot. Thruway buses go to Daytona Beach, 25 miles (40km) east, where the 500 auto races are held each January and February and draw countless fans to the international speedway.

St John's River (↑12/28↓) The *Silver Star* crosses on a steel bridge.

Sanford (↑20/20↓) After the South Florida Railroad arrived in 1884, joining Sanford to Jacksonville, this became a steamboat port and shipping point for the produce of central Florida. The *Auto Train* terminates at 600 Persimmon Avenue, and sidings for dealing with cars can be seen to your left.

You travel on among factories and housing estates with a large cement plant to your left. Urban scenes persist most of the way to Winter Park.

WINTER PARK (↑40/15↓) The train trundles through the streets of one of Winter Park's quiet, leafy neighbourhoods. The park itself is to your left. Rollins College, the oldest in the state, has a Spanish-style campus and the Cornell Fine Arts Centre. A weather vane above the modern station (that opened in 2014) bears the city's official peacock symbol and inside are glass tiles in colours that mimic a peacock's feathers.

You continue through more suburbs to Orlando.

Florida Hospital (↑5/10↓) The imposing structure stands on both sides of the track and is connected by an overhead walkway.

Church Street Station (↑11/4↓) The 1889 South Florida Railroad station on your left has become part of an entertainment complex, complete with 19th-century steam engine and street parties. Look for the high-rise buildings of Orlando ahead.

ORLANDO (↑15/20↓) Tourism has turned a modest agricultural town set among lakes and citrus groves into a 400-square-mile (1,036km²) city of a million people. More than 50 million visitors arrive in this area throughout the year. Don't stray too far from the searchlights of the major attractions or you are almost certain to become lost.

Try to get to the theme parks early – at least half an hour before opening time – when the weather is cooler and fewer people are around. Queues for rides are usually shorter when a parade is on. Take snacks and plastic bottles to fill at the water fountains. Make sure you have a good breakfast before you go to give you energy, and alternate days at the parks with trips to the beach or you may find things too exhausting.

Orlando's daytime temperatures often reach 90°F (32°C) and even the coldest months rarely get below 50°F (10°C). As elsewhere in Florida, humidity can be high.

Orlando basics

Telephone code 407

Station (*Ticket office & waiting room*
08.30–20.15) Amtrak's cheerful white stucco
station is at 1400 Sligh Bd. This splendid 1926
Mission-style building, recently refurbished,
has beautiful columns supporting the platform
canopy. Baggage store, ATM, payphones, vending
machines, newspapers, handcarts, Red Caps,
taxi stand.

Connections Shuttle buses link to all the Disney
resorts & the fare is half that of a taxi. A SunRail
commuter rail station is located just north of the
Amtrak depot.

Local transport Most hotels are some
distance from downtown, & the big attractions
further still, but there is plenty of scheduled
transport. The main companies are Phoenix (574
7662) & Gray Line (522 5911). LYNX buses
operate in Orlando & to the airport (841 5969;
w golynx.com).

Red Line I•RIDE Trolleys (866 243 7483;
w iridetrolley.com) travel to International Dr
every 20mins & serve the south International
Drive Resort area. Green Line trolleys begin & end
on International Dr, arriving every 30mins, but
primarily travel along Universal Bd.

Taxis Mears Transportation 422 2222; Ace
Metro 855 1111

Car rental Avis 851 4656

Greyhound 555 N John Young Parkway;
292 3424

Orlando International Airport 12 miles
(19km) south of downtown by LYNX bus #42 & the
Mears Shuttle (423 5566).

Tours Super Tours 370 3001; w supertours.
com; Gray Line 522 5911; w graylineorlando.
com

Visitors bureau 8102 International Dr,
Orlando, FL 32819; 363 5872 & 800 972 3304;
w orlandoinfo.com; 08.00–21.00 daily

Accommodation Orlando has hundreds of
hotels, especially around International Dr (known
locally as 'I-Drive'). Rooms on Disney property
tend to be more expensive but offer discounts
off-season (*Sep–Dec*). Book well in advance at the
Disney Central Reservations Office, Box 10100,
Lake Buena Vista, FL 32830 (828 3255).

Hotels in Orlando include the Hyatt Regency,
9801 International Dr; 284 1234; w hyatt.
com, **$$$$$**; Renaissance, 6677 Sea Harbour
Dr; 351 5555; w marriott.com, **$$$$**;
Allure Resort, 8444 International Dr; 345
0505; w allureresortidriveorlando.com, **$$**;
Comfort Inn, 8134 International Dr; 313 4000;
w choicehotels.com, **$$**; La Quinta Inn, 5825
International Dr; 915 888 3510; w lq.com,
$$; Ramada, 8342 Jamaican Court; 917 6578;
w wyndhamhotels.com/ramada, **$$**.

Recommended in Orlando

Disney World For information, advance tickets
& a free guide, contact Box 10100, Lake Buena
Vista, FL 32830; 939 1289; w disneyworld.
disney.go.com. This 27,400-acre (11,000ha)
complex opened in 1971 & is the world's most
popular tourist attraction. Over 50 million visitors
come each year & almost all of them ride the
world's largest monorail system. Other highlights
include the Magic Kingdom (rollercoasters, Mickey
Mouse & horrendous queues), the Epcot Center
(cutting-edge technology), Disney's Hollywood
Studios (animation techniques, classic films & the
Star Tours simulator) & 2 water parks: Blizzard
Beach & Typhoon Lagoon. Explore Toy Story Land
with Woody, Buzz & pals, & the new coaster-style
TRON attraction, opening in time for Walt Disney
World's 50th anniversary in 2021. Riders board a
train of 2-wheeled Lightcycles & enter into the
energy, lights & excitement of a thrilling high-tech

universe. Admission is by day ticket or by 'passport'
for several days.

The Animal Kingdom is a fantasy zoo with
an African savannah safari park conjured out of
featureless farmland. Florida oaks have been
pruned to resemble acacias & 40,000 other trees
planted. Among the 1,700 animals are elephant,
black rhino, cheetah & mhorr gazelle, which are
extinct in the wild.

Sea World 7007 Sea World Dr, 20 miles (32km)
southwest of Orlando; 545 5550; w seaworld.
com; daily; admission charge. Features killer
whales, stingrays, sea lions, penguins & some of
Florida's few remaining manatees. You can hand-
feed dolphins & enjoy close encounters with sharks
from the safety of a glass tunnel. Take Greyhound
or city bus #50.

Universal Studios 1000 Universal Studios Plaza;
363 8000; w universalorlando.com; daily;

admission charge. The largest movie studio & theme park in the world has more than 40 rides, shows & film sets, including Volcano Bay & the latest Fast & Furious Supercharged experience.

The adjacent Islands of Adventure site lets you travel back to Jurassic Park & the Lost Continent. Doctor Doom's Fearfall is faster than the space shuttle. Admission to the Islands of Adventure includes entrance to The Wizarding World of Harry Potter with its twin, high-speed rollercoasters.

Lake Eola Park Rosalind & Central; ✆246 4484; w cityoforlando.net/parks/lake-eola-park; ☉ daily; admission free. A favourite picnic & walking place in central Orlando, where you can feed live swans & hire swan-shaped paddle boats on the lake.

Wekiwa Springs State Park 1800 Wekiwa Circle, Apopka, 20mins northwest of downtown; ✆850 245 2157; w floridastateparks.org/parks-and-trails/wekiwa-springs-state-park; ☉ daily; admission free. A beautiful park with fishing, camping, swimming & canoeing on the Wekiva River or Rock Springs Run.

Kennedy Space Center Located at Cape Kennedy (or Cape Canaveral), a 1hr drive to the east; ✆855 433 4210; w kennedyspacecenter. com; ☉ daily; admission charge. Bus tours take in the museum, rocket garden & shuttle launch site. Includes an IMAX film show, the Astronaut Hall of Fame & a 373ft (124m) *Saturn V* rocket saved by cancellation of the *Apollo* project.

ORLANDO: ALL ABOARD! (↑15/20↓)

After suburban Orlando, the *Silver Star* heads west among orange groves, lakes, trees and rivers. Florida has plans for a bullet train which would travel the 250 miles (400km) between Orlando and Miami in 90 minutes.

▟▜ KISSIMMEE (↑20/60↓)

This is Amtrak's nearest station to Disney World, but Orlando provides more hotels and better local transport connections. Kissimmee was originally built on reclaimed swampland late in the 19th century, and this region is served by a network of rivers, canals and lakes. The oldest cattle auction in Florida used to take place in Kissimmee until it closed in 1996 after 58 years. The **visitors bureau** is at 215 Celebration Place (✆407 569 4800; w *experiencekissimmee.com*).

As the train pulls out of Kissimmee note the **Monument of the States** among the downtown buildings to your left. This 70ft-high (21m) structure is made out of rocks from every state in the Union, including one from President Franklin D Roosevelt.

A few minutes later the *Silver Star* passes Lake Tohopekaliga before continuing among orange groves. Look for bald eagles and wading birds such as white ibis, blue herons and egrets.

Auburndale (↑20/40↓)

Look for old citrus juice-processing plants belonging to Minute Maid and the Adams Company. Until the 1970s this entire area in all directions was covered with groves, but freezes in the 1980s caused much of the citrus industry to move further south.

▟▜ LAKELAND (↑60/35↓)

Home of Florida Southern College, many of the buildings here were designed by Frank Lloyd Wright. This is the centre of a vast citrus fruit region and Lakeland has the state's main trading exchange and juice extraction plants. The world's largest phosphate mine is nearby. *Silver Star* trains stop at Lakeland twice, before and after Tampa. Southbound trains disembark only before Tampa and board only afterwards, while northbound trains reverse this order. The train stops at an attractive Art Deco-inspired 1998 station on the north shore of Lake Mirror. This replaced a larger Atlantic Coast Line Railroad station west of town. Lakeland Civic Center is to your right and a power plant to your left.

TAMPA (↑35/35↓) The name 'Tampa' is a Seminole word for 'sticks of fire'. Settlement began when Fort Brooke was established in 1824, but most of Florida's early tourist development concentrated on the east coast. Henry Plant's railway reached Tampa late in the 19th century, when he built the 'world's most elegant' Tampa Bay Hotel. During the Spanish–American War this became a headquarters for Theodore Roosevelt. Florida's state fair takes place in Tampa each February.

St Petersburg, adjacent to the south, is quieter and more residential. From the resorts along this coast you can see a variety of wildlife including cormorants, pelicans, dolphins and, if you are really lucky, a rare and charming manatee.

Tampa basics

Telephone code 813

Station (*Ticket office & waiting room* ⊕ *09.30–18.15*) Amtrak's beautiful Italian-style Union Station opened in 1912. Lockers, ATM, vending machines, handcarts, taxi stand.

Connections Thruway buses connect with Lakeland, Pinellas-St Petersburg, Orlando, Sarasota, Fort Myers, Port Charlotte & Clearwater Beach

Local transport HART buses operate in the Tampa region (254 4278; w gohart.org) & the Pinellas Suncoast Transit Authority (PSTA) (727 540 1900) in St Petersburg

Taxis Yellow 666 6666; Independent 727 327 3444

Car rental Enterprise, 5402 N Nebraska Av; 238 8471

Greyhound 610 E Polk; 229 2174

Tampa International Airport 6 miles (10km) from downtown; you can get there by limousine or HART buses 30, 32 & 60LX. Contact the Super Shuttle (727 571 4220) for transport to St Petersburg's Clearwater Airport.

Tours Swiss Chalet; 985 3601. For dolphin-watching cruises contact Dolphin Landings (727 367 4488; w dolphinlandings.com).

Visitors bureau One Tampa City Center, 201 N Franklin; 223 2752; w visittampabay. com; ⊕ 10.00–18.00 Mon–Sat, 11.00–17.00 Sun. Other information centres are located at 1 Causeway Bd, Clearwater Beach (727 442 3604) & at 100 Second Av N, St Petersburg (727 821 4069).

Accommodation Tampa hotels include the Godfrey, 7700 Courtney Campbell Causeway; 281 8900; w godfreyhoteltampa. com, **$$$$**; Sheraton Tampa Riverwalk, 200 N Ashley Dr; 223 2222; w marriott.com, **$$$$**; Barrymore, 111 W Fortune; 518 7921; w barrymorehotel.com, **$$$**; Holiday Inn, 700 N Westshore Bd; 289 8200; w ihg.com, **$$$**; Quality Inn, 2701 E Fowler Av; 971 4710; w qualityinnandconferencecentertampa.com, **$$$**; Red Roof Inn, 10121 Horace Av; 681 8484; w redroof.com, **$$**; West Wing, 2501 E Fowler Av; 559 8000; w westwinghotel.com, **$$**.

Gram's Place, 3109 N Ola Av, is a combination of bed & breakfast & hostel, inspired by the music of Gram Parsons; 221 0596; w grams-inn-tampa. com, **$**.

Recommended in Tampa

Busch Gardens 3000 E Busch Bd; 884 4386; w buschgardens.com; ⊕ daily; admission charge. The gardens have more than 3,000 birds & animals, with a monorail to transport you among the lions & rhinos. Trek across the wide & wild Serengeti Plain & see animals such as zebras, giraffes & ostriches roaming free.

Ybor City 1600 E Eighth Av; 241 8838; w ybor. org. Tampa's Cuban city-within-a-city features Spanish-style buildings, restaurants & shops. Many of Tampa's first residents were Cuban refugees from the Spanish–American War who brought with them their cigar-making skills. The Ybor

City Museum is at 1818 E Ninth Av (247 6323; w ybormuseum.org; ⊕ daily; admission charge).

Henry B Plant Museum 401 West Kennedy Bd; 254 1891; w plantmuseum.com; ⊕ Tue–Sun; admission charge. Housed in the 1891 Tampa Bay Hotel, a National Historic Landmark built by the railroad magnate, Henry Bradley Plant. This quintessential Victorian hotel was constructed in flamboyant Turkish & Moorish style with minarets, domes, cupolas, horseshoe arches & long verandas. Filled with opulent European furniture & art, the museum tells the story of the hotel & of Florida's tourist industry.

Tampa Bay History Center 801 Old Water St; ☎ 228 0097; w tampabayhistorycenter. org; ☉ daily; admission charge. This history & heritage museum preserves & teaches the history of the Tampa Bay area with exhibits showing the geographical, historical & cultural influences shaping the region from 12,000 years ago to the present.

Tampa Museum of Art 120 W Gasparilla Plaza; ☎ 274 8130; w tampamuseum.org; ☉ daily; admission charge. The museum has a range of 20th-century art as well as a famous collection of Greek & Roman antiquities. Lectures, walking tours & children's activities.

The Dali Museum One Dali Bd; ☎ 727 823 3767; w thedali.org; ☉ daily; admission charge. The museum claims to have the world's most comprehensive collection of the eccentric Spanish Surrealist's work, including paintings, prints, photographs & objects such as the famous *Aphrodisiac Telephone* shaped like a lobster.

TAMPA: ALL ABOARD! (↑35/35↓) You return across central Florida and approach Lakeland again past a huge Publix warehouse.

₩ LAKELAND (↑35/20↓) For Lakeland, see page 242.

₩ WINTER HAVEN (↑20/45↓) The Spanish-style station was built in 1925. Winter Haven's many waterways are the setting for Florida's first theme park, Cypress Gardens.

West Lake Wales (↑8/37↓) Beyond a disused station to your left is a 205ft-high (62m) stone and marble carillon called the **Bok Tower**. This neo-Gothic and Art Deco structure was built in the 1920s and named after E W Bok, an influential editor of *Ladies' Home Journal*. The Singing Tower's 60 bronze bells weigh up to 12 US tons (10.9 tonnes) each and the surrounding subtropical gardens, designed by Frederick Law Olmsted Jr, are a refuge for squirrels and 126 bird species.

Frostproof (↑25/20↓) White beehives can be seen among the orange trees. The town failed to live up to its name in the winter of 1983, when the local crop was severely damaged.

₩ SEBRING (↑45/30↓) Farming, packing and distribution were established here in the early 1900s. The famous international motor racing track is to your left.

Lake Istokpoga (↑7/23↓) The lake is visible among trees to your right before you cross the Kissimmee River, on course between Lake Kissimmee and Lake Okeechobee (the largest lake in the southern United States). On the far side is the swamp wilderness of **Everglades National Park**, where alligators lurk among floating islands of sawgrass and reed.

₩ OKEECHOBEE (↑30/50↓) The town's name is a Hitchiti word for 'big water'. A few minutes later you pass the dykes restraining Lake Okeechobee on your right. The *Silver Star* travels for the next 59 miles (95km) through cattle country at up to 79mph (127km/h) on the longest straight stretch of track east of the Mississippi. It takes an eight-car passenger train approximately 1.13 miles (1.8km) to stop when travelling at this speed.

Indiantown (↑25/25↓) The town was named after the Seminole tribe of Florida.
The train rattles across a bridge over the St Lucie Canal connecting Lake Okeechobee with the Atlantic.

United (↑33/17↓) The airfield is used for testing new Sikorsky helicopters.

⚑ WEST PALM BEACH (↑50/20↓) This is the start of Florida's Gold Coast, with its mansions, condominiums, posh shops and polo fields. Three bridges link West Palm Beach with the island community of Palm Beach. Clear Lake is to your right.

Amtrak's beautiful Spanish-style station on your left at 201 S Tamarind Avenue was a Seaboard Air Line depot that also served the Florida East Coast Railway. The pink-washed Mediterranean-style building opened with the arrival of the Orange Blossom Special in 1925 and is now an intermodal hub for intercity passenger and Tri-Rail commuter trains, local buses and taxis. The Seaboard Air Line (motto 'Through the heart of the South') was the main rival to the Atlantic Coast Line for luxury services between New York and Florida and its *Cherry Blossom Special* was the first air-conditioned train on this route.

The **Flagler Museum** in Palm Beach honours Henry Morrison Flagler, who was visiting Florida 'in retirement' in the 1880s when he came across the quiet, charming and almost dilapidated 'Ancient City' of St Augustine. Flagler immediately saw the potential for creating an American Riviera along the east coast of the Sunshine State, with modern hotels and resorts. In 1885 he bought the assets of the Jacksonville, St Augustine & Halifax River Railway and changed its name to the Florida East Coast Railway, extending into the city of Miami. Many of the hotels he built are still famous: The Ponce de León Hotel, the Royal Poinciana Hotel, and the Palm Beach Inn (later renamed The Breakers). When his line, some of which was built by slaves from the Bahamas, reached the island of Palm Beach he set about creating the most exclusive resort in the country. The luxurious Breakers Hotel featured string orchestras and opera singers such as Dame Nellie Melba were imported to entertain Henry Flagler's rich and eminent friends, including the Rockefellers, Vanderbilts, Astors, Andrew Carnegie and J P Morgan, as well as US presidents and European nobility. The present Renaissance-style hotel is a 'palace by the sea' built on the original site of Flagler's hotel in the 1920s. It boasts more than 500 rooms, 140 acres (56ha) of gardens and two golf courses.

The opulent Flagler Museum is located in his stately Whitehall mansion at 1 Whitehall Way (✆561 655 2833; w *flagler.org*) and features an Italian Renaissance library, Louis XIV music room, Elizabethan breakfast room, Swiss billiard room and a dining room imported from Warwick Castle in England. In Palm Beach you can also find the Estée Lauder mansion, the Kennedy compound, a former home of John and Yoko Lennon, and Donald Trump's Mar-a-Lago estate, built in 1927 for cereal heiress Marjorie Merriweather Post.

You leave West Palm Beach past the airport to your right. Plans to expand the runways were blocked when a population of rare gopher tortoises was discovered.

The train continues among houses and waterways, interrupted by the occasional industrial scene.

⚑ DELRAY BEACH (↑20/10↓) An attractive, low-key resort which began as a settlement for artists, this is the home of the Delray Beach Open tennis tournament and of the **Morikami Museum of Japanese Art,** which shows the history of a daring agriculture experiment that brought George Morikami to the Sunshine State (*4000 Morikami Park Rd;* ✆ *561 495 0233;* w *morikami.org; admission charge*).

Boca Raton (↑4/6↓) Another airport appears to your left. Boca Raton's dusty pink buildings were created by the architect Addison Mizner in a mixture of European styles and have an authentic 1920s atmosphere. Set among palm trees, shady cloisters and herb gardens, this is one of the few places on the coast where beaches and dunes remain in their natural state. Singer Ariana Grande was born here and Ernie Wise, of Morecambe and Wise fame, had a holiday home in Boca Raton.

DEERFIELD BEACH (↑10/15↓) Palm trees line both sides of the track as you approach the station, which houses the **South Florida Railway Museum** (*1300 W Hillsboro Beach Bd in Deerfield;* ✆ *954 698 6620; w sfrm.org; admission charge*). The building is a fine example of Mediterranean-style architecture, with an arched entryway, stucco walls, a barrel tile roof and a two-storey tower. The museum preserves the history of railroads in southern Florida and has two impressive model railroad layouts.

Pompano Beach Racetrack (↑5/10↓) Harness racers and Quarter Horses use the track to your right at the 'Winter Capital of Harness Racing'.

FORT LAUDERDALE (↑15/12↓) One of Florida's main resorts, 'America's Venice' is also well known as a regular port of call for cruise ships. Named after the governor responsible for early Everglades drainage schemes, Fort Lauderdale has 8 miles of beaches. An intricate system of waterways makes yachting a common mode of transport.

The **visitors bureau** is at 101 NE Third Avenue (✆ *954 765 4466; w sunny.org*). Amtrak's romantic station, in Mediterranean Revival style, is a busy stop during summer and in the spring break season for colleges and universities.

You leave past Fort Lauderdale–Hollywood International Airport to your left.

HOLLYWOOD (↑12/20↓) This eastern Hollywood was founded during the 1920s and grew rapidly until the 1960s. Port Everglades is the second-busiest cruise port in the world. Look for the colourful water tower and a Hollywood Boulevard sign to your left. The 1926 Mission Revival-style station also serves Tri-Rail commuter trains, providing frequent services between Hollywood and Miami International Airport.

You continue past the large Opa-Locka flea market and a historic racetrack at Hialeah. Approaching Miami, look for Miami Beach's hotels away to your left beyond an expanse of junked cars. Freight yards sprawl away complicatedly on the right of the line.

MIAMI (↑20) America's Casablanca was founded for growing citrus fruits. Only a handful of people lived here when oil billionaire Henry Flagler's Central Florida Railroad arrived in 1896, following a deal struck in a room above a pool hall between Flagler and the visionary Julia Tuttle, who owned the land. Tourism development in the 1920s and the pretty hotels of Miami Beach (10 miles/16km long and 300ft/90m wide) now attract millions of sun lovers and fashion victims every year. The Four Seasons Hotel downtown was the tallest building in Florida at 789ft (240m) when completed in 2003.

Greater Miami incorporates Key Biscayne (home of President Nixon's winter White House), upmarket Coral Gables, Hialeah and the elegant Coconut Grove. Half the city's two million population is of Spanish-American descent.

Temperatures can reach 90°F (over 30°C) even in winter, which is the peak season and avoids summer's humidity and showers. Spring and late autumn are the best times to visit.

Miami basics

Telephone code 305

Station (*Ticket office & waiting room*
07.00–21.15) Amtrak's station at 8303 NW
37th Av in Hialeah has bus links to downtown
(7 miles/12km south) & Miami Beach (route L).
Amtrak plans to move to the new Miami Central
Station east of Miami International Airport when
this is completed. Lockers, payphones, ATM,
vending machines, newspapers, handcarts, Red
Caps, taxi stand.

Connections Tri-Rail commuter trains (*1 800
874 7245; w tri-rail.com*) go to Fort Lauderdale &
West Palm Beach. You can take one to downtown
from the Metrorail Transfer Station near Amtrak's
depot.

Local transport Metro-Dade buses run
throughout Miami, with free maps & other
information from 111 NW First (*891 3131*).
Metrorail trains operate every day, with transfers
to Metrobus, & a transfer station is close to
Amtrak's depot.

Taxis Metro 888 8888; Flamingo 759
8100

Car rental Avis, 2318 Collins Av; 538 4441

Greyhound 4111 NW 27th St; 871 1810

Miami International Airport Accessed 8
miles (13km) west by Metrobus #7 & Super Shuttle
vans (*871 2000*). Some hotels provide free taxis.
Metrobus, Metrorail & Tri-Rail airport connections will
be available from the new Miami Central Station.

Tours Miami Tour Company 260 6855;

w miamitourcompany.com. Boat cruises on
the *Island Queen* start from Miamarina, Fifth &
Biscayne Bay (*379 5119*).

Visitors bureau 701 Brickell Av; 1 800 933
8448; w miamiandbeaches.com; Mon–Fri.
More information from the Chambers of Commerce
at Key Biscayne (*361 5207*), Coconut Grove
(*446 5150*), Miami Beach (*674 1414*) & the
Everglades Visitor Association (*245 9180*).

Accommodation Miami has an abundance
of rooms, from the economical to the ultra-
luxurious. Top rates & biggest crowds are in winter,
when prices can double.

Downtown hotels include the Hilton, 1601
Biscayne Bd; 855 605 0316; w hilton.com,
$$$$; Hyatt Regency, 400 SE Second Av; 358
1234; w hyatt.com, **$$$$**; Courtyard Miami
Downtown, 200 SE Second Av; 374 3000 or 1
800 319 4927; w marriott.com, **$$$**; Holiday
Inn Port Of Miami, 340 Biscayne Bd; 446 5150;
w ihg.com/holidayinn, **$$$**.

Miami Beach hotels include the Alexander,
5225 Collins Av; 865 6500; w alexanderhotel.
com, **$$$$$**; Sagamore, 1671 Collins Av; 535
8088; w sagamoresouthbeach.com, **$$$$$**;
Days Thunderbird, 18401 Collins Av; 705
6673; w wyndhamhotels.com/days-inn, **$$$**;
Seville Beach, 2901 Collins Av; 786 257 4500;
w editionhotels.com/miami-beach, **$$$**.

Miami Beach Hostel, 810 Alton Road; 538
7030; w miamihostel.net, **$$**.

Recommended in Miami

Art Deco District From Sixth to 23rd sts, Miami
Beach. Over 800 pastel-coloured buildings with
'eyebrow' balconies & Egyptian architraves make
this the world's largest collection of Art Deco
architecture. Walking tours start from the Art Deco
Welcome Center at 1001 Ocean Dr (*531 3484*).

Wolfsonian Foundation 1001 Washington, in
the Art Deco district; 531 1001; w wolfsonian.
org; closed Wed; admission charge. The restored
building contains 70,000 cultural items from the
1880s through to the present, including furniture,
murals & World War II propaganda.

Seaquarium 4400 Rickenbacker Causeway, on
Key Biscayne; 361 5705; w miamiseaquarium.
com; daily; admission charge. The ocean
aquarium stars alligators, dolphins, sharks,
manatees, stingrays & killer whales. The Sea Trek

Reef Encounter lets you explore the 300,000-gallon
reef aquarium without any specialised training.

Vizcaya Museum & Gardens 3251 S Miami
Av, in Coconut Grove; 250 9133; w vizcaya.org;
daily; admission charge. An Italianate palace
built on the bay as a winter residence by the
millionaire James Deering in 1916, with antique
Renaissance furnishings brought from Europe.
Formal gardens & fountains surround the house.

Historical Museum of Southern Florida 101
W Flagler; 375 1492; w hmsf.org; closed
Mon; admission charge. Located in the Cultural
Center, the museum shows Miami's past with
hands-on displays & special exhibits. Walking &
boat tours are available Sep–Jun.

Metrozoo 12400 SW 152nd; 251 0400;
w zoomiami.org; daily; admission charge. This

327-acre (132ha) zoo features over 2,000 animals, including clouded leopards & Komodo dragons – the largest, most powerful lizards in the world. The zoo has over 70 species of birds, 15,000 Italian honeybees, & more than 1,000 species of trees, palms & other plants, including orchids. Most animals are uncaged on small islands made to resemble their natural habitats. The amphitheatre has wildlife shows throughout the day.

Gold Coast Railroad Museum   Near the Metrozoo at 12450 SW 152nd; ☏ 253 0063; w gcrm.org; ☉ daily; admission charge. Among several Pullman cars displayed is the *Ferdinand Magellan*, used by presidents from Franklin Roosevelt to Ronald Reagan. The steam engines here once belonged to the Florida East Coast Railway. Half-hour train rides at w/ends.

Little Havana   Almost a 10th of Cuba's population has settled around Calle Ocho (SW Eighth St) after fleeing Fidel Castro's island, some braving the shark-inhabited Florida Straits on flimsy rafts. Family stores & *cantinas* are named after Havana streets & this is one of the few places in Miami where people still walk.

Key West   Henry Flagler set out to create modern Florida by constructing his East Coast Railway from Jacksonville to the end of the Keys, from where boats would continue to Havana & the Bahamas. He spent $18 million on the railroad, some $12 million on hotels & $10 million on the Key West extension. This continuation – 114 miles/182km long with 17 miles/27km of bridges – was completed in 1912 but a nameless hurricane destroyed the line in 1936.

The right of way now forms the base for a spectacular highway down which Greyhound buses travel from Miami to Ernest Hemingway's old haunts. For visitor information contact the Key West Chamber of Commerce, 510 Greene St, Key West, FL 33040 (☏ 305 294 2587; w keywestchamber.org).

18

The *Silver Meteor*
New York–Miami

GENERAL ROUTE INFORMATION

The Seaboard Air Line Railroad's original *Silver Meteor*, named in a public contest, began services between New York and St Petersburg in 1939. Today's *Silver Meteor* still travels the eastern part of the United States between New York and Florida, visiting Charleston in South Carolina. Like the *Silver Star* and *Palmetto*, it takes in the nation's capital, the Carolinas and Old Savannah.

JOINING THE TRAIN

NEW YORK For New York City and the route to Washington, DC, see page 198. For the route from Washington, DC to Rocky Mount, see pages 233–6.

ROCKY MOUNT: ALL ABOARD! (80↓) North Carolina grows the largest tobacco crop in America and much of it comes here to be traded, along with cotton and other produce.

ESSENTIAL INFORMATION

HIGHLIGHTS As well as New York City, Orlando and Miami, the *Silver Meteor* stops at one of America's loveliest cities, Charleston, South Carolina. This has brightly coloured mansions, cobblestone streets and amazing sunsets to be enjoyed from the historic waterfront.

FREQUENCY Daily. The **southbound** service leaves New York mid-afternoon to arrive in Washington, DC by early evening and Charleston very early next day. You reach Jacksonville early in the morning, Orlando around midday and Miami by early evening. Travelling **north**, trains leave Miami early in the morning to reach Orlando by early afternoon and Jacksonville late afternoon. You arrive in Charleston late evening, Washington, DC early next morning and New York by late morning.

DURATION 28+ hours

RESERVATIONS All reserved

EQUIPMENT Amfleet coaches

SLEEPING Viewliner bedrooms

FOOD Complete meals, snacks, sandwiches, drinks

BAGGAGE Check-in service is available at most stations.

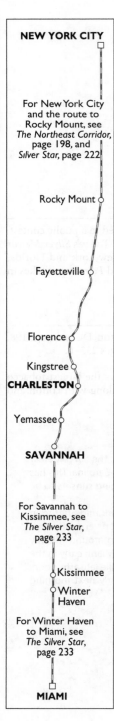

NEW YORK CITY

For New York City and the route to Rocky Mount, see *The Northeast Corridor*, page 198, and *Silver Star*, page 222

Rocky Mount

Fayetteville

Florence

Kingstree

CHARLESTON

Yemassee

SAVANNAH

For Savannah to Kissimmee, see *The Silver Star*, page 233

Kissimmee

Winter Haven

For Winter Haven to Miami, see *The Silver Star*, page 233

MIAMI

Wilson (↑20/60↓) Tobacco warehouses and curing facilities can be seen on both sides of the track.

Selma (↑45/35↓) The *Silver Meteor* continues on the Seaboard Line through tobacco, cotton and soya bean fields.

Smithfield (↑60/20↓) You travel past the birthplace of Ava Gardner then cross the Cape Fear River.

✦✦ FAYETTEVILLE (↑80/80↓) The train crosses Hope Mill Lake at this farming town founded by 18th-century Scottish immigrants. Nearby is Fort Bragg, home of the US Army's 82nd Airborne Division and Delta Force. The Dutch Colonial-style station, which also houses Fayetteville's Transportation Museum, was built in 1911.

Pembroke (↑25/55↓) Home of Pembroke State University, the town is located on the banks of the Lumbee River.

Carolinas state line (↑35/45↓) You cross from North to South Carolina just before the town of Hamer. You then cross the Little Pee Dee River.

Dillon (↑45/35↓) This used to be a haunt of Francis Marion, the 'Swamp Fox' of the Revolutionary War who was one of the fathers of modern guerrilla warfare. The town was named after John W Dillon, an early settler who helped bring a railroad through the area. Dillon is a scheduled stop for the *Palmetto*.

The *Silver Meteor* crosses the Great Pee Dee River 20 minutes later and travels over an area of swampland.

✦✦ FLORENCE (↑80/30↓) General W W Harllee, President of the Wilmington & Manchester Railroad, built his home at the junction of the W&M and the Northeastern and named the town after his daughter. During the Civil War this was an important railroad repair centre for the Confederacy, transporting troops, artillery and supplies. Florence today is the home of Francis Marion College and the extensive Coast Line yards handling mostly cotton, tobacco and corn. Thruway buses link to Myrtle Beach.

Amtrak's modern CSX station was built in the same style as the much larger Atlantic Coast Line depot standing next to it, built in 1910. This was later bought by the McLoud Regional Medical Center and has been returned to its former magnificence. Look for a steam locomotive parked on your right soon after you leave.

You cross the Lynches River 10 minutes from Florence and travel among the farms of the coastal plain. Note the distinctively shaped barns used for storing tobacco.

KINGSTREE (↑30/45↓) Amtrak's station was built by the Atlantic Coast Line Railroad in 1909 and is part of the Kingstree Historic District. The building also houses the Williamsburg Hometown Chamber Offices. A few minutes later you cross the Black River close to where actor Robert Mitchum was born. Mitchum's father was a half Blackfoot Native American who died while working as a train brakeman when two cars collided and crushed him.

Santee River (↑10/35↓)

You cross the river then continue beside **Francis Marion Forest** to your left. Swamps, oak trees, pines and lakes cover an expanse of 250,000 acres (100,000ha). Marion earned his nickname, the 'Swamp Fox', by raiding from these marshlands. He was a master of the surprise attack, never camping in the same place for more than two nights.

Lake Moultrie (↑20/25↓)

The lake is behind the levee to your left, with Lake Marion further inland. You cross the Cooper River on its way from Lake Moultrie to Charleston.

CHARLESTON (↑45/45↓) Founded in 1670 where the Cooper and Ashley rivers meet on the Atlantic coast, Charleston's position made it one of the most prosperous early American ports and for a time the fourth-largest settlement in the American colonies. Further growth came with the start of America's first train service in 1830, which locals called the *Best Friend of Charleston*.

Hundreds of merchants' houses survive and many can be visited during the spring festival. Down on the waterfront you can see spectacular sunsets and watch gulls glide over Battery Park. Charleston's brightly coloured mansions and cobblestone streets have recovered from the hurricane which devastated the city in 1989. For information contact the **Historic Foundation** (*40 E Bay;* ✆*723 1623;* w *historiccharleston.org*).

Charleston basics

✆**Telephone code** 843

Station (*Ticket office & waiting room* ⏱ *04.00–23.45*) Amtrak's station is at 4565 Gaynor Av in north Charleston, 7 miles (11km) from downtown (take the Durant Av bus). ATM, payphones, vending machines.

Connections No Thruway buses

🚌**Local transport** CARTA buses & free DASH trolley services operate downtown (✆*724 7420;* w *ridecarta.com*)

🚕 **Taxis** Yellow ✆*577 6565.* For the Pedicab bicycle cab service, ✆*577 7088.*

🚗 **Car rental** Budget, 2068 Sam Rittenberg Bd; ✆*573 9144*

🚌**Greyhound** 3610 Dorchester Rd; ✆*744 4247*

Tours Charleston Tours Inc; ✆*571 0049.* Talk of the Towne (✆*795 8199*). Carriage rides from The Old South Carriage Company (✆*723 9712*).

ℹ **Visitors bureau** 375 Meeting; ✆*1 800 774 0006;* w *charlestoncvb.com;* ⏱ daily, with film shows

🏨 **Accommodation** Hotels are expensive downtown but reasonably priced motels can be found across the Ashley River on US 17. Downtown hotels include Best Western King Charles Inn, 237 Meeting; ✆*723 7451;* w *kingcharlesinn. com,* **$$$$$**; Days Inn, 155 Meeting; ✆*371 3850;* w *wyndhamhotels.com/days-inn,* **$$$$**; Francis Marion, 387 King; ✆*722 0600;* w *francismarionhotel.com,* **$$$$**; Renaissance, 68 Wentworth; ✆*534 0300;* w *marriott. com,* **$$$$**; Holiday Inn, 425 Meeting; ✆*718 2327;* w *stayincharleston.com,* **$$$**; Meeting Street Inn, 173 Meeting; ✆*723 1882;* w *meetingstreetinn.com,* **$$$**.

Contact Historic Charleston Bed & Breakfast, 55 Broad St, Charleston, SC 29401; ✆*722 6606;* w *historiccharlestonbedandbreakfast.com,* **$$$$**; Rutledge Victoria Inn, 114 Rutledge Av; ✆*722 7551;* w *johnrutledgehouseinn.com,* **$$$$**.

Recommended in Charleston

Charleston Museum 360 Meeting; ☎722 2996; w charlestonmuseum.org; ☺ daily; admission charge. America's 1st museum, begun in 1773, has snuffboxes & silverware among its half a million items. Tickets also give admission to the Joseph Manigault House (an Adam-style mansion) at 350 Meeting & the 1772 Heyward-Washington House at 87 Church.

St Michael's Church Broad & Meeting; ☎ 723 0603; w stmichaelchurch.net. The oldest of Charleston's 181 churches resembles St Martin-in-the-Fields, London. City Hall, the Federal Court, the post office & the County Court House occupy the other '4 corners of law'.

Charles Towne Landing Park 1500 Old Towne Rd, on the site of the 1st settlement; ☎852 4200; w southcarolinaparks.com. The park has trails, a reconstructed village, a sailing ship & an enclosure with wolves & bears.

Fort Sumter 1214 Middle, Sullivan's Island; ☎ 883 3123; w nps.gov/fosu. A short boat ride from the municipal marina. The Civil War began here in 1861 when the garrison surrendered to Confederate general Pierre Beauregard after 2 days of bombardment. Tours of the restored buildings.

Gibbes Museum of Art 135 Meeting; ☎722 2706; w gibbesmuseum.org; ☺ Tue–Sun; admission charge. The collection includes American paintings, prints & drawings from the 18th century to the present, including views of Charleston & portraits of famous South Carolinian citizens. The museum also has miniatures & Japanese prints.

The Best Friend Museum 23 Ann St, behind the visitor center; ☎973 7269; ☺ daily; w bestfriendofcharleston.org; admission free. The museum has a full-size replica of the *Best Friend of Charleston* – the 1st (1830) US train to operate a regular passenger service. The engine was constructed from its original plans in 1928 to commemorate the 100th anniversary of the South Carolina Canal & Rail Road Company.

Old Exchange & Provost Dungeon 122 E Bay; ☎727 2165; w oldexchange.com; ☺ daily; admission charge. Built in 1771 by the British as the Exchange & Customs House, American Patriots were held prisoner here during the Revolutionary War. You can see part of the Charles Towne sea wall built to defend the colony from pirates in the 17th century.

Drayton Hall 3380 Ashley River Rd; ☎769 2600; w draytonhall.org; ☺ daily; admission charge. Completed in 1742, this is the only plantation house remaining on the Ashley River that survived the Revolutionary & Civil wars, & its Georgian Palladian architecture contains much of the original 18th-century craftsmanship. Guided tours & nature walks.

Magnolia Plantation 3550 Ashley River Rd; ☎571 1266; w magnoliaplantation.com; ☺ daily; admission charge. This pre-Revolutionary War plantation house has fine American antiques & the estate boasts America's oldest gardens, dating from 1680 & featuring azaleas & camellias. Boat rides, wildlife observation tower, art gallery & birdwatching walks.

CHARLESTON: ALL ABOARD! (↑45/45↓) The *Silver Meteor* pulls out of Charleston among substantial rail yards. You cross the Ashley River before continuing south along the coastal plain.

Jacksonboro (↑25/20↓) The town was named after its original owner, John Jackson. You cross the Edisto River, then the Salkehatchie, Ashepoo and Combahee rivers en route to Yemassee.

⊷⊷⊷ YEMASSEE (↑45/45↓) The town was named after Yemassee Native Americans. The Charleston & Western Carolina Railroad built the plain-looking station in 1955. Between 1914 and 1964, when the Marine Corps used the Yemassee depot as a gateway to its basic training at Parris Island, more than 500,000 recruits passed through. In 2011, a British reality TV show, *The Week the Women Went*, was filmed in Yemassee. More than 100 women were whisked away via Amtrak to Florida, leaving the men and children to fend for themselves. Part of their time was spent renovating the depot with a new gabled roof and porch.

Interstate 95 (↑5/40↓) The train passes under a highway which runs all the way down the east coast from Maine to Miami.

Savannah River (↑30/15↓) Look right for a concrete highway bridge as the train crosses the river into Georgia.

SAVANNAH (↑45) For Savannah city information and the remainder of the route to Miami, see pages 238–48.

19

The Northeast Corridor
Boston–Newport News

GENERAL ROUTE INFORMATION

Three trains a day make the journey from Boston to Washington, DC, following a route formerly taken by the overnight *Twilight Shoreliner*. You follow the Northeast Corridor route to Washington, DC, then travel through Virginia to the state capital. After Richmond, trains turn east towards Newport News on the Atlantic coast, taking in historic Williamsburg and the tidewater region.

JOINING THE TRAIN

BOSTON: ALL ABOARD! (70↓) For Boston city information, the route to Washington, DC and Washington, DC city information, see page 198. For the Washington, DC to Richmond route, see page 233.

Virginia Science Museum (↑65/5↓) Look right for the museum's dome. Housed in the Seaboard Line's former Broad Street Station is a planetarium and space theatre.

RICHMOND (↑70/65↓) The beautifully restored Main Street station was built in 1901 by the Seaboard Air Line Railroad (SAL) and the Chesapeake & Ohio Railway (C&O).

ESSENTIAL INFORMATION

HIGHLIGHTS This part of Amtrak's Northeast service takes you to America's largest restored town, Williamsburg, where you can recapture colonial days in a reconstruction of 500 public buildings, taverns, gardens and houses. Nearby are Busch Gardens theme park as well as Yorktown and Jamestowne, with replicas of settlers' ships and the foundations of the country's first state house.

FREQUENCY Three trains daily. The **southbound** service leaves Boston early morning, mid-morning or late evening and gets to Newport News by early evening, mid-morning or midday. Travelling **north**, trains leave Newport News late afternoon or early morning to reach Boston by early morning or late evening.

DURATION 12 hours 15 minutes

RESERVATIONS All reserved

EQUIPMENT Amfleet coaches. Business Class.

FOOD Tray meals, snacks, sandwiches, drinks

BAGGAGE No check-in service is available.

Trains continue south from Richmond on the Seaboard Coast Line.

James River (↑2/63↓) You glimpse the James River
to your right before the train crosses a canal and passes through more Chessie (Chesapeake & Ohio Railway) yards at Fulton.

Richmond Airport (↑25/40↓) Aircraft and runways
can be seen to your left. The airport opened in 1927 as Byrd Flying Field, in honour of aviator Richard Evelyn Byrd.

The landscape now becomes flatter as the train continues on into Virginia's tidewater region. Elegant plantation mansions stand next to the river.

New Kent (↑45/20↓) The forestry establishment to
your right produces thousands of fledgling pine trees.

Chickahominy River (↑50/15↓) Seen to your right,
the Chickahominy flows towards the James River.

⚏ WILLIAMSBURG (↑65/25↓) America's largest
restored town was named after King William III of Britain, and the Union Flag still flies on the Capitol Building. The town became Virginia's capital in 1699. You can recapture colonial days in this reconstruction of 500 public buildings, taverns, gardens and houses. Costumed townspeople drive carriages, work as craftsmen and add appropriate atmosphere. To live in the Historic Area, you have to work at Colonial Williamsburg or be an employee at the College of William & Mary.

In summer it can be hot, humid and crowded, so visit during spring or autumn if possible.

Williamsburg basics
☎ **Telephone code** 757
⚏ **Station** (*Ticket office & waiting room* ☉ *08.00–20.30*) Amtrak uses the Williamsburg Transportation Center at 468 N Boundary, located in an elegant restored building formerly owned by the Chesapeake & Ohio Railway (C&O). Lockers, vending machines, handcarts, taxi stand. Greyhound & Trailways buses operate out of the west side of the building.
Connections No Thruway bus
🚌 **Local transport** Buses from the visitor center go to most parts of the historic area, best seen by strolling among the buildings (☎ *220 5493*; w *gowata.org*)
🚕 **Taxis** Yellow Cab; ☎ 722 1111
🚐 **Greyhound** Located next to Amtrak's station; ☎ 1 800 231 2222
✈ **Airport** The airport is 16 miles (26km) by HRT bus # 116 or taxi from the station
Tours Tickets are available at the Lumber House (☎ *888 965 7254*) for carriage rides & walking tours

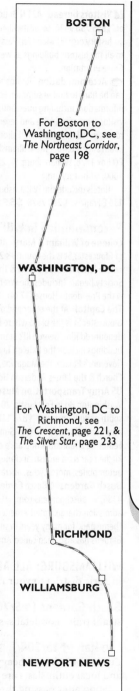

BOSTON

For Boston to Washington, DC, see *The Northeast Corridor*, page 198

WASHINGTON, DC

For Washington, DC to Richmond, see *The Crescent*, page 221, & *The Silver Star*, page 233

RICHMOND

WILLIAMSBURG

NEWPORT NEWS

Visitors bureau 421 N Boundary; 229 6511 or 855 756 9516; w visitwilliamsburg.com or w history.org; Mon–Fri. Passes give admission to all the historic buildings as well as to Carter's Grove Plantation.

Accommodation Rooms are expensive & can be hard to find in summer. For up-to-date information, including guesthouses, contact the visitor center for advice and reservations. Hotel rooms in Williamsburg itself should be booked well in advance. Contact the Williamsburg Foundation, PO Box 1776, Williamsburg, VA 23187-1776; 229 1000; w history.org.

Hotels include the Williamsburg Inn, 136 E Francis; 220 7978, **$$$$**; Fort Magruder, 6945 Pocahontas Trail; 220 2250; w fortmagruderhotel.com, **$$$**; MainStay Suites, 814 Capitol Landing Rd; 229 0200; w choicehotels.com, **$$$**; Comfort Inn Williamsburg Gateway, 331 Bypass Rd; 253 1166; w choicehotels.com, **$$**; Governor's Inn, 506 N Henry; 855 238 4229; w colonialwilliamsburghotels.com, **$$**; Red Roof Inn, 824 Capitol Landing Rd; 259 1948; w redroof.com, **$$**; Rodeway Inn, 309 Page; 229 1855; w choicehotels.com, **$$**.

Hostel rooms are available at the Pineapple Inn & Housing Center, 5437 Richmond Rd, Williamsburg, VA 23188; 259 9670; w pineapplehousing.com, **$**.

Recommended in Williamsburg

College of William & Mary At the end of Duke of Gloucester St is the country's 2nd-oldest college, where Jefferson studied law & the Phi Beta Kappa Society began. Includes the Wren Building (1695) & the President's House (1734).

The Capitol At the other end of Duke of Gloucester St is the place where Patrick Henry denounced King George III's stamp tax. Other buildings include the Raleigh Tavern, the Governor's Palace, the Magazine, Bruton Parish Church & the James Anderson House.

US Army Transportation Museum 300 Washington Bd in Fort Eustis, 20 miles (32km) south of Williamsburg; 878 1180; w ww2. atmfoundation.org; Tue–Sun; admission free. Featuring a railroad ambulance car, a hospital kitchen car & an industrial crane, as well as automobiles, motorcycles, aircraft & a marine park.

Busch Gardens 1 Busch Gardens Bd; 229 4386; w buschgardens.com; Mar–Oct daily; admission charge. Voted 'America's most beautiful theme park' for many years in succession, Busch Gardens has also been called 'America's favourite theme park', edging out Disneyland. The park features roller coasters & Broadway-style shows.

Yorktown On Route 31 S at the Colonial Parkway, 10mins from Williamsburg; 253 4838 or 888 593 4682; w historyisfun.org; daily; admission charge. Settled in 1630, Yorktown became a port & trading centre for the tobacco industry, & the Revolutionary War ended here in 1781 with the defeat of Lord Cornwallis. The battlefield is much visited & many colonial buildings survive or have been reconstructed. The Victory Center has displays & films.

Historic Jamestowne Reached from Yorktown along the Colonial Parkway; 898 3400; w nps. gov/colo; daily; admission charge. Part of the historic triangle, along with Yorktown & Williamsburg. English settlers established the New World's first legislature here in 1619, although the old church tower is all that remains standing. Also featured are the Tercentenary Monument, a Confederate fort, replicas of settlers' ships & the foundations of the first state house. Tours by national park rangers.

WILLIAMSBURG: ALL ABOARD! (↑65/25↓) You depart Williamsburg with the historic district to your right.

Busch Gardens (↑5/20↓) Look right also for this theme park, complete with steam train. For details, see above.

Lee Hall (↑15/10↓) This became a busy station after the establishment of Fort Eustis in 1918, with heavy freight and troop movements. The City of Newport News and local enthusiasts are currently restoring the depot.

Soon after passing through Lee Hall you cross a part of the local reservoir.

NEWPORT NEWS (↑25) Founded in 1619 on a harbour shared with Norfolk, Portsmouth and Hampton roads, this is where the James, York, Elizabeth and Nansemond rivers flow into Chesapeake Bay (14 miles/22km long and 40ft/12m deep). Newport News boasts the world's largest shipbuilding yard and biggest US Air Force and Army base as well as a Naval Station and Naval War College.

The **Mariners' Museum** (*100 Museum Dr;* ✆*757 596 2222;* **w** *marinersmuseum. org; admission charge*) features one of the world's most extensive maritime collections, with more than 32,000 objects as well as several million library and archive items. The **War Museum** has an outstanding collection of personal artefacts, weapons, uniforms, posters and vehicles tracing the development of the US military from 1775 through to the present (*9285 Warwick Bd;* ✆*757 247 8523;* **w** *warmuseum.org; admission charge*). In Newport News Park you can enjoy boating, fishing and camping. For information on attractions throughout the peninsula, contact the **visitor centre** at 13560 Jefferson Avenue (✆*757 886 7777 or* ✆*888 493 7386;* **w** *newport-news.org*).

Amtrak's station is at 9304 Warwick Boulevard, from where Thruway buses link to Norfolk and Virginia Beach in Virginia. There are plans to replace the current depot with two additional train stations in Newport News, one in downtown and one near the Newport News Williamsburg International Airport.

20

The *Cardinal*
New York–Chicago

GENERAL ROUTE INFORMATION

The *Cardinal*'s 1,147-mile (1,844km) journey takes you through some of America's finest scenery, going from New York City to Washington, DC, then across Virginia to the Blue Ridge Mountains and Shenandoah Valley. You travel west through the Appalachians, the Ohio River Valley and Cincinnati, before crossing the cornfields of central Indiana to Chicago. The *Cardinal* operates over a route formerly used by the *Sportsman* train and the stately *George Washington*, the premier passenger service of the Chesapeake & Ohio Railway. The C&O was known as 'George Washington's railroad' as it was descended from a company he founded in 1785.

ESSENTIAL INFORMATION

HIGHLIGHTS The *Cardinal* travels through gently rolling horse country and the natural beauty of the Blue Ridge and Allegheny mountains, Shenandoah Valley, and white-water rivers of West Virginia, which can only be seen by train. After rolling along the banks of the Ohio River through the quaint towns of Ashland and Maysville, the train continues to Cincinnati and Indianapolis, home of the Indy 500 motor race.

FREQUENCY Three trains a week in each direction. The **westbound** service leaves New York early on Sunday, Wednesday and Friday mornings to reach Washington, DC by midday and Charleston mid-evening. You arrive in Cincinnati during the night and Indianapolis early the next morning, reaching Chicago mid-morning on Monday, Thursday or Saturday. Travelling **east**, trains leave Chicago early evening on Tuesday, Thursday and Saturday to reach Indianapolis around midnight and Cincinnati during the night. You arrive in Charleston early in the morning, Washington, DC early evening and New York late on Wednesday, Friday or Sunday evening.

DURATION 27 hours

RESERVATIONS All reserved

EQUIPMENT Amfleet coaches

SLEEPING Viewliner bedrooms

LOUNGE CAR During summer months a CP Huntington Railroad Society guide joins the eastbound train between Charleston and White Sulphur Springs to provide a scenic commentary

FOOD Complete meals, snacks, sandwiches, drinks

BAGGAGE Check-in service is available at some stations. Bicycle racks available (reservation required).

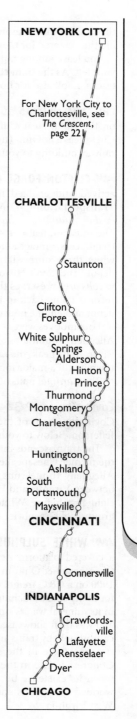

▟▜ NEW YORK For New York City information, see page 205. For the route from New York to Charlottesville, see page 221. The *Cardinal* operates between New York and Washington, DC on Amtrak, between Washington, DC and Alexandria on CSX Transportation, between Alexandria and Culpeper on Norfolk Southern, between Culpeper and Clifton Forge on Buckingham Branch, between Clifton Forge and Dyer on CSX Transportation, and between Dyer and Chicago on Norfolk Southern.

CHARLOTTESVILLE: ALL ABOARD! (55↓) Note the

colonnaded soccer ground to your right as the *Cardinal* leaves through residential and commercial suburbs, passing over the main street on a trestle. You follow US 250 for some way through western Virginia, travelling among farms, orchards and forests and beginning a steep climb into the Blue Ridge Mountains. It was on this highly demanding route that the Chesapeake & Ohio Railway chose to introduce the first of its powerful American-type steam locomotives in 1911.

The idyllic Shenandoah Valley to your right is the home of bear, bobcat, fox and 200 species of birds. Skyline Drive goes along 100 miles (160km) of mountain ridge, where there are spectacular changes of colour during autumn. The train passes through Crozet and East Braham then a long tunnel, the first of many on this route, climbing another stiff bank before beginning the descent towards Staunton.

Waynesboro (↑35/20↓) Following the Civil War, this

became the junction of the Chesapeake & Ohio Railway (running east to west) and the Shenandoah Valley Railroad, which met near Waynesboro and gave the town the nickname of the 'Iron Cross'. After passing this small town beside the river the *Cardinal* continues among cattle and sheep farms with pretty mountains to your right.

Interstate 81 (↑52/3↓) Look for a Neoclassical

building on your right as you pass beneath two highway bridges.

▟▜ STAUNTON (↑55/70↓) Named after English-born Lady Rebecca Staunton, wife of colonial governor Sir William Gooch, Staunton was the birthplace of President Woodrow Wilson. To your right when the train stops on a curve of the tracks you can see colourful Chessie System railcars being used as station architecture. Staunton's altitude (1,359ft/414m) is inscribed on the station's canopy. The town's **Frontier Culture Museum** (*1290 Richmond Av;* ✆*540 332 7850;* w *frontiermuseum.org*) tells

Map (right column)

NEW YORK CITY

For New York City to Charlottesville, see *The Crescent*, page 221

CHARLOTTESVILLE

Staunton

Clifton Forge

White Sulphur Springs
Alderson
Hinton
Prince
Thurmond
Montgomery
Charleston

Huntington
Ashland
South Portsmouth
Maysville
CINCINNATI

Connersville

INDIANAPOLIS

Crawfordsville
Lafayette
Rensselaer
Dyer

CHICAGO

The *Cardinal* New York–Chicago

20

the story of the thousands of people who migrated to colonial America, and of the life they created for themselves and their descendants.

You leave among houses perched on hills, with Victorian buildings seen away to your left. As the train climbs, the tops of the tall trees to your left scarcely reach the tracks. Look also for horses, cattle, sheep and eagles.

Elliott Knob (↑15/55↓) This dark-purple mountain (4,458ft/1,360m) is visible on the right. Near Clifton Forge the *Cardinal* passes through busy yards of the Chesapeake & Ohio (now CSX), with freight trains to your left and a picturesque railway building to your right.

CLIFTON FORGE (↑70/50↓) This area was wilderness until the railroad arrived and enabled lumber and coal to be exploited. Virginia's **Museum of Transportation** (*303 Norfolk Av, in nearby Roanoke;* ☏ *540 342 5670;* w *vmt.org;* ☉ *daily; admission charge*) is housed in a 1917 Norfolk & Western freight depot. The museum features steam, diesel and electric engines, as well as passenger and freight cars, vintage automobiles, trucks and trolleys. Amtrak's waiting room is in a white, three-storey station built in 1902 by the C&O as a coal freight and passenger depot. The C&O Historical Society nearby at 312 E Ridgeway (☏ *540 862 2210;* w *cohs.org*) preserves the railroad's coal mining history with maps, timetables and records going back to the mid-19th century. It also has a signal tower, passenger depot and engine house.

Locomotives were serviced and readied in Clifton Forge for the trip west over the Allegheny Mountains and east over the Blue Ridge Mountains and down the James River. At its peak, the railroad employed over 2,000 people in Clifton Forge and the town is still a major focus for CSX operations in the region.

The *Cardinal* pulls out of Clifton Forge past a hospital and factories to your right.

Covington (↑12/38↓) The town was named in honour of General Leonard Covington, hero of the War of 1812 and friend of James Madison and Thomas Jefferson. Below to your right is Highway 64.

The train ascends into the mountains through more of the many tunnels built by the former Chesapeake & Ohio and Virginia Central railroads in this region. The Allegheny Tunnel runs under the crest of those mountains and marks the boundary between Virginia and West Virginia, as well as the eastern continental divide. Look right just before White Sulphur Springs for a golf course and the immaculate grounds of Greenbrier Spa (see below).

WHITE SULPHUR SPRINGS (↑50/30↓) Amtrak's unmanned station is a covered platform next to the brick Colonial Revival-style depot built for the Chesapeake & Ohio in 1931. The first 'horseless carriage' in these parts arrived in 1900 on a C&O freight car. Greenbrier is a 2,600-acre (1,052ha) resort with facilities for many sports, including ice skating. US presidents and others have come to bathe in its mineral waters since 1778. The Greenbrier Hotel was once owned by the C&O and was their showcase. Tracks behind the station were used for business and private cars brought by trains and parked there by wealthy and famous people using the hotel.

Somewhere in the surrounding hillside is a secret bunker built in 1958 for Congress to use in the event of a nuclear attack. It was decommissioned in 1992 when its existence became known. You can look for the bunker site among the wooded mountains and waterfalls on both sides as the train pushes deeper into West Virginia.

ALDERSON (↑30/30↓) The restored, orange-painted wooden station building dates from 1896 and is typical of the Chesapeake & Ohio designs used between 1890 and 1916. The building high up to your left is a women's federal prison where inmates have included jazz singer Billie Holiday and television host Martha Stewart.

Great Bend Tunnel (↑15/15↓) The Chesapeake & Ohio Line was mostly built by former Virginia slaves supervised by ex-Confederate army officers. According to folklore, one of the ex-slaves was John Henry, the 'Steel-Drivin' Man' who worked on this tunnel, also known as Big Bend Tunnel, in the early 1870s. When a steam-powered drill was introduced, he challenged it to a contest. With the help of a 'shaker' assistant to turn his drill, and swinging 9lb or 12lb (4kg or 5.5kg) hammers in both hands, he made 15ft to the steam drill's 9ft (4.5m/2.7m). He died of a heart attack soon afterwards but his exploits inspired songs such as 'Take This Hammer' and 'If I Had A Hammer'. A statue of John Henry, stripped to the waist, stands next to the tunnel.

Greenbrier River (↑28/2↓) The river on your right is often reduced to little more than a stream.

For the next 120 miles (192km) you follow the New River as it cuts a tree-lined gorge through America's oldest mountains, the Appalachians. Bluestone Lake and Dam are to your left. The beautiful Sandstone Falls is the largest waterfall in the New River Gorge, dropping about 20ft (6m) over a 1,500ft (457m) width of river.

HINTON (↑30/30↓) Elegant houses stand on the hill. Hinton's busier past is revealed by its large brick station to your right, beside an open space where the rail yards used to be. Built for the C&O in 1905, the station and tracks lie along a bend in the New River. Hinton was once a booming railroad town and an assembly point for shorter coal trains to be combined into longer trains to be sent east to the port of Hampton Roads. The city regards itself as a living museum and celebrates its annual Rail Road Days at the end of October, timed to coincide with the popular New River excursion trains that run from Huntington to Hinton to view the foliage in the New River Gorge. The **Hinton Railroad Museum** is located in a former department store building at 206 Temple and contains uniforms, tools and other items from the early days of the C&O (☏ *304 466 6100;* w *visitwv.com/company/ hinton-railroad-museum*).

Bass Lake (↑5/25↓) Look for the rustic holiday cabins to your right.

PRINCE (↑30/15↓) A mountain village with another large depot, from which access to nearby Beckley is by yellow cab. The station dates from 1946, and is a fine example of Art Moderne architecture. In the waiting room, you can see the C&O's original 'Chessie' kitten logo embedded in the floor. L C Probert, public relations official for C&O, saw an etching in a newspaper of a cuddly kitten sleeping under a blanket and used this image with the slogan 'Sleep Like a Kitten and Wake Up Fresh as a Daisy in Air-Conditioned Comfort' to advertise the company's new air-conditioned sleeping-car service. The town's founder, William Prince, was involved in the coal business in the 1890s, when coal was transported across the New River in buckets suspended on a wire cable.

THURMOND (↑15/45↓) The line curves right into Thurmond, which was a classic boom town during the early 1900s, when huge amounts of coal were brought in from local mines. The town was named after railroad surveyor William Dabney Thurmond and had the largest revenue on the Chesapeake & Ohio Railway. The town's banks were the richest in the state and 15 passenger trains a day came through as the depot served as many as 76,000 people a year. With the decline in the coal industry most residents moved away, and Thurmond today is largely untouched by modern development.

The long, narrow, slate-roofed wood-frame depot, built in 1904, originally had three waiting rooms: one for men, one for women and one for African-Americans. Painstakingly restored with authentic furniture, fixtures and equipment from the early 20th century, it now also houses a **railroad museum** (✏ *304 465 8550;* **w** *nps. gov/neri/planyourvisit/thurmond;* ☺ *Jun–Aug*) and a **visitor centre** for the New River Gorge National River.

New River Gorge Bridge (↑20/25↓)
Spanning 3,030ft (924m), this steel-arch bridge carries Route 19 traffic across the valley. When opened in 1977 this was the highest and longest arch bridge in the world. The arch extends 1,700ft (518m) and at 876ft (267m) this is still the second-highest bridge in the Americas, as well as the fifth highest and third longest in the world.

The *Cardinal* continues through dramatically rugged scenery with waterfalls, mountains and a sheer drop to the boulder-strewn river. This forested national park area is pre-dated in geological history only by Egypt's Nile Valley, and is home to many endangered mammals, birds and amphibians. Look for the stone buildings of Hawk's Nest Lodge and the Gauley Bridge, marking the confluence of the New and Gauley rivers to form the Kanawha River. Much of this picturesque country is visible only by rail or white-water raft. Approaching Montgomery, the tracks diverge from the river and the town mayor's office appears among houses to your left.

🚋 MONTGOMERY (↑45/30↓)
By the early 20th century, Montgomery was a shipping centre for 26 coal operations. Christopher Janus's poignant novel, *Goodbye, Miss 4th of July*, tells the story of his Greek family's struggles while growing up in Montgomery.

Kanawha River (↑8/22↓)
The train joins the river to your right and pursues it most of the way to Charleston. Barges can be seen loading coal from a mine on the far side of the river.

You travel through semi-rural scenes, with wooded mountains on the opposite shore and industrial plants below. As you near Charleston, the gold-domed Capitol Building comes into view to your right.

🚋 CHARLESTON (↑30/55↓)
Located on the Kanawha River and surrounded by mountains, state capital Charleston is famous for white-water rafting. Apart from the Capitol, the most impressive buildings are the Cultural Center and the Governor's Mansion. Amtrak stops next to the 1905 Neoclassical Beaux-Arts-style stone and brick depot that is on the National Register of Historic Places and houses offices and a restaurant.

Chemical factories appear on both sides as you cross the river, passing rail yards to your right. During a dispute in 1913 between the United Mine Workers and mine owners in the nearby Kanawha field, formidable 83-year-old organiser Mary 'Mother Jones' Harris – 'the most dangerous woman in America' – took on strike-breakers brought in by armoured train.

Institute (↑10/45↓) This is where Union Carbide used to produce the chemical methyl isocyanate. In 1984, a leak at a similar factory in Bhopal, India, killed at least 3,800 people.

Approaching Huntington, you pass a large CSX yard on the left then a big shopping mall.

⊶⊷ HUNTINGTON (↑55/20↓) Founded by Collis P Huntington in 1870, Huntington was the western terminus for the Chesapeake & Ohio Railway, which initially stretched from Richmond, Virginia, to the Ohio River. The C&O remained the city's largest employer for the next century. Amtrak's modest brick depot on your left was built in 1986. To your right is the historic downtown area of Huntington, with many fine houses. **Heritage Farm Museum & Village**, located at 3300 Harvey Road (✆ *304 522 1244;* w *heritagefarmmuseum.com*), has a huge collection of Appalachian items housed in seven museums dedicated to Progress, Industry, Transportation, Children's Activity, Bowe's Doll & Carriage, Country Store, and Heritage.

Big Sandy River (↑15/5↓) Most of the train comes into view as it crosses the river and takes a long right curve. Look for a concrete highway bridge to your right, linking West Virginia with Kentucky.

⊶⊷ ASHLAND (↑20/55↓) Trains provide a picturesque view for passengers as the rails run between the two central streets lined with shady trees and many Colonial Revival and Queen Anne homes as well as college and commercial buildings. The Richmond, Fredericksburg & Potomac Railroad Company arrived in the early days of railroading when in 1836 the line connected Richmond and Fredericksburg with the Potomac River, providing better trade and transport links than the previous combination of stagecoach, ferries and steamboat routes. Edwin Robinson became president of the railroad in 1846 and invested in building a racecourse here, complete with Jockey Club, grandstand and gambling establishments. Hotels and bars in town made Ashland a popular resort stop. The historic industrial city to your left is noted for oil and steel. Look right for a former Armco (now AK Steel) plant. The 1923 station at 112 North Railroad Avenue also serves Kenova, West Virginia. Inside, the Ashland visitors centre maintains a small museum in one of the old waiting rooms.

The route between here and Cincinnati takes you along the meandering southern shore of the Ohio River, which forms the Kentucky–Ohio border to your right, so the best views are on this side of the train. When travelling east you should have daylight to observe the river's houses, barges, locks, bridges and power stations. Ohio's bluffs are on the far side.

Greenup Dam (↑40/15↓) The dam was built in the 1950s with two locks, the one for commercial barges being 1,200ft long (365m) by 110ft (33m) wide.

⊶⊷ SOUTH PORTSMOUTH (↑55/50↓) The South Portsmouth–South Shore station is a shelter on the platform which Amtrak constructed in 1976 to serve the city of Portsmouth, Ohio, located across the river. The completion of the Ohio & Erie Canal in 1832 brought trade to the Portsmouth area, as did construction of the Norfolk & Western rail yards, leading to growth of the coal mining industry and iron production in this region.

Note the white Presbyterian church to your right as the train leaves and passes beneath a suspension bridge. A highway bridge also spans the river, often busy with freight barges.

Falls City (↑25/25↓) The *Cardinal* makes slow progress through this small town before losing touch with the Ohio for a while, travelling among fields and tree-covered hills. The river and industry return near Maysville.

▟▙▜ MAYSVILLE (↑50/85↓) This atmospheric river city on the edge of bluegrass country was once a centre for the manufacture of wrought ironwork, some of which decorates the buildings of New Orleans. Amtrak's handsome brick and tile 1918 station on W Front & Rosemary Clooney streets (the singer and actress was born and raised here).

Augusta (↑20/65↓) White houses and an imposing grammar school can be seen to your left but the best viewing remains on the right.

Zimmer Power Station (↑30/55↓) A cooling tower and chimneys dominate the Ohio shore. This is the largest single-unit power plant in the United States and was originally intended to be nuclear powered. Problems in construction led to it being converted to coal-fired generation.

Interstate 275 (↑50/35↓) You travel under a highway crossing the river to your right, then cross the Licking River as Cincinnati approaches.

Covington (↑70/15↓) At suburban Covington the train dramatically crosses the Ohio River, scene of an extravagant September festival. Other bridges cross the river on both sides and the Riverfront Stadium is to your right, along with the Cincinnati skyline. The suspension bridge on the right was built by John Augustus Roebling, designer of the Brooklyn Bridge in New York. The *Cardinal* skirts the west side of downtown before easing into Union Station.

▟▙▜ CINCINNATI (↑85/100↓) The 'Queen City of the West' was nicknamed 'Porkopolis' after its pork-packing industry. Another local speciality, Cincinnati chilli, contains not only pork and beans but also a choice of cheese, onions, spaghetti or even hot dog. Many parks, plazas and buildings were created to celebrate Cincinnati's 1988 bicentennial. Procter & Gamble was founded here in 1837 and Jerry Springer, born in a London Underground station, became Mayor of Cincinnati in 1977.

Cincinnati basics

📞**Telephone code** 513

▟▙▜ **Station** (*Ticket office & waiting room* ⊕ *noon–04.00, Tue–Sun*) Amtrak uses the old Union Terminal at 1301 Vine, a superb example of Art Deco design. Lockers, ATM, payphones, vending machines, handcarts, shops, cafés, museum, taxi stand.

Connections Thruway buses link with Indianapolis, Louisville, Gary, Nashville & Chicago

🚌 **Local transport** Metro bus schedules & information are available from the downtown office at 120 E Fourth (📞621 4455; w go-metro.com).

🚕 **Taxis** Yellow 📞486 6747; Taxi Cincinnati 📞549 2469

🚌**Greyhound** 1005 Gilbert Av; 📞352 6012

Tours Ohio River excursions with Celebrations Riverboats at 848 Elm St in Ludlow (📞859 581 2600)

✈ **Greater Cincinnati International Airport** 14 miles (22km) southwest across the river in Covington, Kentucky, reached by taxi. Airport Executive Shuttle (📞1 800 990 8841) & TANK buses (📞859 331 8265).

ℹ **Visitors bureau** 525 Vine; 📞621 2142 or 📞1 800 543 2613 (for the information line); w cincyusa.com; ⊕ Mon–Fri. The Fountain Sq Visitor Center is at 511 Walnut (📞534 5877; ⊕ daily).

🏠 **Accommodation** Hotels include the Summit, 5345 Medpace Way; ☎ 527 9900; w wyndhamhotels.com/dolce, **$$$$**; Blue Ash, 5901 Pfeiffer Rd; ☎ 793 4500, **$$$**; Cincinnatian, 601 Vine; ☎ 381 3000; w hilton.com, **$$$**; Holiday Inn Express, 5505 Rybolt Rd; ☎ 0871 423 4917; w ihg.com/holidayinnexpress, **$$$**; Symphony, 210 W 14th; ☎ 721 3353; w symphonyhotel.com, **$$$**; Comfort Inn Northeast, 9011 Fields Ertel Rd; ☎ 683 9700; w choicehotels.com, **$$**; Quality Inn Downtown, 800 W Eighth; ☎ 241 8660; w choicehotels.com, **$$**.

Clifton House Bed & Breakfast, 500 Terrace Av, Cincinnati, OH 45220; ☎ 221 7600; w thecliftonhouse.com, **$$$**.

Recommended in Cincinnati

Fountain Square E Fifth & Vine. Features interesting architecture, a historic fountain, gardens, shops & free concerts. Contact Fountain Sq management at 1014 Vine (☎ 621 4400; w myfountainsquare.com; ⊕ Mon–Fri).

Contemporary Arts Center 44 E Sixth; ☎ 345 8400; w contemporaryartscenter.org; ⊕ closed Tue; admission free. Includes music events, films & multi-media shows.

Cincinnati History Museum 1301 Western Av; ☎ 287 7000; w cincymuseum.org; ⊕ daily; admission charge. Walk through the city's streets as they used to be as costumed interpreters reveal the lives of early Cincinnatians, or take a ride on the sidewheel steamboat.

Museum of Natural History & Science 1301 Western Av; ☎ 287 7000; w cincymuseum.org; ⊕ daily; admission charge. Explore the Ohio Valley & learn how the natural world works as you travel through a Kentucky limestone cavern. Or visit Cincinnati's Ice Age & experience life 19,000 years ago.

Union Terminal 1301 Western Av; ☎ 1 800 733 2077; w cincymuseum.org. Now partly a museum, this is one of the most opulent railway stations ever built, attracting more than a million visitors each year. It has the highest unsupported masonry dome in the world & the interior of the rotunda (180ft/54m in diameter) features splendid mosaic murals. German artist Winold Reiss, who designed & created the murals, also painted portraits of Blackfeet Native American for the Great Northern Railway from the 1920s to the 1940s. Many were used in the Great Northern's advertisements to encourage travel to Montana & Glacier National Park. The station ceiling has striking silver, yellow & orange plasterwork. The building, which was renovated & reopened as the Cincinnati Museum Center in 1990, has been named one of the top 50 architecturally significant buildings in America by the American Institute of Architects. A 2-year rehabilitation & improvement project costing $213 million began in 2016, during which Amtrak moved to a temporary facility at 1251 Kenner St, on the north side of Union Terminal.

In the late 19th & early 20th centuries, Cincinnati had 5 downtown passenger stations, with Union Terminal, opened in 1933, a co-operative project of 7 railroad companies.

Taft Museum of Art 316 Pike; ☎ 241 0343; w taftmuseum.org; ⊕ Wed–Sun; admission charge, free on Sun. Old master paintings, Chinese porcelains, as well as European & American decorative arts, can be found in the restored interior of the former home of Anna & Charles Taft.

Cincinnati Zoo 3400 Vine; ☎ 281 4700; w cincinnatizoo.org; ⊕ daily; admission charge. Opened in 1875, America's 2nd-oldest zoo breeds gorillas & rare white tigers. More than 500 animal & 3,000 plant species make this one of the largest zoo collections in the country.

CINCINNATI: ALL ABOARD! (↑85/100↓) The *Cardinal* continues north from Cincinnati through scenes of heavy manufacturing.

Hamilton (↑50/50↓) Close enough to Cincinnati still to be industrial, Hamilton! is spelled with an exclamation mark in the local telephone directory! In the 1920s, many Chicago gangsters owned second homes in Hamilton, earning it the nickname 'Little Chicago'. The station was a stop for the *Cardinal* until 2005.

Ohio–Indiana state line (↑80/20↓) You cross into the Hoosier State in darkness.

CONNERSVILLE (↑100/80↓) Founded on the Whitewater River in 1813, Connersville makes everything from auto parts to dishwashers. Automobiles manufactured in the so-called 'Little Detroit' have included Auburn, Cord, Duesenberg, Ansted, Empire, Lexington, Jeep and McFarlan (a favourite car for Al Capone). Amtrak stops at a brick shelter on the platform. Nearby, the original station, built in 1914, is used for freight train operations.

INDIANAPOLIS (↑80/65↓) The birthplace of Kurt Vonnegut and former home town of Steve McQueen is Indiana's capital, located at the geographical centre of the state. The **Indy 500** motor race takes place each Memorial Day Sunday in May, drawing the world's largest sports crowd to the Indianapolis Motor Speedway.

Indianapolis basics

Telephone code 317

Station (*Ticket office* 23.00–12.30; *waiting room* 24hrs) Amtrak shares with Greyhound the modern intermodal station located under a concrete train shed at 350 S Illinois. The imposing red-brick Union Station opened in 1888 as 'one of the finest large-scale public spaces in the city' but the building now mostly houses a hotel & offices; its grand main waiting room is rarely used.

Connections Thruway buses link with Danville, Champaign-Urbana, Bloomington-Normal, Peoria, Galesburg, Moline, Illinois, & Davenport, Iowa

Local transport Indy Go buses (*635 3344; w indygo.net*) operate throughout the city

Taxis Yellow; 487 7777

Car rental Avis, 33 N Capitol Av; 236 1987

Greyhound Next to Amtrak, at 350 S Illinois; 267 3074

Indianapolis International Airport 6 miles (10km) southwest of the city, with a $1.1 billion state-of-the-art terminal. Indy Go's Green Line Express bus travels every 20mins between airport & downtown.

Visitors bureau 200 S Capitol Av 262 3000; 262 3000 or 1 800 323 4639; w visitindy.com

Accommodation The Crowne Plaza Hotel is housed within America's first 'Union Station' at 123 W Louisiana; 631 2221; w crowneplazaindydowntown.com, **$$$$**. Listed in the National Register of Historic Places, this Romanesque Revival-style building has a Grand Hall with distinctive arches & columns. Its soaring stained-glass barrel ceiling is matched by 20ft (6m) stained-glass wagon-wheel windows. Other hotels include the Alexander, 333 S Delaware; 888 384 6866; w wyndhamhotels. com/dolce, **$$$$**; Embassy Suites, 110 W Washington; 236 1800; w embassysuites3. hilton.com, **$$$$**; Le Méridien, 123 S Illinois; 737 1600; w marriott.com, **$$$**; Stone Soup Inn, 1304 N Central Av; 866 639 9550; w stonesoupinn.com, **$$$**; La Quinta Inn & Suites, 401 E Washington; 638 0327; w lq.com, **$$**.

The Indy Hostel is at 4903 Winthrop Av; 727 1696; w indyhostel.us, **$$**.

Recommended in Indianapolis

Children's Museum 3000 N Meridian; 334 4000; w childrensmuseum.org; Tue–Sun, daily in summer; admission charge. The largest museum of its kind in the world, containing the largest water clock in North America. The All Aboard gallery takes visitors back to the age of steam with the original 35ft-long (10m), 55US-ton (50-tonne) steam engine designed by Reuben Wells in 1868 to conquer Indiana's Madison Hill. The museum also features toy trains, rock climbing, carousel rides & a petting zoo.

Motor Speedway 4790 W 16th. For tickets & information, 492 8500;

w indianapolismotorspeedway.com; daily. The Speedway is the largest spectator sporting venue in the world, with more than 250,000 seats. The 2.5-mile (4km) track was built in 1909 & incorporates an entire golf course. Bus tours except in May.

Indianapolis Motor Speedway Museum Located at the Motor Speedway, the museum features 75 historic cars (including the Marmon 'Wasp', which won the inaugural Indianapolis 500 in 1911, & more than 30 other winning cars), films & memorabilia. Exhibits reflect all forms of motorsports, passenger cars & general automotive history.

City Market 222 E Market; ☏ 634 9266; w indianapoliscitymarket.com; ⏲ Mon–Sat. Dating from 1821, this is one of the few original city markets remaining in the United States. The restored 19th-century building contains 15 ethnic sections. Part of Market District is being transformed with a rain garden & bocce ball courts on the east plaza.

Newfields 4000 Michigan Rd; ☏ 923 1331 or ☏ 920 2660 (information line); w discovernewfields.org; ⏲ daily; admission charge. The Indianapolis Museum of Art is one of the oldest art museums in the country, located in a 52-acre (21ha) park with gardens, 5 pavilions, a theatre & a concert terrace. The collection includes ancient bronzes & masks. Paintings are by American & European masters, including Gauguin & post-Impressionist works, with the most significant collection of works by J M W Turner outside the UK. In 2017, the IMA unified its campus under 1 name – Newfields, A Place for Nature & the Arts. This is now also the home of Fairbanks Park, The Garden, Lilly House & the Elder Greenhouse.

Indiana Historical Society 450 W Ohio; ☏ 232 1882; w indianahistory.org; ⏲ Tue–Sat; admission charge. Discover Indiana's past through exhibitions, a library, publications, educational programmes & special events.

Indiana Transportation Museum At Forest Park, Noblesville, 20 miles (32km) north; ☏ 773 6000; w itm.org; ⏲ Sat–Sun; admission charge. Including old vehicles from the Santa Fe, Burlington & Louisville & Nashville railroads, as well as locomotives & Henry Flagler's Florida Coast Line business car. Train rides run on 34 miles (54km) of former Nickel Plate Road track aboard an authentic, historic train.

INDIANAPOLIS: ALL ABOARD! (↑80/65↓) The *Cardinal* departs Indianapolis past the massive Lucas Oil Stadium and adjacent Indiana Convention Center, with the downtown area to your right.

Brownsburg (↑25/40↓) You pass through a less urban landscape as the train makes for the corn and soya bean fields of central Indiana. You go through several small towns and accompany Interstate 74 to your right.

⟋⟍⟋ CRAWFORDSVILLE (↑65/30↓) Home of Wabash College, one of many educational establishments to be seen on this part of the journey. In 1932, the Monon Railroad donated a 300lb (136kg) locomotive bell as a trophy to the winning team each year and the Monon Bell Classic between Wabash College and Depauw University remains one of the most popular games in college football (Monon is a Potawatomi word for 'swift running'). Lew Wallace, Civil War general and author of *Ben Hur*, lived in this 'Athens of Indiana'. America's first official air mail delivery took place in 1859, when John Wise piloted a balloon from Lafayette to Crawfordsville.

You cross Cherry Creek then pass beneath Interstate 74.

Linden (↑10/20↓) The train crosses tracks belonging to the Norfolk & Western line. The New Albany & Salem (later Monon) Railroad opened a station at Linden in 1852. The building was moved to a new location in 1881 when the Toledo, St Louis & Western Railroad was built, crossing the Monon here. This historic depot is now listed on the National Register of Historic Places and houses the Linden Museum.

⟋⟍⟋ LAFAYETTE (↑30/50↓) You accompany an attractive valley with close-up views of this typical mid-American city, where the train used to run directly down Main Street (known as 'street-running') and the old station was simply a storefront. The Romanesque-style Big Four depot has been relocated next to a city park and underneath a bridge now used by Amtrak passengers. Lafayette is the home of Purdue University and was the birthplace of Alvah Roebuck, co-founder of Sears, Roebuck.

Wabash River (↑10/40↓) The train crosses the river then travels beneath Interstate 65 on its way to Chicago.

Tippecanoe Battlefield (↑15/35↓) On your left is the place where, in 1811, General and future President William Harrison defeated the Shawnee brothers, Tecumseh and Tenskwatawa, leaders of a confederacy of Native Americans that opposed US expansion into Native territory.

You continue through the small communities of Brookston and Chalmers.

Reynolds (↑35/15↓) As you cross the former Toledo, Peoria & Western line you change from Eastern to Central Time, so watches go back an hour (forward when travelling east).

♠♦♥ RENSSELAER (↑50/40↓) The *Cardinal* crosses the Kankakee River then proceeds through Shelby, Lowell and Creston as it crosses Indiana's plains.

Cedar Lake (↑30/10↓) The lake is visible to your left just before you reach a town of the same name.

♠♦♥ DYER (↑40/50↓) This became a rail town in 1857 when the Michigan Central established a depot and built a grain elevator, and the Monon Railroad operated here from 1897 to 1971. Amtrak opened a shelter in Dyer in 2014, its design inspired by late 19th- and early 20th-century depots found in small towns across the nation.

You start to enter an industrial environment which will persist most of the way to Chicago as the *Cardinal* transfers to Norfolk Southern tracks from the CSX route used since Clifton Forge.

Eggers Woods Forest (↑24/26↓) Look right for a rare splash of greenery. Originally called Grove Forest, the woodland was named after Frederick Eggers, a German immigrant who started the first Lutheran church here in 1874.

Hammond-Whiting (↑25/25↓) In 1851, the Michigan Central Railroad came through this area and their yards along the lake shore became some of the largest in the world. Whiting got its name from an incident in 1869 when 'Pop' Whiting, a train engineer, ditched his heavy freight train so that a fast passenger train could have right of way. Until 1871 it was called 'Pop Whiting's Siding'. In 1918, one of the worst train wrecks in US history happened near Hammond when the engineer of a World War I troop train fell asleep at the throttle and ran his train into the back of a slower 26-car circus train ahead. The wreckage caught fire, killing 86 people and injuring many more.

This is a stop for Amtrak's *Wolverine* train. Across the former tracks stands the Horseshoe Casino.

Storage tanks belonging to BP, formerly the Standard Oil Company, can be seen on both sides as you depart among freight yards. Watch for grain elevators and ships being loaded as you cross the Calumet River on a steel lift bridge.

Roby (↑35/15↓) The Avalon Regal Theater to your right was opened by Chicago's first black mayor as a centre for African-American culture. Mayor Harold Lee Washington was subsequently buried in Oak Woods Cemetery to your right. Interstate 90 (the Indiana Toll Road) is to your left. The route crosses a now-closed

Rock Island Railroad track at Englewood then crosses the south branch of the Chicago River.

Chicago's Skyway is to your left and the city skyline comes into view on the right, featuring the 110-storey Willis Tower. After crossing the Dan Ryan Expressway, you see the El rail track overhead and Lake Michigan to your right.

Comiskey Park (↑40/10↓) The car park on the right is where White Sox baseball used to be played. A new Comiskey Park stadium (later renamed Guaranteed Rate Field) was completed in 1991 and stands alongside.

Look for Conrail loading facilities to your left, then Amtrak's extensive 21st Street yards on your right. Trains are set up here to travel to every corner of the land.

The *Cardinal* lurches into Chicago, reversing slowly into Union Station through a passage beneath the post office building.

⊷ CHICAGO (↑50) For Chicago city information, see page 83.

21

The *Adirondack*
New York–Montreal

GENERAL ROUTE INFORMATION

The *Adirondack* has been nominated by *National Geographic Traveler* magazine as one of the world's ten best rail trips. It goes from New York to the Gallic charms of Montreal by way of the beautiful Hudson River Valley, the Adirondack Mountains, Lake Champlain, Vermont and the St Lawrence River. This daytime journey is particularly wonderful during autumn.

Adirondack trains operate between New York and Yonkers on Amtrak, between Yonkers and Poughkeepsie on Metro-North Railroad, between Poughkeepsie and Schenectady on CSX Transportation, between Schenectady and Rouses Point on Canadian Pacific, and between Rouses Point and Montreal on Canadian National lines.

JOINING THE TRAIN

NEW YORK: ALL ABOARD (20↓) For New York City information, see page 205. Trains from Washington, DC, connect with the *Adirondack*, which leaves Pennsylvania Station on Empire Corridor tracks. The first 10 miles were opened in 1991 at a cost of $89 million and this part of the route used to be the New York Central's west side freight line. Constructed by the Hudson River Railroad, passenger services had previously operated until 1872.

You emerge from a tunnel with the Jacob Javits Convention Centre (built on the site of the old 30th Street rail yards) to your left. You continue through Riverside Tunnel, then see the Hudson River and Henry Hudson Parkway to your left, followed by Riverbank State Park, which has three swimming pools, a skating rink, sports fields and a theatre. You pass beneath the Hudson Parkway, which continues to your right.

George Washington Bridge (↑8/12↓) Spanning the river to your left is a suspension bridge which was the longest in the world when completed in 1931. Just before the bridge, look for the 'little red lighthouse', officially Jeffrey's Hook Light, which featured in a famous children's book by Hildegarde Swift and is now preserved.

Fort Tryon Park is to your right beyond the highway before you pass Inwood Hill Park. Among the high-rises on New Jersey's Palisades across the river is the cupola of St Michael Villa, run by the Sisters of St Joseph. Dozens of nuns and a priest were rescued after a blaze broke out at the villa in 2016.

Spuyten Duyvil Bridge (↑15/5↓) The *Adirondack* crosses the Harlem River Ship Canal on a 610ft-long (185m) swing bridge, built in 1900 and restored to accommodate this line. One of the world's largest floating cranes was used in

HIGHLIGHTS The *Adirondack* travels through the lush wine country of the Hudson Valley and passes West Point, the nation's oldest military academy. In picturesque Montreal, the world's second-largest French-speaking city, you can enjoy sophisticated food, wine and nightlife, see the gorgeous Notre-Dame Basilica, and visit Mount Royal Park for tremendous panoramic views of the city.

IMMIGRATION FORMALITIES US and Canadian citizens must have a passport, Trusted Traveler card or enhanced driver's licence – **an ordinary driver's licence is not sufficient**. Citizens of other countries must have a passport and in many cases a visa. Visa-exempt foreign nationals need an Electronic Travel Authorization (eTA) to transit through Canada. Passengers aged 15 and under who do not have either a Trusted Traveler card or passport may present a copy of their birth certificate. Passengers aged under 18 and not travelling with both parents require a letter from any parent not present giving permission to cross the border.

For further information, contact the US (☎ *1 800 333 4636;* w *travel. state.gov*) or Canadian (☎ *1 800 622 6232,* w *canadainternational.gc.ca*) government agencies prior to travel. Information on crossing the border between the United States and Canada is also available from Amtrak agents. See also page 37, check with your US embassy or contact US Citizenship and Immigration Services in Washington, DC (pages 39 and 379). Passengers without proper documentation are prohibited from entering the US or Canada and will be detrained before reaching the US–Canadian border. Neither Amtrak nor VIA Rail Canada accepts any liability if you are denied entry or removed from the train.

FREQUENCY Daily. The **northbound** service leaves New York early in the morning to reach Albany by late morning, Plattsburgh mid-afternoon and Montreal by early evening. Travelling **south**, trains leave Montreal mid-morning to reach Plattsburgh just after midday, Albany by late afternoon and New York mid-evening.

DURATION Ten hours

RESERVATIONS All reserved

EQUIPMENT Amfleet coaches

LOUNGE CAR National Park Service rangers from the Roosevelt-Vanderbilt National Historic Sites provide a narrative between Croton-Harmon and Hudson, New York, and the Saratoga National Historic Park between Saratoga Springs and Westport weekends except holidays. Great Dome Car service operates in the autumn.

FOOD Snacks, sandwiches, drinks. The lounge car sometimes serves specialities such as cheesecake baked by nuns of the Canadian New Skete Order.

BAGGAGE There is no check-in service. Ski racks are available.

2018 to move spans of the bridge to a barge for upgrades after it was severely damaged during Hurricane Sandy and had suffered years of corrosion and electrical malfunctions.

The Hudson Parkway Bridge is to your right. Metro-North trains join on the right after travelling from Grand Central Station.

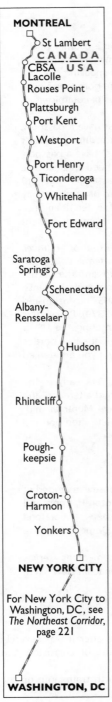

MONTREAL

St Lambert

C A N A D A
CBSA   USA
Lacolle
Rouses Point

Plattsburgh
Port Kent

Westport

Port Henry
Ticonderoga

Whitehall

Fort Edward

Saratoga
Springs

Schenectady

Albany-
Rensselaer

Hudson

Rhinecliff

Pough-
keepsie

Croton-
Harmon

Yonkers

NEW YORK CITY

For New York City to
Washington, DC, see
The Northeast Corridor,
page 221

WASHINGTON, DC

YONKERS (↑20/20↓) This is where Elisha Otis invented the safety elevator and Belgian-born chemist Leo Hendrik Baekeland invented Bakelite. The **Hudson River Museum** (*511 Warburton Av;* ☎ *914 963 4550;* **w** *hrm.org*) includes an 1876 mansion overlooking the Hudson River and Palisades. Other imposing houses can be seen among the hills. The grand Beaux-Arts-style station was built in 1911 and has been comprehensively restored.

Hastings-on-Hudson (↑6/14↓)
This was the home of the promoter Florenz Ziegfeld, whose wife Billie Burke was the good witch in *The Wizard of Oz*. They had a private zoo with bears, lion cubs, buffalos and an elephant, and lavishly entertained the stars of Broadway. The Wizard in *The Wizard of Oz*, Frank Morgan, also lived in Hastings-on-Hudson.

Irvington (↑9/11↓)
Named after Washington Irving, creator of *Rip Van Winkle*, his Sunnyside home in Tarrytown can be seen to your right past the Metro-North station.

Tappan Zee Bridge (↑10/10↓)
Carrying the NYS Thruway 3 miles (5km) across the Hudson River ahead to your left, this new bridge replaced an older one in 2017. Also to your left is Philipse Manor, one of many estates in this region which have belonged to the well heeled or famous.

Ossining (↑15/5↓)
Look for the guard towers of Sing Sing correctional facility, where convicts were sent 'up the river' to do time. The main house is to your left and the annex to your right. A total of 614 men and women, including Julius and Ethel Rosenberg, who were convicted for espionage, were executed by electric chair ('Old Sparky') at Sing Sing until the State of New York abolished the death penalty in 1972.

You continue through the most beautiful part of the Hudson River Valley, where maple trees flourish on steep riverbanks in a lush landscape.

CROTON-HARMON (↑20/35↓) The town was named after Clifford B Harmon, a developer from New York City. Construction of a rail line from New York to Poughkeepsie via Croton-on-Hudson began in 1846. By 1903, electric trains started operating out of Grand Central Terminal and construction began on a steam terminal at Croton Point, where trains could switch from electric to steam power to continue northward. Along with artists, writers and luminaries such as Mary Pickford and Douglas Fairbanks, railroad workers and dam-builders settled here. The 18th-century Van Cortlandt Manor belonged to New York's first lieutenant-governor and was visited by Generals Washington and Lafayette. Across the river are the twin domed towers of Indian Point atomic power station, built on land that originally housed the Indian Point Amusement Park.

Peekskill (↑10/25↓)

Once a frontier trading post, Peekskill was an early American Army headquarters during the Revolutionary War. Across the river is Dunderberg Mountain, at the southern end of the Hudson Highlands. Bear Mountain Bridge carries the Appalachian Trail across the river.

Highland Falls (↑17/18↓)

Singer Billy Joel lived here in the 1970s and wrote 'New York State of Mind' on a Greyhound Bus en route to his home in Highland Falls. The falls cascade 100ft (30m) down cliffs on the far side.

West Point (↑18/17↓)

Cadets at the nation's oldest military academy have included Ulysses S Grant, Robert E Lee, George Custer, Stonewall Jackson, Dwight Eisenhower and Norman Schwarzkopf. The Gothic chapel features stained-glass windows and the world's largest church organ. Washington positioned troops here during the Revolutionary War.

After West Point the river narrows at the eastern end of Constitution Island. Nearby World's End is the river's deepest place at 202ft (62m). The *Adirondack* travels through Breakneck Tunnel then alongside Sugarloaf Mountain, with Storm King Mountain across the river. Look for blue herons, cormorants and flights of geese.

Bannerman's Castle (↑24/11↓)

Situated on Pollepel Island in the middle of the river (which narrows to a quarter of its width between Storm King and Breakneck Ridge), this ruined mock-medieval castle was constructed by Scottish immigrant Francis Bannerman during the early 1900s as a private arsenal, complete with moat and drawbridge.

Beacon (↑26/9↓)

Signal fires on the mountain to your right warned a Revolutionary Army post of approaching British troops. In the 19th century, this was the 'hat-making capital of the US', with around 50 manufacturers. A bridge links Beacon with the larger city of Newburgh across the river.

Danskammer (↑28/7↓)

On the far side of the Hudson are the Roseton and Danskammer power plants, then the red buildings of the Royal Kedem winery, founded in 1848 by Baron Herzog. As you approach Poughkeepsie look for rock quarries on the near shore.

✦✦✦ POUGHKEEPSIE (↑35/14↓)

Founded by the Dutch in 1683, this manufacturing city was famous for making cough drops and ball bearings. Interesting buildings include Clinton House and Glebe House on the corner of Main and N White. The Frances Lehman Loeb Art Center, founded in 1864 as the Vassar College Art Gallery, charts the history of art from antiquity to the present. It has over 21,000 works, including paintings, sculptures, drawings, photographs, textiles, Rembrandt prints and Tiffany glass (*124 Raymond Av;* ✆ *845 437 5632;* w *fllac.vassar.edu*).

Amtrak's splendid four-storey station was completed in 1918 and has a waiting room modelled on New York's Grand Central Terminal, with a gallery lit during daylight hours by five high-arched windows and three original chandeliers. The 14 chestnut benches are also original and above the wood-panelled walls is a ceiling resembling the one in San Miniato al Monte, an 11th-century church in Florence, Italy.

As the *Adirondack* pulls out of the station, note the cantilever Poughkeepsie-Highland Railroad Bridge spanning the river. This was the largest rail bridge in the world when completed in 1889, but was put out of use in 1974 by a fire. In 2009, the bridge reopened as a pedestrian walkway connecting to trails and parks up and down the Hudson. To your right you pass Franklin D Roosevelt's home, where he was born and died, and the enormous mansion of Frederick Vanderbilt. The town of Hyde Park is on the near shore, with Fallkill Creek waterfall to the right.

An old lighthouse nicknamed 'Maid of the Meadows', with a *trompe l'oeil* window, can be seen at the south end of Esopus Meadows in midstream. Completed in 1871, this is the last wooden lighthouse existing on the Hudson. German-style houses on the other side of the water demonstrate why this valley has been called 'the Rhine of America'. You travel through the neat village of Staatsburg.

⋘ RHINECLIFF (↑14/20↓) The station was built by the New York Central Railroad in 1914 in Spanish Mission Revival style. This is Amtrak's stop for the attractive towns of Rhinebeck and Kingston. The Rhinebeck & Connecticut Railroad, started in 1872, carried coal to New England and commodities to growing industries, such as Baker's Chocolate. In the 1890s, when Rhinebeck became the greenhouse-grown violet capital of the world, Rhinecliff was its shipping centre.

Rhinebeck's historic buildings include America's oldest (1776) hotel, the **Beekman Arms**, which was a favourite with Franklin D Roosevelt, who concluded all his political campaigns for governor and president talking from the front porch. An avid stamp collector, President Roosevelt was responsible for building the Rhinebeck Post Office.

Kingston Rhinecliff Bridge (↑4/16↓) The bridge was built in 1957, and on
both sides of the track is the marshland of Tivoli Bays, a haven for fish and birds. Across the river, at the mouth of the Esopus River, stands the oldest lighthouse on the Hudson, the 1869 Saugerties Light. Look also for the Carmelite Sisters' convent.

Germantown (↑10/10↓) First settled by Germans, this is now the centre of a
fruit-growing region. Cement plants and barges appear across the river.

Catskill (↑15/5↓) Fine houses take advantage of dramatic riverbank locations
as you enter a land dominated by the forests and gorges of the Catskills. This recreation area is bigger than Rhode Island and the mountains rise to more than 4,000ft (1,200m).

Roeliff River (↑16/4↓) Docks can be seen to your right as the train crosses the
river and approaches Hudson. The 1874 Hudson-Athens lighthouse, sometimes called the Hudson City Light, to your left, is one of 13 coastguard lights on the river.

⋘ HUDSON (↑20/15↓) Many television shows, including *The Wonder Years* and *Gotham* have been shot locally, as have films such as Steven Spielberg's *War of the Worlds* and Ang Lee's *Taking Woodstock*. Dutch settlers called this place Claverack Landing because of its luxuriant clover fields and the town was renamed after the explorer Henry Hudson in 1785. Among the former whaling port's gardens and estates is the Persian-style Olana, a 37-room extravaganza designed by landscape artist Frederic Church. Hudson is also home to the **FASNY Museum of Fire Fighting** with its unparalleled collection, from primitive handtubs to contemporary motor fire apparatus (*117 Harry Howard Av;* ☏*518 822 1875;* w *fasnyfiremuseum. com*). The red-brick railway station was built in 1874 by the New York Central and is the oldest on this line.

Castleton-on-Hudson (↑11/4↓) The Smith Memorial Bridge appears overhead, followed by a mile-long (1.6km) bridge connecting the New York State Thruway with the Massachusetts Turnpike. As the *Adirondack* nears Albany, look left for the city skyline dominated by the Empire State Plaza. Bethlehem Energy Center, built on the site of the Albany Steam Station, is seen across the river. The new power plant uses gas-fired combustion turbines to produce electricity.

⊶ ALBANY-RENSSELAER (↑15/20↓) The state capital's port prospered greatly with the arrival in 1825 of the Erie Canal, linking Lake Erie with the Atlantic. The railway came six years later when New York's first steam train, the *DeWitt Clinton*, ran on the Mohawk & Hudson line. Amtrak's busy station with its distinctive clock tower was completed in 2002 and is 1½ miles (2.4km) away in adjacent Rensselaer.

Albany's sleek new buildings contrast with the Old State Capitol's Gothic architecture. The Schuyler Mansion is a Georgian house visited by George Washington and Benjamin Franklin. The **New York State Museum** at the Empire State Plaza was established in 1836 and is the oldest and largest state museum in the country (☏*518 474 5877;* w *nysm.nysed.gov;* ⊕ *closed Mon*). Nearby is 17th-century **Fort Crailo**, America's oldest fortress, where tradition says a British surgeon wrote *Yankee Doodle Dandy*.

The *Adirondack* crosses the Hudson River after departing Rensselaer past extensive freight yards. The Romantic buildings on your left once belonged to the Delaware & Hudson Railroad and now house State University headquarters. Albany city centre is to your left.

Approaching Schenectady, look right for the gold dome of City Hall. Red-brick Elston Hall, formerly the Van Curler Hotel, to your left is part of a community college.

⊶ SCHENECTADY (↑20/25↓) 'The city that lights and hauls the world' began in 1661 as a fur-trading station, its name being a Mohawk expression for 'through the open pines'. The American Locomotive Company (ALCO) took care of haulage while Thomas Edison's Machine Works created the light. Edison's first job was selling sweets to railroad passengers, money from which he spent on chemistry sets and building a telegraph system out of scrap metal. He was dismissed from his job when he moved his chemistry lab into a baggage car and accidentally set fire to the train.

Apart from the electric light bulb and power stations, Edison developed or invented, among other things, the phonograph, motion picture camera, high-speed telegraph, typewriter, electric pen, copier and dictation machines, cement mixer and telephone, eventually holding a record 1,093 patents. The Edison factory eventually became General Electric, until recently one of the city's main employers. Some of the biggest locomotives ever to operate on America's rails, including Union Pacific's *Big Boy*, were built here. The city continues to celebrate its history of innovation and connection to the railroad with the arrival of the Canadian Pacific Railway Holiday Train each Christmas season, coinciding with day-long activities (w *cpr.ca/en/community/holiday-train*).

You leave Schenectady with the 17th-century stockade district to your right. After shaking off the factories and power lines you begin to see logging and timber-processing plants among the wooded hills.

▲▲▲ SARATOGA SPRINGS (↑25/20↓)

Before World War I the Vanderbilts and Whitneys came to Saratoga to drink the waters and take curative baths. Mixing only with their own kind, they enjoyed the best hotels, lavish casinos, gardens and America's oldest racetrack. Potato chips (crisps) were allegedly invented by a Native American chef called George Crum when Cornelius Vanderbilt asked for his potatoes to be sliced extra-thin.

No longer an exclusive resort of the rich, Saratoga Springs retains its bathhouses and you can still sample the waters. The 1777 Battle of Saratoga, a turning point in the Revolutionary War, took place 12 miles (19km) to the east and the site is now a military park. Amtrak's station was built in the 1950s by the Delaware & Hudson and reopened in 2004 after extensive renovations. Today, the Saratoga & North Creek Railroad operates excursions over the 57-mile (92km) former Adirondack Railway line between the terminal in North Creek and Saratoga Springs, allowing connections with Amtrak's *Adirondack* and *Ethan Allen Express services* (*26 Station Lane, Saratoga Springs;* ☏*877 726 7245;* w *sncrr.com*).

After the *Adirondack* passes through a cutting lined with evergreens, look for a junkyard to your left then a field containing pheasants. You cross the river with a highway bridge to your left.

▲▲▲ FORT EDWARD (↑20/22↓)

The original fort was constructed during the French and Indian War (also known as the Seven Years War). A sequence of locks later linked the Hudson River to the Champlain Canal, creating a waterway through to the St Lawrence. Note the wood-framed houses on both sides. Amtrak stops next to an elegant Victorian-style Delaware & Hudson Railway depot built in 1900, with a unique polygonal south end forming the waiting room (now used as community meeting space). Restored in 2009, the station also houses a gallery and gift shop. TrainCatcher van/car service is available from Fort Edward to Glens Falls and Lake George Village (☏*518 792 1086 for reservations*). Lake George has cruises, water skiing and winter car races on the ice.

You continue through peaceful country into the heart of the Adirondacks, which were the tallest mountains in the world before the ice ages. Home to eagles, bobcat and deer, they became famous in 1869, when the Reverend William H H Murray published *Adventures in the Wilderness*. His book started a fashion for city dwellers to spend their summers in an area recently made accessible by railroads, and rail companies built many big hotels and lodges to accommodate them. Much of this region can still only be seen by train or on foot.

Champlain Canal (↑10/12↓)

The canal is to your right behind a row of trees, and this is the best side of the train from which to appreciate the scenery ahead.

▲▲▲ WHITEHALL (↑22/25↓)

A lock system connects the canal with Lake Champlain's South Bay. Rutland, served by Amtrak's *Heartland Flyer*, is 20 miles (32km) to the east in Vermont.

You leave Whitehall by way of a short tunnel.

Lake Champlain (↑5/20↓)

Seen to your right as you cross South Bay and enter the six million acres (2.4 million hectares) of the **Adirondack Forest Preserve**, these deep, rocky lakes and shallow-running rivers are favoured by hunters and fishermen.

A few minutes later you pass on your right a channel joining South Bay with Lake Champlain, named after its discoverer, Samuel de Champlain. The *Adirondack* follows the clear waters of the shoreline of America's sixth-largest lake for most of the next 100 miles (160km). In winter, look for ice fishermen fishing from ice houses on the lake. Vermont's tidy farmland is on the far side.

TICONDEROGA (↑25/25↓) The name is Iroquois for 'between two waters'.
Amtrak's station consists of a small brick box and a telephone on Highway 74, some distance from both town and a large 18th-century fort, formerly Fort Carillon. A brick freight house/passenger station, built in 1891, was moved to its current home on Champlain Avenue in 1913 and was used as a passenger station. Visible on bluffs ahead to your right, Fort Ticonderoga was built by the French in 1775. This crucial position on the La Chute River between Lakes Champlain and George was constantly fought over during the Revolution, changing hands several times before the fort was abandoned, destroyed and lately restored.

You leave past the fort to your right and enter a tunnel before continuing through the mountains. Vermont's Green Mountains are across the lake.

PORT HENRY (↑25/20↓) Note the magnificent, ornate town hall to the left of
the quaint chateau-style station, built in 1888 and listed on the National Register of Historic Places. A Canadian Pacific Alco ore car and a Lake Champlain & Moriah Railroad caboose are on display near the station. Abandoned railroad beds appear forlornly to your right before the train travels on among hay fields, forests and hills. Lake Champlain's rocky shoreline continues to the right.

WESTPORT (↑20/56↓) This small fishing town where Thruway buses
connect with Lake Placid is the site of the 1932 and 1980 Winter Olympics. Westport station, originally built in the 1870s, has been restored, winning an Adirondack Architectural Heritage Award for its exemplary historic preservation work. The Depot Theater, founded in 1979, is now the main occupant.

The train keeps to a line between Lake Champlain on your right and mountains to your left, crossing high above the lovely Bouquet River. The tranquil lake boasts its own version of the Loch Ness monster called 'Champ', first seen by Samuel de Champlain in 1609.

Willsboro (↑20/36↓) Trout and salmon fishing are a major attraction on Lake
Champlain and along the dammed Bouquet River. For 25 miles (40km) you travel a route hacked into cliffs 100ft (30m) above the lake, with wonderful views as the train negotiates hundreds of curves among birch trees, tunnels and houses.

Port Kent (↑42/14↓) Trains stop here from May to October, when ferries
cross the water to downtown Burlington in Vermont. Amtrak uses a platform with an open-air wooden shelter built in 1989. Nearby at Keeseville is Ausable Chasm, a 2mile-long (3km) sandstone gorge known as the 'little Grand Canyon of the East'.

Ausable River (↑45/11↓) Watch for herons as you cross the tree-lined
river, which has its source below the state's tallest mountain, Mount Marcy (5,344ft/1,629m).

Valcour Island (↑49/7↓) The *Adirondack* passes several Revolutionary War and French and Indian War battlefields. Benedict Arnold's ships were defeated by the British in 1776 near the island to your right as they competed for control of Lake Champlain.

At this point the train leaves **Adirondack State Park**, the largest state-level protected area in the United States.

Plattsburgh International Airport (↑54/2↓) Seen immediately to your left as you approach Plattsburgh, with yachts moored on your right, the former United States Air Force SAC base is now a civilian airport and industrial complex.

⋙ PLATTSBURGH (↑56/35↓) To your left, as the train enters this industrial city, you can see a Delaware & Hudson Railroad turntable and the Thomas Macdonough Monument. The monument commemorates a victory in 1814 on Lake Champlain which foiled a British attempt to invade New York State from Canada. Amtrak's green-canopied waiting room is to your right. The picturesque French Provincial-style depot was built in 1886 by the Delaware & Hudson to look like a Quebec castle.

The *Adirondack* finally parts company with Lake Champlain before travelling through corn fields and forests towards the Canadian border.

⋙ ROUSES POINT (↑35/45↓) This is the train's last stop before leaving the United States. The station is a platform next to an 1889 D&H depot which now serves as a history and welcome centre.

Owing to its location just south of the Canadian border, Rouses Point also serves as a US Customs and Border Protection checkpoint, housed in the building to your right, for those travelling south. In the days of Prohibition, trains crossing from Canada were known as 'bootleggers', since passengers often tried to sneak a few bottles past the border guards in the shanks of their boots. Look for customs stickers adorning checked freight cars to your right.

You cross the US–Canadian border and pass through St Jean, where a cannon on the right guards a military college.

⋙ CBSA LACOLLE (↑45/30↓) This stop near the village of Cantic is the Canada Border Services Agency checkpoint for people travelling north and is not a passenger stop. After inspection the *Adirondack* proceeds over the flat, nondescript landscape of southern Quebec.

⋙ ST LAMBERT (↑30/10↓) Timber yards and city apartment blocks loom on the right as the train pauses briefly in this residential suburb at a station operated by VIA Rail.

You cross the St Lawrence River on the Victoria Jubilee Bridge, the longest in the world when it opened in 1859. Approaching Montreal through industrial scenes and Canadian national freight yards, the city's high-rise buildings can be seen to your right.

⋙ MONTREAL (↑10) Built on an island where the St Lawrence, Ottawa and Richelieu rivers meet, Montreal hosted the 1967 World's Fair and 1976 Olympic Games. The French settled here in 1642, but explorers had arrived more than 100 years earlier. The British took over in 1760, then (for a short time) American revolutionaries. Montreal today is a centre for commerce, transport, finance, design, culture, fashion and film. Regarded as a Beta-plus 'global city', it is rated the 12th most liveable city in the world by *The Economist* and named best city in the world to be a student in the QS World University Rankings.

Montreal is the world's second-largest French-speaking city, with more than a third of its three million people having English as their first language. Like the rest of Quebec Province, it can be cold in winter, with more snow than Moscow and temperatures well below zero into March, but the city is able to deal with the heaviest snowfall as tunnels link 2,000 downtown stores. July highs can be in the 80°s Fahrenheit (26–32°C).

Montreal basics

Telephone code 514

Station (*Ticket office* ⏱ *07.00–17.00 (Amtrak) & 05.15–19.15 (VIA Rail); waiting room* ⏱ *04.30–00.30; Amtrak reservations & information* ☎ *1 800 872 7245; VIA Rail* ☎ *888 842 7245*) The modernist steel & concrete Gare Centrale (Central Station) at 895 rue de la Gauchetière Ouest is used by Amtrak, commuter trains & Canada's VIA Rail. Panorama lounge, payphones, restaurants, shops, ATM banking, newspapers, Red Caps, taxi stand.
Connections No Thruway bus
Local transport STM runs an efficient bus & subway system throughout the city (☎ *786 4636; w* stm.info; *Le Métro operates 05.30–01.00*)
Taxis Champlain ☎ 271 1111; Diamond ☎ 273 6311
Car rental Budget, Central Station; ☎ 866 7675
Greyhound 1717 Berri; ☎ 842 2281.
✈ **Pierre Elliott Trudeau International Airport** 12 miles (19km) from downtown by Aeroshuttle (☎ 855 628 3883). The 747 bus line runs 24hrs a day between the airport & downtown Montreal.
Tours Gray Line ☎ 398 9769; Old Montreal

Ghost Trail, available in summer ☎ 844 4021; *w* fantommontreal.com/en. Boat trips on the St Lawrence River from Croisières (☎ *866 856 6668*).
🛈 **Visitors bureau** 1255 Peel; ☎ 1 800 230 0001; *w* mtl.org; ⏱ daily
🏠 **Accommodation** Hotels include Le Saint-Sulpice, 414 Saint-Sulpice; ☎ 600 5190; *w* lesaintsulpice.com, **$$$$**; Château de l'Argoat, 524 rue Sherbrooke; ☎ 842 2046; *w* hotel-chateau-argoat.com, **$$$**; Kutuma, 3708 St Denis; ☎ 844 0111; *w* kutuma.com, **$$$**; Marriott Courtyard, 380 René-Lévesque Bd W; ☎ 398 9999; *w* marriott.com, **$$$**; Monville, 1041 de Bleury; ☎ 379 2000; *w* hotelmonville. com, **$$$**; Ambrose, 3422 rue Stanley; ☎ 288 6922; *w* hotelambrose.ca, **$$**.

For bed and breakfast, contact Le Gite du Hu-Art, 1673 Av du Lac St-Charles; ☎ 581 222 0774; *w* legiteduhu-art.com, **$$$**.

International Youth Hostel, 1030 MacKay; ☎ 843 3317; *w* hostellingmontreal.com. Members & non-members, **$**. Auberge Youth Hostel, 901 rue Sherbrooke E; ☎ 522 6124; *w* aubergemontreal. com, **$**. YWCA, 1355 Rene Levesque Bd; ☎ 866 9941; *w* ydesfemmesmtl.org. Women only, **$$**.

Recommended in Montreal

Mount Royal Park Reached via Camilien-Houde Parkway or Remembrance Rd; ☎ 843 8240; *w* lemontroyal.qc.ca. Walk, picnic or take time to admire the views in this natural-looking park, dominated by the modest mountain which gave the city its name. The park was planned by Frederick Law Olmsted, designer of New York's Central Park. Winter activities include tubular slides & ice skating.
Notre-Dame Basilica 110 Notre-Dame St W; ☎ 842 2925; *w* basiliquenotredame.ca; ⏱ daily; admission charge (guided tour included). Located in Old Montreal, this magnificent church was

built in Gothic Revival style & completed in 1843, when it was the largest church in North America. The sanctuary is decorated in blues, azures, reds, purples, silver & gold, with hundreds of intricate wooden carvings. Stained-glass windows made in Limoges, France, show the history of the founding of Montreal. Former prime minister Pierre Trudeau's state funeral took place here, as did the wedding of Celine Dion.
Museum of Fine Arts 1380 rue Sherbrooke; ☎ 285 2000; *w* mmfa.qc.ca; ⏱ Tue–Sun; admission charge. The museum has Quebec & Canadian art, a gallery devoted to Napoleon as

well as European & North American paintings & major international exhibitions. The sculpture garden includes works by Jim Dine, Elisabeth Frink, Antony Gormley & Henry Moore.

Museum of Contemporary Art 405 rue Sherbrooke E; ☎847 6226; **w** mbam.qc.ca; ⊕ Tue–Sun; admission charge. The collection comprises over 7,000 works of art by more than 1,500 artists, covering contemporary art in Quebec in particular & Canada in general, as well as international artists. The museum is Canada's only cultural complex devoted to both the performing & visual arts.

Canadian Centre for Architecture 1920 Baile; ☎939 7026; **w** cca.qc.ca; ⊕ Wed–Sun; admission charge; guided tours Sat–Sun. Founded by the architect Phyllis Lambert, this museum & study centre includes the (1874) Shaughnessy House & a splendid sculpture garden is part of the visit of this outstanding place.

St Joseph's Oratory 3800 rue Queen Mary; ☎733 8211; **w** saint-joseph.org; ⊕ daily; donation. The world's largest church is dedicated to Canada's patron saint. Beneath a green copper dome is the original chapel founded by Brother André, said to have been able to cure the sick.

St George's Anglican Church Pl du Canada, 1101 Stanley; ☎866 7113; **w** st-georges.org;

⊕ Tue–Sun; admission free. Built in 1870, this beautiful neo-Gothic church contains wonderful woodwork, including a double hammer-beam roof, & a tapestry from Westminster Abbey.

Exporail/Canadian Railway Museum 110 St Pierre in Saint-Constant, 1 mile (1.6km) south of Montreal; ☎450 632 2410; **w** exporail.org; ⊕ May–Sep; admission charge. Canada's finest railway museum has over 160 examples of rolling stock, including the country's oldest-surviving steam engines & the *Rocket* (Montreal's first electric streetcar). Train rides on Sun & holidays.

McCord Museum 690 rue Sherbrooke; ☎861 6701; **w** museesmontreal.org/en/museums/mccord-museum.ca; ⊕ daily; admission charge. An introduction to the history of Montreal & its citizens, including toys, photographs & splendid clothes. Inaugurated in 1921, the museum embodies the vision of collector David Ross McCord, & has recently merged with the Stewart Museum & the Fashion Museum, with its collection of over 7,000 garments, accessories & textiles.

Botanical Garden 4101 rue Sherbrooke E; ☎868 3000; **w** espacepourlavie.ca/en/access/botanical-garden; ⊕ daily; admission charge. One of the largest in the world, with over 300 outdoor gardens & 10 exhibition houses, including a butterfly house & an insectarium.

22

The *Vermonter*
Washington, DC–St Albans
(for Montreal)

GENERAL ROUTE INFORMATION

Amtrak's alternative to the *Adirondack* travels from Washington, DC via New York City to St Albans, Vermont. The *Vermonter* follows the Northeast Corridor route before heading north at Springfield. This train replaces the previous nighttime *Montrealer*, allowing you to travel through splendid New England scenery by day and see the sun set over the Green Mountains. The *Vermonter* is financed through funds made available by the Vermont Agency of Transportation and the Massachusetts & Connecticut Departments of Transportation.

Efforts to extend the *Vermonter* to Montreal are underway and in 2014 the freight line between St Albans and the Canada–US border was upgraded.

JOINING THE TRAIN

The *Vermonter* operates between Washington, DC and New Rochelle on Amtrak, between New Rochelle and New Haven on Metro-North Railroad, between New Haven and Springfield on Amtrak, and between Springfield and St Albans on the Connecticut River Line and New England Central Railroad.

For Washington, DC, and the route from Washington, DC to Springfield, see pages 215–17 and 218–20. The *Vermonter* turns north from the Northeast Corridor route after Springfield and travels towards Holyoke.

HOLYOKE: ALL ABOARD! (15↓) Amtrak service to Holyoke began in 2015 after rehabilitation of the Connecticut River Line that parallels the river for 49 miles (79km) between Springfield and Northfield. The new station in Holyoke is located at the crossing of Dwight and Main streets – an area historically known as Depot Square for its railroad associations. Nearby, the historic 1885 Connecticut River Railroad (CNRR) depot originally included an 'emigrant's room' where recent immigrants to the city were vaccinated against smallpox. Situated at a bend in the Connecticut River and at the foot of Mount Tom, Holyoke rose to prominence in the mid-19th century as the United States industrialised. The town prospered, with an opera house, many shops and an impressive Gothic Revival-style city hall that remains a landmark. Although many of the original industries have moved out, the city is still home to businesses in the printing, publishing, electrical machinery and plastics fields. Historic mill buildings have been transformed into homes for new high-tech enterprises.

HIGHLIGHTS The journey begins in Washington, DC, and runs through Philadelphia and New York City to Connecticut, Massachusetts, New Hampshire and Vermont, the Green Mountain state famous for its covered wooden bridges and ski resorts. The charming capital Montpelier has an 18th-century Greek-style State House with a delicately beautiful gold dome.

FREQUENCY Daily. The **northbound** service leaves Washington, DC early in the morning to arrive in Philadelphia by mid-morning and New York before noon. You reach Springfield mid-afternoon and St Albans by mid-evening. Travelling **south**, the train leaves St Albans early in the morning, arriving in Springfield mid-afternoon and New York early evening. You reach Philadelphia by mid-evening and Washington, DC late evening.

DURATION 12 hours 30 minutes

RESERVATIONS All reserved

EQUIPMENT Amfleet coaches. Business Class.

FOOD Snacks, sandwiches and drinks

LOUNGE CAR National Park Service rangers from the Springfield Armory National Historic Site provide a narrative from Essex Junction to Springfield, Massachusetts, on Saturdays

BAGGAGE No available check-in service. Bicycle and ski racks are available (reservations required).

NORTHAMPTON (↑15/25↓) Amtrak service to Northampton began in 2014 to a temporary station consisting of a wooden platform. This is adjacent to historic Union Station, which is currently occupied by commercial firms. Although situated on the west bank of the Connecticut River, early settlement of Northampton grew up along Mill River, the water power of which was used to drive early grist and saw mills. Northampton went on to become an important trade and commercial centre in the 18th century, producing silk, hosiery, cutlery, brushes and caskets.

Before the Civil War, Northampton became a centre for the abolitionist movement, with some homes serving as stops on the Underground Railroad. In 1841, a utopian community called the Northampton Association of Education and Industry was established to promote self-improvement, racial equality, freedom of worship and other public ideals. Calvin Coolidge graduated from nearby Amherst College and began practising law in Northampton in 1895. He married a local teacher, served as mayor, governor of Massachusetts and vice president of the United States before becoming president following Warren G Harding's death in 1923. After leaving the White House, Coolidge and his wife returned to Northampton. The Calvin Coolidge Presidential Library and Museum, located in the magnificent Forbes Library, contains papers, photographs and other memorabilia.

GREENFIELD (↑25/30↓) Amtrak service to Greenfield began in 2014, using a temporary wooden platform within walking distance of shops and restaurants on Main Street. When opened in 2012, this 24,000ft^2 (2,230m^2)structure was the first net-zero transit centre in the country, deriving all its renewable energy needs on site using photovoltaic panels, 22 geothermal wells and occupancy sensors to control lighting. The building takes advantage of natural heating from the sun and cooling from prevailing breezes. Railroad aficionados can pay their respects at the grave of engineer Theodore Judah in Greenfield's Federal Street Cemetery.

Construction of a 4.75-mile (7.6km) tunnel through the mountains lasted from 1851 to 1874 and was a great engineering achievement that allowed for the easy movement of rail traffic between New England and the growing Midwest. Greenfield was connected to eastern Massachusetts in 1850 when a branch of the Vermont & Massachusetts Railroad (V&M) was built from nearby Miller's Falls. Greenfield Energy Park contains sustainable energy exhibits, herb and native plants gardens, public art and a bandstand whose form echoes that of the old depot, including a cupola and spire. A restored B&M caboose functions as a museum and educational space for children.

BRATTLEBORO (↑30/30↓) Named after its original proprietor, William Brattle, the former mill town grew up around Fort Dummer, established by the British in 1724 as Vermont's first permanent settlement. The present Union Station (Brattleboro's first building to be listed on the National Register of Historic Places) opened in 1916 and around 18 trains a day stopped here. Amtrak's small waiting room occupies the ground floor of the former Union Station, the two other levels now being home to the **Brattleboro Museum & Art Center** at 10 Vernon (✆ *802 257 0124*; **w** *brattleboromuseum.org*).

Brattleboro was an industrial city by the beginning of the 19th century, with lumber and paper mills, printing shops, book binders and furniture makers. Grains, maple sugar and other agricultural products and finished goods were shipped down the Connecticut River by flat-bottom boat, or carried overland to cities such as Boston. The city has a large number of art galleries, performing arts groups and artists' studios. Among many festivals is the unique 'Strolling of the Heifers' in June, honouring the region's dairy heritage. A procession of heifers in garlands of flowers parades up Main Street to the Common for a day-long celebration that emphasises sustainable and healthy lifestyles. The **tourist bureau** is at 180 Main (✆ *802 254 4565*; **w** *brattleborochamber.org*).

BELLOWS FALLS (↑30/22↓) The first bridge across the Connecticut River was established here in 1785, and one of the country's first canals was built around the falls. A fish ladder allows Atlantic salmon to pass on their way upstream to spawn. The **Adams Old Stone Grist Mill Museum** (✆ *802 376 6789*) features 19th-century milling equipment, farm tools, machinery and sleighs.

Located at a bend in the river, separating Vermont from New Hampshire, Bellows Falls spreads along a series of terraces carved by the river's waters. A railway station has stood at this crossing of two major lines since the mid-19th century.

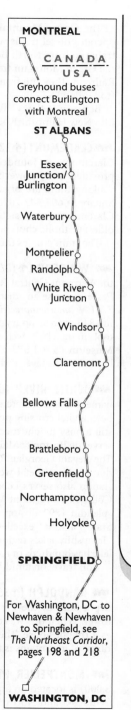

MONTREAL

CANADA
USA

Greyhound buses connect Burlington with Montreal

ST ALBANS

Essex Junction/ Burlington

Waterbury

Montpelier

Randolph

White River Junction

Windsor

Claremont

Bellows Falls

Brattleboro

Greenfield

Northampton

Holyoke

SPRINGFIELD

For Washington, DC to Newhaven & Newhaven to Springfield, see *The Northeast Corridor*, pages 198 and 218

WASHINGTON, DC

The Vermonter   Washington, DC–St Albans (for Montreal)

22

The **Green Mountain Railroad** (*54 Depot;* ☎ *1 800 707 3530;* w *rails-vt.com*) operates diesel trains with vintage coaches from Union Station to Chester. Other trains go from North Bennington to Manchester or White River to Norwich using the Green Mountain freight line and tracks which belonged to the former Rutland Railroad. They run from June to September (to Chester) and September to October (to Ludlow).

Between Bellows Falls and White River Junction you fleetingly cross the border into New Hampshire before returning to Vermont.

🚂 CLAREMONT (↑22/10↓) This is the *Vermonter's* only stop in New Hampshire. Claremont was founded in 1762 on the Sugar River, which drops 300ft (90m) and provided water power for the old cotton and woollen mills. Historic Mill District walking tours are organised by the Chamber of Commerce at 58 Opera House Square (☎ *603 542 7026;* w *claremontnh.com/city-center/Historic-District*). Among Claremont's other sights are a 19th-century opera house and New Hampshire's oldest Catholic church, St Mary's.

The train crosses the Connecticut River again into Vermont.

🚂 WINDSOR (↑10/20↓) The Romanesque Revival Windsor depot, built by the Vermont Central Railroad (VC) in 1901, has been converted into a restaurant. Passengers use an adjacent platform. **The American Precision Museum** (☎ *802 674 5781;* w *americanprecision.org*) is in a historic building at 196 Main, originally opened in 1846 as an armoury. It has the largest collection of historically significant machine tools in the US, as well as products made by them. The **Old Constitution House and Museum** (☎ *802 672 3773;* w *historicsites.vermont.gov/directory/old_constitution*) is located in the tavern where Vermont's first constitution was authored.

🚂 WHITE RIVER JUNCTION (↑20/35↓) Located on the south shore of its namesake river where it joins the Connecticut River, White River Junction has long been a vital crossing point for water, road and rail routes in eastern Vermont, and is still a busy freight train route. Union Station at Railroad Row was built in 1937 to serve the Boston & Maine Railroad, Central Vermont Railway and Rutland Railroad. The elegant Georgian Revival building has an octagonal cupola crowned by a copper dome with a metal weathervane shaped like a steam locomotive and tender. The station also serves Lebanon (another mill city) and Hanover (home of Dartmouth College). A Vermont Visitors' Center is located in the former freight house and a splendid 1892 Boston & Maine steam locomotive stands nearby. **Quechee Gorge State Park** has excellent river fishing and walking trails. Further east is the New Hampshire lakes region, including Lake Winnipesaukee. The 30-mile-long (48km) lake has hundreds of rocky, pine-clad islands and the water is clean enough to drink.

You travel on amid Vermont's hilly forests towards the Green Mountains.

🚂 RANDOLPH (↑35/30↓) Amtrak passengers use a platform across from a depot built by the Vermont Central in Queen Anne style, with a charming clock tower. When this was erected, the old station was moved across the tracks to serve as a freight house. The renovated station now houses a restaurant. The Worcester range of mountains is to your right.

🚂 MONTPELIER (↑30/12↓) Vermont's capital (resident population about 8,000) is located on a pass through the mountains along the wooded banks of the Winooski and North Branch rivers. First settled in 1789, Montpelier was named

after a much larger city in the south of France. The 18th-century Greek-style **State House** (✆ *802 828 0386;* w *vtstatehouse.org*) features a delicately beautiful gold dome as well as many historic exhibits. Among the items in **Vermont's Historical Society Museum** (*109 State;* ✆ *802 479 8500;* w *vermonthistory.org; admission charge*) are a hand-painted atlas dating from the Revolutionary War, a full-sized Abenaki wigwam, a recreation of the Catamount Tavern where Ethan Allen's Green Mountain Boys gathered, and a railroad station complete with working telegraph.

The station that serves Montpelier is located 2 miles (3km) to the west in the town of Berlin, with a taxicab service connection. The current depot, a red-painted wood-frame building opened by the Central Vermont Railway (VCR) in 1934, is the third to occupy the site. Montpelier Junction originally served as a wood stop, where trains loaded up on fuel to power steam locomotives. In the 1870s, the sought-after local granite, known for its superior weather resistance, fine grain and even texture, was shipped to cities across the United States and used in many grand buildings. At 'the granite centre of the world' you can take the Rock of Ages tour to learn about the quarrying and manufacturing processes, browse historical photos and exhibits, and shop for granite gifts (✆ *802 476 3119;* w *rockofages.com/tourism*).

The *Vermonter* continues among green hills, pine trees, rivers and streams, with the graceful orange- and purple-shaded Green Mountains visible ahead as the train climbs.

🚉 WATERBURY (↑12/27↓)
Amtrak's renovated red-brick station was built in 1875 by the Central Vermont Railway and also serves Stowe, a popular tourist destination during the autumn foliage season. The ornate Victorian building with its bell-shaped cupola is next to Rusty Parker Memorial Park – Waterbury's village green. Local ski resorts include Stowe, Sugarbush and Mad River Glen.

Bolton Valley (↑10/17↓)
Another ski area appears to your right as you leave the attractively scattered small town and continue into the 266,000-acre (107,000ha) **Green Mountains National Forest**. Also to your right is the state's highest mountain, Mount Mansfield (4,393ft/1,340m). A toll road from Stowe leads to the summit, from where you can see across Lake Champlain.

🚉 ESSEX JUNCTION (↑27/30↓)
Amtrak's utilitarian station at 29 Railroad Avenue is also the stop for Smugglers Notch ski resort. A white Vermont Federal Bank building features on your left and a graveyard to your right. It was the damming of the Winooski River in the late 18th century which led to the growth of Essex Junction. Six railroad lines converged on this small community by 1853, making it one of the most important rail junctions in the state.

Burlington, 7 miles (11km) west, is the smallest US city to be the largest in its state. During the 1850s, the Rutland & Burlington built an extensive rail yard on the Burlington waterfront with wharves and warehouses. By the mid-1860s, hundreds of ships were operating on Lake Champlain and the lumber industry boomed. Located on a hill above the lake, this resort and industrial centre is home to the University of Vermont and Trinity College. The city retains its old-fashioned downtown area, with beautiful Italianate, Queen Anne and Colonial Revival-style houses and has been voted 'best small town for the arts'; *Forbes* magazine selected it as one of the prettiest cities in America. In 1981 Burlington showed its maverick spirit by electing a socialist mayor.

The Burlington Jazz Festival takes place each June. Except in winter, ferries operate across the lake to Port Kent, New York, served by Amtrak's *Adirondack*. For information throughout the Lake Champlain Valley, contact the **visitors bureau** at 60 Main (✆ *802 863 3489;* w *vermont.org).*

Bed & breakfast accommodation can easily be found in this area but you should book early during the foliage season (peaking in mid-October). Contact the Howard Street Guest House, 153 Howard Street, Burlington (✆ *802 864 4668;* w *howardstreetguesthouse.com,* **$$$**); Willard Street Inn, 349 S Willard, Burlington (✆ *1 800 577 8712;* w *willardstreetinn.com,* **$$$**); Willey's Farm B&B, 5 Red Barn Road, Essex Junction (✆ *802 878 4666;* e *lynnwilley@aol.com,* **$$$**); Willow Pond Farm, 133 Cheese Factory Lane, Shelburne (✆ *802 985 8505,* w *willowpondvermont.com,* **$$**).

The **Shelburne Museum** (✆ *802 985 3346;* w *shelburnemuseum.org;* ☺ *May–Oct; admission charge),* 7 miles (11km) to the south on Route 7, features the 1890 Shelburne railway depot. The station was originally located in central Shelburne to serve passengers of the Central Vermont and Rutland railroads. Passenger service was discontinued in 1953, and the station was moved to its present site in 1959. Waiting rooms for men and women and the station master's office were restored, and telegraphy systems, railroad memorabilia and maps complete a picture of late 19th- and early 20th-century rail travel. A small annex beside the station exhibits hand tools and equipment used by railroad workers and includes handcarts, picks and shovels, and signal lanterns from railroad lines around the country.

Other highlights at the museum include a Central Vermont steam locomotive, an inspection car from the Woodstock Railroad and the *Grand Isle,* a luxurious railcar built by the Wagner Palace Car Company for the Vermont governor Edward C Smith. The *Grand Isle* features mahogany panels, an elegant dining room, staterooms and plush furnishings. The museum has a lighthouse, a 220ft (67m) Lake Champlain steamboat (the *Ticonderoga),* as well as 37 historic houses and exhibition buildings. The Impressionist paintings include works by Degas and Monet, and you can see one of the country's largest collections of Americana, including carriages, furniture, quilts, dolls and weathervanes.

As the *Vermonter* leaves among wooden houses and travels for 30 miles (48km) along part of the Champlain Valley, look for dairy farms, hayfields and logging operations. Warehouses and factories start to intrude on the approach to St Albans.

🚂 ST ALBANS (↑30) The rectangular station at 40 Federal, originally built in 1900 as a switch house by the Central Vermont Railway, is the *Vermonter's* final destination. The previous St Albans station, located opposite Amtrak's facility, is a splendid twin-towered building opened in 1866 and now on the National Register of Historic Places. St Albans developed as a railroad town and more than 200 trains a day were passing through at its peak.

During the Civil War St Albans was raided by a party of Confederates who entered the town from Canada, killed several citizens and robbed the banks of $200,000. They failed in their attempt to burn the place down before fleeing back north of the border. The **St Albans Historical Museum** at 9 Church (✆ *802 527 7933;* w *stamuseum.org)* describes the raid and has a collection of railway exhibits including a century-old waiting room and agent's office from a country depot, railroad lanterns, bells, maps and other paraphernalia.

The *Vermonter* terminates in St Albans but it is hoped that service will soon continue to Montreal, 56 miles (90km) further north. For Montreal city information, see page 278.

23

The *Lake Shore Limited*
Boston/New York–Chicago

GENERAL ROUTE INFORMATION

The *Lake Shore Limited* follows the water-level route once travelled by the luxurious *Twentieth Century Limited*, billed as 'a century ahead of its time' and 'the most famous train in the world'. This fine gentlemen's club inspired a hit 1932 Broadway musical that was successfully revived in the 1970s. The *Twentieth Century Limited* operated for 65 years from 1902 and a 260ft (79m) red carpet would be rolled out for each train departure.

Boston *Lake Shore Limited* trains go through central Massachusetts before crossing the Berkshire Hills to Albany, where they are joined by New York trains which have travelled up the Hudson River Valley. All coaches then accompany the Mohawk River and Erie Canal along a famous Native American highway. The *Lake Shore Limited* touches Lake Erie before hurrying across northern Indiana to Chicago. The *service* operates between New York and Yonkers on Amtrak, between Yonkers and Poughkeepsie on Metro-North Railroad (MNRR), between Boston, Poughkeepsie and Cleveland on CSX, and between Cleveland and Chicago on Norfolk Southern (NS).

ESSENTIAL INFORMATION

HIGHLIGHTS The *Lake Shore Limited* follows a famous Native American highway as it travels alongside the Erie Canal, Mohawk River and south shore of Lake Michigan. The train stops in Cleveland, with its renowned symphony orchestra and Rock and Roll Hall of Fame, as well as South Bend with its attractive River Walk.

FREQUENCY Daily. The **westbound** service leaves Boston late morning (or New York mid-afternoon) to reach Albany by early evening. You arrive in Cleveland during the night and Chicago by early morning. Travelling **east**, trains leave Chicago mid-evening to reach Cleveland early in the morning. You arrive in Albany mid-afternoon and Boston by late evening (or New York by early evening).

DURATION 19 hours 30 minutes (New York City); 22 hours 10 minutes (Boston)

RESERVATIONS All reserved

EQUIPMENT Amfleet coaches

SLEEPING Viewliner bedrooms

FOOD Tray meals, snacks, sandwiches, drinks. Complete meals on New York trains.

BAGGAGE Check-in service is available at most stations.

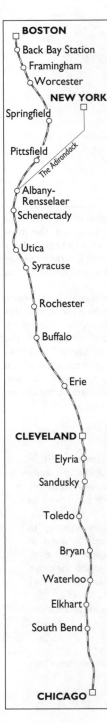

BOSTON
Back Bay Station
Framingham
Worcester
NEW YORK
Springfield
Pittsfield
The Adirondack
Albany-
Rensselaer
Schenectady
Utica
Syracuse
Rochester
Buffalo
Erie
CLEVELAND
Elyria
Sandusky
Toledo
Bryan
Waterloo
Elkhart
South Bend
CHICAGO

JOINING THE TRAIN

◢◣◥ NEW YORK For New York City information, see page 205. For the route from New York City to Albany, see pages 270–5.

BOSTON: ALL ABOARD! (5↓) For Boston city information, see page 200.

The *Lake Shore Limited* departs Boston's restored South Station to travel along the southern edge of the business district before pausing to pick up passengers at Back Bay Station.

◢◣◥ BACK BAY STATION (↑5/27↓) Back Bay Station opened in 1987 to replace a 1899 former New York, New Haven & Hartford station of the same name. This area was once covered by the Charles River and the railroad tracks had to be built on causeways.

As the train leaves Back Bay you glimpse the city skyline before heading into the wooded landscape of central Massachusetts. Fenway Park, the oldest ballpark in Major League Baseball and home of the Red Sox, is to your left.

Newton (↑20/7↓) You go through the suburb of Riverside then cross the Charles River.

Wellesley (↑22/5↓) Prestigious Wellesley College, formerly attended by actors Ali MacGraw and Elizabeth Shue, and by Hillary Rodham Clinton, is to your right.

◢◣◥ FRAMINGHAM (↑27/30↓) The town was named by Thomas Danbury, formerly of Framlingham in Suffolk, England (it is not known why the 'l' was dropped). A study conducted here in the 1940s was the first to link heart disease with smoking.

The *Lake Shore Limited* continues through the small towns of Ashland, Cordaville, Southville and Westborough, where industrial pioneer Eli Whitney Jr was born in 1765.

Lake Quinsigamund (↑25/5↓) The popular watersports area to your right is surrounded by attractive houses.

◢◣◥ WORCESTER (↑30/80↓) Past residents have included the humorist Robert Benchley and Isaiah Thomas, publisher of one of America's first newspapers, the *Massachusetts Spy*. Blue and white Holy Cross College can be seen on the hillside to your left. Old Sturbridge village is located 20 miles (32km) southwest.

Worcester's industrial development began in 1828, when the Blackstone Canal linked the town to Providence.

A railroad replaced the canal 20 years later. Worcester made America's first carpet loom, first liquid-fuel rocket and first calliope (a fairground music device using steam power to play a set of large whistles).

Amtrak operates out of the grand Union Station at Washington Square in downtown. This French-Renaissance-style structure with soaring 175ft-high (53m) twin white marble towers and a cream-coloured exterior was built for the B&A, and also used by the New York, New Haven & Hartford and the Boston & Maine railroads. This impressive 1911 landmark had been quietly decaying for decades before its magnificent towers and main hall were renovated at a cost of $32 million and reopened in 2000.

West Warren (↑45/35↓) A miniature golf course features to your left.

Quaboag River (↑50/30↓) The *Lake Shore Limited* accompanies the river on the right for several miles.

Chicopee River (↑60/20↓) Look right for a waterfall.

☞ SPRINGFIELD (↑80/75↓) Birthplace of Dr Seuss and home of the Springfield rifle and Garand semi-automatic, used by US troops during World War II, Springfield began in the 17th century as a trading post on the banks of the Quinnitukqut River (the longest in New England). When the Western Railroad opened a line between here and Worcester in 1839, the city became industrialised. Springfield is still an important gun-making town and its armoury has one of the world's best military collections. The Basketball Hall of Fame at 1000 Hall of Fame Av (☎ 877 446 6752; w *hoophall.com*) honours the game's inventor, James Naismith. The **visitors bureau** is at 1441 Main (☎ 413 787 1548; w *valleyvisitor.com*).

Amtrak's station sits on a railroad viaduct above street level, across the tracks from Springfield Union Station, which was opened in 1926. In 2017, the rehabilitated station reopened as a $94 million intermodal centre served by local and intercity buses. It will also become a stop for Amtrak trains and the new Springfield–New Haven commuter rail service.

Connecticut River (↑5/70↓) You cross with the stone-arched Memorial Bridge to your left alongside the Eastern States Exposition, which takes place in September. This is the largest agricultural event on the eastern seaboard, also known as 'New England's Great State Fair' or 'The Big E'. The Avenue of States features life-size replicas of all six original New England statehouses.

Westfield River (↑7/68↓) Look for sawmills and logging operations as the train follows the river through Oronoco, Russell, Huntington, Chester and Middlefield. You travel through some of the state's best scenery, including the Berkshire Mountains and **Chester-Blandford State Forest**, where you may see deer, bobcat, porcupine and wild turkey. Approaching Pittsfield you cross the Appalachian Trail.

☞ PITTSFIELD (↑75/65↓) Capital of Berkshire County, surrounded by mountains, forest and lakes, this is where in 1851 Herman Melville wrote *Moby-Dick*. His Arrowhead home is now a museum and the public library includes a room devoted to Melville. Pittsfield was also the home of American poet Henry Wadsworth Longfellow. The Berkshire **visitors bureau** is at 66 Allen (☎ 413 499 1600; w *berkshires.org*). **Hancock Shaker Village** on the slopes of Lebanon

Mountain is an open-air museum dedicated to one of the country's oldest religious sects (☏413 443 0188; w *hancockshakervillage.org*).

On 22 November, 2004, Senator Edward Kennedy and Congressman Olver opened the new glass and brick Intermodal Transportation Center and placed the last two bricks (saved from the original 1914 station) in one of the new station's columns. The **Berkshire Scenic Railway** (☏413 637 2210; w *berkshirescenicrailroad. org*) offers weekend rides along part of the Housatonic Valley. Its museum occupies the restored station at Housatonic and Willow Creek Road in nearby Lenox.

Richmond Pond (↑10/55↓) The lake appears to your left. During summer the Boston Symphony Orchestra plays concerts at Tanglewood, the former home of author Nathanael West.

Massachusetts–New York state line (↑20/45↓) The train enters the Empire State by way of the Taconic Mountains and State Line Tunnel. Look ahead for views of the Catskill Mountains and Hudson Valley.

Chatham (↑55/10↓) A beautifully restored wooden station building stands on your right at 153 Depot Road. This now houses the Chatham Railroad Museum, which has thousands of railroad artefacts, including original and operating Western Union telegraph equipment and vintage models made for the New York Central Railroad for use at the 1939 New York World's Fair (☏ 508 945 5780; w *chathamrailroadmuseum.com*). The 'beefalo' farm on your left cross-breeds cows with buffalo to create a healthier alternative to beef.

The *Lake Shore Limited* rumbles on through small communities such as Niverville, Post Road Crossing, Van Hoesen, Brookview and East Greenbush.

▄▄▀ ALBANY-RENSSELAER (↑65/24↓) For Albany-Rensselaer city information, see page 275.

▄▄▀ SCHENECTADY (↑24/75↓) For Schenectady city information, see page 275.

You cross the Mohawk River on a steel bridge then accompany the river to your left as far as Utica. The Mohawk Trail was the main colonial passage from the East to the Great Lakes. In 1669, Native American Mohawks fought the Mohicans at Kinquariones, situated on the rocky cliff overhanging the tracks.

Erie Canal (↑10/65↓) The train accompanies the canal to your left for much of its route between here and Rochester. Look for the first in a series of locks.

Amsterdam (↑25/50↓) Formerly home of Coleco, the company which created Cabbage Patch Dolls. Among the town's buildings are several associated with Sir William Johnson and family, who joined with the Iroquois against the French and their Native American allies during the French and Indian War. Sir William built the mansion to your left for his daughter. Fort Johnson, seen to your right, dates from 1749. Eight missionaries who were killed attempting to convert Native Americans to Christianity are commemorated by a shrine.

You travel on through an attractive valley of woods, hills and dairy farms.

Nelliston (↑35/40↓) The stone depot with green shutters to your left is now an Elks Lodge. A marker on the other side of the river indicates the site of a Revolutionary army base at Fort Plain.

Palatine Bridge (↑40/35↓) Webster Wagner lived here in the 1800s and is credited with inventing the railroad sleeping car, the elevated roof car and the drawing room coach and parlour car, making him a rich man and later a State Senator. The pretty Old Palatine Church (1770) stands next to Caroga Creek on your right.

Fonda (↑45/30↓) Montgomery County Courthouse is opposite the station, with the town's fairgrounds to your right.

St Johnsville (↑48/27↓) Famous for leather-tanning and dye factories, St Johnsville is the *Lake Shore Limited*'s halfway point along the Mohawk Valley.

Herkimer (↑60/15↓) Theodore Dreiser's 1925 novel *An American Tragedy* was inspired by events related to the 1908 trial and conviction of Chester Gillette in the Herkimer County Jail for the murder of Grace Brown at Big Moose Lake. The town also featured in Walter Edmond's 1936 frontier novel *Drums Along the Mohawk*.

Erie Canal (↑68/7↓) You cross the canal above a sequence of locks. Constructed between 1817 and 1825, the waterway spans New York State from Albany on the Hudson to Buffalo on Lake Erie. It was later enlarged and partly relocated to incorporate Lake Oneida. You approach Utica among factories and junk yards.

⊶ UTICA (↑75/45↓) Located on the Mohawk River and New York State Barge Canal, Utica was called Old Fort Schuyler until it was renamed after a place in northern Africa. Rapid development followed the arrival of the Erie Canal. A monumental, three-storey station is on your left and extensive rail yards stretch away to your right. Opened by the New York Central Railroad in 1914, this was the third station built on this site. The station's interior has an impressive waiting room with a barrel-vaulted ceiling and columns faced with Botticino marble. Amtrak passengers use this restored waiting room, crossing to the platforms via an enclosed aerial walkway.

The Adirondack Scenic Railroad operates regular excursions from Union Station to Thendara, and eventually Lake Placid (☏ *1 800 819 2291; www.adirondackrr.com*). The ASR has carried over 1.5 million passengers and is operated by 350 volunteers who serve as conductors, engineers and board members, as well as helping maintain this 119-mile (191km) former New York Central line.

The train pulls out and continues its journey west. Look right as you near the town of Rome for the Paul Revere brass factory, with its neon sign perched above. The horse and rider measures more than 18ft high and 42ft long (5.5m by 13m), with the company name stretching 155ft (47m). An on/off lighting cycle in the horse's legs created the image of motion, as though it were galloping. The rider is currently out of action but it is hoped that the sign will be relighted.

Rome (↑15/30↓) The Stars and Stripes first flew at the Battle of Oriskany in 1777, inspiring Francis Bellamy to compose the 'Pledge of Allegiance'. Fort Stanwix battle site is now part of downtown. The Erie Canal began in Rome on 4 July 1817, and you catch another glimpse of it off to your right as the train leaves for the northern highlands.

⊶ SYRACUSE (↑45/80↓) Look for long freight trains being set up on your right as the *Lake Shore Limited* enters the city among factories and warehouses. Amtrak uses the modern William F Walsh Regional Transportation Center near the shore of Lake Onondaga.

'Salt City' is where for many years the mines produced most of America's favourite seasoning. Extraction methods are demonstrated in the **Salt Museum** at 106 Lake Drive on the shore of Onondaga Lake (✆ *315 453 6715;* **w** *onondagacountyparks. com; admission free*). The **Erie Canal Museum** is located in the 1850 weigh lock building at 318 Erie Boulevard (✆ *315 471 0593;* **w** *eriecanalmuseum.org; admission by donation*).

LeMoyne College (↑4/76↓) Seen high up to your left, the Jesuit college was named after French missionary Simon Le Moyne.

Onondaga Lake (↑8/72↓) To your right is the place where Father Le Moyne discovered salt reserves.

New York State Fairgrounds (↑13/67↓) The nation's first state fair was held in Syracuse in 1841, and more than a million people now attend the annual event from late August until early September.

Erie Canal (↑32/48↓) You rediscover the canal on your right soon after Weedsport then cross into a more rural landscape. For the next 40 minutes the train travels among orchards, farmhouses and fields of rich, dark earth.

Clyde (↑38/42↓) The town's colonial cemetery is to your left.

East Palmyra (↑58/22↓) Look left for a picturesque church standing on the hill. Nearer to Rochester the dairy farms and greenery dwindle, to be replaced by more factories and freight yards.

Sibley Clock Tower (↑78/2↓) Named after Hiram Sibley, founder of Western Union, the flamboyant tower has Baroque- and Renaissance-style details.

⚞ ROCHESTER (↑80/55↓) Amtrak's busy stop is at the city's $44 million intermodal station opened in 2017. The classic red-brick design was inspired by Rochester's former 1914 New York Central Railroad station, demolished in the 1960s.

In 1837, the Rochester & Tonawanda Railroad was the area's first steam-powered line, connecting the Erie Canal with Batavia to the west then on to Attica and the Allegheny River. By the close of the century, Rochester had five major railroads, making it possible for manufacturers to ship their goods across the country.

The city's largest employer is Kodak (established in 1880) and a turreted, 19-storey Eastman Kodak building appears to your right. The Genesee brewery is on a bluff above the river to your left. Rochester was 'the flour capital of the world' in the early 18th century, when the town grew along the upper falls of the Genesee River, and later became the northern terminal of the Underground Railroad. It has a spectacular lilac festival each May.

The **New York Museum of Transportation** (*6393 E River Rd;* ✆ *585 533 1113;* **w** *nymtmuseum.org;* ⊕ *Sun; admission charge*) in nearby Rush includes a Philadelphia snow-sweeper and a Genesee & Wyoming caboose, along with buses, vintage cars and trolleys. The **Rochester & Genesee Valley Museum** (✆ *585 533 1431;* **w** *rgvrrm.org; admission charge*), in a restored Erie-Lackawanna Railroad station south of the city, has locomotives and cars from the New York Central, Baltimore & Ohio and Erie-Lackawanna railroads.

As the *Lake Shore Limited* crosses the Genesee River, look for a futuristic Times Square building dominating the downtown area to your left.

Erie Canal (↑5/50↓) After you cross the canal for the last time, a massive limestone mine sprawls to your right.

Bergen (↑20/35↓) The train passes Bergen on the right as the rolling landscape gives way to flatter countryside approaching the Great Lakes.

Lancaster (↑47/8↓) Fences surround Alden's Wende Correctional Facility state prison to your left and Lancaster's air park is to your right.

▟▙▜ BUFFALO (↑55/90↓) The city stands next to Lake Erie and is separated from Canada by the Niagara River. After the Civil War many railroads converged here to create important markets and a thriving railroad car industry. Rail businesses included the Gould Coupler Works whose plant was the site of a long and violent strike by unionised workers in 1914. Almost 1,000 workers went on strike and the company responded by hiring strikebreakers. When strikers blocked the tracks and ambushed the train that was bringing in replacement workers, a gunfight between the protestors and guards on the train left one man dead. Buffalo remains a major rail centre and industrial city.

The train pauses at Depew Station on Dick Road, 10 miles (16km) east of downtown Buffalo. A bison statue made of fibreglass stands on the lawn in front of the depot, recalling one that was once inside Buffalo Central Terminal. Made of papier-mâché and covered in a real bison hide, this original statue was put there in the 1930s by the Buffalo Museum of Science to advertise its collections. Look out for the Art Deco clock tower of the old Buffalo Central Terminal, opened in 1929 by the New York Central Railroad, which used to see 30,000 passengers and 200 trains per day. The Allentown area has Victorian buildings, shops and restaurants. For information, contact the **visitors bureau** at 403 Main (↘ *1 800 283 3256;* w *visitbuffaloniagara.com*).

Between here and Toledo, the train lives up to its name by skirting the southern shore of Lake Erie, sometimes visible to your right as you travel through a horizontal land of fields and low hedges.

New York–Pennsylvania state line (↑60/30↓) You briefly enter the Keystone State, founded by William Penn in 1682.

▟▙▜ ERIE (↑90/90↓) Pennsylvania's only port on the lake was named after Eriez Native Americans. During the War of 1812, Admiral Oliver Hazard Perry scored a vital victory over the British and his reconstructed flagship *Niagara*, now used as a sail training vessel, is often moored at the Maritime Museum. Dickson's Tavern, his base before the battle, became a station on the Underground Railroad and escaped slaves hid in its walls before continuing to Canada.

Amtrak passengers wait at the city's Art Deco-style Union Station, opened in 1927. The **Lake Shore Railway Museum** (↘ *814 725 1911;* ⊙ *May–Oct Wed–Sun;* w *lakeshorerailway.com; admission free*) is 15 miles (24km) away at 31 Wall in North East. It is housed in a New York Central passenger station built for the Lake Shore & Michigan Southern Railway. Its collection includes engines, sleepers, refrigerated freight wagons and a wooden business car.

Pennsylvania–Ohio state line (↑30/60↓) Ohio's name comes from an Iroquois word for 'beautiful'. The *Lake Shore Limited* travels through the fishing village of Conneaut before passing the towns of Ashtaboula and Mentor, from where James A Garfield conducted the first successful campaign for the presidency in 1876.

CLEVELAND (↑90/28↓) Founded in the 18th century by General Moses Cleaveland and misspelled by his men on the official document, Cleveland has been the home of President Garfield, millionaire John D Rockefeller and Superman, created by Jerry Siegel and Joe Shuster. Ohio's largest industrial city has lately acquired a less sooty image, helped by cultural institutions such as its world-famous symphony orchestra and the **Rock and Roll Hall of Fame** (see below). In 1967, Cleveland elected Carl Stokes as the first black mayor of any major US city.

Cleveland basics

Telephone code 216

Station (*Ticket office & waiting room* ⊕ *noon–19.30*) Amtrak's excellent Modernist Lakefront Station is at 200 Cleveland Memorial Shoreway, opposite the Cleveland Browns Stadium. Lockers, vending machines, handcarts, taxi stand.

Connections No Thruway buses

Local transport RTA buses operate downtown & to outlying areas (☎566 5100; w *riderta.com*)

Taxis Ace ☎361 4700; Americab ☎881 1111

Car rental Enterprise, 1802 Superior Av E; ☎348 0700

Greyhound 1465 Chester Av; ☎781 0520

Hopkins International Airport 10 miles (16km) southwest by RTA Red Line train from Tower City station

Tours Haunted Cleveland Ghost Tours; ☎903 4892; w *hauntedcleveland.net*; Trolley Tours; ☎771 4484; w *lollytrolley.com*; ⊕ May–Nov. The *Goodtime III* cruises Lake Erie & the Cuyahoga & Rocky rivers (☎861 5110; w *goodtimeiii.com*).

Visitors bureau 334 Euclid Av; ☎875 6680 or ☎1 800 321 1001 (hotel reservations & information hotline); w *thisiscleveland.com*; ⊕ Mon–Sat

Accommodation Hotels include the Renaissance Cleveland, 24 Public Sq; ☎696 5600; w *marriott.com*, **$$$$$**; Crowne Plaza, 777 St Clair Av; ☎771 7600; w *ihg.com*, **$$$**; DoubleTree, 1111 Lakeside Av; ☎241 5100; w *hilton.com*, **$$$**; Drury Plaza, 1380 E 6th; ☎888 324 1835; w *druryhotels.com*, **$$$**; Hampton Inn, 1460 E 9th; ☎855 605 0317; w *hamptoninn3.hilton.com*, **$$$**; Holiday Inn Express Downtown, 629 Euclid Av; ☎0871 423 4917; w *ihg.com*, **$$$**; Residence Inn by Marriott, 527 Prospect Av; ☎443 9043; w *marriott.com*, **$$$**.

For rooms in local homes, contact Cleveland Private Lodgings, 1978 Coltman Rd; ☎291 1209; w *privatelodgings.com*.

Cleveland Hostel, 2090 W 25th; ☎394 0616; w *theclevelandhostel.com*; **$**.

Recommended in Cleveland

Museum of Art 11150 East Bd; ☎421 7350; w *clevelandart.org*; ⊕ Tue–Sun; admission free. An outstanding collection of more than 40,000 works of art, ranging over 5,000 years from ancient Egypt to the present. Includes Picassos, French Impressionists & Rodin's *The Thinker*.

Tower City Center ☎771 0033; w *towercitycenter.com*. An ultra-modern extravaganza of shops, offices & mall located in & around the renovated Cleveland Union train terminal. Amtrak's *Lake Shore* train served Union Terminal briefly in 1971 before the *Lake Shore*

Limited began in 1975 & Amtrak built its new station on Lake Erie.

Rock & Roll Hall of Fame & Museum 1100 Rock & Roll Bd; ☎781 ROCK (7625); w *rockhall.com*; ⊕ daily; admission charge. From Muddy Waters & Little Richard to Bruce Springsteen & Neil Young, you can explore the world's largest collection of past, present & future rock music. The Beatles collection includes John Lennon's Sgt Pepper uniform, Paul McCartney's collarless jacket, the piano on which Lennon & McCartney composed iconic songs such as 'I Want to Hold Your Hand' & 'Eleanor Rigby', the Hofner Senator electric guitar purchased by John Lennon during the Beatles' time in Germany & handwritten lyric manuscripts. Recent inductees honoured include Joan Baez, Tupac Shakur, Pearl Jam, Lou Reed and Green Day.

Cleveland Botanical Garden 11030 E Bd; ✆721 1600; w cbgarden.org; ⊕ Tue–Sun; admission charge. Exotic indoor biomes & some of the finest public gardens in the Midwest, each with its own personality, including a medieval English garden & the largest herb garden in Ohio.

Museum of Natural History 1 Wade Oval; ✆231 4600; w cmnh.org; ⊕ daily; admission charge. Featuring rare prehistoric exhibits, exotic cultures, rare diamonds & a planetarium. The Perkins Wildlife Center has walkways that wind through a forest, giving great views of the animals. The museum preserves more than 9,000 acres (3,600ha) of natural areas throughout the state of Ohio, protecting rare or endangered species.

Great Lakes Science Center 601 Erieside Av; ✆694 2000; w greatscience.com; ⊕ daily; admission charge. More than 400 interactive exhibits make this one of the largest science museums in the country. Permanent exhibits include Virtual Sports, the Indoor Tornado, giant outdoor mazes & one of the largest video walls east of the Rockies. The Rocky Mountain Express takes you on a steam train journey through the Canadian Rockies, highlighting the building of a nearly impossible transcontinental railway.

Cleveland Metroparks Zoo 3900 Wildlife Way; ✆661 6500; w clevelandmetroparks.com/zoo; ⊕ daily; admission charge. 3,000 animals roam 168 wooded acres (68ha) & 2 indoor acres (1ha) of tropics. Including the Rainforest, Wolf Wilderness, Birds of the World & Northern Trek, where cool-weather-loving animals such as bears, deer, tigers & wolves live. The Boomerang Line has a train ride through the zoo's Australian Adventure.

CLEVELAND: ALL ABOARD! (↑90/28↓) The train leaves with the FirstEnergy Stadium on your right before you cross the Cuyahoga River.

Hopkins Airport (↑10/18↓) Cleveland's main airport is to your right. Founded in 1925, this was the first municipality-owned airport in the United States and the first to have an air traffic control tower, ground-to-air radio control and an airfield lighting system, all in 1930.

⊷ ELYRIA (↑28/32↓) This manufacturing city was named after Herman Ely, who founded it on the Black River in the 19th century. Oberlin College became the first in the US to enrol African-Americans (1835) and women (1833) on equal terms with white males. Amtrak uses a shelter put in place in 2014.

Amherst (↑10/22↓) The New York Central depot has been faithfully maintained and old railcars stand proudly to the left of the tracks. The depot was built in 1913 and includes a visitor centre.

Vermillion River (↑15/17↓) Look right for a sight of Lake Erie after you cross a river famous for its fishing fleet. You pass through the fishing towns of Vermillion (with its maritime museum) and Huron (where Thomas Edison was born).

Hudson (↑24/8↓) During the early to mid-19th century, this was a stop on the Underground Railroad used by African-American slaves escaping to Canada. The train crosses the Huron River.

⊷ SANDUSKY (↑32/45↓) Once another stop on the Underground Railroad, Sandusky's busy port today ships coal and local wine. The former post office now houses a museum devoted to merry-go-rounds, with a collection of beautiful carousel animals (w *merrygoroundmuseum.org*). Nearby is the Cedar Point

amusement park, America's fifth largest. The Lake Erie Islands can be reached by ferry from the waterfront.

The **Mad River & NKP Railroad Museum** (*233 York;* \ *419 483 2222;* w *madrivermuseum.org;* ⊕ *May–Oct daily; admission charge*) in Bellevue features a Chicago, Burlington & Quincy Dome car (the first in the country) as well as US Army troop sleepers, uniforms, timetables, lanterns, china, locks and historic buildings. Henry Flagler, builder of the Florida East Coast Railroad, once lived on the property where the museum is located. NKP is the mark for the Nickel Plate Road (New York, Chicago & St Louis Railroad Company) which ran through Bellevue from 1882 until 1964, when it merged with the Norfolk & Western.

You go through manufacturing districts then cross Sandusky Bay before veering east towards Toledo. To your right is the top of one of **Cedar Point's** 18 record-breaking rollercoasters, including the 120mph (193km/h) *Top Thrill Dragster* (\ *419 627 2350;* w *cedarpoint.com*) and the $25 million *Millennium Force* coaster, one of the tallest and fastest in the world. The *Steel Vengeance* is the world's first steel-on-wood hybrid rollercoaster to stand over 200ft (60m) tall.

Lake Erie (↑12/33↓) The lake is visible for the last time away to your right before you cross the Portage River at Port Clinton.

Davis-Bessie Nuclear Plant (↑20/25↓) The 493ft (150m) cooling tower can be seen beneath a plume of steam in the right distance before you continue among vineyards, apple orchards and peach trees.

Clay Center (↑27/18↓) The town is surrounded by a limestone quarry.

Maumee River (↑40/5↓) Scenery becomes ever more industrial as you cross the river, with Toledo's outline to your right. The train curves left among some of the world's largest grain elevators while freight trains gather on both sides.

₥ TOLEDO (↑45/50↓) Ohio and Michigan argued over this valuable harbour, where the Maumee River meets Lake Erie, until President Jackson settled the issue in Ohio's favour. The Toledo Museum of Art's crystal collection reflects the city's reputation as 'the glass capital of the world' and the Libbey glass factory is to your left. Thruway buses connect with Detroit, Dearborn, Ann Arbor and East Lansing from Amtrak's station at 415 Emerald Avenue. Opened in 1950, the striking Union Terminal, now called Martin Luther King Jr Plaza, is the busiest rail station in Ohio. The renovated steel and glass building is also served by intercity bus routes.

The train pulls out on a 68.5-mile (110km) straight of track known as the Air Line route, which doesn't have a single curve. In 1966, the New York Central chose the Air Line to test an experimental high-speed train, mounting a Budd RDC-3 diesel car with turbo-jet J-47 aircraft engines and a streamlined front cowling. This shot down the unmodified track at 183.85mph (295.87km/h), a record that still stands as the highest recorded speed on a North American railroad. Rail fans often come to have their photograph taken next to the marker that commemorates the event.

Holland (↑12/38↓) Neat farms start to replace industry again as the *Lake Shore Limited* continues.

₥ BRYAN (↑50/25↓) A distribution point for agricultural produce, the Fountain City is known for its artesian wells, the Spangler Candy Company (largest

producer of candy canes in the world), and the Ohio Art Company, inventor of Etch-A-Sketch. To your right is WBNO, the first solar-powered radio station in the world.

You cross the St Joseph River and Ohio–Indiana state line.

⚹ WATERLOO (↑25/45↓) This is the highest point on the route, situated 995ft (304m) above sea level and 400ft (120m) above the Great Lakes. In 2016, Amtrak opened Waterloo's upgraded intercity passenger rail station. Waterloo is the train's nearest stop to Fort Wayne.

Elkhart River (↑25/20↓) After crossing the river, the train follows a leisurely course through rolling countryside.

⚹ ELKHART (↑45/22↓) Elkhart has been the world's largest producer of brass musical instruments and mobile homes and is the former headquarters of Miles Laboratories, maker of Alka-Seltzer. Amish and Mennonite Christian communities nearby include Goshen, located 5 miles (8km) southeast. Amtrak's station was built in 1900 by the Lake Shore & Michigan Southern Railroad. Shiny New York Central trains wait beside a steam engine across the tracks to your left.

Elkhart became an important rail centre after the Michigan Southern & Northern Indiana Railway (MS&NI) arrived in 1851. It was a natural location for a rail maintenance complex that included locomotive works, repair shops, a carpenter shop, boiler shop, two roundhouses, freight houses and offices. Rail buffs now visit Elkhart for its rail history and to look at the operating 675-acre (273ha) Classification Yard, one of the largest in the world. This is a 'hump yard', where cars are pushed over a hump and gravity carries them down to the appropriate track.

The **National New York Central Railroad Museum** is located opposite Amtrak's depot at *721 S Main* (✆*574 294 3001;* w *nycrrmuseum.org; admission free)*. Visitors enter through a 1915 passenger coach and exhibits cover Elkhart's place within the regional and national rail system, from the LS&MS in 1833 to the New York Central. Videos show footage of the railroad at work and the rolling stock collection includes steam and diesel-electric locomotives, boxcars, a railroad post office and a 150-US ton (144-tonne) crane.

The *Lake Shore Limited* leaves among factories and warehouses, approaching South Bend past, on your left, the old Studebaker car factory, which closed in 1963.

⚹ SOUTH BEND (↑22/85↓) Situated on a bend of the St Joseph River, this is where settlers negotiated a treaty with Native Americans under the Council oak tree, which still stands in Highland Cemetery. Look right for the gold dome of Notre Dame University above the trees. The first railway train arrived here in 1851, headed by the steam locomotive *John Stryker*. By the 20th century, South Bend hosted eight railroads.

The state-of-the-art Studebaker National Museum at 201 Chapin (✆*574 235 9714;* w *studebakermuseum.org)* celebrates the South Bend area's rich industrial heritage with the display and conservation of Studebaker vehicles. It has the world's largest collection of US Presidential carriages, including the Barouche that Abraham Lincoln used on the night of his assassination and Benjamin Harrison's Studebaker Brougham.

As you travel on you pass from Eastern to Central Time, so watches go back an hour (forward when travelling east).

La Porte (↑20/65↓) Known as the 'Maple City' for its many maple trees, La Porte began in 1832 as a trading centre for farmers.

Gary (↑45/40↓) Long one of the nation's great steel producers, plants on both sides display a mass of complicated pipelines, pylons and storage tanks. With the decline in the steel industry, Gary lost half its population and many homes in the city were abandoned. Gary was the birthplace Michael Jackson and the rest of the Jackson family, astronaut Frank Borman, and noted economists Paul Samuelson and Joseph Stiglitz.

The train continues sedately through the communities of Pine Junction and Indiana Harbor (East Chicago).

Indiana Harbor Canal (↑50/35↓) You cross on a drawbridge. The canal joins the Calumet River to Lake Michigan, seen a short distance away to your right. Look left for more steel mills and a Unilever factory opened by Lever Brothers in 1930.

Hammond-Whiting (↑60/25↓) For Hammond-Whiting and the route to Chicago, see pages 268–9.

🚂 CHICAGO (↑85) Thruway buses connect with Madison, Wisconsin. For Chicago city information, see page 83.

The *Capitol Limited*
Washington, DC–Chicago

GENERAL ROUTE INFORMATION

The *Capitol Limited* takes you through West Virginia, Harpers Ferry and the beautiful Potomac and Shenandoah valleys. You travel among the Allegheny Mountains, visit a revitalised Pittsburgh and see the cornfields of Ohio and Indiana. Some of the splendid views experienced on this 780-mile (1,255km) journey are only available by train and for much of the way you follow the original Baltimore & Ohio line along which the very first *Capitol Limited* ran in the 1920s as an all-Pullman sleeping-car train. In 1938, this became America's first diesel-powered streamliner. Today's *Capitol Limited* travels between Chicago and Pittsburgh with Norfolk Southern (NS), and between Pittsburgh and Washington, DC with CSX Transportation.

JOINING THE TRAIN

WASHINGTON, DC: ALL ABOARD! (25↓) For Washington, DC, city information, see page 215. Thruway buses link with Dulles International Airport and Charlottesville, Virginia.

ESSENTIAL INFORMATION

HIGHLIGHTS This train follows the historic B&O line on a journey through the Potomac Valley, past historic Harpers Ferry and the Allegheny Mountains. In 'Renaissance City' Pittsburgh you can visit the Andy Warhol Museum, the world's largest devoted to a single artist. After crossing into Ohio you travel north to Cleveland and Indiana, the heart of the Midwest.

FREQUENCY Daily. The **westbound** train leaves Washington, DC late in the afternoon, arriving in Cumberland by early evening and Pittsburgh late in the evening. You reach Toledo by early next morning and Chicago by mid-morning. Travelling **east**, trains leave Chicago early evening to reach Toledo by midnight and Pittsburgh early in the morning. You arrive in Cumberland the next morning and Washington, DC by early afternoon.

DURATION 18 hours

RESERVATIONS All reserved

EQUIPMENT Superliner coaches

SLEEPING Superliner bedrooms

FOOD Complete meals, snacks, sandwiches, drinks

LOUNGE CAR Movies, hospitality hour

BAGGAGE Check-in service is available at most stations.

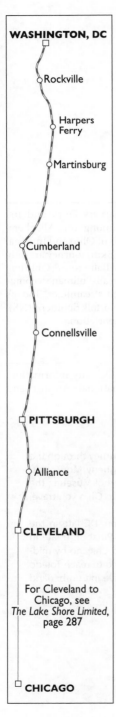

WASHINGTON, DC

Rockville

Harpers Ferry

Martinsburg

Cumberland

Connellsville

PITTSBURGH

Alliance

CLEVELAND

For Cleveland to Chicago, see *The Lake Shore Limited*, page 287

CHICAGO

As the *Capitol Limited* slowly departs Washington, DC, look left for the tiled blue and gold dome of the Greek-style Basilica of the Shrine of the Immaculate Conception (America's largest Catholic church). You travel north through the suburbs of Takoma Park and Silver Spring, then turn northwest and begin to follow Baltimore & Ohio tracks to Pittsburgh. Look left for the gold spires of a Mormon temple just before you cross the Beltway, often crammed with commuters' cars.

Forest Glen (↑12/13↓) The Metro Station here is the deepest train station in the entire DC metro system.

Kensington (↑19/6↓) As you cross Rock Creek Park, look left for the 1891 B&O Railroad station standing beside a row of antique shops.

Garrett Park (↑20/5↓) Named after John B Garrett, President of the Baltimore & Ohio, this was a summer retreat for railway executives. Note the attractive Victorian houses among the trees to your left. Look also for the small white church of St Mary's, where F Scott Fitzgerald is buried.

Approaching Rockville you see the town's original 1873 red-brick Baltimore & Ohio station to your left, along with the Rockville Courthouse. Like many others on this route, the station was designed by Ephraim Francis Baldwin. In 1981, the 400-US-ton (362-tonne) depot was moved 164ft (50m) south of its original location to make way for the current intermodal station. The building is on the National Register of Historic Places and now houses law offices.

⚒ ROCKVILLE (↑25/40↓) An 18th-century Maryland town which has become a Washington, DC suburb. Amtrak stops at a sheltered platform on elevated tracks at the modern concrete-and-tile station. Metro and MARC trains wait on the left.

After Rockville the *Capitol Limited* accompanies the Metro route for a few minutes to the line's final stop, Washington Grove.

Gaithersburg (↑5/35↓) The county fairgrounds and another E Francis Baldwin B&O Railroad Station and Freight Shed can be seen to your right before the train crosses Interstate 270.

After passing through Germantown you begin to shake off suburbia, travelling instead among the farms and gently rolling hills of the Atlantic coastal plain. Ahead are the fertile farms of the Potomac Valley.

Barnesville (↑10/30↓) The station to your left is where the Baltimore & Ohio began a new line in 1866. Look left to see a steam locomotive stranded in the sidings.

Dickerson (↑15/25↓) Sugarloaf Mountain is to your right. Tall chimneys appear in the distance as the *Capitol Limited* eases over to accompany the Potomac along the Maryland–Virginia border. Between the tracks and the river you can see traces of a neglected section of the Chesapeake & Ohio Canal. Trees grow in the cutting and along a towpath which was formerly used by people hauling barges by mule. The canal dates from the mid-19th century, when it carried huge amounts of freight between Cumberland and Georgetown.

Point of Rocks (↑23/17↓) Another picturesque Victorian Baldwin depot stands where the line from Washington, DC joins the original Baltimore & Ohio line from Baltimore. During the Civil War, the B&O Railroad and C&O Canal were targets for Confederate raiders across the Potomac River. In 1861, 'Stonewall' Jackson led a raid at Point of Rocks, shutting off the rail lines east of the town, capturing 56 locomotives and 300 railcars.

You travel 800ft (240m) through Point of Rocks Tunnel, the first of 13 between here and Pittsburgh. The train then loses touch with the river for 15 minutes as it goes through the historic Baltimore & Ohio town of Brunswick.

Appalachian Trail (↑37/3↓) The longest footpath in the world crosses the tracks. This popular hiking trail runs for 2,200 miles (3,500km) between Springer Mountain in Georgia and Mount Katahdin in Maine. Note the canal lock-keeper's white house to your left.

Just before Harpers Ferry you go through a tunnel beneath South Mountain and enter West Virginia's eastern panhandle. The train crosses the canal then the rocky Potomac River on a spectacular long bridge. A second bridge can be seen to your left and beyond it the remains of a third. The Shenandoah River is also to your left.

⟶ HARPERS FERRY (↑40/20↓) A trading post was built in 1733 where Virginia, West Virginia and Maryland meet, and the ferry, first operated by Robert Harper in 1749, was in business until a bridge was built across the Potomac River in 1824. The Baltimore & Ohio Railroad built a 900ft (274m) covered railroad bridge in 1836.

One of the most important events leading to the Civil War occurred here in 1859 when abolitionist John Brown and his supporters seized the government arsenal. Federal troops led by Robert E Lee came by train to force Brown's surrender – the first time a railroad in North America had been used for military purposes. The arsenal ruins can be seen to your left.

During the war itself, nine bridges were built and destroyed. Harpers Ferry today has museums, monuments and several buildings that date from before the Civil War. The **visitor centre** is at 171 Shoreline Drive (✆ *304 535 6029*; w *nps. gov/hafe*). Amtrak's station at Potomac Street, from where MARC commuter trains operate to Washington, DC, consists of a platform with shelter adjacent to a wood-frame B&O depot built in 1894. E Francis Baldwin designed 136 train stations and more than 500 other buildings during a 50-year career. His restored station here was moved from its original location overlooking the confluence of the Shenandoah and Potomac Rivers in 1931 and is now part of the Harpers Ferry National Historic Park.

On your right as you leave are the remains of an early hydro-electric plant fed by water from a dam. Wind-powered irrigation pumps appear to your left.

Nearing Martinsburg look right for the two 1860s roundhouses (one partly demolished) standing beside neglected railroad buildings. The stone mansion next to the tracks on your left once belonged to Revolutionary War general Adam Stephen.

MARTINSBURG (↑20/85↓) To your left can be seen Martinsburg's restored railroad hotel and a historic Baltimore & Ohio roundhouse. The 1847 brick station was the only building in town to survive the Civil War and is the oldest working train station in the country. The B&O built extensive shops and two roundhouses, which are accessible from the station via a pedestrian overpass that crosses the tracks.

In 1863, General Jackson stopped all trains going east at Martinsburg and Point of Rocks, destroying 17 bridges and 36½ miles (58km) of track. His forces also destroyed the Martinsburg roundhouses and rail yards and the town changed hands nearly 40 times during the Civil War. Confederate forces stole 14 Baltimore & Ohio locomotives from Martinsburg, and in 1877 the country's biggest-ever rail strike began here.

Hagerstown, 12 miles to the north, was founded by and named after a German immigrant, Jonathan Hager, and became known as Hub City when many railways converged in the 19th century. It still has two passenger stations, a roundhouse and the largest turntable in eastern America. The **Hagerstown Roundhouse Museum** at 296 S Burhans Boulevard (*301 739 4665; w roundhouse.org*) preserves and restores historic railway equipment, including steam and diesel locomotives, passenger cars, freight cars and other rolling stock. MARC trains travel to Hagerstown from Washington, DC.

The *Capitol Limited* pulls out of Martinsburg and continues past villages, farms, woods and orchards.

Cherry Run (↑10/75↓) Fort Frederick, seen across the Potomac to your right, dates from 1756 and was active during the Revolutionary, French and Indian, and Civil wars. You follow the river for over an hour, with fine views apart from the few tunnels.

Hancock (↑20/65↓) The small town stands on both sides of the river in three states – West Virginia, Maryland and Pennsylvania.

Great Capcon (↑30/55↓) You cross the Great Capcon River. Look right on the far side of the Potomac soon afterwards to see the remains of a Chesapeake & Ohio Canal aqueduct.

Orleans Road (↑35/50↓) The *Capitol Limited* quits the old Baltimore & Ohio main line at this point and enters the 1,592ft (485m) Graham Tunnel. The tunnel is in Maryland but you emerge back in West Virginia and cross Kessler's Bridge.

Mountains and a tree-lined ravine appear to your right as the Potomac River runs through spectacular, sparsely populated country. Much of this region can only be seen from a raft or by travelling Amtrak. Look for deer among the wooded cliffs which sometimes rise sheer from the river. You cross the Potomac three times before leaving West Virginia.

North Branch (↑80/5↓) The Chesapeake & Ohio Canal is visible for the last time before you pass under a highway bridge then under an old railroad bridge. On the approach to Cumberland, coal wagons and trailer trains gather to your left and the *Capitol Limited* leaves the Potomac Valley.

CUMBERLAND (↑85/130↓) Otherwise known as Washington Town, Cumberland has also been called the 'Queen City of the Alleghenies'. Early coal, canal and railway barons built mansions here and many attractive houses can be seen on the hillside to your right. Cumberland was the eastern terminus of the Cumberland (National) Road and the western terminus of the Chesapeake & Ohio Canal. The Baltimore & Ohio Railroad arrived in 1842 and built a maintenance and repair complex in the 1870s. The old B&O shops are still an important centre for locomotive repair work.

This is the northern end of the C&O Canal National Park. Where the canal ends, the Great Allegheny Passage picks up – a hiker–biker path connecting Cumberland with downtown Pittsburgh via abandoned rail rights of way. Part of the Western Maryland route is now operated by the Western Maryland Scenic Railroad at 13 Canal (✆*1 800 TRAIN50;* w *wmsr.com*) which makes a 10 mile (16km) excursion to nearby Frostburg using vintage locomotives and cars, travelling through the Cumberland Narrows and beautiful mountain scenery.

The French and Indian War was sparked in 1755, when General Braddock led his forces 220 miles (350km) from Fort Cumberland towards Fort Duquesne. A thousand men died in the battle. George Washington also made expeditions from the fort, of which his log cabin is all that remains. Look left for a miniature fir plantation as the train departs.

The Narrows (↑5/125↓) This passage through the Alleghenies provided a route for early traders and the military. The railway came later, followed by America's earliest federal highway (US 40, seen to your left).

Mount Savage (↑7/123↓) America's first steel rails were produced at this junction of the Baltimore & Ohio and Pennsylvania railroads.

Maryland–Pennsylvania state line (↑10/120↓) You cross the Mason–Dixon Line and enter the most central of the 13 original colonies.

The *Capitol Limited* climbs laboriously into the mountains, going through Hyndman Station and Falls Cut Tunnel, constructed in 1897.

Wills Creek (↑40/90↓) Look right for anglers fishing a stream named after Indian Will, the last of the Shawnees. A flood here in 1984 damaged several small towns and 18 miles (28km) of track.

The train continues to climb a 2% gradient, one of the steepest in these mountains, rising over 1,000ft (300m) in about 20 miles (32km). You go through the small communities of Mance and Manila by way of a series of curves.

Sand Patch Tunnel (↑47/83↓) Almost a mile (1.6km) from end to end, the tunnel is the longest and straightest on this route.

Sand Patch (↑49/81↓) This pinnacle of the Allegheny Mountains is the route's highest point (2,258ft/685m above sea level). The *Capitol Limited* passes beneath tracks of the former Western Maryland Railroad, now part of CSX Transportation and often busy with freight.

Meyersdale (↑52/78↓) Founded in the 18th century, Meyersdale is famous for maple sugar and hosts the Pennsylvania Maple Festival each March. The renovated Western Maryland station is home to the Meyersdale Area Historical Society and has exhibits relating to the region's history, railroad-themed artefacts and operating model train displays. Look left for Mount Davis (3,213ft/980m) before you continue through the towns of Salisbury Junction and Yoder.

Garrett (↑60/70↓) This is another town named after the Baltimore & Ohio boss, John Garrett. Helper locomotives were based here in the days of steam.

Atlantic (↑65/65↓) The remains of a millstone quarry are visible among the mountains on your right and two abandoned millstones lie in the Casselman River to your left.

As the train continues on a rightwards curve, look left for the boulder called Saddle Rock, shaped like a Western saddle.

Markleton (↑80/50↓) Situated on the banks of the Youghiogheny River, Markleton was a resort for Pittsburgh's elite at the beginning of the 20th century.

Confluence (↑83/47↓) The Casselman River is joined on the left by the Youghiogheny River and Laurel Hill Creek. A bicycle path runs to Connellsville along a former railroad bed beside the river.

Sugarloaf Mountain (↑90/40↓) The mountain's distinctive shape is off to your right as you continue beside the river. Look for canoeists, fishermen, deer and possibly beaver.

Ohiopyle (↑95/35↓) The Ohiopyle Falls are out of sight to your left. Adjacent Laurel Highlands Park is especially beautiful in autumn and has the state's highest mountain, Mount Davis (3,213ft/979m).

Kaufman's Run (↑110/20↓) Frank Lloyd Wright incorporated a small waterfall here inside the house he built and called Fallingwater. It was a weekend retreat for the Kaufman family, owners of a Pittsburgh department store.

Indian Creek (↑120/10↓) You cross the creek by an old stone bridge.

⋘ CONNELLSVILLE (↑130/90↓) Surrounded by coalfields producing the raw material for Connellsville Coke, this was an important railroad town. Rail yards, shops, a roundhouse and bridges across the Youghiogheny were built, as well as several passenger stations. The stylish Union Depot was restored when the Youghiogheny Opalescent Glass Company took over the building. A gallery in the old waiting room has many of the original features. Service trains paused during World War II so that hundreds of female volunteers could serve food to the troops.

Leaving town, the train passes beneath a railway bridge which crosses the river to your left. You depart the Appalachian Mountains at Layton and descend towards the Allegheny Plateau via the attractive suburbs of Versailles and Smithton.

The *Capitol Limited* encounters heavy industrial scenes as it approaches Pittsburgh. To your left is the site of the former Duquesne steel works, home to the largest blast furnace in the world, known as the 'Dorothy Six'. Bob Dylan dedicated his song 'Duquesne Whistle' to the furnace.

Braddock (↑80/10↓) Edward Braddock, a British Army general who died fighting the French in 1755, gave his name to this town. Scottish-born rail and steel tycoon Andrew Carnegie built the Edgar Thomson Steel Works here in 1873 – one of the first American steel mills to use the Bessemer process. The mill continues in operation (now owned by US Steel). Carnegie opened the first of his many US public libraries in Braddock in 1889.

You pass through another tunnel into Pittsburgh.

₩₩ PITTSBURGH (↑90/100↓) The birthplace of Gene Kelly, Gertrude Stein and Christina Aguilera is America's busiest inland port, where the Allegheny and Monongahela rivers meet to become the Ohio. In the 1750s, this strategic position led to the establishment of a fort named after the British prime minister William Pitt (the Elder). Pittsburgh sits on top of one of the largest coal seams in the world and 'Iron City' eventually became so industrial it was known as 'hell with the lid off'. The city had three main rail lines: the Pittsburgh & Connellsville, Baltimore & Ohio and Pittsburgh & Lake Erie railroads. The P&LE was known as the 'Little Giant' because, although small, it carried huge amounts of freight, such as coal, coke, iron ore, limestone and steel, as well as running a passenger service. The Edwardian P&LE station has been restored and now houses shops and restaurants. In 1877, many people died here after soldiers fired on striking railroad workers.

The steel mills have been tamed and the slag heaps eliminated at a cost of $3 billion. Pittsburgh is now a centre for high-tech industry, medical research and development, education, health care and tourism, with smart skyscrapers and clean air. Now that the smoke has cleared, even outsiders are impressed by Renaissance City.

Pittsburgh basics

❧Telephone code 412

₩₩ Station (*Ticket office & waiting room* ☉ *24hrs*) Amtrak's station is at 1100 Liberty Av. Lockers, payphones, vending machines, ATM banking.

Next door is the former Pennsylvania Railroad Station, or Union Station, designed by Daniel Burnham & opened in 1903. This monumental building was constructed from terracotta & brick, with a splendid rotunda & waiting room. It was restored in the mid-1980s, & the office tower was converted into apartments.

Connections Thruway buses serve Columbus, Trotwood-Dayton & Indianapolis. The New Castle Area Transit Authority operates w/day bus services between New Castle in Pennsylvania & Amtrak's station in Pittsburgh.

🚌 Local transport The Port Authority of Allegheny County operates inclines, the 'T' light rail system & bus services throughout the city. For details of routes, a free map & off-peak deals, ❧442 2000; w portauthority.org/paac.

🚕 Taxis People's Cab ❧681 3131; Yellow ❧321 8100

🚕 Car rental Enterprise, 120 Sixth St; ❧325 7042

🚍 Greyhound 55 11th & Liberty, near Amtrak's station; ❧392 6504

✈ Pittsburgh International Airport 15 miles (24km) west. Port Authority W Busway (28X Airport Flyer) serves the airport from downtown Pittsburgh every ½hr ❧442 2000).

Tours Lenzner; ❧761 7000. River cruises (*Apr–Oct*) with the Gateway Clipper Fleet at Station Sq Dock (❧355 7980). Cable railway inclines take you to an observation deck & restaurants on Mount Washington, from where you can see the Golden Triangle formed by the junction of 3 rivers. The Monongahela Incline (❧442 2000) is near Smithfield Bridge & the Duquesne Inclined Plane (❧381 1665; w duquesneincline.org) at Fort Pitt Bridge.

Pittsburgh History & Landmarks Foundation (❧471 5808; w phlf.org) offers a wide variety of tours & events, including walking tours of downtown & historic neighbourhoods. Possible tour themes include architectural landmarks of a particular time period or architect; parks, gardens, & sculpture; historic mansions or rowhouses; & notable engineering works.

▐ Visitors bureau 120 Fifth Av; ❧1 800 359 0758 or ❧281 7711; w visitpittsburgh.com; ☉ Mon–Fri

Accommodation Hotels include the Marriott Pittsburgh, 112 Washington Pl; ☏471 4000; **w** marriott.com, **$$$$$**; Omni William Penn, 530 William Penn Pl; ☏281 7100; **w** omnihotels.com, **$$$$$**; Sheraton, 300 W Station Sq Dr; ☏261 2000; **w** marriott.com, **$$$$$**; Wyndham Grand, 600 Commonwealth Pl; ☏391 4600; **w** wyndhamhotels.com/

wyndham-grand, **$$$$**; Distrikt, 453 Bd of the Allies; ☏855 717 9716; **w** curiocollection3. hilton.com, **$$$**; Parkway Holiday Inn Express & Suites, 875 Greentree Rd; ☏922 7070; **w** ihg. com/holidayinnexpress, **$$$**; Red Roof Inn, 6404 Stubenville Pike; ☏787 7870; **w** redroof. com, **$$**.

Recommended in Pittsburgh

Andy Warhol Museum 117 Sandusky; ☏237 8300; **w** warhol.org; ☉ Tue–Sun; admission charge. Warhol was born in Pittsburgh & this collection (the world's largest devoted to a single artist) includes many films & paintings. Try out some of Warhol's art techniques & star in your own short film.

University of Pittsburgh Bigelow Bd, Fifth Av & Forbes Av; ☏624 4141; **w** pitt.edu; ☉ daily; admission charge. The Cathedral of Learning Tower (☏*624 7717*) is a historic landmark & the 2nd-tallest education building in the world, with 27 'nationality rooms' designed to represent the culture of various ethnic groups that settled in Allegheny County (**w** *nationalityrooms.pitt.edu*) & a 36th-floor observation area. Tours are conducted year-round.

Point State Park Off Interstate 279, near Fort Pitt Bridge (☏*565 2850*). Featuring Fort Pitt Blockhouse, built in 1764 by Colonel Henry Bouquet & now the oldest building still standing west of the Appalachians.

Fort Pitt Museum ☏281 9285; **w** heinzhistorycenter.org/fort-pitt; ☉ daily; admission charge. The museum shows life inside the fort from the 1750s, including a fur trader's cabin, a casemate storage room for munitions, & a British soldiers' barracks.

Allegheny County Courthouse & Jail 171 Fifth Av & Grant; ☏350 5313; tours by arrangement. This wonderful neo-Romanesque building was

designed by Henry Hobson Richardson, with a dominating tower & a 'Bridge of Sighs', where convicts would cross the street from courthouse to prison.

Frick Art & Historical Center 7227 Reynolds, in Point Breeze; ☏371 0600; **w** thefrickpittsburgh. org; ☉ Tue–Sun; admission free. Includes the Frick Art Museum (mainly European works), the Car & Carriage Museum (historic automobiles from 1898 to 1940) & the Clayton Historical House featuring Henry Frick's art collection.

Phipps Conservatory One Schenley Park; ☏622 6914; **w** phipps.conservatory.org; ☉ daily; admission charge. This huge & splendid Victorian conservatory features tropical plants, cacti, orchids & bonsai.

National Aviary 700 Arch St; ☏323 7235; **w** aviary.org; ☉ daily; admission charge. Opened in 1952, the aviary contains more than 500 birds of 150 different species from around the world, including many rare & endangered species.

John Heinz Pittsburgh Regional History Center 1212 Smallman; ☏454 6000; **w** heinzhistorycenter.org; ☉ daily; admission charge. Housed in the former Chautauqua Lake Ice Company Building, this museum's Great Hall features a 1949 trolley, a Conestoga wagon & the huge Pittsburgh city fire bell that was cast after the Great Fire of 1845. Life-size reconstructions show a log home, an immigrant worker courtyard house & a suburban ranch home.

PITTSBURGH: ALL ABOARD! (↑90/100↓) The train travels on through the night via Ambridge, Beaver Falls and Salem.

Garfield (↑60/40↓) Named after President James Garfield, who was assassinated in 1881 in the old Washington, DC, station.

ALLIANCE (↑100/70↓) An industrial city on the Mahoning River, Alliance makes steel and electrical machinery and is the home of Mount Union College. This station is Amtrak's nearest stop to Canton, 7 miles southwest.

Ravenna (↑30/40↓) Founded in 1799, Ravenna has the Northeastern Ohio University College of Medicine.

Hudson (↑45/25↓) The town dates from 1826, and was an important stop on the stagecoach route between Pittsburgh and Cleveland.

CLEVELAND (↑70/110↓) For Cleveland city information and the rest of the route to Chicago, see pages 294–8. The *Capitol Limited* stops at Elyria, Sandusky, Toledo, Waterloo, Elkhart and South Bend.

CHICAGO (↑110) For Chicago city information, see page 83.

25

The *Pennsylvanian*
New York–Pittsburgh

GENERAL ROUTE INFORMATION

After travelling from New York through some of the country's most densely populated areas, the *Pennsylvanian* turns due west at Philadelphia into Pennsylvania Dutch country, home of the Amish people. You follow the Juniata River to the Allegheny Mountains then round spectacular Horseshoe Curve before reaching Pittsburgh.

The prestigious *Broadway Limited* used this route until the mid-1990s. In 1938, the Pennsylvania Railroad's 'leader of the fleet' was re-equipped as a streamliner that can be seen in action in the 1940 film, *Broadway Limited*.

JOINING THE TRAIN

⋙ NEW YORK For New York City, the route to Philadelphia and Philadelphia city information, see pages 205–12.

PHILADELPHIA: ALL ABOARD! (26↓) The *Pennsylvanian* leaves 30th Street Station between apartment buildings on the right and commuter trains to the left.

Overbrook (↑10/16↓) Look left for Victorian buildings beyond the restored wooden station, built in 1860 and currently used by SEPTA (Southeastern Pennsylvania Transportation Authority) trains.

ESSENTIAL INFORMATION

HIGHLIGHTS The *Pennsylvanian* travels between New York City and Pittsburgh, where the Allegheny, Monongahela and Ohio rivers converge. You see the beautiful Allegheny Mountains, the spectacular Horseshoe Curve near Altoona, and Pennsylvania Dutch country, home of the Amish people.

FREQUENCY Daily. The **westbound** service leaves New York late morning to reach Philadelphia around midday and Harrisburg by mid-afternoon. You arrive at Pittsburgh mid-evening. Travelling **east**, trains leave Pittsburgh early in the morning to arrive in Harrisburg by early afternoon. Philadelphia is reached mid-afternoon and New York late afternoon.

DURATION Nine hours 20 minutes

RESERVATIONS All reserved

EQUIPMENT Amfleet coaches

FOOD Sandwiches, snacks, drinks

BAGGAGE No check-in service is available.

Ardmore (↑12/14↓) One of several commuter stops occurring between Philadelphia and Paoli. Some stations have elaborately sculpted canopies.

PAOLI (↑26/40↓) The town is named after Pasquale Paoli, an 18th-century Corsican revolutionary. General Paoli's Tavern was a meeting point of the Sons of Liberty paying homage to the 'General of the Corsicans'. Just to the north is Valley Forge, site of the base camp where George Washington's fledgling continental army spent a cold and hungry winter (1777/78) during the Revolutionary War. You can visit Washington's headquarters and the memorial chapel.

The *Pennsylvanian* continues among residential areas and leafy hills which look especially attractive when dogwoods are in bloom during spring.

Coatesville (↑10/30↓) Industry sprawls to your left before the train enters fertile Pennsylvania Dutch country with its many wooden bell-towered churches. Dutch is a misnomer, since this area was largely settled by Germans whose nationality (*Deutsch*) was mispronounced by English colonists.

Many of those now known as Pennsylvania Dutch are members of the Amish Church. Amish people adhere to strict religious beliefs and run their tidy farms much as they have done for 300 years, using mules and ploughs. The 1985 movie *Witness* was set among these white farmhouses, where Amish men dress in black and the women wear plain frocks and traditional bonnets. The Amish have no electricity or television, although mobile phones are allowed and they can drive but not own cars.

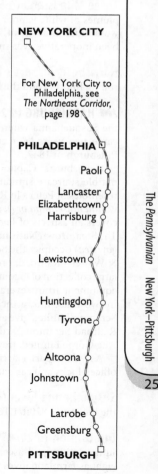

LANCASTER (↑40/18↓) America's oldest inland city was the nation's capital for a single day on 27 September 1777. It was founded in 1718 as Hickory Town before being renamed after a town in England, complete with red rose symbol. The Conestoga wagon and Pennsylvania rifle were made here, and the city was the terminating point of America's first long-distance paved road, the Philadelphia and Lancaster Turnpike. Milton Hershey began his career in chocolate and Frank W Woolworth opened his first store in Lancaster.

Lancaster is where the Amish come to market. You can find information on Amish life at the **Discover Lancaster Visitors Center** (*501 Greenfield Rd;* ☎ *717 299 0470;* w *padutchcountry.com*). Photographs are not allowed but you can visit several families, some of whom make a living selling woven baskets and cookies to 'the English'. Historic Lancaster walking tours depart from 38 Penn Square (☎*717 392 1776;* w *historiclancasterwalkingtour.org*).

The **Railroad Museum of Pennsylvania** (☎ *717 687 8628;* w *rrmuseumpa.org;* ☉ *daily; admission charge*) in nearby Strasburg has one of the world's finest collections of locomotives, passenger cars and freight wagons dating from 1825 up to the present day. The Railroad Weekend in May is one of many special events organised by the museum and the Strasburg Railroad

(✆ *866 725 9666;* **w** *strasburgrailroad.com*) runs daily steam train excursions from April to November.

You continue among factories and refineries, with a park to your left. Between here and Harrisburg, the train follows the path of the first telegraph wires. A short distance to the north is Hershey, founded by Milton Hershey in 1903 and dedicated to all things chocolate.

🚂 ELIZABETHTOWN (↑18/20↓) The town was named after the wife of Captain Barnabas Hughes who purchased the Black Bear Tavern in 1750. The railroad arrived in the 1830s but the town remained mostly agricultural until the early 1900s, when the Klein Chocolate Company opened a factory here and Elizabethtown also became a centre for shoe manufacturing. The granite-walled depot was opened in 1915 by the Pennsylvania Railroad, partly to serve residents of local Masonic homes. The building reflects the architecture of the town's Masonic Grand Lodge Hall, designed in Collegiate Gothic style.

Three Mile Island (↑5/15↓) Two of the power plant's four cooling towers puff plumes of white vapour away to your left. In 1979, this was the scene of America's worst nuclear accident, and the reactor which then suffered partial meltdown has been inoperative ever since.

Harrisburg Airport (↑8/12↓) The international airport is to your left, with rolling hills beyond the Susquehanna River.

🚂 HARRISBURG (↑20/65↓) Pennsylvania's capital stands on the east bank of the Susquehanna where the Pennsylvania Canal arrived in 1834. The first trains came two years later and the main Pennsylvania Railroad linked the city with Pittsburgh in 1847.

Harrisburg's Capitol features bronze doors, stained-glass windows and a marble staircase similar to one in the Paris Opera House. Its 272ft (83m) dome resembles St Peter's in Rome. The **State Museum of Pennsylvania** (✆ *717 787 4980;* **w** *statemuseumpa.org*), situated next to the State Capitol Building at 300 N Street, covers all aspects of Pennsylvania history and has outstanding Civil War exhibits. The **Steamtown National Historic Site** (*150 S Washington Av;* ✆ *570 340 5200;* **w** *nps. gov/stea*) occupies the Scranton railroad yard of the former Delaware, Lackawanna & Western Railroad, one of the earliest rail lines in northeastern Pennsylvania. A large collection of locomotives, freight cars, passenger cars and maintenance-of-way equipment from several historic railroads reveals early 20th-century railroading in two museums, a theatre and a restored roundhouse. Steam train rides on the Scranton Limited give an overview of the former Delaware, Lackawanna & Western Railroad Scranton Yards, including a view over the Lackawanna River. The 'Nay Aug Gorge Limited' travels out of the yards to the entrance of Nay Aug Tunnel.

As you depart Harrisburg, look left for the Capitol's green dome beyond the office blocks and car parks.

Susquehanna River (↑3/62↓) The *Pennsylvanian* crosses on Rockville Bridge, the longest (3,820ft/1,165m) and widest (52ft/16m) stone-arch bridge in the world.

Duncannon (↑20/45↓) For the next 100 miles (160km) you accompany the Juniata River and ascend the Alleghenies. The Susquehanna River fades to your right as farmland gives way to mountains.

LEWISTOWN (↑65/35↓) This manufacturing town has a historic depot on the right. The oldest-surviving structure built by the Pennsylvania Railroad, this station with its unusual tower was constructed in 1848–49 as a freight handling warehouse. It was renovated and converted into a passenger station in 1868. Today, the building has been restored for use as an archives centre and the society maintains a small waiting room for passengers riding Amtrak trains, making this the oldest continually operated train station in America. By the end of the 19th century, the Lewistown area had iron furnaces, tanneries, flour mills, carriage factories and other industrial enterprises. Fifty to 60 freight trains a day run on the former PRR main line, now owned by Norfolk Southern, and branch lines are operated by the Juniata Valley Railroad, a short line with 11 miles (17km) of track in Mifflin County.

In 1909, a lone gunman held up and robbed a westbound PRR express train a few miles south of the station. He shot the conductor and took $5,000 in gold bullion. Police found most of it the next day and the bandit escaped with only a bag of newly minted pennies. Fifty years later, hunters in the mountains stumbled on a stash of 1909 pennies.

As you move deeper into the Alleghenies, look right for Jack's Mountain and left for Blue Mountain.

HUNTINGDON (↑35/15↓) Located next to the Juniata River in an agricultural and fruit-growing region, Huntingdon was the junction of the Huntingdon & Broad Top Mountain Railroad with the PRR, and a port on the main line of the Pennsylvania Canal.

TYRONE (↑15/30↓) This flagstop station is located on the south bank of the Little Juniata River. At the end of the 19th century, Tyrone was the busiest stop on the PRR between Philadelphia and Pittsburgh, serving many industries and nearby Pennsylvania State University as well as visitors exploring the area's natural beauty. A plaque depicts the station as it was in the 1920s. During 2009, scenes for Tony Scott's film *Unstoppable* were filmed in and around Tyrone, with several hundred local residents employed as extras.

The train crosses Spruce Creek, which was fished by former president Jimmy Carter. After negotiating a short tunnel you continue among streams, hills, small towns and rivers. Wooded cliffs appear on both sides.

ALTOONA (↑30/60↓) Founded in 1849 by the Pennsylvania Railroad, Altoona was a supply base for railway construction over the mountains. At its peak in the 1920s, the Altoona Works employed 15,000 people and was almost 5 miles (8km) long with more than 100 buildings, making it the world's largest rail shop complex. The PRR built 7,873 locomotives here, the last one being in 1946, and the town still provides maintenance facilities.

You travel through extensive yards to reach Amtrak's station in the 1986 Altoona Transportation Center at 1231 11th Avenue. The **Railroaders Memorial Museum** (*1300 Ninth Av;* ☏ *814 946 0834;* w *railroadcity.com;* ⊕ *daily; admission charge*) on your left has many engines, coaches and models associated with the Pennsylvania Railroad. Exhibits include historic photographs, life-size dioramas of railroad workers performing typical tasks, and the *Loretto*, a private car that belonged to steel baron Charles Schwab.

Note the domed cathedral to your right as you continue through the middle of Altoona.

Horseshoe Curve (↑15/45↓) This 2,355ft (718m) landmark was carved out of the Logan Valley hillside in 1854, its central curve measuring 220°. Horseshoe Curve was crucial during the early days of westward expansion since it enabled trains to cope with a demandingly steep gradient. To build this engineering marvel, railroad workers had to fill two ravines and carve away part of a mountain. A National Park Service guide is sometimes on board the *Pennsylvanian* to explain the line's history. Look out for an old Pennsylvania Railroad engine to your left next to the modern **visitor centre**.

Gallitzin Summit (↑25/35↓) The train travels through a tunnel to the other side of the Alleghenies. Crossing these mountains was a much more laborious affair during the early 19th century, when the Allegheny Portage Railroad, a system of ten inclined planes and a 901ft (274m) tunnel carved through solid rock, carried train cars and canal boats 36 miles (38km) between the Juniata and Conemaugh rivers. Novelist Charles Dickens, opera singer Jenny Lind ('the Swedish Nightingale') and Civil War General, later President, Ulysses S Grant were among those who braved the Portage system, which injured passengers on a weekly basis. This unique engineering feat is explained at the **Allegheny Portage Museum** at 110 Federal Park Road (✆814 886 6150; w *nps.gov/alpo*) with a full-size model and parts of an original stationary steam engine. The Allegheny Portage Inclined Plane Railroad operated from 1834 to 1854, when the PRR completed its all-rail line from Philadelphia to Pittsburgh, and played a critical role in opening the interior of the United States to trade and settlement. The railroad's National Historic Site covers 1,249 acres (505ha) and includes a visitor centre, the historic Lemon House, Engine House #6 Exhibit Shelter, the Skew Arch Bridge, a picnic area and hiking trails. The Staple Bend Tunnel is located 4 miles (6km) east of Johnstown.

JOHNSTOWN (↑60/45↓) In 1889, a dam burst on the nearby Conemaugh River after heavy rain. John Hess, an engineer on board the Pennsylvania Railroad's *No 1124*, warned the town of impending disaster by sounding the whistle as his train raced down the valley. He and his fireman jumped to safety just before the train was overtaken by the flood. Many lives were saved because of his warning, but 2,200 people still died in the deluge. Before Prohibition, saloons would sometimes have signs reading 'Don't spit, remember the Johnstown flood'. Further floods in 1936 and 1977 killed 25 and 85 people respectively. Since the steel industry's decline, unlucky Johnstown has also been affected by high levels of unemployment.

You travel for 15 minutes through industrial scenes before forests and mountains return. A sinuously curving river follows below to your right.

LATROBE (↑45/5↓) This flag stop is a mostly residential town, used as a training base by the Pittsburgh Steelers football team. Latrobe has been home to professional golfer Arnold Palmer and the Latrobe Brewing Company, which was established in 1893 and is one of the largest breweries in the United States.

GREENSBURG (↑5/42↓) In 1763, Chief Pontiac and the Ottawa Native Americans were defeated by Henry Bouquet and the British at nearby Bushy Run. Fort Pitt was relieved four days later. Following an economic boom in the 19th century created by coal and Greensburg's importance as a retail and industrial centre, the Pennsylvania Railroad commissioned architect William Cookman to design a new Jacobean Revival-style station for the town. This, and rail tracks through Greensburg, were heavily used both for freight and passengers until the late 1940s.

You continue among green hills with occasional houses and factories, including that of the former Westinghouse Air Brake Company. The train slows down as it begins to approach Pittsburgh, seen ahead to your right.

⚙ PITTSBURGH (↑42) For Pittsburgh city information, see page 305.

FOLLOW BRADT

For the latest news, special offers and competitions, subscribe to the Bradt newsletter via the website **w** bradtguides.com and follow Bradt on:

🄵 BradtTravelGuides
🐦 @BradtGuides
📷 @bradtguides
🄿 bradtguides
▶ bradtguides

26

The *Maple Leaf*
New York–Toronto

GENERAL ROUTE INFORMATION

The *Maple Leaf* starts in New York and travels more than 500 miles (800km) before reaching Canada's equivalent city, Toronto. The route takes in the Hudson River Valley, the Mohawk Valley, Niagara Falls and Lake Ontario. Travelling north by day gives you maximum viewing opportunities.

JOINING THE TRAIN

NEW YORK For New York City and the route as far as Schenectady, see pages 270–5; for the route from Schenectady to Depew Station, Buffalo, see pages 290–3. The *Maple Leaf* operates between New York and Yonkers on Amtrak, between Yonkers and Poughkeepsie on Metro-North Railroad, between Poughkeepsie and Niagara Falls on CSX Transportation, and between Niagara Falls and Toronto on Canadian National.

BUFFALO-DEPEW: ALL ABOARD! (10↓) Leaving Depew Station, the *Maple Leaf* picks its way carefully through a mass of tracks. The clock tower of New York Central Station is to your right and a disused evangelical church home on your left. The city skyline appears ahead as you cross Highway 90 before continuing among industrial parks and residential areas. Near Exchange Street Station the eclectic buildings of downtown can be seen to your right.

BUFFALO-EXCHANGE STREET (↑10/30↓) Buffalo stands next to Lake Erie, separated from Canada by the Niagara River. Throughout the 1840s, small lines such as the Attica & Buffalo Railroad were built between Buffalo and Albany. Passengers had to take several trains to reach their final destination until ten separate lines were consolidated in 1853 as the New York Central Railroad. After the Civil War many railroads converged here and this remains an important rail centre where freight trains gather on both sides of Amtrak's Exchange Street Station. In 1952 this served 21 New York Central and Toronto, Hamilton & Buffalo Railway trains daily. The New York Central ceased passenger service ten years later and the station was closed until Amtrak reinstated services in 1978.

Look for older, more elegant buildings in the Victorian Allentown District beyond a derelict factory to your right. The **visitors bureau** is at 403 Main (✆ *1 800 283 3256;* w *visitbuffaloniagara.com*).

You leave Buffalo between houses and high-rise apartments, travelling through several tunnels to emerge with Lake Erie on your left. The lake soon begins to narrow as it forms the Niagara River.

HIGHLIGHTS This train travels between New York City and Toronto via the idyllic Hudson River Valley, New York's wine country and the striking gorges of the Finger Lakes region. The *Maple Leaf* stops on both sides of the US–Canadian border for the dramatic spectacle of Niagara Falls. In Toronto you can find great food at the St Lawrence Market and take a thrilling ride to the top of the CN Tower for dazzling views.

IMMIGRATION FORMALITIES US and Canadian citizens must have a passport, Trusted Traveler card or enhanced driver's licence – an ordinary driver's licence is not sufficient. Citizens of other countries must have a passport, and in many cases a visa. Visa-exempt foreign nationals need an Electronic Travel Authorization (eTA) to transit through Canada. Passengers aged 15 and under who do not have either a Trusted Traveler card or passport may present a copy of their birth certificate. Passengers aged under 18 and not travelling with both parents require a letter from any parent not present giving permission to cross the border.

For further information, contact the US (☏ *1 800 333 4636;* w *travel.state. gov*) or Canadian (☏ *1 800 622 6232;* w *canadainternational.gc.ca*) government agencies prior to travel. Information on crossing the border between the United States and Canada is also available from Amtrak agents.

See also *Red tape*, page 37, check with your US embassy or contact US Citizenship and Immigration Services in Washington, DC (see pages 39 and 379). Passengers without proper documentation are prohibited from entering the US or Canada and will be detrained before reaching the US–Canadian border. Neither Amtrak nor VIA Rail Canada accepts any liability if you are denied entry or removed from the train.

FREQUENCY Daily. The **northbound** service leaves New York City early in the morning to reach Albany by mid-morning, Buffalo mid-afternoon and Niagara Falls late afternoon. You arrive in Toronto by mid-evening. Travelling **south**, trains leave Toronto early in the morning to reach Niagara Falls (Ontario) by midday, Buffalo early afternoon and Albany early evening. You arrive in New York by mid-evening.

DURATION 12 hours 30 minutes

RESERVATIONS All reserved

EQUIPMENT Amfleet coaches. Business Class.

FOOD Snacks, sandwiches, drinks

BAGGAGE No check-in service is available.

Peace Bridge (↑8/22↓) The busy bridge to your left connects the United States with Fort Erie in Canada. Its official opening in 1927 was attended by 100,000 people, including the Prince of Wales (future Edward VIII), Canadian Prime Minister William Lyon Mackenzie King, British Prime Minister Stanley Baldwin and US Vice President Charles Dawes. An estimated 50 million people listened to the ceremony via public radio on the first ever international coast-to-coast broadcast.

Unity Island (↑13/17↓) The island is linked to the mainland by a drawbridge. In 2015, after being petitioned by members of the Seneca Nation of New York, the island's name was changed from Squaw Island to Unity Island.

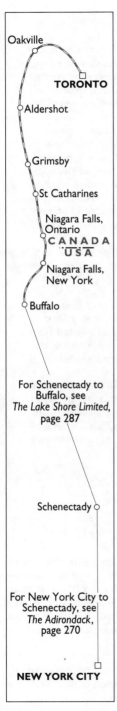

Oakville

TORONTO

Aldershot

Grimsby

St Catharines

Niagara Falls,
Ontario
C A N A D A
U S A
Niagara Falls,
New York

Buffalo

For Schenectady to
Buffalo, see
The Lake Shore Limited,
page 287

Schenectady

For New York City to
Schenectady, see
The Adirondack,
page 270

NEW YORK CITY

You lose touch with the river for a while as the train goes through Tonawanda and crosses the Erie Canal.

Niagara (↑20/10↓) The airport on your left lands thousands of honeymooners from around the world, as well as visitors to the casinos.

As the *Maple Leaf* approaches Niagara Falls, it curves right through ragged-looking yards. Unromantic pylons to your right indicate how much electricity the falls produce. Westinghouse built the world's first hydro-electric plant here in 1896, transmitting power to Buffalo. Nikola Tesla, inventor of the alternating current, has a statue at the top of the falls.

NIAGARA FALLS, NEW YORK (↑30/11↓) Two cataracts pour 600,000 gallons (2.7 million litres) of water a second into the Niagara River below, creating awesome sights and sounds. The American Falls reach 167ft (51m). The Canadian (Horseshoe) Falls are a few feet lower but have a longer, sweeping crest of 2,600ft (790m). The **visitors bureau** is at 10 Rainbow Boulevard (716 282 8992 or 877 325 5787; w *niagarafallsusa.com*). In the past, visitors have crossed the falls on a high wire or gone over the rim in a barrel. Such stunts are now illegal but you can enjoy safe thrills on a *Maid of the Mist* cruise or tour caves under the falls (rented rain gear provided). Not so exciting, although less damp, is the observation tower above the falls.

Amtrak uses the Niagara Falls Intermodal Transportation Center, opened in 2016 next to the Whirlpool Rapids Bridge that spans the Niagara River and links the United States with Canada. Originally chartered in 1846 to transport anthracite coal from Pennsylvania, the Lehigh Valley Railroad became a major carrier of both freight and passengers between Jersey City, New Jersey, and Buffalo, New York. By 1925, ten railroads used Niagara's Union Station, including the Erie, Grand Trunk, NYC and Michigan Central.

US–Canadian border (↑9/2↓) The train crosses the Niagara River on a high bridge with the falls away to your left.

NIAGARA FALLS, ONTARIO (↑11/20↓) Before you are allowed to leave or continue your journey, the train must pause for a customs check. A VIA Rail crew replaces Amtrak staff and even the napkins in the lounge car read 'VIA'.

Like its US counterpart, Canada's town of Niagara Falls makes it easy to see the main attraction. Most people prefer the view from this side, where the 520ft (158m) Skylon Tower offers a terrific vantage point and coloured lights create hypnotic effects on the water by night. The **information bureau** is at 6815 Stanley Avenue (🕻 *905 356 6061 or* 🕻 *1 800 563 2557;* **w** *niagarafallstourism.com*).

After leaving Niagara through Canadian National Rail yards, the *Maple Leaf* continues on towards Lake Ontario, travelling among small farms and vineyards.

Welland Canal (↑15/5↓)

You cross above one of the lock systems which enable ships to be lifted 326ft (almost 100m) between Lakes Erie and Ontario. Just before St Catharines you cross the Old Welland Canal, one of three which pre-dated the present one. The previous canals took much longer for ships to negotiate.

ST CATHARINES (↑20/15↓)

'Garden City' is surrounded by orchards, vineyards and wineries. From a viewing platform you can watch the ships of 30 countries pass through the locks and a museum at Lock 3 includes photographs and models explaining the Welland Canal's history. The pavilion-style station was built in 1917 by the Grand Trunk Railway and acquired by VIA Rail in 1986.

More vineyards appear as you travel through pretty, rolling countryside and cross Sixteen Mile Creek.

Jordan (↑4/11↓)

Lake Ontario is visible for the first time to your right. The train will stay in touch with the lake for most of the next 70 miles (112km) to Toronto.

GRIMSBY (↑15/30↓)

In the late 18th century, Grimsby had Canada's first town government. Founded by United Empire Loyalist settlers in 1783 and named after the English fishing town, it was originally called Township Number 6 or 'The Forty' because of its location at the mouth of Forty Mile Creek.

ALDERSHOT (↑30/12↓)

Connecting VIA Rail trains link Aldershot with London and Windsor, Ontario. Reservations can be obtained through Amtrak.

The train passes through suburban districts until industry returns on the approach to Oakville. You again cross Sixteen Mile Creek.

OAKVILLE (↑12/25↓)

Located at the mouth of the creek, Oakville grew as a harbour for exporting oak timber. It now manufactures cars, chemicals and machinery. Watch for the attractive Victorian houses before you leave past a Ford Motor factory and extensive rail yards to your left.

Port Credit (↑10/15↓)

You cross the Credit River then the Etobicoke and Humber rivers approaching Toronto. The skyline ahead to your right features the giant CN Tower.

Ontario Place (↑15/10↓)

An amphitheatre and Canada's largest 3D cinema appear to your right in a park built over part of Lake Ontario. The government is currently transforming the park from a seasonal facility into a year-round attraction.

Fort York Park (↑21/4↓)

The historic British garrison to your right is where Toronto was founded in 1793. This is Canada's largest collection of original War of 1812 buildings and 1813 battle site (**w** *fortyork.ca*).

TORONTO (↑25)

Ontario's capital claims to be the most liveable big city in North America. Explored by the French in 1615, it became a trading post and later a British colonial town called York. In 1813, during the so-called War of 1812, York was attacked and burned by an American force commanded by Zebulon Pike, a noted Western explorer. The town officially became Toronto in 1834, when it was named after an Iroquois word meaning 'place where trees stand in the water'. It remained a small town until the Grand Trunk Railway (GTR) arrived in 1858 and opened Toronto's first Union Station.

Once scorned as infinitely boring, Canada's largest city has transformed itself into an exciting place of three million people, and among its 70 ethnic groups is the largest Italian community outside Italy. Yonge Street, running north from Lake Ontario, is still known as 'the longest street in the world', although it is no longer listed by *Guinness World Records*. Toronto has acquired a reputation as the Hollywood of the north, with many television series filmed here as well as movies such as *Moonstruck*, *Sea of Love*, *The Fly*, *Chicago*, *American Psycho* and *X-Men*. Freezing temperatures are likely from November to March and midwinter can be very cold, although snow is actually less frequent than in many US cities.

Toronto basics

Telephone code 416

Station *(Ticket office ⏰ 06.00–22.00; waiting room ⏰ 05.30–00.45; reservations & information ☎ 1 888 872 7245)* Clean, efficient & softly lit, the beautiful Beaux-Arts Union Station Building at 65 Front reflects Toronto's character & was designated a National Historic Site of Canada in 1975. Built by the Toronto Terminals Railway (TTR), this superb building was opened by the Prince of Wales in 1927, though it was not fully completed until 1930. Opulent & classically designed, the structure has 40ft (12m) stone pillars weighing around 75 US tons (68 tonnes) each, decorative friezes, arched windows & high Italian tile ceilings above its 750ft-long (228m) hall. Union Station is the busiest public transportation centre of any kind in Canada, including air travel, handling 65 million passengers annually. These include GO train & bus commuters, 20 million subway travellers, & intercity rail passengers.

Lockers, newspapers, Red Caps, restaurants, shops, ATM banking, taxi stand, subway.

Connections Union Station is also used by subway trains & VIA Rail. GO commuter trains operate to Hamilton, Oshawa, Richmond Hill & Georgetown (☎ 869 3200; w gotransit.com).

Local transport City Transit (TTC) buses, streetcars & subway trains allow fast travel throughout the city, with day & monthly passes (☎ 393 4636; w ttc.ca). Toronto has the largest streetcar system in North America.

Taxis Metro ☎ 504 6489; Diamond ☎ 366 6868

Car rental Hertz, at Union Station; ☎ 1 800 263 0600

Greyhound 610 Bay; ☎ 594 1010. The terminal is also used by Coach Canada; ☎ 1 800 461 7661.

Pearson Airport 10 miles (16km) west of downtown by TTC bus, GO Transit or Greyhound. A new Union Pearson Express (UPX) rail service operates every 15mins between Union Station & the airport.

Tours Gray Line; ☎ 1 800 472 9546. Free 90min walking tours start at Union Station with Tour Guys (☎ 1 800 691 9320; w tourguys.ca/toronto). Toronto Harbour tours (Apr–Oct) leave from 145 Queen's Quay Terminal (☎ 203 6994; w harbourtourstoronto.ca).

Visitors bureau 207 Queen's Quay W; ☎ 203 2500; w seetorontonow.com; ⏰ 08.30–17.00 Mon–Fri

Accommodation Hotels include the Hyatt Regency, 370 King; ☎ 343 1234; w hyatt.com, **$$$$**; Bond Place Hotel, 65 Dundas; ☎ 362 6061, **$$$**; Ramada Plaza Downtown, 300 Jarvis; ☎ 1 800 870 3911; w wyndhamhotels.com/ramada, **$$$**; Victoria, 56 Yonge; ☎ 363 1666; w hotelvictoria-toronto.com, **$$$**; Westin Prince, 900 York Mills Rd; ☎ 444 2511; w marriott.com, **$$$**; Radisson Admiral, 249 Queen's Quay; ☎ 203 3333; w radisson.com, **$$**; Super 8 Downtown, 222 Spadina Av; ☎ 1 800 536 1211; w wyndhamhotels.com/super-8, **$$**.

For B&B contact Rose Garden Bed & Breakfast, 1030 Bathurst St, Toronto, ON M5R 3G7; ☎ 289 796 1146; w rosegardenbandb.ca, **$$$$**.

International Youth Hostel, 76 Church; ☎ 971 4440; w hostellingtoronto.com. Members & non-members, **$**. Leslieville Home Hostel, 185 Leslie; ☎ 461 7258. Dormitory beds & sgls, **$**.

Recommended in Toronto

CN Tower 301 Front W; 868 6937; w cntower.
ca; daily; admission charge. In 1995, the CN
Tower was classified as one of the 'Seven Wonders
of the Modern World' by the American Society of
Civil Engineers. Until 2009 it was the world's tallest
tower (1,815ft 5in/553.3m) and it features outside
elevators that rocket you to the Skypod two-thirds
of the way up. Even better views can be achieved
from the Space Deck, another 33 storeys above.
Given a clear day you can see as far as Niagara Falls.
Try to avoid w/end queues. Next to the Tower is
the Rogers Centre, formerly known as SkyDome
stadium, with its unique retractable roof & a hotel
overlooking the pitch.

Royal Ontario Museum 100 Queen's Park;
586 8000; w rom.on.ca; daily; admission
charge. The collection of 6 million objects includes
items from ancient Greece & Egypt, as well as giant
totem poles & a dinosaur gallery. The Gallery of
Canada explores Canadian heritage, from early
European settlement to the present day.

Eaton Centre On Yonge, from Queen to Dundas;
598 8560; w torontoeatoncentre.com; daily.
More than 300 stores & restaurants operate inside
this glittering building, with glass elevators & an
18-screen cinema. The Centre is North America's
busiest shopping mall & Toronto's top tourist
attraction, with almost 50 million visitors a year
(more than Central Park in New York).

New City Hall 100 Queen; 392 9111. Curved
towers enclose a circular council chamber
completed in 1965. Tours of the building are
available by arrangement. Next to City Hall is
Nathan Phillips Sq, a favourite meeting place for
relaxing by the lake (a skating rink in winter).

Art Gallery of Ontario 317 Dundas W; 979
6648; w ago.ca; Tue–Sun; admission charge.
The AGO has more than 79,000 works in its
collection, including masterpieces by Monet,
Cézanne, Van Gogh & Magritte.

First Post Office 260 Adelaide E; 865 1833;
w townofyork.com; daily; donation. Dating
from the 1830s & still in use. Costumed guides
return you to a world of quill pens & sealing wax.

Spadina Historic House & Gardens 285
Spadina Rd; 392 6910; daily; admission
charge. Guided tours. This elegant house has
one of Toronto's finest restored gardens. Built
by businessman James Austin in 1866, Spadina
reflects the Toronto art scene of the late 19th &
early 20th centuries & their Victorian, Edwardian &
Art Nouveau influences.

Casa Loma 1 Austin Terrace; 923 1171;
w casaloma.ca; daily; admission charge. This
Gothic-style castle is the former home of Canadian
financier Sir Henry Pellatt, born to British parents
in Kingston, Ontario. Casa Loma (Spanish for Hill
House) took 3 years & Can$3.5 million to build
& was the largest private residence in Canada
when completed in 1914. 'Toronto's Camelot' has
decorated suites, secret passages, an 800ft (243m)
tunnel, towers, stables & beautiful gardens. Self-
guided multi-media tours are available.

The *Wolverine*
Chicago–Pontiac

GENERAL ROUTE INFORMATION

On a fast trip between Chicago and two of America's largest industrial cities, the *Wolverine* train explores a section of middle America. En route are lakes, orchards and vineyards, together with manufacturing plants belonging to the likes of Kellogg and Ford. Recent infrastructure improvements have reduced travel times considerably between Chicago and Detroit.

JOINING THE TRAIN

CHICAGO: ALL ABOARD! (25 ↓) For Chicago city information, see page 83.

The *Wolverine* eases out of Union Station through a tunnel under the post office building. Trains are set up in Amtrak's 21st Street yards on your left.

Comiskey Park (↑10/15↓) To your left is a car park where the old White Sox baseball stadium used to be. A new Comiskey Park stadium (now renamed Guaranteed Rate Field) was completed in 1991 and stands alongside.

Bronzeville (↑15/10↓) The Harold Washington Cultural Center was named after Chicago's first black mayor, who was buried in the cemetery also seen to

---

ESSENTIAL INFORMATION

HIGHLIGHTS As the *Wolverine* travels from Chicago you can look out over Lake Michigan and head east to the 'Motor City' of Detroit. There you can learn how the automobile changed America at the Henry Ford Museum, relive vivacious Motown sounds at the Motown Museum, or catch an exciting Red Wings hockey game.

FREQUENCY Three trains daily. The **eastbound** service leaves Chicago early morning, early in the afternoon and early evening, reaching Pontiac mid-afternoon, mid-evening and early-morning. Travelling **west**, trains leave Pontiac early morning, mid-morning and late afternoon to reach Chicago late morning, mid-afternoon and late evening.

DURATION Six hours

RESERVATIONS All reserved

EQUIPMENT Amfleet coaches. Business Class.

FOOD Snacks, sandwiches, drinks

BAGGAGE No check-in service is available.

your left. The Center is on the site of the former Regal Theatre, where African-American icons such as Count Basie and Duke Ellington played. Bronzeville has also been home to great musicians such as Scott Joplin, Louis Armstrong, Jelly Roll Morton, Fats Waller and blues legend Willie Dixon.

Interstate 90 (the Indiana toll road) is on the right. You see the El railway track overhead before you cross the Dan Ryan expressway. Chicago's skyline back to your left features the 110-storey Willis Tower. The train crosses the south branch of the Chicago River and a defunct Rock Island line then crosses the Calumet River on a steel bridge. Look below for grain elevators and ships being loaded.

HAMMOND-WHITING (↑25/35↓) The modern yellow-brick station was formerly also a stop for Amtrak's *Capitol Limited* and *Lake Shore Limited* trains.

Several casinos, Lake Michigan and Whiting Park can be seen on your left as the train pulls out. Oil storage tanks proliferate on both sides of the track before you travel east through the towns of Indiana Harbor and Pine Junction.

Indiana Harbor Canal (↑10/25↓) The train crosses the canal on a drawbridge. The canal links the Calumet River with Lake Michigan, a short distance away to your left.

Gary (↑15/20↓) Long one of the nation's great steel producers, Gary has plants on both sides forming a mass of complicated pipelines, pylons and storage tanks. City Hall and the Lake County courthouse are on the right. Gary was the birthplace of Michael Jackson and astronaut Frank Borman.

MICHIGAN CITY (↑35/10↓) Look left for a colourful marina on Lake Michigan, seen just before the train crosses the Indiana–Michigan state line and moves inland through country famous for producing wine and fruit. You pass from Central to Eastern Time, so watches go forward an hour (back when travelling west).

NEW BUFFALO (↑10/20↓) The Michigan Central Railroad terminated in New Buffalo in 1849 and the Chicago & Michigan Lake Shore Railroad built through in 1869. The Chicago & West Michigan Railway arrived in 1882. Amtrak's station opened downtown in 2009, one block from the Lake Michigan shore and harbour. The New Buffalo Railroad Museum at 530 S Whittaker is located across the highway from where Amtrak trains stopped from 1984 to 2009 (☎ 269 469 8010; w new-buffalo-railroad-museum.org).

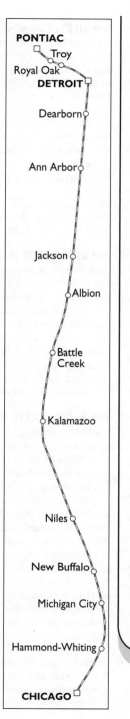

The Wolverine Chicago–Pontiac

27

NILES (↑20/40↓) Probably named after Baltimore journalist Hezekiah Niles, the town has its own small-scale Leaning Tower of Pisa, as seen in the film *Wayne's World*. Note to your left the beguiling Romanesque-style Michigan Central Station and clock tower, which has been a location in films such as *Continental Divide, Midnight Run, Only the Lonely, 8 Mile, Transformers* and *Batman v Superman: Dawn of Justice*. Designed by architects Spier and Rohns, this eccentric brownstone structure was built to impress travellers on their way to Chicago's 1893 World's Columbian Exposition. As well as the 68ft-tall (20m) clock tower, the building has stained-glass windows, elaborate wood panels and a steep, pyramid-shaped roof. The clock faces are each 5ft (1.5m) in diameter.

As the *Wolverine* travels on through grape country, look also for cherry trees, strawberries, plums and cider-apple orchards.

Dowagiac (↑12/28↓) The beautifully restored station was built by the Michigan Central in 1903. This is a scheduled stop for Amtrak's *Blue Water* and one *Wolverine* train daily in each direction.

KALAMAZOO (↑40/30↓) The name is a Potawatomi word for 'place where the water boils', because the river has bubbling springs. Pretty 19th-century houses can be seen to your right. The red-brick and sandstone Romanesque-style station, designed by Cyrus Eidlitz for the Michigan Central, opened in 1887 and originally consisted of three buildings connected by covered walkways. There were separate men's and women's waiting rooms as well as a *porte cochère* (covered carriageway) on the street side of the main building. The city of Kalamazoo bought the depot from Penn Central in the 1970s, and adapted it to serve as a bus/train station. Thruway buses connect with Amtrak's station in Grand Rapids and many other Michigan towns as far north as St Ignace and Sault Ste Marie.

You cross the Kalamazoo River as the *Wolverine* leaves town.

BATTLE CREEK (↑30/25↓) The Kellogg brothers invented flaked cereal in the 1890s and made Battle Creek's fortune. 'The cereal capital of the world' is home to the Kellogg Company, Post Cereals and a Ralston Purina plant, all of which can sometimes be smelt as well as seen. A three-day festival in June features 'the world's longest breakfast table'. The **tourist bureau** is at 34 W Jackson (↘ *1 800 397 2240; w battlecreekvisitors.org*).

Amtrak operates from an intermodal facility opened in 1982 and completely modernised in 2012. This replaced two old stations built by the Michigan Central and Grand Trunk railroads, both now listed on the National Register of Historic Places. Thruway buses connect with East Lansing and Flint. The Michigan Central Depot, now home to a restaurant, opened in 1888 and is another Romanesque-style station constructed between Detroit and Chicago in the late 19th century. The massive Grand Trunk Station, built in 1906, was one of the most elaborate and finely finished depots in the country. Seen on the north side of the track as the *Wolverine* leaves, this was in use as a passenger station until 1971, when Amtrak took over services on the Grand Trunk. Parts of the restored building are open to the public.

Among preserved buildings at the rail town of Coldwater, 40 miles (64km) southeast, are an 1883 depot, freight terminal and railroad granary. The **Little River Railroad**'s 1911 Pacific-type locomotive *No 110* at 29 W Park Avenue makes steam train excursions from Coldwater to Quincy, Michigan (↘ *517 227 5488; w littleriverrailroad.com*).

You depart 'Cereal City' with the Post and Kellogg plants to your right and left then join the Kalamazoo River to your right, following its meandering path through a waterlogged terrain.

ALBION (↑25/22↓) Albion College campus is to your right. The charming Italianate station house was built in 1882 by the Michigan Central, which first reached Albion on Independence Day in 1844. The ornate building was abandoned in 1971 before being restored to its original condition in the 1980s to serve as a bus and train station. A historic freight house is located on the opposite side of the tracks.

The *Wolverine* pulls out and continues among peaceful farming scenes beside the Kalamazoo River.

Jackson Airport (↑18/4↓) Runways of Jackson County Airport, also known as Reynolds Field, appear to your left.

JACKSON (↑22/35↓) Look left to see the solid Italianate Michigan Central station, dating from 1872 and one of the oldest continually operating stations in the USA.

A stone tablet in Jackson marks the spot where in 1854 a meeting of Free Soilers, Democrats and Whigs founded the Republican Party. Jackson was the birthplace of the famous Coney Island hot dog topping (created in 1914 in a restaurant in front of the rail station) and the Bortree Corset Company, maker of crinoline skirts, bustles and the Duplex Corset. The 500ft (150m) Cascade Falls, America's largest manmade falls, were constructed here in 1932.

The train pulls out among freight yards and travels east through the communities of Michigan Center and Leoni, which has many lakes and hosts an annual Carp Carnival each June.

Grass Lake (↑10/25↓) Fire destroyed the station building to your right. You continue through Chelsea then cross the Huron River for the first of many times as it winds between here and Ypsilanti.

ANN ARBOR (↑35/33↓) In 1824, two settlers named the town after a grape arbour and their wives, Ann Rumsey and Ann Allen. The **visitors bureau** is at 315 W Huron (☎*734 995 7281;* **w** *visitannarbor.org*). The Detroit & St Joseph Railway (later the Michigan Central) arrived in 1839, linking the town to Detroit. A former Michigan Central depot built in 1887 stands close to Amtrak's station.

The University of Michigan, one of the country's oldest and largest, moved here from Detroit in 1841. Located mostly downtown, it has America's biggest college football stadium and witnessed the first anti-Vietnam War teach-in in 1965. Note the fine 19th-century Central Michigan building to your right as you leave and cross the Huron River.

Ypsilanti (↑10/23↓) Named after a Greek War of Independence hero, Ypsilanti is the home of Eastern Michigan University. **Depot Town** is a historic district preserving old railroad buildings that were created after the train station opened in 1838 and the railroad connected Ypsilanti with Detroit. The Ypsilanti Automotive Heritage Museum is housed in a former Hudson Motor Car Company dealership at 100 East Cross (☎*734 482 5200;* **w** *ypsiautoheritage.org*). Its collection includes the original Fabulous Hudson Hornet, a 1933 Terraplane

Coach and a Chevrolet Caprice police car manufactured at the nearby Willow Run assembly plant.

Look right just before crossing the Rouge River near Dearborn to see **Henry Ford's Museum** and **Greenfield Village** (↘313 982 6001; w *thehenryford.org*). A million visitors a year come to look at historic cars, a letter from Clyde Barrow and the chair in which Abraham Lincoln was assassinated in 1865. Among nearly 100 buildings are the Wright brothers' workshop, Edison's laboratory and the courthouse where Lincoln practised law – all brought from their original sites and reconstructed. Also on show are a locomotive built by Ford in 1876 and an 1893 replica of the *DeWitt Clinton*. Steam and diesel trains operate from April to October on the Weiser Railroad, with stations that include a relocated Smiths Creek Depot originally built for the Grand Trunk Railway in 1858. There is also a modern replica of a Detroit, Toledo & Milwaukee Railroad roundhouse built in 1884.

DEARBORN (↑33/25↓) Originally a stop for stagecoaches travelling on the Sauk Trail, the village of Dearborn was established in 1836 and named after patriot Henry Dearborn. Amtrak's plain modern station is at 16121 Michigan Avenue.

Henry Ford's 56-room **Fair Lane mansion** is at 1 Fair Lane Drive (↘313 668 3200; w *henryfordfairlane.org*; ⊕ *daily; admission charge*) on 1,300 acres (526ha) of farmland next to the Rouge River. He died there by candlelight after floods cut off the power to the house. Ford's private railcar, also named 'Fair Lane', was kept on standby at the Ford Company's siding of the Michigan Central Railroad in Dearborn. Ownership of the estate was transferred to the University of Michigan-Dearborn and following restoration work it was reopened in phases to celebrate milestones in Ford family history: Henry Ford's 150th birthday in 2013, the estate's 100th anniversary in 2015, and Clara Ford's 150th birthday in 2017.

Soon after Dearborn you see a Ford Company factory to your right and from here to Detroit the *Wolverine* travels through a landscape mostly dedicated to the automobile. As well as factories, look for the many loading docks and rail yards.

DETROIT (↑25/20↓) The Midwest's oldest city grew rapidly in the 19th and early 20th centuries, becoming the world centre of an auto industry dominated by Ford, General Motors, Packard and Chrysler. It was the home of crime writer Elmore Leonard and the birthplace of Joe Louis, Motown music, Alice Cooper, Iggy Pop and Detroit Techno, as well as innumerable cars. Founded by the French in 1701 as Fort Pontchartrain d'Etroit ('of the strait'), Detroit stands between Lakes Erie and Huron. Fought over by French, British and US forces until 1813, it became a staging post on the Underground Railroad for slaves escaping to Canada.

The decline in local industries and the effect of the 1960s race riots drastically reduced the population, but great efforts have been made to repair the city's image. Julien Temple's 2010 documentary, *Requiem for Detroit*, showed that this is a place to create new ideas about urban futures. Detroit's farming movement is growing and there are ambitious plans for the future, with a fundamental rethinking of what a post-industrial city might become. Among nearby scenic railway routes are the **Southern Michigan** (*320 S Division, Clinton;* ↘*517 456 7677;* w *southernmichiganrailroad.com*) and the **Coopersville & Marne** (*311 Danforth, Coopersville;* ↘*616 997 7000;* w *coopersvilleandmarne.org*).

Detroit basics
↘**Telephone code** 313
Station (*Ticket office* ⊕ *06.00–22.00*

daily; waiting room ⊕ *05.30–00.30*). Amtrak's single-storey station is at 11 W Baltimore Av.

Lockers, newspapers, handcarts, taxi stand. It was completed in the 1990s as a replacement for the grand Michigan Central Station, a spectacular 500,000ft^2 (46,000m^2) 1913 building that was abandoned & under threat of demolition. Now a shell of its former self, the station that looms over Detroit's oldest neighborhood was built by the firm responsible for New York's Grand Central Terminal. In its day, the 21-storey building stood proudly with marble floors under an arched 65ft (20m) ceiling. It was the tallest train station in the world when its huge bronze doors first opened to the public. Since closing in the 1980s, this monumental, iconic building has lain empty, losing almost everything inside to looters & nature. In 2018, the Ford Motor Company bought Michigan Central Station, long a symbol of the city's decay, & it could now become the symbol of Detroit's revival as the anchor of Ford's 1.2-million ft^2 (111,483m^2) campus. As well as housing company employees, the building will become a mixed-use facility for up to 5,000 office workers, with space for shops, restaurants & residential housing.

Connections Thruway buses go to Toledo & Port Huron

Local transport The 'people mover' monorail (📞 224 2160) stops at many hotels & attractions. DDOT buses (📞 933 1300) operate downtown. SMART buses (📞 866 962 5515) serve outlying regions.

🚕 **Taxis** Metro 📞 734 216 2510; Mojo 📞 947 517 2702

🚕 **Car rental** Thrifty, 334 Lucas Dr; 📞 877 283 0898

🚌 **Greyhound** 1001 Howard; 📞 961 8011

✈ **Detroit Metropolitan Airport** 2 miles (3.2km) west by SMART bus or AirRide (📞 734 996 0400).

Tours Detroit Tour Connection, 615 Griswold (📞 283 4332; w detroittourconnections.com). Diamond Jack's River Tours, Hart Plaza (📞 843 9376; w diamondjack.com).

🛈 **Visitors bureau** 211 W Fort; 📞 202 1800; w visitdetroit.com; ⏰ Mon–Fri

🏨 **Accommodation** Special rates are available for downtown hotels at w/ends. Hotels include the Courtyard by Marriott at 333 E Jefferson Av; 📞 222 7700; w marriott.com, $$$$; Crowne Plaza Riverfront, 2 Washington Bd; 📞 965 0200; w ihg.com/crowneplaza, $$$$; St Regis, 3071 W Grand Bd; 📞 873 3000; w hotelstregisdetroit. com, $$$$; Dearborn Inn, 20301 Oakwood Bd; 📞 271 2700; w marriott.com, $$$; Rivertown Inn & Suites, 1316 E Jefferson Av; 📞 568 3000; w therivertowninn.com, $$$; Siren, 1509 Broadway; 📞 277 4736; w thesirenhotel.com, $$$; Westin Book Cadillac, 1114 Washington Bd; 📞 442 1600; w hotelstregisdetroit.com, $$$; El Moore Lodge, 624 W Alexandrine; 📞 924 4374; w elmoore.com, $$.

Recommended in Detroit

Detroit RiverWalk This 5½-mile (8.8km) path runs along the river from the Ambassador Bridge to Belle Isle. Free tours from the RiverFront Conservancy (📞 566 8200; w detroitriverfront. org). The east RiverWalk connects an area between Jefferson Av & the river known as Rivertown, which prospered in the 19th century as a centre for railroads, shipbuilding & lumber yards. Historic warehouses have been transformed into restaurants, shops & nightclubs.

Detroit Historical Museum At the corner of 5401 Woodward Av & Kirby; 📞 833 1805; w detroithistorical.org; ⏰ closed Mon; admission free. Displays include the 'Streets of Old Detroit', a fashion library, toy trains, a fur-trading post & an old automobile plant body 'drop'.

Detroit Cultural Center 2 miles (3km) north of downtown along Woodward Av. 3 buildings make up the core of the Cultural Center – the Italianate

Public Library, which has 1 million books & murals showing transport history, the Institute of Arts, & the Horace H Rackham Education Memorial Building. There are also many other museums, galleries, theatres & attractions, as well as Wayne State University & the College for Creative Studies.

Michigan Science Center 5020 John R St; 📞 577 8400; w mi-sci.org; ⏰ daily; admission charge. Exhibits, live shows, an IMAX dome theatre, a planetarium & lab experiences help launch the next generation of Michigan's engineers, scientists & innovators.

Detroit Institute of Arts 5200 Woodward; 📞 833 7900; w dia.org; ⏰ closed Mon; admission charge. The 5th-largest fine arts museum in the country houses Renaissance masterpieces in a 1927 Beaux-Arts building that resembles an Italian palace. The collection also includes Flemish, Islamic

27

& early American art as well as works by Van Gogh & Jan Brueghel.

Museum of African-American History 315 E Warren; ☏494 5800; w thewright.org; ⊕ Tue–Sun; admission charge. The country's largest museum of African-American history & culture includes documents from the Underground Railroad for escaping slaves.

Motown Historical Museum 2648 W Grand Bd; ☏875 2264; w motownmuseum.org; ⊕ Tue–Sat; admission charge. Hitsville USA is the original home of Berry Gordy's Motown Records (derived from Detroit's nickname of 'Motor Town'). Studio A is where Smokey Robinson & Stevie Wonder recorded their hits around the clock in the 1960s.

Fort Wayne 6325 W Jefferson Av, at Livernois; ☏297 8373; ⊕ May–Oct Sat–Sun; admission charge. Built in 1845 as an artillery post to protect the US border, the fort has served as an infantry garrison & induction point for Michigan troops entering every US conflict from the Civil War to Vietnam. During summer, the City's Department of Parks & Recreation hosts historic re-enactments. A Native American burial mound is located at the fort, & ghosts of the Yam-Ko-Desh, the Ottawa name for the mound builders, are said to haunt the site.

Belle Isle Reached via Grand River Bd & the Douglas MacArthur Bridge; ☏852 4078. An island 3 miles (5km) from the city centre, granted to French settlers by Detroit's founder, Antoine de la Mothe Cadillac. Larger than Central Park in New York, this beautiful park has a half-mile (0.8km) beach, the Dossin Great Lakes Museum & the historic Anna Scripps Whitcomb Conservatory.

Ford Piquette Avenue Plant 461 Piquette; ☏872 8759; w fordpiquetteavenueplant.org; ⊕Wed–Sun; admission charge. Walk the plank floors of the factory where the first 12,000 Model Ts were assembled & stand in the secret experimental room where it was created. The museum has a recreation of Henry Ford's office as it was in 1908, plus over 50 historic automobiles. Guided tours.

DETROIT: ALL ABOARD! (↑25/20↓) The *Wolverine* continues through Detroit's northern suburbs and industrial districts. Factories specialise in farm implements, electrical equipment and more automobile products.

ROYAL OAK (↑20/5↓) This mostly residential suburb is the home of Detroit's Zoological Park. The city's name originated in 1819, when a tree reminded Territorial Governor Lewis Cass of the Royal Oak at Boscobel Wood, where England's King Charles II hid after the Battle of Worcester.

TROY (↑5/12↓) Since 2014, Amtrak has used the new Transit Center in Troy, replacing a stop in adjacent Birmingham. Troy Historic Village at 60 W Wattles Road is a collection of 11 19th- and early 20th-century buildings, including a general store, one-room school, wagon shop and church, telling the story of southeast Michigan's rural heritage (☏248 524 3570; w troyhistoricvillage.org).

PONTIAC (↑12) Located next to the Clinton River on the Saginaw Trail, Pontiac was named in 1818 after a Native American Ottawa chief who fought to hold back British forces and is thought to be buried locally. Many parks and lakes are nearby. Pontiac was one of America's earliest industrial cities and it expanded rapidly after the railroad arrived, making cars, trucks, buses and automotive parts, though motor manufacturing has diminished in recent years.

28

Other Amtrak Trains

GENERAL INFORMATION

No reservation or check-in baggage services operate except where stated, and trains run daily unless otherwise indicated.

THE TRAINS

THE *AUTO TRAIN* (LORTON–SANFORD) This is perhaps the world's longest passenger train – over ¾ mile (1.2km) in length with 18 passenger cars, 33 auto carriers and two engines. It transports over 130,000 automobiles and 250,000 passengers per year and is one of Amtrak's finest, much favoured by 'snow birds' escaping the northern winter and by families travelling to Disney World. Being a major money-spinner, the *Auto Train* receives some of the best attendants and best-maintained cars as it operates daily at 70mph (122km/h) over 855 miles (1,376km) of track between Lorton in Virginia and Sanford, Florida. The train is for cars and their passengers only. Amtrak is considering introducing similar services between Chicago and Florida and along the Pacific coast.

The $25 million Lorton terminal at 8006 Lorton Road (just off I-95, Exit 163, 25 miles/40km south of Washington, DC) was opened early in 2000, with a larger waiting room, snack bar and improved facilities. The 1,500ft (457m) platform enables an entire train to be accepted without having to be split as was previously the case. Sanford station at 600 S Persimmon Avenue (about a half-hour drive north of Orlando in Florida) is a smart new building opened in 2010, designed to cope with growing demand for the *Auto Train*. The Lorton and Sanford terminals are for *Auto Trains* only.

Lorton and Sanford ticket offices and waiting rooms open 08.00–16.00. Cars are accepted by Amtrak staff between 11.30 and 14.30, when the train doors are closed and all passengers must be on board. Trains normally depart at 16.00 but if boarding is complete and the track ahead clear they may leave a little earlier. The only stop during the night is in Florence, South Carolina, where the engine is refuelled and the engineer crew and conductor changed. You arrive at 08.58 the next morning. The train is occasionally delayed by problems on CSX's main route along the eastern seaboard but if this happens to any extent there will be extra meals scheduled and movies shown. If the track has been clear and there have been no delays you may arrive up to an hour early – most likely to happen at weekends.

Boarding times are strictly enforced so it is important to allow for possible heavy traffic, especially at weekends and around Washington, DC. All vehicles must be 65 inches (1.65m) or lower and not have temporary luggage or bike racks. Remember to turn off any car alarms because if one goes off en route it could easily drain the battery. There is no check-in baggage except inside vehicles, where you can pack as much as can safely be carried. Personal property left inside your vehicle remains your responsibility. You do not have access to it during the journey so you need to take a small bag of necessities with you when you board.

Northbound fares are lowest between early January and mid-February and from mid-June to mid-December. Southbound fares are lowest between mid-February and late March and from May to December. Special deals are often available, including lodging and tickets to Orlando area attractions as well as your train fare. Amtrak uses Superliner II sleepers and specially designed bi-level lounge cars on this route. The lounge car features improved audio and video systems and booth seating. Complimentary dinner and breakfast in the dining car are included.

Reservations for this daily service are essential and you should allow at least 1 hour prior to departure (preferably 2 hours) for boarding. No pets are allowed and no smoking is permitted on board or at stations. Wi-Fi service is available. For directions and other information call Amtrak's regular number (✆1 800 872 7245) or the special *Auto Train* toll-free number (✆1 877 754 7495).

THE *DOWNEASTER* (BOSTON–PORTLAND)

Amtrak's *Downeaster* operates five-times daily in both directions, travelling between North Station in Boston, Massachusetts, and Portland, Maine, along part of the former Boston & Maine Railroad. The train is named after the strong winds that used to blow ocean-going ships 'downeast' from Boston, and this route through woods, small towns and farmland is a great way to explore the unspoilt coastline. Famous trains such as the *Flying Yankee* used this route from the 1920s until the 1960s, taking passengers on overnight sleepers to New York or Montreal. Amtrak successfully reintroduced services by public demand in 2001, after a gap of 36 years. On its 116-mile (186km) journey, the *Downeaster* stops at Woburn, Haverhill, Exeter, Durham, Dover, Wells and Saco. Three trains a day extend the service further north to Freeport and Brunswick.

All reserved. Business Class available. Great Dome Car service in the autumn. Free Wi-Fi.

THE *CASCADES* (SEATTLE–PORTLAND)

Four European-style trains operate daily in each direction, following the *Coast Starlight* route (pages 55–61). High-tech Spanish-built Talgo 200 equipment provides wider seats and a bistro dining car. The new trains cut almost half an hour from the previous time on this route. Since the introduction of the *Cascades* service, annual ridership has reached a record high of over half a million passenger trips and this has become Amtrak's most highly rated route for customer satisfaction.

Thruway buses connect Portland's Greyhound depot, opposite the Amtrak station, with Hood River, The Dalles, Pendleton, La Grande, Baker City, Ontario, Nampa and Boise, ID. Two trains also travel daily between Eugene and Seattle.

All reserved. Checked baggage. Business Class. Bicycle racks. Wi-Fi.

THE *CASCADES* (SEATTLE–VANCOUVER, BC)

Two trains a day follow the *Empire Builder* route (page 116) to Everett, then continue through north Washington via Stanwood, Mount Vernon and Bellingham before crossing the Canadian border into British Columbia. This train reopened the cross-border Seattle–Vancouver route in 1996 after a gap of 14 years. It is operated by Amtrak in partnership with the states of Washington and Oregon and the Canadian province of British Columbia.

All reserved. Complete meals, snacks, sandwiches and drinks, including Red Hook beer and real coffee. Checked baggage. Business Class. Bicycle racks. Wi-Fi.

THE *CAPITOL CORRIDOR* **(SAN JOSE–AUBURN)** Sixteen trains travel on weekdays between the Sacramento region and the Bay Area, with eight extended to San Jose and one from Sacramento to Auburn. Eleven weekend trains travel between Sacramento and Oakland, with seven extended to San Jose. Trains follow parts of the *Coast Starlight* and *California Zephyr* routes (pages 54 and 82). Many Thruway buses link with places such as Napa, Santa Rosa and Martinez.

No reservations are required for trains but they are required for some Thruway bus services. Free Wi-Fi. Bicycle racks.

THE *ETHAN ALLEN EXPRESS* **(NEW YORK–RUTLAND)** This train follows the *Adirondack* route (page 270) from New York City to Fort Edward, then continues to Castleton and Rutland in Vermont. Buses provide connections from Rutland to the ski resorts at Killington.

Daily. Reservations required. Business Class. Wi-Fi.

THE *KEYSTONE* **SERVICE (NEW YORK–HARRISBURG)** Thirteen trains a day (seven at weekends) travel in each direction, following the *Pennsylvanian* route (page 308) as far as Harrisburg. *Keystone* trains are operated by Amtrak in partnership with the Pennsylvania Department of Transportation.

Reservations are required north of Philadelphia. Business Class available. Wi-Fi.

THE *CAROLINIAN* **(NEW YORK–CHARLOTTE)** This train follows the *Silver Star* route to Raleigh (page 233) then travels west through wooded hills to Charlotte in North Carolina via Greensboro.

Reservations are required, except between New York and Washington, DC. Carolina Business Class service offers complimentary drinks, newspapers, audio and movies between Washington, DC and Charlotte. Check-in baggage. Wi-Fi.

THE *EMPIRE* **SERVICE (NEW YORK–ALBANY–NIAGARA FALLS)** The name of this service originated with the New York Central Railroad in 1967. Six trains a day (four at weekends) travel in each direction, following part of the *Lake Shore Limited* route (page 287) as far as Albany. Some trains travel on to Niagara Falls, New York, formerly known as the Water Level Route. If plans for a high-speed rail service succeed, travel from New York City to Albany will take less than 2 hours.

All reserved. Business Class. Wi-Fi.

THE *PIEDMONT* **(RALEIGH–CHARLOTTE)** Two trains daily follow part of the *Carolinian* route (see above) and serve fresh barbecued food in a refurbished dining car. Some trains operate between Charlotte and Wilson.

All reserved. Complete meals service. Check-in baggage. Bicycle racks. Wi-Fi.

THE *HIAWATHA* **SERVICE (CHICAGO–MILWAUKEE)** Seven trains a day (six at weekends) travel in each direction, stopping at Glenview, Sturtevant and Milwaukee Airport. From Milwaukee, Thruway buses link with Fond du Lac, Oshkosh, Wausau and other towns in Wisconsin. You can also catch the train to and from the new Amtrak station at Milwaukee's Mitchell International Airport. Checked baggage service available at Chicago and Milwaukee.

No reservations required. Wi-Fi.

THE *MISSOURI RIVER RUNNER* **(ST LOUIS–KANSAS CITY)** This route was formerly operated as part of the Missouri Service train network, which included the *Ann*

Rutledge, Kansas City Mule and *St Louis Mule*. Two trains a day travel in each direction via stations that include Jefferson City and Sedalia. Kansas City buses connect to Tulsa and Oklahoma City. As part of the Trails and Rails programme, a National Park Service guide from the Jefferson National Expansion Memorial is on board from St Louis to Kansas City, Missouri.

All reserved. Business Class.

THE *LINCOLN* SERVICE (CHICAGO–ST LOUIS) Four trains a day follow the *Texas Eagle* route (page 175) but also stop in Summit and Dwight, Illinois. An interpretive guide from the Jefferson National Expansion Memorial (consisting of the Gateway Arch, the Museum of Westward Expansion and St Louis's Old Courthouse) provides a narrative on board the *Lincoln* service between St Louis and Springfield.

All reserved. Business Class.

THE *BLUE WATER* (CHICAGO–PORT HURON) An all-reserved train service introduced in 2004, the *Blue Water* runs between Port Huron, Michigan and Chicago, with intermediate stops at Lapeer, Flint, Durand, East Lansing, Battle Creek, Kalamazoo, Dowagiac and Niles. Named after its home region of Port Huron, this train was reintroduced to replace the Chicago–Toronto *International*. VIA Rail continues to operate a service between Sarnia, London and Toronto but it no longer connects with Amtrak at Port Huron. Amtrak's *Blue Water* train, supported by the Michigan Department of Transportation (MDOT), provides daily morning departures to Chicago, with return afternoon service for Michigan passengers.

Reservations required. Business Class. Wi-Fi.

THE *PERE MARQUETTE* (CHICAGO–GRAND RAPIDS) The schedule of this all-reserved Chicago–Grand Rapids train mirrors the operating pattern of the *Blue Water*. The *Pere Marquette* is also operated under a contract with MDOT and has a morning departure to Chicago with an evening return to Grand Rapids, stopping at St Joseph-Benton Harbor, Bangor and Holland en route.

Reservations required. Business Class. Wi-Fi.

Amtrak offers an additional service on this route between Chicago and Holland, Michigan, on two Saturdays in May for travellers to the annual Tulip Time Festival – 'The Nation's Best Flower Festival' and 'America's Best Small-Town Festival', with more than five million tulips in bloom. A stop at Hammond-Whiting is also added, as well as intermediate stops at St Joseph and Bangor. For more information call the Holland Area Visitors Bureau at ☎ 1 800 506 1299, or visit **w** Holland.org.

THE *ILLINOIS ZEPHYR/CARL SANDBURG* (CHICAGO–QUINCY) This daily service follows the *California Zephyr* route to Galesburg (page 82), then continues south to Quincy, Illinois, via Macomb.

All reserved. Business Class. Wi-Fi.

THE *ILLINI/SALUKI* (CHICAGO–CARBONDALE) Morning and late afternoon departures, following part of the *City of New Orleans* route (page 190). These trains also make a stop in Du Quoin, Illinois, named after Chief Jean Baptiste Ducoigne of the Tamaroa.

All reserved. Business Class. Bicycle racks. Wi-Fi.

THE *HOOSIER STATE* (CHICAGO–INDIANAPOLIS) This train operates four days a week along part of the *Cardinal* route (page 258), stopping at Dyer, Rensselaer, Lafayette and Crawfordsville.

All reserved. Business Class.

THE *HEARTLAND FLYER* (OKLAHOMA CITY–FORT WORTH) This train travels daily between Oklahoma and Texas, making stops in Norman, Purcell, Pauls Valley, Ardmore and Gainesville. This service is operated by Amtrak on behalf of the states of Oklahoma and Texas. National Park Service guides from the Chickasaw National Recreation Area are on board the *Heartland Flyer* between Oklahoma City and Fort Worth.

All reserved. Bicycle racks.

THE *PALMETTO* (NEW YORK–SAVANNAH) This is a daily service that starts early in the morning and reaches Savannah or New York by mid-evening. *Palmetto* trains follow the *Silver Meteor* route (page 249), making additional stops in Wilson and Selma-Smithfield (North Carolina) and Dillon (South Carolina). The original *Palmetto Limited*, inaugurated in 1910 by the Atlantic Coast Line Railroad, ran between New York and St Petersburg. Between 1996 and 2002 this service was called the Silver Palm. Currently a day train, in the past the *Palmetto* provided overnight sleeper service to Florida.

All reserved. Business Class. Checked baggage. Wi-Fi.

UPDATES WEBSITE

You can post your comments and recommendations, and read feedback and updates from other readers online at w bradtupdates.com/usa.

Other Amtrak Trains **THE TRAINS**

28

29

US Steam Today

Steam locomotives have always been something special. They seem to possess a soul and to their operators often feel more like living creatures than machines. Early steam engines soon earned people's affection and were given nicknames such as calliope, hog, jack, mill, pig, pot or smoker. Smaller types were called coffee pot, dinky, kettle or peanut-roaster. Their drivers, officially known as engineers, were hog-heads, hog-jockeys, grunts, eagle-eyes or dinkey skinners (if they worked for a logging railroad).

Other words to enter the language were highball (a hand or voice signal to move a train); hostler (someone who services locomotives); shoofly (a temporary bypass track around a damaged track or obstruction); torpedo (an explosive device put on the rail to warn an approaching train of danger ahead); varnish (a passenger train, from the days when coaches were made of wood and varnished); gandy dancer (a track worker named after the Gandy company which made his tools); baby lifter (a brakeman); bakehead, or tallow pot (a fireman); go to beans (go to eat a meal); the brains, or skipper (conductor); brass hat (a railroad executive); car toad (an inspector of freight and passenger cars); crummy (a wooden, two-truck caboose, also called a bean shack when workers lived in them); dead head (a railroad employee travelling on a pass); dinger (a yardmaster); gladhand (metal attachments to which air hoses connect); goat (a yard engine); green eye (a clear signal); kicker (an emergency brake); number dummies (clerks who worked as yard checkers); piglet (a trainee engineer); swing man (a rear brakeman); and yellow eye (a yellow signal).

To 'join the birds' was to jump from a moving engine or car, usually just before it ended up 'in the ditch' (wrecked). Picking up water from between the rails was 'jerking a drink' and a head-on collision was a 'cornfield meet'. Such train language, along with a host of stories, songs and legends, helped railroads become an integral part of American folklore. Even as late as the 1930s and 1940s, being an engineer (driver) was a much sought-after occupation and for some it ranked higher than becoming president.

An engineer earned good money, saw new and glamorous places, and was admired by small boys and women everywhere. It could be hard work, though, and getting the most out of a locomotive, often in difficult circumstances, required artistry as much as expertise. The engineer would use the throttle to 'beat on' the engine, making it run sweetly at maximum power. This was a considerable test of both his skill and the locomotive's strength. The fireman regulated the water and fire box to ensure that the engineer had the right amount of steam pressure to drive the engine.

Steam engine numbers peaked at 72,000 just after World War I. Approximately 180,000 steam locomotives were built in the US altogether, culminating in the Union Pacific's *Big Boys* of the 1940s. These (4-8-8-4) monsters weighed 600 tons, had a capacity of 7,000 horsepower and burned 20 tons of coal an hour. But as technology progressed, lower maintenance costs and safety considerations made the change to diesel increasingly inevitable and no new steam engines were put into service after 1953.

The Norfolk & Western Railroad, centred on Roanoke, was the last steam-powered Class One line. O Winston Link lovingly recorded its demise over a period of six years in the 1950s, making films and sound recordings as well as taking the extraordinary photographs published in *Steam, Steel and Stars*. He even bought his own locomotive, a 1911 Canadian Pacific ten-wheeler. The final Norfolk & Western steam trains ran on 4 April 1960, after which most were scrapped and their metal exported to Japan. The Norfolk & Western merged with the Southern Railway in 1982 to form the massive Norfolk Southern system, with 17,000 miles (27,000km) of track in 20 states.

The age of steam still lives on around the USA though, thanks mainly to the efforts of 40,000 volunteer enthusiasts. It can take up to 30,000 hours of work to restore a single locomotive but more than 200 remain operational out of the 1,875 still in existence in the US and Canada. Most weigh between 100 and 150 tons, but the largest in working order is the Union Pacific *Challenger* (313 US tons/274 tonnes). Some modern reproduction engines have been imported from Europe and China.

Many 'steam chasers' continue to delight in the pungent smell of coal smoke, an echoing whistle and the clickety-clack of the rails. Five million people each year take main-line excursions or dinner trains, visit scenic railways or go to train museums. The leading supplier of books, DVDs and vintage films is **Pentrex** (*PO Box 22283, Indianapolis, IN 46222;* ⟍*1 800 950 9333;* w *pentrex.com*).

TRAINS, ROUTES AND MUSEUMS

'She came at me in sections, more curves than a scenic railway.' – Fred Astaire in *Band Wagon*.

The following are among the most scenic and interesting railways still in regular operation. All are standard gauge except where indicated.

ARCADE & ATTICA (*Mail address: 278 Main, Arcade, NY 14009;* ⟍*585 492 3100 or* ⟍*585 496 9777;* w *aarailroad.com*) Steam trains travel over a historic route to Curriers from the depot in Arcade, New York, using coaches built around 1915. President Grover Cleveland's honeymoon car, complete with original dishes, is on show at the Arcade Station along with other unique items from railroad history, including lanterns, an antique roll-top desk and two wooden telephones. The authentic ticket office has bars in the window.

Trains leave Arcade past the current station and pass a building which used to be a station of the Tonawanda Valley & Cuba Railroad, predecessor to the Arcade & Attica. You cross a bridge giving great views of Cattaraugus Creek and continue through an attractive wilderness area to Curriers. There the locomotive switches and pulls on to a siding to provide photo opportunities before returning to Arcade, pulling the train in reverse.

Steam trains operate mostly at weekends from Memorial Day (last Monday in May) until September, with foliage specials in October. Special event trains also operate in season and there are diesel-powered trips at other times. The nearest Amtrak stops are Buffalo and Rochester, served by the *Lake Shore Limited*.

AUSTIN & TEXAS CENTRAL RAILROAD (*Mail address: PO Box 1632, Austin, TX 78767;* ☏ *512 477 8468;* w *austinsteamtrain.org*) Located at 401 E Whitestone Boulevard in Cedar Park, 20 miles (32km) north of Austin, Texas. A vintage Southern Pacific locomotive and period passenger cars make regular steam excursions into the hill country northwest of Austin, taking a scenic 66-mile round-trip route from Cedar Park through the cedar and oak woods of the South San Gabriel River Valley. You cross the river on a spectacular trestle and climb 500ft (152m) to the top of the valley before descending a steep grade to the town of Burnet.

The Austin Steam Train Association (ASTA) has trackage rights over this route under an agreement with the city and Capital Metro, which manages the line. The track is also used for weekday freight services and has recently been upgraded. Steam engine *No 786* was built by the American Locomotive Company in 1916 and operated over the Southern Pacific's Texas and Louisiana lines until 1956. After more than 30 years on display in downtown Austin, the 143-US-ton (129-tonne) locomotive was restored to working order in record time to operate out of Cedar Park. Engine *No 786* is undergoing a thorough rebuilding that will return it to service as good as new, and as soon as possible. In the meantime, all of ASTA's regular trains are continuing their schedules uninterrupted, using diesel locomotives. Trains run mostly at weekends from March to December. A new railroad museum, located at 401 E Whitestone Boulevard, celebrates the rich history of the American railroad and is open on weekdays. Passengers can also visit the museum an hour prior to each train departure at weekends. Amtrak's *Texas Eagle* serves Austin.

BLACK HILLS CENTRAL (*Mail address: 222 Railroad Av, Hill City, SD 57745;* ☏ *605 574 2222;* w *1880train.com*) Trains travel 20 miles (32km) through forests and mountains between Keystone and a former Chicago, Burlington & Quincy station at Hill City near Mount Rushmore, South Dakota. Vintage coaches and a 1919 Baldwin locomotive (star of television's *Gunsmoke* and Disney's *Scandalous John*) run through the beautiful Black Hills of western South Dakota along part of what was once a Burlington Railroad line. You pass the Holy Terror mine, Old Baldy Mountain (5,605ft/1,545m) and Elkhorn Mountain (6,200ft/1,890m), climbing grades of up to 6% past the old tin mine route to Hill City.

Trains operate daily on a 2-hour round trip from May to October, with a reduced schedule at other times.

BOONE & SCENIC VALLEY (*Mail address: 225 Tenth St, PO Box 603, Boone, IA 50036;* ☏ *515 432 4249 or* ☏ *1 800 626 0319;* w *bsvrr.com*) A 15-mile (24km) round trip from Boone, Iowa, over the historic Dodge, Des Moines & Southern route, crossing the Des Moines River Valley on two great bridges, including the world's largest and highest double-track rail bridge at 156ft (48m). The railroad was begun in the 1890s to transport coal from Fraser to another railroad at Fraser Junction, now called Wolf, before later extending north to Rockwell, Fort Dodge and Des Moines. Passenger cars operated on an hourly basis and freight business flourished. The Boone Railroad Historical Society purchased a section of the defunct line in 1983 for $50,000, and in 1989 the last commercially built steam locomotive made in China was bought for $350,000 to operate services with restored 1920s passenger cars.

For an additional fare you can travel First Class on the Wolf train, making a 22-mile (36km) round trip to Wolf in an air-conditioned *City of San Francisco* Pullman lounge car with roomettes, an observation platform and free refreshments. The depot was built in 1985 in the style of the one in Rockwell, Iowa, using interior oak woodwork from the depot in Tama. The platform was constructed from bricks brought from several other old platforms. Boone also features **Iowa's Railway Museum**, with free displays and exhibits. Steam trains run on weekends and holidays from May to October, with diesels on weekdays. The nearest Amtrak stop is Osceola, served by the *California Zephyr*.

CALIFORNIA WESTERN (*Mail address: 220 S Sierra Av, Oakdale, CA 95361;* ☎ *707 964 6371; w skunktrain.com*) The Skunk line runs 40 miles (64km) between Fort Bragg (*100 W Laurel*) on the beautiful Mendocino coast and Willits on US Highway 101 (*299 E Commercial*). The nickname 'Skunk' originated in 1925, when motorcars (railbuses) were introduced. These had gasoline-powered engines for power and pot-bellied stoves burning crude oil to keep the passengers warm. The combination of the fumes created a pungent odour, and the old timers living along the line said the motorcars were like skunks, 'You could smell them before you could see them'.

A variety of trains and schedules operate from both ends of the line, crossing up to 30 bridges and trestles. From Fort Bragg you can travel with an open observation car along Pudding Creek and the Noyo River, passing through a deep mountain tunnel and seeing splendid redwood trees, wild flowers, grazing cattle and apple orchards. At Northspur you have time to relax before returning to Fort Bragg.

The 90-minute trip from Willits by vintage 1935 M-300 Motorcar begins with a climb into the rolling hills and through a tunnel at the 1,700ft (488m) summit before gently curving down the steep mountain to Wolf Tree then returning to Willits. Steam trains operate Saturdays all year, and Wednesday–Friday during summer. Diesel trains operate daily. Reservations are recommended. Amtrak Thruway buses link Oakland with Willits.

CASS (*Mail address: 242 Main, Cass, WV 24927;* ☎ *304 636 9477; w cassrailroad. com*) The Cass Scenic Railroad uses a splendid switchback route built in 1901 as a logging railroad to haul lumber to the mill in Cass. The locomotives are the same ones that were used in Cass and in the forests of British Columbia for more than 50 years. Old logging flat-cars have been refurbished and turned into passenger coaches, transporting you from the restored buildings of Cass into the mountains of West Virginia.

Cass is home to the world's largest fleet of geared Shay locomotives. Six Shays and two Climax locomotives reside here and the legendary turn-of-the-century class C-80 Shay, #5 has been toiling up Cheat Mountain for nearly 100 years, making it one of the oldest engines in continuous service on its original line, and the second-oldest Shay in existence. A 90-ton Shay locomotive hauls the train out of Cass past an old water tower from which its tanks are filled. The train then rounds the curve up Leatherbark Creek and chugs laboriously into the mountains, reversing up the steepest grades before reaching open fields. At times the train has to cope with a grade of 11% (11ft/3.6m in altitude for each 100ft/30m of track). A logging camp of the 1940s has been recreated at Whittaker Station, including a rare Lidgerwood tower skidder. You can continue from Whittaker to Bald Knob via a stop further up the mountain to take on more water at a spring. The train then climbs to the summit of Bald Knob, the third-highest point (4,842ft/1,477m) in West Virginia, from where you can see across two states and into the valley below.

Trains travel either 8 miles (13km) from Cass to Whittaker (half an hour) or 22 miles (35km) on a round trip lasting 4½ hours to the summit of Bald Knob, operating daily from May to September; weekends in September and October. Amtrak's *Cardinal* stops at nearby White Sulphur Springs.

CONWAY (*Mail address: 38 Norcross Circle, PO Box 1947, North Conway, NH 03860;* 1 800 232 5251; w *conwayscenic.com*) Diesel and occasional steam trains operate from an imposing 1874 station built by the Portsmouth, Great Falls & Conway Railroad in North Conway, New Hampshire. Nathaniel J Bradlee of Boston designed this beautiful structure, housing separate men's and ladies' waiting rooms, ticket office, baggage room and rest rooms. Two curving mahogany staircases lead to offices in metal-sheathed domed towers and an eight-day clock was installed in the face of the building, opposite the park. The station has changed little since it was built, apart from the incorporation of a gift shop, and has been carefully restored in recent years.

Other buildings include a roundhouse, a free museum, a freight house and an original Boston & Maine crossing tender shanty (a shelter for watchmen who protected crossings before automation took over control of the light flashers and gates). There is an outdoor display of restored railcars, operating turntable and roundhouse. The freight house is home to the North Conway Model Railroad Club, open on Tuesday, Thursday and Saturday from July to September.

Some of the 40-plus railroad cars and locomotives are used to take passengers into the White Mountains over part of the Boston & Maine Conway branch line. The Valley train makes a 55-minute round trip from North Conway to Conway (11 miles/17km) or a 1¾-hour round trip from North Conway to Bartlett (21 miles/34km). The Conway route takes you south through farmland, crossing Moat Brook and the Saco and Swift rivers. The Bartlett train travels northwest through fields and woodlands, crossing the East Branch, Saco and Ellis rivers. You can choose Coach Class, the elegant *Chocorua* dining car or the First-Class *Gertrude Emma* Parlour observation car. The *Gertrude Emma* was built in 1898 for use on the *Pennsylvania Limited* and has been splendidly restored with wicker and rattan chairs, rich mahogany woodwork and an open observation platform.

The Notch train crosses two spectacular trestles and many streams, steep bluffs and ravines on its way to Crawford Notch (a 5-hour round trip) or Fabyan Station (5½ hours). Seating options include Coach Class, the First-Class car *Carroll P Reed*, or the Dome car *Dorthea Mae*. Live commentary includes history and folklore of the railroad and area as well as other points of interest. The open-air observation coach is available to Coach- and First-Class passengers.

Valley trains run at weekends from mid-April to mid-May then daily until mid-October, when a weekend service continues until mid-December. The Notch train operates Tuesday, Wednesday, Thursday and Saturday from June until mid-September, then daily until mid-October for peak foliage season.

CUMBRES & TOLTEC (*Mail address: PO Box 789, Chama, NM 87520;* 888 286 2737; w *cumbrestoltec.com*) This is the longest and highest narrow-gauge steam railway in America and is one of the world's most scenic and best-preserved routes, taking you through the Rockies by way of tunnels and breathtaking trestles. There are snowdrifts in May, wild flowers in June and brilliant autumn colours in September and October. The 64-mile (102km) Denver & Rio Grande Western track crosses the continental divide at Cumbres Pass (10,015ft/3,055m), then snakes through the Toltec Gorge of the Los Pinos River before making a precipitous descent towards Chama, New Mexico. Power is provided by Baldwin locomotives and trains sometimes have to use one of two preserved rotary snow ploughs to cope with the weather conditions.

The Cumbres & Toltec is one of the last remnants of a rail empire which began in 1871, with the construction of the Denver & Rio Grande Railroad. The original intention was to build a line from Denver to Mexico City via Santa Fe and El Paso. Financed mainly by British investors, this 'happy little railroad' was constructed to a 36-inch (91cm) gauge to cope with the mountainous landscape, although standard gauge was already the norm. By 1876, it had changed its aim from Mexico to the prosperous silver mines of the San Juan Mountains in southwestern Colorado, reaching Silverton via Cumbres Pass and Durango in 1882. After 1955, only one section of narrow-gauge line remained, running from Antonito through Chama to Durango and Silverton, Colorado, and to Farmington in New Mexico.

The states of Colorado and New Mexico purchased the Antonito–Chama section and created the Cumbres & Toltec Scenic Railroad in 1970. The Durango–Silverton line continued to operate and was sold to a private owner in 1981, becoming the Durango & Silverton Narrow Gauge Railroad (see below).

The *Colorado Limited* travels from Antonito to Osier, Colorado, through Toltec Gorge. The *New Mexico Express* leaves Chama, New Mexico, for Osier via Cumbres Pass. You can make through trips in either direction, returning by road, or make round trips to and from Osier by train.

Trains run daily from late May to mid-October. Dress warmly.

DURANGO & SILVERTON (*Station at 479 Main Av, Durango, CO 81301;* ℡ *970 247 2733 or* ℡ *877 872 4607; **w** durangotrain.com*) Durango was founded by the Denver & Rio Grande Railway in 1880 and the 36-inch (91cm) gauge Durango to Silverton line was completed two years later at a cost of $100,000 per mile (see the previous *Cumbres & Toltec* section, page 336). The 500 construction workers were mostly Irish and Chinese immigrants, earning an average $2.25 a day for often dangerous work as a ledge was blasted from solid granite above the Animas River. Some of them lived in caves dug out of the hillside near Rockwood in preference to the thin-walled railcars provided. This challenging project ranks alongside that of the Central Pacific Railroad's passage through the Sierra Nevada, and the entire line has been designated a National Historic Civil Engineering Landmark.

The **D & SNGRR Museum** is housed in part of a renovated roundhouse and features full-size locomotives as well as elegant Business-Class private cars, railroad paintings, lamps, photographs and books. The original bell from the Union Pacific locomotive *No 119*, present at the Golden Spike ceremony of 1869, is also on display. The **Silverton Freight Yard Museum**, located in the 1882 depot, has more locomotive and freight equipment as well as the *Casey Jones*, a motorised vehicle powered by a 1915 Cadillac engine. Admission to both museums is included in the train ticket price.

Today's Durango & Silverton Railroad has been voted one of the 'top ten most exciting train journeys in the world' by the Society of American Travel Writers. Trains run on a 45-mile (72km) spur of track using coal-fired locomotives built for the D&RGW by the American Locomotive Works (1923) and Baldwin (1925), one of which appeared in the film *Butch Cassidy and the Sundance Kid*. The train has appeared in many other movies, including *Viva Zapata*, *Around the World in 80 Days* and *How the West Was Won*. Robert Royem's book, *An American Classic: The Durango & Silverton Narrow Gauge Railroad*, contains hundreds of original photographs, including several from the 1880s, as well as a historical overview of the train.

Authentic 1880s coaches make a daily 90-mile (144km) round trip from early May to mid-August among wonderful Rocky Mountain scenery, following the Animas River through the remote wilderness of the San Juan National Forest. The fireman shovels 6 tons of coal per day on the round trip to Silverton, where there is a 2-hour layover. Open-sided gondola cars provide panoramic views. Cascade Canyon winter steam excursions operate daily from 22 November to early May. Reservations are recommended at least a month in advance.

EUREKA SPRINGS & NORTH ARKANSAS (*Mail address: PO Box 310, 299 N Main St, Highway 23 N, Eureka Springs, AR 72632;* ✆ *479 253 9623;* w *esnarailway.com*) A 4-mile (6.5km) journey through the Ozark Mountains, leaves from the 1913 Eureka Springs depot built from local limestone. The ES&NA collection of vintage rolling stock, including the elegant 1920s *Eurekan* dining car, is one of the Ozarks' largest. Authentic railroad memorabilia recreate a turn-of-the-century era when the railway first brought visitors to Eureka Springs.

Between trains you can check out exhibits such as the restored turntable, a handcar, vintage locomotives and rolling stock that includes an automobile fitted out to run on the rails.

Trains operate daily (except Sunday) from April to October. Sunday trains operate on Memorial Day, 4 July and Labor Day weekends.

EVERETT (*Mail address: 424 2nd Av, Duncansville, PA 16635;* ✆ *814 695 9628; everettrailroad.com*) The Everett Railroad is located in the borough of Hollidaysburg, near Altoona, Pennsylvania. A 1920 Alco-Cooke steam locomotive, *Old Number 11*, pulls the majority of event trains on excursions lasting 1 hour or more to Brookes Mills, Roaring Spring or Kladder. Vintage 1940s passenger cars have functioning windows to allow for a summer breeze and are heated in the winter. The railroad hauled its first tourists in the early 1970s when the National Railway Historical Society operated several excursions. Expansion occurred again in 1995 with the incorporation of a sister company, the Hollidaysburg & Roaring Spring Railroad (H&RS) which acquired 10 miles of Conrail track that tied together the Everett and Morrisons Cove railroads, creating what is today a 23-mile rail network.

Scheduled trains operate three days per week from March to December. Interchange for the Everett Railroad is with Norfolk Southern at Hollidaysburg (*244 Loop Rd, Hollidaysburg, PA 16648*). Holiday and event-themed rides include trips for 'leaf-peeping', as well as the 'Easter EGGSpress', 'Pumpkin Patch', 'Santa Express' and 'Ice Cream Special'.

FILLMORE & WESTERN (*Mail address: 364 Main, Fillmore, CA 93015; ticket office address: 364 Main St, Fillmore, CA 93015;* ✆ *805 524 2546 or* ✆ *1 800 773 8724;* w *fwry.com*) This 31-mile (50km) journey through the unspoilt Santa Clara Valley in southern California uses vintage equipment and the original 1887 station at Tenth Street in Santa Paula is also a museum.

The Fillmore & Western Railway operates many excursions, dinner trains and other speciality trains. It is also engaged in the restoration of historic railroad cars and its majestic 1913 Baldwin steam engine, originally owned by the Duluth & Northeastern Railroad, is brought out at certain times of the year. The railroad has begun restoring and expanding the track between Fillmore and Piru with a view to running excursions on this route. Steam trains operate mostly at weekends from March to December. Amtrak's nearest stop is Oxnard, served by the *Coast Starlight*.

GEORGETOWN LOOP HISTORIC MINING AND RAILROAD PARK (*Mail address: 646 Loop Dr, Georgetown, CO 80444;* ✆ *1 888 4 LOOP RR (* ✆ *1 888 456 6777);* w *georgetownlooprr.com*) Journey back in time by visiting the Georgetown Loop Historic Mining and Railroad Park. Located 42 miles (67km) west of Denver, the

Georgetown Loop is an engineering marvel originally built in 1884 and refurbished in the 1970s that takes visitors through spectacular mountain scenery, twisting and turning over part of the former Colorado & Southern Railway's 36-inch-gauge (91cm) line.

The narrow-gauge railroad runs 4½ miles (7km), connecting Silver Plume and Georgetown, with tracks scaling an elevation of 640ft (195m) over mountainous terrain. The 300-ft-long (91-m) Devil's Gate Viaduct formed a spiral where the track actually crossed over itself, making the 'Loop' a popular tourist attraction, but with the end of mining it was dismantled and sold for scrap. Today's route includes a crossing of the new viaduct 96ft (29m) high above Clear Creek. Trains can be boarded in Silver Plume (2 miles/3.2km west of Georgetown on I-70) or from the Georgetown depot. Along the route, visitors may stop for guided tours of the historic Lebanon Silver Mine.

Georgetown Loop Historic Mining and Railroad Park is operated in partnership between the Colorado Historical Society (\303 866 3682) and Railstar Corporation. The park includes an 1884 depot, the Morrison Interpretive Center, an early 1870s silver mine mill, and four reconstructed mine buildings. Trains make 70-minute round trips daily between late May and early October. You can also visit the Lebanon Silver Mine until early September (accessible only by the Georgetown Loop Historic Railroad), which has a guided tour that lasts around 80 minutes. Comfortable walking shoes are recommended, and a jacket or sweater is essential. The nearest Amtrak station is Denver, served by the *California Zephyr*.

GRAND CANYON (*Mail address: 233 N Grand Canyon Bd, Williams, AZ 86046;* *1 800 843 8724 or**520 773 1976;* w *thetrain.com*) The 1908 depot is at 518 E Bill Williams Avenue, Williams, Arizona, from where trains travel the 65 miles (104km) through ponderosa pine forest, small *arroyos* and high desert plains to the edge of the Grand Canyon. Watch out for the notorious 'Cataract Creek Gang' robbing innocent passengers and acting out gun fights. The line was built in 1901 by the Atchison, Topeka & Santa Fe Railway and the canyon's 1910 South Rim Station is one of only three log-built depots still in existence. The original Fray Marcos Hotel (a former Harvey House) in Williams is now occupied by the free **Grand Canyon Railway Museum**, with an authentic steam locomotive and caboose on display outside.

Notable passengers here have included Presidents Theodore Roosevelt, Taft, Franklin D Roosevelt and Eisenhower, as well as Clark Gable, Jimmy Durante and Doris Day. Today's restored 1920s Harriman coaches and vintage engines operate daily, with Western entertainment and interpretive guides, and the five classes of service range from Coach to Luxury Parlour Class.

Steam trains run on Saturdays from early March to October. Operating an all-diesel fleet of locomotives year-round saves fuel and manpower, and reduces greenhouse gas emissions and air pollutants associated with steam locomotives. In 2009, the GCR came up with the idea to burn nearly carbon-neutral waste vegetable oil as fuel to keep *No 4960* and eventually *No 29* on the rails regularly. In August 2016, Grand Canyon Railway staged a special event that drew passengers and curious onlookers from all over the United States. A steam double-header featuring *No 29* and *No 4960* pulled the *Williams Flyer* from Williams to Grand Canyon and back, with no diesel locomotive in the consist (formation). Vintage 1950s diesel-powered trains carry over 170,000 passengers a year and you can choose to stay overnight at the rim and return the next day.

GREAT SMOKY MOUNTAINS (*Mail address: 45 Mitchell St, Bryson City, NC;* *1 800 872 4681; gsmr.com*) With 53 miles (85km) of track, two tunnels and 25

bridges, the Great Smoky Mountains Railroad takes you on a memorable journey through a remote and beautiful corner of North Carolina. A variety of scenic excursions are available, departing from Bryson City and ranging from 3½ hours to a full day. The Nantahala Gorge Excursion carries you 44 miles (70km) to the Nantahala Gorge and back again, travelling along the Little Tennessee and Nantahala rivers and across Fontana Lake on a 700ft-long (213m) trestle and into the magic of the Nantahala Gorge. The Tuckasegee River Excursion is a 32-mile (51km) round trip along the Tuckasegee River through old railroad towns and scenic meadows. The historic *No 1702* Consolidation steam engine services both the Nantahala Gorge and Tuckasegee River excursions and is a unique piece of history dating back to 1942, when it was constructed during the official World War II Steam Engine plan. The Consolidation is one of the world's largest engines and this is one of only two remaining in the US. Prior to the departure, the *No 1702* is available for photo opportunities and you can meet and greet your crew, so you get a close and personal view of the fully restored engine. While on your ride, knowledgeable crew members will answer your questions and point out important landmarks along the way. On return to Bryson City, on select days there are live turntable demonstrations, where volunteers will be called upon to assist the crew in the manual turning of the 353,540lb (160,363kg) engine and tender. Steam passengers can watch this exciting activity and receive an exclusive souvenir ticket.

Trains operate five days a week from April and every day during summer and autumn. There are open-air cars, traditional sealed-window coaches and air-conditioned lounge cars.

HEBER VALLEY (*Mail address: 450 South 600 W, Heber City, UT 84032;* ☎ *435 654 5601;* w *hebervalleyrr.org*) This 32-mile (51km) journey is a 3½-hour round trip from Heber City, Utah, starting from a replica depot constructed in 2001 using techniques from the late 1800s. It looks very similar to the New Meadows, Idaho, depot on the former Idaho & Northern Pacific line (later Union Pacific, now abandoned). The original 1899 Denver & Rio Grande Western depot in Heber City still exists and is used by a stonework/monument dealer. Trains cross farmlands of the Heber Valley, follow the shore of Deer Creek Lake and travel down into a majestic canyon, following the beautiful Provo River to Vivian Park. Look out for the abundant wildlife, including bald eagles, deer and elk.

The Denver & Rio Grande Western was built to serve the pioneers who first settled in this valley. The railroad hauled freight in and livestock out, and in the 1930s and early 1940s, more sheep were transported by rail from the Heber Valley than from anywhere else in the country. A new highway eventually took away traffic so in 1967 the line was abandoned, becoming a recreational railroad in 1970.

Today, 1920s coaches are pulled by two 1907 Baldwin steam locomotives and three vintage diesel-electrics. Utah's oldest steam railroad has featured in many television shows, such as *Touched by an Angel* and *Promised Land*, and the engine, along with its ten railroad cars, has appeared in more than 30 films over the past 20 years. Special events include Murder Mysteries, Raft the River, the Vivian Park Dinner Train, the Sunset Special Barbecue Train (a steam service with bluegrass musical entertainment), Cinco de Mayo in May, Haunted Canyon in October and Polar Express in November/December. From December to March the 'Tube 'n' Train' offers snow tubing at Soldier Hollow, site of the 2002 Olympic Winter Games biathlon and cross-country skiing events. The steam train service operates daily from May to the end of October, otherwise at weekends year-round.

HOCKING VALLEY (*Mail address: 33 W Canal, PO Box 427, Nelsonville, OH 45764;* ❧*740 753 9531 (at the depot),* ❧*614 470 1300 or* ❧*1 800 867 7834;* **w** *hvsry.org*) Trains make a 14-mile (23km) round trip to Haydenville or a 22-mile (35km) trip to Logan over a Chesapeake & Ohio route. This was part of the original Hocking Valley Railway and is now on the National Register of Historic Places. You leave from Nelsonville, Ohio, where 11 cabooses are on display, including an ex-Hocking Valley caboose. Trains make a stop at the 19th-century settlers' village of Robbins Crossing. A 1920 steam-powered Baldwin locomotive has also been returned to service.

HUCKLEBERRY (*Mail address: 5045 Stanley Rd, Flint, MI 48506;* ❧*810 736 7100 or* ❧*1 800 648 7275;* **w** *geneseecountyparks.org/crossroads-village*) Despite its name, the Huckleberry Railroad is not a toy ride. The name refers to the first *Pere Marquette*-line trains which often travelled so slowly that passengers could hop off to pick huckleberries (wild blueberries) en route, then reboard before the caboose reached them. Today's ride is somewhat faster as a historic Baldwin locomotive takes open and closed wooden coaches from the old Denver & Rio Grande Western and Rio Grande Southern for an 8 mile (13km) journey.

The Huckleberry Railroad operates in conjunction with Crossroads Village, a collection of 30 historic buildings that includes a working blacksmith's shop and the Davison depot from the Grand Trunk & Western Railroad. The Huckleberry Railroad operates three locomotives, two cabooses, one hopper car and a motor car (Speeder). The train travels over a portion of the original *Pere Marquette* roadbed so you ride along the shores of Mott Lake, with great views and a good chance of seeing deer or other wildlife. During special event weekends such as those at Christmas and Halloween, there are decorations along the track.

Trains operate daily from May to early September. Amtrak's *International* train stops in Flint.

KENTUCKY RAILWAY MUSEUM (*Mail address: PO Box 240, 136 S Main, New Haven, KY 40051;* ❧*502 549 5470 or* ❧*1 800 272 0152;* **w** *kyrail.org;* ⊕ *daily*) Located in the heartland of Kentucky, the Kentucky Railway Museum is one of the oldest rail museums in the United States. Founded in Louisville in 1954, the KRM now owns 17 miles (28km) of the ex-Louisville & Nashville Lebanon branch, with operating headquarters in New Haven and a passenger boarding area in Boston, Kentucky.

Steam and diesel trains operate on alternate weekends between New Haven and Boston, travelling through the Rolling Fork River Valley on a track built in 1857. A fine collection of Kentucky railway history has been assembled, including the only operating Louisville & Nashville steam locomotive and the largest set of L&N passenger equipment anywhere. A new museum building replicates the original New Haven depot.

Steam train and locomotive cab rides take place from late May to the end of October. Diesel trains operate at weekends until mid-December. Dining trips are available from the Louisville, Harrods Creek & Westport Railroad Foundation on the third Saturday of each month except January.

LITTLE RIVER (*Mail address: 29 W Park Av, Coldwater, MI 49036;* ❧*517 227 5488;* **w** *littleriverrailroad.com*) From Coldwater, Michigan, trains travel 10 miles (16km) to Batavia (80 minutes) or 24 miles (40km) to White Pigeon (2½ hours) over tracks of the Michigan Southern Railroad. The engine used, *No 110*, was built in 1911 at the Baldwin Locomotive Works in Philadelphia. It was made specially for Colonel

Townsend's Little River Railroad and is the smallest standard-gauge, Pacific-type steam locomotive ever to be manufactured. Trains operate mostly on Sundays from April to December.

MID CONTINENT (*Mail address: PO Box 358, North Freedom, WI 53951-0358;* ☏ *608 522 4261 or* ☏ *1 800 930 1385;* w *midcontinent.org*) Trains make a 7-mile (11km), 55-minute journey from North Freedom, Wisconsin, along a former branch line of the Chicago & North Western Railroad. This was built in 1903 along the beautiful Baraboo River Valley to an old quartzite quarry. The **Mid Continent Railway Museum** is today dedicated to preserving and interpreting railroad history, especially that of the Upper Midwest during its golden age (1880–1916).

The restored depot was built in 1894 by the Chicago & North Western Railway at Rock Springs, 3 miles (5km) west of North Freedom, and moved to the museum in 1965. Similar designs were used in small communities across the C&NW system in the 1890s, including those at Waunakee and Wonewoc. The interior has two waiting rooms separated by the ticket office, with a freight room on the end, now occupied by the museum gift shop. The exterior has been painted in original C&NW colours. Next to the depot are a dozen steam engines, 33 vintage coaches, 19 cabooses and 33 freight cars, including a wooden tank car for transporting vinegar. Sadly the caboose is now only to be found in museums since it was replaced in the 1980s by the end of train device (ETD), which has a strobe light to mark the end of the train and a radio link to send information to the locomotive cab.

Other structures on site include a Soo Line watchman's tower which formerly stood in Neenah and a tool house for the section crew, moved here from Fond du Lac in 1981. The turntable was removed from an abandoned Milwaukee Road yard and roundhouse in Madison and brought to North Freedom in 1988 but is yet to be installed.

Diesel-powered trains operate at weekends from May to early September, with daily operations from Memorial Day through to Labor Day. There are also autumn and winter special excursions.

NEVADA NORTHERN RAILWAY MUSEUM (*Mail address: 1100 Av A, PO Box 150040, E Ely, NV 89315-0040;* ☏ *775 289 2085 or* ☏ *866 407 8326;* w *nnry.com;* ⊕ *daily*) The 'best preserved shortline in America' and a National Historic Landmark was one of the last great mining railroads built in the early 20th century, carrying millions of tons of ore from the copper mines at Ely. Completed in 1906 by the Nevada Consolidated Copper Company (later the Kennecott Corporation), the Nevada Northern stretched from Ely to the Southern Pacific Railroad line at Cobre, located about 139 miles (220km) to the north. The rails were later extended west to Lane City and Ruth. This railroad provided regular Pullman services until 1920 and carried passengers until 1938. It ceased regular freight operations in 1983, and that year the line was donated to the White Pine Historical Railroad Foundation to run as a working railroad museum.

Two classic steam locomotives are operated by the railway, pulling an original 1882 Pullman coach, a 1907 baggage/RPO (railway post office) and an open-top flat-car with benches. The 14-mile (22km) round trip takes you around downtown Ely then past the ghost town of Lane City to the historic mining area of Keystone. You travel through one of the few curved tunnels in the world and along the scenic Robinson Canyon. Or you might take the 'Hiline' route above the Steptoe Valley, powered by a vintage Alco diesel engine.

You can visit the roundhouse, machine and blacksmith shops and view the historic rolling stock of steam, diesel and electric locomotives as well as turn-of-the-century passenger and freight cars.

Steam and diesel rides take place at weekends from mid-April and in October, November and December. Daily operations begin in mid-May and go through to September. In February the museum offers special photographers' events. There are guided tours daily from May to October and exhibitions include the general office, depot and dispatcher's office.

NEVADA STATE RAILROAD MUSEUM (*Mail address: 2180 S Carson St, Carson City, NV 89701;* ✆*775 687 6953;* w *nevadaculture.org;* ☺ *daily*) The museum houses over 60 pieces of railroad equipment from Nevada's past, including five steam locomotives and several restored coaches and freight cars. Most of this material is from the Virginia & Truckee Railroad, America's richest and most famous short line.

Museum activities include the operation of historic railroad equipment, lectures, an annual railroad history symposium and other special events. Steam trains operate on some weekends from May to December. Amtrak's *California Zephyr* stops at Reno and Truckee.

NEW HOPE & IVYLAND (*Mail address: 32 W Bridge St, New Hope, PA 18938;* ✆*215 862 2332;* w *newhoperailroad.com*) A vintage Baldwin Consolidation coal-fired steam locomotive takes restored vintage coaches over a 9-mile (15km) round trip in about an hour, leaving New Hope's picturesque 1891 station at 32 W Bridge Street for Lahaska along a branch line of the old Reading Railroad. Steam passenger service between New Hope and Buckingham Valley began in 1966, and the New Hope & Ivyland Railroad ran one of the last regularly scheduled steam-powered mixed freights east of Mississippi. The NHIR became bankrupt in 1971, but the line was successfully operated by McHugh Brothers Heavy Hauling Inc until 1989. From 1980, the volunteer New Hope Steam Railway (NHSR) operated weekend excursions.

The railroad was sold to the present owners, the Bucks County Railroad Preservation and Restoration Corporation, in 1990 and since then the New Hope & Ivyland has been completely restored to its original ambience at a cost of $2 million. The New Hope Station, freight house and boarding platform were refurbished and tracks rebuilt before steam passenger services resumed in 1991. Freight services also continue to expand and prosper.

The Lahaska Station features a pretty picnic grove for the exclusive use of passengers and the freight house at New Hope has a gift shop. Narrated trips take you through attractive Pennsylvania countryside by way of Pauline's Trestle and part of the Underground Railroad route. Passenger steam trains operate daily from April to November, otherwise at weekends. A *Fireworks Express* runs on Independence Day and there are other special trains throughout the year, including fall foliage trains, which run the entire length of the railroad, and the *Evening Star Dinner Train*, which runs on two Saturdays during the spring, summer and autumn months. Two other steam locomotives are also being restored to operating condition.

The nearest Amtrak stops are New York, Philadelphia, Princeton and Trenton.

OREGON COAST (*Mail address: PO Box 669, Tillamook, OR 97141;* ✆*888 718 4253 for tickets & 503 842 7972 for information;* w *oregoncoastscenic.org*) The Oregon Coast Scenic Railroad is a registered non-profit museum organisation that operates over the former Southern Pacific and Port of Tillamook Bay railroads.

Regular scheduled trains pulled by a 1910 Heisler or a 1925 Baldwin travel between Garibaldi and Rockaway Beach, with special-event trains throughout the year over the rest of the line, which extends from the Tillamook Air Museum blimp hangar on the south side of Tillamook through Garibaldi, Rockaway Beach and Wheeler where the tracks turn to the east and head up into the coast range along the remote and breathtaking Nehalem and Salmonberry river canyons. Founded in 2003, the Oregon Coast Scenic Railroad has grown from its humble beginnings dodging freight trains in Garibaldi on weekend runs to Rockaway Beach and Wheeler to the sole operator of 46 miles (74km) of the railroad between the Tillamook airport and a point 2 miles (3km) east of the railroad siding of Enright in the Oregon Coast Range.

The 10-mile (16km) 90-minute trips run daily in summer months, with special excursions year-round. You can ride in a flatcar, in the restored 1924 Wilson River coach or, for an extra fee, in the steam locomotive's cab.

RAILTOWN (*Mail address: 10501 Reservoir Rd, PO Box 1250, Jamestown, CA 95327;* ☏ *209 984 3953 or* ☏ *916 445 6645 (recorded information);* w *railtown1897. org;* ☉ *daily*) This California State Historic Park is at Fifth Avenue and Reservoir Road, Jamestown. The Sierra Railway buildings include the only operating steam roundhouse in the west, dating from 1897 and still in original condition. As well as the Sierra's six-stall roundhouse, turntable and main yards, Railtown maintains two operating steam locomotives (with three others located on site) and a wide range of railroad equipment, making this one of the most comprehensive and best-preserved steam railroad sites in the country. Railtown is managed by the **California State Railroad Museum** (CSRM), located at 125 I Street in Sacramento (☏ *916 323 9280;* w *californiarailroad.museum*). The nearest Amtrak stops are Stockton and Riverbank.

The Sierra has appeared in more television shows, commercials and movies than any other railway. The first-known filming was in 1919 for a silent serial called *The Red Glove* and the railroad has featured in *High Noon, Little House on the Prairie, Unforgiven* and *Back to the Future III*. Among the museum's exhibits is a classic Model T purchased in Sonora in 1919, and converted into a railcar for use by the Sierra Railway as a roadmaster's car. Steam trains operate in the 'gold country' of the Sierra Nevada foothills, travelling to the Jamestown Rock siding and back among rolling hills, open pastures and beside a quiet creek. These 6-mile (9.6km), 40-minute excursions take place at weekends from April to October and on Memorial Day and Labor Day.

The award-winning *Polar Bear Express* operates over the holiday season starting the weekend after Thanksgiving and running until mid-December. Pulled by the iconic Sierra *No 3* steam locomotive and headed straight to the North Pole, the staff and volunteers at Railtown 1897 go to great lengths to re-create the holiday experience depicted in the classic children's book of the same name by Chris Van Allsburg. The experience includes souvenir tickets, hot cocoa, festive cookies, Santa Claus sightings and the coveted silver bells – the first gift of Christmas for those who still believe in Santa Claus.

ROARING CAMP & BIG TREES (*Mail address: 5401 Graham Hill Rd, PO Box G-1, Felton, CA 95018;* ☏ *831 335 4484;* w *roaringcamp.com*) This is America's last steam-powered passenger railroad with a year-round passenger service (weekends only during winter). The Roaring Camp & Big Trees Narrow Gauge Railroad was founded in 1958 by F Norman Clark, who restored two railway lines that operated in the Santa Cruz Mountains from the late 1880s to the early 1920s. The Big Trees rail line dates from 1857, and was used by residents of San Francisco and other East Bay cities at weekends and in the summer to take them from their communities to the Big Trees (redwood forests) and to Santa Cruz (the beach). It was often referred to as 'the Picnic Line'. Today the Roaring Camp & Big Trees Narrow Gauge Railroad still operates an old-fashioned steam passenger train service providing visitors with a rare opportunity to ride through some of the country's most beautiful and primitive scenery.

Trains leave the 1880 South Pacific Coast depot on Graham Hill Road at Felton, California, for a 6-mile (10km) excursion lasting 1¼ hours on a 36-inch-gauge (91cm) track between Roaring Camp and the top of Bear Mountain. You travel among the earliest preserved redwoods, then go through Spring Canyon into the Santa Cruz Mountains. On returning to the depot, you can explore an 1880s general store or visit the adjacent **Henry Cowell Redwoods State Park**.

Trains operate daily from April to October, otherwise weekends only. Numerous special events take place throughout the year. The nearest Amtrak stop is San Jose.

SILVER CREEK & STEPHENSON (*Mail address: SCAEC, 2954 S Walnut Rd, PO Box 255, Freeport, IL 61032;*❮*815 235 2198 or*❮*815 232 2306;* w *thefreeportshow. com/scs.htm*) This is located at Walnut and Lamm roads, Silver Creek, just south of the Stephenson County Fairgrounds. The Stephenson County Antique Engine Club purchased nearly 2 miles (3km) of rights of way from the bankrupt Chicago, Milwaukee, St Paul & Pacific Railroad in 1983, and volunteers from the club relaid the track. The shed, which houses Heisler, Brookville and Plymouth locomotives and their maintenance facilities, was erected in 1986. The Silver Creek depot, dedicated in 1993, was built from original plans for the Illinois Central depot in Elroy, Illinois. It contains a large collection of railroad memorabilia, including advertising signs and a working telegraph.

Trains leave the replica depot to travel through Illinois farmland, crossing Yellow Creek on a 30ft-high (9m) stone pier bridge, operating at weekends between May and October. Amtrak Thruway buses stop at Rockford, 15 miles (24km) east.

ST LOUIS, IRON MOUNTAIN & SOUTHERN (*Mail address: 252 E Jackson Bd, PO Box 244, Jackson, MO 63755;*❮*573 243 1688;* w *slimrr.com*) The route goes from Jackson, Missouri, along a Missouri Pacific branch line. Journeys last 1½ hours (to Gordonville), 2 hours (Dutchtown) or 5 hours (Delta). 'The most daring train robbery on record' took place on the railroad in 1874, when Jesse James and his gang held up the *Little Rock Express* at Gad's Hill. In 1902, William Helms, a 72-year-old farmer, was walking along the St Louis, Iron Mountain & Southern Railway where it crosses Big River near Irondale. He saw *No 4* speed northbound over the bridge then heard a strange noise and found an old-fashioned telescoping valise that had fallen from the train. It contained a five-day-old baby, badly bruised after falling 50ft (15m). Helms took the child home to his wife and they nursed him back to health. The story spread throughout the United States and became a folksong ('The Ballad of the Iron Mountain Baby'), and many women claimed to be the mother. The elderly couple later adopted him and he went on to attend Braughton's University and Southwest Missouri State Teachers' College, paid for by the St Louis Iron Mountain & Southern Railway. When he died in 1953, the corpse was carried by train back to Washington County – only the second time William had ridden a train. The story is also the subject of another song, 'Sarah Jane and the Iron Mountain Baby', recorded by Steve Martin and Edie Brickell.

Trains operate at weekends from April to October, and on Saturdays in November and March.

TEXAS STATE (*Mail address: PO Box 1544, Ogden, UT 84402;* \ *855 632 7729;* w *texasstaterailroad.net*) The railroad is located between Rusk (*535 Park Rd 76*) and Palestine (*789 Park Road 70*) on part of the 1896 Texas State Railroad. This line was originally built and run by inmates from the East Texas State Penitentiary to transport iron ore to the prison's furnaces in Rusk. Prisoners were paid 50 cents a day and worked from sunrise to sundown, so the total cost to construct the 32 miles (51km) of track was only $573,724. Prison crews made up the train staff (except for the engineer), but when passenger service was extended to Palestine a crew of nine was employed. With the exception of the superintendent and engineer, staff members were paid $1.01 for each day they worked.

The iron furnace was dismantled in 1913, and the penitentiary converted into a state mental hospital. Regular train service was discontinued in 1921, and the line leased to the Texas & New Orleans (Southern Pacific Railroad Company). The Texas Southeastern Railroad leased the line in the early 1960s and continued operations until December 1969, after which it was conveyed to the Texas Parks and Wildlife Department. State inmates were again brought in to rebuild the track by clearing brush, building bridges and replacing ties and rails. The Texas State Railroad State Historical Park opened to the public on 4 July 1976 as part of the nation's bicentennial celebrations.

There are four historic steam locomotives (including three Baldwins and another) on display, as well as four diesels (including a classic restored FP9 streamlined locomotive). Trains depart from historically accurate stations in either Rusk or Palestine for a 4-hour, 50-mile (80km) round trip among rolling hardwood creek bottoms and flowering dogwood trees, crossing 24 bridges – one over 1,000ft (304m) long. As well as train excursions, the park offers steam engine shop tours and tours of the 1927 Texas & Pacific *No 610* Lima steam engine, plus train seminars and workshops.

Diesel trains operate from Rusk (February–April) and steam locomotives from Palestine (May–July). Amtrak's nearest stop is Longview, served by the *Texas Eagle*.

TWEETSIE (*Mail address: 300 Tweetsie Railroad Lane, Blowing Rock, NC 28605;* \ *828 264 9061 or* \ *1 800 526 5740;* w *tweetsie.com*) The East Tennessee & Western North Carolina Railroad Company was given permission in 1866 for the construction of a railroad from Johnson City, Tennessee, to the iron mines across the state line at Cranberry, North Carolina. The ET&WNC line (sometimes called the 'Eat Taters & Wear No Clothes' Railroad) began operations in 1881 over 50 miles (80km) of track through the Blue Ridge chain of the Appalachian Mountains. The line was extended to Boone, North Carolina, in 1916 to serve passengers and haul lumber.

The railroad was nicknamed the 'Tweetsie' because of the shrill 'tweet, tweet' of its train whistle echoing through the hills. Severe floods damaged sections of the line in 1940, and hastened its closure in 1950. Gene Autry, the movie cowboy, bought engine *No 12*, the last remaining of 13 coal-fired ET&WNC steam engines, intending to use it out West in films. The locomotive was later bought by Grover Robbins Jr for $1 and returned to his home town of Blowing Rock to be restored, along with some of the original ET&WNC railcars. Engine *No 190* is a narrow-gauge steam locomotive built in 1943 by Baldwin Locomotive Works and used in Alaska during World War II by the US Army. It was later put into service on the

White Pass & Yukon Railroad, where it was called the *Yukon Queen*. *No 190* was brought to Tweetsie Railroad in 1960.

These engines are now used on the new Tweetsie Railroad, which had its first run in 1957. Trains follow a scenic 3-mile (5-km) loop through the mountains near Blowing Rock, not far from the original end-of-the-line station in Boone. You can watch cancan girls at the Palace Saloon, chat with cowboys and gunslingers on Main Street, visit the deer park, or ride a chairlift to Miner's Mountain to pan for gold.

Trains operate daily from late May to late August, or on Fridays and weekends from late August to the end of October, plus Labor Day. Amtrak's nearest stop is Gastonia, North Carolina, served by the *Crescent*.

VALLEY (*Mail address: 1 Railroad Av, PO Box 452, Essex, CT 06426;* ❧*860 767 0103 or* ❧*1 800 377 3987;* w *essexsteamtrain.com*) The Valley Railroad was created soon after the Civil War, when steamboats ruled the Connecticut River. The line failed to prosper though, since the Connecticut River was sparsely settled and there were insufficient passengers or freight for it to succeed. The railroad was resurrected in 1971 with the running of a passenger train, 100 years to the day after the first one travelled north from Saybrook on the shore of Long Island Sound up the river to Hartford. In 1871, there had been pauses to finish some stretches of track and to saw off pieces of stations that stood too near the tracks. The Essex steam train takes a 12-mile (19km) trip through unspoiled Connecticut countryside between Essex and Chester on a New Haven Railroad branch line, stopping at Deep River. Optional boat trips aboard the *Becky Thatcher* riverboat can be taken on the Connecticut River.

Trains operate daily from May to October. The nearest Amtrak stop is Old Saybrook.

VIRGINIA & TRUCKEE (*Mail address: PO Box 339, Carson City, NV 89702-0339;* ❧*775 885 6833;* w *steamtrain.org*) The Virginia & Truckee Railroad was built in 1869 to connect Virginia City with the Carson River Valley. By 1874, the 'Queen of the Short Lines' had been extended to Reno and as many as 50 trains a day carried passengers, supplies and silver ore through Virginia City.

Today you can take half-hour rides along part of the Virginia & Truckee line through the famous Comstock mining area, with the benefit of an informed commentary from the conductor riding in the caboose. Look for exposed silver ore along the track and occasional sightings of wild mustangs in the surrounding Flowery Mountains. The route takes you through Tunnel Number Four, one of six tunnels constructed to allow trains to descend nearly 1,600ft (488m) from Virginia City to the valley floor.

The station is at Washington and F, Virginia City, Nevada. Trains operate daily from May to September, or at weekends in October. Amtrak's nearest stop is Reno, served by the *California Zephyr*.

WESTERN MARYLAND (*Mail address: 13 Canal St, Cumberland, MD 21502;* ❧*301 759 4400 or* ❧*1 800 872 4650;* w *wmsr.com*) Trains leave Cumberland's 1913 station (which also has the C & O Canal Museum and Visitor Center) and travel west on Western Maryland and Cumberland & Pennsylvania tracks among the Allegheny Mountains, climbing grades of up to 2.8%. On the 32-mile (52km), 3-hour round trip you go through the Cumberland Narrows, negotiate the spectacular Helmstetter's Horseshoe Curve and travel through the 914ft-long (278km) Brush Tunnel under Piney Mountain. You also pass the castle at Mount Savage and make a stop at Frostburg's historic restored depot. Make sure you watch the locomotive get turned on the turntable.

Steam trains run from Friday to Sunday between May and mid-September, Thursday to Sunday in October and at weekends. Diesel trains operate on Thursdays from May to August, and on Tuesdays and Wednesdays in October. Steam and diesel trains also operate occasionally for special trains and charters.

Amtrak's *Capitol Limited* stops at Cumberland (about four blocks away).

WHITE MOUNTAIN CENTRAL (*Mail address: 110 Daniel Webster Highway, PO Box 1, Lincoln, NH 03251;* ☎ *603 745 8913;* w *whitemountaincentralrr.com*) A half-hour journey through the attractive White Mountains begins at Clark's Trading Post depot near Lincoln, New Hampshire. Among the other entertainments are an 1890s replica railway station, freight car displays, a haunted house, trained bears, a Victorian-style Main Street and a 1920s garage. The 2½-mile (4km) woodland ride takes you from the trading post up a 2% grade and across the Pemigewasset River through the Howe-Truss covered bridge, the only standing covered bridge still in use. Between 1963 and 1965, the bridge was dismantled at its location in East Montpelier, Vermont, before being transported and reassembled here across the river.

The railroad has been in operation for more than 40 years since the Clark brothers began to rescue steam locomotives from the cutting torch to create 'green pastures for Iron Horses'. Salvaged locos now include a 1927 Heisler once owned by the International Shoe Company as well as former Beebe River Railroad and East Branch & Lincoln engines. The restored wood-burning Climax locomotive weighs 42 US tons (38 tonnes) and is one of only three in the world still in working order. The depot opens at weekends from May to mid-October and daily in July and August.

WHITEWATER VALLEY (*Mail address: PO Box 406, Connersville, IN 47331;* ☎ *765 825 2054;* w *whitewatervalleyrr.org*) Indiana's longest scenic railway runs between Connersville and the restored town of Metamora, next to the old Whitewater Canal. The Whitewater River formed a natural trade route for Native Americans and early settlers, and a canal was built in the mid-19th century. In 1863, the Indianapolis & Cincinnati Railroad acquired the right to build on the old towpath and its subsidiary, the White Water Valley Railroad, reached Connersville in 1867. It continued on to Hagerstown in 1868, but passenger service ended in 1933 and freight traffic in 1972.

Today's Whitewater Valley Railroad operates along 18 miles (30km) of track purchased in 1983, plus an additional mile in Connersville. It uses historic diesel locomotives and open-window coaches on a regular schedule from Connersville to Metamora. Another service, the Metamora Shuttle, carries passengers further south on a 2-mile (3.2km) excursion along the restored canal, past the canal boat dock, a working aqueduct and a restored lock. The railroad's *Baldwin Prairie* locomotive is currently out of action and awaiting repairs.

Trains operate at weekends and on holidays from the first weekend in May to the last weekend in October, as well as at Christmas. Amtrak's *Cardinal* stops in Connersville.

WILMINGTON & WESTERN (*Mail address: PO Box 5787, Wilmington, DE 19808-0787;* ☎ *302 998 1930;* w *wwrr.com*) The Wilmington & Western Railroad opened in 1872 to move goods from the mills along the Red Clay Creek to the Port of

Wilmington. Today's railroad operates steam- and diesel-powered tourist trains on 10 miles (16km) of track between Greenbank and Hockessin. Starting from the impressive new Greenbank Station 4 miles (6.5km) southwest of Wilmington, trains travel 10 miles (15km) to Mount Cuba over part of the Landenberg branch line (Sundays, May to December). Or you can travel past Mount Cuba along the Red Clay Creek Valley to Yorklyn or Hockessin (June to October). There are special trains throughout the year, including dinner trains and the *Firework Express*. Amtrak's nearest stop is Wilmington.

YOSEMITE MOUNTAIN-SUGAR PINE (*Mail address: 56001 Yosemite Highway 41, Fish Camp, CA 93623;* ✆ *559 683 7273;* w *ymsprr.com*) From 1899 to 1931, the Madera Sugar Pine Lumber Company operated many miles of narrow-gauge railroad track. Almost 1.5 billion board feet (35,400,000,000m³) of lumber were harvested and transported to the mill on massive log trains by five wood-burning Shay locomotives.

Located south of Yosemite National Park among California's Sierra Nevada, today's Yosemite Mountain-Sugar Pine Railroad is a restoration of the old 36-inch-gauge (91cm) line. A section of the railbed has been reconstructed using the same techniques used originally and two restored Shay steam locomotives were brought from the Westside Lumber Company to provide authentic motive power. *No 15* was built in 1913, and weighs 60 tons (54,000kg). *No 10*, built in 1928, weighs 83 tons (75,000kg) and is the heaviest operating narrow-gauge Shay engine in existence. Railcars which once provided transportation for logging and track repair crews have been refurbished for passenger use on narrated tours. The trains reach 5,000ft (1,800m) before descending through Lewis Creek Canyon and Cold Spring Crossing.

Logger steam trains operate daily from March to October. Antique Model A Ford gas engines power trolley-like 'Jenny' cars over the route every half-hour, except when steam trains are in action. Amtrak's nearest stop is Merced, on the *San Joaquin* route.

29

Part Three

ON CANADIAN RAILS

Location North America, bordering the North Atlantic Ocean to the east, north Pacific Ocean to the west, and the Arctic Ocean to the north

Neighbouring countries USA

Size/area 3,855,102 square miles (9,984,670km²). The second-largest country in the world (after Russia)

Climate Temperate in the south to sub-arctic and arctic in the north

Status Confederation with parliamentary democracy

Population 36,877,687 (April 2018)

Capital Ottawa

Other main cities Toronto, Montreal, Vancouver, Calgary, Edmonton, Quebec, Winnipeg

Economy Canada has the world's 16th-largest economy and the lowest governmental debt among members of the Group of Eight (G8). Agriculture 1.6%; industry 27.7%; services 70.7% (2017).

GDP Cdn$1.64 trillion (2017)

Languages English 58.1% (official), French 21.4% (official), Chinese 3.5%, other 17.8%

Religion Roman Catholic 38.7%, Protestant 17.2%, Orthodox 6.2%, other 37.9%

Currency Canadian dollar; Cdn$1 = 100 cents

Exchange rate €1 = Cdn$1.50, £1 = Cdn$1.72, US$1 = Cdn$1.33 (February 2019)

International telephone code +1

Time Canada has six primary time zones. From east to west these are: Newfoundland Time Zone; Atlantic Time Zone; Eastern Time Zone; Central Time Zone; Mountain Time Zone; and Pacific Time Zone.

Electrical voltage 120V/60Hz standard plugs have two parallel flat pins ('American' type) or have two pins with an earth connector. Adapters cost a few dollars.

Weights and measures Metric system (kilometres, litres, etc)

Flag The Maple Leaf has two vertical bands of red, with a white square between them containing an 11-pointed red maple leaf

National anthem 'O Canada'

National flower Maple leaf

National bird/animal Gray jay/beaver

National sports Ice hockey, basketball, lacrosse, baseball, American football, soccer

RAILWAYS In 2015, Canadian railroads employed about 32,000 people to maintain and operate a total of 38,012 miles (61,174km) of track – the fifth-largest network in the world. This is mostly owned by the Canadian National (20,400 miles/32,831km) and Canadian Pacific (12,500 miles/20,000km) railways. Over 84 million passengers (including 79 million commuters) and 335 million US tons (304 million tonnes) of freight were transported in 2015.

VIA Rail operates most intercity passenger services, with around four million passengers in 2017 and almost 95% of total revenues. Other passenger services include the Algoma Central, Ontario Northland and Quebec North Shore & Labrador. Amtrak serves Montreal, Vancouver and Toronto (the last in conjunction with VIA Rail). The Great Canadian Railtour Company has seasonal services between Vancouver, Calgary and Jasper.

Canada's Trains Today

Canada may be the only country in the world with a written constitution linking its formation to the building of a railway. British Columbia threatened to join the United States if it wasn't given its rail line, so a parliamentary act in 1867 proclaimed the construction of the Intercolonial Railway 'essential to the consolidation of the Union of British North America'. As a result, 4,000 miles (6,500km) of iron road was laid from the Atlantic to the Pacific. In 1871, British Columbia agreed to join the Confederation and trains have been a crucial part of Canada's history ever since.

A short tramway is thought to have been built in 1720 during the construction of a fort at Louisburg, Nova Scotia, and others later opened elsewhere to transport stone, coal and lumber. Canada's first public railway, the Champlain & St Lawrence, opened in 1836 as a 14-mile (22km) route between Dorchester (now St-Jean), next to the Richelieu River, and La Prairie on the St Lawrence. The success of the Champlain & St Lawrence, and rail companies in the United States, encouraged further development, including the Grand Trunk Railway from Montreal to Toronto.

The Canadian Great Western Railway built the world's first sleeping car in 1857, inspiring the American Pullman design which came two years later. The Great Western originally operated between Windsor and Niagara Falls before extending to Hamilton and Toronto. An accident on the Grand Trunk Railway in Quebec in 1864 took 99 lives, making it Canada's worst ever railway disaster. The famous circus elephant, Jumbo (over 12ft/3.65m) tall and weighing almost 8 tons (8,000kg), was killed on the track at St Thomas in 1885 when he was accidentally struck from behind while being loaded into a GTR freight train.

The great transcontinental Canadian Pacific route opened in 1885, having been blasted through some of the world's hardest rock in temperatures as low as –50°F (–45°C). Among the workers were more than 6,000 Chinese, some of whom had remained in California after building the Union Pacific Railway. Working for a dollar a day (which they considered good money), many died from hard labour, disease and careless use of explosives. Others survived to found the first permanent Chinese community in British Columbia. A huge crowd gathered at the Eagle Pass, Craigallachie, for the last spike completion ceremony on 7 November 1885. The hard-drinking CPR president Sir William Cornelius Van Horne made a short speech that amounted to one word for each 200 miles (320km) of railway: 'All I can say is that the work has been well done in every way.'

Despite financial problems and the exceptionally difficult conditions, the track was completed in only 54 months, almost six years ahead of schedule. The first train ran 3,000 miles (4,800km) from Montreal's Dalhousie Square Station to British Columbia in 1886, travelling 139 hours through a harshly beautiful landscape which was then almost uninhabited. The train arrived on 9 November at its final destination, Port Moody, only 1 minute late. The 1949 movie *Canadian Pacific* tells

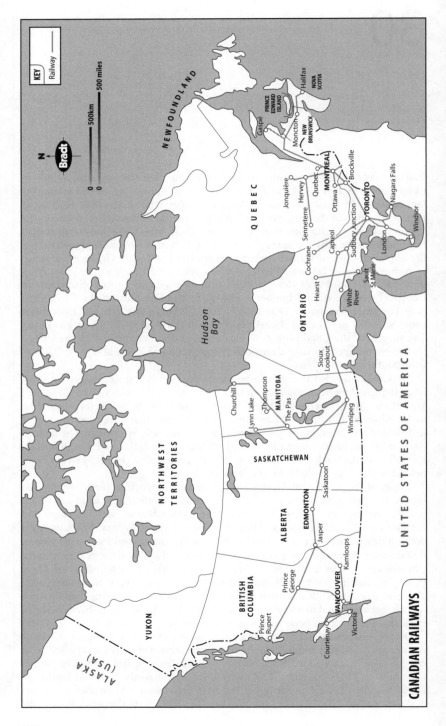

CANADIAN RAILWAYS

the story of the building of the railway rather fancifully but contains many shots of authentic locomotives and rolling stock.

The Canadian Northern line, later to become the Canadian National, reached Vancouver in 1915, going from Montreal via Hawkesbury, Ottawa, Capreol, Fort Frances, Winnipeg, Dauphin, North Battleford and Edmonton. The Grand Trunk Railway formed the Grand Trunk Pacific to run from Winnipeg to the West, reaching Prince Rupert on the Pacific by way of Yellowhead Pass. These railways and others began to open up the land to immigrants, farmers, mineral prospectors, wealthy travellers and land speculators. They created a crucial sense of nationhood in the world's second-largest country, bringing rapid development to what were otherwise isolated settlements along the way.

Sir William Cornelius Van Horne, head of the Canadian Pacific, tempted passengers westward by creating a chain of luxurious chateau-style hotels in spectacular settings. The Banff Springs Hotel (half chateau, half Scottish baronial mansion) opened in Banff National Park in 1886, and was succeeded by the Hotel Vancouver, the Empress Hotel in Victoria and Chateau Lake Louise. A railway surveyor, Tom Wilson, had in 1882 been the first white man to see Lake Louise, which is now one of the country's most popular skiing and tourist destinations. Canadian Pacific remains the largest hotel company in Canada.

Canada's rail network was among the biggest in the world by the year 1900, and more than 40,000 miles (64,400km) of track were in place by the end of World War I. The government took over the Canadian Northern company in 1917 and turned it into the Canadian National Railway, subsequently acquiring the Grand Trunk Pacific and other smaller operations. A transcontinental record was set on 4 November 1925 by the Canadian National with a trip from Montreal to Vancouver in 67 hours, when the engine ran non-stop to average 45mph (72km/h). As in other countries, the 20th century brought increasing competition from airlines, highways and motor cars, but even in the 1950s more than 6,000 locomotives and 200,000 passenger and freight cars were in service.

In 1955, just at the time when air travel was taking over, the prestige *Canadian* train was equipped with glamorous, state-of-the-art stainless-steel coaches. The last Canadian Pacific steam engines ran in 1960. Both CN and CP owned thousands of miles of track and had profitable freight operations, carrying cargoes such as wheat, coal and sulphur, but costs continued to mount for passenger trains. Annual passenger miles fell to around 20 million (one-third of the peak figure) and, like its US counterpart, the Canadian government was compelled to act.

VIA RAIL

Canada's equivalent to Amtrak began in 1977, when it took over most of the country's passenger services. VIA Rail has its own equipment and service personnel but uses tracks belonging to Canadian Pacific and Canadian National. The company employs nearly 3,000 people and operates more than 500 trains weekly, using 7,767 miles (12,500km) of track to serve over 400 communities. The fleet includes 426 passenger cars and 73 active locomotives. In addition to 121 railway stations, VIA Rail operates four modern maintenance facilities. While VIA Rail owns 138 miles (223km) of track, most of the infrastructure used by its passenger service is owned and managed by the freight railways, including ten different national and short-line operators.

Close to four million passengers travel on VIA Rail each year and the company joins Amtrak to operate several trains, including the *Adirondack* and *Maple*

Leaf (pages 270 and 314), connecting with cities in the United States. VIA Rail's equipment, although sometimes older than Amtrak's, is comfortable and has usually been refurbished to a high standard. VIA Rail is acquiring a new train fleet to replace the current rolling stock operating within the Quebec City–Windsor corridor, which serves the majority of passengers. By 2022, it expects to have new trains that are safer, faster, more comfortable, more accessible and more environmentally friendly.

ARRANGING YOUR TRIP

INFORMATION VIA Rail Canada Inc, CP/PO Box 8116 SUCC CENTRE-VILLE, Montreal, Quebec H3C 3N3; ☎800 681 2561 (Canada/USA). For general information and booking from anywhere in Canada, call ☎888 VIA RAIL (☎*888 8427245*) or ☎TTY 800 268 9503 (hearing impaired). From Moncton, New Brunswick, ☎506 857 9830. VIA Préférence, ☎888 VIA PREF (☎*888 842 7733*). Information on VIA Rail is also available online at w viarail.ca/en, and from Amtrak at 400 N Capitol Street, Washington, DC 20001 (☎*888 842 7245*). For Amtrak train information or to make Amtrak reservations when in Canada, call ☎1 800 872 7245. You can book travel online as well as on the VIA Rail mobile app, where you can view reservation details and modify your bookings. The app also offers easy access to all the information you need on boarding and at stations as well as real-time information on departures, arrivals and delays.

TICKETS Information, reservations and tickets can be obtained through the VIA Rail website (**w** *viarail.ca*) or from authorised travel agents and VIA sales offices. See page 382 for details of VIA agents abroad. Reservations may be made up to six months ahead and tickets can be ordered by mail and paid for by credit card at no extra cost. If you have not booked ahead, train conductors are able to issue a fare to a passenger not travelling beyond the end of the train run. Cash (Canadian or US dollars) or credit cards are accepted for payment.

Although VIA Rail does not normally accept responsibility for lost, stolen or destroyed tickets, you can apply for reimbursement by completing a lost ticket indemnity bond obtainable at VIA Rail offices.

Canrailpass The System Canrailpass provides access to the VIA Rail system throughout Canada for 60 consecutive days from the first date of travel, which must be selected at the time of purchase. The Corridor pass allows you to choose between seven and ten one-way trips between Quebec and Ontario for 21 consecutive days. Tickets must be obtained before boarding, and valid photo identification shown if requested by VIA personnel. The number of seats available to Canrailpass holders is limited and bookings must be made at least three days in advance of the travel date. One complimentary stopover (a break in the journey of 4 hours or more) per one-way trip is allowed at no additional charge.

Tickets booked using a pass may be cancelled at any time prior to the scheduled departure of the train, and the credit for the trip will be returned to the Canrailpass for future use within its validity period. Credits are not granted for tickets cancelled after the scheduled departure of the train. Passes are available both inside and outside Canada but are not valid for other Canadian railways. Senior citizens (those aged 60 or more), students and anyone aged up to 25 may qualify for senior/youth rates, saving around 10%.

The following prices (in Canadian dollars) currently apply (2018).

Canrailpass (unlimited)	Cdn$1,429
Canrailpass (unlimited)	Cdn$1,286 (youth/senior)
Canrailpass (7 tickets)	Cdn$761
Canrailpass (7 tickets)	Cdn$692 (youth/senior)
Canrailpass (10 tickets)	Cdn$989
Canrailpass (10 tickets)	Cdn$890 (youth/senior)

Commuter ePass The VIA Rail Commuter ePass is intended for business travellers and allows travel in Economy Class between two pre-determined cities within the Quebec City–Windsor corridor. Valid from the first time you use it for 20 one-way trips (ten round trips) within a 30-day period between the same two stations, the pass can be purchased and used to book train tickets online. An ePass costs Cdn$319 (Toronto–Cobourg), Cdn$327 (Toronto–Brantford), or Cdn$249 (Toronto–Oshawa). For an extra Cdn$100, you can also enjoy added perks like reserved seating and access to the business lounge. A valid rail ticket issued using the ePass credit is required when you travel.

CLASSES OF TRAVEL

Economy Class Economy Class provides adequate space, reclining seats and panoramic views, and is available on all trains. Light meals, snacks and beverages. Most Corridor trains offer free Wi-Fi access and have AC outlets for laptop use. You also have access to the Skyline car with its panoramic dome and lounges.

Business Class Except for short trips, Business Class is available on Corridor services between Windsor, Toronto, Ottawa, Montreal and Quebec City. This First-Class service offers pre-boarding privileges, meals complete with complimentary wine and liqueurs served at your seat, a mobile (cell) phone service, AC power outlets and free Wi-Fi. You also have access to private Business lounges with HD television news as well as complimentary beverages and newspapers in Toronto, Montreal, Dorval, Quebec City, Kingston, London and Ottawa.

On board, you have a reserved, generously cushioned seat and meals are included in the ticket price. On some trains, Business-Class passengers ride in European-designed Renaissance cars.

Sleeper Plus Class Provided to late-night passengers on lengthy routes, Sleeper Plus Class has berth sections and single, double, triple and four-person bedrooms which feature bunk beds, electrical outlet and chairs. Each sleeper car (except in the case of Renaissance cars) is equipped with a public shower. Berth seating consists of wide, sofa-style seats which convert at night into berths, with heavy curtains to ensure quiet and privacy. Passengers travelling alone can choose either an upper or lower berth. All necessary pillows and blankets are provided and Sleeper-Class passengers have access to a shower room with complimentary soap, shampoo and towel. Attendant and turndown service available. All meals and non-alcoholic drinks are included in the dining car, as well as complimentary coffee, tea, fruit and cookies in the lounge cars. You have access to the Vancouver and Toronto lounge upon departure, and to the Skyline, Panorama and (in season) the Park car. Priority boarding and check-in at major stations. Activities for children (games and movies).

Prestige Class Elite Sleeper Prestige-Class accommodation is available on the *Canadian* and *Ocean*. All meals in the dining car are included, with priority reservations and a pre-dining appetiser service. Complimentary coffee, tea, fruit and cookies in the lounge cars as well as all-inclusive alcoholic and non-alcoholic beverages and snacks. Access to the Skyline car, Panorama car (with reserved seating) and unrestricted access to the Park car (year-round, with reserved seating). Activities for children (games and movies).

The *Canadian* has been restored to its sleek 1950s splendour and its Park car, located at the rear of the train, comprises three separate saloons. The Dome gives panoramic views from an observation deck, while the uniquely shaped Bullet lounge below features wrap-around windows, armchairs and a relaxed atmosphere. In the Mural lounge you can admire Canadian artworks or play games such as chess and backgammon.

With the Sleeper Prestige-Class service your private room converts into a bedroom at night. Elegant and spacious cabins have a Murphy bed for two, a private washroom with shower, flat-screen monitor with video selection. Concierge, turndown service and enhanced amenities. You receive expedited baggage handling as well as priority boarding and check-in at major stations, plus access to the Vancouver and Toronto lounges on departure and arrival.

Touring Class Available on the Jasper–Prince Rupert train during peak period from mid-May to mid-October, Touring Class includes meals served at your seat and exclusive use of the Panorama and Park cars. All meals are included in the ticket price.

LRC Economy Class LRC (light, rapid, comfortable) equipment was built for VIA Rail in the early 1980s and is mostly used on VIA's busiest route, the Windsor–Quebec City corridor. Trains travel at speeds of up to 95mph (152km/h).

RESERVATIONS Reservations are required for all First-Class seats and sleeping cars, as well as for certain trains between Ontario, Quebec and the Maritime Provinces. Economy-Class seats are automatically guaranteed on purchase of your ticket. You can obtain reservations up to six months ahead from most travel agents or use the online booking engine on VIA Rail's website (w *viarail.ca*) to book your tickets, reserve hotel rooms and rent a car. Reservations can also be made by calling ☏ 1 888 VIA-RAIL (☏ *1 888 842-7245*) or by using Via Rail's mobile app for iPhone and Android, which lets you buy tickets, modify your bookings, save your e-boarding pass and consult real-time information.

DISCOUNTS A discount applies (except during holiday periods) for local travel in eastern Canada. Similar reductions are available in the Quebec–Windsor corridor every day except Friday, Sunday and holidays (five days' notice required). Between Toronto and Vancouver in off-peak periods there is a reduction on Economy and Sleeper Touring classes, and reductions are available on trains to Canada's more remote regions.

Seniors aged over 60 are entitled to a 10% discount on the Economy Plus fare and on regular Sleeper Plus and Touring fares. Special rates apply for groups of 20 people or more.

CHILDREN Those under two years of age accompanied by an adult (one child per adult) travel free when not occupying a seat. Infants must occupy a seat in Business Class but are entitled to a 25% discount. Children aged two–11 pay half the adult fare in Economy Class and get a 25% discount in Sleeper Class. They also receive a CHOO CHOO CLUB bag containing a fun activity book with games. Children under eight are not allowed to travel unaccompanied. Those aged eight–11 can travel with written permission from a parent or guardian provided certain other conditions are met, such as the signing of a liability waiver form (contact VIA Rail for details). Passengers with children get priority boarding and there are changing tables in the bathrooms, microwaves to heat baby bottles and food. Playpens and pushchairs (strollers) are allowed on board.

STUDENTS Full-time students no longer require an ISIC card – an identity card with your photo and date of birth will suffice. Students and travellers aged 12–25 are entitled to discounts on the Canrailpass, and an Unlimited Student Pass is available for Economy-Class travel for 120 days within one of three regions: Kingston–Windsor, Kingston–Quebec City, or Windsor–Quebec City. Cost is Cdn$549 (or Cdn$449 with some blackout dates). You can also purchase a VIA 6 Pak of tickets giving half-price travel between two pre-determined stations in the Quebec City–Windsor corridor or on board the *Ocean* across Montreal, Moncton and Halifax. VIA 6 Paks can be ordered on VIA's website (**w** *viarail.ca*) for delivery by mail or for collection at a station or travel agent of your choice.

CONNECTIONS Published connections with other trains, buses or ferries are not guaranteed and are subject to change without notice. VIA makes every effort to keep to schedules but does not accept responsibility for delays or inconvenience. You should allow at least an hour between trains when planning your itinerary. If a train is running late, its stopping time at stations may be reduced.

PAYMENT Credit cards can be used for buying tickets and meals or to upgrade accommodation. Debit cards and cash are accepted at most stations. If you purchase a ticket with cash at a VIA Rail station you will need to present either a valid government-issued piece of identification with photograph, showing your full name, or two valid government-issued pieces of identification with no photograph, showing your full name. Self-service kiosks only accept debit cards. You can also purchase with VIA Préférence points online (see below). If you have enough points for your selected trip, you will automatically see the VIA Préférence option as method of payment during your online booking process. Fares and accommodation prices are subject to a 7% goods and services tax.

Refunds If your travel plans alter you should notify VIA Rail as soon as possible. Refunds on most tickets, either unused or partially used, can be provided immediately at any VIA sales office or at the travel agency which issued the ticket. If a refund cannot be made straight away a refund application will be taken, and whatever adjustment is due forwarded by mail. Refunds of the Canrailpass and some reduced-fare tickets may be subject to cancellation fees.

For refunds or credit by mail your original tickets and receipt coupon should be sent to VIA Rail Canada Inc, Ticket Refunds, 895 De La Gauchetière West, Montreal, Quebec H3B 4G1.

VIA PRÉFÉRENCE This is a frequent-traveller programme which lets you earn points to spend on more rail travel, accommodation on the train, car rental and hotels. The VIA Préférence program has three levels, Préférence, Privilège and Premier, each offering exclusive advantages and benefits. Every member begins at the Préférence level and you qualify for a higher level depending on how much you spend and travel with VIA Rail during the 'qualifying period' that runs from 1 April until 31 March each year. If you travel and spend from Cdn$0 to Cdn$999 (before taxes), you will be a Préférence member. Spend from Cdn$1,000 to Cdn$1,999 and you will be a Privilège member. Spend Cdn$2,000 or more and complete at least eight segments (one-way trips) during the qualifying period and you become a Premier member. At the end of the qualifying period, membership levels are calculated and confirmed to each member. Starting 1 May until 30 April of the following year, qualified members enjoy the advantage of a higher level for a 12-month 'benefit period'. Préférence Membership cards can be obtained at most VIA Rail stations and online or by calling ☎888 VIA PREFER (☎842 7733).

FACILITIES AND SERVICES

Language VIA Rail provides a bilingual service in English and French.

Baggage Two large items of personal baggage may be checked in for each adult fare. For Sleeper Class the limits are higher. Each piece of checked baggage should not exceed 50lb (23kg) or measure more than 62in (158cm). Checked baggage includes suitcases, backpacks, sporting goods (golf bags, skis, etc) and musical instruments (restrictions apply). Items weighing more than 70lb (32kg) or measuring more than 71in (180cm) are not permitted, unless they are considered oversized outdoor equipment (bicycles, canoes, skis, etc.). Bags should be labelled with your name and address and handed in at least half an hour before departure.

Free boxes are available for transporting bicycles and their use is mandatory where journeys involve a connection. VIA will adjust the price for carrying oversize items to make sure it does not exceed the fare you have paid for travel, except in the case of children's fares. Infants with a seat reservation are entitled to the checked baggage allowance. For infants travelling on-lap, one stroller (pushchair) and one car seat may be carried free of charge. Other items count as part of the adult baggage allowance and any excess charged accordingly.

Carry-on luggage is limited in Economy Class to one personal item weighing up to 25lb (11.5kg) and one item not exceeding 50lb (23kg) (or two items not exceeding 50lb (23kg) each). Business-Class passengers can take one personal item weighing up to 25lb (11.5kg) and two items not exceeding 50lb (23kg) each. One additional item of up to 50lb (23kg) is allowed in Economy or Business Class for a fee of Cdn$40 (per direction). In Sleeper Plus and Prestige class you can take one personal item per person (max 25lb/11.5kg) and two small items per cabin (max 25lb/11.5kg each). All additional bags must be checked in.

No liability is accepted for loss or damage to carry-on luggage or for articles lost or left on the train, so take out insurance if necessary. Many stations, including Halifax, Quebec City, Ottawa, Winnipeg, Edmonton and Vancouver, have free luggage carts. Red Caps operate in Montreal and Toronto.

Lost property No liability is accepted for items stolen or left behind in a train, although VIA personnel will make every effort to help you find your belongings. Lost or stolen tickets should be reported as soon as possible by calling ☎1 888 842 7245 or ☎TTY 1 800 268 9503 (hearing impaired) or going to the nearest ticket office. Lost tickets can be reissued with no service charge on the departure date by the station's agent. If you have an e-boarding pass, simply print out another copy of your email. If you are departing from an unmanned station, you will be able to board the train without a new ticket. You will have to present a photo ID and the Service Manager will manually validate that you are on the list.

Boarding It is recommended you arrive at the station 30 minutes prior to the scheduled departure time. If you already have a booking but are not yet in possession of your ticket, or if you want to check in your baggage, you should be at the station at least 1 hour prior to departure (30 minutes if travelling Business Class). Those aged 60+, passengers with young children and travellers in Business Class should board as early as possible.

Pets With the exception of service animals for visually or hearing-impaired passengers, pets are not allowed in passenger cars. Only cats, dogs and small rodents are allowed aboard and can be transported in the baggage car on most trains, though passengers are responsible for their feeding and exercise. Baggage cars are heated but most are not air conditioned, so your pet may be exposed to high temperatures. From 1 June to 30 September, baggage cars cannot transport animals due to lack of proper ventilation. However, pets may be transported year-round on the *Ocean*, as all cars are air conditioned. Animals must be claimed immediately on arrival. The cage must be of rigid material (metal or hard plastic), have a padlock to keep it shut, and be high enough to allow the animal to stand. VIA has the right to refuse cages it deems unsuitable (appropriate cages can be purchased at some stations). Be sure to check in your pet at least 1 hour before departure. Service charges for transporting an animal range between Cdn$30 and Cdn$50.

Radios Headphones must always be used when listening to radios, or other electronic devices.

Sleeping Pillows and blankets are not provided for overnight travel in economy accommodation, except on the *Ocean* and *Chaleur* trains. All necessary bedding is supplied in sleeping cars. Roomettes (for one person) and bedrooms (for two people) have a hand basin, mirror, electric razor socket, fold-down table and concealed or separate toilet. Sleeper Class also has showers.

Section accommodation offers two facing couch-style seats which convert at night into an upper and lower berth. Thick curtains provide privacy. A section can be bought separately for one person, either as an upper or lower berth. Toilets are located in each coach.

Smoking All trains offer a completely smoke-free environment, a policy effective everywhere on the network since 1 November 2004. All stations are also smoke-free.

Alcohol Alcoholic and other drinks purchased on board must be consumed where served. The law prohibits consumption of personal supplies (ie: not purchased on the train), other than by passengers travelling in enclosed sleeping accommodation.

Special needs Anyone with special needs will be given additional attention on request (contact VIA in advance). You should give at least 48 hours' notice for special meals (such as diabetic, kosher or low sodium) and 24 hours for a wheelchair. Special meals are not available in Economy and Touring Class.

All VIA trains are wheelchair-accessible and are equipped with wheelchair tie-downs, grab bars in washrooms and narrow wheelchairs for boarding, detraining and accessing the washrooms. The availability of these services may vary according to the train equipment in use. Some trains have baggage cars which can store wheelchairs or scooters during the trip. On transcontinental trains, travellers who are unable to visit the dining car or snack counters can have their meals served at their seat. Passengers unable to care for themselves must travel with an escort, who will be offered free passage in Economy Class (subject to certain restrictions).

The Access to Travel (ATT) website (w *accesstotravel.gc.ca*) provides helpful information on accessible transportation and travel across Canada for people travelling with disabilities and seniors, as well as for their families and carers. The website includes advice on transport between Canadian cities by air, rail, ferry and intercity bus, as well as local transportation and accessibility of airport terminals.

Wi-Fi Complimentary Wi-Fi service is available on board most trains, in Business station lounges and in some stations in the Quebec City–Windsor corridor. It is also available in the following stations: Edmonton, Halifax, Jasper, Moncton, Vancouver and Winnipeg. Travellers on the *Ocean* train can also access free Wi-Fi in service cars adjacent to the dining car. Browsing the internet, checking email and visiting social networking websites are all permitted. However, you are asked to refrain from streaming videos and from downloading or uploading large files. VIA Rail restricts the use of Wi-Fi to anyone using excessive bandwidth and downloading speed will be reduced. If you are using a video conference service, you should wear your earphones. For Via Rail's On-Train Entertainment, turn on your Wi-Fi and connect to 'VIA_WiFi_VIDEO'. Launch your web browser to w viarailwifi.ca and you can watch a wide variety of Canadian programming, including news, films, TV shows and documentaries. Respect fellow passengers by using a headset.

Telephone Personal mobile phones (cell phones) should be used with due consideration and set on vibration mode to avoid disturbing other passengers.

Service If you have any comments or suggestions you should write to Customer Relations, VIA Rail Canada Inc, PO Box 8116, Station 'A', Montreal, Quebec H3C 3N3 (e *customer_relations@viarail.ca*).

If you have a complaint or problem which cannot be resolved by discussion with VIA personnel on the spot, you should call ❧1 800 681 2561 or write to Customer Relations, enclosing ticket receipts if possible. You can also fill in a comments form on the VIA Rail website (w *viarail.ca*).

THE ROUTES

Changes to VIA Rail operations and schedules may take place from time to time, so for the latest information, call ❧888 842 7245. The following passenger services are among those currently operating.

THE *CANADIAN* The government cut the southern transcontinental route through Banff, Calgary and Medicine Hat in 1990, transferring to a more northerly passage via Jasper. At the same time, a Cdn$200 million refurbishment of the *Canadian*'s original 1950s equipment began. Modern comforts such as air conditioning and showers were added to the stainless-steel coaches, and train staff were provided with smart new uniforms. In 2013, the train was honoured by being featured on the back of the Cdn$10 bill.

The *Canadian* now travels three times a week each way (twice a week off peak) between Toronto and Vancouver on the route of the former Canadian National Railway's *Super Continental*, a flagship transcontinental service that replaced the CN's *Continental Limited*. The journey of almost 2,775 miles (4,466km) takes three days and four nights (92 hours) and among its 65 stops are several which VIA calls 'dwell time' – brief pauses giving you a chance to stretch your legs on the platform. The train travels through southern Ontario then over the prairies of Saskatchewan, crossing the mountains and gorges of Jasper National Park before reaching British Columbia. In Jasper it connects with VIA Rail's train to Prince Rupert.

The *Canadian* leaves Toronto late on Tuesday, Thursday and Saturday evenings to reach Capreol early next morning. You arrive in Winnipeg by early morning on the following day and Saskatoon by late evening. Edmonton is reached early on day three and Jasper by mid-afternoon. You arrive in Vancouver on Monday, Wednesday or Friday morning.

Travelling east, trains leave Vancouver mid-evening each Tuesday, Friday and Sunday, arriving in Jasper by mid-afternoon on the second day and Edmonton by late evening. You reach Saskatoon early in the morning and Winnipeg mid-evening on the third day, then Capreol early on day four, before finally arriving in Toronto on Tuesday, Thursday or Saturday mornings.

Check-in baggage is available at all major stations. Complete meals service, lounge car, bedrooms and roomettes. Economy Class, with upgrades to Sleeper Plus and Prestige Class. Passengers travelling in Sleeper-Plus Class are strongly recommended to check in at the VIA ticket counter (or the Business lounge) of their departure city at least 90 minutes prior to departure and to call VIA Rail the day of departure to enquire about possible delays in departure time.

Major stations

Vancouver *(Ticket office ⏲ 06.00–17.30 Mon, Wed, Thu, Sat & Sun, 06.00–20.30 Tue & Fri; waiting room ⏲ daily 05.00–01.00; reservations & information ✆888 842 7245)* Pacific Central Station is at 1150 Station St. ATM, baggage carts, taxis, telephones. Wi-Fi available in the station & in the Panorama lounge. Buses connect with the Amtrak network in Seattle, WA. Amtrak Cascades trains run twice a day between Vancouver & Seattle.

Winnipeg *(Ticket office ⏲ 07.30–13.00 Mon & Wed, 07.30–23.30 Thu, 18.30–22.30 Sun; reservations & information ✆888 842 7245)* Union Station is at 123 Main St. Lockers, newspapers, snack bar, handcarts, taxi stand, Wi-Fi in the station & the Business lounge. VIA Rail Headquarters West is at 123 Main St, Winnipeg, MN R3C 1A3.

Saskatoon *(Ticket office ⏲ 07.30–11.30 Sun, 19.00–midnight Mon, 07.30–10.30 & 21.00–midnight Thu; reservations & information ✆888 842 7245)* Unit 38, 1701 Chappell Drive, 5 miles (8km) west of downtown. Lockers, vending machines, taxi stand.

Edmonton *(Ticket office ⏲ 21.30–midnight] Wed & Sat, 06.00–10.00 Tue & Fri; reservations & information ✆888 842 7245)* 12360-121 St NW, Edmonton, AB T5L 5C3. Lockers, ATM, telephones, newspapers, taxi stand, Wi-Fi in the station & the Business lounge.

Jasper *(Ticket office ⏲ noon–19.00 Mon & Thu, 10.00–17.45 Wed, 10.00–14.15 Sun, 10.00–20.45 Tue & Fri; reservations & information ✆888 842 7245)* 607 Connaught Dr, Jasper, AB T0E 1E0. Lockers, newspapers, Red Caps, restaurant, shop, taxis, Wi-Fi in the station & the Business lounge. For Jasper National Park contact the information centre (✆780 852 6176).

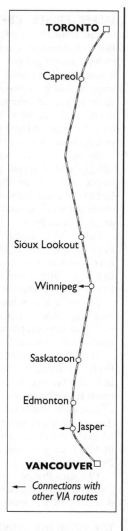

TORONTO

Capreol

Sioux Lookout

Winnipeg

Saskatoon

Edmonton

Jasper

VANCOUVER

← Connections with other VIA routes

JASPER–PRINCE RUPERT Formerly known as the Skeena train, this is a 725-mile (1,160km) journey among British Columbia's spectacular mountains and snow-filled valleys, starting from Jasper in Alberta and following a route formerly used by Canada's First Nation people, trappers and gold prospectors. You accompany the Fraser River to Prince George then the Skeena River ('river of mists' in the native Gitskan language) to Prince Rupert, only 40 miles (64km) south of Alaska. Prince Rupert is proud claimant to the title of 'halibut capital of the world'.

Jasper

Prince George

Prince Rupert

← Connections with other VIA routes

En route are glaciers, forests, salmon rivers, fishing villages and deserted gold rush towns. An hour from Jasper you can see the highest point in the Canadian Rockies, Mount Robson (12,972ft/3,954m). Look for the abundant wildlife, including moose, deer, bald eagles and an occasional bear.

Before the Grand Trunk Railway arrived in 1914, Prince Rupert was an isolated settlement on Kaien Island. Ferry services now operate north from Prince Rupert to Alaska, or south along the British Columbia and Washington coasts to Seattle. Connections can be made in Prince George with the British Columbia Railway service to Vancouver.

The train leaves Jasper soon after midday on Sunday, Wednesday and Friday, reaching Prince George by mid-evening (6 hours). Following an overnight stop in Prince George, trains leave early on Monday, Thursday or Saturday morning to reach Prince Rupert by mid-evening (11 hours).

Travelling east, the train departs Prince Rupert early on Sunday, Wednesday and Friday morning to reach Prince George by mid-evening. After an overnight stop in Prince George, trains leave early on Monday, Thursday or Saturday morning to reach Jasper by early evening.

Complete meals service and bedrooms. Check-in baggage service only available during the peak period (early June to mid-September). Economy Class offers access to the Park car with dome and a panoramic view off-peak (October to end of May). Upgrade to Touring Class for an unobstructed view in the Panorama Dome car.

VIA uses Prince George's First Avenue and Quebec Station, close to downtown. Lockers, vending machines, handcarts, taxi stand. Prince Rupert's historic station is at 2000 Park Avenue. Vending machines, telephones.

THE CORRIDOR SERVICES VIA's busiest routes are between Quebec City and Windsor as well as to Montreal, Ottawa and Toronto, carrying three million passengers at up to 95mph (150km/h). Montreal and Quebec City are linked by five trains on weekdays, and four on Saturdays and Sundays. Economy Class and Business Class are available. The journey takes just under 3 hours, and Montreal to Toronto takes less than 5 hours. There are six departures every weekday from both Toronto and Montreal, with four departures on Saturdays and five on Sundays. Additional services go to Windsor, Sherbrooke (four trains daily in each direction) and Ottawa (five departures every weekday from both Toronto and Ottawa, with three departures on Saturdays and four on Sundays) and Niagara Falls (two trains daily from both Toronto and Niagara Falls, with more added during summer, in addition to Amtrak's *Maple Leaf*). Many trains offer Business Class as well as Economy Class.

Major stations

꫰꫰ Quebec City (*Ticket office* ⊕ *04.45–22.00 Mon–Fri, 06.45–22.00 Sat–Sun*) The refurbished Gare du Palais is at 450 rue de la Gare du Palais (☎ *888 842 7245*). ATM banking, baggage carts, newspapers, restaurant, snack bar, taxis, telephones, Wi-Fi in the station & the Business lounge. Quebec's 600-room Hotel Château de Frontenac was built in French style by the Canadian Pacific. The hotel's turrets & bastions still provide the city with its most recognisable landmark.

꫰꫰ Montreal Gare Centrale **(Central Station)** (*Ticket office* ⊕ *05.15–19.15 daily; waiting room* ⊕ *04.30–00.30; reservations & information* ☎ *514 989 2626*) The station, at 895 rue de la Gauchetière Ouest, first opened in 1943. It is also used today by Amtrak & commuter trains. The Business lounge, for passengers in sleeping-car accommodations on the *Chaleur* & the *Ocean* (☎ *514 871 7759;* ⊕ *05.15– 19.15*). Red Caps, restaurants, shops, taxi stand, ATM banking, bank, exchange office, newspapers, Wi-Fi in the station & the Business lounge. The Canadian Railway Museum (*110 rue St-Pierre, Saint-Constant, Quebec J5A 1G7, located 30mins south of Montreal;* ☎ *450 632 2410 or* ☎ *450 638 1522;* w *exporail.org;* ⊕ *late Jun–early Sep daily, otherwise Sat–Sun; admission charge*) houses over 160 historic locomotives & vehicles in enormous train sheds. The collection includes Canada's oldest-surviving steam engine & a steam-operated snow plough (a Canadian invention) as well as the largest steam locomotive built in Canada & the last to be built for a Canadian railway. A replica steam locomotive operates on summer w/ ends. For Montreal city information, see also page 278.

꫰꫰ Toronto (*Ticket office* ⊕ *06.00–22.00; the Business lounge* ☎ *416 956 7637;* ⊕ *06.00–19.55 Mon, Wed, Fri & Sun, 06.00–22.00 Tue, Thu & Sat; arrivals & departures* ☎ *416 366 8411; reservations & information* ☎ *888 842 7245 or* ☎ *1 800 872 7245 for Amtrak*) Clean, efficient & softly lit Union Station is at 65 Front W & York. GO commuter trains operate to Hamilton, Oshawa, Richmond Hill & Georgetown (☎ *416 869 3200*). Lockers, ATM banking, newspapers, Red Caps, restaurants, shops, taxi stand, subway. For Toronto city information, see page 317.

꫰꫰ Ottawa (*Ticket office* ⊕ *05.00–18.30 Mon–Fri, 06.00–18.30 Sat, 08.00–18.30 Sun; reservations & information* ☎ *888 842 7245*) The station is at 200 Tremblay, 2 miles (3km) from downtown. This iconic building was built in 1966 by renowned Canadian architect John Cresswell Parkin, & won a Massey medal for architecture in 1967. In 2000, it was named one of Canada's top 500 buildings. Lockers, newspapers, Red Caps, restaurants, shops, taxi stand ATM banking, telephones, Wi-Fi in the station & the Business lounge. The Canada Museum of Science and Technology (*2421 Lancaster Rd;* ☎ *613 991 3044;* w *ingeniumcanada.org/scitech/index.php;* ⊕ *daily; admission charge*) is the largest of its kind in Canada & displays historic steam engines & 1890s rolling stock.

THE *OCEAN* The *Ocean* train first ran on 3 July 1904, making it Canada's longest-running train to have operated over the same line. It takes 18 hours to travel 836 miles (1,346km) along the old Intercolonial Railway (ICR) route between Halifax, Nova Scotia and Montreal in Quebec. Trains go via New Brunswick and some of the

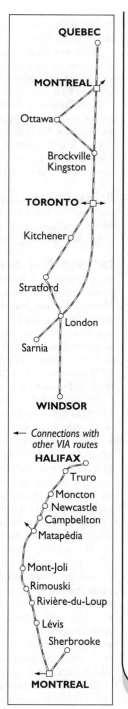

many rural communities of Quebec's south shore, starting out on three days a week in both directions.

You leave Halifax just after midday on Wednesday, Friday and Sunday to reach Moncton by late afternoon, Campbellton in New Brunswick by late evening and Montreal early the following morning. A ferry service connects Levis with Quebec City.

Travelling east, the *Ocean* departs Montreal early in the evening on Wednesday, Friday and Sunday to reach Campbellton early next morning, Moncton by midday and Halifax, Nova Scotia, by early evening.

Check-in baggage at main stations. Complete meals service, bedrooms and Park car. Economy Class, with upgrades to Sleeper Plus Class and access to the scenic dome in the Park car. Free Wi-Fi is available in cars adjacent to the dining car.

Halifax station (*Ticket office & waiting room* ⊕ *09.15–17.30 daily; reservations & information;* ⊸*888 842 7245*). The splendidly restored 1928 station building at 1161 Hollis is adjacent to the Westin Hotel, a former CN property.

Lockers, vending machines, newspapers, Red Caps, restaurant, taxi stand.

THE MONTREAL–JONQUIÈRE AND MONTREAL–SENETERRE The Montreal–Jonquière train, formerly known as the Saguenay, travels 317 miles (510km) between Montreal and Saguenay (borough of Jonquière) in Quebec. It crosses the island of Montreal, heads through the St Lawrence River Valley to Lanaudière, and continues on to the regions of La Mauricie, Portneuf, Haute-Mauricie, Lac-Saint-Jean and Saguenay. The section of track between Rivière-à-Pierre and Chambord was completed in 1888, followed by the Chambord–Jonquière section in 1893. Founded as a train terminal in 1847, Jonquière was merged with Kénogami and Arvida in 1975, and then with Chicoutimi in 2002 to become the city of Saguenay. The journey from end to end takes approximately 9 hours, although it may take longer.

The Montreal–Senneterre train, formerly called the Abitibi, travels 445 miles (717km) between Montreal and Senneterre in the Abitibi-Témiscamingue region of Quebec. Founded in 1919 and located on the bank of the Bell/Nottaway River, Senneterre was a major trading post during the fur trade period. It was named after Lieutenant de Senneterre of the De Languedoc regiment under the command of Montcalm, who defended Quebec against the British in 1759. This train is joined to the Montreal–Jonquière train up to Hervey-Jonction before heading northwest on its own to Haute-Mauricie and Abitibi. The journey from end to end takes approximately 11½ hours.

Stops or points of interest are often indicated only by a black and white sign along the railway track, and the train only stops if a passenger wishes to get on or off the train. Many stops were named after private hunting and fishing clubs (Club Bélanger, Sisco Club, Iroquois Club) that were replaced in 1978 by controlled harvesting zones known as ZECs (*zones d'exploitation contrôlées*) or by outfitters. More than 35 of these outfitters in northern Quebec are accessible by train and offer accommodations, meals, guides and the infrastructure required for a great adventure trip. For information, call ⊸ 877 876-8824 (toll-free), or visit w naturemauricie. com. Unscheduled stops occur deep in the forest where no other transportation is available. The train will stop on request to pick up or drop off a passenger and it is recommended that you let VIA know at least 24 hours in advance by calling ⊸1 888 VIA-RAIL. It is also possible to make a reservation to detrain at an unmarked spot.

Both the Saguenay and Abitibi trains leave Montreal on Monday, Wednesday and Friday mornings. They depart for Montreal on Tuesday, Thursday and

Sunday. Economy Class only. During May, passengers on the Montreal–Jonquière train can enjoy the Skyline car with its panoramic dome for unique views of the wonderful landscapes.

THE *WINNIPEG–CHURCHILL* This train, formerly known as the Hudson Bay and before that as Northern Spirits, is the only dry-land connection between Churchill and the rest of Canada. It travels more than 1,000 miles (1,600km) north from Winnipeg, crossing a bleak desert of ice and snow to sub-arctic Churchill and the polar bear country of Hudson Bay. This is beaver territory, where dams have been known to wash away the track or even wreck a train. The Hudson Bay Railroad opened the line in the 1920s to transport grain for export from Canada's prairies, and the Canadian National's last scheduled steam train (*No 6043*) made its final run between The Pas and Winnipeg in November 1960.

The Winnipeg–Churchill leaves Winnipeg on Tuesday and Sunday mornings to reach The Pas early next day and Thompson by early afternoon. You arrive in Gillam by late evening and Churchill early on Thursday or Tuesday evening (48 hours).

Travelling south, trains leave Churchill mid-evening on Thursday and Saturday to reach Gillam early next morning and Thompson by mid-afternoon. You arrive in The Pas during the night and Winnipeg late on Saturday or Monday afternoon.

The journey takes 48 hours. Book well in advance, especially during summer. Check-in baggage. Complete meals service, bedrooms and roomettes. Economy Class, with upgrades to Sleeper Plus Class. Service between Gillam and Churchill was suspended in May 2017, when unprecedented flooding heavily damaged the track bed and bridges. You should confirm the current situation with VIA Rail before travelling.

Churchill station (*Ticket office & waiting room* ☉ *08.00–08.45 & 19.00–20.30; reservations & information* ☏ *888 842 7245*) This is located on the western edge of town. Left-luggage room, telephones. The station remains open until trains depart.

OTHER VIA RAIL TRAINS VIA Rail's Sudbury–White River train, formerly the *Lake Superior*, departs Sudbury on Tuesday, Thursday and Saturday mornings for a 301-mile (480km) journey via Cartier and Franz to White River in Ontario, arriving by early evening. Travelling east, trains leave White River on Wednesday, Friday and Sunday morning to reach Sudbury by mid-evening. Economy Class only. The train provides flagstop service to many remote locations only accessible by rail on the Canadian Pacific Railway main line in Northern Ontario. Stops include Amyot, Swanson, Franz, Lochalsh, Missanabie, Dalton, Nicholson, Chapleau, Nemegos, Kormak, Sultan, Biscotasing, Metagama and Benny.

Several VIA trains out of Toronto go to Kingston, Windsor, Stratford and London, Ontario.

KEEWATIN RAILWAY In 2006, the Keewatin Railway Company (KRC) completed the purchase of the Sherridon rail line from the Hudson Railway Company (HBR) owned by OmniTrax. Established to help build a strong local economy by offering business opportunities and services to benefit the region, this was the second First Nations railway to be created with the financial support of the Government of Canada and Manitoba. In 2003, following the closure of the mine near Leaf Rapids, HBR announced its intention to abandon the Sherridon rail line. The Keewatin Railway Company was created by three partner nations (the Mathaias Colomb Indian Band, Tataskweyak Cree Nation and the War Lake First Nation) to own and operate the line using Via Rail cars. It currently operates two round trips a week carrying freight and passengers 150 miles (241km) between Pukatawagan and The Pas. First Nation members are involved in all facets of the railway, including management, administration and physical operations. Passenger ticket services are provided by KRC at the VIA rail station in The Pas. To book travel on this route, contact the Keewatin Railway Company (❨204 623 5255; w *krcrail.ca*).

ROCKY MOUNTAINEER A leisurely, all-daylight 667-mile (1,112km) journey among the mountains and forests of the Canadian Rockies and on to Jasper or Banff and Calgary, Alberta, makes this one of the most spectacular train trips in the world. The service, originally operated by VIA Rail and heavily subsidised by the government, became *Rocky Mountaineer* in 1990, when the all-daylight journeys were privatised. Under the ownership of *Rocky Mountaineer* the service has become more popular each year since.

Rocky Mountaineer is the largest privately owned passenger rail service in North America, with more than 550 employees. On 12 September 1996, it made the record books by operating the longest passenger train in Canadian history. A total of 37 cars travelled from Vancouver to Kamloops to beat the previous best of 28, set in Regina, Saskatchewan, by the Canadian Pacific's *Dominion* in 1965. The record was extended to 41 cars in 1999 and is still standing.

The routes The 'Rainforest to Gold Rush' *Rocky Mountaineer* tour uses Canadian Pacific and Canadian National tracks, as well as (briefly) tracks owned by VIA Rail. The entire journey takes place in daylight so that you can absorb the maximum amount of scenery and see animals such as grazing elk, black and grizzly bears, white-tail deer, moose, mountain goats, coyotes, wolves and big-horn sheep. The thick forests of pine and fir are also home to marmots, porcupines and chipmunks. Much of this wildlife has become accustomed to railroad traffic so this is a great opportunity to see more creatures than would otherwise be possible. Bears, for example, have developed a taste for the grain which leaks out of freight cars and ferments beside the track.

William Cornelius Van Horne, first manager of the Canadian Pacific, famously remarked that 'since we cannot export the scenery, we shall have to import the tourists' and this part of Canada has been doing so ever since. *Rocky Mountaineer* leaves Vancouver's Rocky Mountaineer Station and crosses the Fraser River swing bridge before following the Fraser River itself. The passage through the Fraser Canyon was part of the gold rush routes of the late 1880s, when the CN railroad line had to be carved out of the side of the gorge by construction workers using 'dynamite and whiskey'.

At Hell's Gate Canyon, so named because construction work here was so dangerous, a massive rock slide accidentally narrowed the river to 110ft (37m). Look for fish ladders built in the 1940s to allow 40 million sockeye salmon to pass upstream to spawn every year. You continue through a fertile valley of farms and orchards before beginning to climb among snow-capped mountains and glaciers, passing places with names such as Skuzzy Creek, Suicide Rapids and Jaws of Death Gorge. Look for the occasional fields of ginseng, grown under plastic sheets.

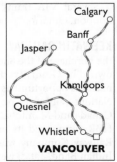

After an overnight stop in Kamloops you continue next morning to Jasper by way of the North Thompson

River, the Monashee Mountains, Pyramid Falls and Little Hell's Gate. You get an overwhelming view of the highest mountain in the Canadian Rockies, Mount Robson (12,972ft/3,954m), and have the option of continuing on VIA Rail from Jasper, travelling across all of Canada to the Atlantic coast. VIA's *Canadian* train uses the same tracks as *Rocky Mountaineer* from Vancouver to Jasper but travels through the night.

The 'First Passage to the West' *Rocky Mountaineer* tour goes from Vancouver to Kamloops and across Glacier National Park to Banff and Calgary. You travel among the ranch lands of the South Thompson River then along the fjord-like shores of the Shuswap Lakes. At Silverdale you pass the spot where in 1904 the American Billy Miner, Louis Colquhoun and 'Shorty' Dunn carried out Canada's first train hold-up, getting away with Cdn$6,000 of gold dust and US$50,000 in US bonds. You also pass the spot where their last train robbery (yielding Cdn$15 and a handful of liver pills) took place a year and a half later. The gang were captured shortly afterwards by the RCMP, although Miner soon escaped from jail and returned to the United States.

At Craigellachie you see a stone cairn indicating where the last spike was driven by CPR financier Donald Smith to complete the Canadian Pacific Railroad on 7 November 1885. This symbolic iron spike was extracted after the ceremony and given to Smith, who eventually donated it to the Canada Science and Technology Museum in Ottawa. It is currently on display at the Canadian Museum of Immigration in Halifax, Nova Scotia, as a tribute to immigrant workers involved in the railway's construction. *Rocky Mountaineer* travels on through Mount Macdonald by way of the 5-mile (8km) Connaught Tunnel, the second longest in North America. Adjacent Macdonald Tunnel is the longest, at 9 miles (14.5km). Both tunnels were built in the early 20th century to protect the tracks from heavy snowfalls and avalanches which had caused over 200 deaths. At Stoney Creek a steel-arch bridge was constructed in 1929 directly above an 1893 bridge which replaced the original wooden structure.

Beyond the Kicking Horse River you go through two unique spiral tunnels located under Cathedral Mountain and Mount Ogden, excavated between 1907 and 1909. These provide a safer and easier route than the original 'Big Hill', an 8-mile (12.8km) stretch which included a 4.5% grade. The upper Spiral Tunnel is 3,255ft (992m) long and turns approximately 250°, emerging 56ft (17m) lower than its entrance. The lower tunnel is 2,922ft (890m) long, turns 230° and comes out 50ft (15m) below. An extra-long freight train may be seen emerging from and entering the tunnel simultaneously.

Rocky Mountaineer leaves Vancouver early in the morning to reach Kamloops by early evening. While in Kamloops, you can enjoy an evening entertainment show such as *Rhythms on the Rails*, a musical dinner show. After an overnight hotel stop you leave Kamloops early next morning for either Jasper or Banff and Calgary. Travelling west, trains leave Calgary early in the morning (or Jasper mid-morning) to reach Kamloops by early evening. After an overnight stop you leave Kamloops early next morning and arrive in Vancouver by late afternoon.

On the 'Journey through the Clouds' tour you travel through scenic valleys, the Coast Mountains range and the Fraser Canyon with its spectacular white-water rapids and dramatic landscape. You follow the route of the Fraser River, pass by the Albreda Glacier, the magnificent Pyramid Falls, and majestic Mount Robson. The 'Coastal Passage' tour is a cross-border route connecting the cosmopolitan cities of Seattle, WA, USA and Vancouver, BC, Canada with the breathtaking Canadian Rockies. On board the *Rocky Mountaineer* you travel along the Pacific Ocean's sparkling coastline through to the Canadian Rockies.

Facilities Each air-conditioned train can carry up to 950 passengers in 22 coaches. Each Dome car cost Cdn$1 million, accommodates 72 passengers and was specially built by the Rader Company in Colorado. These were the first completely new coaches to be put into service on a Canadian train for 40 years. Similar ones operate on the Alaska Railroad.

RedLeaf Service gives you a comfortable reclining seat, large picture windows and open-air vestibules. You get complimentary snacks and non-alcoholic drinks as well as an at-your-seat cold meal service. Attendants supply an enthusiastic commentary on the route's history, geography and wildlife. Choose a seat on the left of the train when travelling east, or on the right if going west.

GoldLeaf Service is well worth the extra cost, offering seating in the bi-level Dome car with uninterrupted panoramic views, pre-boarding privileges, an elegant private 36-seat dining room serving Alberta beef, Pacific Ocean fish, regional game and award-winning local wines, rear observation platform and a hotel for the overnight stop in Kamloops.

Timings and booking The season lasts from April to October. SilverLeaf Service is in a single-level Dome coach with oversized domed windows. Meals are served to your seat. GoldLeaf Service is in a bi-level coach. In the upper level, panoramic views are enjoyed through fully domed windows while gourmet meals from regional cuisine are served in the exclusive dining room lined with large picture windows on the lower level. GoldLeaf Deluxe combines GoldLeaf Service on the train with larger hotels in Kamloops that may have better views. All services offer the same scenery as well as storytelling by the onboard team.

You can book one-way or round trips and the many tours range from two to 13 days, with prices from Cdn$1,799–6,799 (SilverLeaf), Cdn$2,449–9,899 (GoldLeaf), and Cdn$3,549–11,349 (GoldLeaf Deluxe). This includes overnight hotel accommodation. Reduced fares are available for children aged two–11.

You should book at least 30 days in advance for best availability and check in an hour before departure time. For GoldLeaf guests, checked baggage (maximum 66lb/30kg) will be delivered and waiting for you upon arrival at your overnight accommodations in Kamloops. SilverLeaf guests are asked to bring a small carry-on bag as their luggage will be delivered to their final destination. To ensure the preservation of the fragile environment of the areas *Rocky Mountaineer* travels through, no smoking is allowed on board. This includes the vestibules between the coaches and rest room facilities.

Rocky Mountaineer trains are run by Rocky Mountaineer, 101-369 Terminal Avenue, Vancouver, British Columbia V6A 4C4 (🗫*00 800 0606 7372 (UK)*,🗫*0 800 088 5341 (Canada/USA);* w *rockymountaineer.com*). *Rocky Mountaineer's* station at 1755 Cottrell Street in Vancouver was originally built for Canadian National Railway as a locomotive repair shed. It was renovated by *Rocky Mountaineer* Rail Tours and converted into a railway station, with the first train departing in 2005. Before that, the Vancouver terminus for the *Rocky Mountaineer* was the Pacific Central Station.

UK ticket agents include First Class Holidays (🗫*0161 888 5606;* w *fcholidays. com*); Travel Pack (🗫*0208 585 4080;* w *travelpack.co.uk*); Canadian Affair (🗫*0203 424 6305;* w *canadianaffair.com*); Railbookers (🗫*020 3780 2222;* w *railbookers. co.uk*).

THE ALGOMA CENTRAL Trains run for 296 miles (475km) between Sault Ste Marie (pronounced 'soo-saint-marie') and Hearst in Ontario. The Agawa train takes you on a twisting 114-mile (183km) route opened in 1914 among forests, lakes, waterfalls and ravines, where the mountains resemble the Rockies. There are terrific views of the deep Agawa River Canyon and the train makes a 1½-hour stop for you to admire more closely the 1,500ft-high (457m) cliffs, pine trees and waterfalls. Services operate from mid-June to mid-October. During the foliage season (September to October), you should plan a weekday trip if possible and be sure to book early. Dome car service includes breakfast, lunch and a separate bar area with private steward. On certain days you may be able to tour the whole length of the railway, including the flat lands of the Clay Belt region with its countless lakes and conifers.

For information or tickets, contact the Algoma Central Railway (*PO Box 130, 129 Bay St, Sault Ste Marie, ON P6A 6Y2;* ✆ *705 946 7300 or* ✆ *800 242 9287;* w *agawatrain.com*).

THE ONTARIO NORTHLAND In 1932, the Temiskaming & Northern Ontario Railway was built 186 miles (299km) from Cochrane to the Arctic Circle across a demanding physical landscape, opening up the north's mining and forest resources. The railway changed its name to the Ontario Northland Railway (ONR) in 1946, and remains principally a freight line, operating to and from northeastern Ontario and northwestern Quebec. Ontario Northland provides transportation and telecommunications services to the residents and businesses of northern Ontario. Trains cross farmland, bogs, forests and fields of wild flowers. The **Cochrane Railway and Pioneer Museum** (✆ *705 272 4361;* ⊕ *Jun–Sep daily; admission charge*) is housed in several old train coaches at 171 4th Avenue, opposite Cochrane Station.

The ONR's *Polar Bear Express* is a 4-hour, 186-mile (300km) ride down the Arctic watershed, accessible only by rail or plane. This train operates five days per week (six days in summer), year-round. It carries equipment not commonly found on passenger trains, including chain cars (flat-cars) for passenger vehicles and boxcars (enclosed freight wagons, usually with sliding doors on the sides). You go through a sparsely populated wetland of black spruce forests, lakes, muskeg and scrub, known as 'the bush'. The *Polar Bear Express* proceeds from Cochrane over Ontario's fertile clay belt farmland and Cree territory, crossing the Abitibi and Moose rivers to Moosoonee on the edge of the Arctic Ocean near James Bay. Only 3,000 people live in Moosoonee, which was first settled as a trading post by Revillion Frères of Paris in 1903 in competition with the Hudson Bay Company. Winters can be very cold, freezing the Moose River solid enough to make a road to Moose Factory Island.

Before the Temiskaming & Northern Ontario Railway arrived in Moosoonee in 1932, the journey from Cochrane by canoe or snowshoes took ten days. A green railway car on the right of the station houses a museum of the region's natural and cultural history. A short boat ride will take you from Moosoonee to the historic community of Moose Factory, established as a fur-trading post in 1673, and the oldest English settlement in Ontario. Moose Factory's attractions include a Hudson Bay Company staff house, Centennial Park, St Thomas's Anglican Church, and the Cree Cultural Interpretive Centre where you can meet First Nations people who will share the rich history of the area.

The *Polar Bear Express* has a full dining-car service and a Dome car offering spectacular views of the lakes, rivers and waterfalls. You can even sit down and sing along to toe-tapping songs with a live entertainer. In the autumn, winter and spring, the train operates as a passenger and freight train that provides a vital link between Cochrane and Moosoonee as there are no roads to the latter. It is about a 5-hour trip in each direction and this is one of the last flag-stop trains in Canada. It may halt virtually anywhere, perhaps to pick up a canoeist or camper.

The *Dream Catcher Express* is a train excursion which allows you to enjoy brilliant autumn colours through large viewing windows as well as a Dome car for even more spectacular panoramic views. Six trains operate in late September/early October from North Bay to Temagami, home to a spectacular old-growth pine forest. The region is rich with First Nations history and artefacts and stone drawings dating as far back as 6000BC have been discovered here. The famous naturalist Archibald Belaney, born in England in 1888, worked in Temagami as a fur trapper and married an Ojjibwa woman from whom he learned much about the people. He claimed he was adopted by the tribe and given a name meaning 'Grey Owl'.

For information on all Ontario Northland services, contact 555 Oak Street E, North Bay, ON P1B 8L3 (✆ 705 472 4500; w *OntarioNorthland.ca*). Ontario Northland provides comfortable motor coach transportation from Hearst to Toronto, Sault Ste Marie, Ottawa, Sudbury and many points in between. For information on schedules and fares, contact ✆ 1 800 461 8558. Reservations are required and should be made well in advance for the *Polar Bear Express* and *Dream Catcher Express*.

OTHER RAILWAYS AND RAIL MUSEUMS IN CANADA

Royal Canadian Pacific (*201 9th Av SW, Calgary, AB T2P 1K3;* ✆ *403 508 1400 or* ✆ *877 665 3044;* w *royalcanadianpacific.com; for extended stays at one of RCP's landmark hotels,* ✆ *1 800 441 1414*) The RCP is mostly a freight-only railroad but several companies operate over its track, including VIA Rail and *Rocky Mountaineer*.

Based in Calgary, Alberta, the Royal Canadian Pacific was launched in 2000 and carries a fleet of luxuriously appointed 1920s railcars, built by Canadian Pacific Railway (CP). The eight historic coaches are named after people or events from Canada's history, and are 80ft (24m) long. They have carpeted floors, mahogany panelling, inlaid marquetry and cut glass, fine china and white linens to conjure up the service of old. The RCP offers themed tours featuring historic, golfing, fly-fishing and culinary as well as customised private-charter journeys while travelling through the spectacular Rocky Mountains.

As part of their history, these vintage railcars were used exclusively by CP's executives and on occasion by touring dignitaries. These included US President Franklin D Roosevelt, King George VI and Queen Elizabeth, Princess Elizabeth and the Duke of Edinburgh, and Sir Winston Churchill, who travelled by special train from Montreal to Washington, DC in 1943. These cars were the 'private jets' of their time. In 1999, CP built the Canadian Pacific Pavilion to house its fleet of valuable railway cars. In 2007, the RCP moved its offices into a new building located adjacent to the Pavilion in downtown Calgary. The new headquarters has been built with a theme of a historic steel trestle bridge featuring an open-glass concept and housing essential office functions, the sales/booking area and mechanical operations.

The 'Rockies Experience' is a six-day, 650-mile (1,046km) trip from Calgary to Crowsnest Pass and back to Calgary. The fare includes two nights' accommodation at the Palliser Hotel, three nights on board the train, guided tours, meals, baggage handling and admission to off-train tours.

The train heads west from Calgary along the Canadian Pacific Railway main line through the Bow River Valley towards the Rocky Mountains. After a short stop in Banff you continue to Lake Louise and the continental divide, travelling through the famous Spiral Tunnels into Field, British Columbia, where the train stops for passengers to board a motor coach for a tour of Emerald Lake.

You then depart for Golden, British Columbia, where the train leaves the Canadian Pacific Line and goes south along the 'coal route' through beautiful valleys carved by the Columbia River. You also travel through the continent's largest natural wetland, called 'The Rocky Mountain Trench', before making an overnight stop at Invermere. Next morning you travel south to the early 20th-century town of Fort Steele, known as Galbraith Ferry during the 1864 Kootenay gold rush, then to Cranbrook for a visit to the **Canadian Museum of Rail Travel** (page 374). After reboarding the train at Fort Steele, you travel east to Crowsnest Lake at the top of Crowsnest Pass for a second overnight stop.

The following morning, you leave for Fort McLeod and a guided tour of Head-Smashed-In Buffalo Jump before continuing via the Lethbridge Viaduct – the longest and highest bridge of its kind in the world – then on through rolling ranch country to Okotoks. A motor coach takes you to Homeplace Ranch for a guided horseback tour or scenic walk before the train returns to Calgary.

The Quebec North Shore and Labrador Railroad (*100 Retty, CP1000, Sept-Iles, QC G4R 4L5;* 418 968 7805) This line was originally built in the early 1950s to move iron ore from Labrador City to a port at Sept-Iles on the Gulf of St Lawrence, and the line is still used for freight traffic. Construction of the QNSL forms the backdrop for Hammond Innes's 1958 novel *The Land God Gave to Cain*. The author spent some time around Labrador researching for the book when the railway was being built.

QNSL maintained passenger and freight services until 2005, when it sold the Emeril Junction, NL–Schefferville, PQ rail line to Tshiuetin Rail Transportation Inc (*148 Bd des Montagnais, Uashat, QC G4R 5E2;* 418 960 0982; w *tshiuetin. net*). The first ever railway owned by aboriginal people, Tshiuetin means 'North Wind'. Trains depart from Sept-Iles on Monday and Thursday at 08.00 to arrive at Emeril Junction at 15.00. Trains leave Emeril Junction on Tuesday and Friday at noon to arrive in Sept-Iles at 19.00. Passenger trains no longer go to Labrador City so travellers to and from Labrador must take Highway 500 from Emeril Junction, approximately 45 minutes' drive.

White Pass & Yukon Railway (*PO Box 435, 231 Second Av, Skagway, AK 99840, USA;* 907 983 2217 or 800 343 7373; w *wpyr.com*) A daily coach/train service operates mainly between Whitehorse and Skagway, including a steep narrow-gauge route between Skagway and Fraser. The train hugs precipitous cliffs and crosses flimsy-looking trestle bridges as it follows a route used by many thousands during the 1898 Klondike gold rush, passing waterfalls, glaciers and tunnels carved out of solid granite. You travel in an 1890s-style coach on the train but the part of the journey between White Pass and Whitehorse is operated by motor coach. The whole journey takes 4½ hours and services run from May until mid-September.

Summit Excursions take you from tidewater Skagway to the summit of White Pass, a climb of almost 3,000ft (900m) in only 20 miles (32km). The daily round trip takes 3 hours.

The *Yukon Adventure* takes you a further 47 miles (75km) beyond the summit to Carcross, Yukon (passport required). A 2-hour layover at Bennett offers passengers a piping-hot meal and a self-guided walking tour of the historic gold rush town site. At the end of the layover passengers reboard the train and continue on to Carcross. The 6-hour round trips from Skagway take place each Sunday, Wednesday and Thursday from late May to August, and the ticket price includes lunch.

On Monday and Friday there are steam-train excursions on the route to Fraser Meadows, and *the Chilkoot Trail* hikers' service links Bennett, Fraser and Skagway.

Canadian Museum of Rail Travel (*PO Box 400, 1 Van Horne St, Cranbrook, BC V1C 4H9;* ☎ *250 489 3918;* w *crowsnest.bc.ca/cmrt;* ☉ *summer daily, mid-Oct–mid-Apr Tue–Sat; admission charge*) The museum includes a beautifully restored *Trans-Canada Limited* First-Class sleeping-car train built in 1929 for the Canadian Pacific Railway. This has 90,000ft^2 (8,361m^2) of inlaid mahogany and walnut panelling as well as large collections of railway china and silverware. Other trains include the 1907 Soo–Spokane *Train Deluxe*. Expansion plans will enable the museum to display five different trainsets showing passenger travel between 1887 and 1955, along with heritage railway buildings such as the 1901 Elko Station. Begun in 2018, the project will be completed in summer 2019.

Elgin County Railway Museum (*225 Wellington St, St Thomas, ON N5P 4H4;* ☎ *519 637 6284;* w *ecrm5700.org;* ☉ *summer w/ends, by appointment year-round; admission charge*) Located in the 1913 Michigan Central Railway shops on Wellington Street, the collection includes a Hudson locomotive formerly used by the Canadian National Railway on its Toronto–Montreal corridor. Other locos are displayed along with an NYC Pullman sleeper, *Cascade Lane*.

St Thomas has been an important railway town since 1856, and was known in its heyday as the 'Railway Capital of Canada'. Around 26 railway lines then passed through, including the Wabash, Pere Marquette, New York Central and London & Port Stanley.

Winnipeg Railway Museum (*PO Box 48, 123 Main St, Winnipeg, MB R3C 1A3;* ☎ *204 942 4632;* w *wpgrailwaymuseum.com;* ☉ *daily; admission charge*) The museum features major displays and equipment from the CNR, CPR, City of Winnipeg's Railways and others who played a role in the development of Winnipeg. Approximately 37,500ft^2 (3,483m^2) is filled with railway artefacts and exhibits including the dispatch board that controlled CNR Winnipeg, the *Countess of Dufferin* (the first steam locomotive in western Canada), a Midland Railway of Manitoba snow dozer, a large operating HO model layout, and a combine car (colonist's car) which is now the gift shop. The George Hunter Art Gallery has exclusive railway art.

Waterloo–St Jacobs Railway (*50 Isabella St, PO Box 546, St Jacobs, ON, N0B 2N0;* ☎ *519 885 2297 or* ☎ *888 899 2757 (answering machine);* w *waterloocentralrailway. com*) The railway ceased operation in 2000 due to maintenance costs but in 2007 the Southern Ontario Locomotive Restoration Society received approval from the city of Waterloo to revive this tourist train. The renamed Waterloo Central Railway now runs passenger services and leases space in the City of Waterloo Visitor and Heritage Information Centre, formerly owned by the Waterloo–St Jacobs Railway. Trains operate three times a day on Tuesday, Thursday and Saturday, beginning in Waterloo at the station at 10 Father David Bauer Drive, with stops at the St Jacobs farmers' market and the village of St Jacobs. Historic steam train rides on long weekends.

West Coast Railway Heritage Park (*39645 Government Rd, Squamish, BC V8B 0B6;* ☎ *604 898 9336 or* ☎ *800 722 1233;* w *wcra.org;* ☉ *daily; admission charge*) The park is being developed to show a typical railway station of the mid-20th century and an old-style town centre with heritage displays, including more than 90 pieces

of railway cars and artefacts. At 12 acres (4.8ha), it provides the visitor with the opportunity to tour authentic railway equipment in various stages of restoration. Historic exhibits include Brightbill House, a blacksmith forge, a wash house, and a vintage printing press. The collection represents the major railways that have served British Columbia – Canadian Pacific, Canadian National, Pacific Great Eastern, BC Electric and Great Northern. The oldest items are the business car *British Columbia* (1890) and a rare Canadian Pacific colonist sleeping car (1905). West Coast Mini Rail line trains circle the park with sights en route such as the Garden Railway – a large-scale model railway that operates in woods near Sweet Apple Station. The Skeena River railroad car also features model trains, both HO scale and N scale.

Port Stanley Terminal Rail (*309 Bridge St, Port Stanley, ON N5L 1C5;* ☏ *519 782 3730 or* ☏ *877 244 4478;* w *pstr.on.ca*) Services operate over a 7-mile (11km) section of the former London & Port Stanley Railway Line between Port Stanley and St Thomas, which opened in 1856. Over 28 million passengers travelled on the L & PS, many heading for the beach at Port Stanley – 'the Coney Island of the Great Lakes'. Steam trains operated on this route for 59 years, transporting over one million passengers in 1943 alone.

Passenger services were discontinued in 1957 and freight traffic ceased in 1982, but the line was acquired by its present owners the following year and restored by volunteers. Trains again now make over 400 departures each season to cross two bridges and travel the banks of Kettle Creek, where you can see apple orchards and deer as well as plants and trees unique to the north shore of Lake Erie.

Northern Ontario Railroad Museum and Heritage Centre (*26 Bloor St, Capreol, ON P0M 1H0;* ☏ *705 858 5050;* w *normhc.ca;* ⊕ *May–Sep daily, Sep–May by special appointment; admission charge*) This unique museum is a tribute to pioneers who worked along the rails and to settlers who opened up the Sudbury region through mining and forestry. The museum is located in the renovated Canadian National Railway Superintendent's house purchased by the town of Capreol in 1997, and explores the local history of the Capreol area through photographs and stories. Displays include an original steam locomotive that helped open up the North, a caboose and a renovated school car. The 'School on Wheels' was one of seven used to teach children and adults isolated in the northern Ontario wilderness. They began as an experimental joint venture between the Department of Education and the railway in 1926. CN and CP operated school cars on a number of routes throughout northern Ontario, with about six one-week stops at each designated siding. The children would attend school for three–six days and receive further studies to last until the school car returned the following month.

Prince George Railway & Forestry Museum (*850 River Rd, Prince George, BC V2L 5S8 (adjacent to Cottonwood Island Park);* ☏ *250 563 7351;* w *pgrfm.bc.ca;* ⊕ *daily; admission charge*) Located on Cottonwood Island, the museum preserves over 70 pieces of rolling stock, nine historical buildings and many smaller artefacts on its 8-acre (3.2ha) site, displaying the lifestyle of people involved in the railways and industrial development of central British Columbia. The museum's Cottonwood Miniature Railway opened on Canada Day in 2004.

Alberta Railway Museum (*24215-34 St NW, Edmonton, AB T5Y 6B4;* ☏ *780 472 6229;* w *albertarailwaymuseum.com;* ⊕ *w/ends from Victoria Day (the Mon preceding 25 May) to Labour Day, the 1st long w/end in Sep; admission charge*) This is

the third-largest railway museum in Canada, and the largest in Alberta. Operated by the Alberta Pioneer Railway Association, it has more than 75 pieces of equipment, including cars and locomotives formerly owned by Canadian National, Northern Alberta Railways, short lines and industrial railways. The former CN St Albert depot, built in 1909, was moved to the museum grounds in 1980. The station has been completely restored with historic displays and functioning telegraph. Other buildings include a fire hall, bunkhouse and eight-sided water tower. Extensive museum archives are located at the Provincial Archives of Alberta, 8555 Roper Road, Edmonton, Alberta.

Train rides operate on holiday long weekends in May, June, July, August and September. Steam engine *No 1392* or diesel *9000* pull a passenger train depending on availability of volunteers. Diesel locomotives are used on Sundays in July and August.

New Brunswick Railway Museum (*2487 Main St, Hillsborough, NB E4H 2X7;* ⟍*506 734 3195;* w *nbrm.ca*) The museum has the largest collection of railway artefacts in New Brunswick, including cabooses, coaches, a speeder car and locomotives. Until 2004, it was the home of the Salem & Hillsborough Railroad excursion trains that ran over an 11-mile (18km) round trip. The equipment is now on static display at the museum established on the station and shop grounds in Hillsborough. The superb ex-Canadian National steam engine seen outside the museum was used in constructing portions of the National Transcontinental Railroad and other lines. The locomotive was steamed up in 1998 for the movie *Paradise Siding*.

No passenger trains operate in the Northwest Territories.

STEAM TRAINS IN CANADA

ALBERNI PACIFIC (*Mail address: Alberni Valley Heritage Network, 3100 Kingsway, Port Alberni, BC V9Y 3B1;* ⟍*250 723 1376 or* ⟍*250 723 2118;* w *alberniheritage. com*) Operates Thursday to Sunday from late June to early September, with holiday excursions at other times of the year. Trains run along the waterfront from downtown Port Alberni to the McLean Hill National Historic Site, which has a 1926 steam sawmill among its 30 preserved buildings. The trip takes about 35 minutes to wind through a forested valley after starting out from the restored 1912 Canadian Pacific station.

The engine is a 1929 Baldwin ex-logging locomotive and the passenger cars are three converted Canadian National transfer cabooses, one of which is open air. The railway is located on Kingsway at Argyle Street near the Harbour Quay in Port Alberni.

ALBERTA PRAIRIE RAILWAY (*Mail address: PO Box 1600, Stettler, AB T0C 2L0;* ⟍*800 282 3994 or* ⟍*403 290 0980 (in Calgary);* w *absteamtrain.com*) Between May and mid-October the Alberta Prairie Railway operates steam train rides lasting up to 8 hours through central Alberta, complete with staged robberies by the dreaded outlaws 'the Reynold's Raiders'. Different theme trains run throughout the season and an Alberta roast beef dinner is usually included in the fare. A 1920 Baldwin Consolidation locomotive hauls vintage Canadian Northern and Canadian National coaches, including an open-air car and the *Lone Star Saloon*.

Trains travel through Big Valley, the divisional point for the Canadian Northern Railway in the early 1900s when this was a thriving mining centre. Only a few hundred people now live in a community that once numbered 5,000. The restored

1912 station has photographs, blueprints of the gold mine and a complete station master's office.

FORT STEELE (*Mail address: Fort Steele Heritage Town, 9851 Highway 93/95, Fort Steele, BC V0B 1N0;* \ *250 417 6000;* **w** *fortsteele.ca*) Trains travel through the grounds of Fort Steele Heritage Park in British Columbia, climbing a double-loop track to give wonderful views from the Kootenay River lookout point. Locomotive *No 1077* featured in several movies, including Jackie Chan's *Shanghai Noon.*

The train runs hourly during summer, and tours of the roundhouse and restored turn-of-the-20th-century steam engines and equipment are available on request.

KAMLOOPS HERITAGE RAILWAY (*Mail address: #3–510 Lorne St, Kamloops, BC V2C 1W3;* \ *250 374 2141;* **w** *kamrail.com*) The former Canadian National steam locomotive *No 2141* has been fully restored and since 2002, the *Spirit of Kamloops* has carried almost 100,000 passengers on runs during July and August. The locomotive is one of 25 engines built by the Canadian Locomotive Company in Kingston, Ontario for the CNR. The excursion lasts approximately 1 hour, starting from the historic former CNR station (a heritage brick building known as 'The Keg') and is a 5-mile (8km) round trip on which you may encounter feisty saloon girls, seasoned First Nation storytellers and possibly Bill Miner, the gentleman train robber. Other tours operate throughout the year, including the *Canada Day Fireworks Train*, the *Ghost Train* in October, the *Spirit of Christmas* in December and the *Iron Horse Mystery*.

KETTLE VALLEY STEAM RAILWAY (*Mail address: 18404 Bathville Rd, PO Box 1288, Summerland, BC V0H 1Z0;* \ *877 494 8424 or* \ *250 494 8422;* **w** *kettlevalleyrail.org; for details of steam excursions on the Kettle Valley Railway between Summerland & the Trout Creek Bridge*) Enjoy a 90-minute round-trip journey along 6 miles (10km) of track through the scenic rural beauty of Prairie Valley. The KVSR is powered by a 1912 Consolidation Engine called *No 3716* – rolling stock includes two vintage coaches and three open-air cars. The season is from May to October. Special events include the 'Great Train Robbery' train for a taste of the Old West, during which the notorious Garnett Valley Gang rides out of the hills to stop the train and rob passengers of their spare change for local charities.

PRAIRIE DOG CENTRAL (*Mail address: The Vintage Locomotive Society Inc, PO Box 33021, RPO Polo Park, Winnipeg, MB R3G 3N4;* \ *204 832 5259;* **w** *pdcrailway. com*) The splendid Canadian Pacific engine is the oldest (1882) regularly scheduled operating steam locomotive in North America. This or a vintage diesel takes early 20th-century wooden coaches from Inkster Junction in Winnipeg for a 2½-hour, 35-mile (54km) trip over a Canadian National Railways route to Warren, Manitoba, with a stop at Grosse Isle. Other historic Canadian National locomotives are on display in Winnipeg.

Operates on Sundays from May to June, and at weekends from July to September.

SOUTH SIMCOE (*Mail address: PO Box 186, Tottenham, ON L0G 1W0;* \ *905 936 5815;* **w** *southsimcoerailway.ca*) Based in Tottenham, Ontario, the railway uses two former Canadian Pacific steam engines dating from 1883 and 1912, as well as a 1948 Southern Railway General Electric 70-ton (63-tonne) diesel switcher to haul 1920s vintage cars over part of the former Canadian National Line between Tottenham and Beeton. Departures are from South Simcoe Station at Mill Street

West in Tottenham, where there is a gift shop. This old branch line once connected Hamilton with the shipping ports of Barrie and Collingwood.

Operates on Sundays and holiday Mondays from May to October, with special events throughout the year.

Steam trains also operate at:

British Columbia Forest Discovery Centre 2892 Drinkwater Rd, RR #4, Trans-Canada Highway, Duncan, BC V9L 6C2; ☎ 250 715 1113; w bcforestdiscoverycentre.com
Canadian Railway Museum 110 St Pierre S, Saint-Constant, QC J5A 1G7; ☎ 450 632 2410; w exporail.org

FortEdmontonPark PO Box 2359, Edmonton, AB T5J 2R7; ☎ 780 496 7381; w fortedmontonpark. ca; ⊕ May–Sep. A Lima locomotive (*No 2024*) has been saved from the scrap heap & restored to take a passenger train from Midnapore Station.
Heritage Park Historical Village 1900 Heritage Dr SW, Calgary, AB T2V 2X3; ☎ 403 268 8500; w heritagepark.ca

Appendix 1

USEFUL ADDRESSES

USA, GENERAL

American Hotel & Lodging Association 1250 Eye St, NW, Suite 1100, Washington, DC 20005-3931; ☎202 289 3100; w ahla.com

Amtrak Customer Relations Office 60 Massachusetts Av NE, Washington, DC 20002-4225; ☎215 349 1042; w amtrak.com

Bed & Breakfast in the USA & Canada Home Base Holidays, 7 Park Av, London, N13 5PG; ☎020 3695 1123; w homebase-hols.com

BedandBreakfast.com 700 Brazos St, Suite B-700, Austin, TX 78701; ☎512 322 2710; w bedandbreakfast.com

Bed & Breakfast Inns Online 909 N Sepulveda Bd, 11th Floor, El Segundo, California 90245; ☎1 800 215 7365; e info@bbonline.com; w bbonline.com

BnBFinder 55 Broad St, Suite 3F, New York, NY 10004; ☎212 480 0414; e info@bnbfinder.com; w bnbfinder.com

BUNAC Travel Services Priory Hse, 6 Wrights Lane, London, W8 6TA; ☎033 3999 7516; e enquiries@bunac.org.uk; w bunac.org

Camp America 37 Queens Gate, London, SW7 5HR; ☎020 7581 7373; w campamerica.co.uk

Great Rail Journeys Saviour Hse, 9 St Saviourgate, York YO1 8NL; ☎01904 521936; w GreatRail.com. Offers escorted tours across the USA by rail, as well as Eastern Seaboard & West Coast & Yosemite tours, but cannot arrange tailor-made or ticket-only requests.

Greyhound International PO Box 660362, Dallas, TX 75266-0362; ☎1 800 231 2222; w greyhound.com

Hostelling International USA 8401 Colesville Rd, Suite 600, Silver Spring, MD 20910; ☎240 650 2100; e hiayhserv@hiayh.org; w hiusa.org

National Park Service 1849 C St NW, Washington, DC 20240; ☎202 208 6843; w nps.gov

Pentrex PO Box 22283, Indianapolis, IN 46222; ☎1 800 950 9333; w pentrex.com

Rail Passengers Association 1200 G St NW, Suite 240, Washington, DC 20005; ☎202 408 8362; w railpassengers.org

STA Travel 11 Goodge St, London, W1T 2PF; ☎020 3784 7810; w statravel.co.uk

United Airlines Amtrak Penn Station, 8th Av & 31st St, Ticket Lobby, New York, NY 10001; ☎1 800 864 8331; w united.com

US Citizenship & Immigration Services 111 Massachusetts Av, NW, MS 2260, Washington, DC 20529-2260; ☎1 800 375 5283; w uscis.gov

US Customs & Border Protection Service 1300 Pennsylvania Av NW, Washington, DC 20229; ☎877 CBP 5511 or ☎202 325 8000 (outside the United States); w cbp.gov

US Embassy 33 Nine Elms Lane, London, SW11 7US; ☎020 7499 9000; w uk.usembassy.gov

YMCA of the USA 101 North Wacker Dr, Chicago, IL 60606; ☎1 800 872 9622; w ymca.net

YWCA USA 1020 19th St NW, Suite 750, Washington, DC 20036; ☎202 467 0801; w ywca.org

CANADA, GENERAL

Air Canada PO Box 14000, Station Airport Dorval, Quebec H4Y 1H4; ☎888 247 2262; w aircanada.ca

Canada Border Services Agency Ottawa, ON K1A 0L8; ☎1 800 461 9999 or ☎204 983 3500 (outside Canada); w cbsa-asfc.gc.ca

Canadian Tourist Office/High Commission Macdonald Hse, 1 Grosvenor Sq, London, W1K 4AB; ☎020 7258 6600; w canada.embassyhomepage.com

CN North America 935 de la Gauchetière St W, Montreal, QC H3B 2M9; ☎ 1 888 888 5909; w cn.ca
Destination Canada 800-1045 Howe St, Vancouver, BC V6Z 2A9; w destinationcanada.com
Hostelling International Canada 75 Nicholas St, Ottawa, Ontario K1N 7B9; ☎ 613 237 7884 or ☎ 1 800 663 5777; e info@hihostels.ca; w hihostels.ca

Hotel Association of Canada 130 Albert St, Suite 1206, Ottawa, ON K1P 5G4; ☎ 613 237 7149; w hotelassociation.ca
VIA Rail Canada Inc 3 Pl Ville-Marie, Suite 500, Montreal, QC H3B 2C9; ☎ 1 888 VIA RAIL (☎ 888 842 7245); w viarail.ca

Appendix 2

TICKETING AGENTS

AMTRAK INTERNATIONAL SALES AGENTS Amtrak has developed an online booking system that allows for travel agents from anywhere in the world to have access to, and book, Amtrak tickets. The companies that follow have the ability to book Amtrak in these countries but this is not meant to be a comprehensive listing.

Australia Adventure Destinations, 89a Orange St, Bentleigh E, VIC 3165; ☎61 3 9570 4466 or ☎1300 136 330; w adventuredestinations.com.au. International Rail Australia, Suite 6, Level 1, 69–71 Rosstown Rd, Carnegie, VIC 3163; ☎1300 387 245; w internationalrail.com.au. Momento Travel, 10/541 Church St North, Parramatta NSW 2151; ☎1300 300 713; w momentotravel.com.au. Rail Plus, Level 6, 51 Queen St, Melbourne, VIC 3000; ☎61 3 9642 8644 or ☎1300 555 003; w railplus.com.au.

Denmark Check Point Travel, Søren Frichs Vej 42M 8230 Åbyhøj; ☎45 86 137 744; w cpt.dk. Nyhavn Rejser a/s, Nyhavn 31G, 1051 København K; ☎78 767 350; e travel@nyhavn.dk; w nyhavn.dk.

France Comptoir Des Voyages, 2 au 18 rue St Victor, 75005 Paris; ☎33 8 92 23 93 39; w comptoir.fr. Destination SAS, Château de Pourtalès, 161 rue Mélanie, F-67000 Strasbourg; ☎33 3 68 33 41 50; w destination-travel.fr. Discovery Trains, 29 Bd Henri IV, F-75004 Paris; ☎33 1 42 78 37 26; w discoverytrains.net. Fab Travel Troyes, 1 bis rue Cardinal Ancher (Pl de la Libération, Préfecture), 10000 Troyes (en Champagne); ☎33 3 25 70 89 19; w fab-travel. com. Interface Tourism, 16 Ballu, 75009 Paris; ☎33 1 53 25 11 11; w interfacetourism.com. JETSET Voyages, 41–45 rue Galilée, 75116 Paris; ☎33 1 53 67 13 00; w jetset-voyages.fr. Media Voyages, 55 rue Ney, 69006 Lyon; ☎33 4 72 83 04 95; w mediavoyages.fr.

Germany Canada Reise Dienst (CRD International), Stadthausbrucke 1-3, 20355 Hamburg; ☎49 40 300 616 55; w crd.de.

Eberhardt Travel, Zschoner Ring 30, 01723 Kesselsdorf (bei Dresden); ☎49 0352 049 2112; w eberhardt-travel.de.

Italy Gioco Viaggi Srl, Via B Bosco, 57, 16121 Genoa; ☎39 10 553 1169; w giocoviaggi.com

Mexico Trenes Y Otros Servicios S de RL de CV, Oxford # 30, Col Juárez, Mexico, DF 06600; ☎5208 0000; w tyoservicios.net

New Zealand Rail Plus, Level 2, 6 Kingdon St, Newmarket, Auckland, 1149; ☎64 9 377 5415; w railplus.co.nz

United Kingdom American Sky, Tropical Hse, Garland Rd, East Grinstead, West Sussex RH19 1NJ; ☎01342 886501; w americansky. co.uk. Aspen Travel, 175 Washway Rd, Sale, Manchester M33 4AH; ☎0161 755 3081; w aspentravel.co.uk. Complete North America Limited, Colwick Quays Business Park, Private Rd No 2, Colwick, Nottingham NG4 2JY; ☎0115 961 0590; w completenorthamerica.com. Cresta World Travel, Cresta Hse, 32 Victoria St, Altrincham, Cheshire WA14 1ET; ☎0161 927 7177; w www.crestaworldtravel.co.uk. Ffestiniog Travel, Former St Mary's Church, Tremadog, Porthmadog, Gwynedd LL49 9RA; ☎1766 512400; w ffestiniogtravel.com. Haslemere Travel Ltd, 2/4 Petworth Rd, Haslemere, Surrey GU27 2HR; ☎01428 658777; w haslemeretravel. co.uk. Howard Travel, 12/13 Church Walk, Trowbridge, Wilts BA14 8DX; ☎01225 777227; w howardtravel.com. Jetline Travel, Becket Hse, 36 Old Jewry, London, EC2R 8DD; ☎0800 082 2199; w jetlineholidays.com. The Travel Bureau,

The Cottage, High St, Wombourne, West Midlands WV5 9DN; ☎01902 324777; w thetravelbureau. co.uk. Trailfinders, 194 Kensington High St, London W8 7RG; ☎020 7938 3939, + many other UK locations – call for information; w trailfinders. com. Trainseurope Ltd, 4 Station Approach, March, Cambs PE15 8SJ; ☎0871 700 7722; w trainseurope.co.uk. International Rail Ltd, PO Box 153, Alresford, Hants SO24 4AQ; ☎0871 231 0790; w internationalrail.com. Up & Away Holidays, 19 The Mall, Bromley, Kent BR1 1TT; ☎020 8289 5050; w upandawayholidays.co.uk.

VIA RAIL INTERNATIONAL SALES AGENTS

Argentina, Peru, Chile & Columbia   Personal Brasil, Rua Paula Moes, 703 – 4 Andar, São Francisco, Curitiba, PR; ☎55 41 3018 5580 or ☎0800 600 5580; w canadaentren.com

Australia   Momento Travel, 10/541 Church St, North Parramatta, Australia NSW 2151; ☎1300 300 713; w momentotravel.com.au

Austria   Canada Reisen, Buchberggasse 34, 3400 Klosterneuburg; ☎011 43 2243 25994; w canadareisen.at

Brazil   Personal Brasil Tour Operator, Rua Simão Bolivar 210 Alto da Gloria, Curitiba – Paraná, Brasil CEP 80030-260; ☎0800 600 5580; w canadadetrem.com.br

France & Belgium   Discovery Trains, 29 Bd Henri IV, F-75004 Paris, France; ☎+33 (0) 1 42 78 37 26; w discoverytrains.net

Germany   Canada Reise Dienst, CRD International, Stadthausbruecke 1-3, 20355 Hamburg; ☎49 40 3006160; w crd.de

Japan   JTB (Travel Plaza International Inc), HF Monzennakacho Building, Tomioka, Koto-Ku, Tokyo 135-8531; ☎00 813 3820 8040; w tpityo. co.jp. H I S. Shinjuku Head Office, Railway Travel Section, South Gate, Shinjuku Building 1F, 5-33-8 Sendagaya, Shibuya-Ku, Tokyo 151-0051; ☎03 5360 4881; w train-his.com.

Korea   The Pharos Travelartifex Corp, 4F Bukyung Bldg, 183-1, Chungjin-Dong, Jongno-Gu, Seoul 110-130; ☎82 2 737 3773

México   Trenes Y Otros Servicios S de RL de CV, Oxford # 30, Col Juárez, Mexico DF 06600; ☎5208 0000; w tyoservicios.net

Netherlands   Incento BV, PO Box 1067, 1400 BB Bussum; ☎035 69 5 5111; w incento.nl

New Zealand   Adventure World, 101 Great South Rd, Remuera, PO Box 74008, Auckland; ☎64 9 524 5118; w adventureworld.co.nz

United Kingdom   First Class Holidays, Trafford Hse, Chester Rd, Old Trafford, Manchester M32 0RS; ☎0161 888 5636 or ☎0845 644 3553; w 1strail. co.uk

Appendix 3

FURTHER INFORMATION

BOOKS It is obviously impossible to produce any sort of comprehensive reading list on countries so vast as the USA and Canada, and all the more so when they also have such a rich and extensive cultural and literary history of their own. The following suggestions, however, may be of help in providing further information on topics likely to interest rail travellers and those new to North America.

USA
Railways
Ambrose, Stephen *Nothing Like it in the World* Simon & Schuster

Bain, David Howard *Empire Express* Viking

Bell, N J and Ward, James Arthur *Southern Railroad Man* Northern Illinois University Press

Best, Gerald M *Iron Horses to Promontory* Golden West Books

Blumberg, Rhoda *Full Steam Ahead: The Race to Build a Transcontinental Railroad* National Geographic

Broggie, Michael *Walt Disney's Railroad Story* Pentrex

Cook, Richard *The Beauty of Railroad Bridges in North America* Golden West Books

Daniels, Rudolph *Trains across the Continent* Indiana University Press

Drury, George H *The Historical Guide to North American Railroads* Kalmbach

Goble, Paul *Death of the Iron Horse* Aladdin

Hidy, Ralph W *Dining by Rail: A History* Harvard Business School

Holbrook, Stewart H *The Story of American Railroads* Crown Publishers

Kalmbach, Al *Great American Railroad Stories* Kalmbach Books

Kennedy, Ian and Treuherz, Julian *The Railway: Art in the Age of Steam* Yale University Press

Kirby, Lynne *Parallel Tracks: The Railroad and Silent Cinema* Duke University Press

Klein, Aaron E *Encyclopedia of North American Railroads* Bison

Link, O Winston *Steam, Steel and Stars: America's Last Steam Railroad* Harry N Abrams

Mayer, Lyn Rhodes *Makin' Tracks* Praeger

Middleton, William D *Landmarks on the Iron Road* Indiana University Press

Perata, David *Those Pullman Blues* Twayne Publishers

Pindell, Terry *Making Tracks: An American Odyssey* Henry Holt

Potter, Janet Greenstein *Great American Railroad Stations* Wiley

Richmond, Al *Rails to the Rim: Milepost Guide to the Grand Canyon Railway* Grand Canyon Railway

Richmond, Al *The Story of the Grand Canyon Railway* Grand Canyon Railway

Roe, Jo Ann *Stevens Pass: The Story of Railroading and Recreation in the North Cascades* The Mountaineers

Ross, David *The Encyclopedia of Trains and Locomotives* Thunder Bay Press

Sandler, Martin *Riding the Rails in the USA* Oxford University Press

Schwantes, Carlos A and Ronda, James P *The West the Railroads Made* University of Washington Press

Schwieterman, Joseph *When the Railroad Leaves Town* Truman State University Press

Shaughnessy, Jim *The Call of Trains* W W Norton

Signor, John R *Donner Pass: Southern Pacific's Sierra Crossing* Golden West Books

Solomon, Brian *Alco Locomotives* Voyageur Press

Solomon, Brian *American Steam Locomotive* Motorbooks International

Solomon, Brian *Baldwin Locomotives* Voyageur Press

Stiles, T J *The First Tycoon: Cornelius Vanderbilt* Knopf

Stover, John *History of the Baltimore and Ohio Railroad* Purdue University Press

Stover, John and Carnes, Mark *The Historical Atlas of the American Railroads* Routledge

Vance Jr, James E *The North American Railroad* Johns Hopkins University Press

Wegman, Mark *American Passenger Trains & Locomotives Illustrated* Voyageur Press

Welsh, Joe *The American Railroad* Motorbooks International

Welsh, Joe and Holland, Kevin J *Union Pacific Railroad* Voyageur Press

Welsh, Joe, Howes, Bill and Holland, Kevin J *The Cars of Pullman* Voyageur Press

White Jr, John H *The American Railroad Passenger Car* Johns Hopkins University Press

White, Richard *Railroaded* Norton

Wiatroski, Claude *Railroads across North America* Voyageur Press

Wolmar, Christian *Blood, Fire & Steam* Atlantic Books

Wolmar, Christian *Blood, Iron & Gold* Atlantic Books

York, Thomas *North America's Great Railroads* Brompton Books

Young, Gavin *From Sea to Shining Sea* Hutchinson

General travel

Sakach, Deborah E *The Bed & Breakfast Encyclopedia* American Historic Inns

Soule, Sandra W *America's Favourite Inns, B & Bs, and Small Hotels: USA and Canada* St Martin's Press

Tice, Janet *100 Best Family Resorts in North America* Globe Pequot Press

General – history, the country, the people

Bluestein, G *Poplore: Folk and Pop in American Culture* University of Massachusetts Press

Breidlid, Anders (editor) *American Culture* Routledge

Duchak, Alicia *A–Z of Modern America* Routledge

Evans, Harold *The American Century* Jonathan Cape

Garraty, John A *The American Nation* Longman

Holliday, J S *The World Rushed In: The California Gold Rush Experience* Simon & Schuster

Hughes, Robert *American Visions* Harvill Press

Klein, Joe *Woody Guthrie* Faber & Faber

Lozano, Rosina *An American Language* University of California Press

Mauk, David and Oakland, John *American Civilisation* Routledge

McGlashan, C F *History of the Donner Party* Stanford University Press

O'Callaghan, B *An Illustrated History of the US* Longman

Reid, Brian Holden *The American Civil War* Longman

Scheurer, T E *Born in the USA* University of Mississippi

Schweikart, Larry and Allen, Michael Patrick *A Patriot's History of the United States* Sentinel

Skar, R *Movie – Made in America: A Cultural History of American Movies* Random House

Stone, Oliver and Kuznick, Peter *The Untold History of the United States* Gallery Books

Tindall, George B *America* W W Norton
Utley, Robert M *Frontiersmen in Blue* Bison Books

Canada
Railways
Allen, Tom *Rolling Home* Penguin
Berton, Pierre *Steel across the Shield: Canada Moves West* McClelland & Stewart
Berton, Pierre *The Last Spike* Anchor Canada
Berton, Pierre *The National Dream* Anchor Canada
Bohi, Charles *Canadian National's Western Depots* Fitzhenry & Whiteside
Brown, Ron *Ghost Railways of Ontario* Polar Bear Press
Brown, Ron *Rails Across the Prairies* Dundurn
Buck, George *From Summit to Sea* Fifth House
Cruikshank, Ken *Close Ties* McGill-Queen's University Press
Doughty, Geoffrey H *Canadian Treasures* TLC Publishing
Eagle, John A *The Canadian Pacific Railway* McGill-Queen's University Press
Fleming, R B *The Railway King of Canada* University of British Columbia Press
Good, Cherry *On the Trail of John Muir* Luath Press
Graham, Melissa *The Trans-Canada Rail Guide* Trailblazer Publications, 1996
Green, Lorne *Chief Engineer* Dundurn
Guay, David R P *Great Western Railway of Canada* Dundurn
Brown, Ron *Rails Across the Prairies* Dundurn
Harris, Chris *BC Rail* Country Light Publishing
Harris, Lorraine *BC's Own Railroad* Hancock House
Klein, Aaron *The Men Who Built the Railroads* Gallery Books
Leggett, Robert Ferguson *Railroads of Canada* Drake
Lovett, Henry Almon *Canada and the Grand Trunk* Ayer
McDonnell, Greg *Canadian Pacific* Boston Mills Press
Murray, Tom *Canadian National Railway* Motorbooks International
O'Reilly, Susan McLeod *On Track* Canadian Museum of Civilisation
Perry, Lorne and MacKay, Donald *Train Country* Douglas & McIntyre
Pindell, Terry *Last Train to Toronto* Henry Holt
Schneider, Ena *Ribbons of Steel* Detselig Enterprises
Secretan, J H *Canada's Great Highway* Ayer
Solomon, Brian *Railroad Stations* Main Street Books
Taber, Thomas Townsend *Guide to Railroad Historical Resources, United States and Canada* Muncy

General – travel, history, the country, the people
Canada Gazetteer Atlas University of Chicago Press
Canada's National Parks Whitecap Books
Carroll, Donald *Canada Traveler's Companion* Globe Pequot Press
Cheng, Pang G and Barlas, Robert *Culture Shock: Canada* Kuperard
Cropp, Richard *Romantic Days and Nights in Vancouver* Globe Pequot Press
Harvey, R G *Carving the Western Path* Heritage House
Hayes, Derek *Canada: An Illustrated History* Douglas & McIntyre
Kalman, Bobbie *Canada from A to Z* Crabtree
Kranc, Benjamin A *Living and Working in Canada* How To Books
Lechmere, Adam and Catto, Susan *Live and Work in the USA and Canada* Vacation Work
Malcolm, Andrew H *The Canadians* St Martin's Press
McNaught, Kenneth *The Penguin History of Canada* Penguin

Morris, Jan *O Canada!* Robert Hale
Mussio, Russell *The Cariboo* Gordon Soules
Orkin, David *Nova Scotia*, 3rd edition Bradt Travel Guides
Weber, James *Canadian History in 50 Events* CreateSpace Publishing

WEBSITES Some of the most useful websites for those intending to travel by train are as follows:

For the USA

AAPRCO The American Association of Private Railroad Car Owners represents private car owners and publishes *Private Varnish Magazine*. **w** aaprco.com
Alaska Railroad Operates out of Anchorage. **w** alaskarailroad.com
Allplaces Statistics, local links and fun stuff. **w** allplaces.us
Amtrak A comprehensive, award-winning site. **w** amtrak.com
Amtrak California Fare promotions, maps and a quarterly e-zine. **w** amtrakcalifornia.com
Amtrak Capitol Corridor For southern California. **w** capitolcorridor.org
Amtrak Cascades For travel between Eugene, Oregon and Vancouver in Canada.
w amtrakcascades.com
Amtrak/Passenger Railroad For travellers, rail fans and railroaders. **w** trainweb.org/amtrak
Amtrak Unlimited One of the best Amtrak information sources. **w** amtraktrains.com
Coast Starlight Free gifts and historic Parlour cars. **w** coaststarlight.com
CPRR Photographic History Museum Stereoviews, engravings, maps and documents illustrating the history of the Central Pacific Railroad. **w** cprr.org
Friends of Amtrak An internet advocacy supporting funding for Amtrak.
w friendsofamtrak.com
Grand Canyon A railway built by the Atchison, Topeka & Santa Fe Railway. **w** thetrain.com
Great American Stations Information about Amtrak's stations and their fascinating histories. **w** greatamericanstations.com
Green Frog Productions Video, audio and CDs about trains. **w** greenfrog.com
National Rail Page Lists all national and international rail websites. **w** rrhistorical.com
Onroute Guides to more than 200 places in the USA and Canada. **w** onroute.com
Railfan Pictures of trains and other railroad subjects. **w** bfcase.railfan.net
The Railfan Network By rail fans for rail fans. **w** railfan.net
Rail Passengers Association Join and help save America's trains. **w** railpassengers.org
The Railroad Press Railroad magazine and books with exceptional photography.
w alco628.com
RailServe Guide to 19,000 rail-related websites including train travel, model railroading, railfan resources, and industry sites. **w** railserve.com
RailServe Music Page Links to all kinds of railroad songs. **w** railserve.com/music
Silver Rails Resort An expanding railroad-themed resort in La Plata, Missouri, with an exhibition of Amtrak history. Ideal for anyone with an enthusiasm for trains or the history of railroading. **w** silverrails.com
Texas Eagle Full information for *Texas Eagle* country. **w** texaseagle.com
Trainweb Lots of information about North American trains. **w** trainweb.com
Travelinformation Free travel brochures. **w** travelinformation.com
USA by Rail Up-to-date information and tips from other travellers. **w** usa-by-rail.com
USA Tourist The latest tourist developments. **w** www.usatourist.com

For Canada

Algoma Central An unofficial website. **w** agawatrain.com and **w** trainweb.org/algoma
Canada.ca The Government of Canada's official digital presence. **w** canada.ca

CRHA The Canadian Railroad Historical Association preserves and interprets Canada's railway heritage. Exporail, the Canadian Railway Museum, operated by the CRHA, is one of the most important railway museums in the world. **w** exporail.org

Discover Canada General information. **w** discovercanada.com

Ontario Northland From Toronto to the Arctic Circle. **w** ontarionorthland.ca

Rocky Mountaineer Perhaps the most spectacular train route in North America. **w** rockymountaineer.com

VIA Rail Download the latest timetables and request brochures. **w** viarail.ca

White Pass & Yukon Railway **w** wpyr.com

Railroad historical societies

Atlantic Coast Line & Seaboard Air Line. **w** aclsal.org

Baltimore & Ohio. **w** borhs.org

Canadian National. **w** cnrha.ca

Canadian Pacific. **w** cptracks.ca

Chesapeake & Ohio. **w** cohs.org

Chicago & North Western. **w** cnwhs.org

Erie Lackawanna. **w** erielackhs.org

Great Northern. **w** gnrhs.org

Gulf, Mobile and Ohio. **w** gmohs.org

Illinois Central. **w** icrrhistorical.org

Milwaukee Road. **w** mrha.com

Missouri-Kansas-Texas Railroad (the Katy). **w** katyrailroad.org

Monon Railroad. **w** monon.org

Norfolk & Southern. **w** norfolksouthernhs.org

Norfolk & Western. **w** nwhs.org

Pere Marquette. **w** pmhistsoc.org

Reading Railroad. **w** readingrailroad.org

Richmond, Fredericksburg & Potomac. **w** rfandp.org

Rutland. **w** rutlandrr.org

Santa Fe. **w** sfrhms.org

Soo Line. **w** sooline.org

Southern. **w** srha.net

Southern Pacific. **w** sphts.org

Terminal Railroad. **w** trra-hts.railfan.net

Toronto, Hamilton & Buffalo. **w** thbrailway.ca

Toronto Railway. **w** trha.ca

Union Pacific. **w** uphs.org

General

Budget Travel For travellers of modest means. **w** budgettravel.com

Currency Converter Conversions for 200 different currencies. **w** oanda.com/currency/converter

Electronic Embassy Page Includes all foreign embassies in the USA. **w** embassy.org/embassies

Expedia For transatlantic flights and much else. **w** expedia.co.uk

Globetrotters Club For independent travellers. **w** globetrotters.co.uk

GoAbroad Alternative travel with information on studying and living abroad. **w** goabroad.com

Hostelling International Youth hostel associations around the world belong to Hostelling International. **w** hihostels.com

Internet Guide to Hostelling One of the largest directories of hostels in the world. **w** hostels.com

Journeywoman Online Mainly for women travellers. **w** journeywoman.com
Kasbah Travel Information A search engine with 100,000 sites listed. **w** kasbah.com
Maps Available at **w** mapquest.com
Onetravel.com For airfares and accommodation worldwide. **w** onetravel.com
Roadnews Everything you need to stay connected while travelling. **w** roadnews.com
TrainTraveling.com A comprehensive passenger rail guide and news resource.
w traintraveling.com

Index

Page references in **bold** indicate major entries